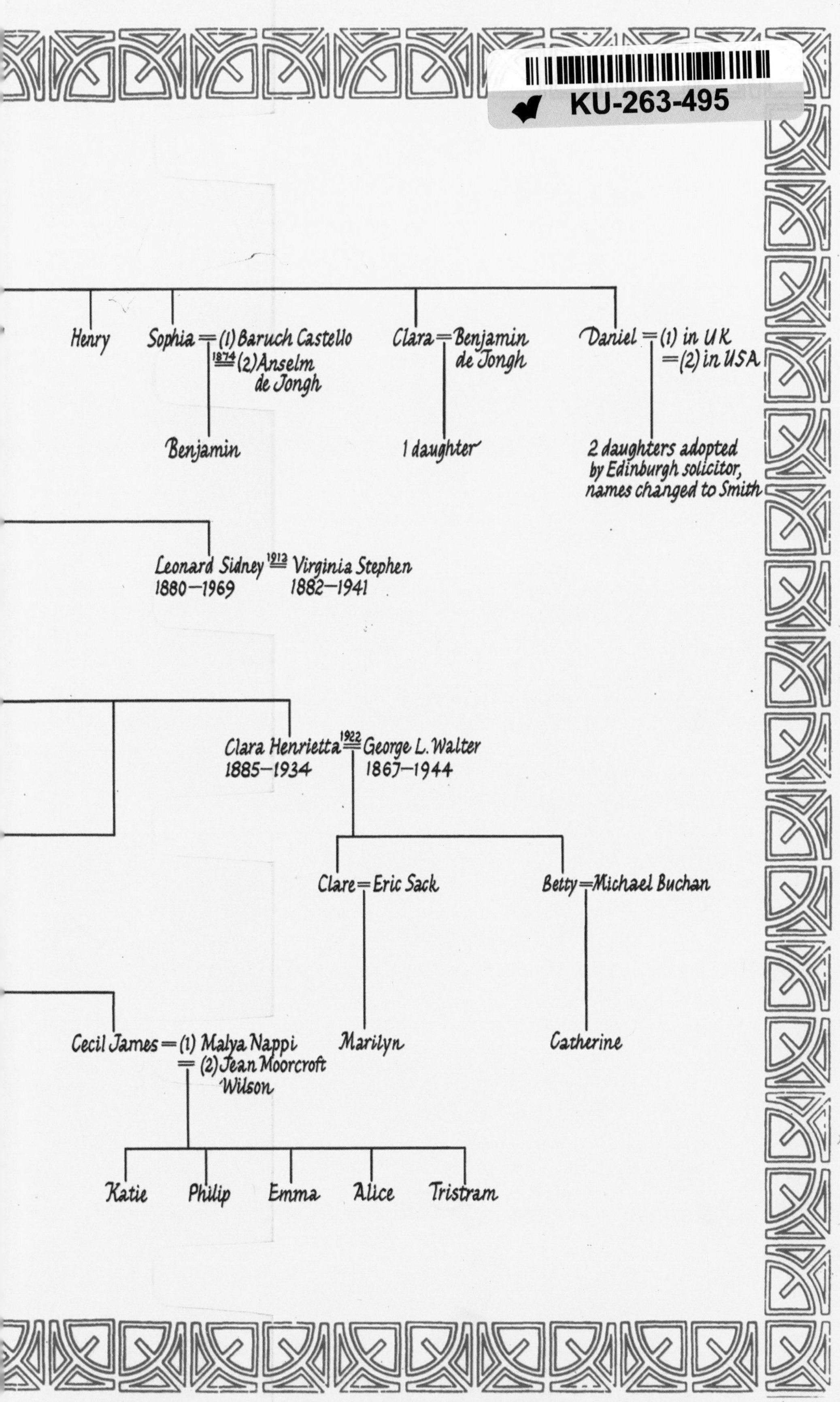

KU-263-495
Henry
Sophia = (1) Baruch Castello
1874 = (2) Anselm de Jongh
Benjamin
Clara = Benjamin de Jongh
1 daughter
Daniel = (1) in UK
= (2) in USA
2 daughters adopted by Edinburgh solicitor, names changed to Smith
Leonard Sidney 1880–1969
1912 =
Virginia Stephen 1882–1941
Clara Henrietta 1885–1934
1922 =
George L. Walter 1867–1944
Clare = Eric Sack
Marilyn
Betty = Michael Buchan
Catherine
Cecil James = (1) Malya Nappi
= (2) Jean Moorcroft Wilson
Katie
Philip
Emma
Alice
Tristram

Also by Victoria Glendinning

Trollope
Rebecca West: A Life
Vita: The Life of Vita Sackville-West
Edith Sitwell: A Unicorn Among Lions
Elizabeth Bowen: Portrait of a Writer
Jonathan Swift
A Suppressed Cry
Hertfordshire
Sons and Mothers (ed., with Mathew Glendinning)

FICTION

Flight
The Grown-Ups
Electricity

I DON'T BELIEVE A WORD OF IT

Leonard Woolf

VICTORIA
GLENDINNING

London · New York · Sydney · Toronto

A CBS COMPANY

First published in Great Britain by Simon & Schuster UK Ltd, 2006
A CBS COMPANY

1 3 5 7 9 10 8 6 4 2

Simon & Schuster UK Ltd
Africa House
64–78 Kingsway
London WC2B 6AH

www.simonsays.co.uk

Simon & Schuster Australia
Sydney

A CIP catalogue record for this book is available
from the British Library.

ISBN 0-7432-2030-7
EAN 9780743220309

Typeset in Baskerville by M Rules
Printed and bound in Great Britain by
The Bath Press, Bath

For O.N.V.G.

CONTENTS

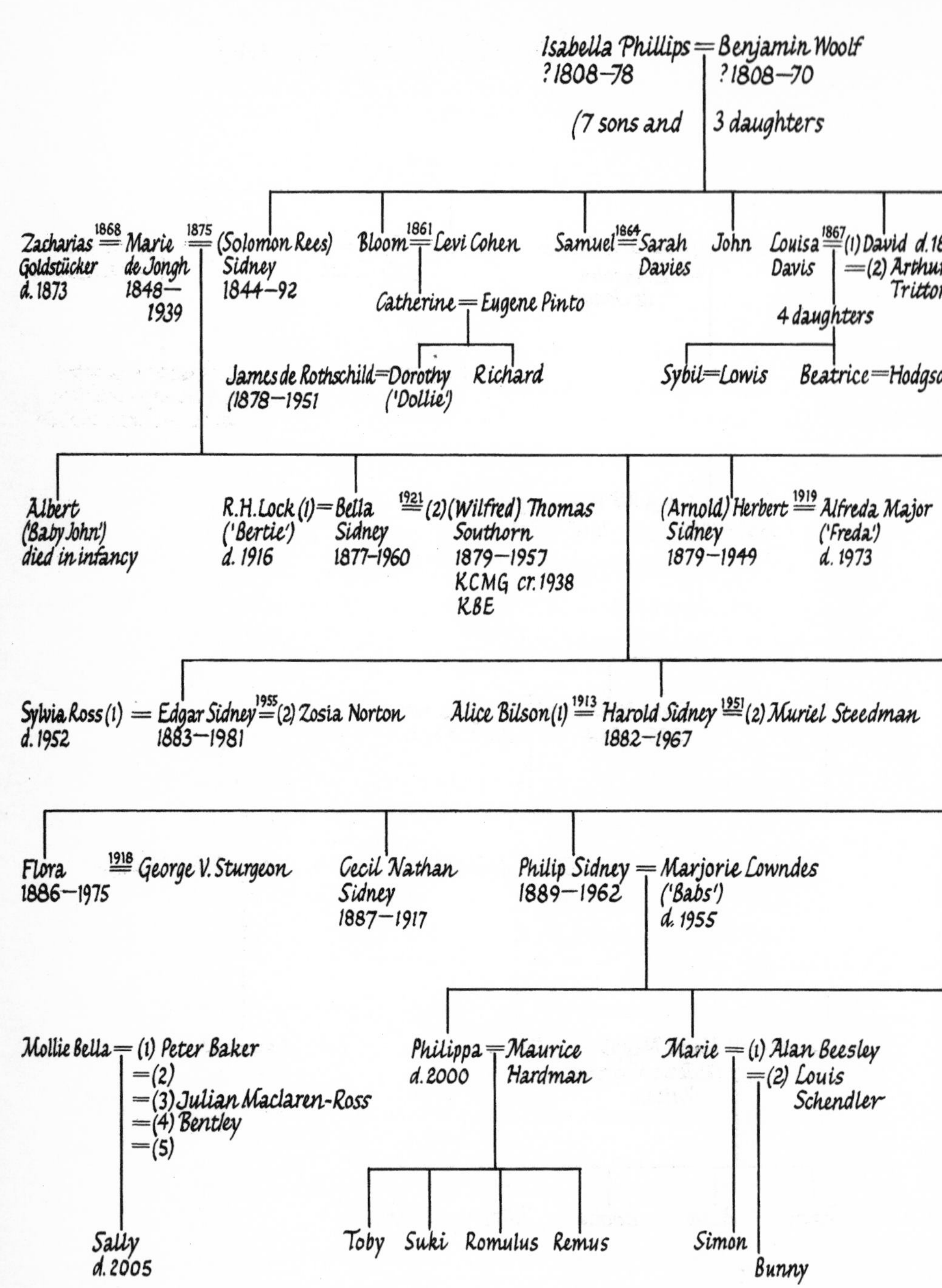

Isabella Phillips = Benjamin Woolf
?1808–78
?1808–70
(7 sons and
3 daughters
Zacharias Goldstücker d. 1873
1868
Marie de Jongh 1848–1939
1875
(Solomon Rees) Sidney 1844–92
Bloom
1861
Levi Cohen
Catherine = Eugene Pinto
James de Rothschild (1878–1951)
= Dorothy ('Dollie')
Richard
Samuel
1864
Sarah Davies
John
Louisa Davis
1867
(1) David d.18
=(2) Arthur Tritton
4 daughters
Sybil = Lowis
Beatrice = Hodgson
Albert ('Baby John') died in infancy
R.H. Lock (1) ('Bertie') d. 1916
= Bella Sidney 1877–1960
1921
(2) (Wilfred) Thomas Southorn 1879–1957 KCMG cr. 1938 KBE
(Arnold) Herbert Sidney 1879–1949
1919
Alfreda Major ('Freda') d. 1973
Sylvia Ross (1) d. 1952
= Edgar Sidney 1883–1981
1955
(2) Zosia Norton
Alice Bilson (1)
1913
Harold Sidney 1882–1967
1951
(2) Muriel Steedman
Flora 1886–1975
1918
George V. Sturgeon
Cecil Nathan Sidney 1887–1917
Philip Sidney 1889–1962
= Marjorie Lowndes ('Babs') d. 1955
Mollie Bella = (1) Peter Baker
=(2)
=(3) Julian Maclaren-Ross
=(4) Bentley
=(5)
Sally d. 2005
Philippa d. 2000
= Maurice Hardman
Toby
Suki
Romulus
Remus
Marie = (1) Alan Beesley
=(2) Louis Schendler
Simon
Bunny

The Woolf Family Tree

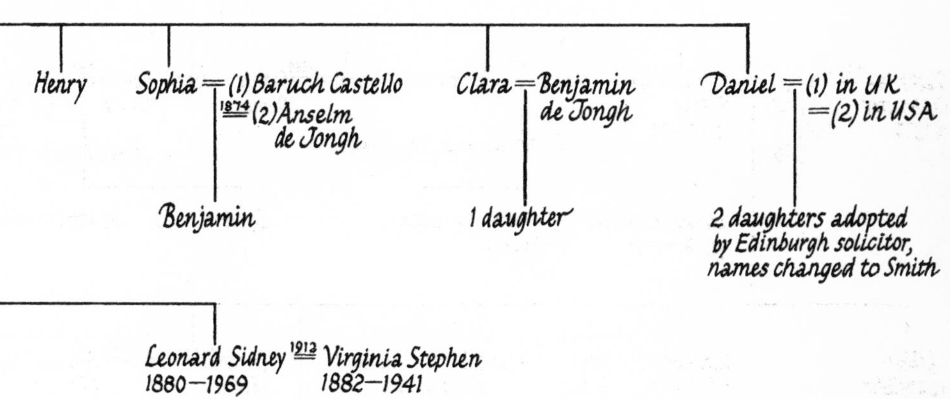

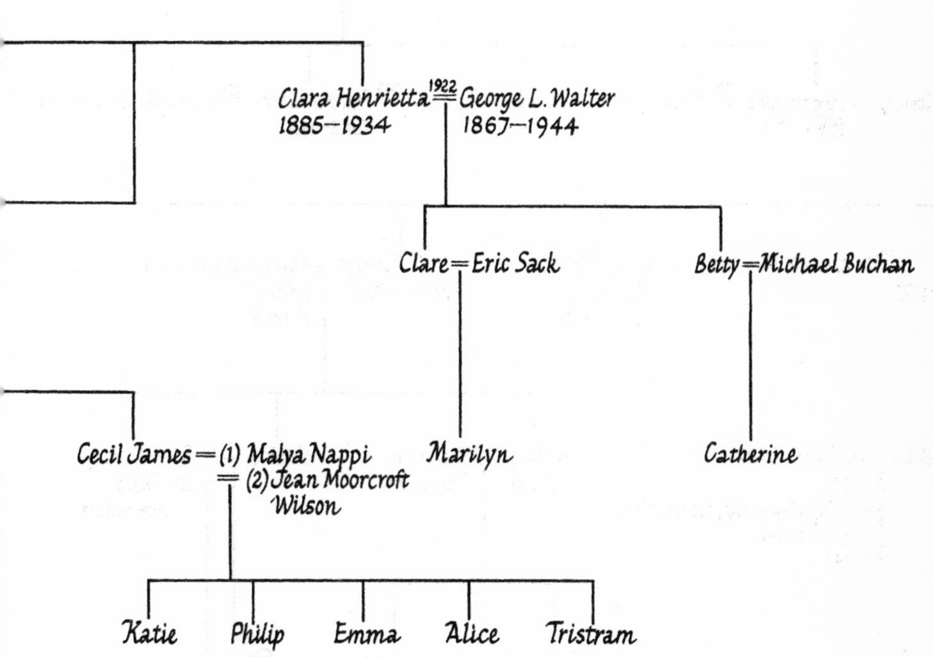

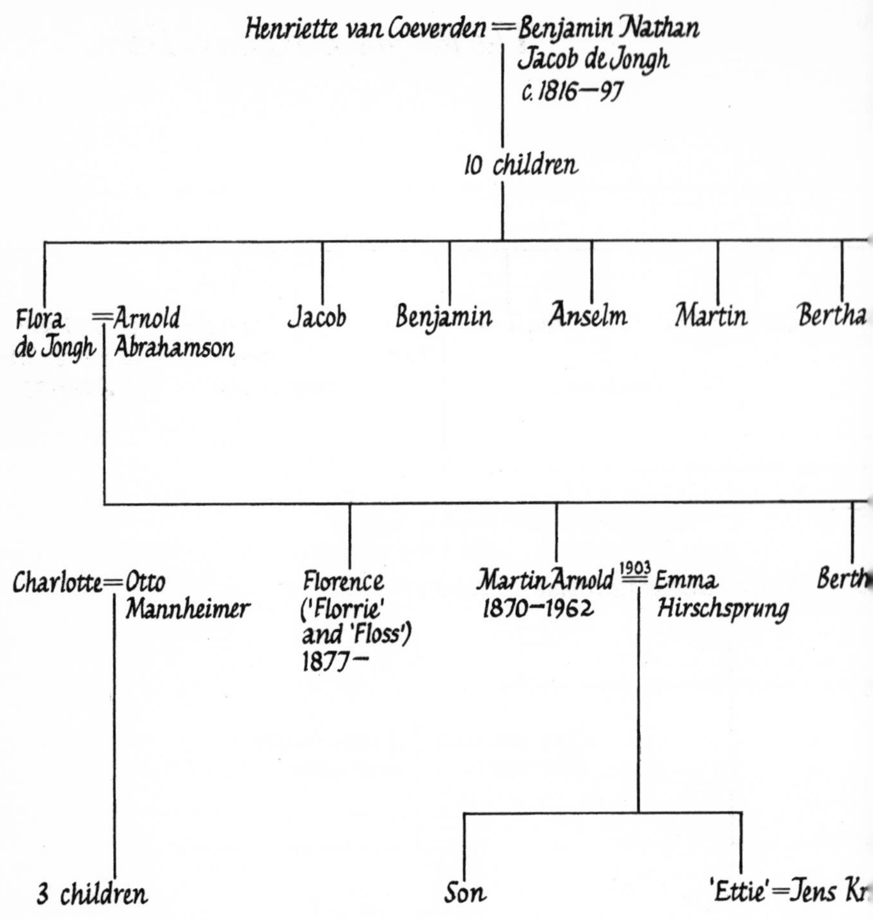

Henriette van Coeverden = Benjamin Nathan Jacob de Jongh c. 1816–97
10 children
Flora de Jongh = Arnold Abrahamson
Jacob
Benjamin
Anselm
Martin
Bertha
Charlotte = Otto Mannheimer
Florence ('Florrie' and 'Floss') 1877–
Martin Arnold 1870–1962
1903
Emma Hirschsprung
3 children
Son
'Ettie' = Jens Kr

The de Jongh Family Tree

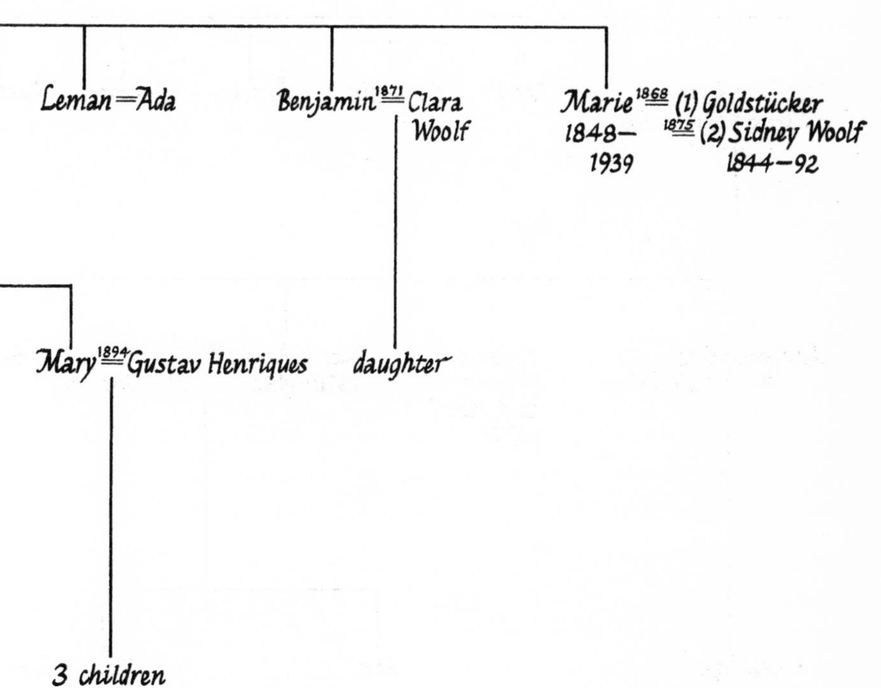

1

In the Beginning

Having a child is problematic, wrote Leonard Woolf when in his eighties, and childless. It concerns the 'new human being' as much as its parents, since this new human being is born without having given its consent. One should think twice, 'from the point of view of the hypothetical child'. He himself was born, without his consent, on 25 November 1880. There he is, Leonard Sidney Woolf, in the Census returns for 1881, a five-month-old baby.

Everyone, holding a baby, has to wonder what life holds in store for him. No one could have foreseen what would happen to this one. He grew up to become a core member of a group of intimate and talented friends who continue to inspire interest and analysis a century later. In his early twenties, as a colonial servant, he administered ten thousand square miles of village and jungle. He became an anti-imperialist, a Marxist 'of a sort' and a socialist, and was an *éminence grise* of the early Labour Party in Britain as it became a party of government. His adult life spanned the two world wars; his writings informed the charter of the League of Nations and, as polemical journalist, as editor and author, his lifelong mission was to prevent the barbarism and insanity of future war through international cooperation and collective security.

His anguished intelligence saw all too clearly both the failure of this great project, and what he saw as the failure of the Left in Britain. He had his own demons to fight in public and in private life, being a man of extremes and contradictions: ferocious and tender, violent and self-restrained, opinionated and non-judgmental. Belief in reason pulled him one way, irrational passion another. He was disconcerting, inner-directed, attractive, always an outsider. The constants in his character were honesty, persistence and energy. He played all games, competitively. He was a dedicated gardener. He had an affinity with animals. Non-stop work – at his writing, at his political activities, in the garden – came naturally to him.

He liked women, and women liked him. ('I have always been greatly attracted to the undiluted female mind, as well as to the female body.') With his wife, he founded the Hogarth Press. He had no idea when he married Virginia Stephen how her mental instability would determine and distort his own trajectory, nor that she would become one of the most famous English authors of the twentieth century. He knew how to love, and she was the love of his life. After her suicide came change and a new attachment. In his last decade, five volumes of autobiography won him respect and recognition. He left not only distinguished books on international relations, but also satirical squibs, a great mass of literary and political journalism, a play, poetry, short stories, and two novels.

Eclipsed in the literary canon, and in the public imagination, by the illustriousness of Virginia Woolf – his family name, when standing alone, commonly signifying her, not him – he is a dark star. 'You cannot escape Fate', he wrote at the end of his life, 'and Fate, I have always felt, is not in the future, but in the past.'[1]

The five-month-old Leonard, dark haired and blue-eyed, had an elder sister, Bella Sidney, aged four; and a brother, Arnold Herbert Sidney, always called Herbert, aged nearly two. Bella, Herbert and Leonard were joined in the nursery at 101 Lexham Gardens, Kensington, by Harold Sidney, Edgar Sidney, Clara Henriette, Flora, Cecil Nathan Sidney, and Philip Sidney. The nine little Woolfs were born within

1 *The Journey Not the Arrival Matters* Hogarth Press 1969

twelve years, the youngest arriving in 1889. There had been yet one more baby, who died in infancy.

Even a rapid overview of Leonard's forebears recalls the remorselessly genealogical chapters of the Book of Genesis.

Leonard's mother, Marie de Jongh, was married at seventeen to Albert Zacharias Goldstücker, a City merchant. Marie's brother Benjamin de Jongh, a stock-jobber, married a young woman called Clara Woolf. When Marie Goldstücker was widowed, aged twenty-two, an executor of her late husband's Will was a brother of her sister-in-law Clara – Sidney Woolf, a recently qualified young barrister. He was Leonard's future father.

Sidney Woolf was living then with two recent widows, his mother and his elder sister Sophia.[2] When Sophia remarried, her new husband was another of Marie's brothers, Anselm de Jongh. In 1875, the following year, Marie Goldstücker and Sidney Woolf were married; she was still in her twenties, and he five years older.

Thus the Woolfs and the de Jonghs were intricately connected. Leonard saw a lot of his maternal grandparents. They too lived in Kensington, at 7 Addison Gardens, and the little Woolfs were taken over to tea once a week. Leonard thought that his de Jongh grandparents 'lived in the cleanest house and they were the cleanest people I have ever seen anywhere.'

Grandfather Nathan de Jongh, a diamond merchant, lived until 1897, when he was knocked down by a horse-drawn omnibus. Leonard was then well into his teens; and his Grandmother de Jongh survived until 1902, when he was at Cambridge. The de Jonghs seemed to Leonard to be 'rather soft' people. Grandfather de Jongh was tall, gentle, quiet, with a long white beard. In the house he wore a brightly coloured smoking-cap, and was never seen without a cigar and a book. Outside he wore the same kind of clothes as 'all the other gentlemen in Addison Gardens', but he nevertheless looked to Leonard as if he had stepped

2 Her late husband was Baruch Costello.

out of a typical picture of 'caftaned, bearded Jews in a ghetto, straight-backed, dignified, sad, resigned, expecting and getting over two millennia nothing but misery . . .'[3]

Leonard remembered his de Jongh grandmother sitting in a high-backed ebony chair in her lace-curtained front window and always knitting, extremely fast. She wore a black lace cap over her white hair, 'and beneath it was the round, pink face of an incredibly old Dutch doll'. She brought the cap with her in a special basket when she came to visit at Lexham Gardens, for putting on after she removed her hat.

Leonard, describing these grandparents in what was to become *Sowing*, had originally written that the cap she wore was of white lace. His elder sister Bella, correcting his draft, insisted it was black. By publishing autobiography, Leonard laid down and pre-empted the family myths. His brothers and sisters regularly and irritably corrected the record. Children born into the same family remember different things, and the same things differently.

Leonard thought Grandmother de Jongh never read a book or 'suffered from an abstract idea' in her life, but he attributed to her special qualities. There are some people, he wrote, 'usually dogs or old women – extremely simple and unintellectual, who instinctively know how to deal with life and with persons, and who display an extraordinary and admirable resistance to the cruelties of man, the malevolence of Providence, and the miseries of existence.'

Grandfather Nathan and Grandmother Henriette de Jongh came to London from Amsterdam in the 1860s. Henriette's maiden name was Van Coeverden ('*not* Katz. Her sister married a Katz', wrote Bella, testily amending Leonard's draft). They had ten children. The eldest daughter, Flora, married Arnold Abrahamson, who lived in Denmark; Leonard had a slew of Scandinavian cousins.

The publication of Leonard's first volume of autobiography in 1960 elicited a small flood of memories and additional information. A Dutchman wrote about the origin of the name Van Coeverden: Coevordon (spelled *sic*) is a small town in the east of the Netherlands,

---

3 *Sowing*

'where there lived for centuries a good kind of Jews, small itinerant traders and small shopkeepers. But of course most of them are gassed now.'

Before they moved to Addison Gardens, the de Jongh grandparents lived at Woburn Lodge, a Regency dwelling like a small country house, off Tavistock Square in Bloomsbury. The house survived until the days when Leonard himself lived in the square. The de Jonghs, in London, must always have been comfortably off.

The Woolfs came up the hard way. Leonard's father, Sidney, was the second youngest of the ten children of Benjamin Woolf and his wife Isabella (*nee* Phillips), both born in London in the first decade of the nineteenth century. Leonard's sister Bella understood that the family had started out in Spitalfields in London's East End, a tight little district of streets, alleys and courts,where the majority of London's poor Jews lodged, earning their livings in small workshops and warehouses, and marrying one another's cousins and in-laws. Nearby is the oldest surviving synagogue in London, Bevis Marks, established in 1701 by the Sephardim community who had come from Spain and Portugal in Cromwell's time and still tended to see themselves as the elite.

It is impossible to establish family trees for families like Leonard's, long-established in Britain, though there are many Woolfs, spelled *sic*, on record. Official registration of Jewish births, marriages and deaths only started in 1837. Some retained Hebrew names, and some were born and died with no public record of their existence. It is estimated that there were around 10,000 Jews in Britain in the 1760s, mostly in London, with a steady influx of those fleeing the persecutions in Europe. By the time Leonard's Woolf grandparents were born, the community had increased threefold. The Jews themselves were alarmed by the impact of the increase. The authorities of the Great Synagogue stopped giving relief to Jewish immigrants who had left their countries 'without good cause'; and the British government offered free repatriation.

No one in Leonard's generation knew where the Woolfs came to England from, or when, though it was probably during this late eighteenth-century influx from Europe. These newly arrived Ashkenazim (from Germany, Holland and Poland) mostly worked in the informal economy of the old-clothes trade, and as peddlers. The Woolfs too worked in the clothing trade – the earliest on record are Benjamin Woolf, a tailor and draper in Soho from 1819, and David Woolf, a clothes dealer in the East End at the same period. Others, including many Benjamin Woolfs, were furniture brokers, or crockery dealers, or cheesemongers. Zadok Woolf, son of a Benjamin,[4] chose Samuel Phillips as a witness to his wedding in 1838. This, since witnesses were by custom either relatives or in-laws, suggests a family relationship between Grandfather Benjamin Woolf and Grandmother Isabella, née Phillips.

It was not until 1830 that Jews were allowed to operate regular businesses. Grandfather Benjamin Woolf moved out of the East End, and acquired a shop at 45 Old Bond Street. He later had a 'waterproof' business in Piccadilly, and by 1835 was living in the apartment above his tailoring premises at 87 The Quadrant, Regent Street, a high-class shopping street.

Sheltered by colonnades, the Quadrant extended on both sides of Regent Street between Piccadilly and Oxford Street.[5] The Woolfs, on the west side, had a chandelier-maker as one neighbour, and a tobacconist as the other. Benjamin and Isabella's first two sons – Israel John, and Maurice – died in infancy. Benjamin subsequently begat Samuel, Bloom, Sophia, David, Daniel, Sidney (Leonard's father) and Clara. Also Henry, who was either an afterthought or a by-blow; he appears in no family record other than in Benjamin's Will. Isabella's unmarried elder sister, Esther Phillips, lived with them. It must have been a terrible squash in the rooms over the shop.

Leonard's father, Sidney, was born on 16 June 1844. He was

---

4 There is a reason for all these Benjamin Woolfs. Many Ashkenazi Jews, required to produce an acceptable surname, often referred to in the community as a 'nickname', adopted animal words – Hart, Bear, Lyon – based on the blessings that the dying Jacob gave to his 12 sons (Genesis xlix). 'Benjamin shall ravin [*sic* for 'is as a ravening wolf in *The New English Bible*] as a wolf: in the morning he shall devour the prey, and at night he shall divide the spoil.'

5 Regent Street was redeveloped and the colonnades removed after World War I.

registered as Solomon Rees Sydney, but called himself Sidney, spelled *sic* – the name that he tacked on to the names of most of his own children, including Leonard's.

By 1861 the family were no longer living over the shop but were installed with three servants at 14 Bedford Square, Bloomsbury, and Benjamin was describing himself as 'Outfitter', a description soon to be replaced by 'Gentleman' in official documents. In the mid-1860s the Woolf family moved to 5 Clifton Gardens, Maida Vale, with four servants, and co-religionists with comfortably large families on both sides.[6]

Large oil portraits of these Woolf grandparents, who died before he was born, hung in the dining room of Leonard's childhood home. He remembered that of his grandfather as depicting 'a large, stern, black-haired, and black-whiskered rabbinical Jew in a frock coat, his left hand pompously tucked into his waistcoat'. Grandmother Isabella in contrast looked 'pretty, roundcheeked, mild, and forgiving.'

The Woolfs were tough. The legend in the family was that Grandfather Benjamin Woolf's mother, Leonard's great-grandmother – not that she born was a Woolf, we don't know who she was – 'used to walk to synagogue with hard peas in her boots in the evening of every Day of Atonement, and she stood upright on the peas in her place in the synagogue for twenty-four hours without sitting down until sunset of the following day, fasting of course the whole time'. Leonard confessed to a sneaking sympathy with her. He had, he said, no sense of sin, but approved of doing things thoroughly.

Three at least of Benjamin and Isabella's children, including Sidney, continued the shift into the middle class. Samuel ran his own tailoring business at the 45 Old Bond Street premises and then moved to Birmingham. Bloom married a stockbroker, Levi Cohen. Daniel married Sarah Myers and had two daughters and a son; but after Sarah died, Daniel got into financial trouble, emigrated with his son to the

6 Charles Dickens, the novelist's son, remarked in his *Dictionary of London* (1879) on the numbers of rich Jews who had taken up residence in Bloomsbury, Maida Vale, and Bayswater; and 'so plentiful are the Jews in the south-west district, that certain streets and terraces where they have formed colonies are playfully called "The New Jerusalem"'.

United States, broke off relations with his parents, and established a new family.[7]

Leonard's uncles Samuel and David Woolf were not fortunate either. Samuel's Birmingham business failed. He took his family to Nuremberg and became German. His widow Sarah (Davis) was interned during the Great War 'as she did not become a German' though her children did; her eldest son died in the Great War fighting for Germany. David, a solicitor, died young. His widow Louisa (Sarah's sister), left with four daughters, and pretty golden hair 'out of a bottle', antagonised the Woolfs by taking as her second husband a Gentile stockbroker, Arthur Tritton.

In Leonard's childhood home there were stacks of gloomy sepia photographs of all these uncles and aunts, printed on stiff cards. Leonard and his brothers and sisters used to play whist with them, the ugliest face taking the trick.

Sidney, Leonard's clever father, was educated at University College School, which he left at sixteen. He qualified as a solicitor at the age of twenty, and four years later left the City practice he shared with his brother David and studied in the Middle Temple for the Bar, to which he was called in 1873. 'Mr Woolf had not long to walk through the valley of brieflessness, but it was only by the most regular attendance in the Temple, by working as hard during the Long Vacation as during term-time, by bestowing unwearied industry upon his cases . . . that he acquired, some few years after his call, a practice that caused his name to be well-known in the profession.'[8] Thus Sidney, by determination, application, and with no social advantages, became successful.

He had the luck, only three years after he was called to the Bar, to be involved in a notorious trial. There was a mutiny aboard an English vessel, the *Lennie*, which was manned by a Greek crew. The mutineers murdered the captain and all his officers, and ordered the Belgian steward to sail towards Greece. Instead, he steered towards France. There

---

7 Daniel's two daughters were adopted by a solicitor friend called MacBeth who lived in Edinburgh, and their name was changed to Smith.

8 *The Law Gazette* 29 Jan 1892

the ringleaders disembarked, sporting their dead officers' uniforms, while the gallant Belgian boarded a British ship lying close by, and effected the arrest of the crew. The ringleaders were tried at the Old Bailey. Sidney Woolf undertook the defence of three Greeks, and got two of them off. The case was widely reported and brought his name before the public.

In 1890, when he was forty-five, Sidney Woolf became a Q.C.[9] Grandfather Benjamin Woolf 'educated his sons out of their class', wrote Leonard, though none of them did as well as Sidney. One at least – whom Leonard did not name, but it was probably Daniel – was 'an extremely brilliant and amusing scoundrel.'

Grandfather Benjamin Woolf was a religious Jew, but a progressive one. As the prosperous members of the community moved out of the East End, new synagogues were established. Benjamin Woolf and his sons had seats in the Western Synagogue, a liberal congregation even before the Reform movement of 1840. In 1851, when Benjamin Woolf was elected a Warden, and the synagogue was re-consecrated after renovations, the event was sufficiently newsworthy to be featured in the *Illustrated London News.* Benjamin held office for many years, and was zealous in his support of the Jewish Free School and of Jewish charities. When he died in 1870, he was praised in the congregation as 'a charitable man of upright character.'

Sidney Woolf, Leonard's father, is the only one of Benjamin's sons mentioned in the records as playing a part in the Western Synagogue's management. The Reform movement caused bitter schisms in the community, even as it sought to bridge the gulf between the Ashkenazi and Sephardic traditions. The Reform Synagogue was consecrated in 1842, after many disputes, as the 'West London Synagogue for British Jews' – an appellation illustrative of the members' desire to affiliate themselves with the national mainstream. It moved in 1870 to a purpose-built edifice at 34 Upper Berkeley Street, in smart Mayfair. Attendance at Upper Berkeley Street was not only a religious but a social and political

9 Queen's Counsel, the elite of the English Bar.

statement. The service was simplified, the music was good, and the leading families, both Sephardic and Ashkenazi, had seats there.

The first three-quarters of the nineteenth century were a propitious time for British Jews, though the improvements – contested at every point – only serve, in retrospect, to highlight the previous disadvantages, and the exclusion from national life which was the price of toleration. One by one, most of the 'disabilities' – the blocks to trading, professional status and participation in public life – were removed by law. In 1827 University College, London, opened as the first English university to admit students regardless of race or religion. In 1833 the first Jew was called to the Bar. In 1837 Benjamin Disraeli entered Parliament, eligible because he had been baptised a Christian; in 1868 he became Prime Minister. Baron Lionel de Rothschild was the first Jew to take a seat in the House of Commons without taking the statutory oath 'on the true faith of a Christian', in 1858. By that time there were around 35,000 Jews in Britain, the majority of them second generation and English-born.[10]

There was a Jewish middle class, much intermarried, in the professions and in business. This is where the Woolfs and de Jonghs fitted in. There was also a wealthy Jewish upper class which included Rothschilds, Montefiores, Goldsmids, Mocattas: the internationally-connected network of Anglo-Jewry known as 'the Cousinhood'. Leonard's family was to make a connection with the Cousinhood when his Aunt Bloom's granddaughter Dorothy (Dollie) Pinto[11] married James de Rothschild.

Being a 'British Jew' was important to the middle classes. Eminent Jews, in the pages of the *Jewish Chronicle*, were praised as great Englishmen, and the doings of the Royal Family were featured with loyal enthusiasm.[12] But assimilation was out of order. Grandfather Benjamin's Will was uncompromising. He left to his youngest daughter

---

10 Like my own great-great-grandparents William Martin Hertz and Fanny Halle.

11 Dollie's father Eugene Pinto was a Sephardic Jew who made enough money to send Dollie's brother Richard to Eton and into the Coldstream Guards, and to take for six years a lease on 1 Carlton Gardens, now the official residence of the British Foreign Secretary.

12 See David Cesarani, *The Jewish Chronicle and Anglo-Jewry 1841–1991* CUP 1994

Clara £1000 for her marriage, plus £200 for a wedding outfit, provided she married 'a person of the Jewish faith'. (Clara took no risks. It was in the year after her father's death that she married Benjamin de Jongh.) Benjamin also set up strict conditions for access to the inheritance of two of his sons, Henry and – in a codicil – Daniel. Sidney, unmarried at the time, was not mentioned in the Will at all, probably because he gave no cause for concern.

Sidney, Leonard's father, remained in the fold through his marriage to Marie (de Jongh) Goldstücker. But after his father died, he transferred his allegiance to the fashionable Reform Synagogue at Upper Berkeley Street. The de Jongh influence may have been a factor; Sidney's sister Clara and Benjamin de Jongh had been married at the Upper Berkeley Street synagogue. Sidney's membership was more than nominal; he became a Warden – a lay official assisting the rabbi with administration – in 1880, the year Leonard was born. The social and professional confidence of British Jews was at its zenith.

Then the demographics changed. In 1881 there was an outbreak of persecution of Jews in Russia and Eastern Europe, which continued until the fall of the last Czar. In one generation, a quarter of a million Jews fled or were displaced.

In London alone, between 1883 and 1905 – when the first Aliens Immigration Act stemmed the free flow – the Jewish population increased to around 150,000. Colonising and expanding the traditional East End districts, earning their livings as old-clothes dealers and tailors like the immigrants of a century before, they had the critical mass to sustain their way of life and their common language, Yiddish. George Eliot's novel *Daniel Deronda*, informed by her romantic perception of Oriental Jews and the aspirations of Zionism, was published in 1876. It was the exodus of Jews from Russia and other points east which gave weight to those nascent aspirations. 'If the Jews of Russia had not existed, neither the case for, nor the possibility of realising, Zionism could have arisen in any serious form.'[13] Many established middle-class

13 Isaiah Berlin in 'Chaim Weizmann', *Collected Impressions* Hogarth Press 1980

Jews were not happy about the conspicuous influx of 'foreign Jews', and made haste to become naturalised British, as Leonard's ageing de Jongh grandparents did in 1889.

A novel called *Reuben Sachs* by a spirited young woman, Amy Levy, published in London in 1888,[14] describes a family in Maida Vale very like the Woolfs. The novel stressed how eager middle-class Jewish people were to 'claim the successful among their number', and the 'scant love' they had for the unfortunate ones. The 'modern' members of this fictional family, like Leonard's family, attended the synagogue in Upper Berkeley Street. 'In the Community, with its innumerable trivial class differences, its sets within sets, its fine-drawn distinctions of caste, utterly incomprehensible to an outsider', the Sachs family 'held a good, but not the best, position.' The women shop at Whiteley's department store in Queensway, a socially neutral zone where 'Bayswater nodded to Maida Vale, and South Kensington took Bayswater by the hand . . .'

Lexham Gardens, the home of Sidney and Marie Woolf, was not in the smart part of Kensington. That was nearer Knightsbridge, in the eighteenth-century streets and squares opposite Kensington Palace and Kensington Gardens – with more recent and grandiose houses in streets close by such as Hyde Park Gate, where Leslie Stephen, man of letters and founding editor of *The Dictionary of National Biography*, was living at number 22. The two young daughters of his second marriage were named Vanessa and Virginia. Sidney Lee, a Jewish professor of English at East London College[15] and Leslie Stephen's collaborator and successor on the monumental *DNB*, lived near the Woolfs in Lexham Gardens. (The geographical distance between Hyde Park Gate and Lexham Gardens is about a kilometre.) Leonard as a child thought Lee was 'a bit stuffy'. Next door to the Woolfs at number 103 Lexham Gardens lived Sir John Strachey, finance minister to successive viceroys of India. Sir John was the uncle of a boy eight months younger than Leonard called Lytton Strachey, living with his large family not far away in Lancaster

14 Reissued by Persephone Books in 2001 with an introduction by Julia Neuberger.

15 Later Queen Mary College. Both Leslie Stephen and Sidney Lee were subsequently knighted.

Gate, north of Kensington Gardens. Leonard's Uncle David and Aunt Louisa had lived in Lancaster Gate, but the Woolfs did not know the Stracheys, any more than they knew the Stephens. Their social circles did not intersect.

Lexham Gardens is off Earls Court Road, which is off the far end of Kensington High Street. It is the last turning before Earl's Court Road crosses busy Cromwell Road and plunges south into the less genteel animation of Earls Court itself. Leonard was born at 72 West Cromwell Road, just round the corner. Lexham Gardens and the surrounding streets were still being built; his parents were buying into a brand-new development.

Their new house, 101 Lexham Gardens, was on the south side, a big stucco terraced house with steps up to a pillared front door, near the corner with Earls Court Road. It was made even bigger by a flat-roofed, single-storey addition which the Woolfs built on to the back of the house, used for children's parties and dancing classes.

Children's parties and dancing classes were the kind of thing that Marie Woolf liked. She was an energetic and hospitable mother. After the dancing classes, with all the mothers looking on, everyone was ushered by Mrs Woolf into the big dining room 'for a wonderful tea of cakes and all good things', remembered into extreme old age by a little girl called Hilda. Mrs Woolf, short and plump, was the sort of woman who is adored. Even the most distant or difficult of the relations wanted to keep in touch with her. Leonard's cousin Sybil, daughter of Uncle David and Aunt Louisa Woolf, wrote to tell Leonard: 'I was very fond of your Mother . . . She was such a Personality'. When Sibyl's widowed mother married Arthur Tritton and cut herself off from the family, 'all us girls kept up with your Mother which [*sic*] we were all very fond of.'

Leonard's best and fullest account of the Lexham Gardens household is not in his autobiography, but in *Principia Politica* (1953). He presented it as an example of a typical, well-to-do, late Victorian way of life, underpinned by an unquestioned social hierarchy and set of values.

The household, when he was nine or ten, consisted of his parents, the nine children, a governess (Miss Amy), a nurse and under-nurse, a footman, a cook with attendant scullery maid, a parlourmaid, two or three housemaids, a dog, a cat, several canaries, two white rats, and a fluctuating population of piebald mice. The coachman, and a horse and two carriages – a brougham and a victoria – were housed in the mews round the corner. Mr Woolf was driven to the Temple every morning and collected in the evening, and Mrs Woolf was taken shopping and for drives in Hyde Park. A tutor came in to instruct the little boys. Three times a week Fraulein Berger came to teach them French and German; a German countess taught Bella to play the piano. 'I have a dim recollection of some of us being taught "elocution"', and for a period the boys had carpentry classes on a bench set up in the basement. There was a man to clean the boots. Mr Tomkins came every morning to shave Mr Woolf in his dressing room. Mr Davies came every Friday to wind and regulate the clocks. Since in *Principia Politica* Leonard was describing a typical well-to-do English household, he did not include the fact that the Woolf children were also, rather ineffectively, taught Hebrew.

If he had analysed the situation, Leonard would have said that he, like his father, was 'a gentleman', and 'that there were a large number of people, including servants and unemployed and plumbers and carpenters, who were not. Gentlemen were superior . . .'

Mr Woolf was a gentleman in character, he lived in the style of a gentleman, he had the professional status of a gentleman. In the microcosm of 101 Lexham Gardens it was not admitted to consciousness that the phrase 'a Jewish gentleman' was, like the phrase 'an Oriental gentleman', for many conservative English gentlemen at best ironic, and at worst an oxymoron. For sure, the Woolfs had been English – always, in any case, a mongrel race – for more than a hundred years. But their acceptability was hardly tested. Though Leonard's parents were acquainted with many Gentiles, they had few close friends among them.

In *Reuben Sachs* the grown-ups do not disapprove of their young adult sons mixing with Gentiles. (Girls were less adventurous and more protected.) They never imagine it might lead to the disaster of their 'marrying out'. What the novel demonstrates is the new self-consciousness, anxiety and self-questioning of young Jewish men as they moved halfway out of the cocoon of the community. Leonard was only eight when this novel was published. He and his brothers and sisters, as young adults, were to move out of the cocoon definitively, and get some benefits – even as they felt, and denied or ignored, the chill.

Leonard, in a later account of the household in *Sowing*, did not endorse the rigid hierarchical structure that underpinned 101 Lexham Gardens: 'it is because I condemn its economic basis and its economic effect upon other classes that I have been a socialist for most of my life.' He perceived the 'snugness and smugness, snobbery, its complacent exploitation of economic, sexual and racial classes'. Nevertheless, 'the actual relations between the human beings living in these large households . . . were, on the whole, in my remembrance extraordinarily human and humane.'

This is borne out by the evidence. Leonard, who kept everything, preserved 'The Leonard Paper', a family newspaper he produced at the age of eight. Here is the issue for 4 August 1889:

MAMA
At the begining of the day Mrs Woolf had a bad head ack.
Sad dis-appointment
In the Woolfs den
A gentleman was expected to dinner but did not come.

He was writing letters, in capitals, when he was four or five, to his brothers and sisters and parents when they were away. He signs himself sometimes 'Lennie', sometimes 'Leonard', and is always demonstratively and confidently affectionate: 'My darling Papa', 'My darling Parents', 'My darling Mother', and ending with 'lots of love and kisses', 'many many kisses' 'xxxxxxx'. Maybe the children were not all as blithe as Leonard. His elder brother Herbert wrote to his parents, when he was six: 'I am a good boy and don't want any cold water.' Harold too was always assuring them that he was 'a good boy'.

Leonard never referred to his goodness or badness. He said he had an acute sense of disgrace, but no sense of sin. He credited his father's personal ethos for this. Sidney Woolf told his children that a complete rule of conduct for a man's life had been laid down definitively by the prophet Micah: 'What doth the Lord require of thee, but to do justly, and to love mercy, and to walk humbly with thy God?'[16]

Leonard had a strong sense of evil, and black epiphanies. The first was when he rushed excitedly out into the small back garden on the family's return from a summer holiday. He loved the garden, and had his own small patch of sooty border, to sow and grow flowers.

The autumnal garden was bounded by walls draped in grimy ivy, and the ivy was covered in spiders' webs. In the centre of each web was a spider. The little boy looked at the spiders, smelled the sour earth and the ivy 'and suddenly my whole mind and body seemed to be overwhelmed in melancholy'. He was experiencing for the first time 'cosmic unhappiness', without knowing what it was.

He knew disgust and terror too, evoked by glimpses of the chaos, violence and poverty beyond the security of the home world: the ragged, cursing, drunken man who tried to 'help' with the family's luggage, before being frog-marched away by a policeman; or, on a walk with his nurse, seeing a 'raging and raving woman' being dragged along by policemen, her hat rolling into the gutter; the shrieks of a demented woman passing along the Cromwell Road behind their house in the night, heard from his bed. Stories of Jack the Ripper, and of a little old woman in black who on foggy nights stabbed Kensington gentlemen with a long knife, penetrated the children's world.

The parents wrote home every day when they were away, and sent flowers and sweets, and left little notes and gifts for the nurse to put under the children's pillows. Leonard told 'My darling Papa' in May 1890, when he was nine, the news of the day: a cat got into the garden under the wire; an overloaded four-wheeler lost its load turning into Kensington High Street, 'a very funny sight'; and a butterfly settled on the grass in the garden and was pounced on by a sparrow 'who took it away leaving one wing on the grass'. There are frequent assurances that 'all the birds and animals are all right'.

---

16 The Book of Micah Chapter 6. 8

That summer the children went on holiday to Whitby in Yorkshire with their mother and Miss Amy, their governess, staying at West Cliff Villa. Papa was not there because he was ill. Papa was often ill, which was why he and Mother went away to south coast resorts so frequently.

In Whitby Leonard had another experience of despair. Just after their arrival he was supremely happy, watching two large newts basking in the sun on the rampart above the sparkling sea. Suddenly afraid, he looked up and saw a big black cloud blotting out the sun. It was in itself frightening; and it elicited again 'that sense of profound, passive, cosmic despair, the melancholy of a human being, eager for happiness and beauty, powerless in the face of a hostile universe.'

There is a bunch of his letters from March 1891, when the parents, with Bella, were in Torquay. While they were away, the de Jongh grandparents took the remaining children to synagogue where there was, according to ten-year-old Leonard, 'a beautiful sermon'. Aunt Bloom came round, and brought 'a nice cake for tea'. Leonard enclosed a piece of Easter egg in one of his letters, 'I hope it won't get squashed by the time it gets to you.' They were going to the Bethnal Green Museum with their tutor, Mr Floyd. They had been to the Indian Museum with Miss Berger. And, over and over: 'I hope Papa is better.'

The children's nurse was Mary Vickary,[17] from a farm family in Somerset, and she was central to Leonard's security and comfort. She brought up all the nine children. (There was always a young nursemaid to help her, and a temporary 'monthly nurse' to care for the new-borns.) She had little education, but lots of imagination. She was a Christian — a strict Baptist – and Leonard shared her entranced reading about the iniquities of the great world in the *Baptist Times.* Similar thrills were provided by her other reading-matter, which was, quite fortuitously, de Quincey's *Confessions of an English Opium Eater*, which she read aloud with difficulty and some mispronunciations in her warm West Country accent. Leonard wrote in old age: 'I can still feel myself physically enfolded in the warmth and safety of the great nursery on the third floor of the house in Lexham Gardens, the fire blazing behind the tall guard,

17 Not 'Vicary', as Leonard has it in *Sowing.*

the kettle singing away, and nurse, with her straight black hair parted in the centre, and her smooth, oval peasant face, reading *The Baptist Times* or the visions of the opium eater.'

Leonard read extracts from *Sowing* on BBC radio in the year before publication, which Bella heard. 'By the way there were many inaccuracies in that broadcast such as the date of our Father's birth.' She thought most of it was excellent: 'I only cavil at your saying Nurse had a "peasant face". You have forgotten her. She had a very aquiline profile – very beautiful in her day.'

Leonard did not change the passage about Nurse Vickary in his book, and no matter how faulty his grasp of historical truth, the emotional truth remains. The curtains would be drawn across the nursery windows, and all they heard was the clip-clop of horses drawing vehicles in the street outside. 'The nursery remains for me the Platonic idea laid up in heaven of security and peace and civilisation.' The nursery world represented the antithesis to the spiders in the garden, the raving, degraded street women, and the ominous mob of the unemployed whom he saw shambling along muddy Kensington High Street in the November fog to a rally in Trafalgar Square, when he was seven. 'Those long lines of marching men, drab and dingy but lowering and grim . . . came into my life from another, unknown world . . .'[18] The nurses hurried the Woolf children away home. There was a note of anxiety in the talk of his parents and their friends.

Leaving the nursery – still occupied by Harold, Edgar, Clara, Flora, Cecil and Philip – Leonard moved into the schoolroom. The first teaching he ever had, at the age of five, was in the kindergarten of the small private girls' school which Bella attended in Trebovir Road, south of the Cromwell Road in a 'wasteland of Victorian middle-class dreariness'. The headmistress, Mrs Cole, was a short dumpy woman in a black bonnet, possessed of terrific energy. All he learnt there was to take an interest in small girls. In class, under the table, he held the hand of a yellow-haired one, and in the hall he kissed a black-haired one.

18 *Principia Politica*

The kiss caused 'an open scandal' and Leonard was removed. He resumed lessons at home, with his elder brother Herbert and the tutor, Mr Floyd.

Mr Floyd was so weird-looking that street-boys used to hoot at him when Herbert and Leonard met him at Kensington High Street underground station after breakfast each weekday morning. Leonard's tame canary, Johnnie, liked to perch on Mr Floyd's head during lessons; Mr Floyd wiped away Johnnie's messes with blotting-paper. Mr Floyd believed in a spell of silence before beginning on the Latin and arithmetic, and wrote 'TACE' (Latin for 'Be silent') in a tiny notebook of Leonard's. He also wrote 'something in Hebrew, which is odd, because I am sure he was not a Jew'. That teasing 'something in Hebrew' which Leonard could never read means 'A fool cannot understand this.'[19]

Like most Jewish families, the Woolfs and the de Jonghs had relations scattered over the world. There were de Jongh cousins in Costa Rica, who came to stay when Leonard was about ten, and whose father subsequently sent each of the Woolf children a gold sovereign at Christmas. (The Woolfs celebrated both Jewish and Christian festivals, without prejudice.) A cousin, Florence Abrahamson of the Scandinavian branch, reminisced about what a relief it had been, when staying with the de Jongh grandparents, 'to escape from the tedium of Addison Gardens into the cheery, cosy atmosphere of Lexham Gardens. Of course, I loved your mother, but I was afraid of your father.' Hilda, the little girl who enjoyed the teas, remembered Bella taking her upstairs to 'a large and very dark library' to meet Mr Woolf. 'He was sitting in a large armchair and looked ill and tired, but he patted me on the head and hoped that I had done well in the dancing lessons.'

During the week, 101 Lexham Gardens was a matriarchal universe. Marie Woolf liked jokes and she was nice-looking, 'we all liked to see her let down her hair, for it reached well below her knees and was

---

19 Book of Psalms Chapter 92.7

extraordinarily thick'. The best time of day for the children was between tea and Father's return from the Temple, when they played with her in the library.

They saw little of their father. It was fun to be with him, because it was a rare treat, and because he was an exciting father, quick-minded and full of energy. Leonard treasured the memory of the time when he, alone of the family, stayed up in London for a night when the rest had started out for the annual summer holiday. He was six, and felt 'terribly proud and important' driving to the Temple with his father, and sitting near him in court while a case was being tried. The opposing counsels – with Leonard – went off and lunched together at the Rainbow Tavern, and Leonard was astonished to find them the best of friends when they had been arguing so heatedly in court. That evening, he dined alone with his father, having received a playfully formal invitation: 'Mr Sidney Woolf requests the pleasure of Master Leonard Sidney Woolf's company to dinner this evening, at 7.30.' For the first time he felt close to his father 'in a grown-up way.'

Leonard inherited his slight physique and modest stature from his father, and was not a robust child. He had scarlet fever and pneumonia when he was three; the Queen's doctor, Sir William Jenner, was called in. (As a reward for taking his medicine, Leonard was offered by Sir William anything he would like. 'I should like to pull your nose', said Leonard.) What he lacked in height and weight, he made up for in determination. On his seventh or eighth birthday he was given a tricycle. He, Herbert and their father, all of them on tricycles, one large and two small, set out on a ride together to Richmond Park. It was a long way for a small boy, and Leonard's tricycle had something wrong with it. He had to work doubly hard just to get the wheels to go round at all. Instead of fun, it was agony. He said no word of complaint to his father, but was so distressed and exhausted when they got home that he collapsed in the hall and had to be put straight to bed.

'I presume that like every other male, I was in love with my mother and hated my father' – but he found no residual trace in himself either of the 'in love' feeling for his mother, nor of hate for his father. 'I admired him greatly and certainly thought I was fond of him, and I think that he was both fond and proud of me, because as a small boy I was intelligent, reserved, and had a violent temper, and so in fact resembled him.'

Leonard all his life suffered from a tremor in his hands, which grew more pronounced when he was nervous. It may have been a type of inherited early-onset dystonia (classified today as DYTI), which mainly, but not only, affects Ashkenazi Jews. He said that his father had it: 'I remember how, as a small child, I noticed that, when he sat in the library reading *The Times* after breakfast, the paper and his hands perpetually trembled a little.' The curious thing is that the generation after Leonard's remembered their Grandmother Woolf as having the tremor, and spraying tea all over the tray as she filled the tea-cups.

Either both Leonard's parents had the tremor, or his mother developed one in the process of ageing, or Leonard preferred to inherit his tremor from his father, feeling as he did so much more his father's son than his mother's. A letter from Mr Woolf to 'My darling little Leonard', when Leonard was seven, suggests great mutual affection: 'I was delighted with your letter and sketch of the dovecote, and thank you very much for them also for the pansy.' Mr Woolf was in Hove to watch a county cricket match, and told Leonard how he had seen the great W.G.Grace go out 'with the large score of 215 [runs]'; 'I send you today's Card which may please you. Give my best love to your darling Mother, Herbert, and your dear little brothers and sisters, and accept a hearty embrace from, Your fond father Sidney Woolf.'

Mr Woolf was tolerant intellectually, but temperamentally irascible, and enraged by stupidity. On Sundays, the atmosphere shifted from matriarchal to patriarchal. Sunday lunch, in true British fashion, was a ritual event. By the late 1880s all the children except the three youngest sat round the table. A cousin called Bennie, who lived alone, had a standing invitation. 'The Jew', to quote *Reuben Sachs*, 'is morbidly sensitive as regards the social standing of the compatriot whom he admits to his hospitality.' It was not Bennie's social status that was the problem so much as his self-presentation, and his stupidity. Leonard recalled him, three-quarters of a century later, with an undiminished vehemence which reflected his father's: 'He was almost, to look at, the comic Jew of the caricature, and he was that curious, but not very uncommon, phenomenon, the silly Jew who seems deliberately to exaggerate and exploit his silliness. He was the Jew so accurately described by one of the Marx brothers: "He looks like a fool and talks like a fool, but don't let him deceive you – he is a fool."'[20]

Bennie never failed to produce, and to insist upon sustaining, some inane generalisation which drove his Uncle Sidney completely wild and brought a torrent of vocal exasperation down on his innocent head. 'I can still see the scene, all of us children sitting round the Sunday lunch table, the great sirloin appearing from under the enormous silver cover, my father with his serious, sensitive face with his carving knife poised over the sirloin as he quoted the prophet Micah, and the rather surprised and sheepish face of my cousin Bennie who was not wont to walk or talk humbly with his God or anyone else.'[21]

The picture of Leonard's first eleven years is of a rich, argumentative, noisy, loving, fully occupied and happy childhood, packed with lessons, pets, walks, visits, excursions, parties, and regular summer holidays, enlivened by constant contact with the extended family.

Leonard already had a deep feeling for birds, beasts and flowers. He had an acute and complex perception of the opposite sex – whether as comfort, or as allure, or as nightmare. His sense of security was shaken by glimpses of the ugliness, violence and poverty outside the home world. He was to hate and fear drunkenness all his life, and the threat posed by any gross disturbance, disorder and loss of control. He was a sensitive boy, 'eager for happiness and beauty', assailed by moments of black melancholy and terror. The significant bad moments he records all have to do with the blighting of expectations: running out into the home garden after absence; the first moments of a longed-for seaside holiday; the new tricycle.

The family's expectations were blighted definitively. Sidney Woolf had always overworked, and had poor health. In its issue of 29 January 1892, *The Law Gazette* published, with a full-page photograph, a

---

20 *Sowing*
21 LW *The Journey Not the Arrival Matters* Hogarth Press 1969

flattering biographical sketch of 'Mr Sidney Woolf, Q.C.' in their series 'Our Portrait Gallery', with the evident purpose of highlighting his next career move. He was a candidate for the post of Recorder of London,[22] and the anonymous author of the article included a quotation from his address to the aldermen: 'I have not, up to the present time, sought a seat in Parliament, but if, in your opinion, the interests of the Corporation are best served by the Recorder being a member of the House of Commons, I should be willing, when an opportunity offers, to seek election to that position.'

Sidney Woolf never became Recorder of London or a Member of Parliament. He must have known how ill he was. He signed his Will on 10 January 1892, shortly before the appearance of the article in *The Law Gazette.* On 12 March 1892 he died, at home. He was forty-seven. The death certificate gave as the cause of death, 'Tubercular disease of both Lungs chronic 2 years. Sudden infiltration of tubercles in both Lungs with great Dyspnoea [breathlessness] & extreme heart weakness 6 days.' He was buried in what Leonard called the 'grim and grimy' cemetery in the Balls Pond Road, which served the Berkeley Street synagogue, and the quotation from the prophet Micah was engraved on his tombstone: 'What doth the Lord require of thee, but to do justly, and to love mercy, and to walk humbly with thy God?'

Sidney Woolf earned around £5000 a year at the Bar, and his income died with him. The gross value of his estate was £6,120. 16s. 1d. The house in Lexham Gardens was held on a lease, not owned. For Leonard, who was eleven, and for his whole family, the world changed overnight.

---

22 The Recorder of a city or borough is a senior legal figure who 'records' or keeps an eye on the proceedings of the courts

2

Ten Thousand Hours

Marie Woolf's first husband, Albert Goldstücker, had left her provided for, but when she married Sidney Woolf her inheritance had reverted to her nephew and niece Charlotte and Martin Abrahamson, who 'did what few people do', as Bella later said, and renounced the capital and its income in her favour. Mrs Woolf hung on at Lexham Gardens for two years, then moved with her children – and a cook, parlourmaid and housemaid – south of the Thames and further west, to the outer suburbs: 9 Colinette Road, off the Upper Richmond Road in Putney. She named the house Lexham, after their lost home, and it was always Lexham, with no mention of '9', on their headed writing paper.[1]

Lexham was smaller than their old home, but capacious – a gravel sweep, a pointed porch, three floors over a basement. All the houses on Colinette Road, built in the 1870s, are detached, with little variation between them except that they were built alternately in red and in yellow brick. The Woolfs' was a yellow one. Marie Woolf found a new best friend at Number 3, in Emma Ross, a fellow widow with three daughters.

---

1 101 Lexham Gardens became a boarding-house after the Woolfs left, and then a hotel. Until in 2004 it was converted into flats, the Woolfs' stark, cube-like back extension remained as it was.

Putney had a celebrity resident. Leonard was having his hair cut in the barber's shop down by the station when in at the door came 'a tiny little man in a black cape and a black sombrero-like hat, below which hung lank curls'. There was 'fear and pain' in his pale blue eyes as he rushed straight out again. The barber told Leonard this was 'Mr Swinburne, the writer', who lived round the corner at The Pines on Putney Hill, with his friend and keeper Theodore Watts-Dunton. Later Leonard and his friends, in their Cambridge days, were to glut themselves on Swinburne's luscious poetical productions, and declaim them at midnight as they strolled back to their rooms across Trinity Great Court:

> Thou hast conquered, O pale Galilean; the world has grown grey from thy breath;/We have drunk on things Lethean, and fed on the fullness of death.

Herbert had started at Arlington House, a boarding preparatory school in Kemptown, a suburb of Brighton, the year before Mr Woolf died. Robert Burman, the headmaster, insisted that Herbert should stay on, and that Leonard should join him, at reduced fees. He was equally generous in taking on Harold, Edgar, Cecil and Philip in their turn.

For Leonard, the most important person at Arlington House was the games master Mr Woolley. 'His attitude to cricket was that of an artist to his art.' Leonard learned the importance of style. He remained small for his age, and slight, and highly competitive. He played, during his long life, virtually every kind of game from contact sports to draughts, and was incapable of taking even the silliest game lightly. At Arlington House he was saved, by his quick temper and by being good at games, from unpopularity as a 'swot'; for to be intelligent and to take lessons seriously was considered despicable.

He was told the facts of sex by a boy who had probably 'the dirtiest mind in an extraordinarily dirty-minded school'. When Leonard's elder brother Herbert became captain of the school he refused to allow practices which had previously been tolerated. Leonard, who succeeded Herbert as school captain, followed his example and, 'as we were both strict disciplinarians', when he left in 1894 'the atmosphere had changed from that of a sordid brothel to that more appropriate to fifty fairly happy small boys under the age of fifteen.'

Leonard was 'half-awake' at this school, his mind insufficiently engaged, as if he were existing in some dreamy, underwater state, always feeling he was about to wake up. He associated this sensation, in *Growing,* with his entranced reading of Jules Verne's *Twenty Thousand Leagues Under the Sea* by the light of gas-jets in the warm school library on Sunday afternoons. He did not discuss in *Sowing* the extent to which he was grieving for his father. Nowhere, in all his voluminous archive, is there any reference to how much he suffered from this loss. There was more dysfunction in the Woolf family than was apparent in their early childhood, and it is probable that depression was a component of their father's ill-health. There was depression in the de Jongh family too. Leonard's 'half-awake' state had a depressive component.

It is impossible to overstress the importance of bicycles. Leonard's boyhood coincided with the last years of an idyllic period, after the development of the rail network, before the coming of the motor car, when suburban roads were quiet and safe, when suburban sprawl did not reach out so far, and the silent countryside was accessible from the cities. Bicycles provided a freedom unknown to all previous and subsequent generations of adolescents. Before they left Lexham Gardens, Herbert had his first two-wheeler – which Leonard, on his first attempt to ride, comprehensively smashed up. Later they became experts, saving up to buy the desired models. 'I got exquisite pleasure from a cycle with handlebars like ram's horns and yellow rims to the wheels.'[2] Leonard won a scholarship to St Paul's School, and bicycled the three miles from Putney in term-time.

St Paul's School is what in England is called for historical reasons a public school – which means a private, fee-paying school. Its significant history dates from 1509. Samuel Pepys was a pupil, as were the first Duke of Marlborough (as John Churchill), and the astronomer Edmund

2 LW in John Lehmann (ed), *Coming to London* Phoenix House 1957

Halley. The school became one of the 'great schools' of England, in the same category as Eton, Winchester, Harrow and Westminster, when in 1884 it moved from the purlieus of St Paul's Cathedral to a building designed by Alfred Waterhouse, architect of the Natural History Museum, on a sixteen-acre site on Hammersmith Road.

Under the High Master, Frederick William Walker, who masterminded this change from charitable City institution to major public school, numbers grew rapidly, turning out a supply of young gentlemen with the confidence and leadership qualities to take high positions in the Church, the Army, Government and Empire. In Walker's day – and Walker was still High Master when Leonard was there – St Paul's also began to admit non-Christians, the majority of whom were Jews.

Just as in families, boys at the same school at the same time remember different things, and the same things differently. It is not from Leonard's autobiography that one learns that the school uniform – an Eton jacket for the younger boys; and a Sunday top hat, a straw hat for summer, and a school cap; a bowler hat instead of the cap, once you turned sixteen – was bought from Barker's department store on Kensington High Street; nor that this gear was laughed at by common boys on the streets; nor that you wore a silver fish on your watch-chain if you were a Foundation Scholar, as Leonard was; nor that the school was divided up into 'clubs', unimaginatively named A,B,C,D,E and F. Leonard did not even bother to record which he belonged to. One learns these things and more from the novelist Compton Mackenzie, who started at St Paul's in the same year as Leonard. Like Leonard, he was to write a multi-volume autobiography. In his second volume[3] – or 'octave', as he called it, because there were eight – he gave his account of the school.

The publisher Victor Gollancz was also at St Paul's, a decade later. From him one learns more than one needs to know about the sordid, stinking lavatories. Gollancz also recorded that when morning and evening prayers were held, the Jewish boys met in the art room for their own prayers, and that there were games on Saturday mornings

---

3 *My Life and Times* Octave 2 1891–1900 Chatto & Windus 1963

in which Gollancz, coming from an Orthodox family, could not take part.[4] Leonard, coming from the Reform tradition, did not have this problem.

Leonard, recalling St Paul's, wrote almost entirely about his educational experience, 'Spartan in its intellectual toughness and severity'. In their first term, scholarship boys were called 'the Special', properly the 'Class under Special Tuition'. Leonard and the other twenty-eight boys in the Special studied Greek and Latin composition, both prose and poetry. 'We did absolutely nothing else.' The ancient languages became part of the 'permanent furniture' of Leonard's mind. The Special worked in the Hall, under Mr Pantin, author of an *Introduction to Latin Elegiacs*, 'a kindly but melancholy master' (with a perpetual cold in the head, according to Compton Mackenzie).

Mr Walker the High Master, the 'Old Man', would erupt into the Hall and flop down on a bench beside one of the boys to inspect his work, growling and grumbling as he assessed his intellectual capacity and the likelihood of his winning a scholarship, or at least an exhibition, to Balliol College, Oxford, or Trinity College, Cambridge. This is how he judged the success of his school; and it was successful.

Leonard described the Old Man as short and solid, 'with a red face, rather bloodshot eyes, a straggly beard, a very wide mouth showing black teeth'. His voice was a raucous bellow. Compton Mackenzie's description was similar: the Old Man was 'the personification of majesty, dominion, ferocity and awe. He seemed [to a small boy] huge of build, with a long grey beard to which adhered stale morsels of food and the acrid scent of strong cigars'. He glared, and he was deaf.

One day he plonked himself down on the bench in the Hall beside Leonard and looked at him 'with a terrifying leer which revealed a satyr's mouth full of black and decaying teeth'. He corrected Leonard's work and then roared at him, in high good humour: 'Boy, your mother has been to see me. Your mother did not like me.' Mrs Woolf, true to form, had called on the High Master to discuss her son's brilliant

4 Ruth Dudley Edwards, *Victor Gollancz* Gollancz 1987

future. She was hectored for ten minutes to the effect that her son had been badly taught, and it was doubtful whether anything could be done with him. 'But Mr Walker, what can I do?' '*Do*, Mrs Woolf? *Do?* You have done enough.' And he opened the door for Mrs Woolf to leave.

After the intensive term in the Special, scholarship boys were drafted back into the mainstream. Leonard took mathematics, French, Divinity and English, though nothing was considered really important except Latin and Greek. Leonard's translations of English poetry into Latin or Greek, or both, were often marked 'Good', or 'Very good', with some sharp comments: 'Do try to put in more words. You cut it down so.' 'Wants more style and vigour.' 'The writing too small and cramped.' But, of a translation of Byron's 'She walks in beauty like the night . . .': 'Your verses are distinctly good, they run well, and read like poetry and [like] Latin. Your chief fault is a tendency to obscurity.'

In his form list at the end of summer 1895 he was ranked just above the halfway mark. A year later, he was third out of eighteen; in 1898, second out of eleven. In his last summer, he had sunk to tenth out of fourteen.

When Leonard was sixteen, he came under the influence of a sympathetic teacher, A.M.Cook. Compton Mackenzie portrayed him as 'Mr Cray' in the first volume (1913) of his successful novel *Sinister Street*: he had his 'favourites and sycophants', to whom he was 'benignity incarnate, purring over his cubs and looking not unlike a mangy old lioness.' Leonard and he used to walk around together, discussing books and life, during the fifteen-minute morning break. Mr Cook talked to Leonard as an equal, and encouraged him to read. Leonard kept a notebook with lists of Mr Cook's recommended authors – Borrow, Montaigne, Sterne – and a few significant quotations: one from Ibsen's *Ghosts*, for example, about 'dead ideas, and lifeless old beliefs' which have no vitality 'but cling to us all the same.' And from Tolstoy's *Resurrection*: 'The animalism of the brute nature in man is disgusting', but when the animalism 'hides under a cloak of poetry and aesthetic feeling and demands our worship – then we are swallowed up by it completely and worship animalism, no longer distinguishing good from evil, then it is awful.'[5]

Mr Cook gave him a prize of Bacon's *Essays* bound in pale blue leather tooled with gold, with an inscription to 'L.S.Woolf, first in written work'. Another quotation in the notebook is from Meredith's *The Tragic Comedians:* 'You meet now and then men who have the woman in them without being womanized; they are the pick of men.' Mr Cook was like that, and if there was a tinge of homoeroticism it did Leonard no harm. Leonard was sexually ignorant. No one, since the 'dirty-minded' little boy at Arlington House, had ever told him anything, and 'no relation or teacher, indeed no adult, ever mentioned the subject of sex to me'. Victorian middle-class boys like himself were 'just left to drift', while, as he grew older, he was continually 'harassed, persecuted and plagued, sometimes one might even say tormented and tortured, by the nagging of sexual curiosity and desire.'

An essay Leonard wrote for Mr Cook was entitled 'Individuality': 'If there be no individuality there can be no great man (for after all a great man is only one who gives his individuality full rein, who allows himself to be different from his fellowmen).' Leonard felt himself to be different from his schoolfellows, and wanted to be. Long afterwards, he wrote in *After the Deluge* (1931) that boys at school were compelled to be 'animated with the right feeling of esprit de corps, a feeling which belongs to the psychology of the herd . . . In such a system there is no place or tolerance for individuality or the consciousness of individuality.'

He wrote a lively essay on 'Political Agitation' which was marked alpha, and his 'Monarchy' won the school's Truro Essay Prize[6] in 1898 (£20 – a fortune – and a gold medal, which he later sold for £15). His conclusion about monarchy was that Britain should dispense with it when, and only when, the population was 'raised high enough' not to need magical thinking and a model 'bathed in mystery'. It sounds as if Mr Cook had set him to read critically Walter Bagehot's *The English Constitution* (1867), in which it is stated: 'Our royalty is to be

5 These two quotations contain the germ of Leonard Woolf's psycho-political philosophy in adult life.

6 Leonard in *Sowing* misremembered it as the Eldon Essay Prize.

reverenced . . . Its mystery is its life. We must not let in daylight upon magic.'

Compton Mackenzie recalled walking with Leonard across the school yard on a summer day. 'Leonard Woolf by now must have been fully sixteen; yet he was still in an Eton jacket and looked not a day more than fourteen.' Mackenzie could not remember what they talked about, 'but I have a clear memory of an emotion of gratitude to know that there were other people near my own age who felt strongly critical of conventional opinion and were able to express that criticism with such lucid eloquence.' Leonard's only recorded memory of encountering Mackenzie at school is, however, quite other – in a football scrum, on a wet November afternoon.

In the summer holidays of their teenage years, Leonard and Herbert took off on long 'bicycle tours' all over the country, once taking their bikes by sea all the way to the Shetlands off the north of Scotland. It says a lot for Mrs Woolf s liberal views or, more likely, for her depressed state, that they were allowed to go. Beneath the liveliness of the large family, there was what Leonard described as a sense of 'fundamental insecurity', reinforced by outside events. His sisters' headmistress at the Earl's Court school, Mrs Cole, became obsessed by the Armenian massacres, and 'descended like a whirlwind of black silk ribbons', fund-raising for the survivors.[7] The terrible stories and Mrs Cole's passionate outrage had a profound effect on Leonard. 'I could almost see the helpless Armenians being bayoneted by the Turkish soldiers and the women and children fleeing and floundering among the snowdrifts.'

He connected these horrors with the trauma of being told to drown five new-born puppies, at about the same age. When he plunged the first tiny blind creature into the bucket of water, it began 'to fight desperately for its life, struggling, beating the water with its paws'. He suddenly realised that it was an individual, an 'I', and that it was fighting for its life just as he would, were he drowning. 'It was', he wrote at the very end of

---

7 In 1894 Turks and Kurds looted and destroyed Armenian villages, slaughtering the inhabitants.

his long life, 'a horrible, an uncivilized thing to drown that "I" in a bucket of water.'[8] By the age of fifteen or sixteen he had 'a fatalistic acceptance of instability and the impermanence of happiness'. Though he felt that some things mattered profoundly, he felt equally profoundly 'in the depths of my being, that in the last resort *nothing matters.*' This was his strategy for avoiding unbearable pain.

The three eldest children became, after their father's death, 'prematurely serious and grown-up' as Leonard described it. Bella, though still in her teens, was earning money for the family by writing children's stories for *Little Folks* magazine, and for the 'Young Israel' page of the *Jewish Chronicle.* Herbert, as the eldest son, could be self-important in a way that annoyed Leonard. In a later and unhappy time, Bella wrote to Leonard: 'I being so near [Herbert] in age, remember of course how he shouldered responsibility from such an early age and was such a tower of strength to Lady and me in those very difficult years after Papa died.'

'Lady' was the children's pet name for their mother. Mrs Woolf was adored, and exacted adoration. They called her 'Lady' all their grown-up lives. All the children except Leonard, that is. He alone never called her 'Lady'. He called her Mother.

During his adolescence, Leonard began to be irritated by Mother. She coped with many difficulties, and 'managed' by upholding what the logical, truth-seeking Leonard saw as a fantasy. He thought she loved him the least of her children, because he was unsympathetic to her fantasy. 'She lived in a dream world which centred on herself and her nine children. It was the best of all possible worlds, a fairyland of nine perfect children worshipping a mother to whom they owed everything, loving one another, and revering the memory of their deceased father.' If anything happened to destabilise this picture, she became agitated.

An example of this was when the boys were discussing at dinner a report from the Boer War about a soldier in the Royal Horse Artillery who saw his brother lying wounded on the ground. It was contrary to orders to stop or swerve, so he shut his eyes and drove his gun-carriage over his brother. Herbert said he was wrong, Leonard said he was right.

---

8 *The Journey Not the Arrival Matters*

In the course of the heated argument Leonard, improvising vividly about what he would feel and do in such a situation, found himself 'unfortunately driving a gun over the body of my brother Herbert'. Mother and Bella burst into floods of tears. It was nearly midnight before calm was restored, principally because Herbert kept bringing the matter up again with more argument. This persistence was a Woolf characteristic. Like poor cousin Bennie at Sunday lunch driving his Uncle Sidney wild by pressing on with his illogical nonsense, they just could not let things go.

The gun-carriage story is like another which, years later, Leonard told E.M.Forster, who told his own biographer.[9] He had been out riding with a man he disliked when their horses bolted out of control towards a gap in a hedge only big enough for one to pass through. Leonard decided that 'I'm more worth keeping alive than he', and prepared to charge at the other man, risking killing him. Fortunately the man fell off his horse in time. Then – and this was the most characteristic touch, thought Forster – Leonard proceeded to tell the man exactly what his reasoning had been. He wished, he told Forster, that it could happen again, only with someone worth sacrificing his life to.

Leonard's revolt against his mother's unreason focused on more than her dream world. 'I was conscious already at the age of 17', he wrote in *Principia Politica,* 'of a particular difference of outlook between me and my mother.' She regarded certain things and behaviours as absolutes, 'natural', when they were purely conventional: that men, for example, should behave in one way and women in another, that only certain professions were possible for middle-class young men, that you should dress in a certain way when you went out to pay calls and that you should pay calls on a Sunday afternoon. Leonard was citing his mother as an example of someone trapped in the 'communal psychology' of her time and class. (One might ask, how could she possibly have been otherwise?)

When Leonard got into the top classical form at St Paul's, it was back to doing nothing except Latin and Greek apart from Ancient History

---

9 P.N.Furbank

and Divinity. He was overwhelmed by what he called 'the greatest masterpiece of historical literature', the famous speech of Pericles in Book II of Thucydides' *History of the Peloponnesian War*, 'a superb statement of Athenian patriotism and of the social ideals and social practices in Periclean Athens'. Pericles' speech became the equivalent, for Leonard, of his father's quotation from the Book of Micah. He knew it was 'one of the most hackneyed passages' in all world literature'[10] and that 'all its associations are wearisome and sordid; dog-eared books, stained desks, the ugly class-room smelling of boys and ink, the bored voice of the master, the slow tick of the malignant clock.' Yet he never read it without an 'uplifting of the heart . . .' This happens to be from *Principia Politica.* But over and over, in his historical and political writing, Leonard was to evoke Periclean Athens in the fifth century BC, and Pericles' speech in particular, as stating 'once and for all, the creed of the civilised man in the language of bare beauty peculiar to the Greeks.' The Athens of Pericles was not as just nor as rational as Leonard saw it, but he invested it with all the values that meant most to him. 'Civilization for Pericles consists mainly in social organization and social objectives of which the most important are mental or spiritual, not material things, and social relations.'[11] The opposite of civilisation, and everything that he feared and dreaded, was 'barbarism'.

During his last year he was one of the promising boys to be tutored in the Walkers' own house by the Walkers' son Dick, a distinguished Balliol scholar, who was grooming him for the university scholarship examinations. Also in his last year, he was formally elected to the school debating society, the Union. Leonard spoke up in the debates: in favour of 'Foreign Immigration'; against 'The Progress of Civilisation' when it raised one class at the expense of others; and against the proposal that cheap magazines had a pernicious moral effect. A more exciting society to which he was elected in his last year was the Junior Debating Society,

10 It is hardly hackneyed now. But in Leonard's generation it was familiar to every educated man.
11 LW *Barbarians at the Gate* 1939

founded by the trio of G.K.Chesterton,[12] E.C.Bentley[13] and Lucian Oldershaw.[14] Cecil Chesterton, G.K.'s younger brother, was in Leonard's year and also belonged, but 'Junior' was a misnomer: the founders, now embarked upon their professional lives, sometimes attended, and on these occasions Leonard heard politics being discussed in an adult way. Leonard thought it 'amusing', in view of the Chestertons' subsequent anti-Semitism, forcibly expressed in print, that three out of the four boys elected during his time 'to this very exclusive society' were Jewish.

Leonard's small pocket diary for his last year at school, 1898, records nothing about the debating societies. It records three occasions when he went to synagogue. He wrote in *Sowing* that when he was fourteen he announced to his mother that he no longer believed and would never go to synagogue again. This caused a family sensation which blew over – as, clearly, did his adamant views on the subject, for the time being.

On his last school report the Old Man wrote: 'Clever and should do well.' The address the High Master gave at that year's prizegiving in July was revealing of his vision. It had been a good year – twenty scholarships to Oxford and Cambridge. Hard work, pronounced the Old Man, does no one any harm, and 'even the excessive strain of the struggle for the scholarships and prizes is not without its adequate compensations. It enforces self-control and self-denial, which are among the foremost of manly virtues.'

Leonard would appropriate the manly virtues of self-control and self-denial all too well, and somewhat to his own disadvantage.

One would suppose, from reading *Sowing*, that Leonard was the only one of his family to have gone to St Paul's. His account breathes singularity and isolation. His elder brother Herbert was educated elsewhere, as

---

12 Prolific author of fiction, poetry, criticism, political journalism, and a self-styled reactionary.

13 Journalist, inventor of the minimalist verse-form the 'clerihew', and author of the prototype modern detective story *Trent's Last Case* (1913).

14 Journalist; lifelong friend and ally of G.K.Chesterton and Hilaire Belloc.

was Harold; but Edgar joined Leonard at St Paul's in 1897, and the two youngest, Cecil and Philip, followed on after Leonard left. Edgar had experience of a different, benign Old Man. Edgar was the brother who liked Leonard least. His letters to Leonard in adult life were like lumps of masonry hurled from an adjacent building. His gloss on Leonard's account of the Old Man was relatively temperate. He said that Leonard was 'quite wrong' about him. The 'point of him' was that he knew every boy in the school, and was always on the lookout for talent in any direction – 'arranging Chinese lessons for one, Egyptology for another, Hebrew for another'. Edgar stayed with the Walker family on holiday in Scotland, where 'meals were hilarious . . . full of wit and repartee.' Leonard knew nothing of this side of Mr Walker, who responded to Edgar's more patent vulnerability.

At St Paul's, Leonard developed what he called his 'carapace' to present to the 'outside and usually hostile world'. Most human beings have something of the sort, though Leonard did know some who seemed 'wonderfully direct, simple, spiritually unveiled'. It made them seem almost like simpletons; they were 'the sillies' whom Tolstoy thought 'the best people in the world'.[15] There was nothing, he believed, maybe with regret, of 'the silly' about himself. The daughter of one of his Cambridge contemporaries, however, suggested that the 'best and most central function' of his carapace may have been precisely to protect and preserve his valuable 'silliness', so rightly 'beloved in you by others'. Leonard 'survived his carapace' and not vice versa, 'as tragically happens to most people'.[16]

Leonard in his autobiography described at length his development of a carapace, but omitted to say why it was so essential for him to have one. He was good at his work, he was good at games. Perhaps he was sensitive about his small stature, his late physical development, the tremor in his hands?

Compton Mackenzie, late in their lives, told Leonard he was one of

15 He thought there was a streak of 'the silly' in this sense in G.E. Moore and in his own wife Virginia.

16 Judith Waterlow to LW. She was a psychiatrist.

the characters in his novel *The East Wind of Love* (1937), set in 1900 in a school based on St Paul's. The hero is John Pendarves Ogilvie, 'a slim youth of seventeen with wavy nutbrown hair and a fresh complexion'. He is friendly with the prodigiously clever, Jewish, Emil Stern, 'a solitary boy without ever being in the least lonely'. Stern is described in Mackenzie's novel exactly as the schoolboy Leonard was later described in Mackenzie's autobiography – with some suggestively lyrical additions: 'He was not developed enough physically to be called a handsome boy, though to proclaim him pretty would be an insult to that finely carved pale face more Greek than Semitic, to those heavy-lidded large lustrous eyes and scarlet up-curving bow of a mouth . . . A Gentile half as attractive as Stern would have won the glances of every ambitious amorist in the school; but being a Jew he was disregarded.' Nor, because he is a Jew, does Stern in his last term become Captain of the School.

Ogilvie and Stern are intimate friends until Ogilvie finds himself teased for being besotted by a Jew, and drops him, to Stern's deep hurt and despair: 'Never to the end of my days shall I feel the least sensitiveness over the attitude of the world to the Jew, for all that could be suffered from such sensitiveness I have suffered already . . .' Stern determines to live from then on without passion. 'I want to see a world ruled by reason not by emotion as it is at present.'

Many of the fictional young Stern's opinions are startlingly like the adult Leonard's. 'Imperialism is more dangerous to the world than nationalism,' says Stern. 'Imperialism can only mean war, and war on a large scale.' Stern says that anti-Semitism is 'an antipathy based on a jealous fear of [the Jews'] superior level of intelligence and of their more realistic commercial sense. To that may be added the distrust of a race which seems parasitic because it lacks a country of its own'; and the doubt their achievements raised in the minds of those who want to believe 'that all Asiatics and Africans are naturally inferior'.

If Compton Mackenzie had not read Leonard's books, either he had the uncanny intuition possessed by some novelists, or Leonard the boy was father to Leonard the man in an unusually coherent way. Emil Stern's mother, in *The East Wind of Love,* says that her son was often difficult, 'but his devotion is limitless'. That too was deeply true of Leonard.

*

One thing Compton Mackenzie did know about was the persecution of the Jewish boys at St Paul's. 'It was my delight to put drawing pins with the sharp end up on the seats of Semitic school-desks. It was my delight to stick the lids of those desks with gelatine lozenges and watch the way the lid would come up with unexpected force and strike a Semitic chin. It was my delight to be a unit in two lines of exuberant young Nordic companions lined up on either side of a corridor in St Paul's School, and when some timid, book-laden young Jew passed along . . . to push him from side to side all the length of those grinning rows of boys until his books were scattered on the floor . . .'

There was more and worse. This kind of bullying is confirmed by G.K.Chesterton's account of how, at St Paul's, he rescued from a gang of tormentors 'a strange swarthy little creature with a hooked nose' who was being 'lightly tossed from one boy to another amid wild stares of wide-eyed scientific curiosity and questions like, "What is it?" and "Is it alive?"' This is from Chesterton's autobiography of 1936, whereas Mackenzie's catalogue of cruelty comes from an unpublished article, also written in the 1930s. Mackenzie wrote it as an act of contrition. 'Looking back at that silly anti-Semitism manifested with all the crudity of savage boyhood, I recognise that the fundamental cause of it was resentment at the way our Jewish schoolfellows used to sacrifice everything to reaching the top of the class.'[17]

That is inadequate, for the same reason that Stern's explanation of anti-Semitism in Mackenzie's novel is inadequate. In all social classes in England, some degree of unthinking anti-Semitism was as normal as class-consciousness, acquired by osmosis from parental attitudes and values: another and different example of the 'communal psychology' which so infuriated Leonard about his mother.

Leonard might well have illustrated 'communal psychology' in terms of anti-Semitism. But he could not, would not, do that, just as he could not, would not, make any link between the construction of his carapace and the reason why he needed one – his Jewishness. Once you have an

17 'How I learned not to hate the Jews' from Andro Linklater, *Compton Mackenzie: a Life*, Chatto & Windus 1987

effective carapace, *nothing matters* and, just as importantly, nothing must ever, ever, be seen to matter. Which is how his youngest brother Philip was able to write to him, after reading the autobiographical passages in *Principia Politica,* that the only criticism he would make was that Leonard 'gave no weight to the effect of our being Jewish, which I believe is all-important.'

Leonard insisted to the end of his life that when he was a boy, he 'never realized I was any different from anyone else for years. I mean, nobody has ever said, "You dirty Jew", or anything like that. I think I once heard somebody say that at school and that was the first time I realized that it wasn't merely that my religion was Jewish and somebody else's was Mohammedan.'[18] Yet, as he wrote in *Sowing*: 'I suspect that the male carapace is usually grown to conceal cowardice. Certainly . . . the character which I invented to face the world with originated, to a large extent, in fear, in mental, moral, or physical cowardice.' (He had every reason to be fearful at St Paul's.) His carapace provided 'the safety of a permanent alibi'. *Nothing matters.*

Leonard went alone to Cambridge to sit the scholarship examination for Trinity College in March 1899. He should have gone up with other candidates from school the previous autumn, but had been ill. He did not get a scholarship, but an exhibition and a minor award which, together, would give him £75 a year.

'I must have spent at least 10,000 hours of my short life sitting in some classroom', many of them in dense boredom. 'My intelligence must have been considerable to have survived this process of desiccation and attrition.'[19] Such arrogance is the flipside of a fear of inferiority. It is also as if he felt his intelligence was something separate from himself, like a very good bicycle.

He was a month short of his nineteenth birthday when he went up to Cambridge, and to his rooms at the top of a staircase in New Court in Trinity College, in October 1899.

---

18 Interviewed by Malcolm Muggeridge for BBC TV 6 Sep 1966.
19 *Sowing*

3

Trinity

'When for the first time as an undergraduate I walked through the Trinity Great Gate on my way to the rooms at the top of a staircase in New Court which was to be my lair for two years, I trod cautiously, with circumspection', his carapace concealing his 'uneasiness, lack of confidence, fear', of which the tremor in his hands was 'in part', he conceded in this context, both the symptom and the cause.[1]

Reading the college notices outside the Hall, he got talking with another first-year man. They walked away together and up to Leonard's rooms. Saxon Sydney-Turner, an ex-scholar of Westminster School and the son of a doctor, was short and thin, with a pale face and pale hair. He was brilliant in a crossword puzzle-solving kind of way. 'He had an immense knowledge of literature', wrote Leonard, but he read books 'rather in the spirit in which a man collects stamps.' He rarely committed himself to any definite opinion. In company, he was either completely silent or, in bursts, immensely voluble.

It is sometimes difficult, hearing someone's great friend described, to understand quite what the attraction is.

1 LW's quoted descriptions of Cambridge life are from *Sowing*.

Leonard and Saxon quickly got to know three other undergraduates who had come up at the same time – Lytton Strachey, Thoby Stephen and Clive Bell – this last somewhat fortuitously, because he lived on the same staircase as Saxon. These five formed an intimate alliance, particularly the trio of Leonard, Lytton and Saxon, 'the trinity of Trinity.'

They did not call each other by their first names. It was not the custom. To signify familiar friendship they used nicknames or abbreviations. Saxon Sydney-Turner was just Turner, though sometimes 'His Majesty', and visits from him 'royal visits'; and, occasionally, he was 'Anne'. Lytton was 'the Strache' and Thoby Stephen was 'the Goth', on account of his physique – six feet two inches tall, broad and already a little heavy, with a handsome head. Leonard was 'the Rabbi', or just Woolf. Towards the end of their time at Cambridge, Leonard graduated to signing himself 'Your L.'

Thoby Stephen, the Goth, had great sweetness of nature. His mind, although 'sound' as Leonard put it, was not brilliant or original, and he was not so stable or robust as he seemed. His mother had died when he was in his mid-teens, and a year before he came up to Trinity, his older stepsister, Stella, who had taken over the maternal role in the family, also died. His Trinity friends loved Thoby for his 'grandeur', his 'magnificence'. This referred to his nature and character, not his intellect or his social poise. He liked, as did Leonard, doing things in the open air; it was with the Goth that Leonard went walking and bird-watching in the countryside around Cambridge, once arming themselves with a rocket so as to have the thrill of putting up a huge flock of starlings – 'thousands upon thousands' of them, which roosted every evening in a clump of hawthorn trees.

Clive Bell had curly red-blond hair, a cherubic face and a cheery manner. He was a 'hearty', from a well-off country family serenely unconcerned with books or ideas, like the Wilcox family in E.M.Forster's *Howard's End*. But even though when he came up to Cambridge he was 'not yet an intellectual' as Leonard put it, he had a lively curiosity and developed an enthusiasm for literature and argument and, later, a passion for art.

Lytton Strachey was an aesthete, and his appearance was singular. He draped his long, limp body and long, thin extremities in eccentric and picturesque garments. He was short-sighted, and never really well. 'I never remember to have seen him run', wrote Leonard. He was the eleventh of the thirteen children of Sir Richard Strachey, an ex-colonial administrator, and was cossetted by his vital and dominant mother and his strong-minded elder sisters. An odd, sensitive boy, Lytton was already 'a very strange character', as Leonard put it, when he came up to Trinity to read history.

His voice was as singular as his appearance. It was a family voice, the 'Strachey voice', with exaggerated emphasis on unexpected words, and the pitch continuously swooping up and down. The voice and the manner were catching; most people who saw much of him, wrote Leonard, acquired the Strachey voice and never completely lost it. Lytton made Leonard laugh. Leonard made jokes and puns, but he was not effortlessly, maliciously funny like Lytton. Part of Lytton' s trick, or manner, which all the friends adopted, was to talk about deeply serious matters with outrageous flippancy, and about trivial matters with elaborate gravity. They analysed one another's characters ruthlessly, and despised all the conventions.

Lytton was unwell, with palpitations, in their first summer vacation, and had to miss the Michaelmas (autumn) term of 1900. Leonard, on the other hand, was full of irritable energy, writing to him in September 1900: 'I suddenly conceived an ardent desire to get away from civilization – so packed up Tristram Shandy and a bicycle and started for Shetland . . . I am seriously thinking of settling down here for good – as a village schoolmaster or something of that kind.' His dream of a retreat from the world of competition and worldly ambition was changing, but recurrent.

During the Christmas vacation of 1900, at Lexham, Leonard drafted a 'syllabus' or proposal for a work about mysticism to be edited by himself in collaboration with Saxon. He made 'a list of Mystics', which he sent on to Saxon. 'I think we ought to hold a general meeting of the contributors next term to discuss the whole work', he wrote. 'Send me any suggestions or ommissions (?spelling). I should be quite willing to resign German mysticism into other hands. I have been reading Novalis and the bible in Portuguese. The latter is harder I find than the former.' Saxon was to write 'a mystical Opera' for the same series, and Lytton would be a contributor.

The idea was to investigate the usefulness of 'the medium of the soul, as part and parcel of the Infinite, for addressing philosophical questions about the First Cause'. Topics to be covered included Platonism, the German, Irish, French, American and Egyptian traditions of mysticism, and the relation of literature, music and art to mysticism. Organised religion was rejected. Many long convivial evenings at Trinity, in Leonard's rooms, were spent on this ambitious project, in the dual spirit of jokiness and intensity; and Leonard took a great many notes. They had no experience of popular culture, or none that they respected; books and ideas were their play as well as their work.

In the Easter vacation 1901, Leonard sat up late in his room at Lexham, smoking his pipe – they all smoked pipes, and they all carried walking sticks – over a dying fire, with his wire-haired fox-terrier Charles beside him, and read and wrote letters until the dawn came up. He missed his friends. He was obsessed by the Book of Job. He identified strongly with Job. One of the amusements of Leonard, Lytton and Saxon during the previous term had been to compile a list of the great books of all time, ranking them in classes as if they were candidates for the Cambridge Tripos, and awarding Fellowships to a select few. Leonard wanted to elect the Book of Job. 'The more I read it the more certain I feel that it is above the first class, that it is absolute perfection and can *only* rank with Plato and Shakespeare. I may be wrong and probably am – perhaps there really is Eastern blood in my veins which answers the cry of an ancestor – how splendid if one discovered that one was descended from Job!' He had, he said, been 'kicking against the pricks' all day and longing to do something outrageous. The worst of it was 'that one never does.'[2]

*

2 20 March 1901. Texas

Back in Cambridge before the start of the summer term, he sent a poem to Saxon, headed '2.30 a.m.', expressive of boredom and disillusion:

I've done with all philosophies
    That tell how God this world has fled
And bowed to Mephistopheles.

I heard thy songs, Parmenides
    With wings of song envelopped, -
I've done with all philosophies.

Some glorious unrealities
    Despairingly were Truth I said,
And bowed to Mephistopheles.

Then, Plato, often spurning these
    I bound thy bough about my head –
I've done with all philosophies.

On intricate inanities
    Of quibbling Germans I have fed,
And bowed to Mephistopheles.

But now with these I finished
And burned my books and gone to bed
    And bowed to Mephistopheles.
    I've done with all philosophies.

He sent the poem to his elder sister Bella. She wrote a warm, consoling letter to 'My dearest Len', encouraging him to seek satisfaction in the everyday. Bella was now twenty-four, and handsome (though she had a cast in one eye), sympathetic and sociable. Leonard invited his friends home to Lexham, to meet the family; he went to Hove, near Brighton, to see Saxon and his parents, and became a familiar visitor at the Stracheys' house in Lancaster Gate. He was fond of Lytton's mother:

'She liked playing billiards with me.' He would also visit the Stracheys *en masse* – thirteen sons and daughters, and some spouses – in the country houses they rented in the summer, all sitting round the table arguing 'at the tops of their Stracheyan voices with Stracheyan vehemence.'[3]

His friendship with Saxon was quieter. They discussed cricket, plays, and Wagner – Saxon's passion – but mostly work (comparing translations of knotty passages of Aristotle), and the reading programme for the mysticism project. 'I see that you have seriously set yourself to Italian', he wrote in August 1901. He himself had been making 'an entry into Spanish'. 'I always feel in a kind of twilight here [at Lexham], just on the borderland of night. I dabble with work in the morning, take a dog – or relations (!) – for a walk, trot people [i.e. his mother and sisters] round to other people or places.'[4]

Before returning to Trinity for the Michaelmas term of 1901, he went to Cornwall with his brother Edgar and a bag of books, walking fifteen miles a day and sleeping eleven hours a night. Again, he rehearsed his fantasy of an alternative life: 'It would be the solution of so many problems to fly it all and become a day labourer and earn one's bread in the sweat of one's brow.' This found no echo in Lytton, who was on a family holiday near Lyndhurst in the New Forest, and seeing the Goth; the Stephen family had rented a holiday house nearby. '2 sisters very pretty', Lytton reported to Leonard – who also visited the Stracheys at Lyndhurst, but missed seeing the Goth's very pretty sisters, Vanessa and Virginia.

Lytton had moved seamlessly from schoolboy crushes into romantic attachments to fellow undergraduates, even though in these early years there was 'a good deal more talk than action', as his biographer put it.[5] Some fellow students were appalled by his indecent conversation, his flamboyant campness, his jeering contempt for religion.

---

3 LW, *Coming to London*
4 11 July 1901. Texas
5 Michael Holroyd, *Lytton Strachey: A Biography* Heinemann 1973 (One-volume version)

Leonard lost a friend because of Lytton. Arthur S. Gaye, whom they had involved in the mysticism discussions, wrote to Leonard that 'your adored Strachey' was one of those who were 'in their several ways the most offensive people I have ever met, and if I had continued to meet them daily, I would not be answerable for what I might do . . . The kind of conversation and habits, which I had with you, had a kind of fascination for me.' It was for his own moral health that Gaye declined to come to Leonard's rooms any more. He was offended by 'the tone of Strachey, and even you', especially on matters of religion.

Others found 'the tone' less threatening. Leopold Douglas Campbell, for example, whom Gaye named as one of the offenders, was actually studying for the Anglican priesthood. Leopold, the son of a general, came from a rich Scottish family. 'I liked him and he liked me', Leonard wrote in *Sowing*, 'although – or perhaps to some extent because – we had so very little in common.' It was reported to Leonard that someone said he was 'sponging' on the wealthy Leopold. Leonard was so angry that he went up to the someone's rooms and challenged him. There was a fearful scene, and some muttered apologies. Leonard lost his advantage, on taking his leave, by falling down the stairs.

From Michaelmas 1901, Leonard and Saxon shared a double set of rooms, M3 Old Court: two bedrooms and a shared sitting room. Even though their college bedmaker, Mrs Carter, serviced their rooms and laid and lit their coal fire, this was not gracious living. The friends had a code phrase, 'filth-packet'. A filth-packet was either a person, or the state of dirt and disorder which he created. Saxon was a filth-packet specialist and his bedroom was a tip. Leonard's speciality was for losing things – books, addresses, his college gown, his walking-stick, bits of clothing.

They hardly went out into the town except to buy books. Trinity made and contained their lives. College societies took up their evenings. When there were no society meetings they went to each other's rooms after dinner in Hall, sometimes keeping fellow students awake by playing rowdy games of catch with candlesticks, or ball games better suited to outdoors; sometimes sitting round the fire in silence punctuated by intense conversation, or playing serial games of chess and draughts, with Leonard religiously – it is the only word – keeping and preserving the scores.

Clive Bell, in his memoirs,[6] claimed to be the founder, in their second term at Trinity, of the Midnight Society, which consisted of himself, Leonard, Saxon, Lytton, and A.J.Robertson, the son of a clergyman. Leonard, however said that 'we' founded it, and that Clive became a member. Whatever the truth of that, it was through the Midnight Society that they came to appreciate Clive. The Midnight met on Saturdays in Clive's rooms. It had to be at midnight because another society, called the X, to which Leonard, Lytton, Saxon and Clive also belonged, met at 8.30.

At the Midnight Society's meetings they read aloud from English poetry and plays. According to Clive, Leonard Woolf was 'the most passionate and poetical' reader. Thoby Stephen was invited to join them. 'Thoby Stephen and I', Clive remembered, 'were deemed worldly because we smoked cigars and talked about hunting. Lytton, however, liked us all the better for that.' Lytton, who read memorably as Cleopatra, was susceptible to manly men.

At the X Society meetings, they read and discussed literature in modern languages other than English, and the minutes were written in rhyming verse. There was also the Sunday Essay Society, with a membership which included Leonard, Thoby, Lytton, George Macaulay Trevelyan, and the philosophy don J.E. McTaggart. Its purpose was 'the discussion of subjects connected with religion'. McTaggart himself entertained on Thursday evenings, in his rooms in Great Court, a select group which, again, included Lytton, Leonard and Saxon. McTaggart was atheistical and republican. He always seemed pleased to see them, and then would lie on his sofa looking at the ceiling, in total silence. When he did speak, it was generally to make a remark which definitively closed off further discussion. Leonard liked him a lot.

Leonard had been grounded and drilled so thoroughly in the Classics at St Paul's that much of the Cambridge syllabus was a repetition of

---

6 *Old Friends Remembered* Chatto & Windus 1956

material he had already covered. He just cruised. There is no reference in his autobiography or letters to any of his supervisors, nor to his attending any lectures or supervisions (tutorials). The memoirs and biographies of his contemporaries are unanimous that the close friendships which developed between some dons and undergraduates were not based on formal teaching; and that the clever undergraduates learnt more from each other than they did from the dons, reading one another's essays and commenting on them.

Several thirty-five-page general essays which Leonard wrote at Trinity have survived. One is a dialogue between Francis Bacon and Dr Johnson about the value of a classical education, Bacon arguing that the Science Tripos had more value for mankind as a whole. Another, 'A Fallacy of History', was sceptical about a 'science' of politics. All the examples and illustrations in his essays come from Greek and Roman history and literature. When he first came up, it was virtually all he knew.

Leonard was, as he acknowledged, 'a really first-class classical scholar' when he arrived in Cambridge, and nothing like so good when, in June 1902 at the end of his second year, he sat the examinations for the Classical Tripos, Part I. A man normally only went on to do Part II if it was thought that he had a chance of being awarded a Fellowship. Leonard got a First Class in the Tripos, but in the third division. He was not surprised. Before the exams, he confessed to Saxon that he was doing 'scarcely any work now . . . I am now quite used to the looming Second Class.' The Master of Trinity, Dr Montagu Butler, encouraged him to stay on and do Part II anyway. Lytton, who had only got a Second Class in his History Tripos, did better in an internal Trinity examination and won a scholarship to continue, and do Part II of the History Tripos.[7]

The group was coalescing with Lytton and Leonard at its core. Leonard was deeply attached to Lytton, unruffled by his foibles, understanding

7 Tripos is the Cambridge term for a course of study leading to a degree. The word implies a three-part course, but part III only applies in certain subjects such as mathematics.

about his ill-health, nerviness and susceptibility, and appreciative of his wit and originality. For Lytton, Leonard was the perfect friend and foil: sufficiently 'manly', unshockable, open-minded, quick off the mark and clever enough to send the verbal balls back over the net with added spin, an ideal confidant and guardian angel. Lytton did not always think to set limits on his malice or his fantastical obscenities and, like a child, needed Leonard to tell him when to stop. Leonard would have liked to break out more than he did; Lytton was iconoclastic enough for the two of them. Leonard was dazzled but not intimidated by Lytton. What Leonard lacked in comedic genius, he made up for with his passion for argument and his granite vehemence. Being Jewish made Leonard interestingly exotic. Lytton was exotic by nature. They did not bore each other.

Leonard and Lytton teased Saxon and sometimes made him their butt. They respected him intellectually, but were frustrated by his reserve which, after a loquacious first term, closed him down like a fog. Yet he supplied some essential element. One could not call it ballast.

Take just one long vacation, the summer of 1902. They were inexhaustibly interested in themselves and each other. Leonard wrote to Lytton from Lexham on 23 June: 'I had an amazing conversation with the Goth and Bell about You ALL. They discussed who were and who were not – you personally, they were unanimous, ARE. The Goth was a little shamefaced as to the eyes during it.'

'You ARE' – what? You just are. You exist, as lesser mortals do not. A Jamesian, Platonic, elliptical locution for the 'real thing', the way they aspired to be. They had a vocabulary of superlatives: 'supreme', 'immense', 'sublime', 'superb', 'the ultimate', 'high up in the snows'. But just to say that someone 'is' (or 'is not') was sufficient.

Leonard, stuck at Lexham, saw a doctor at his family's insistence for his 'delirium-trementic hand'. The doctor, hearing that Leonard was studying Greek philosophy, gave him a lecture on the Greeks as 'filthy paederasts' and some 'probably useless concoctions' for his hands. He was growing a moustache and reading the works of Byron for a university essay prize. 'My god I've never read such trash as those Giaours and Corsairs. I had never read them before and assumed they were nauseous, but I never imagined such feeble banalité as they contain.' He was also working at Aristotle's Ethics and reading Huysman's *A Rebours* – 'diseased magnificence. The words simply dazzle me.'[8]

But it was to Saxon, the doctor's son, to whom he wrote that summer to ask if he knew of a cure for hay-fever, from which one of his younger sisters was suffering. It was Saxon whom he told that his family was having 'a very bad time' because his brother Harold had a worrying 'naevoid place' on his upper lip which continually broke out bleeding, while Lytton in his letters was expatiating on Byron's likely sodomitic practices, and on how he, Lytton, just couldn't feel anything for the beautiful young women among whom he found himself in the Mediterranean. Ought he not to fall in love with one of them?

No, Leonard told Lytton, it wasn't possible for him. Not with a woman.

Leonard began to define himself by discovering his differences from Lytton. Leonard himself did not fall in love with women either, except for a moment, when he glimpsed a lovely face 'in a carriage or bus or gutter'. He had the ability, he said, but it didn't happen. Unlike Lytton, he was by no means repelled 'by what is beneath the girdle in love, although certainly it is not everything'. What repelled Leonard was the frequent discovery that there was nothing above the girdle, and he was left with 'the bare feelings of sexuality, and very often not even those.' Lytton was writing homoerotic, coprophiliac verse and circulating it. Leonard took issue with him: 'You are too obsessed or becoming obsessed by buttocks and genitals . . . I think the buttock-genital-obsession as bad as the fig leaf-trouser-obsession, or rather not as bad because in this case the obsession only is bad while trousers and fig leaves are bad per se.'

His self-protective doctrine that 'nothing matters' fitted comfortably with Lytton's sceptical view of life. But Leonard did want to feel that something could matter. They talked about sex all the time, chiefly in terms of disgust and degradation. Leonard was a virgin. Attracted to women, he was nevertheless affected by the intense relationships of his

8 13 July 1902. Texas

all-male Trinity world, and by the transgressive glamour of Lytton's lusts. He had abandoned his ancestral religion, but could not abandon the quest for transcendence. The longing for something or someone great to devote himself to alternated with moments of bleak nihilism.

All his life Leonard was to include Christ, with Socrates and Shakespeare, in his lists of great people who changed the world. He never forgot that Christ was a Jew like himself. Perhaps, he thought in 1902, he could become a Christian. But when it came to it, he could not. In the last weeks of the long vacation he confessed to Saxon: 'I did become a Christian for a few days and damnably unpleasant it was. Byron had something to do with it and I suppose the Father, the Son and the Holy Ghost.'

It was not quite over. A few days later, to Lytton: 'I wish you would not spread a report that I am now a Christian, as however true – and I have bought a rosary – I only lived on the reputation of not being one.' He knew Lytton would enjoy the thought of the rosary, if nothing else.

The Goth's tall, gangling younger brother Adrian came up to Trinity in October 1902, as did Leonard's brother Edgar. Although Edgar, Leonard and Saxon exchanged competitive versions of Greek iambics at the beginning of term, Edgar did not impinge greatly on Leonard's Cambridge life, which now became momentous.

The ultimate in Cambridge societies was the Society, properly the Cambridge Conversazione Society, known also as the Apostles, because the number of full members was limited to twelve. It was a debating society, not tied to a particular college or colleges, though in practice, in Leonard's day, Apostles were recruited chiefly from Trinity and King's. Lytton was elected to the Society in February 1902. Jack (J.T.) Sheppard from King's – small, white-blond – was elected at the same time, and was for a couple of years the chief object of Lytton's romantic yearnings.[9]

Founded in 1820, the Society was meant to be a secret, and the general run of undergraduates never even heard of it. The strength and

9 J.T.Sheppard became Sir John Sheppard, and Provost of King's.

interest of the Society was that older Apostles, whether dons or those who had left Cambridge for the wider world, continued to attend meetings and read papers – if only from time to time – thus enabling them to remain in touch with the clever young, and enabling the clever young to know older 'brothers' of distinction and experience. Everyone, whatever his age or distinction, was on an equal footing, and addressed by his surname with no respectful prefix.

Election was for life, with annual dinners held in London. The Society was and is self-perpetuating. The 'brothers' scouted for new recruits, 'embryos', whose qualities of mind and body – the latter important, once Lytton's influence became paramount – were scrutinised and discussed. A rejected embryo was 'an abortion'. If an embryo was deemed 'apostolic', he was elected; his first meeting was the 'birth', when he had to agree to uphold the Society's rules and traditions or risk incurring frightful curses. The Society's rituals were silly in the way that masonic or cult rituals are silly, their continuance and significance determined by tradition, exclusivity and, in this instance, a solemn taste for the ridiculous.

The Society met in a member's room on Saturday evenings, and a brother – called for the occasion the Moderator – read a paper, standing 'on the hearthrug'. Freedom of speech was absolute. Taboos were there to be broken. Afterwards there was a discussion, and a vote taken – not on the paper itself, but on some whimsical or subtextual essence suggested by the discussion: what question was *really* being asked? Coffee was drunk and 'whales' – anchovies on toast, later sardines – consumed. The minutes and other records were kept in a cedarwood box called the Ark. Apostles of all vintages were expected to attend every Saturday if they were in Cambridge (sometimes only four or five members were present, and rarely more than ten). They could be released from this obligation by arrangement, in which case they became honorary members; they formally 'took wings' and became 'an angel'.

Lytton became secretary to the Society in October 1902, and immediately Leonard and Saxon were elected. The vote taken on the occasion of their 'birth' was typical in its obliquity, both philosophical and personal: 'Wolf or Shepherd?' (Woolf voted for Wolf and Sheppard for Shepherd.) Clive Bell was never considered to be apostolic, and Lytton and Leonard agonised over whether the Goth was, or was not. They were afraid he might be bored, and show it. Leonard was in favour of electing him; it didn't happen.

Even before Lytton's election, the atmosphere of the Society had become mildly homoerotic, and the discussions, whatever the ostensible topic, were as much concerned with each other's foibles, private jokes, private language, and personal dilemmas as with objective intellectual argument. In March 1900 the philosopher and mathematician Bertrand Russell, as Moderator, had asked 'Should we like to elect women?' He himself had voted 'No', adding 'But I should like to like to.'[10] A regular attender, as an 'angel', was Goldsworthy Lowes Dickinson, known as Goldie, an influential and public-spirited don at King's who lectured in history and politics and was instrumental in setting up the new Economics Tripos. About eighteen years older than Leonard and his friends, Lowes Dickinson was in private a timid boot-fetishist, and given to long serious attachments to men who could never love him back.

Goldie Lowes Dickinson had been an intimate friend of the artist Roger Fry when Fry was in his last year at King's, and he loved E.M.Forster, who was also an Apostle. Lytton nicknamed Forster 'the Taupe' – the mole – not only because he looked like one, but because he seemed to tunnel his way through life invisibly, popping up unexpectedly. Older members – 'angels' – who often attended included Bertrand Russell; the poet Robert Calverley Trevelyan – 'Bob Trevy' to his familiar friends, who included Leonard; Bob Trevy's younger brother, the historian George Macaulay Trevelyan, a Fellow of Trinity and, unusually for this group, fiercely political; G.H.Hardy the cricketing mathematician; and Desmond MacCarthy.

Everybody liked Desmond, who was working as a journalist in London. An old Etonian, clever and athletic, he seemed to have the world at his feet, and planned to write novels. He was a great friend of Clive Bell's, like himself an enjoyer with an easy-going temperament,

---

10 Women were eligible as Apostles from 1971.

and he was close to G.E.Moore, with whom he had read philosophy as an undergraduate.

George Edward Moore, the philosopher, had been an Apostle since 1894; his introduction had transformed the Society. Bertrand Russell wrote to his fiancée Alys Pearsall Smith: 'We all felt electrified by him, and as if we had slumbered hitherto and never realized what fearless intellect pure and unadulterated really means. If he does not die or go mad I cannot doubt that he will somehow mark himself out as a man of stupendous genius.'[11] Moore had a Trinity Prize Fellowship, and in 1902 was giving lectures. He was twenty-nine, sexually innocent, and pure in heart.

Leonard and Lytton were spellbound by Moore. They mythologised him, fascinated as much by his character and personality as by his intellect, and endlessly curious about him. He was not witty, he had no small talk; he was shy and, like McTaggart (also an Apostle), given to long, unnerving periods of silence. 'He had a passion for truth, but only for important truths.' Moore's theory and practice was that until one had something true to say on any subject, one should say nothing. These silences covered deep feeling. Muddled thinking caused him acute distress. 'There was some kind of divine absurdity in Moore.'[12]

When Leonard first knew him, 'his face was beautiful, almost ethereal', with a wonderful smile. He had the single-minded simplicity of the 'sillies' described by Tolstoy in his autobiography. When he laughed, for example at one of Desmond MacCarthy's fantastic stories, he shook from head to foot in uncontrollable paroxysms. His passion was released in his piano-playing and singing, especially of German lieder. The spell he cast was not because he had such a good voice, or was such a good pianist, but because of the subtlety and intensity of his feeling for the music. Under Moore's influence, the Society's debates focused on states of mind, on what one ought to do, ought to feel, ought to find

11 Quoted in Paul Levy, *G.E.Moore and the Cambridge Apostles* Weidenfeld & Nicolson 1979

12 *Growing*

important; and always, on what question was *really* being asked, and always, 'What *exactly* do you mean?'

At the end of the Michaelmas term 1902 Lytton and Leonard went to King's to call on a freshman called John Maynard Keynes, with a view to assessing his apostolic potential. He was initiated into the Society in February 1903. Maynard was an old Etonian, and his family home was in Cambridge, a comfortable, modern house on Harvey Road to which Maynard's friends were often invited at weekends: 'mildly amusing and mildly dull' occasions, in Leonard's view.

Maynard Keynes, in satirical Memoir Club mode,[13] was to evoke a memory of Saxon and Leonard sitting one each side of the fire in basket chairs in their unlit sitting-room, only stopping sucking on their pipes 'to murmur that all good states of mind were extremely painful and to imply that all painful states of mind were extremely good'. Strachey would agree, 'though his sorrow was more fitful than their settled gloom'. At Society meetings, Keynes recalled, each 'brother' argued characteristically: 'Woolf was fairly good at indicating a negative, but he was better at producing the effect that it was useless to argue with *him* than at crushing *you'* – which Lytton and Moore well knew how to do. And then they would all laugh and 'we enjoyed supreme self-confidence, superiority and contempt towards all the rest of the unconverted world.'[14]

The personal dynamics of this very small group were inextricable from the Saturday debates. Leonard went so far as to say that the Society became 'the focus of my existence'. What affected him so powerfully was not only the intimacy of the group but Moore's relentless pursuit of truth, which chimed with his own nature. Leonard's insistence on saying only what he believed to be true, and his abstention from all sentimental half-truths, gush and flummery, became lifelong characteristics. It could sometimes make him seem harsh, even though it was based not on coldness, but on passion.

---

13 The Memoir Club was founded by Molly MacCarthy, Desmond's wife, in 1919. It survived into the mid-1950s.

14 'My Early Beliefs': Memoir Club paper 1938, published in Maynard Keynes, *Two Memoirs* Rupert Hart-Davis 1949

4

Taking Wings

Leonard finished his 20,000-word essay on Byron – his draft all cross-ings-out and insertions. During the Christmas vacation 1902, he was 'in the bottom most gulf, but I really think we are now completely sunk and frozen into an eternal depression. We don't even seem to have enough warmth now to get up and spark a rage, for this time the term just faded out from melancholism into vanishings.'[1]

They were hooked on competitive depression, and a lot of what Leonard called 'Let's all be unhappy together.' 'Sunk' was their word for feeling low. 'Degraded', and the associated 'sordid', was one degree worse, connected with excesses of drink or lust. (Though sex at this time was solitary or in the head.) They vaunted their modernity, but their melancholy – despairing inertia, heightened sensibility, disgust with the everyday, self-absorption – was essentially Romantic, shading palely into fin-de-siècle decadence.

There was a perverse stimulation in exposing to one another the anatomy of their melancholy. It was a semi-literary pose in which they got stuck, and Leonard criticised, from an aesthetic point of view, its dynamic: 'I don't think you know', he wrote to Lytton, 'that there is

1 To Lytton Strachey 14 Dec 1902

never a crescendo when we write to one another. There are bursts of course from you of flame' – and, somewhat incoherently, 'I remember some even fireworks – but as a rule it is a little black – don't you think? – a little too much for crescendo of having nothing to keep up . . . well now I have nothing to keep up, I can go on growling or drivelling as I please.'[2] His Byron essay had not won the prize.

A paper he read to the Society, on 9 May 1903, took as its text Plato's vision of the cave where men sit as chained prisoners, thinking the shadows cast on the wall to be reality, when they are only phenomena. 'Outside blazed the clear sun and the wide world of Reality.' Only the enlightened, in the cave, realise that they are seeing shadows, and only the very few who struggle up out of the cave into the light glimpse what reality is. 'Reality' and the 'real world', in this scenario, mean the exact opposite of what 'reality' and the 'real world' mean for most people. In apostolic language, it was not only the shadows but the prisoners, the unenlightened ones, who were mere 'phenomena'.

Leonard was, by temperament, interested in the world as it was, as well as in states of mind. The discussion after his paper ended with a vote on 'George or George or Both?' One George was George Moore, in the sun outside the cave, on the heights. He knows the cave-dwellers but does not join in their struggles and competition. The other George was George Macaulay Trevelyan, down in the cave, and so concerned with setting things right among the cavemen that he has no time to think of the light up above.

Leonard's question was: 'Can we combine the two Georges in our lives?' He thought they could. Practical politics should not be absolutely divorced from philosophy. Should the George who is on the heights go down again into the cave? Unhesitatingly, Leonard said 'Yes'. While philosophers remain outside the cave, 'their philosophy will never reach politicians or people.' He was challenging the group's aspiration just to 'be', disengaged from any interest in or knowledge of, as he said, 'the Education Bill' or 'the Rating of Ground Values'.

---

2 To Lytton Strachey 17 March 1903. Texas

Leonard already saw it as an imperative, as he always would, for intellectuals to take part in what Morgan Forster in *Howard's End* was to call 'the world of telegrams and anger' and in public life. He described in *Sowing* how important the Dreyfus Case[3] had been to 'us', seeming to mean his Cambridge friends, but more likely his family. The case, with its revelation of virulent and institutionalised anti-Semitism in France and potentially in England, was given enormous coverage in the *Jewish Chronicle*. 'Over the body and fate of one obscure, Jewish captain in the French army a kind of cosmic conflict went on year after year between the establishment of Church, Army, and State on the one side and the small band of intellectuals who fought for truth, reason, and justice on the other. Eventually the whole of Europe, almost the whole world, seemed to be watching breathlessly, ranged upon one side or the other.'[4]

The Dreyfus case jump-started in twentieth-century European politics the role of the public intellectual, and the philosophical stance of (in the French sense) *engagement*, which became central in the 1930s, and with which Leonard Woolf was to align himself. He equated Dreyfus's public vilification with the trial of Socrates and with Christ before Pilate. In old age, he felt that Dreyfus's vindication had given Europe its great opportunity to line up definitively on the side of truth, reason and justice. Instead, there were 'two world wars and millions of Dreyfuses murdered by Russian communists and German Nazis.'

There is no reflection of concern with the Dreyfus case, or any public issue, in the apostolic debates. It was not that they were incurious. They read widely and all the time. Leonard, the list-maker, calculated that in 1902 he read 121 books (unconnected with his degree course). A key novel for him was Samuel Butler's *The Way of All Flesh*, a satire on the complacency, hypocrisy and cruelty of respectable parents, on the falseness of conventional religion, of public school education, and of

---

3 Alfred Dreyfus, a French Jewish army officer, was falsely charged with passing defence secrets to the Germans. Supporters' efforts to prove his innocence provoked further anti-Semitic reactions. The novelist Zola famously defended him in 1898. Dreyfus was re-tried in 1899, found guilty again, but pardoned. The verdict was reversed in 1906. Definitive proof of his innocence came to light in 1930.

4 *Sowing*

maternal solicitude, which was 'solicitude for the most part lest the offspring should come to have wishes and feelings of his own'. Hot off the press in 1903, it was the perfect novel of adolescent revolt. Leonard read Ibsen, Thomas Hardy – and Joseph Conrad, whose protagonists, with their high ideals, their secrets, their fears about failure and faint-heartedness, found a responsive reader in Leonard Woolf.

They read the later novels of Henry James as they came out, and became infatuated by James's manner, talking and writing in the convoluted, allusive Jamesian way and seeing Cambridge through a Jamesian lens. At Trinity, Leonard wrote down verbatim conversations which seemed to him significant or amusing, and thought, when he came across them years later, that the tones and rhythms of Henry James had indeed infiltrated their talk and his manner of reporting it. These conversations do not bear reproducing (though Leonard did so in *Sowing*). One was between the mathematician G.H.Hardy, and another member of the troubled Gaye family, Russell K.Gaye, about their ailing cat.[5]

Another conversation which he recorded verbatim took place in May 1903, in the sitting-room he shared with Saxon. (Neither Thoby nor Saxon, sitting by the fire, said anything at all throughout.) Lytton burst in and paced about, flapping his gown, half-speechless. 'It's reached the ultimate', he finally said . . . He's going – and that of course will be the ultimate – to give me the names.' Lytton had just come from applying 'the method' to some unfortunate fellow undergraduate.

'The method' was invented by Leonard and Lytton, and in Leonard's words, from *Sowing*, 'it was a kind of third-degree psychological investigation applied to the souls of one's friends. Though it was a long time before we had any knowledge of Freud, it was a kind of compulsory psychoanalysis.' It took the form of relentless, probing questioning. The theory was 'that by imparting to all concerned the deeper psychological truths, personal relationships would be much improved'. They derived their technique 'partly from Socrates, partly from Henry James, partly from G.E.Moore, and partly from ourselves.'

---

5 R.K.Gaye, the intimate friend of G.H.Hardy, committed suicide in his room at Trinity in 1909.

Lytton, on the occasion recorded, had gone too far and Leonard told him so. 'But the questions, I said. How could you ask them? Well, you are cruel. I call it sheer brutality.' But Lytton was exalted. 'This has certainly been the most wonderful of all.'

Leonard and Lytton had already applied the method to Saxon, concerned and irritated by the way he had withdrawn from life 'to protect himself from its impact and from the impact of persons, emotions, and things by spinning around himself an elaborate and ingenuous series of cocoons'. One evening after dinner in Hall they began their investigation, 'and continued it uninterruptedly until five in the morning'. When at last the victim staggered off to bed, 'we had successfully uncovered the soul of Saxon, but had disastrously confirmed him in the determination to stifle it in an infinite series of veils.'[6]

Yet he remained their close friend. Maybe the awful intimacy of the experience bound him to them, or he got some gratification from being the focus of their undivided attention. Leonard seems to have seen no connection between Saxon's 'cocoons', and his own 'carapace'. The excitingly risky emergence from his carapace at Cambridge made him eager to prise off other people's.

Shortly after Saxon's ordeal, Leonard wrote to him (at the beginning of the Easter vacation 1903) as 'My dear Anne' – a nickname that he and Lytton used between themselves, but rarely to Saxon directly. 'Are you coming to the Lizard?' If so, he must write at once to Yen How. (That was their private name for G.E.Moore, soon abbreviated to the Yen.[7]) Leonard added a sour postscript: 'We decided yesterday that the only place for you is the Kensington Palace. A suite there where you would could wander from one dreary room to the other leaving trails of filth-packets in your wake.' He never wrote to Saxon again as 'Anne', nor in this vein. Perhaps Saxon, for once, snarled.

*

---

6 LW Memoir Club paper 1952

7 Moore's regular reading party was that year at the Lizard in Cornwall. On his way back, changing trains at Taunton, LW lost his overcoat, three books, a silk scarf and a pair of gloves. 'Yen How' was the name of a philosophical mandarin in the successful musical show *San Toy* then running in London.

Leonard was in Lytton's thrall during 1903, lending himself to his friend's merciless disdains, his infatuations, and to their joint and separate application of 'the method'. 'You are magnificent, supreme', he wrote in a typically incoherent letter from Lexham. 'You say "we" brought it off, but it is surely *you* alone – you are on such heights in such flames this time, that I am, perhaps not dizzy, but certainly wonderfully dazzled . . . For it would be I thought darkness, a real "heart of darkness", pitch if not sulphur. What you say of him completely astounds me . . . That he grasped and was equal to it, lifts him mountains high – though I *do* doubt whether to the heights you at first thought – but after all your "discovery" and *you are* the important thing, I agree.'[8]

This may be about Maynard Keynes. Lytton replied with equal obliquity and extravagance. It should be borne in mind, when impatient with this youthful silliness, that Lytton's flaunting of his homosexual proclivities, and his triumphalism when he forced another to confess to the same, were in a context of risk. It was only eight years since Oscar Wilde's trial and imprisonment.

During May Week in the summer term of 1903, Thoby Stephen's two sisters – Vanessa, who was a year older than he, and Virginia, his younger by two years – came to visit him in his Trinity rooms, where Leonard met them for the first time. In their white dresses and large hats, with parasols in their hands, 'their beauty literally took one's breath away'. It was an awkward occasion. The Goth was not socially adept. His sisters, for all their 'astonishing beauty', were shy and demure. Leonard, more than half a century on, in *Sowing*, fancied he recalled a look in their eyes 'which belied the demureness, a look of great intelligence, hypercritical, sarcastic, satirical'.

Leonard, even then, was an object of interest to the girls. Virginia, in romantic and facetious retrospect, in a Memoir Club contribution of 1921 or 1922, recalled how Thoby used to tell his sisters about his Cambridge friends 'as if they were characters in Shakespeare'. One was 'a man who trembled perpetually all over. He was a Jew.' When

8 20 March 1903. Texas

Virginia asked why he trembled, Thoby somehow suggested that 'it was part of his nature – he was so violent, so savage; he so despised the whole human race'. Most people came to terms with life, but 'Woolf did not and Thoby thought it sublime'. Thoby told her about a dream Woolf had about throttling a man, and that when he woke up he had pulled his own thumb out of joint. 'I was of course inspired with the deepest interest in that violent trembling misanthropic Jew.'[9]

Leonard told Lytton after the end of term that he had been in 'a vague hell' ever since he came home, 'and I only wanted something like this to make it definite.' For he had done worse in Part II of the Classical Tripos than he had in Part I. He was placed in the Second Class. (So, in their Tripos examinations, were the Goth and Lytton. Saxon had a First.) Now he had officially left Trinity, Leonard's exhibition money of £75 a year, augmented by £120 from a scholarship won during his first year, came to an end.

He was virtually penniless apart from what his mother or his elder brother Herbert could spare him. 'I suppose in the end if you never get what you want, you even begin to care when you don't get what you didn't care whether you got or not . . . I want to get out into the open, not to be penned in this swamp of trivialities, having to think twice about spending a penny on an evening paper because one bought a shilling book hardly desired. Curse.' He envied Lytton his 'infinity of desire': 'You have your crises and you feel them, your loves and your hates and your passions . . . I often envy you that, for I am, I feel it, so often a mere spectator with my hands in my pockets. You can't love by desiring an extremely vague desire of a very vague moon.'[10]

What next for the trinity of Trinity? Lytton was trying for a Fellowship. Leonard and Saxon decided to sit for the Higher Civil Service Open Competition. There were twelve examination papers, including some on subjects which Leonard had to get up from scratch, such as Political

---

9 Jeanne Schulkind, ed: *Moments of Being: a Collection of Autobiographical Writing by Virginia Woolf* Harcourt Inc 1985

10 25 June 1903

Economy and Economic History.[11] Most candidates spent the year at specialist cramming establishments. Leonard and Saxon went back to Cambridge in autumn 1903 to study on their own.

That September G.E.Moore's book *Principia Ethica* was published. The Apostles were bowled over, and obliquely flattered. For this was Moore's own voice enshrined in print by the Cambridge University Press, Moore's method of cross-examination, and Moore's hard-won conclusions, just as they had heard them taking shape at Society meetings and late at night in college rooms. The long, agonised and agonising silences, while Moore questioned a question, were mercifully elided, in print. The resulting impression was of striking, common-sense clarity.

The book is an investigation of the idea of 'the Good'. Moore's originality in this unoriginal quest[12] lay in his concept of 'good in itself' – unanalysable, indefinable, an 'intrinsic value'. His chapter 'The Ideal' excited his disciples inordinately. Finding 'the *best* state of things *conceivable*' to be inaccessible, Moore concluded that 'By far the most valuable things, which we know or can imagine, are certain states of consciousness, which may roughly be described as the pleasures of human intercourse and the enjoyment of beautiful objects.'

He stressed that the emotional response should be 'appropriate': if a high degree of emotion is directed towards 'an object that is positively ugly', the state of consciousness may be 'positively bad'. His unquestioning assumption of consensus on what was beautiful or ugly was old-fashioned even in 1903, when the avant-garde was already turning away from conventional ideas of beauty and finding value in new forms. His stress on contemplative enjoyment ignored the pleasure and value of active involvement in life, and his asexual mind-set seemed to preclude the 'intrinsic value' of any 'state of consciousness' elicited by anything more urgent than affection.

---

11 The other papers were English Composition, Greek Language and Literature, Latin Language and Literature, English Language and Literature, Greek History, Roman History, General Modern History, Logic and Mental Philosophy, Moral Philosophy, Political Science, Roman Law.

12 Moore was very strongly influenced by his former professor and fellow Apostle Henry Sidgwick (d.1900) and his book *The Methods of Ethics* (1874), which LW read in 1902.

Nevertheless, the Apostles – in particular Lytton Strachey and Maynard Keynes – pounced on this chapter in delight, disregarding the strictures on the unworthiness of 'states of the body'. It seemed, said Maynard later in a Memoir Club paper,[13] 'the opening of a new heaven on a new earth.' The intrinsic value given to 'the pleasure of human intercourse and the enjoyment of beautiful objects', which to them included beautiful people, exactly met their requirements.

The chapter 'Ethics in Relation to Conduct' was less intoxicating to them. 'What ought we to do?' Moore's answer was, whatever is likely to bring about the best result for the world. A general observance of society's rules would surely be 'good as a means' of preserving civilised society; and the preservation of civilised society 'is necessary for the existence of anything which may be held to be good in itself.'

To the modern mind, the phrase 'civilised society' is in need of being unpacked according to Moore's own method. ('What exactly do you *mean* by . . .?') It did not seem necessary to Moore in Cambridge in 1903; nor to Leonard, for whom the ideal civilisation of Periclean Athens was brought closer by everything Moore held to be 'good in itself'.

Moore did concede that the neglect of an established rule, in individual cases, may sometimes produce a better total result. But rule-breaking by individuals would tend to legitimate general rule-breaking, which would be 'disadvantageous'. Thus Moore came down heavily in favour of social conformity as a guide to practical ethics. That was no great problem to his apostolic readers, whose privileged way of life would suffer if the general population took it upon itself to upset the status quo.

In his summing-up, Moore allowed for more leeway for the individual to comply or not, specifically in the matter of chastity and family values. Here Lytton and Maynard Keynes saw another green light. 'We were not afraid of anything', as Keynes said in his Memoir Club paper. 'We entirely repudiated a personal liability on us to obey general

13 Published as 'Early Beliefs' – exactly as it was delivered, according to LW – in Maynard Keynes, *Two Memoirs* Rupert Hart-Davis 1949. Keynes's paper constituted a repudiation of the value of Moore's doctrines and influence.

rules . . . We repudiated entirely customary morals, conventions and traditional wisdom.'

Principia Ethica seemed to give permission for the complex web of sexual connections for which this group of friends became notorious. Beatrice Webb, in a letter of 1911, let rip about 'the pernicious set . . . which makes a sort of ideal of anarchic ways on sexual questions', setting a bad example to 'our young Fabians'. And as for *Principia Ethica*, 'a book they all talk about as "The Truth"! I can never see anything in it, except a metaphysical justification for doing what you like and what other people disapprove of!'[14]

Leonard Woolf read *Principia Ethica* in his own way and as a whole. In *Sowing* he rejected entirely Maynard Keynes's 'absurdly wrong judgments' about the nature of the influence of Moore and his book. It was just not true that they all became 'rational immoralists'. One might have expected Leonard to respond positively to Keynes's complaint that Moore left out or denied so much of human experience – the possibility of physical love as a 'good', the life of action, 'the pattern of life as a whole'. But Leonard focused on the 'tremendous influence' of the way that Moore 'suddenly removed from our eyes an obscuring accumulation of scales, cobwebs, and curtains, revealing . . . the nature of truth and reality, of good and evil and character and conduct, substituting for the religious and philosophical nightmares, delusions, hallucinations, in which Jehovah, Christ, and St Paul, Plato, Kant and Hegel had entangled us, the fresh air and pure light of plain common-sense'. Moore answered their questions with a voice more 'divine', wrote Leonard, than the voice of 'Jehovah from Mount Sinai or Jesus with his sermon from the Mount.'

Leonard spoke for himself. The green light for him was for spiritual and intellectual freedom, and an end to his search for a transcendent metaphysic or religion.

*

14 Quoted in Paul Levy, *Moore: G.E.Moore and the Cambridge Apostles* Weidenfeld & Nicolson 1979

Staying in Cambridge for this fifth year, he worked for five hours a day, played golf with Keynes and the Yen (who played with passion, and missed the ball a lot), and attended the Society's meetings on Saturday evenings. He gave a paper to the Society on 31 October 1903, 'Othello or Lord Byron', voted on as 'Is Sentimentality a Confusion of Symbolic Parts with Wholes?' Lytton (constantly in Cambridge at weekends) voted against, with the additional note: 'No, a confusion of privy parts with holes.' Leonard's paper was a diatribe against sentimentality, with special reference to a play he had seen, *Little Mary* by J.M.Barrie, with a female 'phenomenon' who had been moved to tears and took offence when Leonard said the play was 'thoroughly bad'.

Leonard's Mooreian point here was the 'inappropriateness' of expending high emotion on unworthy objects. His private fear was that he might never, in the world as it was, find a worthy object – a cause, or a person – to meet his desires and expectations. As he said in another paper, in February 1904, 'The best things and the best people – and we must include among these our best selves – only exist in our imaginations.' Moore was in a similar predicament. He told Leonard privately, on an Easter reading party in Devon that April, that if he could only find 'a female stimulus' who would lift him out of his wretchedness he would marry, 'but he has given up hope, I think, of finding her.'

On 4 May 1904 Leonard spoke to the Society on 'Embryos or Abortions?' – a meditation on the apostolic temperament, in which he made a vehement distinction between reality and realism. 'Merely to give faithful descriptions of things as they are in the world is of no value.' He quoted Emma's deathbed scene in *Madame Bovary* as a wonderful shift 'from realism to reality'; whereas 'to go as Zola does into a Paris slum and give a bare description of all the filth that he can see with his eyes, has about as much value as a photograph of a slum would have.'

Leonard, in this paper, envisaged a modern form of fiction which would demonstrate this distinction between realism and reality – the apostolic reality, a matter of perspective, universal truth, and the perception of links and connections between disparate happenings. (His future wife's fictional aims and methods may owe something to his vision.) Writing, and how to write about writing, was his preoccupation.

In an earlier paper,[15] 'What is Style?' he said that there was almost no worthwhile literary criticism 'because of the vagueness of meaning attached to the critical words which the critic uses'. If criticism were ever to have any value it must become 'scientific', and substitute for 'its present vague and meaningless vocabulary a definite technology' – another idea half a century before its time.

Leonard was no longer in thrall to Lytton, who wrote him an extravagant letter from the British Museum reading-room while working on his Fellowship dissertation: 'If I say that you are the only person I can talk to, will you not be absurd in any of the million ways anyone else will be absurd in? I presume you are noble, I presume you will not imagine too little, or be horrified at too much, that you will understand.' Lytton felt like 'a quavering tongue of fire, a mad ghost searching for a hand of flesh' – and so on.[16] He was, as in so many of his letters, practising arpeggios, with a *basso continuo* designed to check out whether Leonard was still prepared to play the game – which was to play, safely, with fire.

Leonard couldn't do this any more. 'I wonder if I really understand,' he replied. 'At any rate, what I feel is – I must tell you the whole truth – a little sad. Do *you* understand that? You never, I think, understood how a year ago I should have felt far otherwise – and a year is such a long time. I feel sad not for the present, but perhaps for the future, certainly for this absurd combination of the present and past, this silly malignity of fate. *Do* you understand?'

He urged Lytton to abandon the British Museum and come for a walk with him in Richmond Park. The harder you worked, 'the more you want to copulate, and probably the more you ought to. I simply go about wanting to do nothing else. Only, unlike you or, perhaps like you now, I usually want it, when it is that and nothing else, with women. If it wasn't for the paraphernalia [condoms] and their extraordinary foulness, I should work all the morning and engage a

15 24 Jan 1903
16 3 June 1904

whore for the afternoon and copulate among the ferns.'[17] He was still a virgin.

After the Civil Service examinations were over in August 1904, Leonard was to join Maynard Keynes and Charlie Sanger – an older Apostle, married, and a barrister – on a walking tour in Wales. Lytton begged him to come straight on to meet him in Cambridge afterwards, even offering to pay his train fare. Leonard declined. 'I have about £7 & that *must* last me till October at least and I expect I shall spend it all in Wales. I've also vowed to stay with [Leopold] Campbell in Surrey, which however won't cost me anything as I shall bicycle there.' Lytton should write to him at Pwlleli post office, 'but be careful [i.e. discreet] as it may get to the dead letter office and be opened.'[18] On the way back, he lost his luggage on the train with 'all the clothes I ever possessed, except a pair of "knickers" [tweed knee-breeches] and a frayed shirt without a collar.'

A discouraged letter from Lytton which reached Leonard in Wales moved 'my pity rather than my anger'. He reassured Lytton that he was 'only in a trough', and that 'we were and are extraordinarily right' in their values.[19] This elicited another extended verbal flight, designed to recapture Leonard's heart and mind: 'We are – oh! – in more ways than one, like the Athenians of the Periclean age. We are the mysterious priests of a new and amazing civilization. We have abolished religion, we have founded ethics, we have established philosophy, we have sown a strange illumination in every province of thought, we have conquered art, we have liberated love . . . Your letter was wonderful, and I was particularly impressed by the curious masculinity of it. Why are you a man? We are females, nous autres, but your mind is singularly male.'

Leonard was by no means the only one to whom Lytton wrote in such a way. He was increasingly intimate with Maynard Keynes, and perpetually in a tumult over attractive 'embryos'.

*

---

17 28 June 1904
18 29 Aug 1904
19 8 Sep 1904

Moore's six-year Fellowship ran out; he was leaving Cambridge and going north to live with his closest friend Fred Ainsworth, who had a lectureship in Greek at Edinburgh University. Lytton and Maynard Keynes were taking over as the leading lights in the Society, and Cambridge remained the centre of Lytton's social and emotional universe, even though he failed to win his Fellowship at Trinity. But Cambridge, for Leonard, was over. At a meeting of the Society, in Keynes's rooms in King's on 15 October 1904, he became an honorary member and 'took wings'.

The results of the Civil Service examinations came out. Saxon Sydney-Turner was forty-fifth out of ninety-nine listed. Leonard Woolf was sixty-ninth.[20] He had to break the less than good news to his family. His elder brother Herbert, as head of the household, talked seriously to him about money. Herbert had gone straight from school into the City, to work with a firm of stockbrokers. The family finances were worse than Leonard realised. He was required not only to earn his living but to contribute if possible to the home, so there was no question of trying to become a writer, which was what he wanted. The Bar was out of the question too. It cost money to read for the Bar. He could be a schoolmaster. As he told Lytton, 'I have to rush about finding out whether people will allow their sons to be taught by Jews and Atheists.'

But like Saxon, he had an asterisk after his name in the Civil Service list, which meant he would be offered something, though not a plum posting such as the Foreign Office. Saxon was offered the Post Office, turned it down, and accepted a clerkship at the Treasury in the Estate Duty Office. Leonard was offered an 'Eastern Cadetship' in the Colonial Service. 'I shall probably get Ceylon', he told Saxon. 'I am going to have an operation on the scrotum:[21] I shall not be allowed to move for 6 weeks. Amen.'

Ceylon it was. 'I don't know why one doesn't commit suicide, except that one is dead and rotten already', he wrote to Lytton. 'I feel that, in

---

20 For some reason he told Lytton he was 65th.

21 An undescended testicle?

a way, you are lost to me already . . .'[22] (For all the differences and difficulties, he was closer to Lytton than to anyone in the world.) He gave a formal farewell dinner for Desmond MacCarthy, Thoby Stephen and Saxon Sydney-Turner. (Saxon had moved into lodgings at 37 Great Ormond Street – two furnished rooms, with identical oleographs of the same rural scene, one on each side of his bed – where he was to moulder for decades.) Morgan Forster, the Taupe, came for a farewell lunch at Lexham. The Taupe was already publishing stories in the *Independent Review,* a Cambridge journal founded by Goldie Lowes Dickinson, and had started writing his first novel.

Leonard found this lowering. As his sister Bella well knew, her 'dearest Len' would rather 'cast in your lot with Literature with a capital L' than go to Ceylon. But if he felt he could commit himself to the Bar, she would pay the £40 for registration. 'I have a serial ordered by Cassell's[23] for which they promise to pay me £60 and well, there's my offer.' He could not accept. He was running around – so much for not moving for six weeks – buying kit for Ceylon at the Army & Navy Stores, and taking riding lessons. 'My bottom is raw from riding', he told Lytton, and ' I am dressed in completely new clothes. My balls are in a suspensory bandage with four straps round my legs and hips, my calves in sock-suspenders, and my belly in a cholera belt.'

Lytton was in one of his emotional crises, 'drunk and degraded' as Leonard irritably observed. But he went to Cambridge for a last weekend to act as Lytton's 'love surveyor and expert', and to hear, with him and Saxon, Beethoven's Fifth Symphony, the C Minor. He went to Scotland for a couple of days, to say goodbye to his brother Harold, working on a farm near Aberdeen, and to the Yen in Edinburgh.

He also went to dinner with the Stephens, to say goodbye to the Goth. The lovely sisters, Vanessa and Virginia, were there. Their father had died the previous February, and the four young adult children had let the gloomy Hyde Park Gate house and rented 46 Gordon Square, in

22 11 Oct 1904

23 Publishers of *Little Folks,* to which Bella contributed children's stories – hence her reference to 'Literature with a capital L', in ironic acknowledgment of LW's higher aspirations.

Bloomsbury – at least as big, but light and airy – in order to live differently and as they pleased. Virginia was recovering from a severe mental breakdown. The evening that Leonard went to dinner, she was pale and quiet.

Leonard and Lytton agreed to write to each other once a week, and to keep each other's letters. Leonard was taking all the letters he already had from Lytton with him to Ceylon, 'under lock and key in the old cigar box. Do you think it is dangerous?'[24] They were always worried about their correspondence falling into hostile hands.

But what they both had in mind, already, was posterity. When Leonard came to write about his Cambridge years in *Sowing,* he was nearly eighty years old. Thoby Stephen was dead. Lytton Strachey was dead. Saxon Sydney-Turner was dead. Clive Bell was dead. Maynard Keynes was dead. G.E.Moore was dead. Their names were and are famous for whatever it is that each of them became famous for. (Saxon is famous for being their friend. His is the name in a hundred indexes.) What Leonard wrote about Cambridge is discursive and impressionistic, and broken up by fast-forwards to what came after; the world he found there determined so much of his future. He wrote more about the Apostles than, in their memoirs, did any of his contemporaries. He wrote little about his inner life and, writing about his friends, he composed extended 'characters' of them, in the eighteenth-century manner. The actuality of the young men that they were, with their curiosity and desire, their posing, their cruelties and infatuations, their immature authenticities, their terrible arrogance, is irretrievable. It was irretrievable to Leonard, at eighty. Only in the letters that Leonard and his friends wrote to one another, and preserved, can one get closer.

Desmond MacCarthy gave Leonard a miniature edition of Shakespeare, and a four-volume Milton. Leonard also had the works of Voltaire in seventy volumes. His fox-terrier Charles was going too, but

---

24 18 Nov 1904

since the P & O Line did not carry animals, Charles had to travel separately, on a Bibby Line ship.

On the evening of 19 November 1904, Leonard was on board the S.S. *Syria* as it started out on its voyage to Colombo.

5

Serendib

He was leaving behind everything and everyone he knew. His mother and his sister Bella waved goodbye as the *Syria* moved away from Tilbury Docks. The voyage out took a whole calendar month plus one day.

'I feel as if I had been born and lived all my life on this ship', he wrote to Lytton on 26 November, the day after his twenty-fourth birthday. He was thrown in with the kind of people of whom he – the city boy from a large Jewish family, the Cambridge intellectual – had little experience: ordinary English people. His 'carapace' was reimposed during the voyage, and became a fixture. He played chess, quoits, draughts and bridge. He danced and he chatted.

There was a letter from Lytton waiting at Port Said, where Leonard, who had never been further afield than the north of France, had his first experience of the swarming crowds and intense heat of the East. He took to sleeping on deck: 'It's very charming with the stars and the noise of the sea and the waking up at sunrise.' Lytton's letter had been a comfort: 'Do write like that, then I shall not altogether be left high and dry.'[1]

1 4 Dec 1904

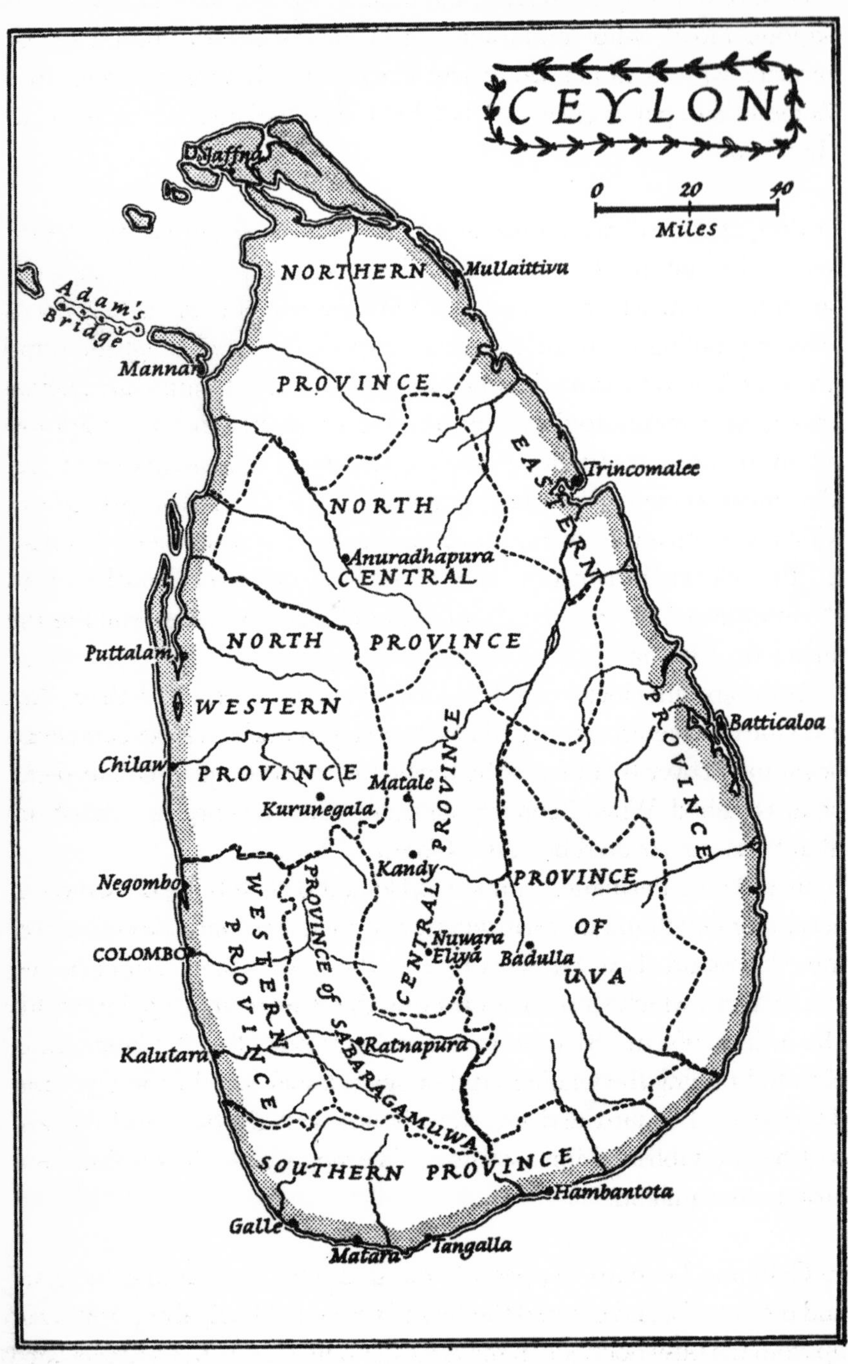
CEYLON
0 20 40
Miles
Jaffna
Mullaittivu
NORTHERN
PROVINCE
Adam's Bridge
Mannar
Trincomalee
EASTERN
NORTH
Anuradhapura
CENTRAL
NORTH
PROVINCE
Puttalam
WESTERN
PROVINCE
Batticaloa
Chilaw
PROVINCE
Matale
Kurunegala
CENTRAL PROVINCE
Kandy
PROVINCE
Negombo
WESTERN PROVINCE
PROVINCE of SABARAGAMUWA
PROVINCE
OF
UVA
Nuwara Eliya
Badulla
COLOMBO
CENTRAL
Ratnapura
Kalutara
SOUTHERN PROVINCE
Hambantota
Galle
Matara
Tangalla

He talked mostly to an Irishman named Scroope and the handsome Captain Lloyd, who reminded him of the Goth, and had a minor romance with 'a rather wonderful female', the Irishman's sister. In a Memoir Club paper given in 1943, he said he had gone so far as to kiss Miss Scroope.

Ceylon, renamed Sri Lanka in 1972, was where Sinbad the Sailor was washed up in *The Thousand and One Nights.* Arab mariners called it Serendib, from which the word 'serendipity' was coined. It is like a tear-drop falling from the southern tip of India, and about the same size as Ireland or Tasmania. Over more than a millennium, an evolved artistic and technological culture was supported by an irrigation system of huge reservoirs – 'tanks' – many of which survive in use. The most ancient Sinhalese kingdom centred on Anuradhapura, which was converted to Buddhism in the third century before Christ. In the eleventh century the capital was moved southeast to Polonnurawa, and the first Tamil (Hindu) kingdom established in the far north at Jaffna.

As the ancient cities were abandoned, the jungle reclaimed them. Not until the nineteenth century did archaeologists and interested amateurs begin to uncover them from the tangled forest through which wild elephants crashed. When Leonard was there, about seventy per cent of the island was still covered by natural forest.

In 1505 the Portuguese landed at Colombo. The King of Kandy, in accepting Dutch military assistance, admitted a second colonial power into the island. Like the Portuguese, the Dutch built churches and coastal forts, which were taken over by the British who supplanted the Dutch in 1796. In 1815 the British gained control of the kingdom of Kandy, bringing the whole island under colonial rule for the first time. Thus when Leonard arrived, what is now called 'the British Period' had been established for a century. The population, in his time, was around four million.

In Colombo Leonard stepped off the ship into the heat and the glare and the crowds, and entered the Grand Oriental Hotel, about 150 yards up from the busy dockside in the area still called the Fort, its streets lined with imperial offices, commercial houses and European stores. There was another letter from Lytton waiting for him. Lytton was lyrically excited by having found the 'perfect embryo' in the form of a blond freshman at Clare College. Leonard was transported back into the world and idiom that he had left behind: 'You are superb: yes, I saw it all unfolding itself as I read your letter and for one moment I felt I was living again.' He himself was not, he believed, 'phenomenal' as yet: 'I'm simply wretched.'[2]

He was reunited with Charles, who was not a classy dog, having been acquired from an advertisement in *Exchange & Mart.* The first thing Charles did on shore was to lift his leg against a bystander's clean white cloth (or sarong). The second was to be sick in the GOH's open-air palm court, the crows swooping to snatch up the vomit. Leonard went for a bicycle ride and felt the beauty of the place and the charm of its inhabitants – 'they are, I feel, either Gods or animals'. The Sinhalese, staring back, probably felt the same about him. Out to dinner with his new civil service colleagues, he was cheered by finding them 'very nice and kind, nearly all from Cambridge and one John Scott of King's' who was a friend of 'Hom', H.O. Meredith.

Leonard was posted up-country to Jaffna in the Northern Province, on a peninsula at the far tip of the island. He set off by train at the beginning of January, with a Sinhalese servant, Charles, the seventy volumes of Voltaire in a crate, and his tin trunk.

The railway line in 1905 only reached as far as Anuradhapura in the central highlands. The British had built Government Rest Houses in the main towns – simple bungalows, for officials in transit or on circuit. Leonard spent the night in the Anuradhapura Rest House,[3] after dining with the local Government Agent, C.T.D. Vigors, and the genteel Mrs Vigors, and the wholesomely pretty Miss Vigors, at the Residency. The conversation was shop, sport and gossip. 'But we were all rather grand, a good deal grander than we would have been at home in London or

2 20 Dec 1904
3 Now called the Tissawewa Rest House

Edinburgh, Brighton or Oban. We were grand because we were a ruling caste in a strange Asiatic country.'

When Leonard returned to the Rest House after dinner, Charles had disappeared. Early next morning two missionary ladies, Miss Case and Miss Beeching, also on their way to Jaffna, looked out of the train window at a station and saw a patently European dog trotting beside the line in the opposite direction. They scooped Charles up and appeared with him at the Rest House just as Leonard was having breakfast. Charles had decided to run back to Colombo to find him.

In *Growing* Leonard described himself on arrival in Ceylon as 'a very innocent, unconscious imperialist'. The Sinhalese had a caste system, which the British trumped by becoming the top caste of all. Leonard, though he had daily dealings with the poor people in their hundreds, and met educated men – lawyers, teachers and doctors – in the course of his work, never made close friends with any of them. He was too uncertain of his own acceptability in the white man's culture, even though he despised it, to think of stepping outside it as did Fielding in E.M.Forster's *A Passage to India* (1924) or Flory in George Orwell's *Burmese Days* (1934). The social divide was mutually sustained. The British were not included in the lively Ceylonese social calendar or in the literary and political circles of Colombo. Many in the Ceylonese middle classes were 'vaguely related, and had Sinhalese, Tamil, Dutch, British and Burgher[4] blood going back many generations.' They saw the English as 'transients, snobs and racists'.[5]

Among the British, the Governor was at the top of the heap. Ceylon was an obscure and small Crown Colony, its governorship frequently shoved on to second-rate men.[6] At the top of the Ceylon

4 Burghers are Ceylonese with some European ancestry, often with Dutch family names.

5 Michael Ondaatje, *Running in the Family* Bloomsbury 1983. Ondaatje was referring to the 1920s, but the same would have been true earlier.

6 One of the exceptions was Sir William Gregory (Governor 1872–77), whose widow was to be the supporter and friend of W.B.Yeats.

Civil Service were the Colonial Secretary and the heads of key departments such as the Treasury and the Judiciary, based in Colombo.

The island was divided in Leonard's time into nine provinces, each run by a Government Agent (GA), supported by officers of the specialist services – legal, fiscal, medical, technical. Under the GAs were the Assistant Government Agents, the AGAs. In charge of a provincial division, a 'district', an AGA fulfilled most of the functions of a GA, working with the chief headmen and a descending hierarchy of local officials. Next in line in each divisional centre came the Office Assistant and, at the bottom of this bureaucratic heap, the Cadets. Leonard when he went to Jaffna was a Cadet, on £300 a year.

The journey onwards to Elephant Pass (the neck of land linking Jaffna to the rest of the island) took '40 hours of hell' in a covered bullock cart, jolting through the endless jungle on rocky earth tracks. The soil in the central hill country is the colour of paprika, shading to turmeric as one proceeds north. Leonard came to love this northern landscape of palmyrah palms and scrub jungle and great stretches of sand. Its austere beauty 'got into my heart and bones.'

In Jaffna, the average mean temperature was 82.2 degrees F. In Jaffna town, population around 34,000, some of the fifteen or so white civil servants lived within the old Dutch Fort on the edge of the sea – a pentagon as big as Trafalgar Square, with a double skin of coral-rock walls separated by a moat. But Jaffna was not a military base. The King's House, where the Governor stayed when he visited, was within the Fort, as were the prison, officials' bungalows and gardens, the tennis courts, and a fine old Dutch church.

Leonard was met by the Office Assistant, W.T. (Tom) Southorn, a year older than himself and an Oxford man – 'brainless', he told Lytton. He was introduced to Herbert Dowbiggin, the Superintendent of Police, and Jimmy Bowes, the Assistant Superintendent of Police, who conducted him into the Fort. Here Charles disappeared over a wall and, after a noisy struggle, emerged with a dead cat in his mouth. A few minutes later he caught a snake. Leonard in *Growing* itemised Charles's exploits with glee: trangression by proxy, as with – on a somewhat different level – Lytton (who was now 'the past and a delightful dream to me'[7]). Charles did much for Leonard's credibility, as did his competent bridge-playing, and even – or so he believed – his green flannel collars. There was a fashion, shortly before he left England, for wearing soft, coloured, detachable collars instead of the usual stiff white ones. Lytton and the Goth were appalled by the green collars, as they were by his brown boots. Leonard was not one of nature's dandies.

On one of the bastions on the Fort's ramparts was the shabby bungalow, overhung by banyan trees, which Leonard shared with Southorn. Outside the Fort was a large open space, a 'maidan', called the Esplanade, leading to the town. Some old Dutch houses stood along the main street, and comfortable villas and bungalows by the lagoon along Beach Road. There were Hindu temples, the bazaar, a Roman Catholic seminary; and streets and alleys of single-storey Tamil homes concealed behind high 'cadjan' fences of woven coconut fronds, bleached by the sun to an ashy no-colour.

The government offices, the kachcheri, were a ten-minute bicycle ride from the Fort. Here Leonard worked in a white-walled room with unglassed barred windows. 'I check the accounts of the province, test weights and measures, and issue orders which I hardly understand', he told Lytton in his first week. His long working days were spent signing letters, responding to official telegrams, issuing licences, taking in revenue.

After a few weeks, mightily bored, Leonard asked Tom Southorn if he could have more interesting work. Interesting work meant more work. Leonard tried and fined miscreants, answered petitions, resolved questions about 'salt and coolies and family quarrels, and irrigation and injustices'. He lived, privately, through letters. He corresponded with Lytton with urgent regularity, and Saxon too wrote often, in well-tailored sentences as if translated from the Latin. Leonard heard from Forster, Keynes, Bob Trevy and MacCarthy. The Yen sent self-deprecatory letters from Edinburgh about not being able to do philosophy or enjoy anything and doubting whether his letters were welcome. The spell he cast over his disciples was weakening. 'The Yen is an old man now', Leonard wrote to Lytton (Moore was in his early thirties), 'he has

7 5 Jan 1905

settled down . . . But we are still drifting: we shall never "settle down", we shall be grey-haired undergraduates in our coffins.'[8]

The British ruled Ceylon not by force of arms but by bureaucracy. Rules and regulations controlled every aspect of life, with penalties for non-compliance. Everything taxable was taxed. The verandah of the Jaffna kachcheri swarmed with jostling humanity, waiting to see Leonard or Tom Southorn in order to pay or contest a fine, buy a licence or permit, fill out a form, air a dispute or grievance, petition for tax exemptions, report crimes.

It seemed to Leonard that the only way to make the system work was to be pedantically strict. The British officials might be disliked, but they must affect to believe implicitly in their religion of rules and regulations, so that the ruled might believe in it too. As George Orwell said, they must 'wear a mask'[9] – not difficult for Leonard. The British also gave Ceylon an infrastructure: roads, railways, schools, hospitals. They developed botanical gardens and game reserves.

The sacred text of the Civil Service in Ceylon was a Minute issued by a former governor, Sir Thomas Maitland, in 1808, which stated that 'the true interests of Government never can be to harass the Natives, with a view to immediate profit, but that on the contrary, the sole object of Government, is and always ought to be considered to be, to ensure the prosperity of the island, solely thro' the medium of generally increasing the prosperity and happiness of the Natives under His Majesty's Government'[10] A modern Sri Lankan commentator's judgement was that the colonial administrators in Ceylon during the British Period were generally 'men of more than average ability, very much like each other, keen on promoting the welfare of the Ceylonese people, but wanting in imagination and sympathy.'[11]

Behind his authoritarian façade, Leonard's imagination and sympa-

---

8 14 Oct 1906

9 'Shooting an Elephant' 1936

10 Quoted by Tisara Prakasakayo, introducing *Leonard Woolf: Diaries in Ceylon 1908–11* Ceylon Historical Journal 1962

11 *idem*

thy were engaged by the people who swarmed on the verandah and stood before him in the kachcheri. He knew them with a paradoxical intimacy, immersing himself daily and with an increasing fascination in their life stories. He appreciated the way their minds worked: their subtlety, suppleness and quick-wittedness, their fatalism.

He had clerks under him and a translator, but the Ceylon Civil Service training programme put stress on learning the vernacular. He had to learn written and spoken Tamil and the Dutch-Roman law under which Ceylon was governed, for the examinations on which promotion would depend. In March 1905, that promotion seemed far away. He was 'nearly dismissed', he told Lytton, for 'a muddle about a travel allowance and I did not answer some letters from the Treasurer'. He was summoned by the G.A. for a ticking-off.

The G.A. was John Penry Lewis, fat and shy and not greatly interested in administration. His true interests were antiquarian and archaeological. His voluble wife Violet, 'Vi' to her intimates, was his antithesis: 'large, plump, floridly good-looking', as Leonard described her in *Growing*.

The GA's residence, The Park, was a large, grey, arcaded Italianate house just behind the kachcheri. Leonard spent many hours in the long drawing room on the first floor. He went over to tea after the office, 'and there sit three women' – Mrs Lewis, her children's governess, and a 'silent, spotty and wizened' Miss Moorhouse. The governess was a 'horrible, painted' forty-five-year-old, 'engaged to a Cadet of twenty-five and who, I quote popular accounts, delights in gentlemen – all Ceylon has done it – putting their hands up her skirts and down her neck but refuses to go any further.' The women 'are always I believe thinking of copulation and if they aren't married and do, they dry up'. Vi Lewis was 'the only amusing person in Jaffna in a curiously vulgar and outrageous way but – Lord! I'm damnably polite and nice and quiet but I feel at any moment I may get up and burst out against the whole stupid degraded circle of degenerates and imbeciles'. Others called in, 'terrible old gentlemen and the wives of cocoanut planters pretending to be grandes dames.'[12] Tea merged into whisky and soda and bridge.

12 To LS 2 July 1905

He found time to read. In March 1905 he read Voltaire's *Dictionnaire Philosophique*: 'The more I read him', he told Lytton, 'the more I see that you are Voltaire on the hearthrug.' But Lytton's ever-changing love life, still focused on Cambridge and the look-out for 'embryos', became baffling. There was another new person – Arthur Hobhouse, 'Hobby'. 'The whole relationship is almost ridiculously parental', commented Leonard. 'Have you – we – grown so very old, or is he so enormously young?'[13] And was Hom quite so wonderful as Lytton made out? 'I don't understand exactly what you want, for I don't understand – as the Yen would say – your state of mind towards him.' He supposed that what Lytton sought was just 'an intimate companionship'. Lytton must remember that Leonard had nearly forgotten how to talk about anything except 'the Service and whores'.[14]

And then, all the warmth of connection, and hope for his own intellectual survival, would flood back. He was sent a copy of the *Independent Review* with a piece he had written about Voltaire in it. 'Wasn't it on the whole rather a distinguished number?' And why did not Lytton come out and see him, 'and forget everything, lying under trees and just talking through the long evenings?' He felt unable to comment on the letters from Hobby to Keynes, which Lytton had enclosed with a book parcel, 'without knowing how far *you* had gone both with Keynes and with him.'[15]

In the late evening he sat out on the verandah of the bungalow, smoking and drinking with the police superintendents, Dowbiggin and Bowes. Jimmy Bowes was in his early thirties, already fat and flabby, and only interested in drink, horses and women. His language, like Dowbiggin's, was filthy. Charles the dog was unable to withstand the torrid heat between monsoons, which grilled the backs of Leonard's hands like bacon and made his eyeballs twitch and jump. 'He is blind now and paralysed.' Leonard sat in on 'the most astonishing and sordid thing' he had yet seen, a case where 'an old hag of a woman' accused an eighteen-year-old of raping her. The rest of his time he spent

13 19 March 1905
14 16 April 1905
15 30 April 1905

bathing poor Charles with warm water. On 26 March 1905 Charles died. 'I was a fool to bring him out', Leonard confessed to Saxon, 'but he would have been just as dead as far as I am concerned, had I left him.'

He went with B.J. Dutton, the Police Magistrate, to the two-room Jaffna hospital to make a man's Will, and witnessed filth and overcrowding such as he could not have imagined. In his bungalow, as he read and wrote his letters, there were cockroaches climbing his legs, a cricket crawling down his back, a huge flying beetle circling, and 'a minor plague of small flies and mosquitoes'. Saxon sent him Conrad's *Nostromo*; and he was thrilled by Sir Richard Burton's *Pilgrimage to al-Medinah and Mecca:* 'Even here in this squalid little place, you have the curious absorbing people, and now and then there is a strangeness and beauty about a place that you could never have dreamt of in England.'[16]

In May 1905 Tom Southorn was transferred to North-Central Province, and as the bungalow went with the post of Office Assistant, the new O.A., J.H. Leak, moved in. Leak had tuberculosis, a 'half naked female child usually dressed in pyjamas, and a grubby looking semiburgher wife dressed in a white dressing-gown very open at the neck'. Since the sick Leak could only work half the day, Leonard added some of the Office Assistant's duties to his own. He was appointed an Additional Collector of Customs and an Additional Police Magistrate.

He went to share B.J. Dutton's bungalow in the town, overhung by trees and infested with mosquitoes. Dutton, the Police Magistrate, was four years older than himself. Leonard became obsessed by Dutton, writing a quite disproportionate amount about him to amuse his friends in Jaffna, in his letters to England, and later in Memoir Club papers and in *Growing*. The combined material constitutes a virtual novella.

Dutton was not a 'pukka sahib' – no public school, no university education. He was physically insignificant. He did not play tennis or bridge. He spent his evenings writing poetry about elves and fairies,

---

16 23 April 1905

and playing, endlessly, an arrangement of Beethoven's Fifth Symphony, the C Minor, on his out-of-tune piano. Leonard too, who did not play the piano, began to pick out the themes, remembering his last visit to Cambridge. Dutton was self-taught, with everything he read and heard mixed up in his mind in an 'undigested, sticky mess of "culture"'. Leonard in a Memoir Club paper called Dutton one of the 'wrecks of civilisation – ruined by education, poisoned by knowledge . . . unhinged by books, art and music'. His poetry had 'a sort of castrated eroticism'. Leonard felt he was a mental and probably a physical eunuch.

The fascination of Dutton for Leonard was that Dutton was a terrifyingly degraded version of himself. 'He always reminded me of Leonard Bast in *Howard's End*', Leonard wrote in *Growing*. There is a trace of the young Leonard Woolf too in Forster's Leonard Bast, who meets intellectuals for the first time at a performance of the C Minor symphony, and has no hinterland of confident, 'establishment' family and friends. Dutton was small and unprepossessing, and a swot, and afraid of sex, and his poetry was terrible.

The basis of Dutton's character, wrote Leonard in *Growing,* was 'timidity, which, as so often, was compensated underneath by boundless self-conceit. His lower-class origin superimposed upon his timidity a deep inferiority complex which burst out in the most grotesque intellectual arrogance.' Substitute 'Jewish' for 'lower class' and one may find a contemptuous description of Leonard as a young man. The saving grace of the obsession was that Leonard was *not* Dutton, and he knew that too. For a start, he had discovered his sexuality.

Leonard was riding home on horseback one evening when he exchanged smiles over a cadjan fence with a Burgher girl sitting on a verandah. A small boy came running out after him to ask whether he would like her to come to his bungalow that night. Leonard said yes. She was the first woman he ever slept with, and visited him thenceforth once a week. 'I am quite sure that every European except Dutton himself, and 90% of the natives knew this and every detail of our conversation, and the number of times that I had her per night and what I paid her. She was – though I did not at that time know it – a most notorious whore.'[17] She was the niece of his own head clerk, and was being kept by a respectable Tamil lawyer.

The next thing was that Dutton as Police Magistrate had a case brought before him against this same girl for standing in the road shouting abuse outside the Tamil lawyer's house. Dutton judged that, although she was technically in the wrong, she was a pure young girl being sexually harrassed by the licentious lawyer. He fined her, and then paid her fine himself. As Leonard recorded in *Growing*, the whole incident gave everyone in Jaffna 'immense pleasure and amusement'.

Since Leonard himself had been hitherto unaware of her other activities, the incident cannot have been very amusing for him. Late in life, he had a letter from an American professor who remembered Leonard telling him that one of his reasons for leaving the Service was 'a realization of the difficulty for you or other Britons to establish normal friendships with the Ceylonese people, because of the risk of blackmail.' That was not, replied Leonard, generally true. 'There was one case in which I felt that unless I was very careful I might have been blackmailed . . .'[18]

Sex with his prostitute was a far cry from evening tennis in the Fort – a social ritual, after which the players sat round with drinks and gossiped. The two missionaries, Miss Case and Miss Beeching, sat apart, disapprovingly. Leonard could not decide whether Rudyard Kipling, in his short stories about amorous intrigues and petty snobberies in Simla, the Indian hill-station, had moulded his characters accurately in the image of Anglo-Indian society or 'whether we were moulding our characters accurately in the image of a Kipling story.'

In July 1905 Leonard and Dutton gave a bridge party, with lemonade and biscuits. Leonard was not keen to invite Miss Case and Miss Beeching, but Dutton insisted, and spent the day, as Leonard told Lytton, 'trying vainly to make his room not the foulest and hugest filth-packet by putting up kind of lodging house curtains of muslin and

17 Memoir Club Paper

18 26 June 1968 to Professor Charles S. Blackstone, the Ceylon specialist, at Colgate University.

terrible pink flowered stuff.' Five females and the GA 'lumbered in'. Dutton played his arrangement of Beethoven's Fifth Symphony in C Minor. After it was over, Leonard wrote a grim poem, 'The C Minor', of which these are the first, and last three, of seven stanzas:

> I laugh, my dear, to see you sitting there,
> Your poor weak eyes blinking into the sun,
> I wonder if for the good God overhead,
> A little shame has crept into his fun . . .
>
> You listen, even as I do, to the notes,
> The awful iteration of Fate's hand,
> Hammered upon the tinkling cracked piano –
> I wonder if you really understand.
>
> You hear him sounding it out in the other room,
> The bitterness, doom and mockery of each thing –
> As you sit there silent, I wonder, do you hear
> The exquisite note of degradation ring?
>
> Your poor pale hair, and queerly puckered mouth,
> And dry skin that fierce suns have marked and tanned,
> Your curious dreary silence makes me think,
> Or like to think, you really understand.

Leonard persuaded Dutton to come to the tennis courts, upon which he was taken up by Miss Case and Miss Beeching. Astonishingly, Miss Beeching and Dutton became a couple. Rumour ran round the small community. 'I *am* engaged', Dutton confessed to Leonard in September 1905. It was generally though to be 'very rum'.

In August 1905 there was a visitation from the governor and his wife, Sir Henry and Lady Blake, and Leonard had to play under-housemaid, as he told Lytton, and see that the King's House was prepared, and 'reckon out how many fishknives and pillowcases and pos he wants'. He had 'counted the linen and put up decorations and shown H[is]E[xcellency] round salt pans and arranged the flowers and sweated in frock coats and helped Mrs Lewis make Lady Blake's bed. (I don't know if you realise how wonderfully vulgar the GA's wife is.)' He confirmed Lytton in his beady suspicion that he was half in love with the GA's wife – because she was the only (white) person in Jaffna not wholly hideous. 'She has superb hair and arms, hideous hands, and a fat "good looking" face . . . When one gets to the heights of unreality, one can be, I think, very nearly supreme.' He was moving house again, having had enough of Dutton's fusty bungalow.

He joined George Dawson Templer, the Assistant Conservator of Forests, in his bungalow on Beach Road. Leonard and Templer got on well. Leonard lent him money when he was short, and Templer missed him when he was away: 'It makes such a difference to me making a male *friend* in this little island.' They played cricket on the bungalow's verandah, Leonard solemnly reporting to Saxon that 'I got his 10 men out for 19 runs principally through the lob bowler. I made 209 for 9 wickets my last man retiring after making his century.' Templer had a tame baby leopard, and Leonard imported a deer. They also acquired five dogs, a monkey and a mongoose.

Leonard had a growing passion for animals. He wrote, describing the menagerie at the bungalow in *Growing:* 'If you really understand an animal, so that he gets to trust you completely . . . there grows up between you affection of a purity and simplicity which seems to me peculiarly satisfactory'. He loved them too for the 'cosmic strangeness' of their minds, their otherness.

But all Lytton wanted to hear about was Leonard's whores. 'I suppose you want to know everything', Leonard wrote in early September 1905, as he lay becalmed in a sail-boat on the lagoon on his way back from Poonaryn, where he had overseen road-building. He was 'worn out or rather merely supine through a night of purely degraded debauch. The pleasure of it is of course greatly exaggerated certainly with a half-caste whore.' Yet he wrote to Keynes in mid-November that the conversation of whores was more amusing than the conversation of bores; and to Lytton that he could envisage living 'alone with a burgher concubine in a long bare whitewashed bungalow overlooking the lagoon, where time is only divided between reading Voltaire on the immense verandah and copulating in the vast and empty rooms where there is a perpetual smell of bats and damp and the paint and plaster peel off the walls and gather on the stone floors.'

The British in Ceylon fell ill constantly. A young colleague died of enteric fever in Jaffna while Leonard was there. Whether a man was 'fit' or not was a matter of grave discussion. Leonard had intermittent attacks of malaria and fever. Always thin, he became seriously underweight. Wounds failed to heal and went septic. He had eczema. He had ringworm: 'Most people do in Jaffna.' When in Colombo for a week to sit his first exams, in Tamil and in Law and Accounts, he had dysentery, but managed to sample Colombo society. The white women gave him the creeps with their 'pale dried-up faces and drawling voices'. He came back 'covered with boils and sores',[19] as he told Saxon, thus more like Job than ever.[20] He passed his exams, which meant a pay rise, 'and people go about saying that I run the Northern Province by myself already'. He attributed his success to his application of 'the method'; it was 'a wonderful instrument and weapon used practically.'

A few days later he fell ill with typhoid. There was no doctor in Jaffna who would treat a European. Even at the American mission hospital at Manippay, six miles away, there was no ward judged suitable, so he was put in an outhouse and nursed by his own servant. He went south to convalesce in the delicious cool of the hill country, in the hotel in Bandarawela, and described to Lytton his joy in walking in a 'sea of hills'. He reassured Saxon that he was improving rapidly, 'except that all my hair is coming out and my hand trembles more than ever.'

At Bandarawela he received a telegram from the GA asking him whether he was fit enough to help to superintend the Pearl Fishery at Marichchukkaddi, off the barren, uninhabited coast of the Gulf of Mannar eighty miles west of Jaffna. Before he left for Mannar, he posted back all Lytton's letters to him in the tin box. He realised, when he was

19 30 Oct 1905

20 'My flesh is clothed with worms and clods of dust; my skin is broken, and become loathsome.' Book of Job 7: 6

away, that it was dangerous to 'keep them in bulk'. 'You must swear to keep them for me until I come back.'

It took a day and a half by boat, in February 1906, to get to the Fishery. A shanty-town built on the desert shore housed twenty to thirty thousand people – divers, traders, dealers, jewellers, criminals – who poured in by sea from all over Asia. Lewis the GA was in charge; Mrs Lewis came along with her gramophone and one record, 'Funiculi, funicula'. John Scott, AGA for Mannar, was there, and Malcolm Stevenson, a convivial Irishman. Arab and Tamil divers shovelled the oysters off the seabed into baskets and hauled them back into their boats. The Government appropriated two thirds of the daily catch, which was auctioned off each evening. The encampment stank, and was infested with flies, for the pearls were extracted by leaving the thousands upon thousands of oysters to rot. Stevenson went down with malaria; he had syphilis, from which he died not long after. Scott too fell ill.

Leonard worked on, overseeing the unloading and selling of the oysters amid the stench and heat, using his walking stick to keep order. He acquired great respect for the Arab divers, for their skill, grace, dignity and lack of servility. His problem was his eczema: 'The irritation is perpetual and the skin continually breaks and bleeds', he wrote to Saxon. 'As it's all over the scrotum you can imagine the result of continually plodding in the sun over loose sand.'[21]

Leonard's account of the Pearl Fishery in *Growing,* lifted from the long, descriptive letters he wrote to Lytton, is among the best sustained set-pieces he wrote. He exploited the material after his return to England in a powerful short story, 'Pearls and Swine',[22] in which the illnesses of Scott and Stephenson were exaggerated to horrific effect. In his story, a brash young Civil Service man new in the colony breaks down, vomiting and weeping, unable to handle the flies, the smell, the violence. Nor can he cope with another white man, a pearl dealer who has fits of DTs, raving about obscene abuses he has inflicted on the natives. There are two deaths – the pearl dealer's, screaming in the

21 26 March 1906
22 Published in LW, *Stories of the East* Hogarth Press 1921

throes of ghastly hallucinations, and an Arab pearl fisher's, handled by his fellow Arabs with quiet, ceremonial dignity. The implication is Conradian: neither white man was any good under pressure – one because he was ignorant and hollow at the core, the other because he had rotted morally and 'gone under' as the phrase was out East.

'Are you ever happy now?' Leonard enquired of Lytton in September 1905. Lytton was falling in love with his handsome artist cousin Duncan Grant; and Walter Lamb, a Cambridge contemporary, had 'made up his fetid mind' to be in love with Lytton's younger brother James. When Lytton called in at Gordon Square, 'Adrian opened the door and told me at once that Lamb had copulated with James. I nearly died.'[23]

The Goth, reading for the Bar in London, had started holding 'Thursday evenings' at Gordon Square. Saxon, attending for the first time, 'was entertained between Goth and Gurth very well. No one else came.' Gurth was the Stephens' dog. ('Your At Homes sound wild', commented Leonard.) Lytton kept in touch, as did Saxon, with the Woolf family, and went to tea with Edgar in Cambridge at his rooms in Market Passage: 'rather gloomy and savage, I thought.' Saxon remarked that 'Edgar looks oddly like you now' and that the similarity had 'quite startled' Henry Lamb when he met Edgar on King's Parade. But maybe Leonard had changed? The Goth often asked Saxon what Leonard would be like when he came back. 'I always answer that I don't know but perhaps your violence will be unimagineable.'

Edgar could indeed be gloomy and savage, being subject to serious depression, and his interests were not Lytton's. He developed 'a mania to see how the working people really lived'; when he left Cambridge, he worked for a year in a tobacco factory, living with his fellow workers 'in the slums of Bristol'.[24] Cecil, the second youngest Woolf brother, came up to Cambridge, to Sidney Sussex College, in autumn 1906, and Lytton called on him too. He wrote to Leonard: 'He's an odd character. I fancy he just misses supremacy, and unfortunately in that case a miss

---

23 7 Dec 1905. Berg
24 Typescript of interview with Edgar Woolf by M.Roe, archivist of St Paul's School

is as good as a mile. But he's very amusing, and very easy to get on with, and very cultivated.' Leonard concurred that 'Cecil, I think, is or was surprisingly unapostolic.'

The Lewises left for Kandy, where Mr Lewis was transferred as Government Agent. The new GA Northern Province, Ferdinando Hamlyn Price, was very different – tall, thin, fit, ruthless. The night Leonard went to meet the Prices at The Park, he got blind drunk, and on his return seriously considered (not for the first time) shooting himself. Mrs Price was reserved and, Leonard thought, unhappy. He gave her a puppy, Twilight, who was snapped up by a crocodile. With the Lewises, Leonard had been expected to visit from teatime onwards. With the Prices, Leonard had lunch (with Madeira wine) at The Park every day.

Like Lewis, Price pushed much of his work on to Leonard. He was 'absolutely cold pure intellect' as he told Lytton, and even 'superb'.[25] Leonard learned two things from him about efficient administration. The first was, never use two words where one will suffice. The second was, answer every letter on the day of its receipt. This was revolutionary in Jaffna, as in his later postings, where bulging files of unanswered letters overflowed every surface. He enforced the rule, and continued to do so in his professional dealings for the rest of his life.

Price was dedicated to golf, so Leonard played golf with him. Price liked to gamble, and so did Leonard. They played bridge for money and had a running wager on the daily rainfall statistics. (Between the monsoons the rainfall was virtually nil.) Price and Leonard also bet on horses. Leonard's biggest win was in the 1908 Calcutta Club Melbourne Cup sweepstake: £690. He sent some of the money home to his family.

27 August 1906, to Saxon: 'I am camping out in a tent in the wilderness.' The AGA of the Mannar division, John Scott, was ill, and Leonard was seconded to take on his duties in 400 square miles of thinly inhabited jungle. Alone apart from his servant and a dog, he

---

25 21 April 1906

acquired a love of solitude which never left him. He rode on horseback ten miles between six and nine each morning 'through a desolation of sand to visit a few huts which are called villages', and lay in a tent reading Dickens during the heat of the day. 'I have forgotten how to talk, after two years of forgetting how to think. It is very pleasant, one glides into the vegetable state of the East,' he told Saxon.

He felt only ironic irritation now about Lytton's love crises. 'You have corrupted Cambridge as Socrates corrupted Athens . . . For it seems to have broken out into open sodomy, or rather into an interminable series of reciprocal flirtations.' In December 1906 Leonard tore up Lytton's latest letter. He said it made him feel sick – though the contents were probably mild compared with the glittering epistolary obscenities then being exchanged between Lytton with Maynard Keynes. Leonard suspected he would hate the new Apostles, such as the old Etonians H.T.J.(Harry) Norton, and Arthur Hobhouse (Hobby), when he met them. He had a letter from Thoby, the Goth, touching on these intrigues with robust dismissiveness. Leonard still revered the Goth: 'He stands, doesn't he?' he wrote admiringly to Lytton.

Thoby Stephen had gone abroad with his brother Adrian, and his sisters Vanessa and Virginia, and wrote to Leonard from Greece, where Vanessa became ill; and Thoby fell ill on their return. Lytton and Saxon assured Leonard that he was recovering.

Thoby Stephen did not recover. He died of typhoid at Gordon Square on 20 November 1906. Leonard's letter to Lytton – 'He stands, doesn't he?' – was written on 4 December. He heard the terrible news from Lytton eight days later. The time-lag of a month between the writing and receiving of letters was always hard, but this was cruel. 'I am overwhelmed, crushed', wrote Leonard. 'If only I had a soul to whom I could speak a word. It was only a week ago that I wrote to you what we had so often written and said, that he was an anchor . . . If I could only see you and talk to you!'

Clive Bell's interest in Vanessa Stephen had been an issue for over a year. Leonard always suspected Bell was in love 'with one of them – though strangely I thought it was the other [Virginia] . . . Do you think he is really wildly in love with her [Vanessa]?' He himself – curiously, as he said – had been in love with Vanessa 'after they came up that May term to Cambridge', and it was 'still more curious that there is a mirage of it still left. She is so superbly like the Goth. I often used to wonder if he [Bell] was in love with the Goth because he was in love with her [Vanessa] and I was in love with her, because with the Goth.' Lytton found this notion 'very, very wild'.

When Lytton wrote again, less than a week after the Goth's death, Vanessa Stephen and Clive Bell were engaged. Leonard was too weary to mind 'the mockery of it all'. He had a fever, he did his work, 'but I seem to see and hear the Goth all day. It is appalling to think that it is only death that makes it altogether clear what he was to us.'[26] He waited a fortnight before writing a formal letter of congratulation to Clive Bell.

Saxon was going daily to Gordon Square to be with Virginia and Adrian. 'Thoby's friends are the only people they want to see.' Virginia asked him to choose one of Thoby's books to give to Leonard: 'I though perhaps a Milton.' 'I should like nothing better than his Milton', Leonard replied. 'Will you thank them for me?' The marriage of Vanessa and Clive took place on 7 February 1907 in St Pancras Registry Office. 'They have invited no one', Lytton reported, 'not their nearest relations[27] and some distress has been caused . . . She's very intelligent: how long will it be before she sees he isn't?'

In May 1907 Leonard was promoted from Cadet to Office Assistant (on £500 a year), and wrote to Lytton: 'Among other things I have been in love lately. I believe really I am mad . . . I am beginning to think it is always degraded being in love.' It was always '99% the desire to copulate, otherwise it is only the shadow of itself, and a particular desire to copulate seems to me no less degraded than a general. One day I shall fall in love with a prostitute.'

Near the bungalow on Beach Road which he shared with George Templer lived two young English girls with their widowed mother. The girls walked on the beach in the evening, and he and Templer would

26 17 Dec 1906
27 Only a slight exaggeration. Clive Bell's father was there.

join them. One of the girls, whom he called in *Growing* Gwen, 'was pretty, lively, sweet-natured and I became fond of her and she of me'. When darkness fell, they lay in one another's arms on the seaweedy sand 'platonically – if that is the right word.'

On the next page of *Growing*, Leonard described a famous local character, old Sir William Twynam, a long-retired civil servant who lived in a large house near the bungalow on the shore. He would have betrayed the girls' identity if he had revealed (as he did in the privacy of the Memoir Club) that Sir William was the girls' grandfather. Their real names were Ethel and Maggie Mortimer, 'very large girls' of eighteen and twenty. 'The smell of stale seaweed is still inseparably linked in my mind with Maggie Mortimer.'

Leonard kept Maggie's letters. On 10 August 1907, about to go up-country, she sent him an urgent note to say that she and Ethel would be at the Fort at seven that evening. 'This may be the last time we shall see you, so *do come* if you can.' While she was away, Maggie wrote to him as 'My dear "Insect"', asking after his dog, and urging him to 'get a bit more flesh on your bones before I come back!'

Leonard re-worked all these Ceylon experiences in diaries, letters, in Memoir Club papers, and in his autobiographies. The boundaries between life as lived and life on the page was everywhere unstable. He was not the only one for whom this was so. In 1907 he was sent Forster's second novel, *The Longest Journey.* Dedicated 'Fratribus' ('to the brothers'), it begins with a parodic approximation of an apostolic philosophical discussion. One of Forster' s biographers',[28] hedging the bets, considered the character Stewart Ansell to be a composite of G.E. Moore, H.O.Meredith, Fred Ainsworth and Leonard Woolf. Ansell is clever, 'not a gentleman', with a 'lean Jewish face'. 'Don't you think it is an astonishing and irritating production?' Leonard wrote to Lytton. 'What a success he will be! For people will think it is all so clever.' Lytton thought it reached the 'depths of fatuity and filth', but agreed that the Taupe would succeed as 'a popular author, and rake in cash. How

28 Nicola Beauman, *Morgan: a Biographv of E.M.Forster* Hodder & Stoughton 1993

horrible!'[29] Lytton, still living with his parents, was reviewing books for the *Spectator*.

Leonard did not tolerate spitting on the verandah of the kachcheri. One of his clerks broke the rule. Leonard ordered him to clear up his spit. The clerk was of a caste that did not wipe floors, and Leonard humiliated him unbearably. The Jaffna Tamil Association (of educated professional men) sent a complaint to the Governor. The Jaffna Tamil Association were also accusing him of having flicked Harry Sanderasekera, a lawyer, in the face with his riding whip when Mr Sanderasekera was driving in his trap down the main street, and Leonard and Mr Price, both on horseback, were going the other way.

Leonard, denying the charge, recalled turning his fidgety horse and pointing something out to Price with his riding whip as Mr Sanderasekera was passing. His explanation appeased the Governor, but no one else. The 'strong measures' of discipline advocated by Price, and adopted by Leonard, made them both unpopular. These incidents shook Leonard's confidence and made him seriously doubt whether he wanted to rule over other people at all. Pro-consular arrogance and 'strong measures', he realised, amounted to much the same thing as a flick in the face.

Leonard longed to be posted back to the solitude of Mannar District. Instead, in August 1907, at very short notice, he was transferred to Kandy, where John Penry Lewis was now Government Agent and had put in a special request for Leonard as his Office Assistant.

The official diary of John Penry Lewis, Government Agent for the Central Province, based in Kandy, 20 August 1907: 'Mr Woolf, the new Office Assistant, took up his duties.' Kandy is built around a lake in the fertile central highlands, with an equable climate, enclosed by thick jungle and by undulating hills covered with tea plantations. A renowned beauty spot, with the attraction of the Royal Botanical Gardens at nearby Peradeniya, Kandy was a destination for passengers from the

---

29 2 May 1907

ships that docked at Colombo. The main tourist attraction in Kandy is the Dalada Maligawa, the great Temple of the Tooth, which houses, in a casket within caskets in a locked shrine, the Buddha's Tooth. In August every year it is displayed in its casket on a caparisoned elephant's back at the great Perahera, the Buddhist festival. The small brick Anglican church, built in 1846, nestles incongruously in the precincts of the Temple.

Leonard, who inspected the three-inch Tooth at close quarters, decided that it was a big dog's. It reminded him of the ferocious upturned canines in carvings and paintings of the yakku (devils) who figure in Sinhalese Buddhism and folk-beliefs. He felt more at home among the Sinhalese than among the Tamils of the north. Soon after his arrival he was sent twenty-four miles up to Urugala,[30] arriving on horseback in a thunderstorm to be greeted by the headmen and villagers with tom-toms and dancers. Every villager in turn prostrated himself before him in the rain. They would have done the same for their feudal chief; it was good manners. Leonard found the Kandyans not only good-mannered but lively and humorous. He felt that their society had a depth and harmony which the western world had lost.

He also saw how difficult, how 'evil' even, life was for them. In relation to himself, they were underdogs. He enjoyed his position – and became more and more 'politically schizophrenic, an anti-imperialist who enjoyed the fleshpots of imperialism'. In Kandy he studied Sinhala with a Buddhist priest, and responded to Buddhism because it was not so much a religion as a philosophy – 'a metaphysic which has eliminated God and gods, a code of conduct civilised, austere, springing from a profound pessimism', as he wrote in *Growing*. He was drawn to the way in which some Buddhists abandoned their life in the world and 'withdrew into solitude and contemplation'. This chimed with his own dreams of withdrawal. The Hinduism which had surrounded him in Jaffna, with 'the multiplicity of its florid gods, the ugly exuberance of the temples', had not appealed to him.

*

30 Now Medamahanuwara

As well as tea-planters and their families, there were British army officers in Kandy, and many more white officials than in Jaffna. Consequently there were parties and dances and picnics and dinners, and a daily routine, for Leonard, of arduous work followed by arduous sociability. In the kachcheri he adjudicated on intimate questions of marriage and divorce; Sinhalese sexual laws and customs were complex, and the administration of them appropriated by the Government, thus in effect by him, 'a young man who had only been two or three years in Ceylon' – and whose experience in this field was nugatory.

He shared a dark old bungalow with Francis – later Sir Francis – Tyrrell, the Superintendent of Police, a reserved, friendly man, on the narrow lane up on the bank behind the Temple of the Tooth, and only a stroll from the arcaded kachcheri and law courts. Leonard got up in the sparkling early mornings and read the day's official mail on the verandah before going over to the kachcheri. After office hours, there was 'the sacrament of tennis' at the Kandy Garden Club. 'Night after night we went up to the head of the lake to the tennis courts',[31] a smarter social ritual that that in Jaffna, with a continual flutter of females.

From the tennis courts they moved on to the Kandy Club. The Club, in outposts of Empire, was the social centre of the white man and woman's world. The Kandy Club atmosphere was 'terribly masculine and public-school', and Leonard once again found himself the 'new boy' – nervous, untypical, essentially unclubbable; and again he found his feet through his competence at bridge and sport. He exercised violently in Kandy – rackets, squash and golf, and risky games of hockey with the Punjabi battalion stationed in the town.

He had hated, in Jaffna, having to supervise floggings. In Kandy it was his duty to go to Bogambara Prison early one morning in mid-September 1907 to see, for the first but not the last time, four men hanged. He had to speak to the condemned men, and then stand on a verandah in the courtyard as they were led to the scaffold. He had to give the signal for the drop exactly as the clock struck eight. The hang-

---

31 The Kandy Garden Club and its tennis courts is still there at the head of the lake.

ings were not always bloodless, nor death immediate. The stoicism of the condemned men astounded him. He performed these duties, as he did his office work, with rigour and a stern demeanour. He grew more and more outwardly severe as, inwardly, his anxieties and reservations increased. He wrote in *Growing* that 'the best chance of getting uncivilised laws abolished or changed is that they should be strictly applied by civilised judges who abhor them.'

Leonard sent Lytton a long, vivid description of the hangings. Lytton, excited and appalled, read it over and over again, sitting over his fire at home. 'Your letter is superb; but if what you describe came into a novel – oh no! Do let's create things that are only dimly real! I want Beauty . . . Isn't it madness your staying out in your ghastly wild?' Leonard should come home, he said. 'England is a nice, quiet, good, sensible place.'

There followed an outpouring of Lytton's most characteristic longing – to be loved: 'I feel that if anyone loved me I should love them. Do you love me? Is it possible? Can one love by letter, memory, and imagination? Wouldn't you love anyone who loved you? Oh! *Really* loved. Isn't that the supreme, the only, thing to be loved? But it all works round in a horrid circle, because who's to begin?'[32]

'No', replied Leonard, to the first part of Lytton's letter, about 'Beauty'. 'I'm all for reality, even in novels, even to hangings and whores.' The differences between them were beginning to grate. As for going home, 'One thing you must understand and that is that I am done for now as regards England. I shall live and die in these appalling countries now.'

He dealt with Lytton's appeal by telling him that 'I am really in love with someone who is in love with me. It is not however pleasant because it is pretty degrading, I suppose, to be in love with practically a schoolgirl.' Since he did not intend to marry her, he had to behave 'like a gentleman', and meanwhile everyone in their little circle knew what was going on. 'Sometimes I think really I am only in love with silly intrigue and controlling a situation, and sometimes merely with two

32 19 Oct 1907

big cow eyes which could never understand anything and look as if they understood everything that has ever been, is or will be.'

The girl was Gladys Jowitt, aged nineteen, the daughter of a tea-planter. In *Growing* Leonard called her 'Rachel Robinson'. Francis Tyrrell[33] was in love with Gladys's elder sister Ethel, and needed someone to take off his hands the younger one, who had to come along as chaperone. The four of them went for gentle rides on horseback in the hills above Kandy, up and down the idyllic drives carved out of the flowering forest above the lake. Leonard and Gladys Jowitt 'reached the maximum of intimacy' allowed by etiquette. He wrote in *Growing* that he had 'a real affection for her without ever at all falling in love with her'. That was not how it felt at the time.

On 29 December 1907 he enlarged to Lytton on his continuing agitation about her. 'I am astonished, almost bewildered, by the niceness of the human mind joined by the imperiousness of human bodies, by modesty which ends in kisses and silence which is a reproach and an avowal.' Women were to be envied because 'they have the niceness and the imperiousness, but they have just the feelings bare, they don't I think have the contortions of introspection afterwards. They just recoil or flame out. I don't think they ever even realise what is happening. They are merely played on.'

He chose this romance to expatiate in *Growing* on what kind of women he liked, and why: 'I have always been greatly attracted by the undiluted female mind, as well as by the female body.' He was not thinking of 'exceptional women with exceptional minds',[34] but of 'ordinary' women, 'undistinguished, often unintellectual and unintrospective.'

Their minds seemed to him so different from men's – 'gentler, more sensitive, more civilised'. It was difficult to gain access to such a woman's mind; it could only be done by listening attentively to what she said. Most men did not listen. They thought about what they themselves

---

33 Disguised as 'Christopher Smith' in this episode in *Growing*.

34 In this passage from *Growing* he cited as 'exceptional women' Cleopatra, Jane Carlyle, Jane Austen, and Virginia Woolf. It was odd but honest of him to include his own late wife in the list; obviously she was not an 'ordinary woman' of the kind he was describing.

were going to say when she had stopped talking. He taught himself to listen, and thus to get every now and then 'a glimpse or rather a breath of this pure, curiously female quality of mind.'

Lytton continued to send Leonard the news: Walter Lamb was now a Fellow of Trinity; there was a new and poetical embryo, Rupert Brooke, 'pseudo-beautiful' with yellow hair, with whom Lytton's brother James was in love; and in addition to the Stephens' Thursday evenings and Vanessa Bell's Friday Club (to discuss the arts) there was also now a play-reading group. Adrian read very well. 'Virginia of course too is very fine.'

Lytton's father died in February 1908, and Leonard ended his short letter of sympathy: 'I wish I could see you and talk to you. I have wished it for 3 years.' And then, defeated by distance and time, and as if conceding that one could not after all love by 'letter, memory and imagination', Leonard and Lytton, for eight whole months, stopped writing to each other altogether.

Leonard had confessed to Lytton in late 1907: 'I have a tremendous desire upon me for England today. It comes upon me in a horrible wave from time to time . . . I work, play tennis, then bridge and billiards at the club and the interminable gossip and filth. I haven't read a book for two months. It all seems to me to matter nothing at all; so much so that I shall never, as you suggest, take the boat to England.'

It was his sister Bella who took the boat, to Ceylon, arriving at the end of January 1908. Tyrrell was on leave, and Bella shared the bungalow up above the Temple of the Tooth with Leonard. She threw herself into the social life. She went to stay with the Jowitt girls on their tea-estate, and reported to Leonard that Mr and Mrs Jowitt spoke so warmly of him that she guessed they would like him as a son-in-law. Bella had already made her own particular friend. She had travelled out on the same ship as Robert Heath Lock, a plant geneticist slightly younger than herself.

Bella was in Kandy when in March 1908 there was a visit from the Empress Eugénie of France, the widow of Napoleon III. She was a friend of Sir Thomas Lipton, one of Ceylon's tea tycoons. Leonard had to meet her at the station. The famous beauty was now over eighty; Leonard just saw 'a tiny little bent old woman' in black. She invited him to tea with her. 'Like nearly all great or very well-known people whom I have met, she asked innumerable questions and would not stay for an answer.'

Hugh Clifford, the Acting Governor and Colonial Secretary,[35] was in Kandy to do honour to the Empress. Leonard, in a letter to Saxon, and later in *Growing*, was resolutely ironic about her visit, but the amount of space he devoted to it in both instances belied his tone. Hugh Clifford had arranged to take the Empress to see the Tooth, and Leonard made the arrangements with the Guardian of the Temple, the Diwa Nilame.

Bella came along too, and made a sketch of the Tooth which came in handy when she wrote her guidebook *How to See Ceylon.*[36] As for Leonard, 'I earned a good deal of unearned kudos from the Colonial Secretary'. Hugh Clifford, a strange and gifted person, had spent twenty years in Malaya, where he had, in the imperial idiom, 'gone native'. In the following years he was to write novels and literary journalism, and in 1913 Joseph Conrad dedicated his novel *Chance* to 'Sir Hugh Clifford KCMG whose steadfast friendship is responsible for the existence of these pages'.

Clifford is said to have been the inspiration for Noël Coward's song 'Mad Dogs and Englishmen'; he never wore a hat on his large bald head. His Ceylonese doctor thought this may have contributed to his lapses into insanity. His second wife, whom he married in 1910, had a hard time with his aberrations, such as appearing to greet a visitor wearing nothing but his socks. As an administrator, when well, Clifford was brilliant, overbearing and intolerant.[37] Leonard was fortunate to have made a good impression on him.

*

---

35 From 1909, Sir Hugh Clifford. He was subsequently Governor of Ceylon, then of the Gold Coast, Nigeria and the Straits Settlements. His career ended in 1929. He died in 1941.

36 Bella Sidney Woolf, *How to See Ceylon*, published by The Times of Ceylon 1914, 2nd ed 1922, 3rd ed 1924., 4th ed, by now much expanded, 1929. Among her children's books are *The Twins in Ceylon* and *More About the Twins in Ceylon.*

37 See H.A.J.Hulugalle, *British Governors of Ceylon.*

On 13 May 1908 there was a great Durbar of Kandyan chiefs at the King's Pavilion. Leonard had his photograph taken with the assembled chiefs and headmen outside the kachcheri, looking small and slight and young in his dark suit, high collar and straw hat, seated in the centre of the front row, surrounded by bearded and moustached Kandyan chiefs in their ceremonial finery. Later that month came the Empire Day Celebrations: sports and tea for two thousand boys and girls, all of whom were given paper Union Jacks to wave. 'It was a pretty sight', wrote Mr Lewis in his official diary, and 'great credit' was due to Mr Woolf and to Miss Woolf 'for having successfully organised it.'

Leonard earned more kudos from Colonial Secretary Clifford, who was between marriages at the time. When Leonard and Gladys Jowitt were out riding, a carriage passed them in which sat Hugh Clifford and a glamorous woman. She was Amy Bonham, in her early thirties; at nineteen, she had been the subject of Edward Burne-Jones's finest portrait.[38] This brief glimpse was enough to show Leonard that the lady had made a conquest. Some days later Clifford asked him to arrange an exhibition of Kandyan dancing in the grounds of the King's Pavilion for Mrs Bonham's delectation. Leonard appealed to his good acquaintance the Diwa Nilame, who produced 'all his retainers and headmen and an enormous company of dancers, tom-tom-beaters, and musicians', with a hundred torch-bearers. It was 'superb'. Clifford was 'immensely pleased'.

It was due to Clifford's estimate of Leonard's capabilities that when the position of Assistant Government Agent for Hambantota (a division of the Southern Province) came up, Leonard Woolf was appointed. John Penry Lewis wrote in his official diary on 25 August 1908: 'This is Mr Woolf's last day as Office Assistant. I am very sorry to lose him.'

---

38 Amy Bonham died two years later. For her sad history see Josceline Dimbleby, *A Profound Secret: May Gaskell, Her Daughter Amy, and Edward Burne-Jones* Doubleday 2004.

6

AGA Hambantota

His bungalow in Hambantota was 'worth having come to Ceylon to live in it', Leonard wrote to Lytton, their correspondence having resumed. 'It must originally have been built by the Dutch with walls of astonishing thickness and an enormously broad verandah and vast high rooms.' When Lytton saw photographs he was dazzled. 'But the beauty seemed to me too intense. I long to pay you a visit. Wouldn't it be heavenly? I could be so lazy, while you were condemning blacks to death.'[1]

The bungalow stood on a promontory, with a view, from the back, of a great curving strand. 'Day and night you hear the sea thundering away almost at the gates of the compound, which is vast with nothing in it but sand and 3 stunted trees.' Bella in *How to See Ceylon* was to describe Hambantota as 'pleasanter to sojourn in than to live in'. Her brother felt otherwise. He wrote in *Growing* that 'I fell in love with the country, the people, and the way of life which were entirely different from everything in London and Cambridge to which I had been born and bred.' He told Lytton at the time: 'I have no connection with yesterday: I do not recognise it or myself of it . . . And I suppose I am happy too, happier I

---

1 11 Dec 1908. Berg

Cartoon by John Kent,
Guardian, 1 December 1979.

expect in terms of quantity than you. I work, God how I work. I have reduced it to a method and exalted it to a mania.'

Along the coast to the west, at Tangalle, were two friends: the District Judge, Tom Southorn from Jaffna; and the Superintendent of Police, T.A Hodson. Leonard would ride the thirty miles to Tangalle to dine with them, sleeping at the Tangalle Rest House on the edge of the ocean. 'If I had to show anyone what God can do in the way of tropical nights, I think I should take him to the Rest House verandah at Tangalle.'

There was also in Hambantota a tall, gaunt, brutal Boer, Henry H. Engelbrecht, who had been in a camp for prisoners taken in the Boer War at Diyatalawa, up in the hills. Because, on his release in 1903, Engelbrecht refused to take an oath of allegiance to the Crown, he was not allowed back to South Africa. Leonard's predecessor as AGA gave Engelbrecht a job as Forest Warden in the Yala Game Sanctuary. 'I think he will die very soon of malaria and curry and rice', Leonard told Lytton. (He was wrong.) When a good-looking Sinhalese woman came before Leonard with a paternity case against Engelbrecht, she unwrapped the baby and indeed it was white. The court was tense; would the white AGA find against his white hunting companion? Leonard awarded the woman a maintenance order against Engelbrecht, apparently on the grounds that since the baby certainly was not his, it must be Engelbrecht's.[2]

Leonard's district, in the south-east dry zone of Ceylon, was a curving strip of land of about a thousand square miles, stretching a hundred miles along the coast, nowhere more than thirty miles wide and in places only ten. It was flat and low, except in the north-west corner, and hot and dry, the low scrub jungle threaded with sandy footpaths. The scattered population of about 100,000 was divided between three subdivisions or pattus: Giruma West Pattu, Giruma East Pattu, and the largest, Magam Pattu, with the Yala Game Sanctuary at its eastern end.

---

2 There is a photograph of Henry Engelbrecht – bald, thin, unsmiling – labelled '1st Camp Warden 1907-1928' in the Visitors Centre at the Ruhuna National Park HQ at Palatupana. His descendants are still living in the area.

Hambantota, the administrative headquarters of Magam Pattu and of the whole district, had a population in 1908 of just over 3,000, composed of Sinhalese (mostly Buddhists), with some Tamils (Hindus), and Moors and Malays (Muslims). Leonard's boss, the GA of the Southern Province, was a married man in his fifties, Charles Morant Lushington, stationed in Galle, sixty miles westwards round the coast.

Leonard's kachcheri was a short way from his bungalow along the promontory, with the Law Courts and the Rest House. His responsibilities as AGA were to collect revenue, dispense justice, and to travel regularly 'on circuit' throughout his district, in order to become familiar with every village and its headman, who acted, unpaid, as intermediary with the colonial administration. The AGA was required to keep 'a most minute diary of his proceedings, and which diary is, at the close of the circuit, to be transmitted to Government.'[3] In practice, Leonard kept a daily official diary, which was duly sent in monthly to his GA in Galle.

Leonard was also obliged to ride out into remote areas of his district whenever there was a serious disagreement between villagers or a suspected murder – in which case he inspected the corpse, held an inquest, and prepared the case for trial. (Serious crimes were referred upwards, to the Supreme Court.) Defendants frequently pleaded that they had mistaken the deceased for a wild pig in the darkness. Leonard often felt, sitting as Police Magistrate in Hambantota, that there was some crucial element in the story which he had not grasped, 'small points which show that I have not got the truth yet', as he recorded on 7 January 1910.

Leonard, twenty-seven when he took up his post, was not comfortable as a judge. His hand tremor sometimes incapacitated him entirely when it came to writing out a 'guilty' verdict. He had to adjourn the court, and calm himself. He always felt that 'the occupational disease' of judges was sadistic self-righteousness. His case was different. 'My hand trembles because in the depth of my being I am physically and mentally afraid.'[4]

*

3 Maitland Memo 1808
4 *Sowing*

His immediate responsibility, and a constant preoccupation throughout his tenure, was the salt collection. Along the coastline near Hambantota were shallow lagoons called 'lewayas', fed from the sea. In the rainy season the lagoons filled up; then the water evaporated, leaving a deposit of salt.

The sale of the salt was a Government monopoly. Determined to maximise the return, Leonard gave himself up to what he called his 'dangerous passion' for efficiency – dangerous, because it can become a 'ruthless obsession'. He reviewed the minutest details of the salt collection, recording his conclusions in his official diary. He thought that the rates paid for carting salt to the stores were too high, and suspected a cartel. So he hired carters individually on his own tough terms and made 'astonishing' savings. The 'watchers', who guarded the salt from thieves, were also being paid too much in his opinion, while the level of wastage was unacceptable. By March 1909 he had changed the system of leaving the salt unbagged and unweighed until it reached the store. He had it bagged and weighed at the lewaya, and weighed once again when it reached the store, and he made surprise visits to check the weight of bags for himself.

The salt gatherers were traditionally paid with chits, but Leonard paid them in cash, thus cutting out the 'harpies' who hung around the lewayas ready to cash chits at a discount. On 26 October 1910, when he calculated that the salt collection for the past year had yielded 224,352 cwts, beating all previous records, he could fairly claim that he 'never had any trouble with labour'. The carters were less complaisant.

Charles Lushington, the GA, was not happy about Leonard's innovations, nor about his manner. In his official diary, supplemented with letters and memos, Leonard was critical and prescriptive. In October 1910 he heard from his friend T.A.Hodson that Lushington had nearly forwarded a letter of Leonard's to the Government in Colombo, 'animadverting delicately on what he believed to be your conduct'. Leonard was against the Government policy of removing some executive powers from administrative officers such as himself, and transferring them to 'experts', such as irrigation engineers: 'I believe the policy to be radically wrong.' 'I see', wrote Hodson in November 1910, 'you are getting fed up with life, Hambantota, and the G.A. The last is the worst by a long chalk. I am getting tired both of doing his work and of taking in his daughter to dinner.'

The first cases of rinderpest, a highly contagious cattle disease, were reported in buffaloes in Leonard's district on 18 February 1909, and the rest of the year was dominated by this disaster. Government ordered mass inoculation, at a small charge to the animals' owners. 'Now anyone who has had any kind of experience with this class of native', wrote Leonard in his official diary, 'knows that one thing to decide him against is if he has to pay.' He made no charge, and achieved some results. But the disease spread, due to the difficulty of quarantining sick animals. When tethered, unable to forage, they died of hunger and thirst. So diseased buffaloes roamed about, and the village headmen did little to prevent them. Next time he dismissed a headman, reported Leonard, 'I shall recommend the appointment of a woman.'

He constantly traversed jungle tracks in intense heat – on horseback, by bicycle, or with a pony and trap – assessing the situation. He recalled in *Growing* returning to a village where earlier in the day he had warned a man to restrain his two straying cows, one of which was diseased. Finding the cows still at large, he shot them both. The whole village turned out in protest, and stood around the dead cows with hostile mutterings. Leonard explained, in vain, why he had to do it. The villagers followed him to his trap, still muttering. As he wrote in *Growing*, it was not a pleasant business to 'shoot the cattle and buffaloes of the villagers whom one knows and likes'. They would have thrown stones, or shot him in the back, if they had dared.

At a place where he found buffaloes loose around the village tank, 'I shot two, one of which was diseased, the whole of one eye and part of one side of the face had been eaten away by maggots but the wretched beast was still straying about.' He went with the headman to check out a water hole around which lay rotting cattle carcasses. Leonard decided to stay there all night to watch for wild animals coming down to drink; the headman wanted him to shoot a leopard which had been attacking the village cattle. They lay up behind a pile of branches, and saw a jackal performing his intricate dance all alone in the moonlight – and then suddenly, there was the leopard, looking straight into Leonard's eyes.

Leonard was never a good shot. His trembling hands made it literally a matter of hit or miss (and he soon lost the desire to shoot anything at all, except game birds for his dinner). On this occasion he was so transfixed by the leopard's magnificence that he did not even think of shooting, and the leopard, startled by a mongoose scuttling out of a dead pig's belly, disappeared as swiftly as it had come. The headman shook his head, thinking Leonard had been too scared to shoot.

Leonard did however get a leopard, out with Engelbrecht and Hodson very early one morning, as he recorded in his official diary on 14 November 1909. Hodson wounded it, and they tracked it to its cave. They could see its tail, which Engelbrecht prodded with a stick. 'Mr Hodson had another shot but unsuccessful and then I had one. It tried to charge but fell dead just outside the cave the shot having gone through its lungs.'

The jungle 'is a cruel and a dangerous place, and, being a cowardly person, I was always afraid of it. Yet I could not keep away from it.' In *Growing* there are magnificent passages, mostly transcribed from his official diary, about being lost alone in the jungle overnight, about elephants fighting head to head, about a crocodile with a tortoise stuck across its throat, about the uncanny homing instincts of jungle people and animals.

In August 1909 rinderpest spread to the Yala Game Sanctuary, which had a special area reserved for British officials and distinguished guests. One of Leonard's duties was to grant licences, provide transport, give hospitality, and generally facilitate their sport. In early 1909 Baron Axel Blixen, a cousin of England's Danish Queen Alexandra, had to be accommodated in this way. Leonard took him out to shoot a crocodile at close range. The Baron missed. 'I have never seen anyone else, even myself, make quite such a bad shot.' Yet when the Baron returned from an expedition made with his own entourage, he proudly showed Leonard his trophies – several deer 'and I rather think a bear'. The implication was that the Baron had a little help from his friends. The Baron was well satisfied and, back home, wrote thanking Leonard for his attentiveness.

In Jaffna, Leonard had become too friendly with a woman in her thirties whom he described to Lytton as 'ugly but terrifyingly and femininely violent'. He allowed an 'idiotic little intrigue' to develop, saw her in Kandy, and established a correspondence.

This was the woman he described forty years on, to the Memoir Club, as 'a small, dumpy, yellowish faced woman, sitting on a camp stool and painting little water-colour sketches or else walking with a particularly hideous mongrel fox-terrier bitch'. She was a German missionary teacher, named Annie Hopfengartner. Jimmy Bowes had a dirty story called 'Miss Hopfengartner's Cunt' which he told when drunk, which was often, and Leonard later retailed Bowes's story to the Memoir Club; it was the kind of thing – risqué, unkind and amusing – which went down well. Leonard had a stock of stories of his own, less obscene but equally cruel.

Miss Hopfengartner was in love with Leonard, and believed he reciprocated. When he did not respond as she expected, she sought reasons: 'When I read your letter I felt exactly what I had felt in Kandy – that you deal wounds when perhaps you would rather do the contrary. Why?'[5] She scrutinised the small differences in the way he signed off his letters to her, assigning to them deep meanings. Not mad, or not very, she was an intense, serious, lonely woman with a great capacity for devotion. Up-country in Badulla, 'Almost every day I see from the Haputale gap the sea and the Hambantota hills in the distance.' She sat in the rain with her fox-terrier Stoffele and thought about Leonard.[6]

She took issue with him over his creed that 'nothing matters', which she rejected in regard to their relationship. She was tormented by seeing his photograph in the *Times of Ceylon,* in the Hambantota cricket team.[7] She sent him telegrams reassuring him about her health, needing to assume that he was desperately worried. Her plan was that he would join her in Badulla for Christmas 1909. He did not go.

Miss Hopfengartner decided to spend some weeks at Mount Lavinia, the tourist hotel on the sea just outside Colombo, and then return to Europe to recuperate. She wanted Leonard to care for her dog Stoffele while she was away – a bid for vicarious intimacy. Leonard told her that

---

5 3 Sep 1908
6 2 May 1909
7 Hambantota versus Tangalle. Hambantota won, but lost the return match.

Hambantota would be too hot for Stoffele; and he already had Judy, Argus, Mermaid, Tiny One, and two or three more dogs. Finally he gave in. Stoffele would be on heat when she arrived, announced Miss Hopfengartner helpfully; and Leonard must meet her at Mount Lavinia before she sailed. She knew that he was coming to Colombo, for his exam in Sinhala, on 16 January 1910.

He did not go and see Miss Hopfengartner at Mount Lavinia. He wrote in *Growing* that in Hambantota he lived 'a life of complete chastity except for one curious night in Colombo when I had to go there for my examination in Sinhalese'. So while Miss Hopfengartner waited and waited, he made love to someone else.

Her disappointment was terrible. 'Has something come between or is it because you know that I love you ever since Jaffna days? . . . There was a time when I thought you wanted it and so I showed it and having gone so far I could and would not go back.' She stood on the sands in the dark on the night of his arrival to see his train go by into Colombo. The morning he was leaving Colombo, she went to the railway station to look for him. ' Please tell me the reasons for your actions.'

In Leonard's Memoir Club paper about Miss Hopfengartner, tacitly identifying Miss Hopfengartner with her dog, he said that this 'hideous fox-terrier bitch' was rejected by his own dogs and never allowed by them to come into the bungalow. Stoffele lived out on the verandah, 'looking very cowed, depressed and ashamed. There too she gave birth to a litter of four dead puppies.' She was not one of the women whose bodies and minds attracted him.

Virginia Stephen wanted Thoby's letters collected and published, with an introduction describing his time at Cambridge. 'You saw I fancy more of him really than Lytton or I', wrote Saxon to Leonard. 'Could you at least write something of those odd walks in search of birds that you used to take with him?'[8] Ever since Thoby Stephen died, the friends had been trying to find a way of putting something in print as a memorial. But Lytton, Saxon and Clive had given up on it.

8 4 Sep 1908

Leonard read this in Kirama during the monsoon, on circuit in his district: 'Some of the foul food which one is obliged to eat travelling like this from day to day in wilderness and jungles must have poisoned me or the cold rain perhaps did it . . . I had to wade through paddy fields and streams to inspect a channel, being violently sick every 100 yards and I rode the last 4 miles into Kirama in the darkness the rain streaming down my back and out of my boots, vomiting over my horse's head every 5 minutes.' In every village crowds of road-tax defaulters were brought before him for trial, 'wild savages from the hills, spectacles incredible to anyone who has not seen them. Naked except for a foul rag round their loins, limbs which are mere bones, stomachs distended with enormously enlarged spleens, their features eaten away by and their skin covered with sores from one of the most loathesome existing diseases called parangi . . .'

Little wonder that Lytton was moved to ask, 'Do you remember Cambridge? . . . Could you find your way from King's to Trinity? Can you draw a plan of the Great Court, and can you visualize the lilac at Clare?'[9]

Finally, in the same long letter to Saxon, Leonard got to the point: 'I thought of writing something about the Goth as you suggest. It ought to be done but the difficulties are immense. Perhaps I'll really try one day. I was reading his letters the other day. They make one weep with bitterness. He is complete in them for anyone who knew him, but I wonder whether they would convey anything to anyone who did not: for after all everything was in his character.'

The truth was that the Goth's dullness had been part of his 'grandeur'. In May 1909 Leonard confessed to Saxon that 'I have written nothing about the Goth and now I don't think I ever shall.' But long after Virginia too was dead, Leonard did honour to her wishes and to the Goth by including in *Sowing* both a letter from him and an account of their 'odd walks in search of birds'.

Fred Ainsworth was marrying Moore's sister; Keynes was giving up the India Office for a fellowship at King's. Leonard was concerned

9 27 May 1909. Berg

about his youngest brother Philip, who had followed Cecil to Sidney Sussex College. He wanted and did not want his brothers to be deemed apostolic. It would be a fine thing for the Society to be serially penetrated by a pack of Woolfs, but gratifying also to be the one supreme Woolf. He told Lytton in January 1909 that he gathered Philip was 'going off on the wrong tack.'

Lytton went to see him, and found degraded imitations of himself. Philip 'seems to move in a queer circle of decadents', talking 'with the Strachey accentuation absurdly exaggerated'. There was a man there whom Lytton had had 'a flirt with last summer', and a freshman, 'more degraded, very Jewish and very stupid, but I imagine more intimate with Philip', who was 'certainly the most interesting and probably the most unpleasant of the group'. These toxic darts can only have glanced off Leonard's toughened carapace. Lytton ended with an antidote, or an appeal: 'If you would only come home and live with me in a small and commodious flat I should be perfectly happy.'[10]

Lytton was seeing almost no one but what he called 'the Stephen group'. His original tranche of golden boys were putting on weight, wearing glasses, taking jobs, getting married. He idealised the absent Leonard as a dangerous, dashing, whoring, man of action. He himself had a wild idea of marrying Virginia Stephen as a way out of his own problems – and, failing that, of Leonard marrying her.

Leonard responded by writing that 'the most wonderful of all would have been [for you] to marry Virginia. She is I imagine supreme . . .' The only problem was that 'I cannot place you in it'. Marrying was 'the only way to happiness, to anything settled, to anything not these appalling alternations from violent pleasures to the depths of depression'. Since he lived on the principle that 'nothing matters', he didn't know why he did not marry. Something always saved him at the last moment 'from these degradations – their lasciviousness or their ugliness probably – though I believe if I did that I should be happy'. Did Lytton think that Virginia would have him? 'Wire me if she accepts. I'll take the next boat home; and then when I arrived I should probably come

---

10 5 Feb 1909

straight to talk with you. You don't know what it's like not to have talked to anyone for four years.'[11]

He ended by saying: 'I wonder if after all Virginia marries Turner', and enclosed a poem (written for Maggie Mortimer):

When I am dead and you forget
  My kisses: in the stirring air
Will you not shudder when my touch,
  Grown nothing now, just stirs your hair?
Will you not shudder when you feel
  My arms about you in the mist;
You will not know the dead man's lips
  You will not know that you have kissed
A dead man. Only there may come
  A memory of a foreign land
Of wind and sun and how you lay
  By the salt marshes in the sand
With someone. Some forgotten name
  May murmur in the wind: but I
Amid the havoc of all things
  Know that our bodies never die.

'You are perfectly wonderful . . . Isn't it odd that I've never really been in love with you? And I suppose never shall', responded Lytton. Then came his bombshell: 'The day before yesterday I proposed to Virginia. As I did it, I saw that it would be death if she accepted me . . .' It was immediately obvious that it was impossible. 'The lack of understanding was so terrific! And how can a virgin be expected to understand? You see she is her name. I think there's no doubt whatever that you ought to marry her. You would be great enough and you would have the great advantage of physical desire. I was in terror lest she should kiss me.'

Lytton had confided in Vanessa, 'who is unparallelled', but who did not quite take in 'the agony of Duncan'. 'I copulated with him again

---

11 1 Feb 1909

this afternoon, and at the present moment he is in Cambridge copulating with Keynes. I don't know whether I'm happy or unhappy. What do you think? If you came and proposed she'ld accept. She really would.'

He added a postscript: he had seen Virginia again. She said she was not in love with him, and he said he could not marry her anyway. 'So things have simply reverted. Perhaps you'd better not mention these matters to Turner, who certainly is *not* upon the tapis. I told Vanessa to hand on your proposal, so perhaps you are.'[12]

Thus was established, notionally, an erotic trinity of Lytton, Leonard and Virginia, alongside Leonard's 'wild' romantic trinity of himself, Vanessa and the Goth.

Lytton reinforced the fantasy. 'You must marry Virginia. She's sitting waiting for you, is there any objection? She's the only woman in the world with sufficient brains; it's a miracle she should exist; but if you're not careful you'll lose the opportunity. At any moment she might go off with heaven knows who – Duncan? Quite possible.'[13]

'Of course', replied Leonard, 'I know that the one thing to do would be to marry Virginia. I am only frightened that when I come back [on leave] in Dec 1910 I may. For though when one had and everything was completed and consummated, life would probably be supreme, the horrible preliminary complications, the ghastly complications too of virginity and marriage altogether appal me.'[14]

Parts of Leonard's arid district only had rain every five or ten years, which meant finding an alternative crop to paddy (rice). In dry years the villagers planted kurrakkan, a variety of millet. Their practice, when the fields round the village became nonproductive, was to burn and clear a swathe of virgin jungle, called a 'chena', and plant there until the soil was exhausted, and then repeat the process.

Government policy was to restrict chenas. Leonard, in July 1909, disagreed. 'I am becoming more and more convinced that the outcry

12 19 Feb 1909
13 21 Aug 1909. Berg
14 14 Sep 1909

against chenas can be overdone', he wrote in his official diary. 'In many villages it means that either the village must cease to exist or chenas must be granted.' The scrub jungle supported no valuable timber. 'Unless this valueless jungle is given to the villagers, they have no means of support in their villages.'

He did not temper his tone: 'Government should face the fact . . .'; Government should recognise . . .'; the AGA 'should, I consider, be allowed to give these persons chenas on the condition that Government takes 1/8 of the produce.' Otherwise the villages would die out. As it was, there were many illegal chenas. By November 1910 he had introduced his own regulatory system: chenas had to be measured out, with the headman's initials cut in a tree at each corner.

Since rinderpest was reducing the buffalo population, and buffaloes were used for trampling the fields for sowing, Leonard hit on the idea of introducing the plough, which required only one or two animals to draw it. He organised trials and demonstrations, trying out one model himself on a piece of ground in front of the kachcheri. He reported progress in his official diary: 'It is a most fascinating occupation at the same time to teach two bulls and oneself to plough.' The problem with the average cultivator was that he was prejudiced against anything new; and walked along 'leaning on the plough handle and making the sort of singing noise which is meant to represent work, and allowing the bulls to wander where they list; the idea of cutting a straight furrow is abhorrent to his nature.'

Leonard introduced forty ploughs into the Tissa area, but cultivators used the ploughs with the nuts and screws loose, so they fell apart; and in May 1910 he noted sadly that they had 'left them out to rust since the last cultivation.'

Leonard made accidental contact with Gladys Jowitt again. He answered an advertisement for a horse for sale, to which Gladys replied by inviting him to come up to Craig – the tea-estate her father managed – and try the horse out. He went to Craig at the end of a month's sick-leave after being 'rotten with fever and with a perpetually bad throat', as he wrote to Saxon from the Grand Hotel at Nuwera Eliya. But by that time Gladys was already spoken for. She had written to tell him she was 'engaged to a Mr [John] Edmonds . . . and somehow I wanted you to hear it from myself – you see I am at last doing the "duty" you so forcibly pointed out to Bella and me do you remember, when you gave us that disquisition on Matrimony.'

Leonard in his autobiography sidestepped this issue; the knowledge that Gladys Jowitt was engaged adds poignancy to what is already a poignant account of his visit. She was as lovely as ever, her parents were charming to him, and he remembered what Bella had said about the Jowitts wanting him for a son-in-law. He went for a long early-morning ride, galloping in the cool sparkling mountain air 'by the side of a young woman of whom I was fond.'

On his last evening Gladys took him for a walk before dinner. 'We had slipped into a long silence and suddenly the narrow path turned round a great rock and brought us out on to a broad ledge with a sheer drop thousands of feet down to the sea level and the low country, and with a superb, terrific view over the miles and miles of jungle to, in the dim distance, the line of the sea and the coast – and somewhere there Hambantota and my bungalow.'[15] He felt he had been taken up into a high mountain and shown all the kingdoms of the earth, the temptation being 'the girl beside me'. He felt – 'I could be quite wrong about this' – that she was waiting for him to speak. (Would she have broken off her engagement for him?) They stood in miserable silence and then walked back to the bungalow and dinner.

He had his bicycle with him, and before dawn said goodbye to the Jowitts, and then 'coasted mile after mile down through the deliciously cool fresh mountain country' until he reached the plains and jungles below, and in the burning midday came to the boundary of his district, 'and there waiting for me by the roadside was my horsekeeper with my horse and my dogs'. He rode on in regret and dejection 'and yet at the same time a kind of relief.'

Bella had written to him in July 1909 advising him to marry as soon as possible to assuage his loneliness. 'You need a very special sort of

---

15 There is no such panorama from the Craig Estate. They may have wandered on to the adjacent Lipton Estate and seen the view from Dambatenne.

girl – if you don't find her, you'd better steer clear of matrimony.' Bella's picture of Leonard's wife was of someone 'strong-minded and clever and [with] a sense of humour . . . If you marry a weak character you'll squash her. You *must* marry someone who can hold her own with you and yet be good-tempered.' Women with brains stood to lose so much in marriage, wrote Bella, 'in nine cases out of ten often it is mere animalism – you *must* love with your *head* as much as with your heart or you're lost.'

Bella knew what she was talking about. In April 1910 she announced her engagement to Robert Heath Lock – Bertie – now Assistant Director of the Royal Botanical Gardens at Peredeniya. In the same month Leonard learned that he would not be getting his leave at the end of the year after all. He was needed in Hambantota to organise the Census returns. Bemoaning this to Saxon, he said he had written nothing for years except administration reports and 'the following which will probably tell you more about my "state of mind" than anything else. I know both are putrid.'[16] 'The following' was a quatrain, 'To Ponamma'.

> O Golden Mother, in this embrace of thine
> Thy fruit of motherhood is bought and sold:
> The cancerous kiss, the ecstasy is mine,
> For then thy womb bears gold, Mother of Gold.

In June 1910, he supervised the great pilgrimage to the Buddhist shrine at Kataragama, a holy place for Hindus and Muslims as well. Kataragama was little more, in those days, than a clearing in the jungle. Leonard described it as 'a kind of Ceylon Lourdes'. The festival lasted two weeks and attracted thousands, travelling on foot from all over the island, dragging sick people. The heat was intolerable: 'One sits in a perpetual sandstorm waiting for the sun to go down and for the mosquitoes to come out and take the place of the eyeflies', wrote Leonard in the official diary.

---

16 12 June 1910

The weather broke and the encampments were inundated. Leonard wrote to the GA strongly suggesting that temporary accommodation should be provided for the pilgrims next time around. Leonard was a good sleeper. The only totally sleepless night of his life was during the Kataragama festival, when the terrible screams of a nearby child kept him awake. The child was blind, and the parents had been pinching and pricking him with pins all night so that the god would hear him and cure the blindness. This incident made a lasting impression on Leonard on account of its mixture of 'pathos and absurdity, kindness and cruelty.'

A crowd of people, petitioning for tax exemptions in the village of Hatagala, included in their list of misfortunes (for which they blamed Halley's Comet) 'a strict Assistant Government Agent'. Leonard's strictness accounted for a sequence of anonymous letters in 1910. One was sent to Lushington, the GA, about the unfairness of allowing his AGA to dismiss a headman.[17] 'Your Asst Sir is a jew brought up by an unconverted jewess, he does not know the love of God, he has not been brought up to live the life that enobles man.' Another accused the AGA of being 'a clever liar, an inhuman beast. He is a ravening wolf seeking whom he may devour.'

Another was to Bella: 'Madam: is Mr Lion Shark Wolf a brother of yours?' She and Bertie Lock were married in September 1910 at the GA's residency at Anuradhapura, and took up their joint life in a bungalow within the Royal Botanical Gardens. Bella was lionised in Kandy as a published author of books for young people, and (like her youngest sister Flora) she contributed stories to *The British Girl's Annual* – typical titles being 'Pat to the Rescue' and 'Wanted – A Heroine'.

Bella had her husband, her household, her writing. Poor Maggie Mortimer, unmarried, was up in the hills at Dijatalawa with nothing to do. 'Ethel and I have had a pretty well abominable time during the four years we have been out here', apart from 'very pleasant intervals', she wrote to Leonard on 27 September 1910. Leonard was a *'nasty mean pig'*

---

17 LW did not have the power to dismiss a headman, only to recommend his dismissal – which he did, on account of the headman's 'slackness and unreliability'.

for neglecting them. They were '*so* bored'. If he came to see them, 'Ethel and I will be fearfully nice to you.'

Young British women, when in the towns, flirted with civil servants and naval and army officers, and were dangled in front of suitable ones by their elders. Marriage was the only way forward, and marrying a 'native' was not an acceptable option. Unmarried European men also had problems finding partners. As Leonard's friend Francis Tyrrell put it, if he could not 'feel passionate' about any from the small pool of European women he met in Ceylon, he could hope to find someone when he went home on leave. If he failed, he would have to wait four or five years until his next leave, by which time he might seem to have been 'too long in the window'. Leonard had written to Lytton that marriage was the 'only way to happiness, to anything settled'. Those of his contemporaries in Ceylon who had wives and babies certainly seemed to find happiness in them.

An exception was the wretched B.J. Dutton from Jaffna days. Leonard happened to coincide with the Duttons, by now four years married, at the Tangalle Rest House. After dinner they 'sat on the verandah with the Indian Ocean a few yards from our toes'. The conversation was 'curious, uneasy', in contrast with the glorious grandeur of the tropical night. Dutton appeared to have shrunk, and Mrs Dutton, the former Miss Beeching, to have swollen. Leonard went off to bed early.

Dutton was now the District Judge at Matara, and when Leonard was visiting the AGA there he called at their house – hygienically clean, 'so different from my bungalow with its immense shadowy grey rooms always smelling of books and dogs'. Mrs Dutton was alone, and even larger, dressed all in white like a huge bride. Her 'neurotic misery' was apparent.

She showed him over the house. The marital bedroom was, 'like Mrs Dutton herself, a mass of white cambric, the two beds being covered with the most voluminous white mosquito nets I have ever seen. It looked as if the whole room were filled with bridal veils, and yet, perhaps owing to the overpowering smell of clean linen, it gave me the feeling of unmitigated chastity.' As they stood one on each side of the beds, Mrs Dutton broke down in floods of tears. Her marriage was a complete failure, and 'Dutton was so queer he ought not to have married'. Keeping the beds between them, Leonard tried to calm her.

What is unspoken here? Married life might not be happiness and a settling, but disaster, and married sex an arid nightmare.

The fifth decennial Census of Ceylon was to be taken on 11 March 1911. Leonard travelled round the villages, appointing and training enumerators from among the indigenous police officers and headmen. He found the villages decimated by malaria, and was struck by the depopulation of the scrub jungle country, especially around the road northwards, towards Badulla. Some villages had just two or three inhabited huts remaining. Others had disappeared altogether. 'I could not want better proof of what I said last year', Leonard wrote pointedly in his official diary on 16 January 1911, 'that the only way in which chenas can really be stopped is by a method which eventually means extermination of the persons who now live by chena cultivation.'

On his way home, he climbed on foot up to a ruined dagoba[18] on a high rock by the ancient tank at Badigiriya. Just as he reached the top a big Asian deer, a sambhur, broke out of a clump of grass about fifteen yards away. 'He went down the rock by the way I had come up like a flash', and then 'turned aside to where the rock drops sheer and with a magnificent bound leapt out and down to the jungle 30 feet below.' He heard the sambhur crashing away through the jungle, unhurt.

On 16 March 1911 Sir Hugh Clifford (he was knighted in 1909), now Governor of Ceylon, came on a four-day visit to Hambantota. Leonard took him shooting and fishing, and accompanied him on inspections of the hospital, jail and schools. Leonard was proud of his new Tamil school for 186 children 'of which 75 are girls'. He financed the building and staffing of his schools through the sale and distribution of opium – another Government monopoly – and was therefore not in favour of restricting supplies.

As he and Clifford were leaving the Rest House to inspect the salt

---

18 Bell-shaped Buddhist shrine

collection, a crowd of angry salt-carters blocked their path, with a petition to the Governor protesting against the AGA's terms and conditions. But the huge and haughty governor, with Leonard in tow, pushed through to his official car and they were driven off – to find, to Leonard's gratification, that 8000 cwts of salt had been collected that day, 'certainly a record for one lewaya', as he claimed in his official diary.[19]

In his last week there was a riot in the town, when a Buddhist procession with loud tom-toms was halted by Muslims as it passed by the mosque. Leonard fined one side for disturbing a religious procession, and the other nearly twice as much for 'tom-toming without a licence'.[20]

A further trouble announced itself in a pompous note from Frederick Bowes (brother of policeman Jimmy Bowes) in the Colonial Secretary's Office in Colombo: 'In your diary last month it is observed that you have adopted a somewhat critical, not to say supercilious tone in alluding to the views of the GA. It is a pity. Whatever you may think, you as his assistant are the one man who must stick up for your chief through thick and thin and therefore when you differ from him you must be most careful to choose your words in order that the jarring note may never be heard.'

This was followed by a copy of a letter from the Colonial Secretary A.N.Galbraith to the GA Mr Lushington, requesting him to inform Mr Woolf that the 'tone' of his comments in his official diary re 'the acquisition of land required for the Public Works Department Store at Tangalle leaves much to be desired. His Excellency [the Governor] accordingly desires you to instruct him to comment with more restraint and discretion upon the orders of his Superior Officer.'[21] Leonard had pointed out in the diary how the absurdly inflated price he had been instructed to pay 'for bare soil' would result in equally absurd prices having to be paid in the future – while the Government regularly refused

---

19 The account of this incident comes from a hostile source in Ceylon following the publication of *Growing* in 1961, and might be discounted had not LW made a brief allusion to it in the book. He did not record it in either his official or his personal diary.
20 13 May 1911
21 19 May 1911

to grant a sum five times less for the improvement of roads 'which would benefit hundreds of people'.[22] His tone was indeed 'somewhat critical, not to say supercilious'. These rebukes, instigated by Lushington, reached Hambantota after Leonard left, and were forwarded to him in England.

Leonard was become increasingly doubtful about his future as a colonial civil servant, not because of the reprimands but because he had lost all faith in the imperial project. He was conspicuously efficacious as an administrator – which meant that sooner or later he would be promoted to central Government in Colombo, to end up as Colonial Secretary or Governor, with a knighthood and a suitable wife. Although power and position tempted him, this prospect made his heart sink. There was a rumour that on return from his year's leave he would be transferred to the Excise Office in Colombo, confirmed by his presence being required at a two-day Excise Conference in Galle shortly before he left. 'Useless', he commented, in his personal diary.

'I hope you'll have a good summer at home, and bring back a wife', wrote Francis Tyrrell, saying goodbye. On 20 May Leonard officially handed over to Lushington, and next morning took the train to Colombo where he met Bella and Bertie; Bella was accompanying him for a short holiday at home. Annie Hopfengartner, after vainly suggesting a rendezvous before he sailed, contrived to meet Leonard by haunting the docks ('Saw Miss H' he noted). She hung on to see the *Staffordshire* move away from the pier and out of the harbour.

Leonard recorded in *Growing* two memories of Hambantota which stayed with him for the rest of his life. One was a visual memory. Every morning, when he had early tea on his verandah, thirty or forty flamingoes would appear from his right, flying in single file along the coast, gleaming black and white. As they came level, 'as each bird in turn wheeled to the left high up in the air above the house, it suddenly changed in the bright sunshine from black and white to a brilliant flash of pink'.

---

22 27 Jan 1911

The other was a sound memory. At any time of day or night, looking down over the bay, he would see 'continually at regular intervals a wave, not very high but unbroken two miles long, lift itself up very slowly, wearily, poise itself for a moment in sudden silence, and then fall with a great thud upon the sand'. The silence followed by the great thud was the last thing he heard before he fell asleep, and the first thing he heard when he woke up; part of the rhythm of his life, 'the rhythm of the sea, the rhythm of Hambantota.'[23]

Bella and Leonard left the ship at Marseille and continued north by train and ferry, arriving on 11 June 1911 at Folkestone, where they were met by Herbert and Edgar.

They were back home in Putney by teatime.

---

23 For further reading and a personal perspective, see Christopher Ondaatje, *Woolf in Ceylon: An Imperial Journey in the Shadow of Leonard Woolf 1904–1911* HarperCollins Canada 2005

7

Aspasia

There they all were, sitting round the table at Lexham in Colinette Road: Mother, Bella, Herbert, Edgar, Harold, Clara, Flora, and Philip. And there they were too in Cambridge: his brother Cecil, Lytton, who had grown a red beard, Henry Lamb, Bertie Russell, Goldie Lowes Dickinson. Leonard met some new Apostles, including Rupert Brooke. When he first saw Brooke's 'sexual dream face', he thought: 'That is exactly what Adonis must have looked like in the eyes of Aphrodite.'[1] But Brooke, after this meeting, enquired casually: 'Was Woolf, who seems very nice, ever more than minor?'[2] On the last day of June 1911 Leonard attended the annual Society dinner in London. He sat between Lytton and Maynard Keynes; G.E. Moore was there. Both in Cambridge and London, Leonard felt as if he were acting in a play.

Desmond MacCarthy was married, and everyone was using first names, talking even more about sex, and actually having sex. Leonard went to Diaghilev's Russian Ballet – a magnet that summer for fashionable and intellectual London. He played tennis, and went riding, and to

1 *Beginning Again*
2 19 June 1911 to James Strachey. King's College

Regent's Park Zoo. He gave his mother lunch at a Lyons Corner House, and took her to a matinee. The Woolfs often went round to his mother's friend Mrs Ross at 3 Colinette Road, where Leonard renewed his acquaintance with the three Ross daughters.

Sylvia, the youngest, was a schoolgirl when he left. She was now twenty-one, a bright, soft, unthreatening young woman. His second novel, *The Wise Virgins*, was to be brazenly autobiographical, contrasting the suburban Putney ('Richstead') world with the world of his Cambridge friends and their families. Sylvia Ross is represented by 'Gwen' – the same alias he gave to Maggie Mortimer in his autobiography. The anti-hero Harry, who is Leonard at his most rebarbative, is torn between Gwen and the cultivated and socially superior sisters Camilla and Katherine, who stand in for Virginia Stephen and Vanessa Bell.

Harry in the novel finds Gwen gratifyingly uneducated – he can hold forth to her on life and literature without fear of challenge – and flatteringly interested in him. The point of life, Harry tells her, is to create – pictures, music, books, children. 'It's the one thing I regret in not being a woman, that I can't bear children.' They see a couple lying in a boat and kissing. 'That's one of the things worth doing', he tells Gwen. She would bring no difficulties into Harry's life: 'things would be marked out for her, just the ultimate events, the great landmarks of life, birth, marriage, child-bearing, death. Yes, one might live simply and happily with someone like that.'

Virginia, telling how her stepsister Stella Duckworth became engaged, only fifteen years before, described how relations between the sexes 'were carried on as relations between countries are now – with ambassadors, and treaties.[3] The Stephen family opened the negotiations. A postcard to Leonard from Saxon: 'Vanessa asked me the other day to bring you to dinner. You needn't dress and you might come here to tea at 5.30 first.' So on 3 July they went round to dinner with Vanessa and

---

3 Jeanne Schulkind (ed): *Moments of Being: A Collection of Autobiographical Writing by Virginia Woolf* Harcourt Inc 1985

Clive Bell at 46 Gordon Square. Afterwards Virginia came in, with Duncan Grant and Walter Lamb.[4] Leonard stayed until midnight.

He always considered Vanessa the more beautiful of the sisters. In her thirties she was a goddess, with something of the 'magnificent and monumental simplicity' of her brother Thoby. Virginia's face, though usually less beautiful, 'lit up with an intense almost ethereal beauty' when she was happy; she was also 'extremely beautiful' when peacefully reading or thinking. Strain or illness made 'the beauty itself painful'.[5]

Virginia made the next move. Five days after meeting Leonard in Gordon Square, she wrote inviting him down to her weekend house in Firle, near Lewes in Sussex. He could not accept the dates she offered; he would be abroad with his brother Edgar. He glimpsed her once more before they left. He was at the Russian Ballet again, with his sister Clara, and Virginia was there with Walter Lamb.

That afternoon Walter Lamb had spoken to Virginia about marriage, after wooing her in an indecisive way for five years. He asked her if she wanted 'to have children and love in the normal way'. (She said she did.) He knew about the Lytton affair, and Clive had told him 'dreadful stories' about her – for there was absolutely no concept of confidentiality within this family or among the close friends. They showed each other intimate letters, and read any that were left lying about, and circulated confidential information, with embellishments. This led to small wars. (Walter complained that they lived in a 'hornet's nest' of intrigue.) Virginia reported to Vanessa that she 'liked [Walter] much better than I ever have done'. She had already turned down several other uninspiring proposals or semi-proposals.[6]

Leonard went to see his Cambridge friend Leopold Douglas Campbell, who had married, and was now rector of St John the Baptist's at Frome in Somerset; and then spent six 'intellectually pretty astringent' days

---

4 Walter Lamb, ex-Trinity, was then schoolteaching. From 1913–51 he was Secretary of the Royal Academy of Arts, and was knighted.

5 *Beginning Again*

6 For the full details see Sarah M.Hall, *Before Leonard: The Early Suitors of Virginia Woolf* Peter Owen 2005

with Lytton and Moore on remote Dartmoor, lodging with a working-man and his family. Lytton was struggling with his first book, *Landmarks in French Literature.* Moore sang in the evenings.

On 22 July he set off with Edgar on their three-week holiday in Scandinavia, visiting relations. Edgar had joined the Fabian Society and the Labour Party while Leonard was in Ceylon. He met Sidney and Beatrice Webb[7] and was invited to their house. (He 'gave it all up in disgust because of their absurd intellectual snobbery'.) In 1964 Edgar, looking at his old diaries, reminded Leonard that it was on this trip that 'I told you about the Webbs and said you ought to read their books on industrial questions, and you told me about Virginia and your difficulty about proposing and the idea of the Ceylon Civil Service'.

Leonard hardly knew Virginia Stephen. Her father Leslie Stephen's first wife was Minnie Thackeray (she died in 1975), daughter of the novelist. They had a daughter, Laura, who did not develop normally. She was thought to be mentally deficient,[8] and in her teens she was sent away to live out her life in institutions. Leslie Stephen's second marriage was to the widowed Julia Duckworth, who became the mother of Vanessa, Thoby, Virginia and Adrian. The Stephens' house, 22 Hyde Park Gate, was also home to Julia's children by her first marriage, George, Stella and Gerald Duckworth.

Julia died when her younger daughter Virginia was thirteen, and the loss precipitated a breakdown. Julia had spent much time away tending the sickbeds of friends and relations, and at home managed a large household of servants and children and an exigent, adoring husband. Virginia could hardly remember ever having been alone with her. In adolescence and beyond, craving affection, she became emotionally attached to older women. She never went to school. Clever and receptive, she educated herself by reading, with some private tuition. Later she went to classes in Greek and Latin at the Kensington

7 Prolific writers and socialist propagandists, founding members of the Fabian Society, founders of the London School of Economics and Political Science (LSE).

8 Laura Stephen may have suffered from a form of autism, or childhood schizophrenia. She lived until 1945. For the best account of Laura's sad life, see Henrietta Garnett, *Anny: a Life of Anne Thackeray Ritchie* Chatto & Windus 2004.

offshoot of King's College, London; and she learned bookbinding.

A second tragedy, when Virginia was seventeen, was the death from peritonitis of her half-sister Stella, who had only recently married. Subsequently, Virginia's father leaned heavily on his two daughters, especially on Vanessa. As the two girls grew up, their older half-brothers George and Gerald insisted on taking them to dances and parties, which they did not enjoy. It was firmly established between the sisters that Vanessa would be a painter and Virginia a writer, and neither was ever to be deflected from her purpose.

Virginia had early success with book reviews and literary articles, but there were setbacks. When their father became terminally ill, she became dependent on Violet Dickinson (unmarried, who had been a close friend of Stella's). After he died, in 1904, she suffered a second and severe breakdown, turning against Vanessa in her psychosis. Violet Dickinson took her into her house at Welwyn with nurses in attendance, where she made a suicide attempt. When Leonard met her at 46 Gordon Square just before he went to Ceylon, she was convalescent.

In 1906 came the third tragedy – Thoby's death, immediately followed by Vanessa's engagement to Clive Bell. With Vanessa's marriage and the birth of her son, Julian, Virginia suffered a loss of intimacy with her sister. She and Adrian set up their own establishment in Fitzroy Square. Clive, also feeling shut out after the baby was born, struck up a close relationship with Virginia – not a full love affair, but something more intense than a flirtation. It was painful for all, although constructive in that Clive encouraged Virginia's writing as she embarked on what was to be her first novel, *The Voyage Out.*

She taught English literature and history part-time for two years at Morley College, an evening institute for working people, and became more independent, while still fragile and subject to insomnia, headaches and anxiety. In summer 1910, when Vanessa was expecting her second baby, Virginia spent several weeks with a Miss Jean Thomas, who cared for mental patients in her small house in Twickenham.

It would have suited Vanessa to see her sister safely married. Virginia needed love and care; and Vanessa, when Virginia broke down, was the primary carer. Vanessa now had children, a husband, her career as a painter and, following a miscarriage in spring 1911, a protracted physical and emotional debility – and, on top of all that, a passionate love affair with the art critic and painter Roger Fry.

This was the precise point at which Leonard returned from Ceylon. Four weeks before he met her after dinner at 46 Gordon Square, Virginia had written to Vanessa: 'To be 29 and unmarried – to be a failure – childless – insane too, no writer.'[9]

But what was she like? She was self-absorbed, highly sensitive and vulnerable, and waspishly observant of others. She was childlike, and could be childish. At her best, she was quick, funny, outstandingly clever, unscrupulous, affectionate and playful, with a grace and a star quality which could light up a room, and which bewitched virtually everyone who knew her. She was an original, 'supreme', like no one else. She lived most authentically in her imagination, and in her reading and writing, already for her the most important thing of all.

In August 1911 Leonard accompanied his mother, Bella, Clara and Flora on the annual Woolf summer holiday at the comfortable, well-upholstered Burlington Hotel at Boscombe, on the south coast. Mrs Woolf's idea of a holiday was very different from the rentals of spartan cottages or farmhouse rooms with minimal amenities which were normal for Leonard and his Cambridge friends. Mrs Ross and Sylvia were also holidaying in the area, and the two families went on excursions. On 23 August, Leonard and Sylvia went off for a three-mile walk on their own along the cliffs.

That holiday was to feature largely in *The Wise Virgins*. Harry, in Leonard's novel, empathises with Gwen's sexual arousal on the cliff walk: 'It surprised Gwen to feel the keen pleasure which Harry's inexpert kiss gave her. A sort of thrill passed through her body . . .' Their kisses become passionate. She tells him she loves him. Harry feels detached. '*Could* he marry her? . . . It might be comfortable with Gwen – but God! How tired he would grow of that child's face at the breakfast table, and the lunch table, and the dinner table.' That night Gwen comes to his

---

9 8 June 1911

hotel room. 'A little movement of desire, cruel and brutal, ran through him.' He does not send her away. Since the Rosses were not staying in the same hotel as the Woolfs, this scene at least has to be fictional.

Leonard was keeping up his Sinhalese, knowing that he wanted to write something about Ceylon. He knew he wanted to be a writer, but was not sure what else he could do. He went with an ex-Cambridge friend, now a surgeon, to watch him perform operations. He went with his brother Philip to the Heatherley School of Fine Art, where Philip was a student, and took some classes himself.

At the end of an inconclusive summer, on Saturday 16 September 1911, he finally took a morning train to Lewes, to stay for three nights at Firle with Virginia Stephen, in her rented red-brick semi-detached villa on the village high street. 'It would be much nicer to use Christian names', she wrote, confirming the date. The first afternoon, they went for a walk on the South Downs. Later, Lytton's sister Marjorie Strachey arrived, as chaperone. Leonard recorded, on his last evening, 'Talked w. V. until 1.' Marjorie presumably went off to bed.

After a visit he made on 11 October to Vanessa on her own, Vanessa reported to Clive: 'I like him very much. He is of course very clever and from living in the wilds seems to me to have got a more interesting point of view than most of the "set" who seldom produce anything very new and original. He thinks we ought to visit the East. The colour is amazing and one's animal passions get very strong and one enjoys one's body to the full.' Two days later, Adrian, too, was reporting that 'I like him very much' (to Duncan Grant, with whom he was having an affair). 'He seems very like what he was at Cambridge except that he has become rather mellower and he was very amusing about Ceylon. His descriptions of hanging were very interesting.' No one in what Vanessa called the 'set' had experiences to match Leonard's. He captured Virginia's imagination as Othello the Moor, 'with all my travel's history'[10] captured Desdemona's.

---

10 Shakespeare's *Othello* Act I Scene 3

Virginia and Adrian had left a concert early so as to meet Leonard and Saxon at Gordon Square and go on to a party. 'It was too funny', Adrian continued to Duncan, with the exasperation of a younger brother. Virginia rushed upstairs to change for the party into her 'best Turkish cloak and satin slippers and so on', keeping them all waiting. 'She made great eyes at Woolf whom she called markedly Leonard which seems to be a little forward. Her method of wooing is to talk about nothing but fucking and [illegible] which she calls with a great leer copulation and WCs and I dare say she will be successful, I hope so anyway.' Vanessa was really the one for talking about sex, encouraged by Lytton. The inexperienced Virginia's talk had an element of attention-seeking, like a knowing child using 'bad words'.

There was a cycle of Wagner's *Ring* at the Royal Opera House; Leonard grandly took a box. Virginia had her own tickets, but came to his box to hear *Siegfried* with him. After each opera in the cycle he went to supper with Virginia and Adrian, leaving so late that the trains had stopped running and he had to take a costly taxi home. He needed to move out of Lexham, which grew more oppressive after Bella, taking Clara with her for a holiday, went back to her husband in Ceylon, leaving Leonard as Mother's preferred escort on her ruminative walks around Harrods. From the end of October 1911, he was writing, with total commitment but in adverse conditions, what was to be *The Village in the Jungle*.

'I have been wandering in the rain ever since I saw you, looking at landladies, prostitutes and rooms', he told Lytton on 30 October 1911. There was a bedroom to let in Saxon's dim lodgings: 'Do you think this would be fatal?' Leonard wrote poems about these wanderings, and the street-walkers under the gaslights. This one was in Southampton Row, close to where Saxon lived:

> . . . You stood I think near a tobacco shop
> And first I saw the whiteness of your face
> And then I saw the halo of black hat,[11]

11 Earlier in this poem, big black hats are described as 'the symbol of their trade'.

I thought, what shall I do in case
I see the question in the whiteness of your face?
And then you smiled. I thought you really smiled
And then I thought it must have been the leer
Which I had seen so often. Anyway
Doubt made me answer, 'Not tonight, my dear'.
I was afraid the smile might prove a leer.

Virginia and Adrian too were moving house, and Leonard inspected 38 Brunswick Square with them. They suggested Leonard might be their top-floor tenant. 'I see it will be the beginning of hopelessness', Leonard wrote to Lytton on 1 November. 'To be in love with her – isn't that a danger? Isn't it always a danger which is never really worth the risk'? I expect after two weeks I shall again take the train not to Morocco[12] but Ceylon.'

The Stephens moved into 38 Brunswick Square on 20 November. Maynard Keynes (in Cambridge much of the time) and Duncan Grant had the ground floor. Adrian had the first floor, and Virginia the second. Leonard called in daily for tea and talk, and momentously wrote in his diary for 4 December 1911: 'Went live Brunswick Sq. V. there.'

Mrs Woolf was not pleased about her dearest Len moving out. He was back in Colinette Road two days later: 'Sylvia there.' He took his mother shopping and to see Phil in his studio the next day, and to a matinee the day after that. Then he felt he had given her enough reassurance. 'Put her on the bus and walk off— to dine w Lytton, go to *Swan Lake,* call on Saxon.' Immediately, Brunswick Square became 'home' in his diary. But his diary also records that he returned to Colinette Road on Sundays, noting 'Sylvia there' every time.

The five months after he returned from Scandinavia were 'the most exciting months of my life'. It was then, he wrote, that '"Bloomsbury"[13] really

12 'Morocco' was code for apostolic or homoerotic friendships – originally from 'Moore-ish'.

13 The term 'Bloomsbury' to indicate a group of people was first used, in a geographical sense, by Molly MacCarthy, to distinguish it from Chelsea, where she and Desmond lived.

came into existence and I fell in love with Virginia. I felt the foundations of my personal life becoming more and more unstable, crisis after crisis confronting me . . .'[14] To ensure concealment from prying eyes, he began writing parts of his diary in code, in Tamil and Sinhalese characters and sometimes a numerical code.[15] Thus on 8 December 1911, dining alone with Vanessa and Clive: *'Talked about syph, art, Walter* [Lamb] & *Virg'*. Leonard knew he was lucky not to have caught syphilis in Ceylon. But 'syph', here, is about Adrian Stephen. 'Either just before or just leaving Cambridge, Adrian contracted tertiary syphilis from a woman prostitute.'[16] Illness accounted for much of Adrian's habitual lethargy.

'Dear Leonard – as Virginia says I may call you', wrote Vanessa, inviting him to dine for her 'Friday Club' at Gordon Square – another little move towards incorporating Leonard into the inner circle. That morning he worked at his novel as usual, and then, that evening: *'talk Virg. Clive & Keynes came. Talk art syph etc.'* And the next night, 'Talked w. Virg Lytton Sax till 1.0'. In Putney as always on Sunday, he called on the Rosses. *'Gloomy'*. All the next week he had fever and stomach-ache, and over Christmas 1911 shuttled back and forth between Brunswick Square and Colinette Road. On Boxing Day, 'Talked w Keynes & Duncan *about sodomy'*; on the twenty-seventh, *'Wrote & saw Virg Made my will Lytton came lunch . . . read and read Sinhalese.'*

As Leonard fell terminally and unconditionally in love with Virginia, he began to call her 'Aspasia' in his diary. The real-life Aspasia was the intelligent, cultivated mistress of Pericles, the ideal leader who, in Leonard's view, made Athens in the fifth century before Christ the universal model for civilised society.

His 'Aspasia Papers' included a whole cast of characters, under classical names. Marjorie Strachey, for example, was 'Sophia', who has 'a good analytic mind', but 'lank and untidy' hair, a 'pinched and grubby'

---

14 *Beginning Again*

15 The words written in code are given in italics. They were decoded and transcribed by Anne Olivier Bell.

16 Jean MacGibbon, *There's the Lighthouse, A Biography of Adrian Stephen* James & James 1997

face, a 'loose and awkward' body. Knowing she longed for love and babies, 'I feel a strong desire to throw myself at Sophia's feet and swear to her that I love her. Unfortunately I am in love with Aspasia and have already flung myself at her feet.'

Raptly in love with Virginia's looks, her manner, her mind, the way she talked and moved, Leonard attributed to 'Aspasia' the highest of high qualities:

'When I think of Aspasia I think of hills, standing very clear but distant against a clear blue sky; there is snow upon them which no sun has ever melted and no man has ever trodden.' But the sun is within her, 'in her hair, in the red and the gold of her skin, in the bow of her lips and in the glow of her mind'. Most wonderful of all was her voice, 'which seems to bring things from the centre of rocks, deep streams that have lain long in primordial places within the earth'. In company , 'Aristotle [Saxon] spins his webs around her, Aristophanes' [Lytton' s] wit and obscenities flash about her.' He wrote poems too, about Virginia as a clean, ethereal creature, a spirit at one with the wind and the wide sky over the Downs.

Aspasia did not know that 'nothing matters': she asked too much of life. Yet she was 'one of possibly three women who know that dung is dung, death death and semen semen. "And her heart?" you ask. Sometimes I think she has not got one.' She seemed aloof, 'and then the spring bubbles up – is it wit or humour or imagination?' – and life for a moment seems to go faster . . . The things that come out are strange, often fantastic.' But was she, as some said, 'vain and a liar?'

'He heard someone say, "She doesn't really understand life because you see she's a virgin. They can't."' There was a side of life which 'she does not see, cannot understand, the meanness and sordidity of it. She would not have the strength to walk through the valley of shadow where all that is low and mean in human feelings crawl. If they touched her she would go mad as some women go mad at the touch of a caterpillar.' She swooped like a bird between reality and romance, 'which join inextricably to form her.'[17]

*

17 Give or take the emotional rhetoric, this is an astute summation of VW's nature, from which few subsequent commentators would diverge.

Nevertheless, Leonard had qualms about whether to throw in his lot with the Strachey/Stephen 'set'. After seven years away, he saw his apostolic friends, 'the Olympians' as he called them in the Aspasia Papers, with an outsider's eyes: 'The Olympians live in ordinary houses except for an enormous number of books and sometimes some queer pictures.' The Olympians sit in their houses, 'in ones or twos or threes. I should not be surprised if you thought them rather dull and the silences rather uncomfortable for very often they sit and don't even talk. They are however thinking and very often feeling. They think a great deal and talk a great deal of what the others of them think and feel. You would probably call this gossip.'

He wrote a vicious sketch in the Aspasia Papers of Goldie Lowes Dickinson as 'Europroktus', 'a lascivious male old maid . . . an effete and rotten old lecher in the body of a eunuch frog . . . I would rather touch a decaying dogfish than his body'. Leonard, in love with a lovely woman, violently repudiated the homoerotic world. 'There is nobility in the form and spirit of virility, and god in the breast and womb and fertility of woman.' Even Moore, 'Socrates', could seem ridiculous, 'with his remorseless reasoning, with his questions "What exactly do you mean by this or by that, by beauty by truth by God?" and they run about with their tongues wagging out of their mouths and there is nothing but blither blither blither . . . about the is-ness of is and the wasness of was and the willness of will and the everythingness of everything.'

Leonard wrote a 'character' of himself in the Aspasia Papers as 'Namus', who was 'wonderfully intelligent' but 'lustful, a whorer, a gazer after women, vicious because he loves the refinements of vice. He sees the filth of the brothel, knows it to be filth, but lies very romantically with the ugliest whore.' Yet when Namus heard that Kymon (Clive Bell), married to 'the most beautiful and intelligent woman in Europe' (Lysistrata/Vanessa) was unfaithful to her (as he was), he 'feels quite sick with disgust and disillusionment' and tells Aspasia. She is shocked. 'I knew you would feel like that! Thank God.' But next day Namus hears about something 'ignoble and treacherous' that Aspasia has done. 'Namus feels quite sick with disgust and disillusionment and goes to a brothel.'

What had Virginia Stephen done? Read other people's letters, and told Leonard what she had gleaned about Vanessa's affair with Roger Fry. Leonard revered Vanessa, and still felt her attraction.

As for the author of the Aspasia Papers, 'I was born at Jericho and like most of the inhabitants of Jericho I have a long nose and black hair . . . I should like to live on Olympus but all Syrians are wanderers, and I doubt whether any of them are really Olympians. There is some taint in their blood, and blood you know has a great deal to do with the heart. You want a strong heart to live among the Olympians.'

His leave was up in May 1912, and he was due to sail for Ceylon in April. In a wretched state of indecision, he took refuge again with Leopold at Frome. From there, on 10 January 1912, he sent Virginia a telegram saying he was coming to London the next day. He had to see her.

He wrote to her, on his return to Frome that night: 'I never realized how much I loved you until we talked about my going back to Ceylon. After that I could think of nothing else but you. I got into a state of hopeless uncertainty, whether you loved me or could ever love me or even like me. God, I hope I shall never spend such a time again as I spent here until I telegraphed.'

He had declared himself to her that afternoon. It amounted to a proposal, even though they were interrupted by the arrival of Walter Lamb. He then listed, by mail, the risks any woman ran who was to marry him: 'I am selfish, jealous, cruel, lustful, a liar and probably worse still.' He feared he could never control these things 'with a woman who was inferior and would gradually enfuriate [*sic*] me by her inferiority and submission.' Virginia was different: 'You may be vain, an egoist, untruthful as you say, but [your faults] are nothing compared to your other qualities: magnificence, intelligence, wit, beauty, directness. After all too we like one another, we like the same kinds of things and people . . .'

Vanessa advised her sister not to marry Leonard unless she was in love, but not to worry about his Jewishness. She promoted the match, letting Leonard know that Virginia had told her about 'her talk' with him, 'and also to say how glad I shall be if you can have what you want. You're the only person I know whom I can imagine as her

11 Jan 1912

My dear Virginia, I must write to you before I go to bed & can, I think, probably think more calmly.

I have not got any very clear recollection of what I really said to you this afternoon but I am sure you know why I came — I dont mean merely that I was in love but that that together with uncertainty drives one to do these things. Perhaps I was wrong, for before this week I always intended not to tell you unless I felt sure that you were in love & would marry me. I thought then that you liked me but that was all. I never realised how much I loved you until we talked about my going back to Ceylon. After that I could think about nothing else but you. I got into a state of hopeless uncertainty, whether you loved me or could ever love me or even liked me. God, I hope I shall never spend such a time again as I spent here until I telegraphed. I wrote to you once saying I would speak

LW's passionate letter to Virginia Stephen, 11 January 1912.

husband, which may seem to you a rash remark. However I have faith in my instincts.' She hoped he would be coming to Asheham 'for our house-warming party.'[18]

Asheham House was discovered by Leonard and Virginia when walking on the Downs. It was off the road from Lewes to Newhaven, with a field running down to the river Ouse: a yellow-washed Regency farmhouse with gothic windows, and single-storey additions, like little pavilions, at each end. Virginia rented it for seven years, sharing it, and the costs, with the rest of the set. Asheham House had a ghost, was always damp, and never comfortable. It also had charm and a magic, and was much loved by them all.

Vanessa had promised to keep Leonard's proposal secret. She told Clive – who was much *too* interested – that Leonard apparently 'had the offer of a job and wanted to consult with her whether to take it or go back to Ceylon . . . Do you think this looks as if he were in love with her? Tell me all you know.' This was a way of testing how much the inquisitive Clive did know.

Leonard's proposal proved too much for Virginia, who took to her bed. 'It was a touch of my usual disease, in the head you know', as she wrote to her good friend Ka Cox[19] on 7 February, after the glacial weekend at Asheham for which 'housewarming' was a misnomer. There was no useable lavatory, and the water-pipes froze. There was a second Asheham weekend in late February, equally cold. Leonard talked to Saxon long into the night, and returned yet again to his trusted confidant, Leopold, in Frome.

The Colinette Road contingent was in the dark about his intentions, and there is no way of knowing how much he had seemed to commit himself to Sylvia Ross, if at all, nor at what stage he disabused her, if at all.

Moore was back at Trinity with a lectureship, and asked Leonard to choose a place for an Easter reading party, and to invite the usual

---

18 14 Jan 1912

19 Katherine Cox had been at Newnham College, Cambridge and was in love with Rupert Brooke.

people. 'Wouldn't you, perhaps, undertake the whole business of arranging, instead of me?'[20] This was the last thing that Leonard needed. He replied tersely that he did not want to do it in the least, 'but if you really want me to do so I will.'

He still did not know what to do about Ceylon. At Christmas he had sent cards and presents of money to the kachcheri clerks in Jaffna, Kandy and Hambantota. His colleagues, looking forward to his return, sent him all the news. His dog, Mermaid, had had four pups. George Templer had married, as had T.A.Hodson, who already had a baby. 'I had hoped to hear you were married by now', Hodson wrote to Leonard. 'It is an excellent institution for keeping a man cheerful, to say the least.'[21]

Even if Virginia Stephen would not marry him, Leonard was in two minds about pursuing his career in the Colonial Service. That had been the case even before he came on leave. He knew that his alternative notion of immersing himself in the life of Hambantota, living with a Sinhalese woman, was total fantasy.

If Virginia Stephen did marry him, he would not be able to go back anyway. Another kind of woman – a 'Gwen', a Sylvia – would naturally have returned to Ceylon with him. There was never any question of that with Virginia. 'First of all it would have killed her – the climate. It was absolutely impossible.'[22]

Between the two icy housewarming weekends at Asheham, Leonard wrote to the Secretary of State for the Colonies, asking if he could extend his leave for private reasons for another four months. A prompt reply invited him to state what the private reasons were. This Leonard felt unable to do. The Secretary of State could not have been more accommodating. The next letter emphasised that his reasons would be treated in strictest confidence; but that if he still felt unable to divulge them, then the Secretary would ask the Governor of Ceylon whether an extension might be granted 'on grounds of service'.

Meanwhile Virginia's insomnia, headaches and anxiety overwhelmed

---

20 26 Feb 1912
21 11 March 1912
22 LW in interview with Malcolm Muggeridge for BBC TV recorded 6 Sep 1966

her, and Dr Savage sent her to Jean Thomas's house in Twickenham for a couple of weeks' bed-rest. Vanessa asked Leonard not to communicate with her at all. It was not looking good. Leonard wrote again to the Secretary of State, saying that if the Governor of Ceylon granted him extra leave 'on grounds of service', he would not take it up unless his private affairs 'absolutely necessitate it', but would resume his duties in May.

Even when Virginia returned to Brunswick Square, Vanessa let Leonard know it would be best if he kept away. 'I think she is worrying a good deal about you just now and can't make up her mind what she feels.' Leonard took himself off and walked alone in the West Country in pouring rain, scouting for a base for Moore's Easter reading party. Moore, not satisfied, urged him to further research, fussed about sleeping arrangements and whether there would be a piano, and instructed Leonard to 'write to the station master at Paddington' about trains. But Charlie Sanger and Bob Trevy pulled out, as did Lytton and James Strachey. MacCarthy could not afford to come, and Maynard Keynes never intended to come. Leonard wrote to Moore. 'Will you think it beastly of me that I'm not coming either?'[23]

On 5 March 1912 Virginia told Leonard that she felt 'very clear, calm, and move slowly, like one of the great big animals at the zoo'. She had taken up knitting. He was allowed to write to her now, but only on impersonal matters. Her semi-invalid life continued through March.

This was Leonard's first experience of her mental collapses. Its chief effect on him was the unhappiness of being forbidden to see her. Perhaps he should have stood up to Vanessa and Dr Savage.

> How long how long ago is it since I
> Saw your face hover about me night and day
> Smile in the darkness to take my sleep away
> Smile between bare earth and wintry sky
> Hanging above me unreal intangible

---

23 12 March 1912

Among real clouds, real trees and real hills
The day and darkness heaven and earth – ah well
For ever was a few days, and then I saw
You sitting in your chair by the fire,
I could have kissed the lips that I desire
But only words came from those lips, and we
Talked and talked and talked, until the spell
Returned: your face, unreal, intangible.

He saw her at last on 21 March, for a walk and dinner, after going alone with Vanessa for a consultation with Dr Savage. George – soon to be Sir George – Savage, that elderly and eminent specialist in mental diseases, had dismissed in a recent (1911) article, 'Insanity and Marriage', the notion of marriage as a 'cure' for neurasthenia in women. Though he came out in favour of the marriage, he cannot have been wholly sanguine, privately, about Virginia's chances with Leonard. 'He was very friendly to me', wrote Leonard, 'but impressed me more as a man of the world than as a doctor.'[24] Neither Dr Savage nor the Stephen family were candid with Leonard about the seriousness of Virginia's previous breakdowns. 'Of course the Goat is mad', Vanessa and Adrian would say; but as if it were a joke. Virginia too made a joke of being 'mad'. That was the way they dealt with it.

Savage knew the family history. He had treated Vanessa and Virginia's father for depression. He had treated their first cousin James K.Stephen, who committed suicide in 1892. He had known Virginia since she was a child, and had looked after her since the breakdown following the death of her father. He administered what were called quietening drugs, and followed the humane psychiatric mainstream in prescribing seclusion, bed-rest and nourishing food. He was against terms such as 'asylum', and 'lunatic'. Where young women were concerned, he was against 'over-education', and ascribed much disturbance to 'the stress of sexuality'. Savage was, in short, a decent man but a product of his era. Virginia did not like him, and never had.

---

24 *Beginning Again*

Leonard turned for advice to Roger Fry – a generation older, with experience of a mentally ill wife. After two years' marriage and two children she had recurrent breakdowns. From 1910, on Dr Savage's advice, she was confined in mental hospitals from which she never again emerged. Though 'dried up and hardened by the utter tragedy of my love',[25] Roger Fry became passionately involved with Vanessa in 1911. At his suggestion, Vanessa was being treated by the 'nerve specialist' Maurice Craig, whom he recommended to Leonard for Virginia.

From the beginning of April 1912 Leonard was at Asheham nearly every weekend with Virginia, Ka Cox (as helper and minder), Vanessa, Roger and others. In London, the life of theatres, opera, walks, dinners, visits to Putney, picked up again – with the difference that on evenings at home in Brunswick Square, he and Virginia sat together in his room or hers after dinner.

Leonard heard that the Governor of Ceylon was not, after all, prepared to grant an extension of his leave 'on grounds of service'. On 25 April he sent in his resignation. The next day he wrote in his diary: *'Worked at terrace*[26] *w Virg & talked late w her about what we should do if we married.'* They went to Eastbourne and walked on the cliffs: *'She was extraordinarily gentle I kissed her . . .'*

The kiss resolved nothing. Leonard sensed that 'something seemed to rise up in you against me'. This, written on 29 April, was in a long, inchoate letter of love. 'God, the happiness I've had by being with you and talking with you as I've sometimes felt it mind to mind together and soul to soul . . . I don't think much of the physical part of it though it must come in . . . If one happens to be born as I am, it is almost certain to be very strong, but even then it becomes so merged with one's other feelings.' She was the best thing in life. He would never now be content with 'second best'.

The Secretary of State for the Colonies did not give up on Leonard. He was invited to come into the office and explain his difficulties in person. 'They now obviously want to grant me the leave', he told

---

25 Quoted in Denys Sutton (ed): *Letters of Roger Fry* Chatto & Windus 1972
26 They were levelling the ground and laying tiles.

Virginia, seeking from her some sign, or some sign of a sign. He was rewarded by a quick response, Virginia fully realising, not without some satisfaction, 'what a career you're ruining!' She considered the 'obvious advantages of marriage' for herself – 'companionship, children, and a busy life – then I say By God, I will not look on marriage as a profession.' She did indeed feel 'angry sometimes at the strength of your desire. Possibly your being a Jew comes in at this point. You seem so foreign. And then I am fearfully unstable.' She kept coming back to the problem of sex: 'As I told you brutally the other day, I feel no physical attraction in you.' When he kissed her, she felt 'no more than a rock'. But his caring for her meant everything to her. 'I feel as if I must give you everything; and that if I can't, well, marriage would only be second best for you as well as for me.'[27]

This was enough, for Leonard. He declined the offer of the Colonial Office and confirmed, definitively, his resignation.

The news reached his former colleagues in a seven-inch item in the *Times of Ceylon* on 8 May 1912: 'At the time of his going on leave he was drawing £650 as salary. He has served the Government for 8 years, and his many friends will be sorry to hear of his early retirement from the service in which he has been very popular.' Tom Southorn, hoping his resignation did not mean 'that your health has given way',[28] sent him a clip from another paper: 'Mr Woolf was a civil servant of great promise, and we have not yet heard of the reason for his resignation.' For Annie Hopfengartner it was 'a fearful shock and I feel there must be something terribly wrong.' She was sending a telegram urging him to come back. 'I hope you will take notice because I love you and am fearfully anxious about you.' The news unleashed, as Bella reported from Peradeniya, a spate of rumours.[29] Leonard had inherited a fortune from

27 1 May 1912

28 8 May 1912

29 Pablo Neruda in the 1920s was told in Ceylon that Leonard Woolf had been ordered to burn down a peasant's hut, in order that his land might be appropriated. Woolf had refused, and therefore been dismissed. (Pablo Neruda, *Memoirs* Souvenir Press 1977) This is nonsense.

someone drowned on the *Titanic*; he had made such a killing on the race-course that he was set up for life; a letter in a bottle picked up on the shore in Hambantota had contained a promise of untold wealth.

Leonard, having just about finished *The Village in the Jungle,* wrote a short story, 'A Tale Told by Moonlight'.[30] It was about the 'flame of passion' evoked in a man by a woman, 'not for her body or her mind or her soul but for something beautiful mysterious everlasting – yes that's it the everlasting passion in her which has flamed up in him', so that he can find his way now 'even among the stars'. 'Not one man in ten thousand feels it and not one woman in twenty thousand.' It is not just being 'in love', which is about the body. 'The body's damnably exciting . . . It's only when we don't pay for it that we call it romance and love.'

His Cambridge-educated protagonist becomes overwhelmed in Colombo by his feelings for a young prostitute, believing he can find 'the same passion, the same fine strong thing he felt moving in himself'. Realising she is just 'a simple soft little golden-skinned animal with nothing in the depths of the eyes at all', he contemplates suicide. But his passion at least is authentic, and he buys her out of the brothel and lives with her. By the time he faces up to how much her mindlessness gets on his nerves, she has grown to love him 'like an animal, as a bitch loves her master', and the end is tragedy.

Leonard was working out to its logical conclusion his own fantasy, in an extreme version of the dilemma he had with prostitutes and even with the 'Gwen' girls. He idealised and desired them, while knowing they could not meet him intellectually and had not 'the power to feel, the power that so few have, the flame, the passion, love, the real thing'. The 'real thing' was what he felt for Virginia. But what did she feel? And what about the desires of the body, so 'damnably exciting' – or 'damnably exacting'?[31]

*

30 Published in LW, *Stories of the East* Hogarth Press 1921. The theme of Conrad's *Almeyer's Folly*, 1924, is very similar.

31 It is 'damnably exacting' in LW's manuscript. 'Exciting' in the printed text is either a change of mind or a misprint.

Adrian Stephen was very thick with Clive Bell, reporting on 12 May: 'Nothing seems to be happening here. I don't know what may not be happening upstairs between the Goat and Woolf, but if there is anything they certainly manage to keep very quiet about it.'[32] Clive, pursuing Molly MacCarthy with amorous intent, wrote to her on 22 May: 'Virginia had been at infinite pains to throw dust in my eyes – Vanessa had been sworn to secrecy etc etc – so, of course, I have been at as many to keep them open.' Virginia 'still vacillated, uncertain of her feelings but enjoying them immensely; within a few weeks she will come down heads, and it will all be very satisfactory' – except, Clive wrote, for Woolf's Jewishness, 'and Woolf's family are chosen beyond anything.'[33]

Lytton had his own agenda, hoping that Leonard might combine the supreme marriage with an attachment to 'Morocco': 'If there was a fine morning, and you got into a train, with or without a companion, and arrived [in Cambridge] for a light lunch, and then sank into the punt among cushions, chocolates, poetry-books, cigarettes, and penises – wouldn't you enjoy yourself?'[34]

This was the last time Lytton made a bid to re-engage Leonard in 'the dialect of their intimacy'. Nevertheless Leonard had a sharp sense of the limits that marriage set on life. An unpublished short story, probably written in Ceylon, tells of a dull man in a dull Kensington house, with a wife in the process of giving birth upstairs. The first-person narrator, sitting with the husband, recalls to him the days when he was young and handsome and in love with 'a divinely beautiful and divinely foolish' fellow student. He sees his friend redden and start. 'There was a moment of complete silence in the room and then we both heard quite distinctly from the floor above the dreary wail of a new born child. Then I fled from the house.' But that was before he fell in love with Virginia Stephen.

*

32 12 May 1912. King's College

33 'chosen' as in 'the Chosen Race'. Letter quoted in Hugh and Mirabel Cecil, *Clever Hearts: Desmond and Molly MacCarthy* Gollancz 1990

34 nd. From internal evidence May 1912

1. LW's mother dressed for presentation at court when her husband became QC.

2. LW's father, Sidney Woolf QC, shortly before his death at the age of 47.

3. LW's elder sister, Bella.

4. 101, Lexham Gardens.

5. Lexham, 9, Colinette Road, Putney.

6. Woolf family in 1886: Herbert, Harold, Marie, Nurse Vickary with Flora, Clara, Edgar, Bella, Sidney, Leonard.

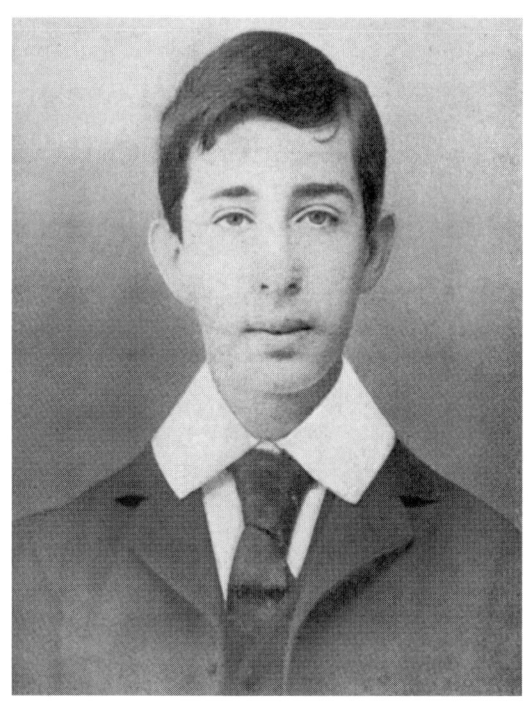

7. LW when a schoolboy.

8. Leonard and Herbert, c. 1885.

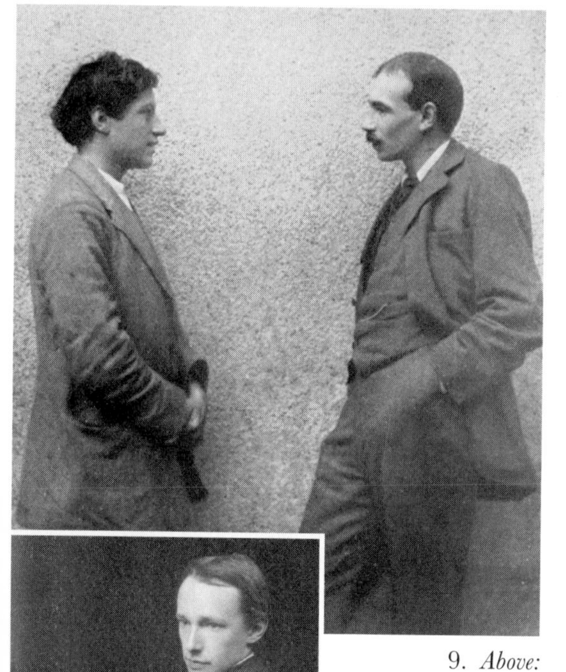

9. *Above:* Duncan Grant and Maynard Keynes.

10. Lytton Strachey at Cambridge.

11. *Left:* George E. Moore.

12. The Shakespeare Society, Trinity College, Cambridge. In the back row Thoby Stephen is second from the left, and on the extreme right Walter Lamb, later one of Virginia's suitors. In the front row on extreme left is Lytton Strachey and on extreme right LW; second from the right is R.K. Gaye.

13. LW in Jaffna.

14. Sir Hugh Clifford, LW's patron in Ceylon: a very eccentric Governor.

15. The Fort at Jaffna in the 1940s.

16. LW introduced ploughs into his district.

18. A village in the jungle.

17. Interior of LW's bungalow.

19. The bay at Habantota from LW's bungalow.

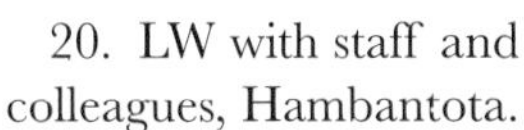

20. LW with staff and colleagues, Hambantota.

21. Virginia Stephen, 1902.

22. Vanessa Bell, 1912.

23. Clive Bell.

24. Virginia and Leonard during their engagement, 1912.

25. Lytton Strachey.

26. Oliver Strachey, G.E. Moore, Maynard Keynes.

27. LW and G.E. Moore at Asheham House, 1914.

28. Saxon Sydney-Turner and Duncan Grant at Asheham.

29. Virginia Woolf.

30. Clive and Julian Bell, Roger Fry, Duncan Grant and Saxon Sydney-Turner.

31. Asheham House.

On Wednesday, 29 May 1912, Leonard wrote in his diary: 'Wrote morn. Lunch w Virg talking after she suddenly told me she loved me went on river Maidenhead dined there.'

It was a beautiful afternoon. They seemed, he remembered in old age, to drift in a dream of happiness. On the train, on the river, in the restaurant, they seemed alone together in the universe.

She loved him. They were going to be married.

In the morning, they broke the news to Adrian. Vanessa was in Italy, so they agreed to keep it secret. But Leonard lunched with Morgan Forster that day, and with Saxon the next. He probably told them. Vanessa returned, and on Sunday 2 June they went to Gordon Square and told her. She was taken aback by the great step having been taken in her absence. 'Well, I'm afraid I was very inexpressive today', she wrote that evening, 'but although I had expected it, it was somehow so bewildering and upsetting when I actually did see you and Leonard together that I didn't know how to say what I felt.'

There were some 'tiresome side issues', which she recounted to Roger Fry. Leonard and Virginia seemed 'very happy', but Adrian had, typically, shown them Clive's 'bitter and abusive' letters to him about Virginia, 'which naturally made both her and L very angry', and they 'worked themselves up into a fury'. They walked off their fury on the Embankment, and that night Leonard wrote to tell Lytton the good news: 'I'm so happy that that's the only thing I can say to you, simply that I am. Lord, it is so difficult to put one's happiness into words and it was so easy to put the miseries of life into them from Ceylon. At any rate after 13 years and the silences in them, youre [*sic*] the person I turn to first in the world to try to tell you of either.' Leonard and Virginia also sent Lytton a triumphant note:

> Ha! Ha!
> Virginia Stephen
> Leonard Woolf

And Lytton, privately to Leonard: 'It is magnificent. I am very happy, and je t'aime beaucoup.'

Walter Lamb, noble in defeat, wrote at once to Leonard: 'You have the love of the finest person I know of in the world . . . I am sure you will do all in your power to make her happy, and that I can count on your lasting friendship as well as hers.'[35] There was some predictable malice, of which Leonard would not have known. Rupert Brooke wrote to James Strachey, on hearing the news: 'No doubt you've a heap of funny stories about it. I *thought* the little man 'ld get her. Directly he began saying he was the only man who'd had a woman she knew,[36] and telling tales about prostitutes – oh, you should have seen the love light dance and dawn in her eyes! *That* gets them.'

The friends in Ceylon had simpler reactions. Annie Hopfengartner buried her love and conveyed her congratulations. J.A.Wilson, the Irrigation Engineer at Tissa, while urging Leonard to 'think again' about resigning, wished 'you and the little lady the best of luck and happiness'. Maggie Mortimer sent an affectionate note: 'We shall never forget you dear old friend Stick Insect. Please don't forget us.'

Lytton, a little piqued by not being in Leonard's confidence throughout, wrote to Lady Ottoline Morrell on 12 June: 'I've not seen either of them yet; but I know that he is in ecstasies of happiness.' Virginia, he heard, was disappointed that everyone took the news so calmly. 'She hoped that everyone would be thunderstruck. Duncan alone came up to her expectations – he fell right over on the floor when she told him: and of course he had been told all about it by Adrian before.'

On the day Lytton wrote that, Leonard was taking Virginia to Lexham to meet his mother. 'Work and love and Jews in Putney take it out of one', Virginia, with a headache, wrote to Violet Dickinson that evening. She transcribed a bit of the dialogue:

"A sandwich, Miss Stephen – or may I call you Virginia?".
"What? Ham sandwiches for tea?".

---

35 4 June 1912

36 The poet's prose is clumsy. He means, 'the only man she knew who'd had a woman . . .' Letter quoted in Keith Hale (ed): *Friends & Apostles: The Correspondence of Rupert Brooke & James Strachey 1905–1914* Yale University Press 1998

"Not *Ham:* potted meat. We don't eat Ham or bacon or Shellfish in this house."
"Not Shellfish? Why not shellfish?"

And so on, with Virginia at her most mischievous. To Madge Vaughan, an older cousin with whom she had convalesced after her last breakdown, she sent a colourful account of her fiancé: 'First he is a Jew: second he is 31; third, he spent 7 years in Ceylon, governing natives, inventing ploughs, shooting tigers, and did so well that they offered him a very high place the other day, which he refused, wishing to marry me, and gave up his entire career there on the chance that I would agree. He has no money of his own I've only known him 6 months, but from the first I have found him the one person to talk to.' Her account grew extravagant: 'he has ruled India, hung black men . . .' Virginia told Violet that Leonard 'wants to find out about labour and factories and keep outside Government and do things on his own account.' Meanwhile he had some journalism, and she had nearly finished her novel (she did not mention his), and was thinking of another: 'but next year I must have a child.'

The next weekend at Asheham Leonard could not sleep, and went for a long walk before dawn. He had had to put off a visit from Lytton, because Dr Savage was against their having visitors. In London he bought an engagement ring, and they all played tennis in the gardens of Gordon Square, 'even w Virg who was not well'.

They paid a visit to the MacCarthys in Wellington Square. Desmond came home to find them sitting side by side on the sofa, Molly introducing them as 'Mr and Mrs Woolf'. 'Virginia has a bad headache, the consequence of excitement, and has gone to bed and no one sees her.'[37] This was in early August, not much more than a week before the wedding.

Privately, they had begun to carve out the idiom of their own intimacy. Virginia gave herself and those close to her animal nicknames. Loyal,

37 Hugh and Mirabel Cecil, *Clever Hearts: Desmond and Molly MacCarthy: A Biography* Gollancz 1990

kind Ka Cox was Bruin. In her tender excesses to Vanessa (Sheepdog, or Dolphin) and Violet Dickinson, she called herself not only Billy or Billy Goat, but the Wallaby, the Barbary Ape or, in the plural, 'the apes', or the *singes,* or the *singerie,* as if she were a whole squealing pack of monkeys. During their engagement, Leonard became Mongoose. He had kept a mongoose as a pet when he was in Ceylon, and had mongoose characteristics: 'The motto of all the mongoose family is, "Run and find out."'[38] Although a mongoose is carnivorous and solitary, 'No one can imagine the affectionate nature of a mongoose.'[39] Virginia became Mandril. 'I hope the Mandril went to its box early and isn't worried by anything in the world', Leonard wrote to her on 24 May. 'The end is as the beginning was and as it always will be, that it's for me the dearest and most beloved creature in the world.'

This was a marriage brought about by Lytton and Vanessa – and by Leonard's absolute love.

They were married on Saturday, 10 August 1912 at St Pancras Registry Office. Leonard described himself, under 'Rank or Profession', as 'of independent means'. He had almost no means at all. Virginia's half-brother George Duckworth had asked him, since he could not settle any money on Virginia, to take out life insurance in her favour. 'Virginia will be a most adorable wife', he added, man to man. George was acting *in loco parentis*; he and Vanessa were the witnesses at the wedding.

It was a small wedding. The only other people there were Roger Fry, Gerald Duckworth, Virginia's Aunt Mary Fisher, Duncan Grant, Saxon Sydney-Turner and the young artist Frederick Etchells, a friend of Duncan and Roger's. Adrian was away in Germany. Lytton was enduring a long wet holiday in Scotland and Ireland with Henry Lamb, brooding on his friends' amatory arrangements – including those of 'Woolf and Virginia' – and 'the wildest Dostoyevsky novel seems to grow dim and ordinary in comparison'.[40] Vanessa, deep in her own

---

38 Rudyard Kipling, 'Rikki-Tikki-Tavi', a story in *The Jungle Book* (1894)

39 Pablo Neruda, *Memoirs* Souvenir Press 1977. Neruda too kept a mongoose as a pet in Ceylon, in the 1920s.

40 To Lady Ottoline Morrell, 14 Aug 1912. Quoted in Michael Holroyd, *Lytton Strachey* (one-vol version) Heinemann 1973

concerns, interrupted the proceedings by enquiring how one went about changing the name of a child. She did not like 'Clement', the name she had given her second son. (She was to add the name 'Quentin.') 'One thing at a time, please, Madam', said the registrar. They all went back to 46 Gordon Square. After lunch 'Clive sat down and wrote a short, painful letter to Virginia, declaring his love for both her and her husband.'[41]

There was no one at all at the wedding from Leonard's family, not even his mother. Leonard and Virginia were agreed that his chief fault was cowardice, and hers was snobbery. The exclusion of Mrs Woolf proves them right. He wrote explaining that they were getting married quietly, with no party, and hoped she would not be hurt. 'My dear Len', she replied, 'To be quite frank, yes, it has hurt me extremely that you did not make it a point to have me at your marriage.' To be present at his wedding, the most important day of his life, 'would have compensated me for the very great hardships I have endured in bringing you all up by myself.' She ended her letter generously: 'With very much love, Ever, my dear Len, Your devoted Mother.'

Leonard was the sambhur who leapt from a high rock and crashed away into the jungle. 'Nothing matters', he always said. Yet he had been seeking, without much hope, someone to whom he could devote himself wholeheartedly and passionately, without cynicism or degradation. It was Virginia.

---

41 Frances Spalding, *Vanessa Bell* Weidenfeld & Nicolson 1983

8

Mongoose and Mandril

Leonard and Virginia spent their wedding night at Asheham, then went to the Plough Inn at Holford in Somerset. After a week, they crossed the Channel, took the train south, and meandered for two months through France, Spain and Italy, sleeping in primitively simple lodgings. Leonard loved this but acknowledged, in retrospect, that it was too tiring for Virginia. They stopped in Venice for a rest at the end of their trip, from where Leonard wrote to Molly MacCarthy, who had expressed curiosity about how they were getting on: 'I don't feel like a married man which I think is a good test of happiness.' It would be easier to satisfy Molly's curiosity if 'we had quarrelled and bored one another. It would be so much more amusing.'

The friends and relations were indeed curious, chiefly about how Leonard and Virginia were getting along sexually. Vanessa, at Asheham making curtains (orange, lined and bordered with mauve), wrote to her sister, when the new couple were still at the Plough Inn, as if to the animal (male) that Virginia played at being. Her facetiousness grates: '*Of course* I should have expected him [Leonard] to be in the 7th heaven of delight . . . As long as the ape [Virginia] gets all he wants, doesn't smell too much and has his claws well cut, he's a pleasant enough bed-fellow for a short time. The whole question is what will happen when the red undergrowth sprouts in the autumn? Are you really a promising pupil? I believe I'm very bad at it. Perhaps Leonard would like to give me a few lessons.'[1] And a week or so later, to Leonard: 'I am happy to say it's years since I spent a night in [the apes'] company. And I can't conceive of anything more wretched than it sounds. It would be bad enough to know they were in the next bed with all their smells and their whines and their wettings, but to have to change beds with them and all the rest of it – a coal hole would be more to my taste.' To Leonard again: 'Ask him [the ape, Virginia] if he really feels more attracted by the male than by the female figure. Does he like manly strength and hardness? Also do tell me how *you* find *him* compared to all the others you have had? I suppose that is really a foolish question.' Vanessa, beset by physical and nervous symptoms, was unnerved by Virginia's marriage, even though she had worked to bring it about.

They were both 'marrying out' and both 'marrying in'. Virginia, announcing her engagement, had written repeatedly that Leonard was 'a penniless Jew', maximising the social *frisson* this would cause. It was not a match anyone would have predicted for the well-connected daughter of Sir Leslie Stephen KCB. She added in every case that Leonard had been a great friend of Thoby's. Everyone knew how much she had loved Thoby. She even said that Leonard reminded her of Thoby. But marrying Virginia Stephen did not reinforce Leonard's sense of belonging. It emphasised his difference. 'I was an outsider to this class, because, although I and my father before me belonged to the professional middle class, we had only recently struggled up into it from the stratum of Jewish shopkeepers.' He had no foothold in the 'intricate tangle of ancient roots and tendrils' which connected upper-middle-class families to one another and to the aristocracy. He disliked many of their assumptions while 'envying and fearing' their assurance and manners.[2] Yet he was also marrying in – to the ex-Cambridge world of which he was a part, and to the makers of the match, Lytton and Vanessa. The link with Thoby, for him too, was crucial. In his Aspasia Papers, excoriating the Gordon Square group, he wrote how

1 12 August 1912. Berg
2 *Beginning Again*

'one towers up clear above the mist, a rock to hold by, just as he was in life.'

Virginia committed herself to the penniless Jew, but not to his family. She shared the unthinking habits of most English gentiles, expressing freely her distaste for Jews, including her in-laws – their accents and voices, their clothes and food, their physical characteristics. It was legitimate to find Jews comic. Her brother Adrian was specially good at 'imitating Jews'.[3] Marrying a Jew was part of her rebellion against the conventions in which she was raised. Her airy references to Leonard's Jewishness can be read sometimes, but not always, as flying the flag of liberation.

Virginia's sexual experience was minimal and not encouraging. When she was about six, her half-brother Gerald Duckworth lifted her on to a ledge and explored her body under her clothes. 'I remember how I hoped that he would stop; how I stiffened and wriggled as his hand approached my private parts. But it did not stop. His hand explored my private parts too. I remember resenting, disliking it . . .'[4] In their late teens, both she and Vanessa were subjected to the fondlings of their other half-brother, George Duckworth, sixteen years older than Virginia. He would come into her room when she was in bed and throw himself on to (but not into) her bed, cuddling and kissing her. All girls have to have some first experience of male sexuality, and George's late-night petting, however unsavoury and unwanted, was no worse than most. Virginia made a good story out of it for the Memoir Club; and though she despised George for his conventionality, she always remained on cheerful terms with him.[5]

She seems to have reached the age of thirty without having experienced sexual desire. She had felt 'like a rock' when Leonard first kissed her, and there was something granite-like in her rejection of the male principle. Morgan Forster described how in later life she refused to sit on committees or sign appeals, however good the cause, 'on the ground that women must not condone this tragic male-made mess'. Like Lysistrata,

---

3 Jean MacGibbon, *There's the Lighthouse: a Biography of Adrian Stephen*

4 'A Sketch of the Past', *Moments of Being: A Collection of Autobiographical Writing by Virginia Woolf* ed Jeanne Schulkind. Harcourt Brace 1985

5 'Old Bloomsbury', *Moments of Being*

she withdrew.'[6] The genetic, psychic and physical components of her blocked sexuality – if her sexuality, in regard to men, was sufficiently developed to be blocked – cannot be disentangled. Some people, as the Apostles would have said, just 'are'.

What marriage to Virginia seemed to offer Leonard was the sharing of passion and a creative life with a woman who was 'supreme', light-years away from the (to him) repellent, hungry womanhood of an Annie Hopfengartner or a Mrs Dutton. He knew sexual ecstasy, but was ill equipped to initiate Virginia. Prostitutes know their business and do not put up any resistance, unless required to do so. The 'Gwen' girls were responsive up to the point where their or Leonard's scruples called a halt. He did not have the confidence and light-heartedness to negotiate the physical seduction of someone so highly strung and ambivalent as Virginia.

The marriage was consummated, not infrequently, but incompletely. During their honeymoon, Virginia wrote to Ka Cox from Saragossa as one who had 'lost my virginity' wondering why everyone made such a fuss about it. 'Possibly my great age makes it less of a catastrophe; but certainly I find the climax immensely exaggerated. Except for a sustained good humour (Leonard shan't see this) due to the fact that every twinge of anger is at once visited upon my husband, I might still be Miss S.' This tallies with what Leonard told Molly MacCarthy about not feeling like a married man. They were proclaiming their inalienable individuality; the less glorious subtext is, that they had not become one flesh. The only report from Leonard comes filtered through a letter from Gerald Brenan, written more than half a century later: 'Leonard told me that when on their honeymoon he had tried to make love to her she had got into such a violent state of excitement that he had had to stop, knowing as he did that these states were a prelude to her attacks of madness.'[7] If Leonard did use the word 'excitement', it was not in the sense of sexual excitement. It was the word doctors used routinely to

6 EMF in Joan Russell Noble (ed): *Recollections of Virginia Woolf* Peter Owen 1972. Lysistrata, in Aristophanes' comedy, rallied the women of Athens to put a stop to the war with Sparta by refusing sexual relations.

7 Brenan to Rosemary Dinnage, 4 Nov 1977

express what we would mean by agitation or acute anxiety. Rumours and anecdotes about what the Woolfs did and did not do in bed circulated freely, mostly spread by Clive and gleaned from Vanessa. These are in the public domain.[8]

In a jaunty exchange between Virginia and Ethel Smyth in 1933, Ethel told Virginia she had been told that 'lots of girls get themselves operated on nowadays so as not to endure tortures on marriage nights . . . Why not try it now? (It's never too late to rend).' Virginia replied: ' For god's sake tell me about the maidenhead removal – what a lark! Shall we go and be done together? Side by side in Bond Street?'[9]

Leonard, in early days, may have wondered whether such a procedure might help their own marriage. How else to interpret Vanessa's letter to him of 1 December 1913, about Sydney Waterlow[10] and his wife? 'He failed to penetrate her! And she's had to go to a nursing home to be penetrated or enlarged or something! You were right you see.' Leonard and Virginia, a couple of months after their return to London, were taking counsel with her about what she called 'the Goat's coldness'.

'Coldness' is wrong. Virginia liked soft things and silky stuffs, she loved to be stroked and petted and kissed – on her arms, her feet, her neck – and made extravagant demands for such shows of affection from the women and children who were her intimates. Leonard and she achieved an emotional and physical intimacy in which Mongoose and Mandril exchanged caresses and small tendernesses in total trust. There was a poem called 'Luriana Lurilee' which meant something to them both – Leonard quoted a stanza from it in *Growing*, and Virginia in *To the Lighthouse*.[11] It conveys the spirit of the private Garden of Eden inhabited by Leonard and Virginia when all was well. These are the first stanzas of five:

---

8 See Hermione Lee, *Virginia Woolf* Chatto & Windus 1996

9 VW *Letters* 26 Aug & 6 Sept 1933

10 Sydney Waterlow was a friend and contemporary of LW's at Cambridge, and had proposed to Virginia Stephen before he was divorced from his first wife.

11 Leonard had known it since the summer of 1899, when Lytton had produced a manuscript copy; it was by Charles Elton, a Strachey connection by marriage. The poem was included in *Another World Than This*, an anthology compiled by V.Sackville-West and Harold Nicolson, 1945.

Come out and climb the garden path
Luriana, Lurilee.
The China rose is all abloom
And buzzing with the yellow bee.
We'll swing you on the cedar bough,
Luriana, Lurilee.

I wonder if it seems to you,
Luriana, Lurilee,
That all the lives we ever lived
And all the lives to be,
Are full of trees and changing leaves,
Luriana, Lurilee.

How long it seems since you and I,
Luriana, Lurilee,
Roamed in the forest where our kind
Had just begun to be,
And laughed and chattered in the flowers,
Luriana, Lurilee.

They rented a set of rooms up seven flights of stairs in old Clifford's Inn,[12] off Fleet Street, had dinner every night at the Cock Tavern across the street, often with friends, and went to Asheham for weekends.

Desmond MacCarthy was hard up, and writing for Hilaire Belloc's anti-Semitic *The Eye Witness.* When in 1912 the paper collapsed, owing him two month's money. Leonard organised a whip-round. 'Dearest', Desmond wrote to Molly, 'I found a letter from Woolf containing – you'll open your eyes – a cheque for £30! . . . Just think of it and not a rich one among them!'[13]

Leonard needed paid work himself. Virginia had an income of

12 Destroyed by bombs in World War II
13 23 Oct 1912, quoted in Hugh and Mirabel Cecil, *Clever Hearts: Desmond and Molly MacCarthy, a Biography*

around £400 a year from investments, which was about enough for them to live on, but he had returned from the honeymoon with less than £20 in the world. He too looked to journalism. *The Eye Witness* was born again as the *New Witness,* to which Leonard contributed an article on economics on 7 November 1912. He worked with Roger Fry at the second Post-Impressionist Exhibition at the Grafton Galleries, which had opened the previous autumn. He helped to re-hang it, and then acted as secretary for two months. He sat at a desk, fielding comments from the people who came to see, and mostly to sneer at, paintings by Cézanne, Matisse, Picasso, Bonnard, and some English painters – including Duncan Grant and Vanessa Bell. 'I used to think, as I sat there, how much nicer were the Tamil or Sinhalese villagers who crowded into the verandah of my Ceylon kachcheri than these smug, well-dressed, ill-mannered, well-to-do Londoners',[14] who hated anything new, and abused the pictures and Leonard indiscriminately.

Leonard had his own thoughts about modern art, and wrote an (unpublished) critical riposte to Clive Bell's concept of 'significant form',[15] which elicited a thoughtful response from Vanessa and an angry one from Clive. Leonard replied, apostolically, that he still felt Clive's ideas were 'muddled'. It was unclear what exactly Clive *meant* by 'form and significance and significant form. You sometimes make it incompatible with representation and sometimes you don't.'[16] Peace did not break out between them.

Bob Trevy gave him an introduction to Bruce Richmond, the editor of the *Times Literary Supplement,* for whom Virginia had been reviewing for years. Leonard asked to review books on industrial questions, and was sent new French poetry – Stephane Mallarmé, Paul Claudel – which he proceeded to address 'more thoughtfully' and, one might add, more wittily, 'than any of the other poetry critics of the paper at this time.'[17]

---

14 *Beginning Again*

15 See Clive Bell, *Art,* 1913

16 24 Jan 1913. Huntington

17 Derwent May, *Critical Times: A History of the Times Literary Supplement* HarperCollins 2001

He also began writing articles about Co-operation for the *Daily Citizen* and *Co-operative News*. Before he married, he met Margaret Llewelyn Davies[18] on the occasion of a 'Suffrage play' put on by Lytton's suffragist sisters Pippa and Marjorie. Margaret was a close friend of Janet Case, who had taught Greek to Virginia. When Virginia, back in 1909, first met Margaret with Janet, she had described how these 'women who have worked but not married come to have a particular look'; there was something 'schoolgirlish', she thought, about the way they talked about their activities, but she saw that they were altruistic and competent.[19] Margaret enlisted Leonard in the Co-operative cause, and there was no resisting her.

The Women's Co-operative Guild was an offshoot of the Co-operative Society and movement, founded in 1844 as a socialist system of economic enterprise, to protect working-class consumers against capitalism by cutting out the middleman. Any surplus was returned to the members in the form of a dividend. Leonard was convinced by Co-operation as a democratic system which, 'if extended and developed, would place large sections of the economy in the control of the community.' The public image might be of drab Co-op grocery shops in back streets. But behind the retail was not only the Co-operative Wholesale Society, but Co-operative insurance, banking, medical services and an ambitious programme of education and political activism.

Margaret Llewelyn Davies was the Secretary of the Women's Co-operative Guild, which combined socialism and feminism. The health and social conditions of working-class women were key issues, and women were encouraged to join trades unions and to lobby for a minimum wage and equal pay, as well as for the vote.[20] The stronghold of the Women's Guild, as of the whole movement, was in the industrial north. When Leonard became involved it had about 30,000 members, operating through more than a thousand local branches.

Had Margaret Llewelyn Davies not lived at a time when telephoning

---

18 The elder sister of Cambridge friends, Crompton and Theodore Llewelyn Davies.

19 VW, 'Hampstead' (1909), *Carlyle's House and Other Sketches* Hesperus 2003

20 See University of Hull Archives website, 'Women's Co-operative Guild and the International Women's Co-operative Guild'

was for emergencies only, she would have been constantly on the phone. She was relentless. For the next few years she wrote Leonard eight-page, eleven-page, letters in her clear, flying handwriting, opening her mind to him on the policies and progress of the Women's Co-operative Guild, with strong suggestions as to what he should write about next and for whom and by when. She had a terrific appetite for committees, congresses, conferences, rallies, and 'long talks'. Leonard admitted that like all fanatics she could be a bore. Twenty years older, she grew fond of him, and he of her, admiring unreservedly her 'quicksilver eagerness' and her dedication. 'If she had been a man', he wrote in *Beginning Again*, 'her achievements would have filled probably half a page in *Who's Who*'. That she was not included at all was 'the kind of fact which made – and makes – feminism the belief or policy of all sensible men.'[21]

Virginia was revising her first novel, *The Voyage Out*, for the umpteenth time 'with a kind of tortured intensity',[22] and was sleeping badly. Leonard went with Vanessa to consult Dr Maurice Craig, Vanessa's 'nerve doctor', at 87 Harley Street. Craig advised Vanessa against seeing much of Virginia, for the sake of her own mental health. Virginia had discovered, to her fury, on honeymoon, that Vanessa had broken her word by telling Leonard that Walter Lamb too had proposed to her. There was a distancing between the sisters.

Leonard's question was: although both he and Virginia badly wanted children, should she, given her mental vulnerability, have a child? Dr Craig was doubtful: 'Thought gr[eat]. risk', wrote Leonard in his diary. 'Bed early, bad night.' Vanessa was inclined to agree with Craig: 'Not that I think Virginia any worse. For I quite agree with you in thinking her certainly better since you married.' But 'one does plunge into a new and unknown state of affairs when one starts a baby and once it's started there's no going back . . . I suppose he thinks the risk she runs is that of another bad nervous breakdown and I doubt if even a baby would be worth that.'

---

21 *Beginning Again*
22 *ibid*

The day after he saw Craig, 17 January 1913, Leonard went to see Jean Thomas at Twickenham. She too 'thought gr. risk'. Vanessa was 'rather surprised . . . for she certainly told me the opposite'. On 21 January he went to see Dr Maurice Wright, whom he consulted about his hand tremor. Wright was 'thoroughly in favour'. On 23 January he saw Dr Savage, who was also in favour ('Do her all the good in the world'), and went on to a Dr Theophilus Bulkeley Hyslop, a man who had written in 1905: 'The removal of woman from her natural sphere of domesticity to that of mental labour not only renders her less fit to maintain the virility of the race, but it renders her prone to degenerate and initiate a downward trend which gathers impetus in her progeny.'[23] Dr Hyslop recommended their waiting for a year and a half before starting a baby.

Anyone who runs around as Leonard did from doctor to doctor has to be in a distraught state. He lost his equilibrium, and leaned far too much on Vanessa whose own equilibrium was shaky. It is extraordinary how readily doctors gave their opinion without meeting the patient. But then Virginia did not like 'nerve doctors'. She was to express her loathing and fear in the depiction of their insensitive approach to the mentally ill Septimus[24] in *Mrs Dalloway.* Leonard reported back, and Jean Thomas had a talk with her. No wonder she was sleeping badly.

But there is a glimpse of them at Asheham in January 1913 – a cheerful glimpse, unless one chooses to load it with symbolism – of Virginia reading aloud to Vanessa and Leonard, who are making her 'a pair of pale blue drawers', Leonard making one leg while Vanessa made the other.[25] And she was well when Leonard took her off for a weekend in Dorset shortly after. 'Have you settled anything about your plans for the future now you've had all the conflicting advice?' Vanessa asked her on their return. 'Or are you still vague?'[26]

*

23 Quoted in Stephen Trombley, *All That Summer She Was Mad* Junction Books 1981

24 Virginia was a 'Septimus' – the seventh in age of the younger generation at 22 Hyde Park Gate (counting in Laura).

25 Vanessa Bell to Clive Bell, January 1913

26 Feb 6 1913. Berg

The intellectual climate was against their having children. Selective breeding for humans, on the analogy of stock-breeding, was nothing new. It was advocated in Plato's *The Republic*[27] and practised in many modern cultures, from the arranged marriages of India to the socially exclusive mating rituals of European aristocracy. At the time of the marriage of Leonard and Virginia it was receiving a scientific boost, and in 1911 the first international conference on eugenics[28] took place in London. A bequest from Francis Galton, a cousin of Charles Darwin and founder of the movement to check the birthrate of the 'unfit', had established a chair at University College, London, with a requirement for the teaching of eugenics.

Eugenics was a radical, progressive ideal, supported in Britain by the left-leaning *bien pensants* with whom Leonard was to be working – the Webbs, G.B.Shaw, the young academics at the London School of Economics. Maynard Keynes was a supporter, as was the young Winston Churchill. Jews generally favoured eugenics, owing their own hereditary capabilities to a voluntary eugenic mating system. The Mental Deficiency Act of 1912 in Britain provided for mandatory segregation of the feebleminded (but not sterilisation, as in some states of America). Other European countries enacted their own legislation. The eugenics movement is one of those historical 'hinges', which have greater and different consequences than were ever envisaged. No one could then know what concepts such as 'racial hygiene' would lead to. Nazi ideology did not spring fully formed from Hitler's brow.

The status conferred on this neo-Darwinism explains how Leonard and Virginia could both express what seems today an atrocious callousness about the mentally handicapped.[29] No one was of the opinion that Virginia was 'feeble-minded'. Obviously the reverse was true. But attitudes to mental illness were determined by antiquated legislation which

---

27 Part VI Section 2

28 Eugenics is defined as 'a science which has the objective of improving the inherited characteristics of humans by controlling genetic transmission' (*The Oxford Medical Companion*).

29 'It was perfectly horrible. They should certainly be killed', Virginia wrote in her diary 9 Jan 1915, about 'a long line of imbeciles' whom they met on a walk along the Thames towpath.

meshed with current concepts of degeneracy, tainted heredity, the 'bad seed'.

In this context, her medical and family history were problematic. But the question Leonard was asking necessarily predicated another, about full penetrative sex. Should Leonard persist and insist? What effect on her might that have, quite apart from the strain of bearing and rearing a baby?

In early March 1913 he took her finally completed novel to Gerald Duckworth, who had started his own publishing firm. Then, with Virginia accompanying him, he went to the northern industrial centres – Liverpool, Leicester, Manchester, Bolton, Leeds, Carlisle, Glasgow – to learn about Co-op factories and wholesale businesses: a bakery, a tailoring and a shoe repairing business, a biscuit factory, a jam factory, a shirt factory, a soap works, cabinet-making, flour mills, a tobacco factory, a printing works, a slaughterhouse, laundries, a boot factory.

Margaret Llewelyn Davies snowed him with instructions. 'At Crumpsall [the biscuit factory], don't omit the basement where the candid [*sic*] peel barrels are, and see what you think of the conditions of the girls on the wet pavements . . . and if you could manage to find out what the bottle-washers are paid it would be good.' At Middleton, 'in the jamjar *stacking* department, see what you think about the lifting of weights in doing the stacking.'

Leonard came away impressed by the quality of the people, but appalled by the monotonous manual labour and drab, dirty environment imposed by modern industrial civilisation. Immediately on their return he and Virginia fled off to hear Beethoven's 5th Symphony, and retreated to Asheham, which was for Virginia 'far the loveliest place in the world'. They were a close little unit, in a way that no other couple in their circle was. Adrian and Vanessa fell out with 'the Goat' that March on precisely that point. They did not like it.

On 8 April Leonard heard from Edgar that Herbert had had a riding accident and was in Richmond Hospital with a fractured skull. Leonard rushed away to see him, staying in Putney overnight. His brother-in-law

Bertie Lock was there with Bella; Lock had retired, and they were living in Streetly, just north of Birmingham. That afternoon Leonard wrote to 'My dearest dearest Mandy [for Mandril]: 'I am miserable without you. I have been wanting you all day, and I shan't be happy till I see you tomorrow . . . I love you and adore you and worship you Mandy and I never want anything else in the world but you.' Virginia walked all the way to Lewes railway station to meet him off the train.

The good news was that Gerald Duckworth liked *The Voyage Out* and would publish it. On 11 April 1913, the day before they heard this (Leonard rang Gerald up, to bring an end to uncertainty), Virginia wrote to Violet: 'We aren't going to have a baby, but we want to have one, and 6 months in the country or so is said to be necessary first.' In *Beginning Again*, Leonard wrote that while waiting for Gerald's verdict she suffered from 'intense bouts of worry and insomnia', and that 'some time in the spring it was definitely decided it would not be safe for her to have a child.' His diary confirms her agitation, with many entries such as 'V n.v.w. b.n.' (V not very well bad night); and his bald statement of fact smooths over what was a devastating decision for them both.

Quentin Bell, in his biography of Virginia Woolf, phrased it thus: 'In the end Leonard decided and persuaded Virginia to agree that, although they both wanted children, it would be too dangerous for her to have them.' Bell's book was written with Leonard's full co-operation, and the early chapters were read aloud to him in the last months of his life. There can therefore be no doubt that Leonard took the responsibility for deciding. Childlessness was to be a lasting if intermittent source of grief – as, for Leonard at least, was the lost hope of shared passion, or even of a full sexual relationship: Virginia confessed in late life to Ethel Smyth that she had been 'a sexual coward'. Whatever his reasoning, his courage too failed – though it took courage of a different kind to make the decision he did, for them both. He had to deal with his own double sorrow in his own way. He knew that Virginia, being as she was, gave him all that was in her to give.

During the period of medical consultations in March 1913, Leonard's novel *The Village in the Jungle* came out from Edward Arnold, who was E.M. Forster's publisher. Leonard wrote his story from the point of view and from within the consciousness of Sinhalese villagers. He found a register for their speech in English which was neither archaic nor modern and reflected the cadences and idioms of Sinhala; the Sri Lankan writer Mervyn de Silva commended Leonard's command of Sinhalese speech patterns, and his sensitivity to nuance in the mixing of Buddhist thinking with both Hinduism and with 'primitive ritual devils and jungle gods' in the popular consciousness.[30] Leonard Woolf could have written a work of social anthropology; he wrote a unique and extraordinary novel.

He placed Beddegama (which means 'the village in the jungle') thirty miles from Hambantota, between the sea and the mountains. In his introduction to the second American edition,[31] he described how, in the north-eastern part of his district, he would ride on jungle tracks all day, occasionally coming upon traces of villages which had died out completely, overgrown by the jungle. These sad vestiges captured his imagination. There is no shortage, in Sri Lanka, of assertions as to the exact location of the fictional Beddegama,[32] though Leonard himself told his Sinhalese friend Shelton C.Fernando that he had no particular village in mind, but any one of a whole group in the north of Magam Pattu.

There was little scholarly interest taken in *The Village in the Jungle* before the early 1970s, after Leonard's death.[33] The main foci of interest have been its correlation with Virginia's first novel *The Voyage Out*, and the question of whether his is an anti-imperialist text, or a paternalistic and imperialist text. This may be a category error, though readers may find the former view the more convincing. The story centres on Silindu

30 Mervyn de Silva, article in *Ceylon Observer* 14 Feb 1960

31 Harcourt Brace 1925

32 Believed variously to be Pallemattala, Beddawewa, Katagamuwa or Malasnegalwewa.

33 Only recently has *The Village in the Jungle* become available again in the UK, reprinted by Eland Publishing, with an afterword by Christopher Ondaatje, 2005; and for a scholarly edition, see Yasmine Gooneratne (ed): *The Village in the Jungle by Leonard Woolf, Revised and Annotated in Accordance with the Original Manuscript* Edwin Mellen Press 2004. The manuscript was given to the University of Peradeniya by LW's executor Trekkie Parsons.

the hunter, his two daughters, their marriages, and the village embroilments of lust and spite which finally destroy them.

It is not the East that is mysterious here, but the West. Silindu and his son-in-law Babun, brought from the jungle to the courthouse in town charged with theft and murder, understand nothing. The questions they are asked make no sense to them, though Silindu feels 'vaguely encouraged' by the white magistrate, the AGA. He had spoken Sinhalese to him; he had 'not spoken in an angry voice'. The white magistrate, in his turn, feels – as Leonard often did – that 'there is almost certainly something behind this case which has not come out'. But the gulf between their mentalities, and the malice of Silindu's enemies, are insuperable obstacles to understanding. The courthouse, the view of the bay, the big high room in the AGA's house, the AGA himself – this is all Leonard's Hambantota, and Leonard. The AGA is not a realised character, nor a hinge between cultures. Seen through Silindu's eyes, he is from another planet.

Leonard used in the novel, verbatim, episodes from his official diary and from his letters to Lytton: about the tracker whose corpse was found in the jungle with his axe, inexplicably, stuck in a tree; the tragic elephants searching for water; the pilgrimage to Kataragama. There are urgently vivid passages evoking the jungle, that 'evil' world 'of bare and brutal facts, of superstition, of grotesque imagination . . . a world of hunger and fear and devils, where a man was helpless before the unseen and unintelligible powers surrounding him', where everything alive is either predator or prey, death comes quickly, and 'the blank wall of fate' makes resistance useless.

He did not have to make an effort to enter into the mentalities of the unscrupulous commercial middleman and village headman, who bring ruin to Silindu and his family. The plot turns on the cruel human price demanded by the headman for granting a permit to 'chena', without which, a family must starve or leave the village, as Leonard made vehemently clear to his superiors when he was in Hambantota. Leonard's feat of empathy was his seamless slither into the unreflective unawareness of the abused Silindu and his family: not stream of consciousness, but stream of unselfconsciousness.

As if by direct transmission, he entered into their unmediated terror, or hate, or lust, and into the meaninglessness, to them, of anything outside their own world. Credulous, without speculation, they fall sick from disease or grief or terror, from curses or spells, or from being removed from the village. The message from a god transmitted by a corrupt and cynical holy man can heal. Driven to extremes, like an animal at bay, Silindu will kill. The supernatural is natural. The *yakka*, the devils who haunt the jungle, are no less real than the buffalo and the leopard.

Towards the end – for reasons which have everything to do with man's inhumanity to man – the village is abandoned. The huts are smothered one by one by encroaching jungle and 'its impenetrable disorder of its thorns and creepers'. Only Silindu's youngest daughter remains, herself now 'one of the beasts of the jungle', and her fate is horrifying.

The rational man buries his impulse towards irrationality. Leonard Woolf was the civilised man, the bureaucrat, the imposer of order. In his extraordinary novel he launched himself into the jungle of unreason. Magical thinking with its different logic is accessed in modern Western civilisation only by children, artists, poets, and the mentally deranged. Writing at this level shows that Leonard was supremely the right man to be with Virginia – and not only in the way that their contemporaries supposed him to be. His intuitive capacity is nakedly demonstrated in *The Village in the Jungle.* He was burning to write about Ceylon, for its own sake; and he was released into something greater, at that time of risk and heightened sensibility, facing his own demons and hers as he fell unconditionally in love with Virginia Stephen.

'Falling in love' is a misleading phrase. Love is an ascent. 'Only connect the prose and the passion, and both will be exalted, and human love will be seen at its highest.' The prose of life would have the upper hand, with him; his passion had to be redirected outwards, and he became comfortable in the world of 'telegrams and anger'.[34] But the jungle was always around and within. In his maturity, his life's work was

34 Both quotations from E.M.Forster, *Howards End*, 1910. Forster's fiction, for the student of Leonard Woolf, is shot through with echoes and pre-echoes.

to combat the irrational savagery of nation towards nation, and to try and keep his wife from being overwhelmed by her devils, her 'madness' – which, he knew, shared its tangled roots with her creativity. He dedicated the novel 'To V.W.':

> I've given you all the little, that I've to give;
> You've given me all, that for me is all there is;
> So now I just give back what you have given –
> If there is anything to give in this.

The publisher Edward Arnold gave Leonard, as was normal, no advance on royalties, ten per cent on the first 1,000 sold and fifteen per cent thereafter. *The Village in the Jungle* received good reviews, the best and best-informed from his old boss Sir Hugh Clifford, in *Blackwood's* magazine. He also had personal letters from Sir Hugh, written from Government House, Accra: 'My sober judgment is that your book is the best study of Oriental peasant life that has ever been written – or that I have ever read.' He specially praised Leonard's skill in showing 'the effect which natural environment has had and is having on the moulding and formation of Oriental character. That is the point at which it outstrips its precursors, and which stamps the book as a really philosophical and original piece of work.'

By 1929 *The Village in the Jungle* had sold 2,149 copies, which was not disgraceful for those days. (Virginia's *The Voyage Out* had sold just under 2,000 copies by the same date.) It was published in the United States in the same year, and Edward Arnold was eagerly anticipating Leonard's next novel. The book was well received in Ceylon, where it has never been out of print since, in English, in Tamil and in Sinhala. It has been a set book in Sri Lankan schools. Everyone with the habit of reading in Sri Lanka has read it, or heard of it.

What is not understood in Sri Lanka, and not only in Sri Lanka, is why *The Village in the Jungle* has not found a canonical place in the tradition to which it belongs and which it transcends – novels about the East and Empire, from Kipling and Conrad to Woolf to Forster and Orwell. One commentator from Sri Lanka has found a positive value in this omission: 'Mercifully, the novel has managed to escape the dire fate of being annexed to the rapidly enlarging province of "Commonwealth Literature."'"[35]

His friends' reactions were characteristic. Margaret Llewelyn Davies admired 'the merciless simplicity with which you let facts speak for themselves'. Charlie Sanger praised the 'beautiful sympathy with the things that matter'. Hom (H.O.Meredith) 'thought it just about as good as the subject-matter made possible. Savages are clearly when one knows about them less interesting than civilised people.'

Lytton, embarrassed, put off writing, and then went further than Hom: 'I think I'm in a particularly difficult position for judging of it, because my tastes are not at all in the direction of the blacks etc. I'm sure most people have more of a fellow-feeling for them. As for me, the more black they are the more I dislike them, and yours seem to be remarkably so. I did hope for one bright scene at least with some fetid white wife of a governor . . .' He found some aspects to praise – 'the general atmospheric description and psychological drawing' – and 'the restraint of it all is I think very supreme'. He ended with a hope and a plea for Leonard's next novel: 'Whites! Whites! Whites!'

When Leonard went up north for the three-day Women's Co-operative Congress in Keswick in June 1913, Virginia went with him, but spent most of the time in their hotel. Leonard was fascinated by this 'parliament of 650 working-class women'. One of the most gross common errors, he wrote in *Beginning Again*, 'is that women are more emotional than men and more flighty'. The women at the Congress were 'much more unemotional, stable, quiet, matter of fact than any similar male assembly'. They also had much more patience, 'a kind of intensity of patience', learned perhaps 'over babies, saucepans, frying-pans and coppers'. He respected, almost idealised, these women, who were the exact opposite of his wife. She was in a category of one, and the one whom he loved.

At Margaret Llewelyn Davies's prompting, he wrote a lively report on the Congress which was taken by the *New Statesman* and published under

35 Dr A.J.Gunawardena, 23 Nov 1980 (unidentified newspaper cutting)

the heading 'A Democracy of Working Women' on 21 June. It was read by Sidney and Beatrice Webb, always on the look-out for new writers to enlist in the Fabian Society's research projects, and they invited him to lunch. 'On July 12, I ate my first of many plates of mutton at Grosvenor Road.' The *New Statesman* had been founded by the Webbs the previous summer, with the support of G.B.Shaw, as a socialist weekly, and immediately became a platform for the reformist Left. Leonard met at that first lunch Clifford Sharp, the surly and, as it turned out, alcoholic editor, and the literary editor Jack Squire, 'a gay, casual, good tempered, generous Bohemian.'[36]

Margaret Llewelyn Davies rushed round that evening to hear how he had got on. She was jealous of the Webbs. '*Can* you read the ponderous Webb articles on Socialism?' she had written to Leonard. 'You see you mustn't mention the Webbs to me, or you will get a downpour!' She had a scheme for a Co-operative College to rival the London School of Economics and the Fabian Research Department. Like the Webbs, she was always on the look-out for new talent, and read the young G.D.H.Cole's *The World of Labour* : 'Who is he? We must get to know him.' She did, to no avail. 'It *is* odd how the Fabians are somehow all wrong. But how are we to get Univer[sity] people to work inside Movements, in the right way?'

Cole, then a don at Magdalen College, Oxford, was one of the young intellectuals who were to make their mark on the Fabian Society, sidelining the Webbs in the process. The Webbs were in their mid-fifties when Leonard met them, and still at their peak. They co-founded the Fabian Society in 1884; the purpose of Fabianism was to infiltrate democratic socialist ideas into the thinking of the political and governing classes by means of research, fact-finding, discussion, education, lobbying and propaganda. They founded the London School of Economics and Political Science – LSE – in 1895, to train students in the scientific collecting of social and economic facts, which would influence public policy, and whose graduates who would make their careers in public administration and the social sciences. Within a decade, LSE had won

36 *Beginning Again*

academic acceptance as a degree-awarding faculty in the University of London; Sidney Webb was professor of Public Administration.

The Webbs were childless, and lived plainly. They were so eccentric, and so blinkered to anything in life except their work, that many people found them absurd. Sidney was squat and quite ugly. Beatrice was thin and distinguished-looking. She came from a privileged background. Sidney had left school at sixteen and educated himself at evening classes. They were a united couple, their partnership endlessly productive of books and pamphlets on trade unionism, labour history, local government, social reform. They were not primarily party-political, but pragmatic, seeking to influence whoever had influence. 'Permeation' was the key word, and 'the inevitability of gradualism' the dogma.

Leonard had to make a living. He was not paid for his many contributions to *Co-operative News*, and it was not read in the corridors of power, nor even in the industrial heartlands, where it piled up in Co-op stores unbought. 'I can't get over the wonder and pleasure of having such a sympathetic supporter of the work and cause', Margaret wrote to him. '*You must make us a charge.*' At the same time she bemoaned the movement's lack of funds. She wanted him to go to the Leicester Congress: 'If you offered to pay your own expenses, they wd. almost certainly let you be a delegate.' No doubt they would. She told him how the Woolwich Labour people 'want an educated man to help them without pay . . . It wd be splendid experience for anyone.' Leonard needed money as well as experience. But life was opening out for him. At the same time, Virginia's illness was closing in on them both.

A week after his July lunch with the Webbs, her anxiety and headache became acute. On the morning of 25 July, according to his semi-shorthand diary, 'Went Savage w V morn said she ought to go Jean. Took her to Twickenham even & had dinner there. Better when I left.' Vanessa begged Roger to 'please be *very* careful not to say a word to *anyone* about her worrying over what people will think of her novel, which really seems to be the entire cause of her breakdown.'[37] While she was at Jean

---

37 26 July 1913

Thomas's, Leonard worked in the mornings and spent the afternoons and evenings with his troubled wife – except for one day, when he went to Wimbledon to watch the tennis, and in the evening dined with James Strachey and Herbert (recovered from his accident) at the Cock Tavern, and played poker afterwards with a large group at 46 Gordon Square.

He wrote to Virginia every day, sometimes twice; short letters of love and reassurance signed 'M': 'Only rest quietly and don't worry about anything in the world, and it won't be any time before we're again having the best time that any two people can have.'[38] She wrote equally loving notes to her 'darling Mongoose', remorseful at giving him so much misery. 'Never talk again, dearest, of causing me anything but the most perfect happiness', he wrote to her on 27 July, 'because literally and honestly that is what I get merely from sitting quietly reading by you.'

Leonard's own family's affairs evolved at what seemed a great distance. Herbert wrote with an odd casualness on 26 July from Bournemouth, where Mrs Woolf and her unattached offspring were on their summer holiday: 'I suppose you heard that Harold was married at Whitsun . . .[39] I suppose it is a good thing that Mother has accepted the fait accompli' – adding that National Mexico Stocks were still going down. He managed Virginia's investments, and his communications, like his interests, were normally confined to dividends and share-prices.

On the last day of July Dr Savage said Virginia was well enough to come home. But the nightmare continued back at Asheham. Leonard noted in code in his diary the 'dreadful' nights, her agitation, scenes about food – and days when she was 'cheerful'. Dr Savage had unfortunately made her a promise – that if she spent two weeks at Twickenham, she and Leonard could still go back to the Plough Inn at Holford for their first wedding anniversary, as they had planned. Leonard was apprehensive. Holford was an isolated village, ten miles from a railway station. Dr Savage thought the situation would be even more dangerous if Virginia were told they must not go. Roger Fry

38 25 July 1913

39 Harold Woolf, who worked with Herbert at a stock-jobbing firm in the City, married Alice Bilson.

introduced Leonard to yet another doctor,[40] twenty years younger than Savage: Henry Head, a neurologist with literary interests. Dr Head and Dr Craig agreed with Savage that more damage would be done by not going to Holford than by going, even though they thought that Virginia was potentially suicidal.

On top of this, there was a typical Bloomsbury bust-up – 'one of our usual embroilments', as Vanessa put it. 'Lytton gave Leonard a lot of Clive's letters to read, in one of which Clive wrote that as soon as Virginia was well enough he meant to have an affair with her.'[41] Clive, faced by Leonard in a towering rage, insisted he was only joking. But under the much-discussed circumstances, the implications of his letter, for Leonard, were intolerable. As Margaret Llewelyn Davies wrote to him, 'It must be *horrid* living in such a callous crowd.'

Vanessa saw the Woolfs off at Paddington station, both looking wretched. Virginia 'worries constantly, and one gets rid of one worry only to find that another crops up in a few minutes', and she had 'definite illusions about other people'. Ka was going down to stay with them, she told Clive, 'which may help matters as I don't think Woolf can go on for long alone, the strain of looking after her is so great.'

On their honeymoon, Leonard had begun a second novel, and before they left for Holford he sent his family the unfinished draft of what was to be *The Wise Virgins*.[42] This was *un*wise. His mother read it first, and was shocked. In it she was described, as Mrs Davis, as someone whose 'semitic features' would have seemed very fine 'if she had been squatting under a palm tree with a white linen cloth thrown over her head', instead of sitting in an overfurnished English suburban drawing-room. Bella read it next, and responded to 'My dearest Len' in Holford with a nine-page critique. 'It will give extraordinary pain to a few people whom I cannot imagine you have a particular desire to hurt.'

---

40 For the careers and professional orientations of the doctors consulted, see Stephen Trombley, *All That Summer She Was Mad* Junction Books 1981

41 Vanessa to Roger Fry Aug 7 1913

42 The novel's full title is *The Wise Virgins: A Story of Words, Opinions and a few Emotions*. It was reissued by Persephone Books, with a preface by Lyndall Gordon, in 2003.

But he had a particular desire to hurt, whether he knew it or not. *The Wise Virgins* is like a book by a gifted adolescent in revolt, as he lashed out at his family's vulgar and commonplace values and attitudes, at Gordon Square's snobbish, over-critical values and attitudes, and at the young Jew, himself, bitter, angry and displaced, in between the two worlds and fitting in nowhere. His extreme vehemence may have been historical, i.e. what he used to feel, without realising that he had in fact moved on, or it may have been the displacement of another conflict. He was aware of this as a phenomenon, for in the tendentious letter to Clive about 'significant form', in which he questioned Clive's insight into his own psychology, he wrote: 'It is a common thing for people to think they feel something which they don't feel at all and to think that one thing is causing them to feel something when all the time it is another thing . . . I suppose it has happened to everyone who has ever written about his own thoughts and feelings.' Whatever spurred him, his 'thoughts and feelings' demanded harsh expression.

What horrified Bella was that he had given the Richstead/Putney characters 'distinguishing outward signs and idiosyncracies' that rendered them 'as if deliberately' recognisable, 'right down to their gardens and the arrangement of their furniture.' As for Harry, 'in him I trace all your less pleasant characteristics magnified to the nth power.' She conceded that the novel was well-written, 'vivid and virile, when it doesn't become foul.' She agreed with their mother that the Gordon Square set 'appear to be a set of drones' and no happier than the 'suburbans': 'They simply make me scream with boredom.' (Harry, in spite of his love for Camilla, despises them too. There was no life in them, 'no dark hair, no blood'. They never *did* anything. Jews had to *do* things, just because they were Jews.)

His brother Philip's reaction, which also reached Leonard in Holford, was that family could not be critics, 'it is bound to be either too interesting or too painful'. The problem was, how to 'convince Lady that Mrs Davis's most annoying characteristics aren't – what they really seem to me – a very exact picture of her own, few as they may be.'

Thus Leonard had worries of his own, as well as about Virginia. The process of eating and digesting, and her 'delusions' that people were laughing at her, were agitating her unbearably. Vanessa tried to rally her sister by letter: 'No one will tell you to eat if it's not necessary. Why should they? It *is* most necessary and is the only way of preventing you from getting really bad. Now Billy do be sensible and don't make things difficult for Leonard, and realise that at this moment he is far more sensible than you are, and trust him to get things right.'[43] She confided to Roger Fry that 'I shouldn't think if this goes on that Leonard would be able to stand the strain of it all alone for long.'[44] Ka Cox came down, as arranged, to help him.

Night after sleepless night, he gave her the prescribed drugs: bromide, and 10 grams of Tripinal at 3.30 a.m. one particularly bad night. He thought they should go home, but Virginia was against it. 'Promised to do everything if we stayed. Very happy at first then difficulty w food at dinner.'[45] With Ka, they returned to 38 Brunswick Square on 8 September. The next morning, Leonard took Virginia to see Dr Wright and then Dr Head, who tried to convince her that she really was ill and advised a 'rest-cure', with professional care.

What follows is reconstructed from Leonard's diary for the same day. Vanessa came round, and Virginia 'became more cheerful and rested'. Leonard went off to their lodgings in Clifford's Inn to collect what Virginia needed, came back for tea with her, and then left with Vanessa to try and arrange a joint consultation with Dr Head and Dr Savage who, understandably, was feeling sidelined.

After visiting Savage in his office at Devonshire Place, Leonard and Vanessa sat on a bench in Regent's Park to discuss the way forward before returning to Savage at 6.30. While they were there, Ka telephoned. 'V had fallen asleep.' Leonard took a taxi to Brunswick Square and found her unconscious. Vanessa came back, bringing Dr Head. 'Found V had taken 100 grains of Veronal.' Dr Head and Geoffrey Keynes (Maynard's brother, a surgeon, who happened to be staying at Brunswick Square) and nurses worked until 12.30. 'I went to bed then. V very bad 1.30. Better at 6 when Van came to me.'[46]

---

43 Aug 27 1913. Berg
44 Aug 27 1913.
45 7 Sept 1913
46 9 Sept 1913, all in code

Leonard thought in retrospect that it was the dread of the doctors which drove her over the edge. He took on himself the responsibility for the catastrophe. 'At Holford I had always kept my case containing the Veronal locked. In the turmoil of arriving and settling in at Brunswick Square and then going to Head, I must have forgotten to lock it.' He did not suffer the additional agony of remorse. He clung to common sense as to a raft, in order to survive the flood of unreason in which he might drown. What was done could not be undone, and 'it was almost impossible sooner or later not to make a mistake of this kind.'

Short of twenty-four-hour supervision, you cannot prevent a potential suicide from doing what that person is set on doing. Leonard had been on watch for two months. He knew people might find it a 'psychological black mark' that after that 'appalling day and night' he had gone to bed when the doctors had done their rescue work. It was the best thing he could have done. He had to keep well. As Lytton wrote to Henry Lamb, 'Woolf has been having the most dreadful time for the last month or two, culminating in this.'

The sociologist Emile Durkheim's *Le Suicide*, published in 1897, represents the collective wisdom of the immediately pre-Freudian years. (We produce the symptoms and behaviours peculiar to our times.) Neurasthenia was the contemporary word for most mental instability. The doctors called Virginia's illnesses neurasthenia. Neurasthenics, wrote Durkheim, 'seem destined to suffer . . . Every impression is a source of discomfort to them.' The neurasthenic's nerves 'are disturbed at the least contact, being as it were unprotected; the performance of physiological functions which are usually most automatic is a source of generally painful sensations for him . . . To be sure, he may live with a minimum of suffering when he can live in retirement and create a special environment only partly accessible to the outer tumult . . . But if forced to enter the mêlée and unable to shelter his tender sensitivity from outer shocks, he is likely to suffer more pain than pleasure. Such organisms are therefore a favourite field for the idea of suicide . . . Now today neurasthenia is rather considered a mark of distinction rather than a weakness. In our refined society, enamoured of things intellectual, nervous members constitute almost a nobility.' The neurasthenic has an important role, 'for he is superlatively the instrument of progress.

Precisely because he rebels against tradition and the yoke of custom, he is a highly fertile source of innovation.'[47] It could have been written about Virginia Woolf.

Virginia was out of danger the next day, though unconscious. Vanessa, back at Asheham, wrote Leonard a minatory letter with just a suggestion of blame: 'You will of course have done this, but to satisfy my own mind, will you tell the nurses . . . to turn out the room carefully and remove everything that *could* be dangerous. Knives etc and of course drugs . . . It will all become a routine soon and you will feel safe, but it mustn't be relaxed.'

Leonard had to decide what to do next. On the morning after the overdose, he went to see George Duckworth in his office. George had a large and comfortable country house, Dalingridge Place, at Tye's Cross near East Grinstead in Sussex. He offered it, fully staffed, to Leonard and Virginia. Suicide was a crime (until 1961) and a suicide attempt rendered a person 'certifiable', that is, liable to be detained in a mental institution by a magistrate's certificate on the recommendation of a doctor. Leonard wrote in *Beginning Again* that he went to see one or two recommended mental hospitals – his diary makes no mention of it – and found them too awful to contemplate. Vanessa consulted Roger Fry, who had been through all this for his own wife, and reported on 13 September: '[Roger] says that if they see you are doing all you can and have good advice they are anxious not to interfere. So if Savage *should* be difficult I should simply write to Craig who was we know in favour of nurses and not complete isolation – and as Head is also strongly against any kind of asylum I don't see what else can be suggested but a house with you and nurses.'

On 20 September, Leonard hired a motor car and driver and took Virginia down to Dalingridge. George Duckworth and his pregnant wife Margaret settled the Woolfs into the house, from which they themselves retreated for as long as necessary. Duckworth wrote from London,

47 Emile Durkheim, *Suicide*, edited by John Simpson, translated by John A.Spaulding and George Simpson, The Free Press, Glencoe, Illinois, 1951

on 23 September, that 'the strain on you must be so hard that I hope Miss Cox may be able to stay on with you – the longer the better. Let Virginia pick all the flowers she likes' – and had Leonard found the croquet set? Somehow Leonard found time to write the first book review that Jack Squire commissioned from him for the *New Statesman*. He could not take on another for a long time.

They were at Dalingridge Place for almost two months. Virginia's weight went down to eight stone-seven (119 pounds. She was five-foot ten inches, about the same height as Leonard.) Leonard and the nurses shared mealtime duty, the nurses calling him in when they could not manage. Leonard's diary is a catalogue of bad nights and better nights, of numbingly painful scenes, of Virginia physically attacking the nurses, of excruciating 'difficulty', of her agitation and unpredictability. There were four nurses – two for the daytime and two for the nights. He had no intimation of how long this breakdown would last. For all he knew, it might never end. They were in luxurious surroundings, but she was in torment, and his life and their marriage was on hold.

He received support by mail from all their friends, who tried to reassure him of her obvious happiness with him when she was well. Virginia was too disturbed to see visitors. She had something against everyone. Vanessa did not come, on Dr Craig's advice. Margaret Llewelyn Davies wanted to visit Virginia 'but I can't help feeling she is not sufficiently used to me – or that the mere sight of me might suggest things that wd excite'. This suggests that Virginia resented Margaret's demands on her husband's time and attention. Margaret did come down for a day, to be with Leonard.

Ka Cox was at Dalingridge as much as she could, herself unhappy after the break-up of a love affair with Rupert Brooke. 'You really are rather a fine creature, you know,' she wrote to Leonard. 'I'm sure any other husband would have done something either selfish or stupid.' (Like what? Like sending Virginia to a mental hospital, or having an affair.) He bicycled across country to Asheham one day, after which Vanessa wrote: 'To tell you the truth I am rather worried about you, for you looked to me fearfully tired.'

The day after Virginia, for the first time, was well enough to come out for a drive with him on her own, followed by eight hours sleep without medication, he took a couple of nights off. He stayed at Gordon Square and saw everybody, went to the Hippodrome with Desmond, dined at the Eiffel Tower. By mid-October Virginia's weight had gone up to nine stone seven.

Her recovery gave space for his own collapse. Utterly exhausted, he went to London to see his mother, Flora and Clara, who had moved from Putney back into a London flat in Earls Court, close to long-lamented Lexham Gardens. Then he went for a couple of nights to Lytton in his cottage in Wiltshire. 'Poor Woolf!' Lytton wrote to Lady Ottoline Morrell. 'Nearly all the horror of has been and still is on his shoulders.' Everyone said, 'Poor Woolf', but there was nothing they could do.

The improvement continued, and the four nurses became three. On 27 October Leonard and Virginia played croquet together. It was time to think of leaving for Asheham. On 18 November, 'V bad day, gr tr[ouble] w f[ood]', they left Dalingridge, with two nurses.

Nothing much changed at Asheham. Leonard arranged with Gerald Duckworth to postpone the publication of *The Voyage Out* until Virginia was more stable. He was still in balk himself, where outside work was concerned. He had to miss appointments, pencilled hopefully in. On 29 November he got to the Co-operative Education Conference, returning the same evening, having left his bike at Lewes station.

By then, they were down to one nurse for night duty, at a guinea a night. The medical bills were mounting up. (They owed Dr Belfrage alone £88.19s.11d, 'a curious sum' as Vanessa commented.) But Dr Craig, Vanessa reported, said Virginia should always have someone in her room at night, 'and he thought it most important that you should not be with her by night as well as by day'. Leonard had not been able to share a bedroom with her when she was so ill at Dalingridge. From now on, they always slept in separate rooms.

Virginia, whose fluctuating emotions controlled their relationship, wrote – wonderfully, from his point of view – while he was in London for a couple of days in December to pack up their books at Clifford's Inn and arrange for storage: 'Would it make you very conceited if I told you that I love you more than I have ever done since I took you into service, and find you beautiful, and indispensable? . . . Goodbye Mongoose, and be a devoted animal, and never leave the great variegated creature. She wishes to inform you delicately that her flanks and rump are now in finest plumage, and invites you to an exhibition. Kisses on your dear little pate. Darling Mongoose.'

On 16 February 1914 the last of the nurses departed. 'So we really seem to be getting out of the wood at last', Leonard wrote to Violet Dickinson. 'V has been very well lately.'[48] Leonard wanted her to get back in control of her own life. Their general practitioner, Dr Belfrage, agreed in principle, so long as she recognised the necessity to order her life carefully – 'the hours of rest, immutability of mealtimes and of going to bed', as he wrote. 'She should take life very quietly in the early hours of the day and be in bed no less than 10 hours out of the 24.'

He had finished and revised *The Wise Virgins*, and sent the manuscript round his family all over again. Bella was still outraged. If what he had done was the price to pay for being a great writer, 'I'd sooner remain inglorious.'[49] His mother, in her firm, spiky handwriting, left herself out of it, and lambasted him for the 'insult' to the Ross family. 'How anyone with a spark of good taste and feeling could have dealt such a blow to people and near neighbours who had never shown you anything but interest and friendship is beyond me to grasp.'[50] She told him how she had knitted a jacket for Phil, 'a gigantic piece of work that took me several months. I went by a published pattern but found, when it was done, that it was so unsatisfactory that I undid every stitch . . . I meant to have it right and set to work.' If it had not been right 'I should have done it again until I could pass it on as a decent piece of work.'[51] Leonard should do the same.

Leonard sent his problematic 'knitting' to Lytton, for a candid opinion. 'I am so sick of the whole affair . . . I shall never write another book

48 4 Feb 1914. Berg
49 19 Nov 1913
50 11 Dec 1913
51 16 Nov 1913

after these damned Virgins.' Lytton composed a long and encouraging critique ('very acute, never boring'), with one reservation: 'In a novel of that sort – depending so much on plot – there is bound to be a point of crisis', which is the 'test' of the whole book. 'In yours the crisis comes after the fucking of Gwen', and the treatment of this central point was 'not strong enough'; it was actually 'ambiguous', because the author stopped analysing Harry's feelings at this point. 'One isn't prepared to feel his decision to marry is inevitable, in his character, from what we know of him.' Was he only 'falsely superb'? Why did he not insist on 'having Camilla'? Didn't he think of it? And didn't she desire it?'

Lytton privately felt that Leonard was not 'in his right assiette', writing fiction: 'Perhaps he should be a camel merchant, slowly driving his beasts to market over the vast plains of Baluchistan.' It would be more appropriate than 'Fabianising and novelising, and even than his past one of ruling blacks'.[52] Naturally it was 'the Camilla set' who interested Lytton, in *The Wise Virgins*. He told Leonard that he didn't see how 'eminent' women such as Camilla and Katherine would have bothered with those men. Shouldn't there have been some figure 'not second-rate'? 'It's rather marked, isn't it? That I'm omitted?' He liked Katherine, '(though if you think she's Vanessa I don't agree with you).'[53]

Katherine/Vanessa was indeed Leonard's idea of Vanessa, 'calm and beautiful and wise', in comforting contrast to the sneers and 'critical hostility' of her friends. For Harry is conscious every minute he is with them of being a Jew, braced against insult, but superior by reason of twenty thousand years of civilisation. Leonard told the truth about himself in fiction, conceding what he never conceded elsewhere.

Just as he went from doctor to doctor about Virginia, Leonard sent the manuscript to friend after friend. No wonder his family were upset, said Vanessa, 'when the superficial things are copied so exactly . . . it's almost impossible not to think that the character does to some extent convey your idea of the person'. Even the relations between them 'are

---

52 To Henry Lamb 19 Jan 1914. Quoted in Michael Holroyd, *Lytton Strachey* Heinemann 1973

53 Dec 14 1913. Berg. Vanessa, with Lytton, was not a Madonna figure: racier and more open than with Leonard, enjoying Lytton's indecent conversation and poems.

more or less copied'.[54] But writers, Vanessa opined, should be able to hurt people's feelings if they have to. 'The feelings, after all, *aren't* very important.' She was in the process of transferring her own from a devastated Roger Fry to Duncan Grant. Her comment chimes with something Ka Cox wrote to Leonard about the Gordon Square set: 'Their amazing entanglements are very absurd it seems to me! They really struck me as so infinitely unimportant!'

The reactions of all Leonard's siblings are not recorded. Cecil, for one, had his mind on other things. Seven years younger than Leonard, he had done better academically than any of his four brothers. He may not have been an Apostle, but he won the Thirlwell Prize Essay at Trinity in 1913 for *Bartolus of Sassoferrato: his position in the history of mediaeval political thought*, and was a Fellow of Trinity. His work on Bartolus was expanded into a 400-page book, with an affectionate dedication to his younger brother Philip, with whom he was collaborating on a translation of Stendhal's *De L'Amour*.[55] Like Edgar (briefly), and like Leonard, Cecil was scooped up by the Webbs, and gave some lectures at LSE.

Leonard decided to publish, and Edward Arnold accepted *The Wise Virgins* warmly, on condition that Leonard made some 'concessions to the reading public'. He wanted Leonard to cut the cliff-top conversation with Gwen about making babies. Leonard, in his adamant reply, gave a good account of what he meant his novel to be about, and of his own position. If the conversation about the creative life and having babies were cut out, 'Gwen's act [coming to his bedroom] at the crisis is one of mere lust, an act completely incongruous with her character'. The moral significance of the book was this: 'Harry is living in a circle of somewhat unnatural cultured persons and like them he indulges in a habit of wild exaggerated talk which he believes that he believes. The effect of such talk upon Gwen who is half in love with him is that her *imagination* (not her mere desires) is fired and she really believes and proceeds to act on her belief. When the reality is as near to Harry as that,

54 14 Jan 1914
55 Through Leonard, their translation was published by George Duckworth.

he finds that *he* dare not act up to his talk, because it was more talk than belief.'

Still debilitated and in the grip of a low-level depression, it was now Leonard's turn to get crippling headaches. On 7 March 1914 he went back to Lytton in Wiltshire for ten days, arranging for Janet Case, Ka Cox and Vanessa to take turns staying with Virginia, to make sure she ate.

Leonard and Lytton walked and talked in icy rain. Lytton was writing about Cardinal Manning, the first of the essays in his *Eminent Victorians*, and Leonard was in bed by half-past nine every night. Lytton handed him a bundle of his private correspondence to read, which did not enhance his mood. He wrote to Virginia every day: 'Sweetest Mandy, do you know that I almost cried when I got your letter just now? Merely from longing for you . . . I've been depressed and wanting you so much today', he wrote on 13 March. 'You can't realize how utterly you would end my life for me if you had taken that sleeping mixture successfully or if you ever dismissed me.'

'The poor fellow has been in rather a bad way', Lytton wrote to Clive after Leonard left. 'Anyone more angelically good tempered I've never known. Not a word of complaint and not the dimmest sign of snottishness from start to finish. Is it the result of Jewish training do you think? . . . After 1900 years of persecution I daresay the last shreds of peevishness have been worn away' – or perhaps it was 'the result of being happily married'.[56] Leonard went on to Bella and her husband in their 'comfortable villa house' at Streetly for a few days, against Virginia's wishes. She missed him. Bella decided his liver was upset, because he yawned so much.

'Leonard is better, according to him, and to me too',[57] Virginia reported to Janet Case on his return to Asheham. Dr Craig prescribed medicine for him; he had lost more weight. ('I love your little ribby body, my pet', Virginia wrote while he was away.) They went to Cornwall

56 14 March 1914
57 ?20 March 1914

for three week's holiday. Virginia had violent mood-swings, but it was a great step forward. Life at Asheham became almost normal. He could work again.

At the beginning of the year 1914 he read a paper on education to the Guild, and another on the control of industry. He wrote for *Co-operative News* about the minimum wage, fired up by reading R.H.Tawney's *Minimum Rates in the Chain Making Industry.* He began writing a book commissioned by the Home University Library, with Margaret Llewelyn Davies at his back, on Co-operation, and told Margaret on 21 May that he was dividing it into two halves, the first historical and the second on 'the development of the movement to the present day . . . I'm beginning to think it's got into rather a tangle. I should so much like to have your criticism of it.' Margaret thought that to have half the Co-operation book on the historical background was too much. He should have heeded her. In his polemical writings, he could never resist starting so far back in time that by the time he reached the present, and the policies which he passionately wished to promote, reader-fatigue had set in. Constant readers of Leonard Woolf learn to fast-forward.

He had two reviews in the *New Statesman* and four in the *New Weekly* between February and June 1914. Two of the books he wrote about became classics in their field, drawing Leonard deeper into areas which would interest him most, written by men he would come to know: J.A.Hobson's *Work and Wealth*[58] and Noel Brailsford's *The War of Steel and Gold: a Study of Armed Peace.* He wrote in his diary, in the space for 12 May, the title of the book he read that day. This is unique; normally he just listed 'books read' in the spare pages at the back. It was Freud's *Interpretation of Dreams,* and he was reading it in preparation for reviewing Freud's *The Psychopathology of Everyday Life* for the *New Weekly.*

Given that in Britain there was as yet, except among specialists, little knowledge of Freud, Leonard's review was astute. 'Whether one believes in his theories or not, one is forced to admit that he writes with great

58 J.A.Hobson's prescient *Imperialism* was published in 1902, when LW was still at Cambridge.

subtlety of mind, a broad and sweeping imagination more characteristic of the poet than the scientist or medical practitioner.' Freud's work was 'often a series of brilliant and suggestive hints . . . There can be no doubt that there is a substantial amount of truth in the main thesis of Freud's book, and that truth is of great value.' His judgement was exceptional in a year when the *British Medical Journal* was ranting about Freud's 'excessive sexual probing' and his work as 'the new pornography . . . Sex, sex, sex, in its grossest aspect'. English psychologists, as members of a civilised nation, were advised by the *BMJ* to give Freud a miss.[59]

Leonard's diary entries began 'Work morn', as they would in normal times for the rest of his life. In the afternoon he worked in the garden. They had visitors at Asheham again, though Lytton declined, pleading fear of dogs. (The Woolfs had two.) But Moore and MacCarthy came. Leonard walked with Moore, and bathed with him at Seaford. Leonard loved sea-bathing, riding off to the coast by bicycle; that summer of 1914 he bought a bicycle for Virginia, at the Lewes Co-op.

His fear of losing his lovely Aspasia, and the whole fine world she made, seemed over.

On 18 July 1914, like a footnote to *The Wise Virgins*, Leonard's brother Edgar married Sylvia Ross. The family legend is that for both of them it was second-best. Leonard went to London for the wedding reception.

It may or may not be coincidence that the following night he had to give Virginia, sleepless, a dose of Veronal at two o'clock in the morning. It was certainly unfortunate that he had arranged to go up to Keswick in the Lake District for two nights, for the Fabian Summer School, where he talked with the Webbs, and met for the first time George Bernard Shaw and Douglas Cole (the young academic whom Margaret wanted to snaffle for her Guild). He was invited to open the discussion on the Co-operative Movement, 'and tried to show that there were no limits to the movement in the control of industry', as he reported to Margaret Llewelyn Davies on 27 July. But he found the Summer School

59 Quotations from *BMJ* in Daniel Pick, 'The Id comes to Bloomsbury', *Guardian* Review, 16 August 2003

'a vague and a rather dreary affair', and could not think how the Webbs and Shaw endured it, year after year. Still, Leonard the ex-imperial administrator had things to learn. Shaw ticked him off for referring to Indians as 'natives'. Margaret had already ticked him off about another solecism, to which he replied: 'I really do try to remember to put in "and women" because I know that in practice it never is understood as included in "men"'. In his mind, it was. 'So I always forget to put it in.'[60]

He returned to Asheham, bringing with him from London his sixteen-year-old cousin Gertrude Mannheimer, on a visit from Denmark. At Asheham they found 'V not v well owing prob. to overdose of Veronal'.[61] In 1964, living in Israel and reading *Beginning Again*, Gertrude reminisced to Leonard: 'Virginia was very pretty, frail and sleepless. She, her dress, her blue veils – all impressed me, and books everywhere, even on the floor! You took me for a walk on the Downs . . .' After this Veronal episode Leonard was 'naturally', as Vanessa wrote to Roger Fry on 2 August, 'rather gloomy about the future. He said [Virginia] was bent on coming to London', where it would be impossible to persuade her to rest. She added: 'I wish Woolf did not irritate me so.'

The previous day, 1 August 1914, Leonard was swimming at Seaford when, coming up from a dive, he emerged face to face in the water with another swimmer who told him that Britain had declared war on Germany. 'Millions of men, most of them young, suddenly began to try to kill one another.'[62]

60 16 Jan 1914
61 LW diary 22 July 1914
62 LW, *After the Deluge* Hogarth Press 1931

9

Great War

Leonard and Virginia had a holiday in Northumberland and the Scottish borders planned, and went ahead. Virginia was well and happy. Leonard was preoccupied by events.'I still don't believe that Germany wanted war.' He blamed 'the small mad war party' and 'experts' on both sides.[1]

After the holiday they saw an empty house in Richmond which they liked – Hogarth House, in Paradise Road – but it was not yet available. So they moved into a boarding-house nearby, at 17 Richmond Green. Vanessa thought her sister seemed 'amazingly well', as she told Roger Fry. 'She was very charming and quite herself, though not as beautiful as she used to be – in fact so much changed to look at that it's quite odd talking to her.' Illness took its toll.

Leonard sat on a committee for the relief of the Belgians, on another about the war-time employment of women, and applied for a job with the government's Refugees Committee. It was just as well he did not get it. In November 1914 Beatrice Webb asked him to undertake a comparative study of the organisation of the legal profession 'in England, America and as many of the continental countries as you can get hold

1 To Margaret Llewelyn Davies 13 Aug 1914

of', inviting him and Virginia to come to dinner[2] and discuss the project. 'I am sorry to say I have not your Wimbledon [*sic*] address.'

The Webbs had a second project for him: an enquiry into 'international control over Foreign Policy, Armaments and methods of warfare', to be published by the Fabian Research Department. Joseph Rowntree, the Quaker chocolate magnate and philanthropist, was willing to subscribe £100, of which Leonard would get £50. This, which started as a report, was to form the core of Leonard's book *International Government*, 'one of the few books on politics written during the War that are not ephemeral', as the historian Arnold Toynbee told him.[3] Leonard, aware of the Webbs' habit of reshaping their protégés' research material, accepted the proposal with the stipulation that the Fabian Executive Committee 'would not require anything to appear over my name of which I was not the author or with which I did not agree.'

This letter exists in draft, jokily signed 'LSW (M's M)' – for 'Mandy's Mongoose'. Virginia, like Margaret, disliked Leonard's involvement with the Webbs and would have sabotaged it if she could. Lytton, while loyally following Leonard's progress in the public prints, was bored by international arbitration. Maynard Keynes, rising fast in the Treasury and on familiar terms with the Prime Minister, Herbert Asquith, thought Leonard's poorly paid work was a dreary waste of time. When Virginia, in January 1915, went with Leonard to a Fabian meeting where he spoke, she thought everyone looked 'unhealthy and singular and impotent'.[4]

Reactions like these were depressing for Leonard.

Over Christmas 1914 Leonard and Virginia took their usual kind of modest lodgings, in Marlborough, Wiltshire. On 27 December Leonard, on his own, walked the few miles west to Lytton's cottage, and found a houseful of noisy young guests playing snap. (One of them was David Garnett, known as Bunny, soon to become Duncan Grant's lover.) 'It

---

2 Virginia did not go. She found the Webbs' dinners 'dismal'. She asked friends – Ka Cox and Walter Lamb – to dinner with her instead. This became the usual pattern.

3 8 July 1924

4 VW Diary 23 Jan 1915

made me feel very old', Leonard told Janet Case, 'especially when I noticed that they were inclined to treat me rather respectfully and very kindly.' He described Lytton to Janet, who had never met him: 'He is the most particular of the particular in wit, taste, literature, race, music, humour, art, brilliancy. He has an immense and immensely beautiful russet beard, an immense black broad-brimmed felt hat, a suit of maroon corduroys, and a pale mauve scarf fastened with a Duke's daughter's[5] cameo brooch. He is the most charming and witty of human beings since Voltaire.'

The Woolfs' landlady was thrilled when Lytton came over to tea the next day, having spotted this amazing creature shopping in Marlborough. She had heard that he was editor of the *Sporting Times*.

When after Christmas Leonard gave a series of lectures to the Women's Co-operative Guild, his wife wrote in her diary: 'No one except a very modest person would treat these working women, & Lilian[6] & Janet & Margaret, as he does. Clive, or indeed any other clever young man, would give himself airs . . .'[7] The Woolf family visited them in Richmond, and after Flora came to tea Virginia wrote in her diary: 'I do not like the Jewish voice; I do not like the Jewish laugh' – but there was something to be said for Flora. 'She can typewrite, do shorthand, sing, play chess, write stories which are sometimes accepted, & she earns 30/- [shillings] a week as the Secretary of the Scottish Church in London.' At this point in their lives, she shared her diary with Leonard – an opportunity to be kind, and to be unkind.

Many of Virginia's ailments may be read as solicitations for affection and attention. Women in her youth tended to be rewarded for being unwell. Although she railed like a child against being restricted in her activities, or against drinking the milk that the doctors prescribed, she also responded like a child to being cosseted. On her birthday, 25

5 Lady Ottoline Morrell was the half-sister of the Duke of Portland.

6 Lilian Harris was Assistant Secretary to the Guild, and shared a house in Hampstead with Margaret.

7 6 Jan 1915

January 1915, Leonard crept into her bed with a present, and took her out for a day of treats, ending with a packet of sweets to bring home. 'I don't know when I've enjoyed a birthday so much', she wrote in her diary, 'not since I was a child anyway.' Childlike herself, she spotted that quality in others. 'Mrs W[oolf] has the mind of a child. She is amused by everything, & understands nothing – says whatever comes into her head – prattles incessantly . . .'[8]

On the last day of January 1915 the Woolfs quarrelled all morning. 'I explode: & L. smoulders.'[9] Perhaps it was about his coming home late the previous evening, after reading his new story 'The Three Jews' to Janet Case in Hampstead. Perhaps it was because while he was out Virginia read *The Wise Virgins* straight through – for the first time, although it had been out for some months. It had not made a splash on publication. Leonard said that the outbreak of war killed it, but it died a natural death. Because of the predominance of the Jewish theme, it just fell short of slotting into the genre of 'shocking' fiction on modern sexuality to which it rightly belonged – exemplified by H.G.Wells's *Ann Veronica* (1909) and *Marriage* (1912).) Virginia passed judgment the night she read it, in her diary: 'My opinion is that it's a remarkable book; very bad in parts; first rate in others. A writer's book, I think, because only a writer perhaps can see why the good parts are so very good, and why the bad parts aren't very bad . . . I was made very happy by reading this: I like the poetic side of L. & it gets a little smothered in Blue-books, & organizations.'

That was carefully distanced, written for his eyes. Leonard's novel was as scathing about her family and friends as it was about his own. It cannot have been agreeable reading about the bloodlessness of gentile women, or Harry's attraction to the calm, complete womanliness of Katherine/Vanessa, or Harry's (unwilling) marriage to the 'normal' and sexually ardent Gwen. The impact may have contributed to what happened.

Virginia was taking cookery lessons – 'a godsend', Leonard told Janet

---

8 VW Diary 25 Jan & 27 Jan 1915
9 VW Diary 31 Jan 1915

Case, 'as she makes us the most delicious omelette every night for dinner'. He was pitifully pleased when she took any interest in domesticity, as he was when she helped him with his work (note-taking, copying etc). She also kept household accounts at 17 The Green. Precisely detailed in most respects, when it came to food (they bought their groceries at the Richmond Co-op) she at first just wrote the bald word 'Food'. No doubt at Leonard's request, she began itemising 'Food' in detail. On 15 February 1915 she wrote just 'Food' again, which in context has a rebellious or despairing note. It was her last entry. On 18 February Leonard consulted Dr Craig before going to LSE and then meeting his mother. When he got home, his diary records, 'found V w headache. Bad night. Ver[onal].'

Virginia was relapsing. On 4 March 1915, after consulting with Dr Craig and Vanessa, he hired nurses. He wrote to Jack Hills, Stella's widower (now an MP) who had made over Stella's wedding settlement, after her death, to Vanessa and Virginia – £100 a year each, due at the end of March – and asked whether under the circumstances the £100 could be advanced straight away. He wrote to Beatrice Webb offering to give up the international arbitration project, explaining why. She replied kindly on 16 March: 'I hope your anxiety will not be too long drawn out . . . I myself would certainly wish you to go on – at your leisure.' She suggested it was best for him 'not to give up thinking about outside things however anxious and saddened you may be'. She and her husband had been reading his novels: Sidney preferred *The Village in the Jungle*, she was 'more interested' in *The Wise Virgins*.

On 25 March Virginia went to be cared for by Jean Thomas in Twickenham – conveniently close to Richmond – while Leonard organised the move to the house on Paradise Road, which had at last become available. He negotiated a five-year lease at £50 a year. Hogarth House was half of a large Georgian house divided in two, with four bedrooms on the top floor, two bedrooms, bathroom and WC on the first floor, and a drawing-room and dining room on the ground floor. The kitchen was in the basement, and there was a garden. A good house, then – except Paradise Road was noisy and, as Leonard's surveyor said, 'the sanitary fittings are not of a modern character'. Leonard loved Hogarth House.

It was 'the perfect envelope for ordinary life' in its combination of 'immense solidity with grace, lightness and beauty'.[10]

There was no 'ordinary life' at first in Hogarth House. Margaret sent a coffee cream for Virginia: 'it has eggs too in it and ought to be very nourishing.' Leonard was not to say who had sent it. 'I hope your cold has gone. Be on your guard in moving – it is the most chilly of processes.' Leonard brought down a cook, Annie, and a house parlourmaid, Lily, from Asheham. He fetched Virginia to their new home on 1 April 1915: 'V bad day V. exc[ited]' – meaning agitated, with great pressure of talk. On 28 April Leonard reported to Violet Dickinson that 'she is worse than I have ever seen her before. She hasn't had a minute's sleep in the last 60 hours.'

So it all began again. Bad days and better days, quiet days and shouting days, bad nights, better nights and worse nights. There was a new 'nerve doctor', Dr Ian Mackenzie, in addition to Dr Craig in whom Leonard was losing confidence. Vanessa warned Clive that Virginia was 'much worse, very violent as she was at Dalingridge and having to have 3 nurses and quite incoherent'. For Leonard it was not like the Dalingridge time, when he had been inexperienced and bewildered. This time he was assuming a burden whose weight he knew all too well. The one person who could assuage his unhappiness was the cause of it. It was like when, in his childhood, the cloud blotted out the sun. He drugged himself with work.

There is a sub-plot to this unhappy time which concerns Lily, their house parlourmaid. Leonard had a tenderness for girls of this kind – simple without being simpleminded. 'Lily was one of the persons for whom I feel the same kind of affection as I do for cats and dogs.' This is foully condescending, but less so, coming from him, than from anyone else. He felt she was like a damaged girl out of a novel by Dostoevsky, a divine 'silly'.

---

10 *Downhill All the Way* (1967), LW's fourth volume of autobiography. The title refers to the descent into World War II, but may also be a playful riposte to the title of his friend Mary Agnes (Molly) Hamilton's second book of memoirs, *Uphill All the Way* (1953).

A country girl with a 'long, pale, weak, rather pretty, sad face', Lily had been 'in trouble' and had an illegitimate child. Leonard devoted more than three pages of *Beginning Again* to Lily, whom he caught one night 'in some disarray' in the kitchen with a soldier. His account carries a stronger charge than, as it stands, it merits. There may be something left out. If Leonard were to seek sexual solace with anyone, it would be with someone like Lily, or one of the working girls he met on his Co-operation tours in the north of England. It is legitimate to wonder how he accommodated his strong sexuality. Any liaison would have had to be covert, and outside the circle of Virginia's friends. The merest suspicion of his unfaithfulness would have been catastrophic for her mental health.

Perhaps he made a triumph of self-denial. Perhaps he just thought about Lily, or someone else, and made love to his mattress. The novelist Anthony Powell told a story about a conversation with Leonard and 'a bunch of chaps' late one evening about how they would spend their last hours on earth. 'Leonard Woolf said he'd like to spend his fucking. We were all rather embarrassed because we knew Virginia wasn't all that keen.'[11]

Vanessa to Clive again, in May 1915: Virginia was 'so violent and unmanageable, attacking one of the nurses, that they say they can't control her at all, and want her to be moved into a home. The doctor also thinks she ought to be, and Leonard can do nothing with her himself as she is now angry with him. Also he is afraid of the neighbours complaining of the noise.' Margaret wrote to Leonard, 'I am very anxious to hear if she accepts the idea of a Home.' The answer was obviously in the negative. Leonard, as before, decided to hang on. This time around he himself was the object of Virginia's rages. (He did not record what the rages were about.) On 20 June 1915, for the first time, 'Did not see V.' For her sake and his own, he had to keep away from her, for weeks.

A week after his banishment, Bella's husband Robert Lock died of a heart attack. Leonard went to the funeral. The only upside of not being able to see Virginia was that he was not housebound. He could attend meetings, do his research for *International Government*, see friends, and

---

11 Private information

sometimes go to Hampstead in the evenings, to Margaret Llewelyn Davies, the one person in whom he fully confided. Morgan Forster came, for walks in Richmond Park. Leonard set up a routine of dining on Saturday nights at the Cock Tavern in Fleet Street with Saxon, and playing chess afterwards, and went for three days to Liverpool for the Women's Co-operative Guild conference.

But he was unable to go north to the Lake District for the annual Fabian get-together, where he would have heard his own report on international arbitration for the new Fabian Research Department being presented by Sidney Webb 'with great lucidity and urbanity', and G.B.Shaw contributing his 'perversely brilliant criticism and paradoxical proposals'.[12] Leonard's report was published as a special supplement of the *New Statesman* on 15 July under the title 'An International Authority and the Prevention of War'. From early 1915 onwards he was also knocking off political articles and book reviews every week for the *New Statesman,* to make money – sometimes two or three pieces (mostly unsigned) in the same issue.

On 12 July 1915 he wrote to Violet Dickinson that Virginia was still 'very opposed' to him. 'Craig says it's very common and will pass away.' Dr Craig was right. A week later, she was talking to him again, and during August he wheeled her out in an invalid chair, took her for a boat-trip on the river, and to Kew Gardens. She was not well but she was getting better, and her weight had gone up to twelve stone, the heaviest she had ever been.

In September they went to Asheham. Leonard wrote to Margaret, the day after they arrived: 'I should like to tell you what you've done for us both these last months and what we feel about it and you but it's impossible.' He said 'we' because it would have been hurtful to Margaret to know how little Virginia knew about it. Virginia lazed and read and made blackberry jam. Leonard was able to go to a meeting in Bristol to hear the wily, radical Liberal MP David Lloyd George speaking against the conduct of the war; the following year Lloyd George became Prime Minister in the wartime coalition government.

---

12 Margaret I.Cole, ed: *Beatrice Webb's Diaries* Vol 1 Longmans, Green 1952

Sidney Webb, in his large sprawling handwriting, wrote to Leonard in October enquiring about the international study of the legal profession which Leonard had taken on. Assuming he had been unable to work on it recently, Webb offered to 'take it off your hands', suggesting that Leonard should send him 'any notes you have made'. Webb explained that 'it is a habit of ours – perhaps a disease – to do these elaborate, detailed studies, in preparation for a work of larger scope', in this case the Fabian Research Department's Report on the Control of Industry. He took a further *fifteen* pages to say a) that they would be expanding on Leonard's work and inserting more detail and b) that they would not need more than a 'paragraph or two about Lawyers' anyway. Might he 'take the liberty of cutting your MS about, in order to amplify and complete it in my own way – and in fact, use it as my own? – putting in, of course, the fullest possible acknowledgment of your having furnished the basis . . .' Leonard sent what he had written, which was a lot, and was milked for supplementary material.

Leonard Woolf was drawn back into the politics of Ceylon when, at the end of May 1915, rioting broke out between Sinhalese and Muslims. The colonial government, misinterpreting the riots as seditious revolt (instead of inter-ethnic disturbance), over-reacted, and imposed martial law. Eighty-three people were condemned to death, and sixty to life imprisonment. Public servants were dismissed and professional men harassed. Armed police and soldiers patrolled the streets and people got shot. When Ponnambalam Ramanathan, a member of the Legislative Council of Ceylon, sought an interview with his good friend the Governor, he was instructed by the private secretary – who was Leonard's former colleague Tom Southorn – to send in a representation in writing. 'It was plain that the Governor did not want my advice.'[13]

---

13 P.Ramanathan KC CMG, *Riots and Martial Law In Ceylon*, St Martin's Press 1916. Other material from unidentifiable contemporary newspaper clippings in the National Archive, Colombo. The correspondences between LW and the two Sinhalese delegates, E.W.Perera and D.B. Jayatilaka, with accompanying papers, are in the National Archive in Colombo; there are copies in the Leonard Woolf Papers at Sussex University and in the Centre for South East Asian Studies in Cambridge.

Resentment at the mismanagement and injustice escalated, and delegates from Ceylon travelled to London to demand an official enquiry. The Colonial Office brushed them off. The two principals were the lawyers and future statesmen E.W. Perera and D.B. Jayatillaka,[14] who had been one of those arrested. Perera contacted Leonard, sending the relevant documentation. Leonard wrote articles about the situation in the *New Statesman*, edited the delegates' pamphlet, and sent it to all the MPs he knew. But the government in Ceylon also had representatives in London, spinning the story their way. A replacement governor compiled a report, which was a whitewash.

On 14 January 1917, Perera and Jayatillaka were invited for the first time to Hogarth House. Leonard liked them very much; and Mrs Jayatillaka sang Sinhalese songs after dinner 'more beautifully than I had ever heard singing in Ceylon'. Virginia, shackled by racism, misread as bribery the visitors' gift-giving and formal courtesies and, recording the visit, perpetrated the grossest discourtesies in her diary. Leonard could not hope to modify her attitudes. There were areas even in his marriage where it was necessary to preserve a carapace.

The campaign wore on. In summer 1917 the *Manchester Guardian* published a letter from the Ceylonese delegates alongside a supportive editorial.[15] But in the autumn, Perera was informed that the Colonial Office was not even prepared to continue corresponding with him. Leonard, however, continued to use his columns in the *New Statesman* to good effect, and the *Daily News* and the *Yorkshire Post* picked up the story as new documentation came in from Ceylon, revealing the sexual abuse of Sinhalese women in the crack-down after the riots. No official report by Leonard's former colleague, the foul-mouthed Herbert Dowbiggin, now Inspector General of Police in Ceylon, had been forthcoming until 'a considerable time after the riots and it is not inaccurate merely in details but was found to be false in material and vital points', as Jayatillaka wrote to Leonard. (Dowbiggin was later knighted.)

Perseverance, and the power of the Press, had an effect. Finally, the

14 Sometimes spelled 'Jayatilaka'
15 28 Aug 1917

Secretary of State for the Colonies agreed to receive a deputation, and on 16 January 1918, the Sinhalese delegates met at the Colonial Office with the Under-Secretary of State for the Colonies and his permanent officials. The Ceylonese delegates were supported by the Bishop of Lincoln, Gilbert Murray,[16] and Leonard Woolf, who had drafted the points each should make and also spoke himself, requesting an official enquiry and a revision of sentences. 'We all did our best, but all we got . . . was the inevitable and expected refusal.'[17] So far as Leonard was concerned, this was another nail in the coffin of imperialism. Posterity was to agree with him. It was a 'watershed of Empire': 'Sinhalese nationalism suddenly came of age.'[18]

Over the years, Leonard met frequently with groups such as the Ceylon Reform Society, in London. As adviser to the Labour Party, he reported on a meeting with Sir Ponnambalam Ramanathan and other Tamil leaders concerned with safeguarding their constitutional position, and he was to press repeatedly for equivalence between India and Ceylon on the route to independence. Forty years on, he would still be consulted by students from Ceylon doing research on the notorious riots of 1915.

The men in Leonard's and Virginia's circle were virtually all conscientious objectors (C.O.s)[19] in the Great War. Only young unmarried men were called up at the beginning of the war. Those C.O.s exempted by a tribunal from military service had to do approved war-work, and most opted to labour on farms. (Morgan Forster worked in Alexandria helping to trace missing soldiers.) In May 1916 Virginia sent Vanessa an enthusiastic description of Charleston Farmhouse, up a lane in the lee of Firle Beacon and only four miles from Asheham; Leonard took photographs of it with his new Kodak. So Charleston became home, during

---

16 Professor of Greek at Oxford, translator of Greek plays, committed internationalist and worker for peace.

17 *Beginning Again*

18 Charles S.Blackton, 'The Action Phase of the 1915 Riots', *Journal of Asian Studies* Ann Arbor, Michigan, 1970.

19 A pacifist is against all war. A conscientious objector is against a particular war.

the war, for Vanessa and her two children, for Duncan Grant and Bunny Garnett – who worked for the farmer – and, part-time, for Clive and Maynard.

Thus the war scattered the Brunswick Square/Gordon Square circle into the countryside. Bloomsbury was over, as a strictly geographical grouping, before the word 'Bloomsbury' became common currency. Vanessa took 'Old Bloomsbury', real Bloomsbury, to have existed only in the years 1904-1915. Leonard, solipsistically, was of the opinion that Bloomsbury 'did not exist in 1911 when I returned from Ceylon; it came into existence in the three years 1912 to 1914.'[20] When Clive Bell in 1917 proposed a 'great historical portrait of Bloomsbury'[21] he included himself, Roger Fry (who would paint it), Lytton, Duncan, Maynard, Vanessa and Virginia, the MacCarthys, and – a long shot, this – his new lover, Mary Hutchinson. (Not Adrian, not Saxon, not Leonard.) Bloomsbury, to Bloomsberries, was what they chose to make it.

The war was also a period of emotional realignments. The Bells had established separate sexual lives. Clive Bell had his relationship with Mary Hutchinson, a quiet, clever woman, a second cousin of Lytton's and the wife of barrister St John Hutchinson. Vanessa was in love with Duncan Grant, who was in love with Bunny Garnett. Adrian Stephen married Karin Costelloe – Irish-American, deaf, large, and the sister of his elder brother Oliver's wife Ray. (Leonard could not abide Karin and was habitually uncharitable about her.) Lytton, exempted from army service on health grounds, formed an attachment to Dora Carrington, a vivacious, bi-sexual, blonde-bobbed, ex-art student with china-blue eyes whom he had met with Vanessa at Asheham. Carrington – as she was always known – fell deeply and permanently in love with him, and it was with her that Lytton went to live at the Mill House at Tidmarsh in 1917. Carrington ran the household and cared for Lytton among the ebb and flow of his and her visiting friends and lovers and, while the war lasted, unlikely agricultural workers.

---

20 *Beginning Again*

21 Roger Fry to Vanessa Bell, 12 Dec 1917. *Letters of Roger Fry* ed Denys Sutton, Chatto & Windus 1972

Saxon Sydney-Turner fell madly in love with pretty Barbara Hiles, an art-college friend of Carrington's; she married Nick Bagenal, who served in the Irish Guards. She envisaged that Nick and Saxon might share her. Whatever the details of the arrangement, Saxon remained passionately attached. James Strachey had a relationship with Alix Sargant-Florence, a brilliant young woman who had just come down from Newnham College, Cambridge, and who married him – it was that way round – in 1920.

G.E. Moore surprised everyone. Leonard had a letter from him in October 1916 saying he was going to be married to a Miss Ely; she was 'very young', said Moore, 'compared to me'. He was forty-two. Dorothy Ely was twenty-two, and had been a classics student at Newnham. She called him 'Bill' and they had two sons. 'Moore had a positive vocation for marriage and fatherhood.'[22]

There were shakings of the kaleidoscope in the Woolf family too. Harold, the only Woolf brother who could be described as jovial, married to Alice, established their home in a house called the Boreen, in Laleham-on-Thames. Edgar, whom few would describe as jovial, started his married life with Sylvia in Putney – in Luttrell Avenue, a mere step from Colinette Road. Mrs Woolf had a new home, the strangely named Hygeia House, in Staines, outside London to the west.

'In order to keep as much in L.'s company as I could', Virginia went with Leonard to Hygeia House on one of his regular Sunday visits at the end of October 1917. 'Pink arm chairs were drawn up round a crowded but not luxurious tea table; a multiplicity of little plates, minute knives, people told to help themselves.' Alice, Flora, Clara and Sylvia all trooped in: 'malice suggested the whole of Kensington High Street poured into a room.'[23] There was a flurry when 'Mr Sturgeon' was announced. George Sturgeon, a schoolmaster, and an old schoolfriend of Philip's, was courting Flora.

Five months later, at the end of March 1918, Leonard had a

---

22 Paul Levy, *G.E.Moore and the Cambridge Apostles* Weidenfeld & Nicolson 1979
23 VW Diary 28 Oct 1917

querulous letter from his mother, complaining that he had not answered Flora's invitation to her imminent wedding at St Columba's, Pont Street. Mother was not well. 'But it is good to see Flo so happy, though poor child it will be hard enough for her to see George [Sturgeon] go off to the Front next day.' There was going to be 'a little luncheon' at Grosvenor House Hotel afterwards. Leonard and Virginia did not attend. Under difficulties as to a sufficiency of fuel and food, they had Lytton (ill in bed), Noel Olivier[24] and James Strachey staying with them at Asheham.

Herbert married Alfreda (Freda) Major in 1919. Virginia, knowing the predilection of Woolfs for dogs, wrote that Freda was 'merely a toy dog wrapped in human flesh, but retaining the pretty, plaintive, rather peevish ways of her canine existence. She has stimulated Herbert to talk with greater fluency & enthusiasm than usual . . .'[25] Leonard (but not Virginia) did go to that wedding, and stayed overnight at Hygeia House. Herbert and Freda had a modern house in Cookham Dean, Berkshire. Thus the male Woolfs dispersed themselves along the Thames Valley, within easy reach of London, of their mother, and of each other.

The Woolfs were neither pacifists nor conscientious objectors. Bella was decidedly pro-war, and published in 1914 *Right Against Might*, a rousing call to arms. Cecil and Philip joined up, and were in the Twentieth Hussars, a cavalry regiment.

'Well, this is an odd war and an odd life!' Cecil wrote to Leonard in February 1916. 'I wouldn't have missed it for anything. It all defies description. As you get nearer the firing-line, the country becomes more and more gloomy . . . until you come to utter desolation.' Philip, in December, when he and Cecil were resting up after two months in the trenches, told Leonard they had a little dog who stuck to them 'through all the horrors of war'. Edgar joined up in the Bedford Yeomanry, and Harold in the Army Service Corps. There were family gatherings, which

---

24 Noel Olivier had just qualified as a doctor. Rupert Brooke, Adrian Stephen and James Strachey all fell in love with her.
25 VW Diary 28 Oct 1918

Leonard attended, before each departure. Herbert, holding together his depleted stock-jobbing business,[26] did special police work.

Under the Military Service Act of 1916, conscription was widened to include married men aged between sixteen and forty-one. Leonard was thirty-five. Virginia still had recurring headaches which were only relieved by withdrawing from social life, though she continued to maintain a more than healthy weight – 'even larger than usual' as Lytton reported to Lady Ottoline, 'she rolls along over the downs like some amphibious monster.' Leonard, he added, was a good deal alarmed 'at the prospect of being forced either into the army or gaol,[27] and obliged to leave Virginia to her fate.'[28]

'I shall of course apply for exemption', Leonard wrote to Margaret Llewellyn Davies, 'on grounds of health (shaking hands) and domestic hardship . . . but I am not hopeful of the results. I feel I am a conscientious objector – for I loathe the thought of taking any part in this war – and yet I feel very much the difficulty from the point of view of reason.' Dr Craig gave him a typed letter, dated 10 May 1916, to present to the tribunal in Richmond Town Hall:

> I hereby certify that I have this day seen and examined Mr L.S.Woolf.
>
> He first consulted me in March, 1914, when I found that he was suffering from marked nerve exhaustion symptoms. He had a general tremor which I regarded as a permanent one, which was most marked in the hands and arms; sleep was defective and he had severe headaches . . .
>
> Owing to his highly nervous state I have no hesitation in saying that I regard him as quite unfit for military service, and that if he attempts it, he will almost certainly break down within a short time.
>
> I may further add that his wife has had several severe mental breakdowns during the last sixteen years, and I have been

---

26 Herbert's firm was Woolf, Christey & Co, 4 Copthall Court EC2.
27 Would-be C.O.s who did not convince the tribunal were sent to prison.
28 23 April 1916

> consulted about her on many occasions since 1913. Her husband, Mr L.S.Woolf, has personally nursed her through these attacks, and she is still in a highly unstable condition and if his care is removed, I am of opinion that the effect will be highly detrimental to her and may bring about a severe mental breakdown. I may add that it is only in cases where I know the personal element to be of vital importance that I am willing to express such an opinion to a tribunal.

Leonard was granted a temporary exemption.

In mid-June 1916 they went for a weekend to the Webbs at Wyndham Croft in Sussex where G.B. Shaw and his wife were fellow guests. Leonard recalled how the Webbs card-indexed everyone in their minds: Virginia was 'the novelist', so anything connected with writing was referred to her; Leonard was 'the ex-colonial civil servant', so anything connected with foreign parts was referred to him; Shaw was the all-purpose artist, so the name of the flowers on the dining-table (flowers 'so common or garden', he said that everyone in Europe except the Webbs would know what they were) was reckoned to be his field. Charlotte Shaw seemed to have nothing on her notional index-card.

Leonard always found Shaw charming and friendly, 'though if you happened to look into that slightly fishy, ice-blue eye of his, you got a shock'. He was never looking at you, or even speaking to you, personally. That blue eye 'was looking through you or over you into a distant world or universe inhabited almost entirely by G.B.S., his thoughts and feelings, fancies and phantasies.'[29] That weekend contributed to the apocalyptic Shavian fancies and phantasies of his play *Heartbreak House*; Leonard remembered him writing it in the garden on a pad on his knee.

G.E.Moore came to Asheham for a night shortly after, and returned for four nights in mid-August. His visit gave Leonard enormous

---

29 *Beginning Again*

pleasure.[30] It was like old times. Every afternoon he and Moore went for long walks. Photographs were taken – Moore portly now, Leonard stick-thin and glossy-haired.

In October 1917 Leonard was called up before the tribunal again. Craig examined him again, and wrote another letter: 'His body weight, which was always low, is now half a stone lower than it was 18 months ago.[31] I have no hesitation in saying that he would not stand any form of service which entailed mental or physical fatigue. Further I am of the opinion that if he were called upon to serve, he would certainly break down within a short space of time.'

He had a letter from Dr Wright as well, which referred to the 'inherited tremor', adding that 'Mr L.S.Woolf has a markedly Neuropathic Temperament and suffers readily from symptoms of Nervous Exhaustion.' 'Rejected' Leonard wrote in his diary. Since 'His Majesty's Army has decided that I am totally unfit to be used in any way by my country', he told Violet Dickinson, 'I shall be unable even conscientiously to object.'[32] Apart from the humiliation of hearing an army doctor referring to his condition as 'senile tremor', he was relieved, though taken aback by the opinions about himself expressed by his doctors.

Leonard was, as it were, shell-shocked already. It is sobering to realise the depleted state of the young man who had a few years previously been administering a thousand square miles of Ceylon. His attitude to fighting in the Great War, not having been tested, fluctuated until the end of his life. He wrote in *Beginning Again* that 'I have never been a complete pacifist; once the war had broken out it seemed to me that the Germans must be resisted and I therefore could not be a Conscientious Objector.'

A fortnight after the tribunal he was off by train to industrial Lancashire for five days, lecturing on 'Sanctions and Disarmament' to branches of

---

30 Reading over his diaries in old age, he marked the days of this visit in pencil with the word 'Moore', not wanting whoever came after to miss the reference.

31 Leonard weighed 133 pounds at this time.

32 23 June 1916. Berg

the Co-operative Society. He enjoyed staying in the members' homes, some of them local worthies but most of them working-class, consuming fish and chips and quantities of tea after his lecture, sitting up late with the children not put to bed, talking and arguing about 'politics and classes and the war and education and what the children would do or wanted to do', and finally finding a hot-water bottle in his bed.[33]

He wrote daily letters to 'My dearest dearest Mistress . . . You don't know how many times a day I think of you and always with a longing to see you, talk to you, and kiss you.' Saxon meanwhile kept Virginia company at Asheham, ' and said how our marriage seemed the best of any he knew . . . It's no good repeating that I adore you, is it? That seems to be a well known fact.' Saxon's indecisiveness seemed odd to Virginia 'after my rapid bold Mong'.[34] Leonard longed to be back with her. 'We'll go and fetch poor old Tinker[35] from the vet in the afternoon and walk by the river and then we'll come back to tea and sit over the fire and talk.'

He was still the Servant and she the Mistress, still and always his Aspasia. He remained in love with her. It was part of his sense of himself. He never really 'had' her – neither sexually, nor in the periods of her illness, which were like abandonments. She was never a captured butterfly. He knew by now how vitally important unconditional love (it happened to be his) was to her well-being. Her hostility swung ninety degrees, into dependency. To please him, but not only to please him – she supported wholeheartedly the causes of women, even though the Guild's earnestness was not her cup of tea – she attended with him the Women's Co-operative Guild Congress at Toynbee Hall, presided at Guild Social Evenings, and for four years chaired the small Richmond branch of the Guild.

His *International Government* came out in July 1916. Shaw offered a supportive introduction, which Leonard declined for the British edition, but

---

33 *Beginning Again*

34 VW Letters 30 Oct 1917 & 31 Oct 1917

35 Tinker was a new dog given to them by Herbert. He was a problem dog and kept running away.

accepted for the American one. Leonard had made himself 'an authority' on international relations, coming to believe that if one worked with the 'laborious pertinacity of a mole or beaver',[36] any intelligent person could acquire in a few months the knowledge necessary for a thorough understanding of any subject.

International Government was the right book at the right time, and a major contribution towards providing a solution to the most important problem facing Europe. Soon after the outbreak of the Great War there grew up a multiplicity of groups, unions and societies, bristling with acronyms and, like all voluntary organisations, with internal dissensions. All were dedicated to the question of how to bring about a permanent peace in Europe, post-war, as was the Fabian Society; and all produced plans or programmes to ensure that this would be the war to end wars.[37] The establishment of some form of international arbitration between nations – Leonard's core topic in *International Government* – was, in every plan, the key issue. Leonard saw the already existing institutions for European co-operation – in postal services, commerce, international law, finance, the professions, international Trades Unionism – as a main plank on which to build. But in Britain each union was fighting for itself, 'which means that Trades Unionism might just as well not exist at all.'[38]

He did not belong to the Bryce Group, named for its chairman, an Oxford professor and former ambassador to the United States, and the most 'establishment' of the peace organisations. Goldie Lowes Dickinson was its most influential and active member; the phrase 'League of Nations' may have originally been his. Leonard remained ambivalent about Goldie. 'There was a weakness, a looseness of fibre, in Goldie and in his thought and writing, which was subtly related to the gentleness and highmindedness.'[39] The Bryce Group's plan was like all the others in leaning heavily on the American President Woodrow

---

36 *Beginning Again*

37 The familiar phrase comes from the title of H.G.Wells's book *The War That Will End War* (1914).

38 To Margaret Llewelyn Davies 21 Aug 1915

39 *Beginning Again*

Wilson's League to Enforce Peace. It was largely through Goldie, who had a relentless quality, that Leonard was drawn into other groups; Goldie belonged to them all.

As the idea of a League of Nations took hold, the Government put its oar in, and the Phillimore Committee was established, centring on a putative 'Conference of Ambassadors'. Leonard would have nothing to do with this one, either. He loathed secret diplomacy and 'those subterranean regions where the evil spirits guide diplomatists towards inevitable war'.[40] But in 1915 Leonard did become heavily involved, as a co-founder, in the League of Nations Society. J.A.Hobson, whose book *Towards International Government* preceded Leonard's – Leonard reviewed it critically in the *Nation*[41] – was on the executive, as was the *Manchester Guardian* writer, H.N.Brailsford. Goldie Lowes Dickinson constantly exploited Leonard to write pamphlets for the Society, to send 3000 words 'about providing for change without war', to 'get up' some detailed research about 'the international control of trade concessions and loans', to write an article which he needed 'within a week or two . . . Could you not squeeze it in immediately after the pamphlet on Constantinople, and before you tackle the Fabian book?'

A similar group emerged in late 1917, called the League of Free Nations Association, with Gilbert Murray and H.G.Wells among its founders. The significant difference between them and Leonard's League of Nations Society was their conviction that Germany must be excluded from the post-war consortium of nations, while the League of Nations Society was equally adamant that Germany must be included. Leonard was one of the four representatives of the Society which met representatives of the League for a series of working dinners. He became friendly with H.G.Wells in the process, and had some good lunches with him at Boulestin's. After the war, Wells learned that 'There's a Mrs Woolf, I believe. Somehow I hadn't thought of you in that way.' (Because of the Lowes-Dickinson connection, he assumed Leonard was homosexual.) 'But last night when I

---

40 *International Government*

41 7 Aug 1915

was discoursing on your goodness and wisdom somebody told me you are married to Virginia Woolf. I used to write novels in the dear old past. Will she come?'[42] H.G.Wells was a warm creature and possibly the best-known author in the world, but the Woolfs never did go and stay with him.

The working dinners and discussions became bogged down in acrimony and high-principled pettifogging. 'Don't resign', Goldie begged Leonard. Finally, the two groups formally amalgamated as the League of Nations Union, at a meeting in Caxton Hall in November 1918. Leonard was at the top table, elected on to the Executive Council along with Lord Grey of Falloden (a former Foreign Secretary), Herbert Asquith, Arthur Balfour and David Lloyd George.

Leonard joined yet another peace group, the Union of Democratic Control (UDC), and contributed to their journal *War & Peace*, dominated by the ideas of Norman Angell, author of the anti-imperialist, anti-war *The Great Illusion* (1911). The UDC's main aims, which Leonard shared, were the replacement of traditional diplomacy with an International Council, and disarmament. Hobson and Brailsford were founder members. A key figure in the UDC was Ramsay MacDonald of the Independent Labour Party (ILP), a charismatic figure who refused to support the war. Leonard wrote parliamentary reports for the ILP organ *The Labour Leader* – until he was sacked for, he suspected, not featuring Ramsay MacDonald with sufficient adulation.

Completely exasperated by the overlapping multiplicity of organisations, Leonard made the time in 1917 to edit a collection of seven of the more responsible programmes for international arbitration post-war, under the title *The Framework of a Lasting Peace*. 'Everyone', he wrote in his introduction, 'has some "scheme" or "plan" or "league", and all seem to differ profoundly.' In fact the reverse was true. Mostly, they squabbled over procedure and nit-picking minutiae. Leonard went on to demonstrate what they had in common.

*

42 HGW to LW 19 March 1920. The Hogarth Press was to publish 4 minor works by Wells in the late 1920s and 30s.

It is a relief to read in Virginia's diary about even a wet summer holiday that she and Leonard had at Asheham in 1917 – picking mushrooms, making jam, collecting wild flowers, having Vanessa and her boys for tea; and to hear of Leonard chopping wood, mending bicycle punctures, gardening, picking apples. His work took him away from Asheham once or twice a week. 'I am going to try to get up to London on Friday for the Labour Party Conference', he wrote to Margaret on 4 August 1917, 'as it seems to me much the most important thing that has happened to Labour during the war.'

The 'most important thing' was that the Government refused to allow Arthur Henderson, a Labour MP and member of the War Cabinet, to attend the 2nd International of Socialist Parties in Stockholm – basically, in case he might get talking with Germans. Conference voted by a large majority to send Henderson to Stockholm; he resigned from the War Cabinet, and went. Leonard was delighted by the unusual unity of the Labour Party conference, and made a new friend there – S.S. Kotelianski, always called Kot, a Jew from the Ukraine working in London as a translator. But the harmony of the Labour Party was short-lived. The ILP were showing themselves 'so bitter and truculent that they can see nothing except a tiny segment of the horizon', complained Leonard. 'What a bore it all is: extremists hopeless because they are as blind as mad bulls, and moderates hopeless because they are moderates!'[43]

Arthur Henderson was drafting a new Labour Party constitution, to bring together the two wings of the party and make it capable of mounting a serious electoral challenge to the Conservative and Liberal parties. Most Labour MPs, coming from the working class and from the provinces, did not have the education, the experience, or the information available to MPs of the two long-established parties. Henderson (with Sidney Webb at his back) proposed the establishment of advisory committees, to brief, inform and advise.

The first of these was the Advisory Committee on International and Imperial Questions, a 'think-tank' which Webb chaired and for which he

43 To Margaret Llewelyn Davies 25 Aug 1917

recommended Leonard Woolf, who became its secretary. He was a full member of the committee in addition to setting the agenda, drafting the minutes, and circulating papers and recommendations. In the inner circle of Labour policy-making, he was wanted on all sides as a facilitator and provider of information. R.H. Tawney[44] approached him in 1918 asking him to advise Norman Leys, who was working on making British war aims intelligible to the neutral Irish. Leys's real subject was Africa, and he was helpful to Leonard over the research for his next book, *Empire and Commerce in Africa.*

Empire and Commerce in Africa was a result of the success of *International Government,* selling steadily on both sides of the Atlantic. Sidney Webb asked Leonard whether he had any ideas for another book. The Fabian Society could perhaps pay for 'any good study.' Leonard suggested something on international trade.

Webb kept Leonard on a tight rein. He was not allowed to borrow books from the LSE Library himself, but only through Webb, who insisted he ask the librarian 'to let *me* have on loan anything that *you* indicate to him'. Leonard could have £15 to buy materials which would, ultimately, be put at the Fabian Society's disposal, and he should borrow books rather than buy them. Leonard soon found that to take on a study of worldwide trade was impracticable, and narrowed his researches to the case of Africa.

His research was primary and his material raw. As for *International Government,* for *Empire and Commerce in Africa* Leonard embarked on a crash-course of self-education. He interviewed civil servants and union officials, tracked down and filleted government reports, blue books, white books, trade figures, annual reports of international organisations, company balance sheets, minutes of conferences and congresses. Facts, uncovered with difficulty, had to be assessed and quantified. New narratives had to be constructed from the materials, at an angle to the traditional top-down political and diplomatic record. The Webbs were perfect terriers when it came to unearthing facts on their own subjects, but they knew little about foreign affairs and did not pretend to. As

44 Economic historian, Fellow of Balliol, social reformer.

Webb said to Leonard, 'as to methods and scope we must leave it to you. It is an adventure.'

'The Russian revolution in 1917 was a tremendous event for me'. As he said, one did not have to be very far to the left to dislike Tsarism, and Leonard was quite far to the left. He went as a delegate to Leeds on 2 June 1917 to what was billed as a 'Great Labour, Socialist and Democratic Convention', and was 'one of the most enthusiastic and emotional that I have ever attended'. He said in his old age that he would still and again welcome the Russian revolution of 1917 which, whatever horrors came after, was 'essential for the future of European civilization'.[45]

The immediate change to Leonard and Virginia's daily lives was the celebratory founding of the 1917 Club as a socialist forum. The idea was Leonard's and Oliver Strachey's. Premises were found in a house in Gerrard Street in Soho, financed by Maynard and others, and the club opened in December. Leonard was on the committee, to which he was regularly re-elected, and the club was a success from the beginning.

The membership was primarily political, and met over lunch. In the afternoons, for tea, the club was taken over by art and culture, and would often include Lytton with a coterie of young persons. Virginia felt comfortable at the 1917 Club, and she and Leonard used it as a rendezvous. Political members included Ramsay MacDonald, J.A.Hobson, H.N. Brailsford and Mary Agnes (Molly) Hamilton, a Labour activist and writer who later became an MP, with whom Leonard is said to have had a special relationship. Virginia was certainly extremely curious about her. At the club, 'I went upstairs, hid behind a door, & saw Mrs Hamilton for the first time, or rather heard her, holding forth like a jolly club man; for I didn't dare look.'[46]

How splendid to have acquired the PRESS!' wrote Margaret Llewelyn Davies. 'Now we may have reconstruction in art and literature and

---

45 *Beginning Again*
46 VW Diary 27 July 1918

morals.' Leonard and Virginia had planned to have a printing-press even before the recurrence of her illness. Printing would be something they could do together, it had always interested Virginia, and it would give her an absorbing occupation as a complete change from her morning's writing: 'I have never known anyone work with more intense, more indefatigable concentration than Virginia . . . the novel became part of her and she became part of the novel',[47] and it was hard for her to detach her mind from it even when she had stopped writing for the day. They thought of apprenticing themselves to a school of printing, but apprenticeships were a closed shop, not open to middle-class adults.

One afternoon in March 1917, walking up Farringdon Street, they passed the Excelsior Printing Supply Co. They went in and, taking advice, ordered a small hand-press, some Old Face type, and the attendant implements and materials, for £19.5s.6d. When it was all delivered, plus a sixteen-page instruction book, they set it up in the dining-room at Hogarth House and began to learn how to use it. (You worked the press by pulling down a handle which brought the platen and paper up against the type in its chase. It could only print one demy octavo page at a time.)

After a period of experiments and inky fingers they began on 3 May 1917 to print a hundred and fifty copies of a thirty-two-page book, which they stitched into paper covers. It took them over a month. Leonard's customary diary entries, 'Work morn. Walk aftn.', became 'Work morn. Print aftn.' They sent out a circular to everyone they knew inviting them to become subscribers to what they called the 'Hogarth Press'. The little book was *Two Stories* – one by each of them. His was 'The Three Jews', hers 'The Mark on the Wall.'

'The Three Jews' starts with a man enjoying Kew Gardens on a sunny Sunday in the 'quiet orderly' English springtime. He goes into a tea-shop on Kew Green where he is joined at his table by a stranger – instantly identifiable as a Jew from his gait, voice and physical features,

---

47 *Beginning Again*

described dispassionately and not kindly. This stranger recognises the first-person narrator as a fellow-Jew and they get talking. 'We show up, don't we, under the apple-blossom and this sky. It doesn't belong to us, do you wish it did?'

They establish that neither is a believer. Yet 'we belong to Palestine still'. Then the second Jew embarks on a story about someone else who 'belongs to Palestine still':[48] a third Jew, the keeper of the cemetery where the second Jew's wife lies. The third Jew is, like the others, a religious sceptic, while regretting the loss of the old spirit, kept alive 'hot and vigorous' over centuries of persecution. He has come down in the world; all that remains is pride of family. But he disowns a son, for marrying a Christian servant girl working in the family house. 'Times change: I might have received his wife, even though she was a Goy. But a servant girl who washed my dishes! One must have some dignity.' Expressing his outrage, his pride of race and family seems restored.

It is hard to know what the story signified for Leonard. Was his point that the traditional Jewish exclusivity of race and religion becomes transmuted, when faith no longer prevails, into an exclusivity based on social class? Or was it that traditional Jewish family feeling has a brutal and punitive aspect? Or something else entirely?[49]

'The Three Jews' was based on a Woolf family story, and seemed tragi-comically sufficient to its author. Philip, writing in August 1917, said he read it 'with great amusement'. It could not 'possibly be much more true to life, but at the same time I shouldn't have thought there was much danger of a libel action – considering the real person concerned. As to the propriety of such very intimate revelations – that I think far more questionable.'[50]

48 References to Palestine had a special resonance in 1917, the year of the Balfour Declaration: On 2 November Arthur Balfour, as Foreign Secretary, pledged British support for the establishment of a Jewish National Home in Palestine.

49 Freema Gottlieb sees the third Jew as 'a symbol of humanity who only in adversity comes into full grandeur': in 'Leonard Woolf's Attitude to his Jewish Background and his Judaism' (The Jewish Historical Society of England: *Transactions* Vol XXV 1977).

50 Remembering Grandfather Benjamin Woolf's rebarbative Will and its codicils, it seems probable that the outcast son was one of Leonard's and Philip's uncles, perhaps Henry.

Philip's strictures were, justly, about the story's structure. 'I believe I should have liked an absolutely simple construction – the visit [to the cemetery] a first-hand experience.' Leonard used the 'framing' technique of authors he read in his youth, such as Conrad and Wells. The first Jew's walk in Kew Gardens, and the second Jew in the teahouse, are a long introduction to the 'real' story, about the third Jew. The framing is incomplete, since we never return to the first and second Jews in the tearoom.

Morgan Forster wrote Leonard a similar critique of an early version of his story 'A Tale Told by Moonlight', advising him to simplify the introduction; and identical advice, on a postcard, after reading the draft of his story 'Pearls and Swine': 'Shorten the introduction. That is a real technical defect. Present the scene as a blur out of which the I[ndian C[ommissioner] emerges.'

'Present the scene as a blur': E.M.Forster, Lytton Strachey, Virginia Woolf, alive to the plasticity and suggestiveness of language, could do that. Leonard could do a lot with language, but he could not do 'blur'.

Virginia's story 'The Mark on the Wall' was in a different league. To describe it as a woman's free-floating meditations as she contemplates a mark on the wall which she can't quite make out is accurate, but it is an attempt to pin down running water. 'I want to sink deeper and deeper, away from the surface, with its hard separate facts.' 'The Mark on the Wall' is an underwater reverie made up of old conversations, memories, images, resentments and longings, within a vision of a fluid world 'without professors or specialists or house-keepers with the profiles of policemen, a world which one could slice with one's thought as a fish slices the water with his fin . . .'

Everyone who knew Virginia well knew how she would sometimes, in conversation in familiar company, suddenly 'leave the ground' as Leonard put it, taking off from some mention of a person or place into a fantastically fluent verbal flight or fugue, giving rise to an entrancing few moments (except to those few who found it affected or irritating). Reading 'The Mark on the Wall' is as near as one can get to experiencing what her conversational flights were like. They were the brilliant middle stretch of a continuum which began in rills of wickedly creative gossip and free association and ended in the dark waters of incomprehensible gabble, when she was insane. If Leonard believed in the link between her creativity and her insanity, so did she. One of the reasons that she was so sensitive to the reception of her novels was her fear that people might find them insane.

After reading *Two Stories*, Lytton wrote that 'Virginia's is, I consider, a work of genius. The liquidity of the style fills me with envy . . . How on earth does she make the English language float and float? And then the wonderful way in which the modern point of view is suggested! *Tiens*!'[51] This was in a letter to Leonard, in which Lytton said not one single word about 'The Three Jews'. From then on there was a compass-correction. Lytton communicated with Leonard as one grown-up friend to another, not exercising his fantasy or opening his heart. He transferred to Virginia the 'dialect of their intimacy'. He and she were alike – hungry for praise and affection, supersensitive, observant and critical, impatient, fantastical, exigent, amused by glamour and glitter.

Virginia was finding her fictional voice just as Leonard was realising the limitations of his own. He, who thought creation and creativity were among the greatest of life's values, lost his confidence for writing stories or novels. He would always write exquisitely about real things in the real world which moved him. Among the welter of political articles he so professionally produced for the *New Statesman*, there is an article in the issue of 6 January 1917 entitled 'The Gentleness of Nature':[52]

> The other day there was a hard frost upon the Sussex downs; a bitter, north-east wind raced across the bare, whitened hill-sides. Late in the evening I came upon a green plover sitting on the ground, ceaselessly turning its head from side to side.

---

51 17 July 1917. Berg

52 Reprinted in L.S.Woolf, *Essays on Literature, History, Politics etc.* Published by Leonard and Virginia Woolf at the Hogarth Press, 1927

He expanded into a discussion of how in England we have tamed nature so that 'her ruthless ferocity, her dark and gloomy ways' are normally hidden, contrasting this with the pain, disease, destruction and death everywhere apparent in the East. The writing is spare and unmannered. His ideal was the style of the early nineteenth-century journalist and radical reformer William Cobbett: 'If ever England becomes a civilised country, 90 per cent of the population will write like William Cobbett. His English is plain, absolutely unaffected, vigorous and supple, beautiful . . .'[53]

Walking on the Downs above Asheham, they heard the pounding of the guns across the Channel. On 2 December 1917 Leonard heard by telephone that Cecil had been killed, and Philip wounded, in the inconclusive fiasco of the Battle of Cambrai.

'In the muddle of Bourlon Wood they were sent dismounted to support the guards and there [Cecil] was killed and another of my brothers who was in the same regiment wounded by the same shell', he told Violet Dickinson.[54] Edgar was in the same 'show' and not far away. Cecil and Philip left their trench together during the night of 27 November to bring in a wounded colleague, and a shell burst between them. By the time Edgar reached the field hospital, Cecil had died (on 29 November) and Philip been evacuated. It is not known what happened to their little dog.

Lieutenant Philip Woolf was brought back to a temporary hospital for war-wounded in Fishmonger's Hall, beside London Bridge, and later convalesced in the country. He was sent back to the Front and fought in France till the end of the war. He managed to find Cecil's grave. 'I do not think that Philip ever completely recovered from Cecil's death', wrote Leonard.[55]

The second and private publication of the Hogarth Press, in 1918, was a small booklet – four inches by three – of fifteen poems by Cecil

---

53 'An Englishman', *The Nation & Athenaeum* 4 Aug 1923. Reprinted in *Essays . . . etc*, 1927

54 15 Dec 1917. Berg. Bourlon is about 5 miles from Cambrai.

55 *Beginning Again*

Woolf, written before the war. They are no good. Philip wrote in his touching preface that they might, had Cecil lived, have been 'revised and re-polished'. Philip wrote to thank Leonard and Virginia: 'There's no book now which means more to me.'

A new friend in 1918 was the Jewish painter Mark Gertler, depressive, self-obsessed and tubercular, who had been Carrington's lover. He came for an Asheham weekend – when the rain came in through the ceiling on to his bed – and to dinner at Hogarth House, with Leonard's other new friend, Kot. Gertler said afterwards that most of the conversation had been about 'Jews, Judaism, the relation of Jews to other people, their differences, their faults, and virtues, evolution, etc etc.'[56] Some shred of the evening may survive in Leonard's eloquent description of Kot in *Beginning Again*. Kot was an 'uncomfortable' man, like an Old Testament prophet. 'There are some Jews who, though their ancestors have lived for centuries in European ghettoes, are born with certain characteristics which the sun and sand of the desert beat into the bodies and minds of Semites. The heat of the desert burns their bodies until they are tempered like steel; it tempers their minds until they seem to be purified of all spiritual grit, leaving in mind and soul only pure, undiluted, austere, fanatical passion.' This is Leonard's myth of himself as well as of Kot.

Kot was a friend of Katherine Mansfield, whom the Woolfs met with Lady Ottoline Morrell at Garsington Manor. They agreed to print Katherine's sixty-eight-page story *Prelude*, in an edition of three hundred copies. Leonard machined it on a larger, borrowed machine belonging to a jobbing printer round the corner from them in Richmond, and Barbara Hiles came for three days a week to help with the type-setting, in return for her fare from Hampstead, lunch, and a share in the profits, if any.

Barbara was put in a room at the top of Hogarth House to set up the type. It was winter (early 1918) and the room was icy. Coal was rationed and Leonard was careful with it. When Barbara caught a bad cold,

---

56 To Mary Hutchinson 23 June 1918. Texas

Lytton intervened,[57] and from then on Barbara had a 'small fire' in her room every day. When there was a bad air-raid Leonard would not let her risk the journey back to Hampstead. She huddled with the whole household in the basement kitchen: the servants Lottie Hope and Nelly Boxall in a single camp-bed on one side of the range, Virginia in a camp-bed on the other, Barbara under the table – and Leonard on top of the table, silencing Virginia's jokes about his precariousness, and the young servants' giggles, with a stern 'Be quiet!'[58]

The Woolf's next assistant was Alix Sargant-Florence, who had just graduated from Newnham and was helping Leonard with the research for *Empire and Commerce in Africa.* She too on her first day was put in the top room, to continue with the setting of *Prelude.* Once they had shown her what to do, the Woolfs went out for a walk. When they came back, 'I told them, to their astonishment, that I could not possibly carry on, it was much too boring'.[59] So that was the end of that.

Virginia had a close but subtly rivalrous friendship with Katherine Mansfield. Leonard liked Katherine but thought she did not like him. In fact, she envied Virginia for having Leonard to care for her, as she told 'Jack', her husband John Middleton Murry – who was sentimental about Katherine, who was seriously ill, and at the same time neglectful of her.

Leonard loved the 'cynical, amoral, ribald, witty' side of Katherine. No one, he said, made him laugh as much as she, which is saying something, as although his dead-pan humour always made other people laugh, he no longer laughed out loud much, as he had in Cambridge days. He was more likely to respond to a joke with a gruffly approving 'Huh huh', or a grunt of appreciation. Morgan Forster could still make him laugh aloud: 'Dear Leonard, I would gladly make you laugh again, but one cannot write the word f—— every time, and I'm sure that was the reason.'[60]

*

57 Barbara was Carrington's great friend, and therefore a friend of Lytton's.

58 Barbara Bagenal in Joan Russell Noble (ed): *Recollections of Virginia Woolf* Peter Owen 1972

59 Alix Strachey, *idem*

60 EMF to LW 2 Jan 1924

In a catch-up letter written from Asheham on 8 September 1918, Leonard told Margaret that Virginia was well, and that the garden had produced '1 cwt potatoes, some broad beans, French beans, Japanese anemones, nasturtia, phlox & dahlias & a forest of weeds'. He had corrected the proofs of his *Co-operation and the Future of Industry*, and 'it is going to be a nasty-looking book'.[61] The 'output of his mind' was 500 words a day, and the output of Virginia's 300. (She was writing her second novel, *Night and Day*, as well as reviews.) The next weekend was to be 'the culminating glory of the Woolfs & Asheham', as the Webbs were coming to stay.

Margaret enquired jealously whether Leonard and Virginia had ended up 'wrecks' after the visit. No, replied Leonard, and 'the Webbs were really rather nice and human – in a strange inhuman way'. Their conversation was incessant; Beatrice Webb fell asleep after dinner and Sidney talked gamely on through her snores. They brought a spirit lamp with them, and at six on the Sunday morning Sidney made tea in his room and took it along to Beatrice's, and then read to her until breakfast time. On Sunday afternoon they all went for a walk on the Downs, and Sidney, waiting for their wives to catch up, bet Leonard that Beatrice was telling Virginia that marriage was the 'waste-paper basket of the emotions'. He was right.[62]

'At anyrate today I am the wife of an editor', Virginia wrote in her diary on 8 September 1918. Leonard had deputised for the editor of *War & Peace* for a few months, commissioning reviews from Lytton, whose *Eminent Victorians* was the publishing sensation of 1918. Leonard now had the wildly ambitious idea of transforming *War & Peace* into an international socialist review under the aegis of the Labour Party, with an international board, to be published in two or three languages. The scheme was put to Arnold Rowntree,[63] who financed *War & Peace*, and he seemed keen. Ramsay MacDonald,

---

61 It came out from Allen & Unwin the following year.

62 Virginia recorded it as 'waste pipe' of the emotions. But then, as Leonard wrote, she was never 'an accurate reporter of what people said'.

63 A nephew of Joseph Rowntree, Arnold Rowntree looked after the family's magazine business, Westminster Press and Associated Papers.

leader of the parliamentary Labour Party, appeared to be equally enthusiastic.

But at the last moment MacDonald brusquely withdrew his support, which meant the project had no Labour backing. Leonard never forgave him for this piece of treachery.[64] Rowntree decided that the only way forward was to abandon the international socialist aspect, and Leonard agreed to edit a straightforward journal to be called the *International Review*.

On 11 November 1918 the Prime Minister, David Lloyd George, announced to the House of Commons: 'At eleven o'clock this morning came to an end the cruellest and most terrible war that has ever scourged mankind. I hope we may say that thus, this fateful morning, came to an end all wars.'

Leonard and Virginia, at home in Richmond, heard the maroons which signalled the war's end. Virginia had an appointment in London. Leonard's diary: 'Trains packed streets crowded. V had gone to dentist I could find no one I wanted to see so walked Wigmore St & met V there . . . Then [underground] trains so crowded we could not get in at all. Eventually got to Waterloo and so home.'

They did not feel the war was properly over until, a few weeks later, they saw that the Belgian confectioner on Richmond Hill had chocolate creams in the window. After four years of chocolate deprivation, this was heaven. They ate the chocolate creams sacramentally, sitting over the fire.

Although he had not suffered as those who fought in France and Flanders had suffered, Leonard Woolf had cared for the wife he loved through a severe breakdown and, with her, started the Hogarth Press. He had worked fanatically, committing his energies to the one topic:

64 MacDonald probably did not trust the Rowntrees, who were Liberal not Labour. He was to be out of Parliament anyway for the next four years, losing his seat in the General Election of December 1918.

how to prevent future war. Public figures who had been just great names to him were now colleagues and friends. He was an established documentary journalist and political propagandist, an experienced public speaker, and the author of distinguished books. He was an eminence – a grey eminence – in the evolving Labour Party. Approaching his thirty-eighth birthday, he was well-placed for any career in public life that he might choose. Just before the end of the war, he was invited by an independent left-leaning group, the Seven Universities Democratic Association,[65] to allow his name to go forward as their prospective parliamentary candidate. He cavilled, and did not commit himself.

For this was the man of whom Virginia, during their engagement, had written that 'he wants . . . to keep outside Government and do things on his own account',[66] and that had not really changed.

65 The universities of Birmingham, Bristol, Durham, Leeds, Liverpool, Manchester and Sheffield elected collectively their own MP.
66 To Madge Vaughan, June 1912

10

Editor

In early 1918, the Woolfs heard about an extraordinary and indecent manuscript by James Joyce in the hands of Harriet Weaver, for which she sought a publisher; and on 14 April, a Sunday, Leonard recorded that Miss Weaver, 'a very mild blue-eyed advanced spinster', came to tea, bringing with her the incomplete manuscript of *Ulysses* wrapped in brown paper. They read 'this remarkable piece of dynamite', and would have published it, but neither of the printers to whom Leonard showed the manuscript was prepared to take it on for fear of prosecution.

Miss Weaver was the friend and patron of T.S.Eliot, and through this connection Leonard was emboldened to write to the poet, on 19 October 1918: 'My wife and I have started a small private Printing Press, and we print and publish privately short works which would not otherwise find a publisher easily. We both very much liked your book, Prufrock.'[1] He wondered whether Mr Eliot would care to let them see more of his poems. 'I should add that we are amateurs at printing but we could, if you liked, let you see our last production.'

T.S.Eliot came to tea. Originally from St Louis, he had been settled

---

1 *Prufrock and Other Observations* was published by Harriet Weaver's Egoist Press in 1917; Eliot inscribed Leonard's copy for him at the time when *Poems* was being printed by Hogarth, probably when he came to dinner on 2 Feb 1919.

in England since his marriage to an Englishwoman, Vivien[2] Haigh-Wood, in 1915. He edited Harriet Weaver's *The Egoist*, and earned his living as a clerk in the foreign loans department of Lloyds Bank. At first the Woolfs found him stiff and inhibited, but he quickly got on sprightlier terms with Virginia. They printed seven of Eliot's poems in paper covers. Generally, Leonard got 'terribly irritated' by what he was printing, seeing the lines appear again and again as they came off the machine. 'But I never tired and still do not tire of those lines which were a new note in poetry and came from the heart of the Eliot of those days.'[3]

By the beginning of November 1919, 140 copies of *Poems* had been sold, and Eliot recevied a cheque for £1.13.10d. Virginia was asked to review *Poems* for the *Athenaeum* (anonymously), even though she was the co-publisher. She got into difficulties, and Leonard picked up where she left off, 'and then we cobbled the two parts of it together hoping no one would recognise either of us'.[4] Literary incest can hardly go further, though it frequently did: Virginia also reviewed for the *Athenaeum* the Hogarth Press's essay *Critic in Judgment* by J.Middleton Murry – who was editor of the *Athenaeum*.

Vanessa had her third child, a daughter named Angelica, at Charleston on Christmas Day 1918. Angelica's father was Duncan Grant, though Bloomsbury truth-telling did not extend so far as to acknowledge this. Vanessa had confided in Virginia the previous May; Virginia did not tell Leonard for some time. Clive generously behaved as if Angelica were his own daughter. Angelica herself was not told until she was seventeen.

The Bells' two boys, Julian and Quentin (aged ten and eight) were to come to stay with the Woolfs at Hogarth House for a while after the birth, to relieve the pressure on Vanessa. 'I hope Leonard won't mind having them', she wrote to Virginia, 'but I think he likes brats and they'll be thrilled by anything he can tell them about his Cingalese

---

2 Or Vivienne, or Vivian
3 *Beginning Again*
4 VW to Philip Morrell, 30 June 1919

adventures.'[5] Although children always loved Virginia, the boys' fortnight at Hogarth House was a disaster. She had 'a fit of melancholy', and although she was 'divinely reassured by L.'[6] she was not well. She had trouble with her teeth, and over the years had most of them out. Extracting teeth was thought to be therapeutic. On 2 January 1919 she had another removed, and afterwards stayed in bed with an ominous headache. Leonard took Julian and Quentin out – to the Natural History Museum, to Hampton Court – but he was too busy, and Virginia too unwell, for the arrangement to be sustainable. On 9 January he took them to 46 Gordon Square, to be cared for by Maynard's cook and maid. He felt badly about it, and apologised to Vanessa.

Tom Eliot came to dinner, with Marjorie Strachey and Walter Lamb as fellow guests, in early April 1919, and brought with him his wife Vivien, 'a washed out, elderly & worn looking little woman' in Virginia's view.[7] (Vivien was six years younger than Virginia, as was Eliot himself.) Eliot became a familiar guest, generally without Vivien. Later that April there was another dinner, for Douglas Cole and his new wife Margaret[8] – though Leonard's political friends and Fabian colleagues were never Virginia's.

She felt that 'the only honest people are the artists, & that these social reformers & philanthropists get so out of hand, & harbour so many discreditable desires under the disguise of loving their kind, that in the end there's more fault to find with in them than with us'.[9] Leonard, towards the end of his life, voiced exactly the same thought. 'I am sure that if one could look deep into the minds of those who are on the Left in politics (including myself), Liberals, revolutionaries, socialists, communists,

5 13 Dec 1918. Berg
6 VW Diary 3 Dec 1918
7 VW Diary 10 April 1919
8 Margaret Cole nee Postgate, writer and political activist, had a First Class Degree in Classics from Girton College, Cambridge, and met her husband when working, unpaid, for the Fabian Research Department. They were married in 1918. She was to edit Beatrice Webb's diaries.
9 Diary 19 July 1919

pacifists, and humanitarians, one would find that their political beliefs and desires were connected with some very strange goings on down among their ids and their unconscious', evidenced by the patent dissonance between their 'gentle highmindedness' and their 'absurd verbal violence'.[10] He included himself in this.

While Leonard was comfortable among the artists, he preferred sometimes to stay behind when Virginia went for weekends with the Morrells at Garsington, or to dinner with society hostesses such as Sybil Colefax or Emerald Cunard.

In January 1919 the owner of Asheham House warned the Woolfs that he would be giving them notice. 'Ah but how happy we've been at Asheham! It was a most melodious time.'[11] In March they leased, sight unseen, three tiny, conjoined cottages in Cornwall. Katherine Mansfield had lived there with Middleton Murry; D.H.Lawrence and Frieda had occupied them too, and Ka (Cox), who had married Will Arnold-Forster, had a cottage nearby. The Woolfs never went down there even once, and in November Leonard surrendered the lease. Virginia finished her second novel, *Night and Day*; Leonard read it in two mornings and evenings and pronounced it melancholy but, to her relief, very good.

In June their offer for the Round House, the relic of an old mill in the centre of Lewes, was accepted. Immediately, and by chance, they saw on a hoarding an advertisement for the auction of Monks House in Rodmell. Virginia bicycled over, and fell in love with it. Leonard looked it over, and felt the same. They sold the Round House on, and on 1 July cycled into Lewes to bid – through their solicitor – for Monks House at the auction at the White Hart Hotel, and secured it.

The village of Rodmell slopes down to the water meadows of the river Ouse. It is across the river from Asheham; Leonard and Virginia were familiar with the outside of their new house, as they often walked over to the shop in Rodmell, crossing the Ouse by the bridge at Southease.

---

10 LW, *Downhill All the Way*
11 VW Diary 5 May 1919

Monks House stood on a track leading out of the village across the wide flat marshland called the Brooks and towards the river, against the backdrop of the Downs.

It was the luxuriant, overgrown garden that attracted them, cluttered with sheds and outhouses, backing on to the churchyard and overlooked by the tower of the twelfth-century St Peter's Church. Monks House had belonged to the Clear family for most of the eighteenth century, and then to the Glazebrooks, who were millers. (Broken millstones were still in the garden when the Woolfs took over, and Leonard had them set into paths.) Monks House was the name given to it by the farmer Jacob Verrall who bought the house from the last Glazebrook executors.[12] He had recently died, and Leonard and Virginia paid his sister Lydia Brand £580, plus £120 for the freehold. 'I hope you and Mrs Woolf will learn to love the little house as much as our brother did, he simply adored it', wrote Mrs Brand.

On 14 August there was an auction sale in the garden at Monks House of the Verralls' miscellaneous accumulation of forty-two years. Leonard bid successfully for curtains, blankets, table-linen, a table and chairs, cutlery and crockery, glassware, an oil stove, a mincing machine, apple trays, a wheelbarrow, a garden roller, garden tools, and the contents of the garden shed. He also bought three pictures painted on wood by, he imagined, some early nineteenth-century Glazebrook – stiff, dark, 'primitive' paintings, unframed, one of them a line-up of five children; they all three hang in the house to this day.

On Monday, 1 September 1919 they spent their first night in Monks House. Leonard, experienced now in tying up books and papers into bundles, organised their transport across the Ouse from Asheham in two trips by horse-drawn wagon. Virginia was saddened by the loss of the 'flawless beauty' of Asheham. She disliked the chilliness of Monks House, but it improved, she thought, 'after the fashion of a mongrel who wins your heart'.[13] Leonard was captivated. He thought that the

---

12 Verralls had previously lived at Monk's Gate in Horsham (though Jacob and his sister had been brought up in Iford), which explains the naming of the house in Rodmell. See letter from Stanley Godman, *West Sussex Gazette* 31 Dec 1964.

13 VW Diary 28 Sept 1919

house one inhabits was 'the most powerful moulder' not only of one's life but of oneself – and Monks House was to be where he, who thought of himself as the Wandering Jew, found home.

There was no electricity, no mains water or drainage. They had an earth closet in the garden, and indoors they put a chair, with a cut-away cane seat over a bucket, up in the loft. Rodmell was an agricultural village, with a pub, a post office, a forge and the shop. Because of changes in farming practice, the rural population was falling.[14] Before the Woolfs came, a rector of Rodmell recorded that 'the walls in the village are crumbling and broken – the cottages are in a sad state'[15] The decline was to be arrested by weekenders, retirees and country-loving incomers, but in 1919 the only other middle-class residents were the rector, Mr Hawkesford, and his wife, who 'suffered intensely, but not silently, from the boredom of village life'. No one in Rodmell had a motor car, and the only means of transport into Lewes, four miles away along an unmetalled road,[16] were legs, or bicycle, or pony and trap.

There were at Monks House, in 1919, three and a half bedrooms. The ceilings were low, and the downstairs crudely partitioned into a series of small rooms It was a brick and flint cottage, set into the side of a slope, and the uneven brick floors sweated moisture. When it rained heavily, a stream flowed down the eight steps from the garden into the kitchen, continued across the sloping floor, and exited through cracks at the front.[17] At the foot of a parallel set of steps from the garden, water welled up as if from a spring. Mr Dean[18] assured them that the damp was a mere matter of blocked gutters.

---

14 Nevertheless there would still have been far more people about in the Sussex countryside than there are now, their large families often sharing accommodation in small cottages.

15 *Victorian Rodmell* – pamphlet sold in aid of St Peter's Rodmell Restoration Fund.

16 A road not then bisected by the roaring and congested A27.

17 The depth of the step made after Leonard's death in order to level the kitchen floor gives an indication of the steepness of the original slope.

18 C.C.A. Dean's business in Rodmell included that of builder-handyman, farrier, blacksmith, wheelwright and undertaker. See Frank Dean, *Strike While the Iron's Hot*, privately published by Susan Rowland 1994.

The Woolfs had neither the money for nor the concept of 'making over' a house. What this socially and intellectually sophisticated pair, like others of their kind, were content to have, in 1919, would be condemned in Britain nowadays as unfit for human habitation. They seem privileged, because they had servants. But cooking, washing and cleaning were labour-intensive to a degree unimagineable today. Leonard, as early as the 1950s, described the change in living standards in his lifetime as a 'revolution'.[19] In *Beginning Again*, he commented that when he first came to Rodmell, village life and the village people 'were probably nearer to Chaucer's England than to the England of 1963.'

Lytton visited, and was amused, telling his brother James: 'They strike one as being absolutely happy; he looks more gaunt and eminent than ever, and she a school girl, almost, in cheap red beads.'[20] By this time Leonard had improved the kitchen by incorporating into it the coal store and scullery, but until they installed a solid-fuel range, their meals were cooked and brought in by Mrs Dedman, who lived round the bending lane in Pear Tree Cottage. Her husband William, the church verger, had been Jacob Verrall's gardener for twenty-one years. Before the Woolfs even moved in, he offered his services, at nine pence an hour, enquiring in beautiful handwriting whether he should go round and plant out vegetables, 'it is quite time they was in if they are to be ready in the winter and the spring.' William Dedman initiated Leonard into the garden; and Leonard weeded, sowed a promiscuous selection of flower seeds, and harvested the apples and pears. He had to make an agreement with Virginia to take regular afternoon walks with her, twice a week on set days, otherwise he would never have left the garden.

In November, they went to see Lytton and Carrington at Tidmarsh, where Saxon was also visiting, 'mute & sealed until Sunday night, when he flowered for a time & talked of Greek'.[21] Lytton, a little invalidish,

---

19 LW, *Principia Politica* 1953
20 19 Sept 1920. Quoted in S.P.Rosenbaum, *The Bloomsbury Group* University of Toronto Press 1995
21 VW Diary 15 Nov 1919

and writing his *Queen Victoria* (to be dedicated to Virginia), was enamoured of Ralph Partridge, a handsome classicist in his twenties. Ralph was falling in love with Carrington, and gradually a *ménage à trois* was established at Tidmarsh. Leonard described Ralph as apparently a typical public-school type, but with an 'extraordinary childlike emotional vulnerability'[22] beneath the surface.

Ralph needed a job. At Lytton's request, he became the next in a series of part-time assistants at the Hogarth Press. In May 1919 they finished printing Virginia's story 'Kew Gardens', 'in its own small way and within its limits perfect', in Leonard's opinion. For the first time, they sent a copy of their new production to *The Times Literary Supplement*, where it received a rapturous review,[23] which resulted in orders for the little book flooding in through the letter-box of Hogarth House. This was a significant straw in the wind, both for Virginia and for the Press. They then printed a second edition of Virginia's story 'The Mark on the Wall', from *Two Stories*. Leonard ordered a brass plate – 'The Hogarth Press' – to fix on the front door.

Leonard's 'The Three Jews' was not reissued; but they set and printed themselves his *Three Stories of the East*[24] with a ravishing paper cover: a woodcut by Carrington of a tiger surrounded by palm trees, which they printed in coral and amber-gold. He received on 2 May 1921 a rave review by H.Hamilton Fyfe in the *Daily Mail*, in particular for the Ceylon pearl-fishing story, 'Pearls and Swine', which should find a place 'among the best short stories of the world'. This review elicited a visit to Rodmell from the literary agent Henry Holt, offering to sell stories by Leonard Woolf to magazines in the United States for £200 each.

Holt had not even read 'Pearls and Swine' when he made his pitch. When he did he had a shock, as did his corresponding agent in America, Ann Watkins, who wrote to Holt: 'You see, we in the States . . . veer from

22 *Downhill All The Way*

23 Unsigned, as were all *TLS* reviews. It was by Harold Child, an Oxford classicist and *Times* writer of light leaders.

24 All three had been written when he first returned from Ceylon: 'A Tale Told by Moonlight', 'Pearls and Swine' (already discussed) and 'The Two Brahmans', the retelling of a Sinhalese folktale, a fable about the destructive yet socially supportive pride of caste, not unconnected with the theme of 'The Three Jews'.

the shocking, the revolting – the truth. But holy, suffering cats! How Woolf can write!' Holt tried to persuade Leonard to tailor stories for the American market. 'I may never again have patience to bully a man into making several thousand pounds a year, so, for the last time, *do think it over.*' He even sent Leonard a plot outline. Leonard just let it lie. Holt gave up.

Virginia's *Night and Day* was published by Duckworth. The Hogarth Press had never tackled a full-length work. They had to decide whether printing was their hobby, or a growing business. In November 1921 Leonard invested in a bigger printing machine, a Minerva, 'a formidable monster, a very heavy, treadle, platen machine'. After treadling away at it 'for fours hours at a stretch, as I often did', Leonard felt that he had taken a great deal of exercise.[25] It was too heavy for the dining room of Hogarth House; it would have broken the floorboards. So they put it in the larder in the basement.

The Woolfs' Minerva printing machine, now at Sissinghurst.

1919 was the year of the Paris Peace Conference. All political life revolved round it. There was a suggestion that Leonard should attend, as Gilbert Murray's secretary, but he remained in the background. In April, Sidney Webb asked him to provide the chairman of the Parliamentary Labour Party, a Scots miner, with notes and documentation for a speech responding to what Lloyd George was 'likely' to say on his return from the Peace Conference, 'as soon as you can'. In May, Beatrice Webb asked him for references 'containing apt quotations' in

25 *Downhill All The Way*

French or English 'demonstrating the close connection between the greed of markets and the arming of nations and the outbreak of war.'

As well as negotiating the Treaty of Versailles, conference approved the setting up of a commission on the proposed League of Nations, chaired by President Woodrow Wilson. The British Prime Minister Lloyd George was not really an enthusiast. He had pinned the General Election of 1918 on beating the Germans, with little discussion of the peace; Leonard was disgusted when he was returned with a big majority. Clemenceau, the ageing Prime Minister of France, never really believed in the League either. Sir Robert Cecil[26] was the chief British Foreign Office advocate of the League, with Philip Noel-Baker[27] and the Woolfs' friend Sydney Waterlow on his team; Molly Hamilton and Helena Swanwick[28] attended as female representatives of the British Empire.

While this was going on in Paris, Leonard was editing the *International Review*, lecturing to Co-operative Quakers and at the South Place Ethical Society, and having 'Trouble w censor over Lenin's speech'.[29] The trouble, and the speech, came through Theodore Rothstein, who had in his possession the Russian text of a number of Lenin's speeches, and offered one to Leonard for publication in the *International Review*. Rothstein was a young Russian Jew and the unofficial ambassador of the unrecognised Bolshevik government. He was the first fanatical communist Leonard ever met: 'Communists, Roman Catholics, Rosicrucians, Adventists, all those sects which ferociously maintain a divine or absolute truth', filled Leonard all his life with 'melancholic misery'.[30]

It was a cloak-and dagger affair. Rothstein instructed Leonard to walk up the Strand on the inside of the pavement, timing himself so as

26 Husband of Eleanor (Nelly) Cecil who was an old family friend of Virginia's.

27 Leonard knew Philip Noel-Baker, a campaigner for disarmament and a passionate supporter of the League, as plain Phil Baker; during the war he married Irene Noel, a valued friend of Virginia's, and in 1922 he joined his name to hers. A Fellow of King's, Cambridge, from 1914, he was chief organiser of the Friends' Ambulance Unit during the war.

28 Suffrage activist, feminist, pacifist, and journalist, member of UDC and ILP. She committed suicide after the outbreak of World War II in 1939.

29 LW Diary 19 March 1919

30 D*ownhill All the Way*

to pass under the clock on the Law Courts at precisely 2.30. Rothstein, coming from the opposite direction and on the outside of the pavement, would pass him at precisely 2.30 and slip an envelope from his right hand to Leonard's. The plan worked perfectly. But fantastic though it seemed to Leonard, Rothstein must have been trailed by a Secret Service man, because the police raided the printers of the *International Review* and stopped publication.

Within a year of the Bolsheviks seizing power, reports of their brutal methods were filtering through. Leonard's disillusionment was all the sharper because of the elation he had felt in 1917. He remained an active campaigner for Britain to trade with the new regime, and 'I hope you don't think I'm anti-Bolshevik', he wrote to Margaret Llewelyn Davies in April 1920. 'I'm not, I think they're the only people who've made an honest and serious attempt to practise what I believe in. But I can't help seeing their faults and mistakes which, if persisted in, will undo the good they've done. Perhaps however it's only the original sin of Governments.' He was against the anti-Bolshevik hysteria which gripped Britain, and against intervention. But as time passed the 'senseless barbarism' of communist society appalled him, as did Soviet foreign policy – which was not only to fish in troubled waters, but to 'make the waters troubled so that they could fish.'[31] His clear-eyed rejection of the Soviet regime was to isolate him from the hard core of the British Left.

In Paris, a final draft of the Covenant of a League of Nations was agreed and adopted. The League of Nations was born. President Wilson went home, leaving foreign ministers and diplomats to tie up loose ends, which included the intractable problem of feeding homeless refugees in chaotic, post-war Europe: Leonard joined the Fight the Famine Council.

By the end of the twentieth century it was acceptable to marvel how 'such a project as the League of Nations could be taken seriously . . . Its very name evokes images of earnest bureaucrats, fuzzy liberal supporters, futile resolutions and, above all, failure'.[32] It is too easy to disregard

31 *Downhill All The Way*
32 Margaret Macmillan, *Peacemakers: the Paris Conference of 1919 and its Attempt to End War* John Murray 2001

the high hopes which were invested in the League in the aftermath of the terrible war. It seemed to many that 'under the League of Nations the reign of freedom and brotherhood must prevail.'[33] The historian Asa Briggs, born in the north of England in 1921, was taught in his elementary school to believe in the League of Nations as a previous generation had been taught to believe in Empire.[34]

Although Leonard was not present at the Peace Conference, his work and his ideas emphatically were. His *International Government* was reprinted, and available in the French translation. Sidney Waterlow had already condensed the book for the Foreign Office and, preparing a paper for the British delegation in Paris, wrote that 'where a mass of facts has been collected and sifted with great ability, as is the case with Mr Woolf's work, it would be folly to attempt to do the work all over again . . . My detailed descriptions of the various existing organs of international government are therefore for the most part lifted almost verbatim . . . from Mr Woolf's book.'[35]

Lord Robert Cecil 'incorporated virtually the whole of Woolf's ideas into the British Draft Covenant which he gave to Woodrow Wilson in Paris.'[36] Lord Robert however gave Leonard – privately – a cogent criticism of *International Government*. 'I need not say I read your book . . . with great pleasure and admiration.' But it seemed to Cecil that a lot of what Leonard advocated had more to do with international co-operation than with international government.

Alfred Zimmern, son of German Jewish immigrants, a fellow of New College, and head of the League of Nations section at the Foreign Office, also acknowledged in his book *The League of Nations and the Rule of Law* (1935) 'the masterly analysis of Mr Woolf'. Zimmern received a knighthood, whereas Leonard's backroom influence did not bring him public recognition.

Lytton had public recognition, as the author of *Eminent Victorians*;

33 Malcolm Muggeridge, *Tread Softly Because You Tread Upon My Jokes*
34 In conversation with VG
35 F.O.Confidential, 3 Jan 1919. Quoted in Duncan Wilson: *Leonard Woolf: A Political Biography* St Martin's Press 1978
36 From Philip Noel-Baker's obituary of LW, *The Times* 21 Aug 1969

Leonard joked drily that his own prestige was much enhanced when people learned that they were acquainted.[37] From 1919 Maynard Keynes, too, was a public man. He attended the Peace Conference as chief Treasury representative. Finding the terms of the Treaty of Versailles so outrageous that he walked out and left Paris, he wrote *The Economic Consequences of the Peace* in two months flat at Charleston (taking time out to go to the races at Lewes with Leonard, who lost £2). It was published in December 1919 and a month later in the USA. More than 100,000 copies were sold, and it was translated into eleven languages. He believed that the sums demanded in reparation from Germany were inhumane and unrealistic, and that Germany's humiliation and bankruptcy would have a disastrous political effect; he saw the way to European peace through stable economic integration.

Leonard had come out publicly against the terms of the Peace Treaty before Keynes, as soon as the text became available in June 1919. In a leading article in the *International Review* he excoriated a document founded on 'military guarantees, vindictive punishment, subjection and economic discrimination'. But the *International Review* did not have a large circulation. Some people became self-important in 1919. Morgan Forster stayed the night at Hogarth House on 5 November, when Sydney Waterlow came to dinner, 'full of boyish delight at the various expeditions he is making, in special trains, to all the capitals of Europe for the promotion of international amity. Woolf hissed "Ridiculous" and poor Sidney collapsed.'[38]

Leonard never got to go in special trains to all the capitals of Europe. He never got to go anywhere. He had written his book on Africa without setting foot in Africa. The Webbs in 1922 wanted to send someone to Russia, to investigate 'the Soviet system of government and its later developments'. Was there, Beatrice asked Leonard, 'the remotest chance of your being able to do it?'[39]

---

37 To LS, 18 Aug 1921, re LS's *Queen Victoria*

38 EMF to Florence Barger, *Selected Letters* ed Mary Lago and P.N.Furbank Vol I, Collins 1983

39 Beatrice Webb to LW 26 June 1922. Norman Mackenzie (ed): *The Letters of Sidney and Beatrice Webb* Vol III, Cambridge University Press 1978

No, there was not. Virginia could not be left for long. Their close companionship, and the alternating routines of Hogarth House and Monks House, provided the loving and secure base which made it possible for her to take risks with herself and with her writing, and to make scintillating forays out into the world of people and parties. It was becoming a co-dependency. Leonard had grown to need her need of him.

Even though he had violent opinions and expressed them on occasion violently, there was something withheld about Leonard Woolf. He did not use Virginia's vulnerability as an excuse not to do things, but her vulnerability legitimated an existing tendency in him towards self-limitation. (He might have called it cowardice.) From his early middle-age, he had an aura of controlled or reserved potency.

At the end of November 1919 Arnold Rowntree told Leonard that the Trust was no longer prepared to finance the *International Review.* There was not the public for it. Leonard was producing for every issue an 'International Diary', covering the main events of the month, and 'Facts and Documents', which consisted of thirty or forty pages of abstracts – of international treaties, military pronouncements, foreign government initiatives and, for example, the full text of the new German constitution. Rowntree incorporated the *International Review* into another journal in his stable, the venerable *Contemporary Review*, for which Leonard agreed to compile sixteen pages of 'Facts and Documents' for the same salary, £250 a year. Less than a year later, on Leonard's forty-first birthday in 1921, Rowntree axed 'Facts and Documents' in favour of a single signed article by Leonard on foreign affairs. Leonard left at the end of that year.

In December 1919 both the Woolfs, exhausted, and temporarily without domestic help, became ill at Hogarth House; added to which, 'all our drains are exposed', as Leonard reported to Lytton.[40] They went to Monks House for the New Year: 'Pruned trees and my finger. Rain & wind.' Leonard calculated in the back of his diary that he had earned £578.7s.8d during 1919, and Virginia £163.17s.0d.

*

40 LW to Lytton Strachey 24 Jan 1920. Texas

Leonard's *Empire and Commerce in Africa: A Study in Economic Imperialism* was published in London and in New York in January 1920. In that book he let rip. Some sections read like machine-gun fire crackling out of his typewriter, aimed at the whole imperial project, and particularly at Captain F.T.Lugard, later Lord Lugard, who collared Uganda as a British Protectorate: 'Psychologically there is no difference between Captain Lugard and the people in past centuries who burnt and tortured men and women from the highest of religious motives.' The *Manchester Guardian* reviewer who said the book would irritate most old Africa hands was right.

Lytton did not read it for five months – and then found that, at last, his friend had written something he could admire. 'It seems to me a most important work, done with superb power, perfect clarity, and marvellous, devastating detachment. Those final pages on Uganda really remind one of Swift and Voltaire.'[41] No praise could have been better designed to please Leonard. Goldie Lowes Dickinson's praise of the book was lapidary: 'I like your fierce and somber irony.'

Leonard was still writing for the *New Statesman*, which had doubled its circulation during the war years, and also for the *Nation* (which Rowntree merged with the *Athenaeum* in 1921). He went twice a week into the *New Statesman* office, and political journalism kept him in the loop, as on 9 February 1920: 'Phil Baker asked me come League of Nations re Trial of German War Criminals. Discussed it w a Norwegian and w Lord R. Cecil.' Philip Snowden, a leader of the Labour Party from 1919, asked Leonard in 1920 to write something for the ILP. He knocked off a short book, *Socialism and Co-operation*, for which he was paid £25.

Leonard constantly changed gear between his different worlds. On 19 February 1920 he went to tea at the 1917 Club to hear Roger Fry speak on modern art to a group that included Vanessa and Duncan, Clive, Arthur Hobhouse, James Strachey and Alix – and then on to a meeting at Central Hall, Westminster about the importance of trade with Russia, with Helena Swanwick in the chair, at which he spoke. He proposed the toast to 'the Sinhalese Nation' at a Ceylon Reform Society dinner, and introduced their

41 14 June 1920. Berg

deputation into the House of Commons to meet MPs. Leonard had access.

The Seven Universities Democratic Association came back to him in spring 1920 with their invitation to stand as their parliamentary candidate. In his capacity as Secretary to the Labour Party Committee on International and on Imperial Questions (the original committee was divided in two in 1924, with Leonard appointed Secretary to both), he observed at close range the life of backbench Labour MPs, which seemed to him 'the acme of futility and boredom'. But he agreed to stand. He knew he had little chance of getting in; and the next General Election did not come up for another two years. He was committed to private life and to the disposition of his own time. After Virginia abandoned the household accounts in 1915 he took over, keeping a record of every day's expenses – everything from Nelly and Lottie's wages to a pair of shoelaces – and totting up the weekly, monthly, yearly totals. It was a fat account book, his writing was small, the last page was not filled until 1955. He kept a record of his personal expenses in even smaller writing, in the back of his diaries. He had a talent for small pleasures, punctuating their hard-working lives with treats. To please himself, he took the odd afternoon off to watch county cricket.

In summer 1920, to replace Noel Brailsford (who was on the tour of Russia that Leonard might have taken), he took on, temporarily, the writing of leading articles on foreign affairs for the *Nation*. Leonard went into the *Nation* offices in Adelphi Terrace, off the Strand, on Monday mornings to discuss with Massingham, the editor, what he would write for Saturday's paper, sometimes staying on for the regular Monday office lunch. It was a Liberal weekly – Rowntree, the proprietor, was a Liberal MP – and Massingham, in his sixties, was swinging sharply towards Labour. This made for dissension.

Molly MacCarthy was the moving spirit behind the Memoir Club, which brought together the old Bloomsbury friends[42] plus some attach-

42 The original 13 members were VW, LW, Molly and Desmond MacCarthy, Vanessa Bell, Clive Bell, Mary Hutchinson, Duncan Grant, Roger Fry, Lytton Strachey, Maynard Keynes, Sydney Waterlow, Morgan Forster. Bertrand Russell was also elected, but never came.

ments, and was intended to encourage Desmond to write the book he was not writing. (It was she who had produced a novel.[43]) Saxon Sydney-Turner, though elected, did not come. The Memoir Club met in the members' houses, and after dinner a number of them read aloud stories and memories from their joint or separate pasts. With time, the readings grew longer, the number of readers fewer – usually just two – and the meetings less frequent. Satire on personalities was well-received and frankness was encouraged, although – as Leonard wrote in this context – 'absolute frankness, even among the most intimate, tends to be relative frankness.'[44]

Leonard and Virginia were at the first Memoir Club meeting on 4 March 1920,[45] in Desmond MacCarthy's study in Wellington Square in Chelsea. At the second, in June, the meeting was at Hogarth House, and both the Woolfs read. 'Leonard was objective & triumphant', Virginia wrote in her diary, 'I subjective & most unpleasantly discomfited.' She soon found her voice, and shone more brightly than anyone – except, thought Leonard, for the occasional memorable contribution from Maynard Keynes.

Apart from Molly MacCarthy,[46] Leonard was the only member to fulfil one of the initial objectives: each person's collected papers were intended to contribute to an autobiography. Many of Leonard's papers for the Memoir Club were incorporated word for word, with minimal editing in the interests of clarity or discretion, into the autobiographies which he wrote in the 1960s: the account of his voyage out to Ceylon, the saga of the unfortunate Dutton, and the story of Annie Hopfengartner;[47] another was about his family and their antecedents,

---

43 *A Pier and a Band* Chatto & Windus 1918

44 *Downhill All The Way*

45 LW's diary, like VW's, confirms the date as 4 March, at Wellington Square; though in *Downhill All The Way* he wrote that the first meeting was on 6 March, and in Gordon Square.

46 Molly MacCarthy's contributions to the Memoir Club were published in the *Nation* under LW's literary editorship between Sep 1923 and June 1924, and published as *A Nineteenth-Century Childhood* by Heinemann.

47 There survives yet another and unpublished version, entitled 'The Story of Miss Gulbranson's Dog'.

another about 'the method' which he and Lytton had evolved at Trinity, and a later one about his childhood intimations of doom.

Another late Memoir Club story which went into his autobiography was about spending, with Virginia, a weekend with the Webbs, when Leonard got into an argument with Beatrice about the teaching of religion in schools. Leonard was adamantly against it. 'She seemed to get angry that I mildly[48] maintained my opinion, and marched up and down the room arguing almost violently. Indeed, up and down she marched faster and faster, and as she whisked herself round at each turn faster and faster, talking all the time, suddenly at one of the whisks or turns something in her skirt gave way and it fell on the floor entangling her feet. She stopped, picked it up, and holding it against her waist, continued her march up and down, never for a moment interrupting her passionate argument in favour of the teaching of religion in schools.'

In 1919 Maxim Gorky sent Kotelianski, from Moscow, his newly published memoir of Tolstoy, giving him the English translation rights. Kot brought it to the Woolfs with the suggestion that he and Leonard should translate it and the Hogarth Press should publish it. This was the beginning of a collaboration which included Virginia. The Hogarth Press published *Reminiscences of Leo Nicolayevitch Tolstoi* in 1920, selling 1,700 copies in the first year which was, for the Press, an unprecedented success. It was followed by *Tchekhov's Notebooks* in 1921, Dostoevsky's *Stavrogin's Confession*, Bunin's story *The Gentleman from San Francisco* and the *Autobiography* of Countess Tolstoy in 1922, and Tolstoy's *Love Letters* in 1923.

Leonard and Virginia taught themselves the basics of Russian. Kot would produce a handwritten draft translation, leaving spaces between the lines where Leonard (or Virginia) inserted a revised version. The next stage was to go back to the Russian and scrutinise the translation again, sentence by sentence. Kot was as much a perfectionist as Leonard. 'We would sometimes be a quarter of an hour arguing over a single word.'[49]

48 LW never maintained any argument 'mildly'. He put this story into *Sowing* (in the notably un-mild section on his attitude to religious belief).
49 *Beginning Again*

An attempt to get Desmond MacCarthy down on paper was made in May 1921. Costive as an author, Desmond was a famously entertaining talker. Leonard arranged for his stenographer from the *International Review*, Margaret Green, to sit in the corner during dinner at Hogarth House, and to take down Desmond's conversation in shorthand. Roger Fry was invited and, next day, wrote to Vanessa: 'We had a most successful party last night – got Desmond well on after two bottles of Chablis and he told some of his stories with great style and Miss Green (whom Virginia calls the chest of drawers – it's a terribly exact description) managed to take it all down. I'm sure Desmond suspected nothing.'[50] But 'Desmond's Table Talk' came out on paper as supremely dull; when Leonard sent Molly the transcript, he admitted defeat, and there was no 'next time'.

Molly was depressed by her deteriorating hearing, and by Desmond's chronic infidelities. Leonard thought of her as charming, amusing, and incompetent. 'Her vagueness and fluttering indecision must have been perpetually nourished by a lifetime of waiting for Desmond to return to dinner to which he had forgotten that he had invited several friends.'[51] In the letter to her with which he enclosed the disappointing transcript, he wrote: 'I hope you have now realized that NOTHING MATTERS and have also experienced the exhilarating effects of that belief. I should have liked to continue my diagnosis and therapeusis. *Nothing* matters.'

Virginia, in June 1921, collapsed again with depression and headache, and had three more teeth out. Leonard and Dr Ferguson, their Richmond GP, looked after her without recourse to 'nerve doctors' or professional nurses. Experience suggested to Leonard that it was these intrusive figures who had triggered Virginia's psychotic rage in the past. She might recover more quickly without them. It was, as Leonard conceded, 'a severe bout'. Virginia, when she resumed her diary in August, wrote that 'all the horrors of the dark cupboard of illness' had been

50 Denys Sutton (ed): *Letters of Roger Fry* Chatto & Windus 1972
51 *Beginning Again*

revealed to her once more – but also the compensations. 'To be tired & authorised to stay in bed is pleasant . . . I feel I can take stock of things in a leisurely way. Then the dark underworld has its fascinations as well as its terrors'; and she compared 'the fundamental security' of her present life, favourably, with its 'old fearfully random condition'.

All this Leonard could understand and accept, as he steered her, and himself, through her 'dark underworld'. After a month, he was writing to Lytton: 'Virginia is being allowed gradually to return to life and see visitors, the two terms being apparently synonymous. She would very much like during the next week to see any day at 2.30 the particle of life going about under the name of G.L. Strachey.'[52]

Lytton was just back from honeymoon – no, not his own, but Ralph Partridge and Carrington's. The three of them went together to Venice after the wedding. Ralph wrote to Leonard: 'We are both very happy and hope to emulate you and Virginia.' To which Carrington added: 'Indeed I don't,' and indeed she didn't. That same summer she embarked on a love affair with Ralph's friend Gerald Brenan.

The Woolfs went to Monks House (in a hired car, so as not to tire Virginia) for the long summer break of 1921. Leonard put brick edging to the flowerbeds, and had a toolshed made into a garden room, with an apple store above it. They bought the strip of land between their side-entrance path and Church Lane, making up their holding to one acre. In November Virginia was able to finish her novel *Jacob's Room.* But her temperature (Leonard kept a chart) was volatile, with unexplained highs and lows.

In connection with his parliamentary candidacy, he had been to Manchester in mid-March 1921 and spoke at the university on Africa and on the League of Nations. Virginia went with him; next day they went to the art gallery and Belle Vue Zoo. On the writing paper of the Queen's Hotel, Manchester, Leonard wrote a fairy tale for her, about the filthy city, the ugly people, the grinding of the mills: 'In the midst of this sat one day the fairest of God's creatures, a mandril, which in the perfumed forests of the East swung herself from bough to bough above the canopy of the

52 LW to Lytton Strachey 17 July 1921. Texas

jungle.' Virginia wrote in her diary[53] that Leonard in Manchester was 'emphatically first rate'. 'I don't mean his clothes; nor yet his speech; but it's a question of being the master.' He went north again, alone, in December 1921 to address his constituents. 'I do not think I made a very good impression, partly because I did not always succeed in concealing the fact that I was not really very eager to be an MP.'[54]

His printed election address made a plea for electing 'new men' and for no longer trusting in the two ancient parties who had 'brought us war and a peace which has proved hardly better than war.' Labour had 'ideals and principles which are real and alive, based not upon the possessions and privileges of classes . . . but upon the generous hopes and vital needs of millions of ordinary men and women'. The 'pivot of its programme' was threefold: the creation of 'a real League of Nations'; disarmament; and 'an equitable settlement of the reparation problem'. He argued for recognition of the Russian Government and for trade with Russia; for 'close co-operation with the USA'; also for 'complete abandonment of the policy of imperialism and economic penetration', the immediate granting of self-government to India and Ceylon, and the fundamental revision of Britain's exploitative government of 'the so-called backward races of Africa'. At a time when unemployment and economic downturn at home were exercising both Government and electorate, this was less an election manifesto than a personal statement. As such, it was cogent and eloquent.

Virginia finished *Jacob's Room* in early November 1921. The abrupt cessation of the all-absorbing rush towards completion could plummet her into an abyss of despair. Her agitation continued until the book was out and the reviews were in. Worries about hostile reviews were her 'thorns'. She would come to Leonard and say, 'I have a thorn', and he would help her to get rid of it. She was again ill in bed in January 1922, still with a fluctuating temperature. Dr Ferguson referred her to a heart specialist. Incurable and probably fatal inflammation of the heart was diagnosed. Nonsense, said Dr Ferguson. They went to a lung specialist, who said her

53 18 March 1921.
54 *Downhill All the Way*. In old age, he said in a TV interview with Malcolm Muggeridge that he regretted not having been an MP.

lungs were in a serious state. Nonsense, said Dr Ferguson. Consultations with specialists, at three guineas a visit, continued off and on throughout the year. On 26 May, Virginia had three more teeth out.

Leonard attended the Apostles' annual dinners in London every June. In 1920 Lytton was president – an office which involved sending out invitations to all brothers, planning the menu, arranging the placement, hosting the dinner, conscripting after-dinner speakers to propose toasts, and recruiting a president for the following year. In 1922 Ralph Hawtrey was president, and wrote telling Leonard he was having three toasts: to the Ark, to the Whales, and to the Hearthrug; would Leonard propose the Whales?[55] Leonard's diary 15 June: 'I spoke whales'. Facetiousness and reminiscence were the normal formula for the speeches. Leonard did not break with this custom, as those of his speeches which he preserved confirms.(He was president in 1925.) He felt impelled after his 1922 speech to write to Moore hoping that he had not taken amiss the references to himself. No, replied Moore, 'and it is very nice to know for certain that your feelings towards me haven't changed, though indeed I never suspected that they had.'[56]

Fellow Apostle Morgan Forster, recently back from his second visit to India, was having trouble with his novel in progress. He had taken the opening chapters of *A Passage to India* out with him, but the 'gap between India remembered and India experienced was too wide.' He tried to get on with it when he returned. 'But I still thought the book bad, and probably should not have completed it without the encouragement of Leonard Woolf.'[57] He spent several nights of discussion at Hogarth House in the first half of 1922, and Leonard 'took on the role, one that had never previously been played [with Forster], of literary confidant and supporter (the kind of role that is often fulfilled by a spouse or lover)'.[58] In 1937, considering what had been most worthwhile in his life

---

55 Readers may have forgotten that 'whales' were the sardines on toast traditionally consumed at the Saturday evening meetings of the Apostles.

56 20 June 1922

57 E.M.Forster, *The Hill of Devi* Edward Arnold 1953

58 Nicola Beauman, *Morgan: A Biography of E.M.Forster* Hodder & Stoughton 1993

'and ruling out Bob[59] on the ground that he is not in a cheap edition', Morgan Forster came to the conclusion that it was *A Passage to India.* It was 'only owing to Leonard that I was encouraged to finish it, but ever since publication I have felt satisfied.'

Leonard's 'nothing matters' echoes through the mysterious central episode in the Marabar Caves. What the booming echo seemed to say was: 'Pathos, piety, courage – they exist, but are identical, and so is filth. Everything exists, nothing has value.' Nothing matters. What had spoken in the cave was 'something very old and very small . . . the undying worm, itself.' And all it says is 'boum'.

There is a passage where Forster's central character, Fielding, assesses his success as a human being. He had 'learnt to manage his life and make the best of it . . . had developed his personality, explored his limitations, controlled his passions – and he had done it all without becoming pedantic or worldly.' But he felt 'he ought to have been working at something else the whole time . . . and that was why he felt sad.' Did Leonard, in the 1920s, feel that his busy and useful life was just displacement activity? What might one not miss, Forster is asking, by controlling the passions, allowing nothing to matter?

Leonard reviewed *A Passage to India* for the *Nation.*[60] He was to advise Forster in the practical management of his career, to the extent that in 1927 Forster suggested, unseriously, that Leonard should take a percentage of his royalties from his New York publisher. Leonard also enabled Morgan Forster 'to be Apostolic again, to detach himself mentally from Weybridge',[61] where he had lived in a cosy cocoon with his mother for more than fifteen years. *A Passage to India* consolidated Forster's reputation and made him financially secure. Like Lytton Strachey and Maynard Keynes, he became famous. He was never

---

59 Bob Buckingham, the love and mainstay of EMF's life from 1930. Quotation from EMF to Christopher Isherwood, 4 July 1937, in Mary Lago and P.N.Furbank (ed), *E.M.Forster: Selected Letters* Vol II, Collins 1983

60 Students of early twentieth-century literary reputations do well to check out personal links between canonical authors and those reviewers who piled the first bright pebbles on the cairn of celebrity, and to speculate on the implications.

61 Nicola Beauman, op. cit.

entirely comfortable with Virginia; he and Leonard always remained close.

The Hogarth Press undertook a dozen books for 1923. Leonard and Virginia were running the Press in their exiguous spare time, and 'printed in the larder, bound books in the dining-room, interviewed printers, binders and authors in a sitting-room'. They needed more assistance than Ralph Partridge gave. Setting type bored him, and his private life was distracting. Leonard's diary, 12 June 1922: 'Ralph told us about C[Arrington] and G[erald] B[renan].' Ralph had just found out about the affair and had a terrific bust-up with Gerald.[62] Lytton begged the Woolfs to keep his beloved Ralph on, but their own position was barely tenable. They were briefly tempted by the publishers Heinemann, who made an offer to buy the Hogarth Press out. They also turned down a cultured American, James Whittall, who offered partnership.

Then Marjorie Thompson[63] virtually fell into their laps. In the 1917 Club, they overheard 'one of those usual shabby, loose, crop-haired, small faced bright young women'[64] saying she wanted to become a printer. They asked her to tea, and arranged that she would start full-time at the Hogarth Press on 1 January 1923. Before he left the Press, Ralph had fallen for Frances Marshall, a pretty Cambridge philosophy graduate who was working in Bunny Garnett's bookshop, so there was a reconfiguration: Carrington with Gerald Brenan, Ralph Partridge with Frances Marshall, and Lytton loving Ralph, and Carrington loving Lytton.

The Woolfs regrouped too. Towards the end of the war, the widowed Bella had informed Leonard that she had 'seen Mr Southorn twice lately and had some very amusing yarns . . . I think he is a very remarkable person and much more amusing than he used to be.' In

62 Carrington and Brenan were betrayed by Valentine Dobree. She was in bed with Ralph at the time, having just been dumped by Brenan. See Jonathan Gathorne-Hardy, *The Interior Castle: A Life of Gerald Brenan* Sinclair-Stevenson 1994.

63 She was about 22 at the time, and living with the philosopher, civil servant and, later, radio personality C.E.M.Joad as his common law wife, he already having a wife and children.

64 VW Diary 27 Nov 1922

1921 Bella, now in her mid-forties, thin and birdlike, married Leonard's former colleague Tom Southorn and went back to Ceylon.

Clara Woolf, in her late thirties, went to the United States in summer 1920, and two years later married, in America, George L. Walker, a widower in his sixties, a journalist with a special interest in copper. Mrs Woolf, left with no obliging unmarried daughters, was 'a very tattered old eagle, poor woman.'[65]

Philip Woolf went to India in 1921 for a job that did not work out, and where he was excluded from the white man's club. He was open about the setbacks he suffered because of his Jewishness, as Leonard was not – though no one could be more expressive than Leonard in *The Wise Virgins* or 'The Three Jews'; and Leonard told his wife on a Sunday afternoon walk in April 1921 about another book he was planning, 'a revised version of the Wandering Jew'.[66] This late-mediaeval legendary figure was the Jew who insulted and spurned Christ as he carried his cross to Calvary. The Jew's punishment was to wander over the face of the earth until the Day of Judgement. The Wandering Jew fell into a trance every hundred years and woke up each time as a man of thirty: there were sightings of him in Europe from the thirteenth to the last quarter of the eighteenth century. This would have been the perfect subject for Leonard Woolf, whether framed as cultural history or as time-travelling fiction. It might have been his masterpiece. So far as is known he never wrote a word of it.

Philip landed safely into the arms of the Cousinhood, when James (Jimmy) de Rothschild MP offered him the post of land agent at Waddesdon Manor, his vast house and estate in Buckinghamshire. Jimmy Rothschild knew the Woolfs through his much younger wife Dorothy (Dollie), the granddaughter of Aunt Bloom, one of Marie Woolf's sisters. When Leonard turned up at the Savoy Hotel in the Strand on 22 March 1922 for tea with 'Mother, Phil, Babs, Edgar and Sylvia, and Flora', it was to celebrate the marriage of Philip to Marjorie Lowndes, known as Babs, and ten years his junior. His new job at

65 VW to Philippa Strachey 5 March 1922
66 17 April 1921

Waddesdon, which included the provision of a beautiful and ancient house on the estate, called The Wilderness, made marriage practicable.

All nine Woolfs were now married. They all married Gentiles, and only three of them – Clara, Flora and Philip – produced children. There were various physical and psychological reasons why the others did not. Philip, observing his elder brothers' marriages, assumed that his generation of male Woolfs was infertile. In the event, he and Babs had their three children quite quickly – Philippa, Marie, and then Cecil, named after the beloved brother.

In the run-up to the General Election in mid-November 1922, Leonard hung out in the office of the ILP journal the *New Leader*, in the congenial company of its editor Noel Brailsford, and Bertrand Russell, Harold Laski, Molly Hamilton, and other kindred spirits of the Labour Left. (Communists and fellow-travellers were known as the Extreme Left, though their correct placing, Leonard came to think, was on the Right of the Extreme Right). He made one last visit north to Liverpool on the ninth to meet his electors.

Diary, 16 November: 'Heard results of election.' Leonard came bottom of the poll. The two elected members were Virginia's pompous cousin Herbert Fisher (Liberal) and Martin Conway (Conservative). Leonard had a soapy letter from Conway, expressing certainty that the author of *The Village in the Jungle* 'would have found the H. of C. a most unattractive place . . . especially if he had been obliged to associate intimately with the rank and file of the Labour Party – tho', of course, among them are some delightful simple souls'. Leonard quoted this in *Downhill All the Way* as an illustration of the 'social and political snobbery of those days.'

Diary, 20 November 1922: 'Met Ramsay MacDonald at lunch at New Leader.' The Conservatives had won the 1922 election, and Ramsay MacDonald, back in Parliament, was officially the leader of the Opposition, since Labour had won twenty-five more seats than the Liberals. Sidney Webb had been elected to Parliament for the Seaham division of Durham. The Labour Party had, at last, a realistic vision of itself as a future party of Government.

*

'I expect you have heard', Leonard wrote to Lytton on 4 May 1923, 'that, having failed as (a) a civil servant, (b) a novelist, (c) an editor, (d) a publicist, I have now sunk to the last rung . . . literary journalism. I am now Literary Editor of The Nation and Athenaeum.'[67]

Rowntree, the Liberal, was no longer prepared to finance a journal which, after the editor Massingham's shift to the Left, had become a Labour organ. The survival of the *Nation* was discussed, as Leonard's diary attests, over many gloomy lunches. But he was taken by surprise: Maynard Keynes acquired an interest in the *Nation*, with overall control as chairman of the board. Leonard's diary, 23 March 1923: 'Went Maynard tea. Asked me to become Lit Editor Nation.' Maynard wanted him to write the foreign affairs leaders as well, but Leonard had no desire for full-time office life. He agreed to write a weekly review article under the heading 'The World of Books' and to run the literary pages, in two and a half office-days a week.

Keynes put in as editor Hubert Henderson, an economist, and an ex-pupil of his at King's.[68] This was a hinge-moment for Leonard. He was ten years older than Hubert Henderson. It was the first time he had been accountable to a member of the younger generation. Henderson's son confirmed that his father was 'on easy terms' with Leonard Woolf.[69] Henderson questioned Leonard's use of young reviewers, and the irreverent tone of their reviews, which caused affront. He thought beginners should only be offered minor books, and that contentious pieces should be rejected.

Two of the youthful reviewers who nettled Henderson were George (Dadie) Rylands, a handsome blond ex-Etonian from King's, an Apostle and Maynard's protégé; and Raymond Mortimer, puckish, ex-Oxford. Leonard defended them in a heated row with Hubert Henderson in the office, and in a lengthy letter of afterthoughts: 'If you don't mind me saying so, your life will be impossible if you pay too much attention to every criticism of every review and article which is in *The Nation* . . . It

67 4 May 1923. Texas

68 (Sir) Hubert Henderson became Drummond Professor of Political Economy at Oxford, and Warden of All Souls. He was married to a sister of Nicholas Bagenal

69 Nicholas Henderson, *Old Friends and Modern Instances* Profile Books 2000

is simply that if I think a piece of writing good, I think that I am right – and that's an end to it.'[70] If Hubert wished, he would send in his resignation at the end of the year.[71] His resignation was not required.

The salary – £500 a year – put him on track financially, and coincided with the beginning of the most prolific and successful period of Virginia's writing life. *Jacob's Room* was published by the Hogarth Press (they did not print it themselves) in October 1922, with a jacket illustration by Vanessa, who also designed the wolf's-head colophon which henceforth graced all Hogarth Press publications. Gerald Duckworth let them buy back from him the rights in her first two novels. Virginia Woolf was from now on her own co-publisher, and was saved the agony of submitting her manuscripts to alien eyes. She was also publishing volumes of stories and criticism, and had started the slow process of writing what would become *Mrs Dalloway*.

In 1922 T.S. Eliot launched and edited a new magazine, the *Criterion*. He and Leonard became conspiratorial fellow editors, passing the names of likely contributors between them, sometimes attempting to dump unwanted material on each other. By the end of that year the Woolfs and Eliot were on first-name terms, and Tom Eliot was answering Virginia's invitations in Old Possum-style verse. The thirty-seven pages of *The Waste Land* were set and printed in the larder of Hogarth House, to Eliot's warmly expressed satisfaction as to spacing and paging, and was published in September 1923. Eliot was in a strange phase, and his marriage, as *The Waste Land* attested, the source of a savage unhappiness. His face seemed to be powdered greenish-white, and his lips to be painted. He wanted to come round and see the Woolfs more often than they could always manage. A prim man, he was shocked when, on a walk with Virginia, Leonard dropped back to relieve himself. Eliot said his wife had never even seen him shaving.

Desmond MacCarthy meanwhile had taken on the literary editorship of the *New Statesman*. He and Leonard each thought the other stole his

70 Both Rylands and Mortimer became extremely distinguished figures on the British cultural scene.

71 26 Sept 1923

reviewers, which was true. Leonard's young reviewers Dadie Rylands and Raymond Mortimer – who also wrote for Desmond – became neo-Bloomsbury, like Bunny Garnett[72] and his partner in the bookshop Francis (Frankie) Birrell. Bunny married Frances Marshall's sister Rachel (Ray) in 1921. Duncan Grant had loved Bunny, and Lytton had a fling with him; it was natural that he and his friends should merge with Bloomsbury.

Vanessa Bell, like everyone else, was enchanted by Lydia Lopokova, a principal dancer with the Russian ballet with whom Maynard Keynes fell in love in 1922 – until, that is, Maynard announced he intended to marry her. Vanessa responded grandly: 'Clive says he thinks it is impossible for any one of us . . . to introduce a new wife or husband into the existing circle . . . We feel that *no one* can come into the sort of intimate society we have without altering it.'[73]

Vanessa, artist and mother, was in her early middle age a domestic deity while claiming many freedoms. Duncan was her permanent partner but no longer, to her grief, her lover. He conducted elsewhere his amatory life with his boyfriends. Vanessa spent time in Italy and France, so was able to recommend to the Woolfs a hotel in Paris: the Hotel de Londres in the rue Bonaparte. For two days after Leonard agreed to take on the literary editorship of the *Nation*, and even though Virginia's temperature was still unstable, they went abroad for the first time since their honeymoon more than ten years before. They went to Spain.

72 David Garnett (Bunny) published his first and successful novel *Lady Into Fox* in 1922.
73 VB to MK 20 May 1922, King's College Cambridge

11

Prime Time

They went to Andalucia to visit Gerald Brenan in the village of Yegen, four thousand feet up in the foothills of the Sierra Nevada. 'All yesterday', Leonard wrote to Margaret Llewelyn Davies, 'we sat on the back of two mules, on the top of all our luggage, from 9 in the morning to 9 in the evening, and crawled up the bed of a torrent among orange trees and olives and almonds and pomegranates to reach this village where Brenan, aged 28, lives alone with 3000 books on £60 a year, the son of a retired army officer who has disinherited him because he refused to go into the guards.'[1] In an article Leonard wrote for the *Nation and Athenaeum* while in Spain, he claimed that it was 'modes of transport' which determined how men lived: 'In London we are made in the image of the Tube and Underground, but here on the Sierra Nevada it is the mule who makes man in his image. Anyone who has sat for many hours on a mule's back, picking his meditative way through along a rocky mountain track, will know that to say this is no slur on any Spaniard.'[2]

Gerald Brenan, though much younger, found 'steady, masculine, pipe-smoking' Leonard quite boyish, and Virginia like a schoolgirl

1 5 April 1923
2 13 April 1923. The journal henceforth will be referred to just as the *Nation.*

(always Lytton's impression of her too, when she was happy). Because the Woolfs knew about the Carrington affair, there were intimate confidences. Virginia told Gerald that their marriage was chaste; and Leonard told Gerald about her dangerous 'excitement' when he first tried to make love to her, which persuaded him it would be better to desist. 'Since then he had given up all ideas of sexual satisfaction "because she was a genius"'. He never flirted with another woman, 'only expecting that she would not either with a man'.[3] He apparently told Gerald that in Yegen he was having two wet dreams a night instead of one, because of the beauty of the scenery.[4] Brenan 'was told' that 'some time later' Leonard had relations with the parlour maid in London on occasions when Virginia was at Rodmell. Brenan's recollections[5] were recorded decades afterwards, but he did keep a diary.

On their way home, in Alicante, Virginia boasted to Mary Hutchinson of discomforts bravely borne: 'Last night I did not sleep till 4, because of bugs. At 4 Leonard extricated a camel shaped lump of purple tissue from the hairs of my blanket. It burst with an odious smell into thick blood.'[6] Virginia remained in Paris for a few days, while Leonard went straight back to London. 'Do come back Friday', Leonard wrote to her from the train home to Richmond, 'for your Mongoose misses you.'

The friendship with Brenan did not, for Leonard, develop deep roots, blossoming too fast in the heady air of Yegen. Gerald however admired Leonard greatly. In London in 1924, he wrote to Carrington (who moved that year with Lytton to Ham Spray House, in Berkshire between Newbury and Hungerford): 'When you told me that [Leonard]

---

3 It was true that LW was not flirtatious; and was unmoved when literary socialite Nancy Cunard settled herself in his lap at a Bloomsbury party.

4 Gossip. Brenan told Bunny Garnett this, who told Frances Partridge, who told VG 14 Sept 2001.

5 See Jonathan Gathorne-Hardy, op. cit., and letter of 1977 from Brenan to Rosemary Dinnage already quoted on page 190/191. As Frederic Spotts wrote in his editorial remarks in *Letters of Leonard Woolf* (Harcourt Brace Jovanovich 1989), the 'talk' that he had an affair with Nelly Boxall has neither 'evidence not plausibility'. But Lily?

6 VW Letters 18 April 1933

liked cactuses, you threw a great deal of light on his character . . .' The reader might expect this sentence to end, 'because he is like a cactus himself'; but it ends, 'for what interests him in men is what they share with these plants'. Leonard, Gerald thought, would always be the most intelligent person in a room 'because, having a head so clear that no one could have a clearer, he has energy to spare for watching and comparing the speakers and their psychological motives.'[7]

Leonard had 'energy to spare' for the mundane, too. As well as keeping the household accounts, he kept a list of the clothes that he and Virginia bought. This was customary; with no universally acceptable cheap clothing, garments were bought or made with forethought, and meant to last. What was unusual was a husband keeping the tally. In 1923 Virginia had three new hats, two pairs of drawers, two pairs of shoes, two cloaks, one coat, one dress, one skirt, and one jumper. She was too old in the 1920s for short skirts and 'flapper' fashions, and too young to retain the Edwardian gowns which some older women never discarded. Her longish, loose, compromise garments could be eccentric, but she looked graceful and distinguished. Her fine face, with its changing expressions, could still startle with its pure beauty. Photographs do not capture her gaiety, or the 'schoolgirl' quality.

Leonard, in 1923, had two new silk shirts, one flannel shirt, a pair of breeches, two pairs of pants and two vests, boots, shoes and socks, and a rucksack for Spain. They both had new nail-brushes. The awe-inspiring meticulousness of these lists is relieved by a merciful category called 'Misc'. Leonard kept accounts and made lists because he was by nature utterly disorganised; thus he kept chaos at bay. It was Virginia who was subject to money panics in the small hours. 'Like my father, I can always conjure up bankruptcy. But unlike my father Leonard has no money complex.'[8] Until 1927, Leonard regulated her personal spending for her, giving her 'pocket money'.

Sometimes he bought clothes for her on his own initiative. He came

---

7 6 May 1924. Copied by Gerald Brenan into his *Personal Record: 1920–1972* Jonathan Cape 1974

8 To Ethel Smyth 12 Jan 1941

back from the Richmond Co-op, while she and Barbara Hiles were having tea, carrying a large paper parcel containing 'two enormous pairs of thick woollen combinations for Virginia. They had long, long sleeves and an array of buttons. Virginia and I laughed at these extraordinary garments until there were tears in our eyes.' Leonard gazed 'long and thoughtfully' at the combinations and then joined in the laughter.[9]

Virginia longed to move from Richmond into central London and into the mainstream of literary and social life. The Woolfs were being 'sucked into' (Leonard's phrase) more parties. He went sometimes to Garsington Manor with Virginia and other assorted weekend guests: socialites, bohemians, artists and underdogs. No one had a bath; there was, in spite of the sumptuousness, no hot-water system. Their hostess Lady Ottoline Morrell, thought Leonard, 'was herself not unlike one of her own peacocks, drifting about the house and terraces in strange brightly coloured shawls and other floating garments, her unskilfully dyed red hair, her head tilted to the sky at the same angle as the birds' and her odd nasal voice and neighing laugh always seeming as if they might at any moment rise into one of those shattering calls of the peacocks which woke me in the morning at Garsington just as so often I had heard them blare in the jungles of Ceylon'.[10] In London there were parties of the kind which Virginia liked best, such as the Oriental fancy-dress party given by Maynard at 46 Gordon Square in January 1923, where Lydia Lopokova danced. The Woolfs coloured their faces and went as Indians, Leonard wielding a sword he had brought back from Ceylon.[11]

---

9 Barbara (Hiles) Bagenal in Joan Russell Noble (ed): *Recollections of Virginia Woolf* Peter Owen 1972

10 Lady Ottoline's daughter Julian Vinogradoff took exception to this virtuoso description in *Beginning Again*, finding it cruel and unfair.

11 It was after another, later party, walking home after an evening with Vanessa in her studio in Fitzroy Street, that Leonard and Virginia came upon a drunken woman being bullied by a policeman. Leonard lost his temper and intervened on behalf of the woman. A crowd gathered and backed Leonard up. In Bloomsbury lore, this evening became conflated with the night when Leonard, with blackened face, was wielding a sword. It made a better story.

Leonard worried that London life would exhaust Virginia; yet it would suit him, too, now that he had to be at the *Nation* office in Great James Street for two and a half days every week. On 9 January 1924 he signed a ten-year lease on 52 Tavistock Square in Bloomsbury, at £140 per annum. Virginia was delighted, with 'music, talk, friendship, city views, books, publishing . . . now within my reach, as it hasn't been since August 1913, when we left Clifford's Inn, for a series of catastrophes which very nearly ended my life, & would, I'm vain enough to think, have ruined Leonard's.'[12] Her health was 'as good as it ever would be in this world, and a great deal better than it had ever been', as she recorded two days later.

Leonard rented out Hogarth House, and after two years sold it to a local solicitor for £1,350. He went to say goodbye to the house, with his sister Flora, before it was sold. He retained his feeling for it, and sneaked in twice more, long afterwards, to find that it had fallen on evil days. The first time 'it was inhabited by Mosley's Fascists', the second time by the Conservative Association.[13]

At 52 Tavistock Square, the Press machine was installed in the basement scullery. The kitchen, with a big dresser still in place, was the Hogarth Press office. Towards the back of the basement there was a larder, and a dark stone passage leading to a windowless, lightless WC. (The staff had to use cut-up galley proofs in the WC, until they rebelled, taking money for toilet paper from the petty cash.) Then came the stairs up to the Woolfs' flat and, at the very back of the basement, a bigger room which became the book-store and packing room, where Virginia worked at a small table, surrounded by shelves and piles of book-parcels.

The Woolfs' sitting tenants, the solicitors Dollman and Pritchard, occupied the ground and first floors. Leonard became very friendly with old Mr George Pritchard and his staff; there was no Mr Dollman. Every day, according to Rose Talbot, who came as a young clerk in 1924, he 'had a little chat, then went in to see Mr George', like a com-

---

12 VW Diary 9 Jan 1924

13 LW to Ann Thwaite 17 June 1961. Hogarth House was the local office of the British Union of Fascists 1934–5; Suffield House was the Richmond and Barnes Conservative Association office.

bination of 'landlord, client and friend'; he gave the staff a huge box of Fortnum & Mason chocolates every Christmas. Nelly Boxall would alert the clerks when 'important people' were coming to see the Woolfs – and then they would leave open their waiting-room door, from which they could see the door up to the Woolfs' flat.[14]

Leonard and Virginia lived on the two top floors. Their sitting room was 'shabby but elegant',[15] with lamps each side of the fireplace, painted panels and a painted screen by Duncan and Vanessa, and two Knole sofas.[16] Leonard waged a war with the developers of a hotel on Woburn Place, directly behind their house. The noise from the building-site was atrocious and, when the hotel was finished, so was the noise of dance music from the ballroom at the back. Leonard wrote letters of protest, and invited the manager round to hear the din for himself. He called on the company secretary. He canvassed the neighbours. He employed Mr Pritchard downstairs and took legal action, winning his case.

Before the move back to London, Virginia met the rich, aristocratic Vita Sackville-West, with whom she made the second-closest relationship of her life. Vita, already a successful published author, and her husband Harold Nicolson were a devoted couple with two young sons at Eton. They led separate sexual lives – he with men, she with women. Harold was in the diplomatic service, and also wrote. Vita had no intention of being a diplomatic wife, and just visited him at intervals when he was *en poste* abroad.

The husbands, Harold Nicolson and Leonard Woolf, were both deeply interested in politics, and they knew a lot of the same people; Raymond Mortimer was Harold's current boyfriend. But Harold was worldly and sophisticated in a way that Leonard was not. While Virginia was becoming closer to Vita, Leonard had perforce to see a great deal of the Nicolsons – excursions, dinners in restaurants, visits to their house Long Barn in Kent, and to Knole, the magnificent and ancient house

---

14 Rose (Talbot) Schrager to L.A.Charlier 17 July 1973

15 Angelica Garnett, *Deceived with Kindness* Hogarth Press 1984

16 Knole sofas, named after those in Vita Sackville-West's ancestral home, have let-down ends, secured with tasselled cords.

where Vita lived until she married and which was her adored ancestral home.

Leonard's life, from the time they moved to Tavistock Square until the end of the 1920s, was dominated by his literary editorship of the *Nation*, as well as by his political work and the expansion of the Hogarth Press. He liked to tell people that everyone should change occupation every seven years, as he did: seven years in Ceylon, seven or eight years of varied journalism, and the same on the staff of the *Nation*. The two and a half days in the office were just part of what was a full-time job, bolted on to his other commitments. He did much of his *Nation* work at 52 Tavistock Square, writing his weekly 1,200-word article, plus items for 'Books in Brief', and for the feature 'On the Editor's Table'. He had to drum up 'middles' under the heading 'From Alpha to Omega', on theatre, music, painting, science. Often he wrote even these himself. A fluent and pithy reviewer, he had a talent for seductive openings: 'In 1618 Ben Jonson, aged forty-six years and weighing just under twenty stone, an inveterate Londoner, decided for some mysterious reason that he must walk to Edinburgh.'[17] A trenchantly dismissive piece on Robert Louis Stevenson ('quite a good imitator of great writers') provoked the fury of the elderly Edmund Gosse,[18] who wrote to a friend describing Leonard Woolf, whom he had never met, as 'a perverse, partially educated alien German.'[19]

In 1927 the Hogarth Press published a collection of Leonard's recent articles and reviews, which the Woolfs set and printed themselves.[20] Virginia, much later, wrote a pamphlet about the demoralising effect of reviewing upon the sensitive author, and proposing a dual system: just symbols – an asterisk or a dagger – to signify approval or disapproval in the newspapers, with considered criticism to be available to authors privately, from paid specialists. Leonard, finding this too eccentric, just

17 *Nation* 23 June 1923
18 Author and critic, librarian of the House of Lords
19 To Sir Sidney Colvin. National Library of Scotland
20 L.S.Woolf, *Essays on Literature, History, Politics etc*. Published by Leonard and Virginia Woolf at The Hogarth Press, 52 Tavistock Square, London WC. This style was restricted to those books which they set and printed themselves.

as eccentrically appended a 'Note' at the end, stressing that reviewing was a service to the public, 'talking to the reader', not to the author, and reformulating the problem Virginia identified – which was, indeed, the growing split between reviewing and literary criticism.[21]

He was to call into question the value of much of his life's work, but remained satisfied with what he achieved at the *Nation*. Thomas Hardy, a literary idol of his youth, sent him a poem for the paper, after which he and Virginia, on a weekend trip to Dorset, went to have tea with the old man. Leonard's old Cambridge and Bloomsbury friends wrote for him, as did rising stars such as Osbert Sitwell, Arnold Toynbee, Aldous Huxley and Robert Graves. Leonard spotted the quality of the Scots poet Edwin Muir, who became a regular reviewer for the *Nation*, and a Hogarth Press author. It was a lifelong association; the first two books of Muir's poems[22] the Woolfs set and printed themselves; and his last and posthumous book, *The Estate of Poetry*, was published by Hogarth in 1962.

At the end of 1924 he wrote over Hubert Henderson's head to Maynard Keynes, as chairman, complaining that he was letting the paper become more and more political, and 'materially deteriorating the literary side'. In late March 1926, according to his diary, he went to see Maynard and resigned. Maynard talked him round, but Leonard reduced his two-and-a-half days in the office to two. He had books to write. Speaking from experience, he had the strongest possible opinion on the deleterious effect of regular journalism on a writer's work.

He was increasing, too, his involvement in Labour politics. In 1924, under Ramsay MacDonald's triumphant but short-lived first Labour administration,[23] the party's Advisory Committee on International and

21 VW *Reviewing, with a Note by Leonard Woolf*, Hogarth Sixpenny Pamphlets Number Four 1939. VW's idea of symbols for approval and disapproval was adopted by some broadsheets half a century later.

22 *First Poems* (1925) and *Chorus of the Newly Dead* (1926)

23 For an intriguingly personal account of how and why MacDonald's government fell, see M.A. (Molly) Hamilton's *J.Ramsay MacDonald (1923–1925)* published under the pseudonym 'Iconoclast' in 1925. It is evident from this short book that Molly Hamilton was more intimate with MacDonald than she ever was with LW, or than LW ever was with MacDonald.

Imperial Questions was divided into two (known as A.C.Int.Q and A.C.Imp.Q, the latter chaired by Charles Buxton). Both committees met in the House of Commons fortnightly, on alternate Wednesdays, and Leonard was secretary to both. Even though he felt that the achievement of the advisory committees was 'nothing commensurate with the amount of work we did',[24] he thrived on it. In collaboration with Philip Noel-Baker, he drafted the Labour Party's foreign policy section for the election programme of 1929, and worked to reinforce the centrality of the League of Nations.

A.C.Imp.Q, the imperial affairs committee, pressed the Labour governments of 1924 and 1929 to meet Indian demands for self-government. Looking back, Leonard was to feel that if successive British governments had been prepared to grant in 1920 what they granted in 1940, and to grant in 1940 the transference of power which was granted in 1947, 'then nine-tenths of the misery, hatred, and violence, the imprisonings and terrorism, the murders, floggings, shootings and assassinations, even the racial massacres might have been avoided'.[25] One of the many lectures he gave was to Indian students in London, in June 1925. That may have been when he first met the aspiring novelist Mulk Raj Anand, who had just arrived to study philosophy at University College.

An ardent nationalist, Mulk Raj Anand was nevertheless ambitious to make his way in literary London. At a party at Harold Monro's poetry bookshop, he encountered in a single evening T.S.Eliot, Aldous Huxley, D.H.Lawrence and Leonard Woolf, deep in a conversation about big-breasted women. 'In the Kandyan hills', said Leonard, 'we can still see lovely, big-breasted women', working naked to the waist in the tea-gardens, 'the opposite of the flat-chested Miss Quested in Morgan Forster's novel [*A Passage to India*]'. Leonard was an aficionado of big breasts. 'As for Naomi Royde Smith', Morgan Forster wrote to him, 'even my eyes could not leave her breasts, so I had no doubt as to the destination of yours.'[26]

24 *Downhill All the Way*

25 *Downhill All the Way*

26 18 Aug 1921. Naomi Royde Smith was literary editor of the *Westminster Review*. When the Woolfs and Forster first met her at one of her parties, Virginia described her as having 'a body that billows out but perfectly hard' (Diary 5 June 1921).

Mulk Raj Anand wanted to meet the author of *A Passage to India*, so Leonard asked them both to drinks. They sat in the central garden of Tavistock Square, Leonard carrying out a sherry bottle and glasses from the flat. The talk centred on British prudery and sexual repression, which led, Leonard said, to the British 'compensating for our guilts by going and bossing other people', and to young Englishmen on tea plantations behaving appallingly when they got the chance; they had been brought before him for rape in Ceylon. D.H.Lawrence had it right, said Leonard, about sex. Mulk made copious diary notes. He saw the two friends that evening as 'two pioneers of freedom and intimacy' ... 'without the bluff of white Sahib superiority'. In the smoky London sunset, he thought he saw Leonard's eyes 'filled with nostalgia for the tropical light of Ceylon evenings . . . his forehead lined with furrows of doubt.'[27]

Freud's theories had been filtering into British intellectual life since the Great War, and Leonard's talk of sexual repression reflected Bloomsbury's interest in psychoanalysis. In 1924 the Hogarth Press, in conjunction with the newly founded Institute of Psycho-Analysis, took over from Stanley Unwin the publication of the Psycho-Analytical Library. 'If I end up without loss, profit, or lawsuit', he wrote to Unwin, 'I shall congratulate myself. But I shall have had a good deal of amusement.' By the end of July 1924 Virginia was bewailing 'all the psycho-analyst books . . . dumped in a fortress the size of Windsor Castle in ruins' on the floor of the basement in Tavistock Square.[28] In the event the Hogarth Press kept on with the Library for forty years, and was still the publisher of Freud in English well after Leonard's death.

James Strachey, who was to translate with the assistance of his wife Alix the *Complete Psychological Works of Sigmund Freud* (Frances Partridge indexing all twenty-four volumes), had, with Alix, been analysed by Freud in Vienna, and encouraged Leonard in this new enterprise. Both

27 Mulk Raj Anand, *Conversations in Bloomsbury* Wildwood House 1981. Anand became a distinguished writer of novels, stories and essays and a major figure in Indian English literature. E.M.Forster wrote a preface for his best-known novel *Untouchable* (1935).

28 VW Letters: to Marjorie Joad , ?20 July 1924

James and Alix became analysts. Adrian Stephen and his wife Karin were also deep in the politics and practice of psychoanalysis in England, deciding that they too would be psychoanalysts, and qualifying as medical doctors before going to Vienna to be analysed by Freud.

Leonard grew resistant to much of the Freudian dogma. After a dinner given in 1966 by the Institute of Psychoanalysis to celebrate the completion of the Freud publishing programme, he mentioned to Alix Strachey that there was one emotion – she couldn't afterwards remember which[29] – that he never felt. 'How do you know you don't in your unconscious mind?' she asked him, hoping for an 'interesting discussion'. He moved away.[30] Mentioning that dinner in *The Journey not the Arrival Matters*, Leonard said that he did not find psychoanalysts 'in private life – much as I have liked many of them – altogether easy to get on with'. As he wrote late in life, in the course of an intense correspondence with a Hogarth novelist, 'I certainly do not agree that the unconscious mind reveals deeper truth about someone else than plain common or garden sense does.'[31] As a young man, though he always preferred to see emotion and reason as the significant and conflicting poles, he was more receptive: 'The most modern psychology teaches us that the more obvious manifestations of the emotions are no clue to their real nature or strength, that it is what we do with our emotions in the inner recesses of our minds that is most important.'[32] 'We are all psychoanalysts now', as the *New Statesman* put it in 1923;[33] and the unconscious and Leonard's 'inner recesses of the mind' seem much the same thing.

James Strachey wondered why Leonard did not persuade Virginia to see a psychoanalyst. Leonard believed that her mental and nervous disturbances were functionally linked to her genius, and that to tamper with that link could be disastrous for her and for her writing. In any case, depressives with histories of psychosis and suicidal tendencies are not

29 It was probably guilt or remorse

30 Alix Strachey in Joan Russell Noble (ed): *Recollections of Virginia Woolf* Peter Owen 1972

31 To Esther Salaman 1 June 1964

32 'The Character of Herbert Spencer', *New Statesman* 10 March 1917

33 Daniel Pick, 'The Id comes to Bloomsbury', *Guardian* 16 Aug 2003

generally considered suitable subjects for psychoanalysis. Another counter-indication was that the foibles and frailties of the analysts in their circle, leaders in the field though they might be, were all too familiar. Virginia observed that analysis did not seem to have made *them* any better or happier. When Barbara Strachey,[34] the niece of both the Bloomsbury psychoanalytic couples, was asked the family's view of them, she replied that 'they would not have sent a dog to either pair'.[35]

Leonard, who respected dogs more than he respected many humans, would have agreed, and when Tom Eliot asked him: 'Now could you give me the name of the best M.D. there is with psychoanalytical knowledge – if there is one? . . . This is obviously *not* for V[ivien] but for myself if for anyone', Leonard replied, 'I should think that the best English psycho-analyst is probably James Glover.'[36] The terminology and usages of psychoanalysis were certainly part of Leonard's mental furniture: anti-Semitism, for example, was 'so irrational that a long course of psychoanalysis alone would uncover its origin in any particular case.'[37]

This last was in the context of an enquiry about T.S.Eliot's anti-Semitism, one of many which Leonard received from scholars in the 1960s. He always answered in the same way: he did not know why Eliot was anti-Semitic, and he had never shown any sign of it in his presence. He could not remember whether they had ever even discussed it. (No one liked to enquire what he felt about the expressions of anti-Semitism in his wife's fiction.)

Leonard's strategy of not noticing anti-Semitism, and his mantra that 'nothing matters', were frequently necessary. In 1929 Hugh Dalton, parliamentary Under-Secretary at the Foreign Office, came to dinner with the Woolfs, along with Harold Nicolson. They discussed current Labour Party plans, in which Leonard was involved, for reorganising the selection for the Foreign Office on more democratic lines. Harold

---

34 Daughter of Ray and Oliver Strachey

35 Susan O'Cleary, 'Bloomsbury and Psychoanalysis', *Charleston Magazine* No 16

36 8 May 1925. Berg. Adrian and Karin Stephen were in analysis with James Glover, who died this same year, 1925.

37 To Lyall Wilkes 31 Nov 1968

Nicolson's diary: 'The awkward question of the Jews arises. I admit that is the snag. Jews are far more interested in international life than Englishmen, and if we opened the service it might be flooded by clever Jews. It was a little difficult to argue this point with Leonard there.'[38] No one would disagree with that. Nicolson would have attributed to Leonard the sophistication not to take anything personally.

In November 1924 the Hogarth Press published, through Virginia's friendship with her, a novel by Vita Sackville-West, *Seducers in Ecuador*, and subsequently two of her travel books. Vita later produced poetry, non-fiction and novels which made big profits for the Press. After *The Edwardians* (1930) and *All Passion Spent* (1931), both best-sellers, she could have gone to any publisher she chose for more money, but remained loyal – as she sometimes liked to remind Leonard. Another valued author did however move elsewhere. In 1925 the Woolfs were sent from South Africa a novel, hand-written in pale pencil, called *Turbott Wolfe* by William Plomer. The Hogarth Press published it, and Plomer subsequently wrote copiously to Leonard about his emotional and professional difficulties, apologising for treating him as 'a sort of moral clearing house for a person you've never even seen'.[39]

Plomer was less forthcoming in the flesh, 'a compressed inarticulate young man',[40] as Virginia described him when he first came to England. After publishing ten volumes of prose and poetry with the Hogarth Press, Plomer left them in 1932 – 'a half-unwilling desertion',[41] the not uncommon reward of small publishers. The friendship with the Woolfs was not broken. The welcome they had given him, 'and their subsequent friendship, I value as much as anything in my life'.[42]

In November 1924 Dadie Rylands left the Hogarth Press to take up a fellowship at King's. He was replaced by Angus Davidson, a young

---

38 11 July 1930. Nigel Nicolson, ed: *Harold Nicolson: Letters and Diaries* Vol 1 1930–1939, Collins 1966
39 11 Jan 1929. Huntington
40 VW Diary 19 Aug 1929
41 Plomer to LW 4 April 1933. Huntington
42 William Plomer, *At Home* Jonathan Cape 1958

intimate of Duncan's. As well as series of Hogarth Essays, Hogarth Letters, Hogarth Lectures (in pamphlet form), the Press brought out twenty to thirty books a year throughout the 1920s and 1930s in editions of between 150 and 30,000 copies – 'never', Leonard asserted in retrospect,[43] running out of stock or failing to supply an order. He ascribed this efficiency to the discipline he learned in the government offices of Ceylon.

His discipline included obsessional time-keeping. If Angus Davidson turned up even marginally after nine-thirty, he would find Leonard 'fuming, a bundle of papers in his hand, looking at his watch'. On one 'absurd occasion' their watches varied by two minutes, 'and we ran out up the basement steps together to look down the street at the immense clock that projected above the door of Pitman's in Russell Square'. It was only later that Angus realised that Leonard's 'extreme nervous irritability' must have been 'largely due to the strain imposed upon him by Virginia's illnesses'- though when she was well, and sometimes helped 'not very efficiently' to make up book parcels, the whole atmosphere lightened.[44] Leonard did not lose his temper with Virginia. His assistants at the Press received the fall-out of his strain.

On 20 August 1925, the fifteenth birthday of Vanessa's son Quentin, the Woolfs cycled to Charleston. Leonard's diary: 'V. fainted.' He typed a taut memo describing that hot evening in the Charleston garden, and another occasion when she fainted in the Ivy restaurant, with all attendant details, like clinical notes. He had reason for concern. The mutual fascination of Vita and Virginia became a love affair towards the end of December 1925. Leonard did not know the full truth, though Harold Nicolson did. Leonard was apprehensive about the effect on Virginia of this intense relationship. He wanted her to be happy, but he felt excluded, even though Virginia took pains not to make him feel so. Some deception of him was involved. Vita would enclose intimate letters to Virginia inside anodyne ones which could safely be shown to him.

---

43 *Downhill All the Way*

44 Angus Davidson in Joan Russell Noble (ed): *Recollections of Virginia Woolf* Peter Owen 1972

When the Woolfs spent Christmas 1925 at Charleston, Virginia stayed on one day more than Leonard. 'I thought she'd stay longer', Vanessa wrote to Duncan, 'but she really can't bear to be parted from him [Leonard] for a moment.' Vita had driven over to lunch at Charleston, and 'Virginia held forth in her usual style which you know and I cannot describe, very amusing but also most uneasy, at least to my mind . . . It was brilliant of course and I suppose one sounds curmudgeonly for finding any fault, but one simply gets exhausted and longs for some quiet talk that will lead nowhere for a change.'[45]

Her sisterly irritation had a core of sense, in that Virginia was perilously high (and subsequently in bed with 'influenza' until mid-January 1926). On the level of gossip, and of servant and family problems, art and décor, the sisters were in harmony. Yet each envied the other for what she did not have. Only sibling malice can have fuelled Vanessa's letter to her sister about her own maternal instinct, suggesting that Virginia might write a book about it; the maternal instinct was 'animal and remorseless'. 'But how can one avoid yielding to these instincts if one happens to have them? Perhaps you manage to.'

Vanessa knew that Virginia sometimes suffered badly over her childlessness, seeing herself as incomplete, not 'a real woman', in comparison with her sister or Vita. 'My own fault too – a little more self-control on my part, we might have had a boy of 12, a girl of 10: this always makes me wretched in the early hours.'[46] Virginia would grieve for Leonard too; overhearing a boy talking excitedly with his father about stamp-collecting, 'I thought of L. if he had a son.'[47] Thinking of the Webbs, and of herself and Leonard, she felt 'the pathos, the symbolical quality of the childless couple; standing for something, united.'[48]

The Webbs had a country home, Passfield Corner, at Liphook in Hampshire, where the Woolfs were invited (two months in advance) to spend a weekend in early 1926. Beatrice Webb wrote a long diary entry

---

45 Dec 27 1925. *Selected Letters of Vanessa Bell*
46 VW Diary 5 Sept 1926
47 VW Diary 8 March 1937
48 VW Diary 23 Oct 1929

about the visit of 'this exceptionally gifted pair', remembering the first time she met them as a couple, when Virginia was 'on the borderline of lunacy, he struggling desperately to keep her out of a mental home'. Leonard, she thought, had 'matured and lost his nervous shyness'. (He was forty-five.) Beatrice Webb deplored the Woolfs' rigid secularism. 'Here his Jewish blood comes in . . . the anger of a Jew and an apostate from the Judaic faith . . . He is an anti-imperialist fanatic but otherwise a moderate in Labour politics.' She described their 'raging argument about denominational education and the validity of religious mysticism', but did not record that this was the famous occasion when her skirt fell off.[49]

Beatrice followed up the visit with a long letter to Leonard, her argument being the very one that Leonard consistently refuted – that religious belief 'does bring peace and inspire effort to many human beings'.[50] As he wrote to his former secretary Margaret Green, 'the mere fact that a very large number of people believe such a thing and that the world would be a better place if it were true, is no reason for believing that it is true.'[51]

Eliot continued to consult Leonard, as an expert on mad wives, about his own state of mind and that of his unhappy and disturbed wife Vivien, who was also trying to write. Leonard revered T.S.Eliot as a poet, but not slavishly. In his review of Eliot's *Poems 1905–1925*, he wrote: 'My only criticism of him is that the theme which he plays on these subtle strings is always the same and is very old.'[52] Eliot took this humbly, describing the collection to Leonard as 'an ejection, simply a means of getting all that out of the way'.[53] The two lunched together about once a week, exchanging letters in between the lunches, during a crisis with Vivien in 1925. Tom, deeply grateful for Leonard's support,

49 Margaret I.Cole (ed): *Beatrice Webb's Diaries* Vol 2 1924–1932 Longmans, Green 1956
50 31 Jan 1926
51 26 Oct 1960
52 *Nation* 5 Dec 1925
53 17 Dec 1925. Berg

was wondering whether he should try and limit Vivien's writing; she was 'naturally immoderate'.[54] Leonard advised him to begin by 'limiting and regularizing and watch very carefully to see whether as a matter of fact the writing seems to do good or harm. The main thing to go by, I think, is excitement and depression' – the slightest increase of either, after a session of writing, being bad signs.[55]

In October 1928 Tom Eliot told the Woolfs that he had a new poem which he would like them to criticise. On the seventeenth, they went over to the Eliots at 57 Chester Terrace. Mary Hutchinson, who was close to Tom, and the graphic artist McKnight Kauffer were also there. 'We all sat solemnly on chairs round the room and Tom began the proceedings by reading the poem aloud in that curious monotonous sing-song in which all poets from Homer downwards have recited their poetry.' Then they each in turn had to comment on it. It was rather like an examination, Leonard thought, 'not of the examinee, but of the examiners . . . Virginia passed with flying colours'.[56] Vivien remained upstairs, occasionally shouting down at them.

The poem was *Ash Wednesday*, which Eliot revised before the Hogarth Press published it. (Leonard kept a copy of the first version.) On holiday with Virginia in the West Country, he wrote on impulse to thank Eliot for *Ash Wednesday*, which he was reading and re-reading. 'It is amazingly beautiful. I dislike the doctrine, as you probably know, but the poetry remains and shows how unimportant belief or unbelief may be.'[57] The only value which transcended reason for Leonard Woolf, apart from love, was art.

During the 1920s Leonard was working on his next 'big' book, but he threw off two satirical squibs as Hogarth Essays. The first, in 1925, was *Fear and Politics: A Debate at the Zoo*. The super-civilised Zoo animals hold a debate after closing time to discuss Man – after a skirmish about Woman, and the animals' preferences as to their hairiness and

54 30 April 1925. Berg
55 1 May 1925
56 *Downhill All the Way*
57 5 May 1930

nakedness. The Mandril – a private reference, this – is a Bolshevik, eats shrimps out of a paper bag, and is not a true monkey: 'You have only to observe the coloration of my face and backside to see this. I belong to the intelligentsia.' The animals deduce from Man's appalling behaviour that he is still uncivilised, in the jungle, afraid of others and of his own shadow. 'These human beings delude themselves that a League of Nations or Protection or armies and navies are going to give them security and civilisation in their jungle. But they are the savagest race of carnivore known . . . and the world will never be safe for democracy or for any other animal, until each human animal is confined in a separate cage.' *A Debate at the Zoo* reflects Swift and Kipling, and casts a beam ahead towards Orwell's *Animal Farm* (1945). It is the other voice in Leonard's head – pessimism in fabulous guise, undermining the thesis of the book on which he was then working.

Leonard described himself as 'an unredeemed and unrepentant intellectual', a creature distrusted by many in the Labour Party and an appellation which many British people, uniquely in Europe, used derogatively. His second Hogarth Essay, in 1927, was *Hunting the Highbrow.* Still in zoological mode, he discerned five distinct varieties of which the most significant are '*altifrons aestheticus* var. *severus*' and '*altifrons altifrontissimus*'. The highbrow is most hated when he applies his intellect to popular 'illusions and prejudices' such as religion, the party system, or patriotism. The highbrow can become dangerous. He may want to change the world. So he is laughed at, in order to render him harmless.

Norman Leys, a colleague on A.C.Imp.Q., took Leonard to task for evading the fact that highbrows were often wrong. 'There have been many cases where the whole body of highbrows and all their aunts and cousins have been wrong and the great heart of the people right.'[58] Leys also quarrelled with Leonard for not pushing the government harder over the implementation of the trenchant report on the Empire in Africa which the advisory committee provided for the Labour Party.

But Leonard was fighting his corner. Fabian gradualism no longer convinced Leonard Woolf. In 1929 he brought the Labour

---

58 24 March 1927

Government's budget for Kenya before the committee, who concluded that it was grossly unfair: more money was being proposed for the education of white children *per capita* than for black children, and more money for roads serving the white settlers' estates than for roads serving the 'native reserves'. Sidney Webb, Secretary of State for the Colonies, having been elevated to the peerage as Lord Passfield, chose to hold what Leonard called 'an absurd meeting' about the injustices in Kenya in the chamber of the House of Lords, 'completely empty except for the tiny Secretary of State and the humble chairman [Buxton] and secretary [LW] of the Advisory Committee sitting one on either side of him.'

Leonard followed up the meeting with a letter[59] deploring the Labour Party's 'lax' sense of trusteeship in Kenya, and advocating the appointment of a governor 'who would not be afraid to stand up to the planters if necessary'. Leonard cited as a possible model the governor of Hong Kong,[60] whom he did not know personally, 'but my brother-in-law is Colonial Secretary there and I have heard a good deal about [the governor] from my sister. I must admit that I do not set great store by her judgement.' His brother-in law Tom Southorn was moving smoothly up the imperial career ladder rejected by Leonard. His last posting before retirement was to be Governor of the Gambia; he was knighted, and Bella became Lady Southorn. The poet Sheila Wingfield recalled lunching with them in the Gambia, and Bella retailing her problems with the local Girl Guides: 'I have to be very strict, very strict. *Of course* I can't object to them wearing their uniforms at night to solicit men, because to them it's a most glamorous dress. But I've *had* to put my foot down and tell them they must *not* give birth to their babies on the parade ground.'[61] Bella was awarded the Order of the British Empire (OBE) for services to the Girl Guide movement.

*

59 24 Oct 1929. The 'absurd meeting' with Lord Passfield was on 23 June 1929. LW in *Downhill All the Way* dated it in 1930, probably because it was the 1930 Kenya budget that was being considered.

60 C.C.Clementi

61 Sheila Wingfield (Lady Powerscourt) to LW 25 Jan 1960

In domestic politics, the General Strike of 1926 seemed to Leonard Woolf 'the most painful, the most horrifying' event.[62] The mine-owners combined to reduce coal-miners' wages and, when the miners went on strike, imposed a lock-out. A strike of all its members in sympathy with the miners was called by the Trades Union Council, to bring the country to a standstill. Leonard was on the side of the miners and strikers, even though he felt it was a mistake in policy. Politicians and the press represented the strike as unpatriotic and 'political'; it was widely believed that the Bolsheviks were behind it. Leonard collaborated in soliciting the support of prominent writers and artists in an appeal to the government to negotiate with the TUC, despatching relays of people round London on bicycles collecting signatures. The telephone rang non-stop at 52 Tavistock Square.

What Leonard found 'painful and horrifying' was what the government's attitude suggested to him about the 'communal psychology' of Britain. Why was it more 'unpatriotic' for miners to strike than for the mine owners to lock them out? 'The idea that the employee ought to be in an inferior and subservient position in his relations with his employer, though rarely admitted or expressed, is still deeply rooted in the psychology of all classes except that of the manual workers . . . For the working of our industrial organisation we rely upon a complicated system of privilege, monopoly, and class war', with absolutely no concept of the co-operation of 'free and equal individuals' for a common object.[63]

Leonard was invited again the following year to stand for Parliament, this time for the Labour Party in the London University division. Another path not taken, among many. This was one he was to regret. Nor did he pursue what might seem a natural connection with the London School of Economics. Though he gave seminars on economic imperialism at LSE in 1928, standing in for Philip Noel-Baker, he never was on the staff, though his qualifications and experience were as good as many that were, and his *International Government* was on the reading-list.

---

62 *Downhill All the Way*
63 LW, *After the Deluge* Vol 1 Hogarth Press 1931

Leonard Woolf was not one of nature's academics, nor an organisation man.

One result of Virginia's relationship with Vita was acquaintance with Lady Gerald (Dorothy) Wellesley, wife to the heir of the Duke of Wellington and one of Vita's sentimental attachments. Dottie Wellesley was dotty, and wrote poetry much admired by W.B. Yeats. Leonard could not stand her. After a visit to her country house, Penns-in-the-Rocks, he drove home at forty miles an hour (i.e. *very* fast), 'furious at her vanity, conceit, egotism, vulgarity; ill breeding, violent temper etc'.[64] But Dottie was rich and generous, and subsidised the Hogarth Living Poets series, with the title of Series Editor; and Lady Gerald Wellesley was a name to shelter behind when a rejection letter was in order.

A differently beneficent result of Virginia's relationship with Vita was a spaniel puppy. The Woolfs' old dog, Grizzle, contracted mange, then fits, and had to be put down in December 1926. They fetched Pinka, or Pinker, from Long Barn on 5 January 1927.

The modern thing for women in the 1920s was to have their hair cut short. Vita had hers shingled, and Virginia followed suit. Leonard's diary, 9 February 1927: 'Bobo Mayor[65] and Clive dined. V shingled.' Bobo did the cutting, urged on by Leonard and Clive, during an evening at 52 Tavistock Square enlivened by Spanish wine. Vita had a motor car – a Rolls Royce. She was 'a very good, but rather flamboyant driver'; to hear her 'put an aggressive taxi-driver in his place, even when she was in the wrong, made one recognize a note in her voice that Sackvilles and Buckhursts were using to serfs in Kent 600 years ago'. Her aristocratic lineage 'had put into her mind and heart an ingredient which was alien to us and at first made intimacy difficult'.[66] Leonard was disingenuous in his use of 'us'. Virginia was amused and enchanted by Vita's careless magnificence.

---

64 VW *Letters*, to Vita S-W 8 Sept 1928

65 Bobo (Beatrice) was the wife of Robin (Robert) Mayor, Fellow of Kings and Apostle, and the daughter of one of Beatrice Webb's eight sisters, who married the banker Daniel Meinertzhagen.

66 *Downhill All the Way*

Even Vanessa had a motor car. In the *Nation*'s 'Books in Brief' section on 14 July 1928 Leonard reviewed *The Car Buyer's Annual.* His diary, 15 August 1927: 'Bought Car. Drove Car Hampstead.'

This first car, for which they paid £275, was a second-hand Singer with 7,500 miles on the clock. It was nicknamed the Umbrella. The next day Leonard drove it to Richmond, the day after that he drove Virginia to Long Barn to stay with Vita. On all his early excursions he was accompanied by Mr Tate, the garage man. On the last day of July, when Virginia was away, he drove to Charleston by himself for the first time.

Nothing, for years, had given him so much pleasure. 'Certainly nothing ever changed so profoundly my material existence, the mechanism and range of my every-day life, as the possession of a motor-car.'[67] No one now can properly empathise with the unprecedented freedom that a car provided in those early traffic-free years. As he had written in connection with Spain, it is modes of transport which determine how men live. 'Did Leonard tell you', Virginia wrote to Tom Eliot, 'how our entire life is spent driving, cleaning, dodging in and out of a shed, measuring miles in maps, planning expeditions, going on expeditions, being beaten back by the rain, eating sandwiches on high roads, cursing cows, sheep, bicyclists, and when we are at rest talking of nothing but cars and petrol?'[68]

By late September 1927 Leonard was confident enough to drive Virginia down through France to Cassis, a small fishing village on the Mediterranean between Marseille and Toulon. They took a week each way over the journey, with one puncture on the way down and four on the way back. Cassis was a spot so quiet 'that men might have risen up at the sound of a bird'.[69]

Duncan and Vanessa too were there, discovering the loveliness of Cassis and its potential for painters. Vanessa's elder son Julian reported

---

67 *Downhill All the Way*

68 VW *Letters* 24 Aug 1927

69 Twenty-six years later Leonard was to find Cassis 'submerged in cars and villas', the rocky shore black with people, loud with transistors, littered with bottles and paper bags.

to his brother Quentin that 'Leonard had continual quarrels with Nessa and Duncan as to the exact shares each should pay for a litre of petrol. Virginia was quite dotty and asked perpetual questions.'[70] Vanessa negotiated a ten-year lease on a cottage outside the village, La Bergère, where she would establish 'Charleston in France'. Cassis became identified, in Bloomsbury lore, with Vanessa; but Leonard made a point, in *Downhill All the Way*, of stressing that 'Vanessa followed us to Cassis' (the Woolfs had gone there by train, the previous spring), and that he and Virginia had introduced her to the retired Indian Army colonel who owned La Bergère.

This was the first of many touring holidays abroad, and Leonard thought that nothing they ever did gave Virginia such an 'intense pleasure, a mixture of exhilaration and relaxation'.[71] They had endless breakdowns and punctures. It seemed to Leonard 'that there was hardly any road in France on which I had not grovelled in the mud changing wheels.'[72] Yet the liberation of the long, white roads of France stretching ahead confirmed for him one of his favourite sayings of Montaigne, that 'it is not the arrival, but the journey which matters' – from which he derived the title of the last volume of his autobiography. He recorded in his diary his daily mileage, the accumulated mileage and, in early years, even the occasions when he filled up with petrol.

Maynard Keynes (who of course had a motor car), after he married Lydia Lopokova in 1925 acquired Tilton farmhouse, just up the lane from Charleston, as a weekend and holiday house. Maynard, the richest of the friends, could afford to make Tilton, already more imposing than the average farmhouse, comfortable to a degree hitherto unknown to either Charleston or Rodmell – electric light, central heating, and every modern convenience. For this he was both mocked and envied.

Maynard had influence. When Vita Sackville-West dined at Tilton on 10 July 1927, Maynard told her that a peerage for Leonard was on the cards; and Leonard had apparently told Virginia he would style himself

70 22 April 1928. King's College Cambridge
71 *Downhill All the Way*
72 *Downhill All the Way*

'Lord Leonard Woolf'.[73] 'Went Maynard re peerage', Leonard noted in his diary on 27 November. Nothing more is heard of this. Leonard was to turn down every honour he was offered. But he too had influence. Sydney Waterlow of the Foreign Office, in 1929, asked him to use his contacts in the Labour Party to get him an 'alpha' diplomatic posting. Leonard replied gently that such a move could only be counterproductive.

In 1926 Virginia, for the first time, earned more than Leonard, thanks to the success of *Mrs Dalloway* and *The Common Reader* in both Britain and America. In 1927 her novel *To The Lighthouse* was even more successful. 'Leonard says its my best book; but then he has to.'[74] (He did have to. Anything less would have thrown her into disarray.) Her income for 1928 was £1,540, while Leonard's was £394. The Press also made twice as much profit as ever before. 'After 1928 we were always very well off',[75] wrote Leonard, especially as they always lived on less than they earned.

In 1926 partitions downstairs at Monks House were removed, making one large sitting room, which they painted green. The alterations provided a narrow hall, entered from the garden, and a small dining-room. The year 1926 also saw the installation of a new cooker, a piped hot-water system, and an upstairs bathroom with bath, basin, and a flush lavatory with a mahogany seat. There were new drains, a new cesspool, and an outside lavatory with a flush. They bought Park Cottage No 1, and Park Cottage no 2, one for Nelly and one for the gardener, who from November 1928 was Percy Bartholomew. He had the cottage rent-free, and was paid £2 a week.[76]

The outbuildings in the garden were cleared away, their flint standings serving to make interlocking enclosures and garden 'rooms'. In the

---

73 A solecism, more defiant than it seems today. Strictly, only the younger son of a duke or a marquess incorporates his first name into his title.
74 VW Letters: to Vanessa Bell, 8 May 1927
75 *Downhill All the Way*
76 Mr Bartholomew's wages did not rise much over the years. In the early 1940s he was paid £2.7s.6d. a week.

summer of 1928 they bought the six-and-a-half acre field called the Croft which abutted their garden to the north. The level part was incorporated into the garden as lawn, and the sloping remainder let out to Mr James the farmer. They had beehives against the churchyard wall, a fishpond, and Leonard had his first greenhouse. A new vegetable garden was planted. (Lists of vegetable seeds jostled for space with book-titles and reviewers in the back of Leonard's diaries.). The next innovation at Monks House was a gramophone, in January 1929; and he contributed an occasional feature 'New Gramophone Records' to the *Nation*. They did not yet have a wireless set, though both were giving live broadcast talks from 1927.

Morgan Forster, staying at Rodmell in March 1928, got drunk with his hosts as they discussed 'sodomy, and sapphism, with emotion', in connection with a new lesbian novel, Radclyffe Hall's *The Well of Loneliness*. Forster thought that being homosexual was like being a Jew – you were an outsider – which explains why Leonard asked him that evening: 'Would you like to be converted?' Morgan said he preferred to stay as he was. He encouraged Leonard later in the year to mount a protest on behalf of *The Well of Loneliness*, which was likely to be banned.

As Leonard wrote to Tom Eliot, 'the book is perfectly decent and it is monstrous to suppress it'.[77] Leonard's review in the *Nation*,[78] voicing the opinion of most critics – that *The Well of Loneliness* was not pornographic, although it was not a great work of art – was placed first in a collection of reviews as evidence for the defence. Radclyffe Hall's solicitors asked Leonard to give evidence in court; but the magistrate refused to take oral evidence, the prosecution was successful, and a subsequent appeal failed.

Vita, unlike Radclyffe Hall, was a closet lesbian, maintaining a conventional social front with her husband. In September 1928 she and Virginia went away together for a short holiday in Burgundy. The morning they left, Leonard and Virginia had a 'small and sudden row'. Both

---

77 25 Oct 1928
78 4 Aug 1928

husbands were anxious lest Virginia became over-excited and ill, but Vita was well aware of her responsibility. Both women wrote home every day. Leonard, at Rodmell, 'was terribly sad to see you go and moped with the Pinka family[79] for a long time – it was the summer dying out of the year, and the chill of autumn in fact immediately descended and today I woke up to a regular grey, damp Rodmell autumn with the clouds at the foot of the Downs and the smell of dead leaves burning.' He had been 'tinkering with the car'; Quentin had come to paint the new gramophone (with Charleston-type decorative motifs), and they went for a walk 'and discussed his change of character and view of life'.[80] Leonard picked apples, and listened to gramophone records for his *Nation* review. 'It is very dreary here without you and the minor animals – I could not live without them despite their curious ways . . . I hope you won't make a habit of deserting me.'[81] He knew Vita's history of extended fugues with her lovers, which had caused Harold much misery. But Vita and Virginia came back a day earlier than arranged. When anxious about Virginia and Vita, Leonard would walk all the way to Hampstead to see Margaret Llewelyn Davies, still his confidante; he went often to the Zoo; he made more frequent visits to his mother and to his brothers and sisters.

His mother, in her late seventies, was living in a hotel in Barkston Gardens, Earl's Court, with a bedroom, a sitting room, and a paid companion. She came for a weekend to Rodmell at the end of August 1928. After her visit, Virginia wrote to Vanessa a virtuoso letter of about two thousand unparagraphed words approximating to her mother-in-law's inconsequential talk, there being no filter between what flickered through Mrs Woolf's mind and what came out of her mouth – a 'stream of consciousness' in the flesh. A sample: 'Len is a splendid man. He should have gone to the Bar. He has such a clear brain in so many directions. His father thought the world of Len. Have you read Radclyffe Hall's book? I have got it from Harrods. She was a friend of

79 Pinka had four puppies.
80 25 Sept 1928. Quentin Bell was nineteen years old.
81 27 Sept 1928

Bella's. They went to Mrs Cole's school together and she used to come to our house sometimes – a regular society girl. Bella never liked her; but Bella did not dislike her. And now she has written this book. Of course I cannot say all that I would like to say if we were alone together. I may be foolish, but I cannot speak to you and Len as if Len were not there.'[82]

Virginia never called her husband Len. She called him Leo.

In January 1929 the Woolfs went to Berlin to visit Harold Nicolson, with Vita and her two boys Ben and Nigel. Harold was Chargé d'Affaires at the British Embassy. Duncan Grant, Vanessa and her younger son Quentin joined them, as did Vita's cousin Eddy Sackville-West. The group was too big to all want to do the same things, and the weather was wet and icy-cold.

Vita was bad-tempered because she loathed both the Germans and Harold's diplomatic career. Leonard was bad-tempered because when they went to see Pudovkin's film *Sturm über Asia*, Vita kept asking him stupid questions. He was bad-tempered again when Harold expected him to go to a diplomatic lunch party, arranged specially so that he might meet German politicians – though he did go, as his diary attests. Vita took Virginia off alone one afternoon, which made everyone else bad-tempered. Duncan was interested in Eddy Sackville-West. Harold and Eddy were interested in the gay bars. Vanessa was bad-tempered because she could not see why they had to be with the Nicolsons at all, and thought the Woolfs did not know how to behave abroad: 'they walked miles to avoid the difficulty of getting a cab', and ate in the hotel restaurant, whereas Vanessa and Duncan prided themselves on finding small places where they got better food for a third of hotel prices.[83]

Despite the bad tempers, Leonard and Harold Nicolson dined together alone one evening in Berlin, and Harold consulted 'My dear Leonard' privately, later that year, about whether he should leave the diplomatic service as Vita wished, and accept an offer from Lord Beaverbrook to write for the *Evening Standard*. It would pay well. But if it

---

82 VW *Letters* 2 Sept 1928
83 Frances Spalding, *Vanessa Bell* Weidenfeld & Nicolson 1983

did not work out, would he be damaged by the association with Beaverbrook?[84] Soon afterwards he did leave the diplomatic service – an unhappy time for him – and wrote to Leonard again. He was getting panic attacks when he went to the theatre. Should he stick it out, or stop going to the theatre? Leonard advised him to try sticking it out for six months and, if it was just as bad, 'give in and not go to the theatre.'[85]

On the night-crossing, returning from Berlin, Virginia took too much Somnifene (against seasickness). 'When I woke her in the morning', Leonard wrote to Vanessa, 'she was in a curious state, so giddy that it was only with the greatest difficulty I got her off the boat and on to the train, as she could hardly walk and was in a kind of drugged state.' She went to bed once they got home 'and now has one of the old-fashioned headaches and rather a bad one.'[86] She was in bed for three weeks. Leonard wrote rather pointedly to Vita that Virginia had been near 'breaking-point' – nothing to do with 'influenza' (the customary label for Virginia's collapses) or the Somnifene, 'but simply to her over-doing it', with seven or eight late nights in a row in Berlin. 'It was mad.'

He wrote in a PS: 'I knew the danger', but decided it had to be risked, and 'that to interfere, as I always do in London, would do no good and only spoil things with the continual nagging which that kind of shepherding always involves.'[87] Some of their friends saw Leonard as tyrannical where Virginia's social life was concerned. But another bad breakdown was such a nightmare prospect for them both that he walked a perpetual tightrope between under and over-watchfulness, giving her, as she herself said (even as she complained), the 'maternal protection which . . . is what I have always most wished from everyone.'[88]

Vita replied to Leonard, equally pointedly, that '*I* had not taken her to any galleries etc, and had only twice been with you in the evening.' She had referred to 'influenza' when writing to Virginia 'because I thought she would be less likely to worry about herself if she could

---

84 22 July 1929
85 LW to Nigel Nicolson 8 May 1968
86 28 Jan 1929
87 15 Feb 1929
88 VW Diary 21 Dec 1925

attribute it to a (so to speak) "normal" cause.'[89] In fact, what Vita had sportively written to Virginia was that 'SUPPRESSED RANDINESS', as well as influenza, was the probable cause of her illness.

The best account of Leonard at the Hogarth Press in the late 1920s is by Richard Kennedy,[90] who came as an 'apprentice' aged seventeen, and left after a year to go to university. At the interview, with Pinka at his feet, Leonard looked 'very like a wolf in human form – but an extremely intellectual wolf, a kindly wolf – a very Socrates of wolves', his hand trembling slightly as he bit into an apple, giving the impression 'not of infirmity, but of the vibration of a powerful intellectual machine'. In spite of his tremor, Leonard could feed paper into the printing machine at high speed, and 'very delicately' adjust a full stop which came adrift from its bed of type.

Richard Kennedy's letters of reminiscence to Leonard, when he was reading *Sowing*, were evocative: 'I can see you setting out for the *Nation* on a wet Friday afternoon with your pipe at right angles to your jaw and Pinker trailing behind not liking the weather.' Kennedy had been reading Leonard's description of his 'carapace' in *Sowing*: 'I doubt whether your carapace was so thick and impenetrable. The fact that your heart was often at war with your head caused chinks.' Nobody, he said, took Leonard's rages at the Press very seriously 'as it was so easy to flannel round you, and I expect the inhabitants of Hambantota found the same thing'. The trick was 'to switch planes to that of the heart rather than the head'. It had seemed 'quite natural when there was a great frost that you should take me skating at Richmond instead of the usual afternoon's business'. (Leonard used the same pair of skates with curling ends that he had when he was a boy.)

Richard Kennedy recalled how fat Mrs Cartwright, the office manager, 'slipped down the frozen area steps grasping her basket of shopping'. In *A Boy at the Hogarth Press*, written in the present tense like a diary in spite of being published more than forty years later (and after

---

89 20 Feb 1929
90 *A Boy at the Hogarth Press* Whittington Press 1972, illustrations by the author.

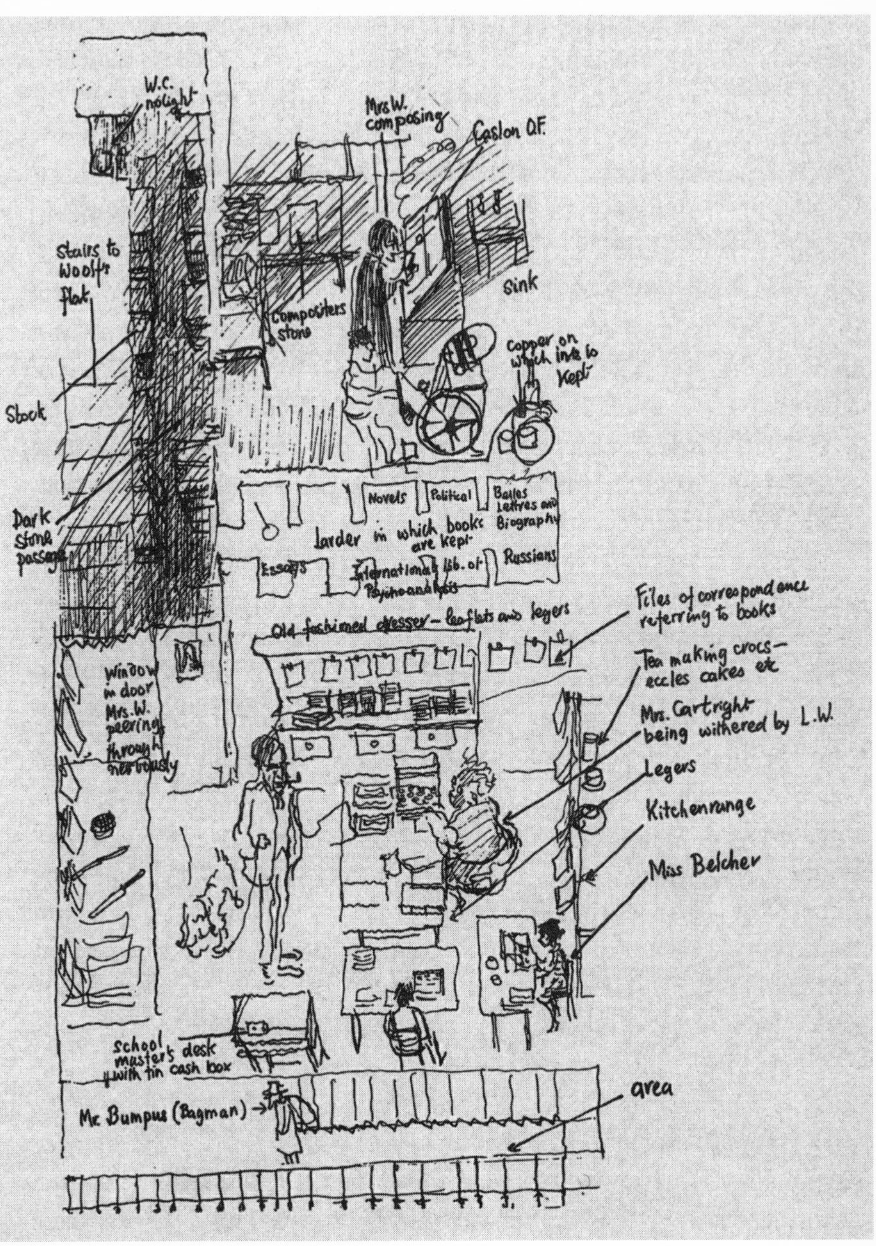

Richard Kennedy's sketch of the Hogarth Press offices in the basement of 52, Tavistock Square, LW on lower left, with Pinka.

Leonard's death), he recalled Virginia making a cruelly funny story of Mrs Cartwright's fall; and himself asking Leonard, on those same area steps, if he believed in the existence of the soul. 'Obviously not!' said Leonard. Another employee was Miss Belcher, dangerously pretty; Leonard told Richard Kennedy and Miss Belcher they must lunch separately. When annoyed by the shortcomings of Mrs Cartwright or Miss Belcher, he would let out an exasperated wail, 'saying words like "Why???" and "Absurd!!!"'.

For this observant boy, Leonard was 'the magician who keeps us all going by his strength of will . . . and Mrs W is a beautiful magical doll, very precious, but sometimes rather uncontrollable'. Richard Kennedy had modelled himself on Leonard, he confessed in his letter, kindly not reminding him that when he recommended the manuscript of Ivy Compton Burnett's first novel as a work of genius, Leonard turned it down flat. Richard Kennedy wondered how Miss Belcher, Mrs Cartwright, and Miss Ritchie had fared. 'I can see Miss Belcher stumping out of the office in her high heels and flowered overall with a mole on her cheek holding the towel from the towel service which this strong-minded girl had forced you to except [*sic*] the services of. I am getting like Marcel Proust.' In Kennedy's book, it was Leonard who became a Proustian figure 'rather like Swann . . . Of course, Mrs W is not at all like Odette, but they are both rather wayward creatures, worshipped by their husbands.'

The 'Miss Ritchie' to whom Kennedy referred to was Alice Ritchie; she and her younger brother and sister were brought up in South Africa. Her father returned to serve in the Great War, and the family followed. Alice went to Newnham College, Cambridge, and then to Geneva to work for the League of Nations Secretariat. She was sacked for some insubordination, and came to Leonard with a recommendation from Philip Noel-Baker; he gave her the job of sales rep for the Hogarth Press. 'Alice Ritchie was, I think, the first woman to travel for a publisher and some booksellers did not like the innovation. She was not only a very good traveller, but also a good and serious novelist.'[91] The Hogarth

91 *Downhill All The Way*

Press published Alice's first novel *The Peacemakers*, based on her experiences with the League, in 1928. In *Downhill All the Way* Leonard picked out two Hogarth novels published in the late 1920s, long out of print, which still seemed to him remarkable. One was F.M.Mayor's *The Rector's Daughter* and the other Alice Ritchie's *The Peacemakers*.[92]

Alice Ritchie, who was seventeen years younger than Leonard, became dear to him. He could give himself a long rope with the young women authors of whom he grew fond, establishing an intimacy based on mutual attraction which was all the more free because of the impossibility of the attraction having physical expression – and Leonard was attractive. Frances Marshall described the 'enormous charm' of Leonard's blue eyes with their marked black lashes, his illuminating smile, his boyish build, his musical baritone voice, his hair standing up in tufts.[93] Alice Ritchie often stopped by the office for a cup of tea, and brought with her, to meet Leonard, her beautiful art-student sister Marjorie, known as Trekkie.[94] She was five years younger than Alice, and married from 1926 to a fellow-student, Peter Brooker. Alice persuaded the Press to use Trekkie's design for the jacket of her second novel, *Occupied Territory* (1930).

Alice Ritchie first came to dinner at Tavistock Square on 2 May 1928. Virginia could be unkind to young aspiring females, such as Elizabeth Jenkins – 'poor little grey mouse Jenkins',[95] straight out of Newnham College, who was invited in March 1928 to Tavistock Square on the recommendation of Lytton's sister Pernel Strachey, the Principal of Newnham. Elizabeth observed the way Leonard attended to Virginia, 'his whole attention fixed on her', and it seemed to her that

---

92 Leonard, over-cautious, only published *The Rector's Daughter* 'on commission', the author bearing costs of printing, binding, publicity and distribution, and Hogarth charging 10% on each copy sold. It sold well, and has been reissued by Penguin Modern Classics (1973), Virago (1987), and Wordsworth Editions (1996). Neither of Alice Ritchie's novels has been reissued.

93 Conversation with VG 14 Sept 2001.

94 From Afrikaans 'trek', which has a secondary meaning denoting determination and a strong desire. See Judith Adamson (ed): *Love Letters: Leonard Woolf & Trekkie Parsons 1941–1968* Chatto & Windus 2001

95 VW Diary 12 May 1929. Elizabeth Jenkins became a successful novelist and biographer.

Virginia 'adored' him too. She overheard Leonard saying to a bumptious young man, 'You are quite right, but you can't say that to her [Virginia], she can't take it.'

When Virginia, that evening, was 'disagreeable and sarcastic' to Elizabeth, saying she could be doing without young people 'fished out of the blue', Leonard took the young woman by the elbow, went downstairs with her, and found her a taxi. He told her he hoped she would come again: 'Virginia is not always like that, she has a lot to put up with.' Elizabeth was filled with a sense of his 'deep kindness', and also of his cheerfulness.[96] Thus Leonard stood up for his wife while reassuring their young visitor. Virginia afforded Alice Ritchie rather more latitude, at least outwardly, and she frequently came to Monks House; though after several years of Alice, Virginia referred to her to Pernel Strachey as 'that formidable and to me slightly repulsive – no only acutely unhappy like a beast that gets its paw in a trap – figure . . . Add to that a head which can fit no hat, feet which are impossible to cover, and a nature that expects insults.'[97]

Leonard wrote several pages about Alice Ritchie in *The Journey Not the Arrival Matters*, the fifth and last volume of his autobiography. 'She had the mind of a novelist and the temperament of an artist'; but there was some 'psychological twist' in her which made her unable ever to finish her third novel, an 'artificial sterility' arising from her own impossibly high standards. He encouraged her, reading and commenting on this novel in progress, chapter by chapter, in the early 1930s.

Alice had, he wrote, 'a streak of melancholy'. One of her surviving letters to him from this time, which has with hindsight a grim resonance, confirms this. 'I think your anti-suicide recipe ['nothing matters'] is admirable', she wrote to him, 'for a stoic. It needs a little modification for novelists because it's precisely when we get the feeling that nothing matters that the river looks most attractive at its deepest.' Virginia declined to enter into an anguish which reflected her own. Her tone to

---

96 Conversation with VG 16 Nov 1902
97 VW Letters 30 Dec 1931

Alice could be aggressively jocular: 'How is the novel? Are you in the process of jumping out of the window, as I advised?'[98]

Virginia's *Orlando* was published shortly after her trip to France with Vita, and she gave Vita the manuscript. *Orlando* is the fruit of their love affair. The flower of it was already spent. They were lovers, tentatively, for about three years; but Vita was predatory and passionate and, knowing Virginia's nature and her own, made new conquests. Virginia – more mentally agile than Vita, and subtle, ironic, teasing– was not however one of Vita's victims. Passion faded, but affection remained, and the Woolfs and Nicolsons continued to see each other regularly.[99] *Orlando* was like a love letter to Vita, a game played with biography and history, a time-travelling, gender-morphing phantasmagoria fuelled by infatuation, by the splendour of Knole, and by Vita's romantic sense of her heritage.

Leonard read *Orlando* in May 1928, at Rodmell, and took it more seriously than Virginia expected him to. 'Thinks it in some ways better than the Lighthouse; about more interesting things, & with more attachment to life, & larger . . . He says it is very original.'[100] He categorised it as a satire, which is part of what it was. His response is typical of his self-control, as of his respect for Virginia as an artist. Vita's younger son Nigel, who knew the Woolfs from the time he was about seven years old, thought that there was 'no question' that Leonard knew the realities of the affair, and accepted it without jealousy, while privately thinking it 'rather a bore'.[101] If he was right on that last point, which sounds emotionally unintelligent, it would be because Leonard would not have chosen to spend so much time with the Nicolsons; and because seeing Vita, writing to Vita, took up such a lot of Virginia's time.

Orlando was the turning-point in Virginia's career, commercially

---

98 VW Letters 8 Aug 1932

99 For details of the relationship between V and V see their published letters; and Victoria Glendinning, *Vita: The life of V. Sackville-West* Weidenfeld & Nicolson 1983, and Hermione Lee, *Virginia Woolf* Chatto & Windus 1996.

100 VW Diary 31 May 1928

101 Nigel Nicolson in conversation with VG 13 Dec 2001.

speaking. Though the Woolfs' investments lost half their value in the crash of 1929, *Orlando* paid for more work on Monks House. They put a brick fireplace in the big downstairs sitting room; Leonard provided a sketch for the contractors of what he wanted, as he did for the new garden gate at the front of the house, to be 'absolutely plain oak, without any ornamentation at all'.

Then the local builders, Philcox Bros, constructed for them an extension of box-like charmlessness, which the Woolfs thought was just fine, consisting of a new bedroom for Virginia at ground level, with no bathroom and no access to the house other than going out into the garden and in at the kitchen door; and another room above it. The garden room beside her new bedroom was improved and re-floored. Leonard had a new, heated greenhouse. The coach-house, now the garage, was lined with asbestos and fitted with sliding doors. The weatherboarding on the front of the house was repainted in Virginia's preferred bluish-green: trade name 'Pompeian Pale Turquoise'.

They pooled their earnings and the profits of the Press, and shared out equally between them the surplus, after all expenses had been met. This seems unfair to Virginia, but they were a partnership, and Leonard had substantively supported the household and her novel-writing by his earnings from journalism until she began to make money in her forties. Virginia, from her 'hoard', paid for the work on the house (£454.12.7), and he from his, for the outside work and the garden (£80.12.7).

Just before Christmas 1929 Leonard wrote to Maynard Keynes formally resigning from the *Nation*. They could manage without his salary. Virginia's *A Room of One's Own*, published that October, sold 22,000 copies in the first six months in Britain and the United States.

If *A Room of One's Own* was Virginia's most compelling statement of her feminist position, Leonard's feminism was manifest in practice, not only in regard to his marriage and his friendships, but in his respect for unconsidered women in the workplace. There was something he wanted to say, he wrote, which was 'never said about the history of weekly journals'. There was always a secretary to the editor, 'who played an extraordinarily important part in the fortunes of the paper. Mrs Mason of Sharpe's *New Statesman*, Miss Crosse of Massingham's *Nation*, Mrs

Jones of Henderson's, all deserve to be mentioned when one is praising famous men and women.'[102] To this list he might have added Louise Matthaei, his assistant on the *International Review*, and Margaret Green, whose letters prove that the esteem was mutual. He had 'trained and taught' her, she wrote, and she had 'lasting gratitude for all that I learnt through working under you.'[103]

---

102 LW, 'The Prehistoric "N.S. & N.", *New Statesman* 12 May 1956. Reprinted in Edward Hyams, *New Statesman: An Anthology* Longmans 1963

103 17 Dec 1961

12

The Spring has died out of our lives

In 1931 Leonard was appointed to the executive committee of the New Fabian Research Bureau, a young breakaway group from the Fabian Society, spearheaded by Clement Attlee and Hugh Gaitskell, with Douglas Cole as honorary secretary. Leonard chaired the International Section. He had turned fifty, but was not perceived as one of the old guard. The Webbs saw no betrayal. After the Woolfs stayed a night with them at Passfield Corner at the end of March 1931, Beatrice redefined Leonard as 'a saint with very considerable intelligence; a man without vanity or guile, wholly public-spirited . . .'[1] He was one of a Labour group who met privately with Gandhi at the time of the Round Table Conference on India in London in 1931. 'At first sight he presented to one a body which was slightly inhuman, slightly ridiculous.' But when he spoke, Leonard felt his 'strength, subtlety, humour', and 'an extraordinary sweetness of disposition'. Leonard was about to begin co-editing another new journal, the *Political Quarterly*. But before that took shape, there was a game of editorial musical chairs.

*

1 Diary 1 April 1931

Kingsley Martin was a part-time junior lecturer at LSE in his mid-thirties, the son of an impecunious nonconformist minister. He had a First from Magdalene College, Cambridge, and just missed a Fellowship at King's. Socially naïve, he never, as an undergraduate, even heard of the Apostles. He had a long, craggy face, and was the epitome of plain living and high thinking: bike-rides and lemonade and no sex.

Emerging from that background of dissenting Christianity from which most social reform sprang, Kingsley Martin repudiated religion in favour of Socialism. G.B.Shaw became one of a series of 'father figures', and Harold Laski a close friend. A late link in the long chain of clever young people invited to lunch with Sydney and Beatrice Webb at Grosvenor Road, he broke a taboo there by asking to use the lavatory. Harold Laski told him that no one, not even the Prime Minister, had ever dared ask that before. Maynard Keynes invited Kingsley Martin to review for the *Nation*, which was how Leonard first became conscious of him, and the Hogarth Press published Kingsley's short book *The British Public and the General Strike*, which reflected Leonard's own views, in November 1926.

At LSE Kingsley Martin met another junior lecturer, W.A.Robson, who conceived with him the idea of launching a serious political journal. The background of William Robson, two years older than Kingsley Martin and fifteen years younger than Leonard Woolf, was closer to Leonard's. His father was a dealer in pearls in Hatton Garden, and the family lived in middle-class comfort until his death when William was fifteen, when he went to work as a clerk for Hendon Airport. He was soon a manager, and the author of *Aircraft in War and Peace*, published when he was twenty-one – by which time he was a fighter pilot with the Royal Flying Corps.

Robson's book caught the attention of Shaw, which led to the inevitable introduction to the Webbs; he was encouraged to take an undergraduate place at LSE, where he got a First in economics, and then a doctorate, while simultaneously reading law. He was called to the Bar in 1922 and wrote two more books before being taken on to the staff of LSE. His chief interest was public administration, which his work and career established as an academic subject.

Leonard wrote a full-page signed review in the *Athenaeum* of Robson's seminal *Justice and Administrative Law*.[2] In 'Trial by Whitehall', his lively review of a sober book, Leonard summarised Robson's arguments, stressing that the separation of executive and judicial functions, 'believed by all patriotic Britons to be part of their birthright', had never really existed, and that the growing judicial power of government departments threatened to supersede the courts of justice and the common law. Leonard and William Robson met soon afterwards. Robson was a natty dresser, always wrote with green ink, and seemed rather an 'old young man',[3] of austere demeanour but with a charming smile.

William Robson and Kingsley Martin envisaged their *Political Quarterly* as left-leaning, but with no party affiliation. They called a private meeting at LSE of 'forty or fifty leading intellectuals'[4] and issued a prospectus, which doubled as an appeal for funds, with twenty-eight signatories. Leonard Woolf's name was among them. William Robson persuaded a reluctant G.B.Shaw to stump up £1000, and Harold Macmillan was to be *PQ*'s publisher – a shrewd move, as Macmillan, in his mid-thirties, was a progressive Conservative MP, thus reinforcing the image of *PQ* as politically broad-based.

Robson and Martin wanted a famous name as editor, and one who would not frighten non-socialist backers. Leonard, on the launching committee, unsuccessfully tried to persuade the social historian J.L.Hammond to take it on, perhaps in partnership with himself or Harold Laski. The idea of a co-editorship took root. Leonard was rather keen to co-edit, while assuring Kingsley Martin that he was *not* keen, but prepared to do it, and that 'of all the suggestions Robson would be best as joint editor with me. I have not suggested it to him as I thought it might come better from you or someone else.'[5] It is unusual to find Leonard politicking on his own behalf. He was trumped by Maynard

2 25 Feb 1928

3 But he became, as Sir Sydney Caine said at a Memorial Meeting held at LSE 20 June 1980, 'a very young old man'. LW too frequently used green ink.

4 W.A.Robson, *The Political Quarterly in the 30s* Allen Lane The Penguin Press 1971

5 23 Feb 1929. Quoted by Bernard Crick in the first chapter of his unfinished history of *PQ*, from which most of the detail of the gestation of *PQ* is taken.

Keynes, who 'had a talk' with him, reporting to William Robson that 'on personal grounds he [Leonard] would be perfectly happy if your colleague were to be Martin rather than himself.'[6] Robson preferred Kingsley Martin to Leonard, maybe fearing that Leonard would be a 'bossy nanny'[7] to his baby. But when Keynes offered Kingsley Martin the editorship of the *New Statesman and Nation*[8] in summer 1931, he withdrew as co-editor of the *PQ*, and Leonard took his place.

Kingsley Martin remained editor of the *New Statesman*, contributing articles and surveys to *PQ*, and on its editorial board, for the next thirty years. Leonard remained joint editor of *PQ* with William Robson for the next twenty-seven years, and was a regular contributor. He maintained his connection with the *New Statesman*, writing reviews and articles for Kingsley, and from 1942 he was on its board. These arrangements attained a triangular stability. In spite of the age difference, William Robson became Leonard's most trusted male friend, in the undemonstrative fashion natural to both of them. William Robson was married to Juliette Alvin – French, and a professional cellist;[9] the first of their three children, Elaine, was born in 1931. The Woolfs became friends of the whole family. 'Call me Willie', Robson said to Virginia when he came to tea at Monks House in August 1935.

Leonard's relationship with Kingsley was equally close, but stormy. They had snapping rows, like an old dog and a younger one in the same basket. Kingsley Martin found Leonard 'as I still do, the most companionable of men. He was always ready to advise me, and became, I think, something of a Father Figure to me. No one was ever so ready for argument and, I may add, so obstinate and so loveable.'[10]

---

6 28 June 1929. Quoted in Bernard Crick, op.cit.

7 Bernard Crick, op.cit.

8 Henceforth referred to as the *New Statesman*. (Maynard Keynes merged the *Nation* with the *New Statesman and Athenaeum*). The 'new' weekly first appeared 28 Feb 1931. From January 1934 the *New Statesman and Nation* acquired a subtitle: 'The Weekend Review'. The '*and Nation*' was dropped from the masthead in 1957, and 'The Weekend Review' in 1964.

9 Juliette Alvin founded the British Society of Music Therapy in 1958. She published *Music Therapy* in 1966 and *Music Therapy and the Autistic Child* in 1978.

10 Kingsley Martin, *Editor: A Second Volume of Autobiography* Hutchinson 1968

He veered between modelling himself on Leonard, and contesting him violently, as one does with a father figure. He cited Leonard Woolf as exercising 'a powerful influence on the policy and character' of the new *New Statesman.* Leonard collaborated with him for several years on the unsigned 'London Diary' column, although he hated having his paragraphs 'hacked about'. When he wrote a parody of a *Times* leading article, and the paper's cautious printers insisted on changing '*The Times*' to 'Britain's leading newspaper', he was furious.

PQ business – less hectic, being a quarterly, and not office-based – was conducted over lunches each Wednesday with William Robson, and sessions at 52 Tavistock Square, which was used in early days as the address on *PQ*'s letter-head. Leonard started by writing book reviews for *PQ*; his first long article was on the future of British broadcasting. He and Robson had a policy of publishing whatever was of importance, whatever the provenance – a prime example being a translation, 'The Political and Social Doctrines of Fascism', by Mussolini. They fulfilled the *PQ* promise to be progressive and radical, publishing Hugh Dalton's plan for abolishing the House of Lords, and the Webbs' scheme for the devolution of England, Scotland and Wales.

The Hogarth Press reissued *The Village in the Jungle* in September 1931; and *After the Deluge: A Study in Communal Psychology* the following month. This was Leonard Woolf's 'big book', and the first of a projected trilogy. He set out to analyse, through a study of history, the psychological dynamic of violent social upheaval. His premise was that 'the old is always stronger than the new, and the dead than the living. Thus you have the tyranny of the dead mind', against which extreme misery or outrage will finally revolt; but those in revolt themselves become in time the old guard, with their 'communal psychology' (a constellation of irrational, unquestioned attitudes, derived from the past) out of sync with the new.[11]

They published Virginia's novel *The Waves* in the same month. Leonard read it in typescript over a weekend in mid-July. '"It is a

11 Graham Wallas's *Human Nature in Politics*, 1908, had covered some of the same ground.

masterpiece", said L. coming out to my lodge this morning. "And the best of your books."'[12] He did tell her that he found the first hundred pages extremely difficult, which was rather a lot since it is a short book. But he always cited *The Waves* as the one incontrovertible work of genius that Virginia wrote, and was ready to concede that the character of Louis in the novel was based upon himself.

He felt that the reception of his *After the Deluge: A Study in Communal Psychology* was disappointing: 'Half a column of belittlement' in the *TLS*,[13] as Virginia put it in her diary. Leonard told her 'that his ten years work are wasted, & that he sees no use in going on'. This was irrational. Many column inches throughout the anglophone world were filled by notices of *After the Deluge*, virtually all of them respectful even when they disagreed on points of detail. Notably enthusiastic were Harold Laski's in the *New Statesman* and L.B.Namier's in the *Observer*; and the *Melbourne Age* praised the book as 'an outstanding contribution to social psychology, and, like the psychology of William James, as exciting to read as a novel'.[14] The book was translated into German.[15]

Leonard's despondency was due to his 'curious pessimistic temper', Virginia thought, forgetting her own hypersensitivity to reviews – 'something deeper than reason, strangling, many coiled, that one can't deal with'. It was the 'irrational despondency which I see in all Woolves, & connect with centuries of oppression'.[16] Marital supportiveness was not all one way. Virginia's tenderness and respect for Leonard, when she was not preoccupied with her own processes, were given full expression, and her 'untarnished' happiness in being at home alone with him, and their sensitivity to one another's sadnesses, are evident from her diary. 'If it were not for the divine goodness of L. how many times I should be thinking of death.'[17]

*

12 VW Diary 19 July 1931
13 TLS 22 Oct 1931. The reviewer (anonymous) was Harold Stannard, who dealt regularly with books on foreign affairs.
14 30 April 1932
15 By F.O.Keller
16 VW Diary 23 Oct 1931
17 VW Diary 28 May 1931

The Hogarth Press published thirty-one books or pamphlets, prose and poetry, in 1930, and thirty-four in 1931. Leonard had consuming outside commitments, and was working on the second volume of *After the Deluge* and other books. Virginia remained joint proprietor, and was the chief reader of literary manuscripts, but day-to-day it was Leonard's business. Since Angus Davidson had left, Leonard was thinking of taking on a partner.

John Lehmann came down from Trinity College, Cambridge in 1930. He was a friend of Dadie Rylands, who suggested he might work for the Press. John was also a close friend of Julian Bell's, who was at King's. As a partner, John Lehmann would be expected to put money into the firm. Lytton was horrified: 'The latest scandal is that the Woolves (aided and abetted by Dadie, of all people) are trying to lure John Lehmann to join the Hogarth Press, and put in all his capital as well as to devote his working hours to doing up parcels in the basement.'[18]

Julian Bell too was doubtful: 'The point is, Leonard has had very little success as an employer . . . I know that he's apt to lose his temper, and also to be rather interfering and overbearing, also obstinate and argumentative.' The job would involve 'an enormous amount of very hard drudgery'. The Woolfs told Julian that even if John did not go for the partnership idea, they would like him as manager: 'Only then of course you would have no decisive voice in the books published – I think you may anyhow find Leonard slightly dictatorial about that.'[19]

John Lehmann opted to be manager. This arrangement lasted just two years. John Lehmann – a gifted but a touchy person – later milked his time at the Hogarth Press in two volumes of autobiography and (after Leonard's death) in a whole separate book, *Thrown to the Woolfs*. He was not literary capital for the Woolfs as they were for him, and Leonard was more measured about those two years: 'Poor John, like Dadie a product of Eton and Cambridge, only 24 years old when he came to us, was put in a small, dark, basement room, from which he was expected,

---

18 Lytton Strachey to Roger Senhouse. Quoted in John Lehmann, *Thrown to the Woolfs* Weidenfeld & Nicolson 1978

19 Quoted in John Lehmann, *Thrown to the Woolfs*

under my supervision, to "manage" the publication of 22 books to be published by us in the spring of 1931.'[20] John's room was actually the former larder, with an ancient gas-fire which gave no heat 'and in front of which Leonard on his regular morning visits would try to warm his hands, without any marked success'.[21] Leonard stood an optimistic pot-plant on the sill of the dirty, jammed window.

The arrangement was nevertheless mutually beneficial. Leonard was patient in initiating John into the business, and 'devastatingly, caustically funny' about the vagaries of authors, reviewers, booksellers and printers. 'In fact I learnt the essentials of publishing in the most agreeable way possible: from a man who had created his own business, had never allowed it to grow so big that it fell into departments sealed off from one another, and who saw it all as much from the point of view of an author as of someone who had to make his living by it.'[22]

Leonard, in his turn, was put in touch with the rising generation of writers. The Hogarth Press published John Lehmann's own first volume of poems, *A Garden Revisited*, in September 1931. John was responsible for *New Signatures*, published in the Hogarth Living Poets Series in February 1932, edited by Michael Roberts and recognised as the collective opening blast from the key British poets of the 1930s. Through Stephen Spender, he brought Christopher Isherwood to the Press with his novels *The Memorial* (which had been rejected by Cape), and *Mr Norris Changes Trains.* Then there was a falling-out, when Isherwood's long short story *Sally Bowles* was offered to Hogarth as a full-length work – with the idea of extinguishing Hogarth's option on his third novel. Leonard was adamantine with authors and their agents who engaged in what he called 'sharp practice'.[23] He published *Sally Bowles* but refused to pay an advance, and enforced his option on the new novel, *Lions and Shadows.*

When Virginia first thought of writing *Flush*, her novel about

20 *Downhill All the Way*
21 John Lehmann, *Thrown to the Woolfs*
22 John Lehmann, *The Whispering Gallery* Longmans, Green 1955
23 To Isherwood's agent Spencer Curtis Brown 23 March 1937. Hogarth Press Archive, U of Reading

Elizabeth Barrett Browning's dog, the Woolfs came to John and explained the idea, and how they wanted to illustrate it with photographs of Pinka. Virginia began to tell John some of the episodes she had thought up. 'Leonard stood watching her and chuckling in the background. She soon became so carried away and almost hysterical with laughter, that she was red in the face and tears were streaming down her cheeks before Leonard led her off, incapable of going on.'

This tableau, or something similar, was witnessed by others. Barbara (Hiles) Bagenal was laughing and joking with the Woolfs at lunch 'when suddenly [Virginia] began to flip the meat from her plate on to the table cloth, obviously not knowing what she was doing.' Leonard quietly asked Barbara not to comment. 'Then he took her upstairs to rest and stayed with her until she fell asleep and the danger was past.' Reappearing at teatime, Virginia did not even remember the incident.[24] Nigel Nicolson remembered a visit to Monks House with his mother Vita, when he was a young boy: 'Virginia, standing by the fireplace, was arguing excitedly, when Leonard slowly rose from his chair and gently touched her on the shoulder. Without enquiry or protest, she followed him from the room, and they were absent for about a quarter of an hour.' Everyone, except Nigel, understood why. He remembered the incident, all the same. 'The tenderness with which he touched her on the shoulder was almost biblical, and her submission to him indicated a trust that she awarded to no other person.'[25]

John Lehmann loved and revered Virginia, and 'worshipped' Vanessa, who became his confidante as his dissatisfaction with his job grew. 'All last night', Virginia wrote in her diary on 19 May 1932, 'Nessa put his case for him & against the irascible Leonard & the hard work & the underpay. And today we have to discuss with him his "feelings."' Leonard was generous with holidays, and displayed 'a sage-like calm' over major disasters. What John found intolerable was the way he was upset by trifles – a minor discrepancy in the petty cash at the end of the

---

24 Barbara Bagenal's memories in Joan Russell Noble (ed): *Recollections of Virginia Woolf by her Contemporaries* Peter Owen 1972

25 Nigel Nicolson, *Virginia Woolf* Weidenfeld & Nicolson 2000

day driving him into 'a frenzy that often approached hysteria', with a marked worsening of his tremor.

John found both the Woolfs' attitude to the Press over-emotional, 'as if it were the child their marriage had never produced'. When Dottie Wellesley, still subsidising Hogarth Living Poets, was against taking on Louis MacNeice, Leonard backed her up. MacNeice went to Faber & Faber, where Eliot was now in charge of the poetry list, and John left the Hogarth Press. Leonard took on new managers, preferring women, but they did not stay long. He was overworking. Yet to Virginia he could seem splendid, coming in from some meeting 'in his grey suit & blue tie, sunburnt; & I felt that we are still vigorous & young'.[26] They 'drifted on, as one does',[27] and only occasionally thought of giving the Press up.

A Hogarth coup the following year was the acquisition of Laurens van der Post's first novel, *In a Province*. Van der Post, an Afrikaner, was a young friend of William Plomer, through whom the manuscript reached Leonard. Van der Post kept Leonard's brief but warm letter of acceptance for the rest of his life, 'and never forgot his gratitude to the Hogarth Press'.[28] *In a Province* was well-reviewed but not a big seller. The W.H.Smith chain refused to stock it, on account of a sexually vivid conversational exchange, and earned themselves one of Leonard's caustic letters. The big dividends on this investment did not begin to pour in until after World War II, with Van der Post's *Venture to the Interior.*

After Labour lost the 1931 General Election to the National Government, there was a bitter split in the party, with Ramsay Macdonald leading the new coalition and Arthur Henderson remaining out. Morgan Forster wrote to Leonard: 'I have been thinking over your remark, that we shall now all move to the left or to the right.'

Where now was 'right' and where was 'left'? The extremes of both were authoritarian, and reliant on a powerful leader. Sir Oswald Mosley was not unique in his quest for a new direction. One of the generation

26 VW Diary 29 June 1932
27 *Downhill All the Way*
28 J.D.F. Jones, *Storyteller: The Many Lives of Laurens Van der Post* John Murray 2001. LW's letter written September 1933.

of clever thirty-somethings, Mosley was a Conservative MP, and an enthusiastic member of the executive of the League of Nations Union (while arguing that the League, if it was to be effective, must be prepared to exert force). He switched to the Labour Party, as MP for Smethwick. Mosley was ambitious and fertile with ideas. When he was frozen out by the cautious Labour Party, he founded his own 'progressive socialist' New Party, basing his programme for industrial recovery and social renewal on Keynesian economics, a strong state with strong leadership, the strengthening of the British Empire as a self-sufficient bloc, and rearmament.

Leonard knew Mosley as a younger colleague from 1920, when he was secretary of the Peace with Ireland Council, of which Leonard was a member. Harold Nicolson knew Mosley much better, was a Mosley supporter, and edited the New Party's newspaper, *Action*. Nicolson was recruiting left-wing intellectuals while Mosley set about establishing a working-class youth movement involving uniforms (Nicolson touchingly suggested grey flannel trousers) and stirring public meetings. In 1932 Leonard and William Robson published in the *Political Quarterly* an article by Mosley, in which he warned of Britain's terminal decline unless a new strong spirit in politics could be found in opposition to Communism, to which the radical young were tending.

The Communist Party of Great Britain was from 1929 fielding candidates at General Elections, and though it never won more than two seats at any one time, many socialists, including writers, dons, and other professionals, joined the Party or became sympathisers – 'fellow travellers' – during the 1930s. The international model of Soviet Communism seemed to many the best if not the only bastion against Fascism. Many of the LSE intellectuals were moderate or theoretical Marxists. A Fabian group, which included the Webbs and Kingsley Martin, visited Russia in 1932, and were impressed by the absence of unemployment. There was also an absence of political freedom – but did the West perhaps over-value political freedom? The Webbs became 'quite silly about the Soviet Union'.[29] They saw in the planned economy

29 Kingsley Martin, *Editor: A Second Volume of Autobiography* Hutchinson 1968

of the USSR a model for Britain, by a process of gradual transition from capitalism to socialism.

Leonard Woolf was never remotely inclined to join the Communist Party, though the Press published CP material, such as R.Palme Dutt's pamphlet *The Political and Social Doctrine of Communism.* Victor Gollancz, the left-wing publisher, commissioned him to edit *An Intelligent Man's Way to Prevent War* (1933), the editorial strategy being to argue for the efficacy of international co-operation and international socialism. *Does Capitalism Cause War?* was the title of an argumentative collection of letters to the *New Statesman* by Leonard and others, published in February 1935. Leonard, at an angle to the radical Left, held that while war between capitalist, imperialist states was inevitable, two socialist states might equally well go to war. 'For a Socialist to refuse to admit and to combat these non-economic causes seems to me blind and absolutely disastrous both to peace and to Socialism.'

Meanwhile Mosley came off the fence after going to Rome in April 1932 (Harold Nicolson went with him) to meet Mussolini, and see Fascism at first hand. Six months later he disbanded the New Party and founded the British Union of Fascists, with an opening rally in Trafalgar Square on 1 October. With drums, communal singing, spotlights, and their uniform of black shirts, the Mosleyites made their presence felt, funded not only by British supporters but with money from Mussolini channelled through the Italian Embassy in London. Harold Nicolson disengaged himself at this point, and resigned from *Action.*

From 1932, street confrontations between Fascists and Communists became frequent, and a whiff of anti-Semitism entered the Mosleyite rhetoric. Many poor East End Jews were Communists or anarchists, partly in protest against Fascism and partly against the sweated labour imposed by their employers (generally, less poor Jews). In Germany, economic depression and unemployment were attracting more and more members to the National Socialist German Workers' Party – the Nazis. Adolf Hitler was imposing himself, and his anti-Semitic 'master-race' vision of Germany, on the Nazi Party. John Lehmann's diary, end of June 1932: 'Leonard very difficult today, haggard, abrupt, twirling bits of string, a touch of hysteria in his voice, in fact suffering from a severe nervous crisis, cause unknown. This manifests itself in repeated invasions of the office, anxious examinations of work being done, nagging tirade and unnecessary alarms.'[30]

Lytton Strachey was ill towards the end of 1931. Lytton was often ill, but this time he could not eat and was wasting away. He managed to finish Leonard's *After the Deluge*, finding it important and 'quite readable', but did not have the strength to immerse himself in *The Waves*. None of his doctors diagnosed the cancer that was killing him.

The Woolfs went to see him at Ham Spray on 14 January 1932. Carrington hardly slept, and let it be known that she would not choose to live if Lytton died. 'Suicide seems to me quite sensible',[31] Virginia wrote in her diary. Carrington attempted to kill herself in the garage with the fumes from the exhaust pipe of the car while Lytton still lived.

Leonard's diary 21 January 1932: 'Work Press Heard news Lytton's death Van's party.' They did not hear of his death until after the party. Lytton carried away with him the old intimacies, and Leonard's youth. 'It was the beginning of the end, for it meant that the spring had finally died out of our lives.'[32] He wrote a tribute to Lytton Strachey for the *New Statesman*[33] in which he indicated, but did not stress, his long personal connection. He wrote of Lytton's contradictory qualities, and how his iconoclastic biographical writing was a result of these contradictions. He wrote of Lytton's intellectual integrity and of his courage in the face of death. Marjorie Strachey was touched: 'One saw that you understood and cared. I think in the end the thing that will explain him best will be his letters, but I suppose we shall have to wait another fifty years at least for them'.[34]

Tragedy was interrupted by tragi-comedy. Immediately after Lytton died, Leonard became embroiled in the affairs of the *soi-disant* Count, Geoffrey Wladislaw Vaile Potocki de Montalk, a poet from New

---

30 Quoted in *Thrown to the Woolfs*
31 30 Jan 1932
32 *ibid*
33 30 Jan 1932
34 2 Feb 1932

Zealand whose customary street-wear was a long scarlet cloak and sandals, his hair flowing down his back. He had written indecent poems, printed up as Christmas cards, and was sent to prison for publishing obscene material. Leonard, always anti-censorship, drummed up support for an appeal, making up the £50 shortfall himself. 'As you know, de Montalk's appeal failed',[35] he wrote to Tom Eliot, reminding him that he had pledged £5. Eliot was sympathetic: 'We had to have a director's meeting [at Faber & Faber] of over three quarters of an hour a couple of days ago to deal with fuck and bugger in a book of verse.'[36] Montalk showed no gratitude, publishing a nasty article about the Woolfs in his notoriously anti-Semitic magazine, mocking Virginia's cut-glass accent; and as for the 'wizened' Leonard, 'it seems to be natural to him to take up what one might call a distinguished Simian attitude.'[37]

Three days after the Montalk appeal, on 10 March 1932, Virginia and Leonard drove to Ham Spray to see Carrington. 'It was one of the most painful days I ever slowly suffered', Leonard wrote. 'I remember most vividly Carrington's great pale blue eyes and the look of dead pain in them.' As they were getting into the car, Virginia asked her to come to see them next week – or not, just as she liked. Carrington said, 'Yes, I will come, or not.'

The next morning Carrington shot herself. She bungled the shooting, but was mortally wounded, and died that afternoon. When Mary Hutchinson spoke of Carrington's death as a beautiful gesture, Leonard said it was 'histrionic': the only real thing was, that they would never see Lytton again.

Frances Marshall and Ralph Partridge got married and stayed on at Ham Spray for the next three decades. They called their son Lytton Burgo.

Soon after Carrington's suicide, the Woolfs travelled in Greece for nearly a month with Roger Fry and his sister Margery. Leonard had

---

35 16 March 1932.

36 18 March 1932. University of Reading

37 'Social Climbers in Bloomsbury', *The Right Review* 1939. Quoted in Jean Moorcroft Wilson, *Virginia Woolf and Anti-Semitism*, Bloomsbury Heritage Series pamphlet, Cecil Woolf 1995. For more about Potocki de Montalk see Stephanie de Montalk, *Unquiet World: The Life of Count Potocki de Montalk* Victoria University Press (NZ) 2001

never been to Greece before. Like all vehement anti-sentimentalists, he was subject to major bouts of sentimentality, as happened in Athens, the city of Pericles. He was sitting alone on the parapet of the Acropolis overlooking the Agora when a tout selling photographs came up and spoke to him, commented critically on a walking stick he had bought in Sparta, and sat down beside him. An hour later they were still sitting there talking. 'The intelligence, knowledge, humanity of this man were extraordinary. I do not think that there is any other country in the world, except perhaps Israel, in which it would be possible to have the kind of talk and relationship which I had with a tout selling photographs.'[38]

'Yesterday L. came to my room at Breakfast & said Goldie is dead.'[39] Goldsworthy Lowes Dickinson was seventy years old. On their return from Greece, Leonard visited his fellow Apostle and companion in so many political campaigns in hospital. He died on 3 August. His last letter to Leonard praised *After the Deluge* as 'a new view of history' – while chiding Leonard for his 'excess of repetition' and 'excess of bitterness', especially in regard to the General Strike.[40] Tom Eliot asked Leonard to write a 'sizeable' appreciation of Lowes Dickinson as a writer, for the *Criterion*. Leonard advised him to ask Morgan Forster, candidly admitting that 'The difficulty is that I do not know many of Lowes Dickinson's books.'[41] Forster, whom Goldie had loved dearly, wrote to Leonard: 'I expect I shall have to do a short memoir, and the problems are most tiresome, also I miss him dreadfully, like everyone else.'[42] 'So people will go on dying until we die', Leonard said. 'Lytton, Carrington, Goldie . . .'[43]

*

38 LW, *The Journey Not the Arrival Matters: An Autobiography of the Years 1939 to 1969* The Hogarth Press 1969. The fact that this story was only told in this last volume is an illustration of the discursive and non-chronological nature of his autobiographies.
39 VW Diary 5 Aug 1932
40 29 Oct 1931. King's College Cambridge.
41 18 Aug 1932
42 21 Sept 1931. EMF wrote a full (but discreet) biography of Goldsworthy Lowes Dickinson, published 1934.
43 VW Diary 5 Aug 1932

In the New Year of 1933 Leonard had a bad recurrence of what Virginia called 'his incurable and disgusting skin disease',[44] which itched intolerably as if, he said, he had black insects crawling on his neck. At the end of January, Hitler became Chancellor of the German Reich, and the following year was declared Führer. Germany began to re-arm. The poet Stephen Spender thought that the Woolfs were among the few people in England who understood the dangerous state of affairs – 'Leonard, because he was a political thinker and historian with an almost fatalistic understanding of the consequences of actions.'[45]

'Leonard is caballing with the Labour Party as usual', Virginia wrote to her nephew Quentin. 'They think Mosley is getting supporters. If so, I shall emigrate.'[46] It was thought that he might be in power within five years. Shaw taunted the Fabian Society with Mosley's courage and dynamism: this was a man who intended actually to 'do something'.[47] On 22 April 1934, aping Hitler, Mosley held a mass rally of 10,000 at the Albert Hall, entering under a spotlight to cheers of 'Hail Mosley!' On 7 June Mosley held an even bigger rally, at Olympia, where the presence of many left-wing and liberal intellectuals (but not Leonard) was noted, drawn by a need to know and by the lure of spectacle. It ended in a pitched battle provoked by protesters hell-bent on provocation. Because many of the anti-Fascists were Jews, Mosley saw the green light for openly promoting anti-Semitism, already endemic among his supporters.

Tom Eliot was breaking with his wife Vivien during the early 1930s. He went to Harvard for a year without her, and they both came to see the Woolfs at Rodmell before he left. Leonard gave Vivien flowers from the garden. When after two years Eliot returned, he told Viven the marriage was over, and made financial arrangements for her, making Leonard her executor; but Leonard never became involved, or took responsibility for her.

---

44 VW Diary 19 Jan 1933
45 Stephen Spender, *World Within World* Hamish Hamilton 1975
46 24 Jan 1934
47 Quoted in Jan Dalley, *Diana Mosley: A Life* Faber 1999

Vivien, deranged and in grief, behaved erratically. She joined the Fascists. Eliot refused to see her. She stalked him and made public scenes. Virginia found her appalling, and sympathised with Tom. Vivien was 'cast off by those who aligned themselves with her husband, and this meant almost everyone whom they had known as a couple.'[48] Eliot became once more a regular dinner guest at 52 Tavistock Square, and a weekend guest at Monks House. He was part of the Woolfs' lives.

Leonard's mother was often ill, but as Virginia put it, she entirely refused to die. She even had an admirer, an old gentleman in Worthing where now she spent her summer holidays. 'Tonight', wrote Virginia to Ethel Smyth, 'I slip on a magnificent dress of purple velvet and old lace and dine with 22 Jews and Jewesses to celebrate my mother in laws 84th birthday. And it'll be as hot as a monkey house. And tomorrow I shall have a headache and shan't be able to write.'[49] Leonard, Herbert and Harold contributed to their mother's medical expenses and to her hotel bills, which involved terrific Woolfian calculations on Herbert's part as to who had paid how much and for what, provoking Leonard into sending more than his share: 'It is very good of you to calculate against yourself',[50] wrote Herbert.

The next death, in a nursing-home in Surrey,[51] was that of their sister Clara, on 4 January 1934. She was forty-eight, and the cause of death was a stroke following infective endocarditis. Clara left her husband George Walker with two young daughters, Clare and Betty. Leonard, Herbert and Philip went to Balls Pond Road cemetery; women under the Jewish rite did not go to funerals. Virginia meanwhile sat with Mrs Woolf: 'She asked so little of life', she said of her dead daughter.[52] 'It was all very interesting, as the Jews dress up in black, wear top

48 Lyndall Gordon, *Eliot's New Life* OUP 1988
49 VW Letters: 29 Oct 1933
50 4 April 1933. Herbert and Freda were living at Cookham Dean in Berkshire.
51 Clara and George Walker, returned from America, were living in Ashley Road, Epsom, Surrey.
52 VW Diary 16 Jan 1934.

hats, and look exactly like Hebrew prophets. My brothers in law sat round cursing, and entirely righteous and hopeless.'[53]

When he listed the deaths of the 1930s in *Downhill All the Way*, Leonard did not mention Goldie's. He did not mention Clara's either, but then he was extremely selective in what he wrote about his family in his autobiographies.[54]

The next death was Roger Fry's, on 9 September 1934. It was Vanessa who felt it most keenly. The news came on a Sunday afternoon. Vanessa, Clive, Angelica and a schoolfriend were with Leonard and Virginia in the garden at Monks House when Micou Diamand (the husband of Roger's daughter Pamela), telephoned. Vanessa fainted. Angelica heard her mother 'howling in anguish'[55] in her bedroom the next day. Both the Woolfs were at Roger's funeral and cremation with all the old friends at Golders Green, and Leonard served as a trustee of his estate.

Virginia's letters and diary reveal how stricken she too was by the loss of Roger, and by how sadly and gently she and Leonard spoke of the inevitability of death, including their own. On the last day of September 1934 she finished the first draft of what was not yet called *The Years*, and the idea was taking root that she should write Roger Fry's biography.

In spite of the economic depression, the rise of Fascism, the threat of war and the deaths of friends, the accounts of Leonard and Virginia in the early 1930s convey happiness and harmony. Virginia was commercially and critically successful. Vita Sackville-West was still a beloved friend and, to both Vita and Harold Nicolson, the Woolfs represented purity and clarity: 'Their sky is as wide and clear as the sky above the downs', Harold wrote in his diary after a visit to Monks House; they left 'feeling as usual lightened and inspired.'[56]

---

53 VW Letters, 10 Jan 1934

54 The same is true of the family letters in his archive. There are so many of these that it is not at first apparent that he culled nearly all which related to illness and death, except a few from later life.

55 Angelica Garnett, *Deceived with Kindness* Chatto & Windus/The Hogarth Press 1984

56 Nigel Nicolson (ed): *Harold Nicolson, Diaries & Letters* Vol 1 Collins 1966

Vita's role as chief adorer of Virginia was taken over by the deaf composer Ethel Smyth – a lesbian feminist, brave, garrulous, combative and demanding. (Virginia was forty-eight in 1930, when they got to know one another; Ethel Smyth was seventy-two.) Virginia joked about old Ethel, but enjoyed the adoration. Ethel's immensely long letters were love letters; and Virginia wrote freely, sometimes indecently, in reply.

Leonard was not at all keen on Ethel. She was recounting an interminable tale of grievance to young Quentin Bell, in a taxi with him and the Woolfs, when Leonard, trusting to Ethel's deafness, asked Quentin if he could not get her to shut up. She heard what he said, and the atmosphere became strained. Ethel, when they got back to 52 Tavistock Square, goaded Leonard by being rude about Socialists, abusing Shaw's *The Intelligent Woman's Guide to Socialism*, until he could not resist saying: 'Perhaps it was not addressed to you, Ethel.' This time he had to repeat himself again and again before she heard – and understood.[57]

Virginia was ill in the hot summer of 1932, and fainted again, falling on the grass at Leonard's feet. (He rushed to get ice from their new Frigidaire.) 'L. fetched and carried & hardly let me walk upstairs carrying my own body.'[58] Sometimes she woke Leonard in the small hours, wanting a cool drink, or comfort. Her temperature still fluctuated, and she had an irregular heartbeat. Yet she and Leonard were happy together. 'I don't think we've ever been so happy . . . And so intimate, & so completely entire, I mean L. and I. If it could only last like this for another 50 years . . .'[59]

They played their part in Vanessa's annual parties, which combined the celebration of Angelica's birthday with Christmas. In 1932 it was fancy dress, and the Woolfs went as Queen Victoria and the Prince Consort. In January 1935 there was a performance of Virginia's play *Freshwater* for Angelica's birthday; Leonard took the part of the husband of the photographer Julia Margaret Cameron. The Woolfs never attended the big family Christmases laid on by Philip and Babs at

57 Quentin Bell, 'Ethel Came to Lunch', *Charleston Magazine* No 4
58 VW Diary 20 Aug 1932
59 VW Diary 10 Nov 1932

the Wilderness. Flora and Clara (while she lived) did not go either, as they had children of their own; and Bella was usually abroad. But as Philip's younger daughter Marie remembered it, old Mrs Woolf was always there, as were Uncle Herbert and Aunt Freda, Uncle Harold and Aunt Alice, Uncle Edgar and Aunt Sylvia – three childless Woolf couples, though Edgar fussed over his dachshunds as though they were children. Marie thought that Leonard would have enjoyed it, but that Virginia 'apart from Harold seems to have disliked the Woolf family and therefore would probably have hated our Christmas.'[60]

Vanessa's sons had grown up; in 1935 Julian went to China as professor of English at Wuhan University, and Quentin to the pottery town Stoke-on-Trent to learn pot-making. The Woolfs and their circle were the older generation, observed by the clear-eyed young – and the odd clear-eyed contemporary. Morgan Forster penned an anti-Bloomsbury riff to Sebastian Sprott,[61] its tone perhaps influenced by a wish to amuse an exciting younger friend: 'Oh the Bells, the Woolves – or rather Virginia, for I do like Leonard! . . . But to turn one's backside to them is the only course – they will never have the grace to penetrate it, their inquisitiveness never had any spunk, that is why one loathes it so.'[62] Gerald Brenan was between the generations and, writing of 'Bloomsbury', felt 'already by 1930 it was pot-bound. Its members were too secure, too happy, too triumphant, too certain of the superiority of their Parnassian philosophy to be able to draw fresh energies from the new and disturbing era that was coming in.'[63]

This was not true of Leonard Woolf. In his alertness to the international situation, his polemical journalism, his books, and his work for the Labour Party he was supremely concerned with the 'new and disturbing era that was coming in'. He was, to use the term just then coming into currency, *engagé*. Nor, in his home and marriage, was he pot-bound. He was embedded at Rodmell, as when a plant in its pot is put out to stand

60 Marie (Woolf) Beesley, 'The Wilderness', unpublished memoir.

61 Born 1897, an Apostle and protégé of EMF's who became Professor of Philosophy at Nottingham University.

62 16 July 1931 *Selected Letters* Vol I

63 Gerald Brenan, *Personal Record 1920–1972* Jonathan Cape 1974

in the open garden, and the roots find their way out of the holes in the base, down into the earth. He became a manager of Rodmell's (Church of England) village school in the 1930s, and a member of the local Rural District Council. Both the Woolfs belonged to the Rodmell Labour Party – five or six people, meeting at Monk's House or in the school classroom. He was agitated by the potential ruination of the open downland around the village by housing development, writing to the Prime Minister about the possibility of 'a scheme under which special areas would be scheduled and protected at no great cost to the country'.[64] Not until after World War II, following a Report chaired by Sir Arthur Hobhouse (Lytton's 'Hobby' from Cambridge days), were 'National Parks' designated.

Gerald Brenan's picture of Bloomsbury was discoloured by his view of Saxon Sydney-Turner, 'one of the greatest bores I have ever known'. What was more, Saxon seemed to enjoy 'dealing out his death packets' of boringness to people whose greater vitality he despised. Gerald was amazed by the loyalty that made the Woolfs continue to ask Saxon to Rodmell. 'I can only conjecture that every group or society feels the need for a private bore of its own, who belongs solely to them.'[65] His failure to be promoted at the Treasury was either 'because he saw so many sides to any question that he was quite incapable of making up his mind' or because he did not want to have to move from his office, which had a beautiful view.[66]

Old friends do not have to justify their existence, and Saxon's attachment had an intensity of which they were aware – as Leonard was twenty years earlier, when Saxon sent to him in Ceylon some verses he wrote for Lytton's birthday, about the trinity of Trinity:

> Time cannot make it false that he and you
> Walked, once with me along fair flowery ways
> Not though all time and times be past and over.

---

64 LW to Ramsay MacDonald 3 Jan 1930. A Town and Country Planning Act, which enshrined the desirability of rural planning, was duly passed in 1932.

65 Gerald Brenan, *Personal Record 1920–1972* Jonathan Cape 1974

66 Nicholas Henderson, 'Child of Bloomsbury', *The Charleston Magazine* No. 13

When Lytton died, his brother James wanted no one at all to go with him to the cremation. Only Saxon, roused from quietude by a fierce sense of entitlement, insisted on accompanying him.

In July 1931 Stephen Tomlin was working on a bust of Virginia,[67] and in the early 1930s at Rodmell she was at her most enchanted and enchanting, with Leonard moving slowly in his contentment, emerging from the garden on the arrival of visitors 'in shirt-sleeves, with clay on his boots and a pair of secateurs in his hand'.[68] Bobo Mayor told Leonard, years later, how Virginia, at some time between 1930 and 1936, asked what was the happiest moment in one's whole life and, with a shining face, answered her own question: 'I think it's the moment when one is walking in one's garden, perhaps picking off a few dead flowers, and suddenly one thinks: "My husband lives in that house, and he loves me."'[69]

Virginia bought new beds from Heal's in Tottenham Court Road; Leonard said that the undulating downs around Mount Caburn were 'like a Heal bed'[70] Mains water was connected to Monks House in 1932, and also the telephone: Lewes 382.[71] They remodelled the shed beyond the orchard, against the churchyard wall, to make a 'writing lodge' for Virginia with a view towards Mount Caburn, and a terrace for sitting out. Monks House remained problematic; the weight of their thousands of books threatened to bring down the ceilings, rainwater still flowed through the kitchen, and in March 1934 Nelly Boxall, after months of rows and glooms, was dismissed with difficulty and painful scenes, refusing to shake hands with Leonard on her departure. 'No I really couldn't Sir.'[72]

Yet the summers and weekends of the early thirties seem, like that earlier time before world war sent Europe reeling into ruins, one long

67 The original is at Charleston. Copies are in the National Portrait Gallery in London and in the garden at Monks House.
68 Angelica Garnett, *The Eternal Moment* Orono, Maine: Puckerbrush Press 1998
69 26 May 1964
70 VW Diary 8 Feb 1932
71 They had a telephone at 52 Tavistock Square by the mid-1920s: MUSeum 2621.
72 VW Diary 11 April 1934

golden afternoon. 'There was electricity in the air', Frances Partridge remembered – appositely, since electric power was connected at Monks House in 1931 – 'engendered by Virginia's tense and erratic genius', while 'Leonard was a powerful influence of calm and order, with his slow deep voice, steady gaze and trembling hands. The lawn was always beautifully mown, his roses and dahlias grew to supernatural size, and his doting dogs obeyed his grumbled commands and affectionate kicks.'[73]

The Woolfs' routine was unbroken even when they had guests. Morgan Forster, as he told Christopher Isherwood, felt neglected. On an April Sunday in 1934, Leonard read the *Observer* and Virginia the *Sunday Times* and then both retreated to write until lunchtime, leaving Morgan sitting in the garden. 'At least L. has just come out, but I, piqued, continue my letter to you, and he, not displeased, cuts the dead wood out of a Buddleia with a small rusty saw . . . I am fed up with these two-day visits where I am left to myself.' Then Virginia came out, and suggested taking a photograph of Morgan. 'L.thinks it a good idea, and continues to saw the buddleia.'[74]

When Vanessa and Virginia were young, the tea-table was 'the very hearth and centre of family life' at Hyde Park Gate. The girls, as Virginia wrote, learned 'a certain manner' of light, unbroken conversation, with rules, like a game. 'We still play the game.' Tea-time for the Woolfs' generation remained a ritual, its fixity creating a recognised period called 'after tea', during which one might visit or be visited.[75] Tea-time at Charleston was when, at weekends, the Woolfs most often called in, Virginia 'pacing through the house, followed by Leonard and Pinka'. Angelica, as a teenager, was embarrassed by Virginia's whimsical 'demanding of her rights' on arrival, from both herself and from Vanessa – 'a kiss in the nape of the neck or on the eyelid, or a whole flutter of kisses from the inner wrist to the elbow'. Virginia seemed to the

73 Frances Partridge, 'Bloomsbury Houses', *Charleston Newsletter* 11

74 7 April 1934. Mary Lago and P.N.Furbank (ed): *E.M.Forster: Selected Letters* Vol II Collins 1985

75 This space, in a teatimeless age, has become attached to the next meal: 'a drink before dinner'.

young girl 'ingratiating, even abject'. Vanessa did not enjoy this carry-on either, and bought her sister off with a single kiss. 'Leonard, like a vigilant and observant mastiff, remained unmoved by this behaviour.'[76]

Leonard seemed to the young Angelica to be made of some different material than the others, something which 'inevitably suggested the rock of ages'. Had he been a parent, he would have imposed on his children a more structured regime that that which prevailed at Charleston. Angelica never forgot the occasions (only two) when she was ticked off by Leonard. 'These contacts with a sterner reality impressed me – he seemed to be the father figure who was missing from my life.' Yet if he had been her father, she might have 'resembled one of his dogs, never beaten but always intimidated by the force of his personality'. But she never forgot, either, the Christmas when he gave her an illustrated copy of *Pilgrim's Progress.* 'For some reason this book meant a great deal to me, and my eyes met Leonard's over the festive tea-table in a moment of intense understanding. For once I felt limpid and transparent, purged by emotion of all the dross of puerile secrecy and prevarication that usually submerged me. I had unwittingly come into contact with the passion in Leonard's character . . .'[77]

Tea-time at Monks House was Virginia's private theatre. She could make her nephews Julian and Quentin laugh uncontrollably. Christopher Isherwood, introducing an evocation of Virginia's teasing, incandescent conversation, set the scene 'at the tea table',[78] in the green-painted sitting-room. The porch and walls on the garden side of the house were covered by climbing plants which 'knocked at the small-paned windows as though longing to come in',[79] making the room cool even on the sunniest day, the low light giving an underwater feeling enhanced by Leonard's tank of fish. There were always pot-plants, exotic, brilliant, double varieties, from Leonard's greenhouse. The Woolfs each had their own sweets for handing round after meals: Leonard's were always striped humbugs.

---

76 Angelica Garnett, *Deceived with Kindness* Hogarth Press 1984
77 Angelica Garnett, op.cit.
78 Christopher Isherwood, *Exhumations: Stories, Articles, Verses* Simon and Schuster 1966
79 Angelica Garnett, op.cit.

Philip's daughters, Philippa (Pip) and Marie, staying without their parents at Monks House at the ages of twelve and ten, were amused and shocked to be told not to say 'Uncle Leonard' and 'Aunt Virginia' – the latter 'draped in flowing grey clothes'[80] – but to just call them by their names, and by being offered cigarettes in the evenings. Adrian's daughters Ann and Judith, by now in their teens, came to stay at Rodmell, and in London were taken to the Zoo and to the theatre. The word 'bowls' occurs for the first time in Leonard's diary on 30 August 1931; playing bowls on the top lawn after tea became a regular fixture, the guests young and old trooping out in Leonard's wake. He was fiercely competitive, and had to win.

Natural life thrived at Monks House, whether outside, inside, or in between. One spring, the hall door could not be closed for fear of disturbing a nesting swallow. The garden spilled into the house. House and garden were a single habitat, because of Leonard.

Louie Everest came to work at Monks House in summer 1934. She and her husband Bert had, rent-free, the cottage next to Percy Bartholomew's, plus seven shillings and sixpence a week; she thought it good money. Leonard made the breakfast coffee himself, and he and Louie carried the two trays round to Virginia's bedroom, even when it rained, so that Virginia and Leonard could breakfast together. The only thing that seemed strange to Louie at the beginning was that 'when Mrs Woolf was having her bath before breakfast I could hear her talking to herself. On and on she went, talk, talk, talk.' Leonard explained to her that Mrs Woolf was trying out the sentences she had written in her head in the night to see that they sounded right.[81] Virginia talked to herself on her solitary walks, as well. It was this obliviousness, and her sometimes careless clothes, which made some people in the village think of her as 'quite mad'.[82] Louie learnt to know when Mrs Woolf was having

---

80 Marie (Woolf) Beesley, 'The Wilderness', unpublished memoir.

81 VW was not alone in doing this. When Julian Jebb went to stay with Elizabeth Bowen he was startled to hear her talking to herself at night, and for the same reason.

82 Private information

one of her bad headaches, because she would wander into the garden and sometimes bump into trees, 'not really knowing what she was doing'.[83] Louie, young and adaptable, became indispensable.

'Leonard is feeding Mitzy on a grasshopper he caught on an apple tree at this moment or he would send love.'[84] Mitzy, or Mitz, was a black and white marmoset belonging to Victor Rothschild. In December 1933 Victor married Mary and Jack Hutchinson's daughter Barbara; he was working for a Fellowship in zoology at Trinity. An outstandingly wealthy youth, he drove a Bugatti and leased a magnificent Elizabethan house, Merton Hall, on the Backs in Cambridge. When the Woolfs visited Merton Hall in July 1934 they found a heavily pregnant Barbara, a litter of kittens, and 'a sickly pathetic marmoset'[85] who climbed into Leonard's lap. Leonard agreed to look after the marmoset, just for a while, as the Rothschilds were going away; he nursed the little creature back to health, and she never went back to Cambridge.

Leonard fed her on meal-worms and fruit, and she loved macaroons and tapioca pudding. A marmoset is a small monkey – 'bigger than a squirrel, smaller than a cat'[86] – native to Brazil, with a long hairy non-prehensile tail, big eyes, and tufted ears. Mitz sat on Leonard's shoulder, or on his head, or inside his waistcoat. Mitz was jealous. Whenever she ran up a tree and would not come down, Leonard only had to kiss Virginia at the foot of the tree to have Mitz scrambling down in a frenzy to reclaim him. Mitz 'obviously adored him', wrote Kingsley Martin, 'and threatened to bite anyone who approached. His coat was permanently stained because the marmoset lived on his shoulder and performed his natural functions down his back.'[87]

Mitz was fond of Pinka, and in cold weather spaniel and monkey snuggled together in front of the fire. During the day Mitz rarely left

83 Louie (Everest) Mayer's memories from Joan Russell Noble (ed): *Recollections of Virginia Woolf by her Contemporaries* Peter Owen 1972
84 VW Letters: to Dadie Rylands, 27 Sept 1934
85 VW Diary 21 July 1934
86 The description is Elaine Robson's.
87 Kingsley Martin, *Father Figures*

Leonard, but as soon as it grew dark she 'scuttled across the room into a large birdcage which I kept full of scraps of silk. She rolled herself into a ball in the middle of the silk and slept until next morning – the moment the sun rose, she left the cage and came over to me.'[88] Though Leonard, as Kingsley Martin observed, wrote in his books about his love of animals, he 'had not said as much as he might about their apparently instinctive love for him.'[89]

Many animal-lovers abhor zoos, but Leonard could not keep away. He was a member of the Zoological Society of London, and often took his nephews and nieces, and the children of friends, to London Zoo. 'I have an uneasy feeling that one should not keep animals in cages, but I never get tired of watching animals anywhere.'[90] It was through animals that Leonard faced up to his own violent impulses and to the sadism of intimate attachment.

The incident with the drowning puppy, when he was a boy, had taught him that every living creature is an individual 'I'. But Leonard did not understand or control animals, in a good way, before his tenderness for his wife and the horror of war taught him to understand and control himself. The potential for domination was part of the fascination of Leonard's connection with animals, and so, in his youth, was the potential for cruelty. The painter Henry Lamb's wife Pansy (Pakenham), who never met Leonard, told a story she had from her husband. Leonard [before his marriage] told Henry 'how he had once been nipped by a horse in the balls . . . & how he had done nothing *at the moment*; but quietly leading the horse home ten or twenty miles, he then proceeded to tie it up hard & fast to the loose box & then beat & belaboured it until it was in a *lather*, & hardly had a bone unbroken left in its body!'[91]

That, at second hand, may be apocryphal, but the violence which his friends perceived in him at Cambridge was not a figment. In a notebook dating from his first year in Ceylon, there is a short story called 'The Cat', about a lonely old woman. One day, after having 'prickly stinging

---

88 *Downhill All the Way*
89 Kingsley Martin, op.cit.
90 *Downhill All the Way*
91 Julia Strachey to Carrington 25 Nov 1929. Berg

horse chestnuts' thrown in her face by jeering children, she goes home and is greeted with purrs by her pet cat. 'In a sudden fit of blind fury against all things she seized it by the neck and twisted its paw backwards and forwards. The cat screamed and scratched and bit with fright and pain, and though she flung the animal from her, with that scream there fell upon the woman's heart a sense of peace and satisfaction – she felt that she too could inflict pain, and that her own fled before it.'

There is no certainty that Leonard's insight – that the infliction of pain assuages one's own pain – reflected his experience. But what jeers and what attacks from 'prickly stinging horse chestnuts' (which have a striking particularity, not like something invented) might Leonard as a schoolboy have suppressed? 'Nothing matters.'

When he first began to keep animals, he admitted in *Principia Politica*, he controlled them by means of 'fear, force, and [with dogs] a sense of sin'. But he learned that an animal made civilised by means of force and pain is only superficially civilised. Fear and hostility remain just below the surface. 'The other way of training animals is through their potential affection. You must never hurt them or use unnecessary force upon them. You must establish from the earliest moment the things which . . . they are never under any circumstances to do; and you must prevent them doing these things with the utmost patience and gentleness.'

The thirty-two intense and fluent pages of his chapter 'Freedom and Authority' in *Principia Politica* are overwhelmingly about training animals, in the context of a discussion about the civilising of humans and of societies, in which he represents authoritarianism as dysfunctional. 'It astonishes me that religion and philosophy, psychology and sociology have almost always ignored the existence of animals.' If he had an immortal soul, which he did not believe, then 'there is something indistinguishable from an immortal soul in my dog and my marmoset'. Leonard did not treat his cats and dogs as pets. 'They were just sharing the house and garden together, and this respect was absolutely mutual.'[92]

*

92 W.A.Robson in *Leonard Woolf 1880–1969*, BBC Radio 3, 17 Feb 1970, producer Virginia Browne-Wilkinson.

In September 1934 Leonard heard on the radio the broadcast of Hitler's Nuremberg Rally – three hours of the thud of marching boots, and drumbeating which reminded him of the tom-toms of Ceylon, and a German announcer 'with the voice of a man participating in a religious ceremony, a ritual dance of his tribe in the primeval jungle before his god incarnate in the form of his Chief.'[93] Lapped in domestic harmony ('And I have L.', Virginia wrote, '& there are his books; & our life together. And freedom, now, from money paring'[94]), he took out his feelings on his typewriter. 'L. has today finished a book called Quack Quack', Virginia wrote to Quentin on 27 February 1935.

Quack, Quack![95] is a short, fierce demonstration of how tyrants and dictators are the magicians, witch-doctors and rain-makers of primitive superstition, who reappear – 'the great quacking of the quacks' – when civilisation is failing, reason and intelligence go by the board, and animal savagery resurfaces. Leonard illustrated it with photographs of Hitler and Mussolini in full declamatory mode in apposition to effigies of the Hawaiian war-god Kukailimoku, all wearing the same terrifyingly aggressive expressions.

Dictators apart, Leonard's relation to power and authority, including his own, was Janus-faced – not hypocritical, but unresolved. In June 1935 he upset Mabel Haskins, the cook at 52 Tavistock Square. 'L. is very hard on people', Virginia wrote in her diary, 'especially on the servant class. No sympathy with them; exacting; despotic. So I told him yesterday when he'd complained about the coffee.' She was always surprised by his 'extreme rigidity of mind' – towards others, not to her. 'What does it come from? Not being a gentleman partly: uneasiness in the presence of the lower classes: always suspects them, is never genial with them. Philip & Edgar are the same. His desire, I suppose, to dominate. Love of power. And then he writes against it.'[96]

93 *Quack, Quack!* Hogarth Press 1935

94 VW Diary 2 Nov 1934

95 LW first used the phrase 'Quack, Quack' as the heading of a review in *New Statesman and Nation* of a book by C.E.M.Joad on the philosophy of Radakrishnan (2 Dec 1933)

96 VW Diary 25 June 1935

'Not being a gentleman', in the sense that Sir Leslie Stephen's daughter meant it, is another key. Leonard, through long days spent with members of the Women's Co-operative Guild and of the Labour Party, and his experiences in the industrial north, was perfectly comfortable with working people. Marginal, and imperfectly slotted into the English class system, he had no sense of *noblesse oblige*. He related to everyone in the same way, and hectored poor Mabel just as he might contradict Kingsley Martin or rail at the staff at the Press. He was no respecter of persons. He discussed politics with Mr Fears, the Rodmell postman, in exactly the same engaged and engaging manner as with an MP. Three days later Virginia was writing: 'L's book selling now; & he is cheerful, & very contrite, in his way, about Mabel.'[97] She dreaded his glooms; she liked it when he was 'charming, affable, urbane'.[98]

Quack, Quack! did not come out from the Hogarth Press until June 1935, which was just as well, because in May of that year Leonard made an extraordinary decision. En route to Italy to meet up with Vanessa, the Woolfs were going to drive through Germany. He wanted to see the situation for himself.

He was at the time in daily heated speculation about what was to come, attending anti-Fascist meetings and joining yet more committees. But when he came to write his autobiographies, he never mentioned Oswald Mosley,[99] or the BUF, or any manifestations of anti-Semitism in England, in all his thoughtful analysis of the years leading up to World War II. He could not acknowledge for posterity the possibility of rejection and worse in his own country. He kept fear on a tight leash. To go to Germany was an act of defiance and denial. The Foreign Office was advising British Jews not to go to Germany. Leonard insisted that as a British subject, he could surely expect to travel safely.

He became annoyed during a farewell evening with Vanessa, 'suddenly turning stony in the way that I know', as Virginia wrote in her

---

97 VW Diary 28 June 1935
98 VW Diary 15 June 1935
99 He mentioned Mosley in *Quack, Quack!* as filling the position 'previously held by a long line of kings, magicians, witch-doctors'

diary, '& cut up rusty, when we got back, ostensibly because I suggested staying not 7 but 10 days [with Vanessa] in Rome.' He resented the way her family always seemed to take precedence over everyone else. She told him it was all 'silly rot', and 'so we went in [to the house] and laughed'.[100] In every marriage, one partner's family 'wins'. With Leonard and Virginia, there was no contest, and sometimes he resented it. Virginia could navigate a way through his moods and had the upper hand when it came to families, coolly observing that he was touchy about her relations because they were so much more 'vigorous and interesting' than his, about whom she continued to record her dismissive opinions. Leonard was getting 'more and more addicted to solitude & astute – the old wretch – at finding good reason for it. But then his hand trembles; mine doesn't.'[101]

They set off, with Mitz, on 1 May 1935, in their convertible Lanchester 18 hp, two-tone grey and green, with green leather upholstery, via Holland. Mitz attracted indulgent attention wherever they stopped: 'We hope even Hitler will soften to us',[102] Virginia wrote to Ka (Cox) Arnold-Forster.

At the frontier with Germany, a farmer at the Customs Office was given a hard time because he had not removed his cap in front of the photo of the Führer hanging on the wall, and Leonard felt 'with some disquiet that I had passed in a few yards from civilisation into savagery'.

Leonard drove to Cologne and on towards Bonn, feeling uneasy because there was no traffic, and a soldier with a rifle every twenty yards. This, they learnt, was because 'Herr Präsident' – Hermann Goering[103] – was also on his way to Bonn. When they crossed the Rhine, it got worse: the road was lined with Nazi stormtroopers and singing children waving Nazi flags and banners with anti-Jew slogans. He had to drive painfully slowly, trapped in precisely the sort of situation he had been warned by the Foreign Office to avoid. They were driving with the sun-roof down, and Mitz perching on Leonard's shoulder.

---

100 VW Diary 15 April 1935
101 VW Diary 17 April 1935
102 8 May 1935
103 'Präsident': the term for the Speaker of the Reichstag

When the crowds saw her they shrieked with delight all along the route, shouting 'Heil Hitler!' and giving the Nazi salute – to Mitz and, by extension, her owners. Mitz saved the day, but it was not pleasant. They stuck to their itinerary – Mainz, Darmstadt, Heidelberg, Stuttgart, Esslinger, Ulm, Augsberg, Munich, over the Austrian frontier, and thence into Italy. Everywhere in Germany, Mitz was their passport – '*das liebe, kleine Ding*', was she a rat, was she a bat? – but there was menace in the air, and notices outside the villages informing them that Jews were not welcome: '*Die Juden sind hier unwundscht.*'

Not even Mussolini and his Fascists, in Leonard's opinion, could make the Italians as uncivilised as the Germans. They stayed five days in Rome, where they duly met Vanessa, Quentin and Angelica. On the way home through France, having left Mitz overnight in the car at Draguignan, they found her in the morning sitting up at the steering-wheel being observed by a French soldier, who asked Leonard all about her 'in an adult, intelligent way',[104] confirming Leonard's positive view of France and the French. He never went to Germany again.

When they got home they found Pinka dead in her basket, and an upset Percy Bartholomew. She had expired the night before, from an unknown cause. 'Leonard is so unhappy.'[105] But he was capable of a jaunty note to Tom Eliot: 'If you would like an article for the Criterion on Europe through the Eyes of a Marmoset, let me know.'[106] And within a few days they bought for £18 a thirteen-month-old black and white pedigree cocker spaniel, Sally. She subsequently declined to breed in spite of repeated matings. She had phantom pregnancies – Leonard would prepare a bed behind screens in his study – but there were never any puppies. She could only love Leonard: 'It's a curious case of hopeless erotic mania – precisely like a human passion',[107] Virginia told Ethel Smyth.

In autumn 1935 the German Reich passed the Nuremberg Laws on citizenship and race. Jews were no longer citizens, and might not vote.

---

104 *Downhill all the Way*
105 VW Letters: VW to Vita Sackville-West 5 June 1935
106 6 June 1935
107 VW Letters 2 July 1935

Sexual relations between Jews and German subjects were forbidden. Jews might not hold public office, and would be 'retired' from their posts. In London, the Woolfs saw Fascist slogans and the BUF symbol – a swastika-like design within a circle – chalked on the walls.

In the last issue of *PQ* for 1933 Leonard had contributed an article on Labour's foreign policy which William Robson found 'profoundly disturbing . . . utterly realistic and utterly merciless in its analysis of the inevitable failure of the League [of Nations] in the Sino-Japanese dispute, in the Disarmament Conference, in the World Economic Conference, and above all in retaining the confidence of peoples, the loyalty of governments or even the lip-service of politicians.'[108]

On 2 October 1935 Mussolini invaded Abyssinia[109] with the aim of establishing an Italian empire in East Africa. This was another major test of the League of Nations. Economic sanctions were imposed on Italy, and Leonard was exalted: the League was not a failure after all. 'Abyssinia, I think, is one of those political miracles which happens occasionally', he wrote to Julian Bell in China. It seemed accepted that 'the League is the only faint hope of preventing a world war', and the 'bulwark' against the Fascist powers.[110]

As oil, steel and iron were excluded from the boycott, and non-League countries (which included the USA, Germany and Japan) were free to trade normally with Italy, the sanctions were a complete waste of time. What is more, a few weeks later the British government made a deal with the French to allow Italy almost all Abyssinia. 'I did not meet one solitary person who did not think the thing outrageous', Leonard wrote to Julian. It made nonsense of all the 'League of Nations blather from Government speakers at the election'.[111]

The General Election on 1 November 1935 had been another 'wretched disappointment'. In drizzling rain Leonard drove Labour voters to the polling station, to little effect; in the Woolfs' constituency the Conservative candidate won easily, and the National Government

108 W.A.Robson (ed), Introduction, *The Political Quarterly in the Thirties*
109 Modern Ethiopia, Eritrea and Somalia.
110 24 Nov 1935
111 16 Jan 1936

was headed by a Conservative, Stanley Baldwin. Leonard attributed Labour's failure to its lack of a credible leader, its lack of unity on the League and sanctions, and its pusillanimous Socialism: 'Nine tenths of the Trades Unionists even are not socialists and are indeed as much scared of socialism as the old ladies of Balham & Tooting.'[112]

Leonard was not a pacifist, but he had devoted his professional life to arguing that war could be avoided by international co-operation and a system of collective security. He wrote in *Downhill all the Way* that towards the end of 1935 he faced up to the fact that 'the League was to all intents and purposes dead and it was fatal to go on using it as a mumbled incantation against war'. Therefore the Labour Party should take the line that it was necessary for Britain to 'make herself strong enough on land and sea and in the air to defeat Hitler'.[113] He argued the case for re-arming, he recalled, in his memoranda to the Advisory Committees.

But he telescoped, in *Downhill All the Way*, months of ambivalence and soul-searching. He had arguments which degenerated into rows with Kingsley Martin. To oppose rearmament and support the League was the traditional Labour position, and Kingsley was among the minority of convinced pacifists in the party – involving, in Leonard's view, much muddled thinking. But his own thinking was confused too.

The National Government believed in 1935 that rearmament could no longer be postponed. The crunch came for Labour at the three-day Party Conference at the end of September that year, which both Woolfs attended. George Lansbury, the leader of the Parliamentary Party, was annihilated by Ernest Bevin, a working-class Trades Unionist, who argued that if you were going to oppose Hitler you had to have arms with which to do it. This was when the ground shifted beneath Leonard's feet. He had to agree with Bevin, even as he shrank from the 'almost indecent cruelty' with which Bevin destroyed the pacifist position and Lansbury himself, who was 'essentially with Pericles, Aristotle and Theophrastus' and in their terms 'a good man'.[114]

*

112 To Julian Bell, 16 Jan 1936
113 *Downhill All the Way*
114 *idem*

'Last night L. was woken at one, by a man shouting abuse at Woolf & Quack in German under his window. Ought we to tell the police? I think it was a drunken undergraduate.'[115] A week later, on a walk on Hampstead Heath, they discussed, yet again, giving up the Hogarth Press.

Tom Eliot brought Emily Hale – an old love, and his confidante and muse – to tea at Tavistock Square on 26 November, the day after Leonard's fifty-fifth birthday; the cake which his mother sent every year was on the table. Miss Hale, a Bostonian, was thrilled to meet Virginia Woolf, but found it easier to connect with her husband. Mr Woolf's face, she reported to a friend, 'is almost emaciated, the features very aquiline but not necessarily Hebraic, the expression warmer than hers, especially the eyes which to me revealed a number of qualities, [such] as patience, weariness and isolation'. Sally sat at his feet and Mitz on his shoulders, 'peering out at one, first from one side, then the other', her tail hanging down his neck.[116]

The Woolfs went to Rodmell for Christmas 1935, and it rained.

115 VW Diary 21 Nov 1935

116 Emily Hale to Ruth George 6 Dec 1935. Quoted in Lyndall Gordon, *Eliot's New Life* OUP 1988

13

Life and Death

Leonard's diary, 19 March 1936: 'Fainting girl in Press.' There was a tap on the window, and out on the steps a girl, hardly able to stand, asking for a drink of water. Leonard heated up some soup for her. Virginia's diary: ' [She] Said you look like brother & sister, both have long noses. I'm a Jewess – a curious stress on the word as if a confession. So's he I said. Then she perked up a little.'[1] They sent her off with a bun, some cold tongue, two eggs and £5, and Leonard met her again to help her find work.

No one has expressed what it was like to be Jewish in England in the 1930s better than the twenty-four-year-old Betty Miller in *Farewell Leicester Square.* She submitted it to Victor Gollancz in 1935, but he was 'too squeamish' to publish it.[2] The protagonist, Alec Berman, is like Leonard's Harry Davis from *The Wise Virgins*, twenty years on – less angry but more fearful. He is in love with Catherine – assured, immaculately *English* – and tells her what it is like, 'hearing your own race casually vilified; and allowing the remark to pass . . . smiling even.'

1 VW Diary 20 March 1936
2 Jane Miller, preface to Betty Miller's *Farewell Leicester Square* Persephone Books 2000. It was first published by Robert Hale in 1941.

Catherine says, 'But this is England.' He replies: 'Yes. The concentration camp is only *spiritual* here.'

No one has expressed the 'spiritual concentration camp' better than Virginia Woolf in *The Years*, in the passage where Sara, in her lodging-house room, is nauseated by the sounds made by the Jew in the shared bathroom, imagining the line of grease and the hairs which he will leave in the bath. 'The Jew . . . the Jew . . .' Sara reiterates the word until the individual, 'Abrahamson, in the tallow trade', engaged to a pretty girl in a tailor's shop, is reduced to an emblem of pollution.

This is not all that contemporary fiction suggests. Jews had a romantic allure for some English non-Jews. Lewis Eliot, the narrator of C.P.Snow's *The Conscience of the Rich*,[3] was in the years leading up to 1939 dazzled by his close friendship with a rich, well-established, Jewish family who, like the Woolfs, think of themselves as English. Eliot, the gentile, with his thinner, cooler heritage, expands in the warmth of their communal life. The plot turns on a campaign to implicate in an arms deal a family member who is also a member of the government. As scandal threatens, and Hitler rants, the patriarch (whose name is Leonard) cries out: 'I wish the *Jews* would stop being *news*!'

Being news is less terrible than being dead. In Germany, Hitler had already liquidated 'the Communists, Social Democrats, Jews . . .', as Leonard wrote in *PQ* in January 1936. His long 'Meditation on Abyssinia' was an interim report on the prospects not of the League, but of the League system. He was careful to distinguish between the two: even if 'the League did not exist', there would still be international arrangements to take its place. 'We are', he wrote, 'spectators and participants in a long drawn-out struggle between two methods or organizing relations between states, the method of violence and war and the method of settlement and agreement.' On 6 March Hitler's troops occupied the demilitarised zone of the Rhineland, in breach of the Treaty of Versailles. Leonard, unwilling to war-monger, wrote in *PQ* ('The Ideal of the League of Nations Remains') that 'No one knows why

3 Published in 1958. C.P. Snow wrote in an 'Author's Note' that this novel should have come second, and was 'out of place', in his novel sequence *Strangers and Brothers*. He did not explain why.

we re-arm except that everyone else is re-arming.' History was made not by wickedness but 'by stupidity'.

For the rest of 1936 Leonard was able to contribute only book reviews, for personal reasons. Virginia was 'much nearer a complete breakdown than she had ever been since 1913.'[4] She herself wrote, about this 'catastrophic illness', that she had 'never been so near the precipice of my own feeling since 1913'.[5] She was planning out what was to be *Three Guineas* and revising *The Years*; they were getting the latter set in galley-proofs as she went along, which she then revised yet again. In an attempt to help by setting a limit to her rewriting, Leonard gave her a deadline, which made her even more agitated. She lost half a stone in weight.

In May he took her off on holiday to her beloved Cornwall. They went to St Ives, taking a look at Talland House, where Virginia's happy childhood holidays had been spent. But returning to the proofs plunged her back into the pit, and she spent three and a half months at Rodmell over the summer unable to work at all – months which were for Leonard 'filled with endless nightmare'.

He left her in Louie's care once a week to drive up to London, cramming in Hogarth Press business with his editorial and political commitments. He wrote in *Downhill all the Way* that he was rarely home until nine in the evening; but he must often have been later, as his diary shows him having dinner with his mother, or with Bella and Tom, home on leave. He saw Alice Ritchie. Leonard wrote in *The Journey Not the Arrival Matters* that 'although Virginia and I liked her very much', Alice Ritchie passed out of their lives after she gave up her job at the Hogarth Press, until he saw her again in 'mid-1941'. This is forgetfulness, or fudging.[6] In January 1936, he and Virginia dined with Alice, returning via Buckingham Palace where the death of King George V had just been announced. Her name occurs in his diary that September, and again in December. While contact was infrequent, it was unbroken.

---

4 *Downhill All the Way*

5 VW Diary 11 June 1936

6 Any fudging would have been to avoid stressing his friendship with Alice, in view of his subsequent relationship with Trekkie.

Back in March 1932, the Woolfs had dined with Alice in company with her younger sister Trekkie and husband Peter Brooker. This marriage broke up soon after. Trekkie met Ian Parsons, a young director of the publishers Chatto & Windus, and in 1934 they married. Trekkie published an anthology with Chatto in 1935, *English Drawings*. She had commercial work, but her ambition was to succeed as an easel painter. Alice wrote to Leonard in 1936 'as the only person I know in the inner circle in these matters and a friend to art – what does a painter do to get its paintings shown? I'm worried about Trekkie', who went on from year to year 'without the smallest scrap of encouragement from outside'. Leonard offered to ask Vanessa Bell or Duncan Grant to take a look at Trekkie's work, but Trekkie was unwilling.

Civil war erupted in Spain in 1936, with General Francisco Franco's armed revolt against the socialist and anti-clerical Republican government. The Germans and Italians materially aided the insurgents, while the Russians sent technical help to the Republicans. It was a European conflagration in microcosm. Some Labour MPs urged the British government to send military aid to the Republicans, but a policy of non-intervention prevailed. 'The League is dead; collective security is dead and rotten', Leonard wrote to Julian Bell. 'Meanwhile the Spaniards are shouting: "Long live Death."' He was glumly in favour of isolationism for Britain. 'It is too late to stop a European war by an alliance; in fact it would probably precipitate a war.'[7]

In autumn 1936 Hitler and Mussolini recognised Franco's government as the government of Nationalist Spain, and in London Mosley's blackshirts staged a deliberately provocative march through the Jewish East End, which became 'the battle of Cable Street'. The *Jewish Chronicle*, in its editorial for New Year's Day 1937, urged the community to deflate British anti-Semitism by stamping out the 'vice of vulgar display', not something which had ever tempted Leonard Woolf – unless he were to be condemned for his predilection for showy, gaudy flowers.

During Virginia's collapse of 1936, Leonard again relied on hard-

---

7 15 Nov 1936

won experience, and on Dr Ellie Rendell's support. No authoritarian 'nerve-doctors', no nurses, no nursing-home. Just Monks House, peace and quiet, sedatives, and no pressures. It could not prevent, but did not exacerbate, her suffering. The risk he took was that her illness might escalate. She described their 'peaceful, lonely life . . . extremely soothing', to Vanessa, and was well enough on 30 August to go to a Charleston party with fancy dress and theatricals. The Woolfs went as bookcases, labelled 'Fact' and 'Fiction'.

Leonard wrote to Margaret Llewelyn Davies at the end of 1936 saying that 'Virginia was not really well for the first three-quarters of the year . . . The last three months she has been ever so much better and has now finished her book.'[8] Margaret was too old now to be burdened with his miseries. The garden was his best solace, and an opportunity for solitude. 'I'm always losing him in the garden', Virginia told Ethel Smyth. 'He's up a tree, or behind a hedge.'[9]

Leonard had started to read *The Years* in April 1936, when Virginia was too depressed for them to talk about it. In early November he read the finished manuscript. 'I knew that unless I could give a completely favourable verdict she would be in despair and would have a very serious breakdown.' Waiting for his verdict, Virginia was on tenterhooks. Then: 'The miracle is accomplished. L. put down the last sheet at about 12 last night; & could not speak. He was in tears. He says "it is a most remarkable book – he *likes* it better than The Waves", and has not a spark of doubt that it should be published.'[10]

His tears were caused by release from tension, and relief that the novel was not as bad as she feared. He praised it 'more than I should have done if she had been well', but was truthful about its inordinate length. So Virginia had to make cuts and more revisions, but was 'vigorous and cheerful' after Leonard's reassurance: 'How I woke from death – or non being – to life! What an incredible night . . .!'[11] She was sufficiently herself again to take a lively interest in the gossip about the

8 30 Dec 1936.
9 VW Letters 18 Sept 1936
10 VW Diary 5 Nov 1936
11 VW Diary 24 Nov 1936

new King Edward VIII and Mrs Wallis Simpson, and his abdication on 19 December. ('I imagine that we cannot now go further in romantic idiocy', Leonard wrote to Julian.[12]) The proofs of *The Years* went back to the printer on the last day of 1936.

Leonard's own health then gave way. He was not at all well throughout 1937 and 1938. Again, during those two years, his journalism was confined to reviews, and to contributions to the *New Statesman*'s 'London Diary', apart from two big pieces in the first issues of *PQ* for 1937. In 'Arms and the Peace', which spelled out the confusion in political circles (and in his own mind) about the arguments for and against re-arming, he came out in print for the first time with the statement that, in the war that was surely coming, 'I do not believe that it is psychologically possible to stand aside from the conflict.' This was for him a huge and alarming step.

He expressed anguish and dread physically. On 4 February 1937 he saw a Harley Street specialist with symptoms suggesting either a prostate problem or diabetes. Virginia paced up and down Harley Street for an hour when, a week later, he went back to hear the result of tests: 'At last just before 5 L. came out in his new light overcoat, & smiled.' The specialist thought it was a question of diet – less sugar – and later in the month gave him a sugar-tolerance test, which was normal.

His chronic skin irritation flared up at the same time. When it erupted on his face it affected his eyes. As usual, different creams and unguents were tried. He consulted Dr Leo Rau, an Orthodox Jew from Berlin who settled in Highgate in 1933, a good friend of the Woolf family. Dr Rau too suspected either prostate trouble or diabetes, and sent him for another sugar-tolerance test. He went on seeing Dr Rau and returned to the specialist (at five guineas a consultation) who gave him his third sugar-tolerance test.

Seeking relief from his worsened hand tremor, Leonard also consulted Frederick Matthias Alexander, founder of the 'Alexander technique', on the recommendation of the Shaws, and began a course

---

12 13 Dec 1936

of exercises with him. Leonard could believe that Alexander's theory – that many disorders were caused by people holding their head, neck, shoulders and spine in the wrong position – held 'an important truth'.[13] He thought Alexander was an 'honest, inspired quack'.

The Years was just coming out, and Virginia was tormented by worries about what her friends and unknown critics would write, and how her reputation would stand. The reviews were good, and it was, commercially, her most successful novel, even though Leonard privately thought it 'the worst of her books'. Her agitation over its reception, and what she called 'T of L',[14] and Leonard's continuing illnesses, made them scratchy with each other. She was ungracious about his inviting the Robsons to Monks House; he was irritated, as so often, by the 'self-centredness' of her family.

Julian Bell came back from China determined to go to the war in Spain. Before his return, Leonard was among several people who put out feelers for him. No one who loved Julian wanted him to go, and Leonard reported that 'they do not want untrained men'. But Julian went off to Spain to drive an ambulance for Spanish Medical Aid in the first week of June 1937. Guernica, the capital of the Basque country in the north of Spain, was destroyed by German bombs in April, causing terrible casualties; on 24 June, Leonard and Virginia were among artists and writers on the platform at a fund-raising event in the Albert Hall on behalf of refugee Basque children, at which Paul Robeson sang.

John Lehmann had come back into the Woolfs' lives. He founded and edited a twice-yearly journal, *New Writing*; his contract with the publishers ran out, and *New Writing* needed a new home. Leonard and Virginia were still indecisively talking of divesting themselves of the Hogarth Press, and Leonard offered to sell the Press to John for £6,000, retaining for himself 'an advisory interest'. At this point in the negotiations, there was terrible news.

On 20 July 1937 Leonard was in London for his appointment with

13 *Sowing*
14 Time of Life i.e. the menopause.

Dr Alexander, and then: 'Heard Julian killed Drove Charleston [taking Vanessa] fetch Quentin.' Julian was hit by a fragment of shrapnel and died a few hours later on the operating table. He was twenty-nine. 'There's nothing to be said', Leonard wrote to John Lehmann the next day, 'except about the sheer waste and futility of it all. It is the war all over again, when one was rung up to be told that Rupert [Brooke] was dead, or that one's brother [Cecil] was killed, and one knew that it was only to produce the kind of world we are living in now. Horrible.' Discussions about the Press were put on hold. Vanessa was utterly shattered. Virginia showed her strength and her quality by putting aside her own concerns for weeks to be with her sister, going down to Charleston when the ailing Leonard had to remain in London. 'Thus I left L. alone: have I the right to leave L. alone, & sit with Nessa?'[15]

Leonard wrote in *Sowing* that he stopped going to Dr Alexander because he did not have the patience to practise the 'abominable exercises' at home. Circumstances played their part: he could not, in the immediate aftermath of Julian's death, keep his appointments; and having stopped, he went no more. But in July Virginia was recording a marked lessening of his tremor, thanks, she thought, to Dr Alexander. A 'disease' was cured, she wrote, which had, 'I guess, moulded his life wrongly since he was five. All his shyness, his suffering from society, his sharpness, & definiteness, might have been smoothed.'

The improvement did not last, and he was not better in other ways. Dr Rau prescribed calamine and zinc oxide cream and 'eczema powder' for his skin, tablets for his kidneys, Benzedrine, and a week's course of testosterone. Virginia, thinking of joining the Bagenals and Saxon in Paris for a weekend in October 1937, decided not to go when Leonard showed dismay. His illnesses made him dependent. So far from being resentful, Virginia was 'overcome with happiness'. They walked round Tavistock Square 'love-making – after 25 years can't bear to be separate . . . you see it is enormous pleasure being wanted: a wife. And our marriage so complete.'[16]

---

15 VW Diary 11 Aug 1937
16 VW Diary 22 Oct 1937

This happiness, which she called a 'fiction' – not in the sense that it was untrue, but that it was a state of mind – was overtaken by the 'fact' that on 25 October John Lehmann came to dinner and they discussed the future of the Hogarth Press again. Leonard had the idea that the trio whom he called 'the young Brainies' – Spender, Isherwood and Auden – might buy it collectively, with John as manager. The young Brainies had neither the cash nor the inclination. John however could offer £3000 for a half-share, buying out Virginia. The deal was completed in spring 1938. John reported to Virginia that Leonard was 'very rugged the other day when I signed the Partnership Agreement, and to my proposal that the event be marked by a mutual health-drinking, replied that he had only cold water.' Leonard wrote apologising for being 'gruff' over the signing. 'It was emotion.'

Alice Ritchie, close to Trekkie and Ian Parsons, heard a rumour that Leonard had sold the Hogarth Press, which he had to contradict. 'The thing is', she wrote, 'that Ian has always had a day-dream of some sort of amalgamation between Chatto and the Hogarth Press. He often talked to me about it and when he heard, in the way of gossip, that the Press was sold he was in despair and begged me to ask you if indeed all hope for him was over.' The timing was not right, but a seed was sown.

Leonard was ill in bed for more than a week at Monks House as 1937 became 1938, and Dr Rau sent him to the Royal Northern Hospital for an X-ray on 31 December, in case he had cancer. He went straight back to bed afterwards, dictating to Virginia in a formal letter to John Lehmann the terms and conditions of his partnership in the Press.[17] Morgan Forster thought Leonard should be seeing a kidney specialist: 'You have none of the ordinary symptoms of prostate trouble.' The X-ray was clear, but Leonard was threatened with physical investigations of a kind that he dreaded. 'The catheter is not a thing to worry about',

17 JL was to have the title of managing director, to be entirely responsible for the management of office and staff, to put in at least three days a week, with August and September off, plus two further three-week periods. His salary would be £500 a year, and LW's £200 a year, before the division of profits. 'Each of us would have an absolute veto against the publication of any book.'

Morgan reassured him. 'Insist they pump the local anaesthetic in first.'[18] He began to recover, and they went down to Rodmell – where Virginia fell ill with 'influenza'. They were on a marital see-saw, as regards their health. Virginia thought Leonard's trouble was the result of a blow to the kidney area of his back from the handle of a car door.

Leonard's various doctors do seem to have understood, if vaguely, his skin and kidney problems. The likely diagnosis is constitutional vasoatopic eczema, which can be precipitated by sudden changes between heat and cold, as when in Ceylon he was baked by the sun one moment and chilled to the bone in the rain another. Curries and spicy food, alcohol, and fever are also known triggers. Psychological stress too can cause the blood vessels to dilate and redden the skin. The itchy rash increases the stress, and scratching adds to the inflammation. There is also a connection with the prostate and kidneys. Prostatic enlargement obstructs the bladder. The pressure builds back to the kidneys, which produces itching of the skin, since sweat glands share, in a small way, the functions of the kidneys. These are physiological explanations.[19] Another way of putting it is that Leonard's 'carapace', on which he relied, periodically cracked up. He was more thin-skinned than he acknowledged.

At the beginning of February 1938 Leonard read the typescript of Virginia's *Three Guineas*. She noted that he 'gravely approves. Thinks it an extremely clear analysis'.[20] This short book is an anti-war companion volume to Leonard's *Quack, Quack!* – with a lethal injection of gender hostility, and photographs of pompous, bedizened British generals, judges and archbishops instead of foreign dictators and primitive war gods. Leonard stood up for *Three Guineas* in terms of what, in a lovely phrase, he called Virginia's 'impeccable feminism', but Morgan Forster

18 28 Jan 1938

19 LW may also be a candidate for Sulzberger-Garbe syndrome, described in 1937 by two refugees from Nazi Germany: an itchy skin eruption peculiar to middle-aged Jewish men (and some Jewish women), chiefly involving the genitalia, the chest and the mouth, and, like vasoreactive or atopic eczema, believed to be psychogenic.

20 VW Diary 4 Feb 1938

thought it cantankerous, Maynard Keynes thought it silly, and Vita Sackville-West thought it unpatriotic. It came out in June 1938, and sold well. Virginia had started on her biography of Roger Fry, and embarked on a new novel.

On 1 March 1938 John Lehmann started at the Press under the new regime. It was never plain sailing; there were endless tiffs with Leonard about details, such as the punctuation in the collection of Julian Bell's letters and essays which the Press published in November. John again lodged his grievances with Vanessa, who relayed them to Virginia, who defended Leonard. The worst disagreements were about *New Writing*, which Leonard did not value as highly as John did (or so John felt), and which made no money.

On 8 March the Woolfs had a new radio 'installed' as Leonard put it, at 52 Tavistock Square. Leonard was a regular broadcaster and took a furious interest in the medium, drafting a letter signed by himself, Virginia and others[21] to the Director General of the BBC, Sir John Reith, complaining about the 'very meagre provision of music by the great classical composers'. The BBC was 'contemptible', he wrote to the editor of the *Listener*, his friend J.R.Ackerley: 'they habitually choose the tenth rate in everything, from their music hall programmes and social lickspitlers [*sic*] and royal bumsuckers . . .'[22] He had just had one of his reviews for the *Listener* censored on account of a disrespectful reference to the Princesses Elizabeth and Margaret Rose.

The new radio was installed in time to 'listen in', three days later, to the news of the German invasion of Austria, the *Anschluss*. Within hours, a Nazi government was proclaimed in Vienna. Leonard was in no doubt now about what had to be done. The next day, at the Labour Party Executive, he argued strongly that the Party should enter into a coalition with the Conservatives (under Winston Churchill) and 'agree to an immediate introduction of conscription

---

21 Jan 1936. Signatories included Kenneth Clark, M.S.Amos, Margery Fry, Duncan Grant, Vanessa Bell, W.A.Robson, R.C.Trevelyan, Aldous Huxley, Ethel Smyth. Reith addressed his acknowedgment to 'Mrs Woolf'.

22 6 Nov 1937. The *Listener* was the BBC's weekly magazine, carrying transcripts of broadcast talks, original articles, and book reviews.

and rearmament'. But insufficient support was forthcoming from the Parliamentary Party.

Lady Ottoline Morrell died, after a long illness, on 21 April 1938. Ka (Cox) Arnold-Forster died suddenly, of a heart-attack, on 22 May. But Leonard had the final all-clear from his doctors. He immediately took on yet another commitment, as a member of the Whitley Council.[23] Civil servants did not go on strike; the Whitley Council provided an arbitration system for the settlement of disputes, with representatives from the Treasury and from the Civil Service Clerical Association, in whose interest Leonard served.

Ever since Ceylon, anything to do with administration fascinated him. He wrote, with startling lyricism: 'Administration must be regarded as the most precious flower and fruit, the essential mark and prerogative of the independent, sovereign state.'[24] He enjoyed, in the course of the tribunals, learning about different worlds of work – from prison officers, and 'the women who clean out the government offices in Whitehall, foresters in the north of Scotland, the men who talk down aeroplanes . . . in fog, and a small and peculiar class of men in the secret service.' The more he learned, the more 'crazily irrational' and in need of reform the structure of the Civil Service seemed to him. In another life, he would have been the man to do it.

As if in defiance of the international situation, in spring 1938 the Woolfs undertook another extension of Monks House. The Press, even as they were partly unloading it on to John Lehmann, was making more money than ever: £6,000 in the tax year April 1937–April 1938. The new room built in 1929 up in the attic, reached by steep stairs from the kitchen end of the house and officially Virginia's private sitting room, was regularly used by both of them, in spite of its smallness and its

---

23 Properly, the National Whitley Council for Administrative and Legal Departments of the Civil Service. LW's enthusiasm for this work sits oddly with his earlier perception that official tribunals exercised an inappropriate judicial power over the lives of individuals.

24 *International Government*

slanting ceiling, for listening to music in the evenings. It was brighter than the big ground-floor room, and not damp. At the other end of the house, over Leonard's bedroom and up another steep flight of stairs, they now built a room which became Leonard's new study – long and narrow, made even narrower by bookshelves, but full of light from three windows, with a balcony built off one of them, overlooking the garden. As with their other extensions, the new room did not improve the appearance of the house from the outside.

The garden too had a makeover, with a built-up paved terrace replacing the sloping lawn to the back doors (which children had liked rolling down). Vita spent a night at Monks House in August; it was maybe on this occasion when, asked by Leonard what she thought of his new garden, she grandly replied that one could not create Versailles in three-quarters of an acre of Sussex. (He was not trying to create Versailles.) Yet Vita, in her way, appreciated him: 'I know he is tiresome and wrong-headed and sometimes Jewish but really with his school-boyish love for pets and toys (gadgets) he is irresistibly young and attractive.'[25]

Vanessa painted a portrait of Leonard the following year, writing at an inconveniently small table with his typewriter pushed aside, and Sally the spaniel lying with her chin between her paws on a chair close by. Thin as a blade, Leonard looks, as Vita said, young and attractive – in spite of his illnesses, and the grey in the thick, boyishly-cut hair, and his nearly fifty-nine years. John Lehmann, renewing his intimacy with Leonard at the Press, found him 'well preserved', although 'his lean and narrow face (which always reminded me of a Red Indian chief) was heavily lined. His energy was still formidable . . .'[26] In September he had another greenhouse built in the garden, to Virginia's disapproval; she called it his Crystal Palace. But he needed more frost-free space to grow more of the double scarlet and yellow begonias, the gloxinias and the lilies, which he brought up to the top sitting-room and placed among the piles of papers and journals on the table.

*

25 Quoted in VG, *Vita: The Life of V. Sackville-West* Weidenfeld & Nicolson 1983
26 John Lehmann, *Thrown to the Woolfs* 1978

That August of 1938 T.S.Eliot's wife Vivien was certified insane, and committed to a mental hospital; 'and Eliot never visited her in the asylum, where she remained for the rest of her life'.[27] Nothing has survived of what Leonard thought about this. Tom Eliot was moving a little apart from the Woolfs, into Tory dining clubs and the Anglican Church. Leonard and he exchanged densely argued letters in 1939 following the publication of Eliot's *The Idea of a Christian Society*, Leonard's point being that a society governed on a basis of Christian dogma, where the majority was not truly Christian, would be authoritarian if not actually fascistic.

Apostolic dogma was challenged at a Memoir Club meeting at Tilton on 11 August 1938, where Maynard Keynes read his astute, revisionist paper on the nature of the influence that G.E.Moore had on them all at Cambridge. Something had perhaps been put in its proper place; something was becoming history. Afterwards, Maynard had to go and lie down. He had had a heart-attack the previous year. The next day, after an afternoon game of bowls, Leonard and Virginia listened to Hitler's rantings at Nuremberg on the wireless, those 'savage and insane ravings of a vindictive underdog who suddenly saw himself as all-powerful.'[28]

Leonard had been writing a play, and did not like Virginia asking him when it would be finished: 'He has, amusingly [*sic*], all an artist's sensibility.'[29] His play, *The Hotel*, is set in the foyer of the Grand Hotel de l'Univers et du Commerce. Through its revolving doors come and go the British Secretary of State for Foreign Affairs, an Italian Fascist agent, a German Nazi agent, the leader of the Irish Communist Party, a member of the British Communist Party, a French hooker, a Jew – all stereotypically named and characterised. *The Hotel* is a short black farce on the Shavian model, into which Leonard discharged his pessimism.

On 13 October 1938 Leonard read *The Hotel* to Maynard and Lydia, at Tilton. Maynard appeared impressed. Leonard was excited. Virginia was envious. The theatrical agent Walter Peacock sent it to the Group

---

27 Lyndall Gordon, *Eliot's New Life* Oxford University Press 1988. Vivien Eliot died in 1947.

28 *Downhill All the Way*

29 VW Diary 4 Aug 1938

Theatre company, who did not find it 'suitable'.[30] Nor did the Stage Society, the Unity Theatre, or the Westminster Theatre. 'I will try the play elsewhere and let you know the result from time to time.'[31] All authors know what that means. Leonard published *The Hotel* at the Hogarth Press and bit on the bullet.

Leonard contested Fascism in England in the later 1930s through his writing and through committees and pressure groups, overlapping in their membership and aims, as in the period of the Great War. He spent hours with what seemed to his wife 'dirty unkempt, ardent, ugly but entirely impractical but no doubt well meaning philanthropists at whom I should throw the coal scuttle after ten minutes if I were in his place'.[32] She hated hearing the drone of committee meetings in the next room, but 'that's Leonard's hobby, and passion'.[33]

As before, Leonard deplored the proliferation. When Morgan Forster, as vice-president of the National Council for Civil Liberties, sent him an appeal for core funding, Leonard wrote a formal reply: there were three organisations concerned with civil liberties – the Council, the UDC and FIL[34] – with three separate offices and staffs. 'They all do much the same work and tap much the same sources (I subscribe myself to all three). They ought to be amalgamated.' When this was not seriously considered, he resigned from the executive of FIL, while remaining a member of all three 'largely from sentimental reasons, I suppose'.[35]

Kingsley Martin, emotionally overwrought, declared in the *New Statesman* at the end of August 1938 that the likely breaching by the Germans of the Czechoslovakian frontier to claim the Sudetenland must not be made the occasion for a world war. The Conservative Prime

---

30 The Group Theatre was founded in 1932 by Rupert Doone with Ormerod Greenwood and Tyrone Guthrie for the performance of poetic and socialist drama. It produced first performances of works by Eliot, Auden, Isherwood and Spender.

31 31 May 1939

32 To Janet Case VW Letters 24 Dec 1936

33 To Ethel Smyth VW Letters 3 Aug 1936

34 UDC: Union of Democratic Control. FIL: For Intellectual Liberty, an un-catchy name thought up by LW, a co-founder.

35 20 Aug 1939

Minister (since 1937) Neville Chamberlain was of the same mind; he flew to meet Hitler, Mussolini and Daladier at Munich on 29 September. If they did not arrive at an accommodation, there would be war.

Leonard was in the lavatory on the morning of 30 September when he heard on the wireless that agreement had been reached at Munich: Hitler was to have his way over the Sudetenland, and the Czechs must submit. In return, Hitler expressed 'a desire' that Britain and Germany should never go to war again. 'Peace with honour', 'peace in our time', as Chamberlain said. Leonard rushed out into the garden to let Percy Bartholomew know. At Kingsley's panic-stricken request, he went to London and into heated discussions on editorial policy. Leonard's opinion was that there would be 'peace without honour' for about six months, and then war. He was not an appeaser.

The countryside was calmer than the city, and Leonard was impressed by the good sense of the older Rodmell inhabitants. Why not stay at Monks House for ever, thought Virginia, in their peaceful routine of writing and reading and walking and music, 'enjoying this immortal rhythm, in which both eyes and soul are at rest? So I said, and for once L. said; Youre not such a fool as you seem. We were so sane; so happy . . .' She made a new loaf, and was about to call Leonard in to tea 'from the ladder on the high tree – where he looked so beautiful my heart stood still with pride that he ever married me',[36] when they were invaded by uninvited visitors who stayed four hours – eliciting from Virginia afterwards a diatribe of rage and contempt. Leonard thought she was being harsh. She thought he was being sentimental.

That autumn of 1938, the full horror of what was happening in Germany was brought home to Leonard. In Paris, on 7 November, a seventeen-year-old Polish Jew, Herschel Grynszpan, shot a German diplomat.[37] When the diplomat died two days later, Nazi stormtroopers

36 VW to Vanessa Bell, Letters 8 Oct 1938

37 The Nazis claimed that the shooting was part of a Jewish conspiracy against Germany. It was a protest against the deportation of Polish Jews from Germany to Poland, which would not accept them.

were unleashed to attack Jews and destroy their homes and businesses. The rampage continued overnight, becoming known as *Kristallnacht* – the 'night of broken glass'.

'I saw a photograph', wrote Leonard, 'of a Jew being dragged by storm troopers out of a shop in one of the main streets in Berlin; the fly buttons of the man's trousers had been torn open to show that he was circumcised and therefore a Jew. On the man's face was the horrible look of blank suffering and despair which from the beginning of human history men have seen under the crown of thorns on the faces of their persecuted and humiliated victims.' What was even more horrible to Leonard was 'the look on the faces of respectable men and women, standing on the pavement, laughing at the victim.'[38] (The only image that made a stronger impression on him was published after the war: 'a long line of Jews, men, women and children, being driven naked down a path into a gas chamber'.[39])

Virginia recorded in her diary a fortnight later that Leonard had a new outbreak of his rash, on his back. Thinking it was connected with his bladder problem, he sent for Dr Rau, who 'says no its your new pyjamas'. Leonard nevertheless underwent physical investigations. Morgan Forster was sympathetic: 'I hope the examinations are not very fidgety and wretched – if they are of the sort I had, you may care to know that one gets indifferent to them.'[40]

Walking home through Russell Square on 10 December from a performance of *The Merchant of Venice*, with Peggy Ashcroft as Portia, Leonard told Virginia he had taught himself not to think about death, though two or three years previously 'fear of death became an obsession'. (That would have been when Virginia was ill.) Virginia said she would not wish to live if he died. Meanwhile life was 'what? exciting? Yes I think so. He agreed. So we don't think of death.' The next day 'L. lacerated with his rash'[41] was hobbling painfully round St James's Park.

*

38 *The Journey not the Arrival Matters* (1969)
39 *ibid*
40 Nov 1938
41 VW Diary 16 Nov 1938, 11 Dec 1938

During the icy night of Christmas Eve 1938, Mitz died. She crept on to Leonard's bed and when he woke she was lying on his foot, her tail wrapped round her neck, her eyes closed. Leonard buried her in the garden in the snow against the churchyard wall. She had been with him for five years – a year longer than London Zoo had ever succeeded in keeping a marmoset alive.

On 29 December 1938 Leonard wrote in his diary: 'Finished After the Deluge Vol 2' – the first and last time he ever noted the finishing of a book. Virginia read it straight away and described it in her diary as 'very good; full; moulded; subtle'.[42] (Leonard had not read her diary, in an open and ordinary way, for many years. But there was always the possibility that he might. What she wrote in it was therefore potentially for his eyes. Sometimes she twisted the knife, sometimes she offered balm.)

The first volume of Leonard's *After the Deluge* established his concept of communal psychology, and discussed the Enlightenment ideas of the eighteenth and early nineteenth centuries. It was grounded in the recent fact of the Great War, and in his burning desire to demonstrate the psychological and sociological processes by which wars came about, in order that further wars might be avoided. His second volume, eight years on, concentrated on the effect which the ideas of liberty, equality and fraternity had on the communal psychology of the years up to 1830-32, as a historical link between the first and final volumes. It was reviewed respectfully by friends: Leonard received an anonymous letter (posted in Northumberland), sneering at 'the way Bloomsbury scratches one another's back'. Published in September 1939, it sold pathetically few copies. Even Barbara Wootton, an admirer, admitted she was disappointed by the narrow time-scale.[43] The first volume was issued as a Penguin paperback; this second one was not. For all its success in Britain, Leonard's American publishers, Harcourt Brace, had done poorly with *Before the Deluge* Volume 1[44] and declined to publish Volume 2.

*

42 VW Diary 9 Jan 1939
43 27 Nov 1940
44 It appeared in USA as *The Horns of Our Dilemma*

The Woolfs befriended a refugee lawyer, Robert Spira, and his wife Mela, who fled from Austria after the *Anschluss.* When war broke out and Robert Spira was interned on the Isle of Man as an 'alien', Leonard managed to get him released, and to find work at the BBC. And on 28 January 1939, a Saturday, the Woolfs went to tea with a particularly distinguished Jewish refugee, the eighty-two-year-old Sigmund Freud.

Freud was living in Hampstead at 20 Maresfield Gardens, with his daughter Anna. Leonard, as his publisher, had corresponded with him, but they had never met. 'I feel no call to praise the famous men I have known', he wrote in *Downhill all the Way.* 'Nearly all famous men are disappointing or bores, or both. Freud was neither; he had an aura, not of fame, but of greatness.' They sat round a table in the room overlooking the garden. Freud's son Martin, whom they already knew – he managed the business side of the Hogarth publishing programme for his father – was with them. Freud was suffering from cancer of the mouth, and 'it was not an easy interview.' But Leonard found Freud 'a formidable man', 'an extraordinarily nice man'. He presented Virginia with a narcissus. They did not see him again – he died later that year – but he wrote a charming note to Leonard after the visit: 'Handicapped in the use of your language I think I could not give full expression to my satisfaction in having met you and your lady.'[45]

It was to Leonard that Anna Freud turned when her brother Martin was interned as an alien, and Martin's nineteen-year-old son deported to Australia. 'After all, it is so very clear that we came to England as friends and not as enemies', as she wrote to him.[46] Leonard wrote to Clement Attlee, a Labour member of Winston Churchill's war cabinet: 'Freud and his family, when they came here, were welcomed as distinguished guests and victims of the Nazis . . . That any of them should now be interned as dangerous and that a grandson of Freud should have been sent off to Australia by the Government seems to me amazing.'[47] Attlee took the matter up at once with the Home Secretary.

*

---

45 1 Feb 1939
46 21 Aug 1940
47 24 Aug 1940

On 15 March 1939 German troops marched into Prague, and Hitler declared that Czechoslovakia as an entity had ceased to exist. One week later, Virginia recorded: 'L. all rash. Rau says it will go in time.'[48] In mid-April he was running a temperature, and Virginia had 'influenza'. Leonard told Virginia that 'he was fonder of me than I of him'. This led to another discussion as to which of them would mind the other's death most. Leonard said he hoped he would die first. 'He said he depended more upon our common life than I did. He gave the garden as an instance. He said I lived more in a world of my own . . . I was very happy to think I was so much needed.'[49]

That was Leonard's aim: to make her happy. What Virginia loved was Leonard's unconditional love. That was his gift to her. She accepted his love and returned it, insofar as it was in her. That was her gift to him. She loved no one – or rather, no one was essential to her – apart from Vanessa, Vita and above all Leonard. 'I have no circumference; only my inviolable centre: L. to wit.'[50] But his citing the garden as a binding agent in their 'common life' was dubious. She loved their garden, but not as he did. If Virginia was jealous of anything or anyone in Leonard's life – and she may have been, a bit, of the young women about whom she made biting comments in her journal – it was of the garden.

They had Mark Gertler to dinner on 14 May; Virginia wanted his opinion on Roger Fry's paintings, for her biography. On 23 June Gertler committed suicide by gassing himself in his studio.

Two weeks post-Munich, Victor Gollancz had written to Leonard, stating that 'tolerance, the open mind, freedom of thought and discussion' were endangered, and inviting him to write a book to be called something along the lines of 'The Defence of Western Civilisation', for the Left Book Club. Leonard agreed unwillingly. The 60,000-strong membership of the Left Book Club included many British Communists and fellow travellers. What Leonard would want to say could never please these last factions. He asked therefore for a guarantee of 'complete

---

48 VW Diary 22 March 1939
49 VW Diary 28 April 1939
50 VW Diary 30 Oct 1938

freedom' in the expression of his opinions. Gollancz's co-selectors in the Left Book Club, John Strachey and Harold Laski, were away; Gollancz took it upon himself to give the guarantee, and offered Leonard £500.

Leonard sent in his lucid and lively book to Gollancz on 9 May 1939. He called it *Barbarians at the Gate.* Having no response after a month, he wrote to Gollancz, who replied ominously that there were 'a number of complications'.[51] While the Woolfs were on holiday in Brittany, what Virginia called a 'letter war' rumbled on. 'L. very calm; & how sane, compared with me.'[52]

Gollancz, in a six-and-a-half-page letter, said he wanted to postpone publication. He, John Strachey and Laski felt that he had used phrases which could be used out of context by 'reactionaries and indeed, fascists as propaganda against the Soviet Union'. Would Leonard 'modify' his text with alterations and some additions? Strachey was proposing to write a corrective ten-thousand word 'review' for *Left News*, to be published perhaps before the book appeared.[53]

Leonard was angry. Because, he wrote to Gollancz, 'I deal in a book of which the subject is tolerance, with tolerance', he was accused of hostility to the Soviet Union. 'Woolf is cutting up nastier and nastier', Gollancz reported to John Strachey. 'When can you get your memorandum done by? Then we can reckon three to four days for Laski and myself to prepare our points, and then we will have the bloody meeting . . . If Woolf gets any nastier I shall break the contract and refuse to publish it.' John Strachey sent Leonard twenty-seven pages of notes, and the letter war raged on.

Leonard's mother, with Edgar and Sylvia, visited Monks House in August 1938, on a hot sultry day when tanks with gun carriages were mustering on the Downs. Old Mrs Woolf maundered on about the

---

51 June 5 1939

52 VW Diary 29 June 1939

53 Gollancz to LW 22 June 1939. John Strachey, who had been an associate of Mosley's, and a Labour MP, was never a member of the Communist Party, but a supporter of CP views and policies until 1940.

past, mulling nostalgically over all the 'lovely furniture' she had had at 101 Lexham Gardens.

'The Jews obsess her', observed Virginia, as if that were not, in the circumstances, quite reasonable.

Mrs Woolf would no longer have a paid companion, preferring to depend upon her adoring children. But adoration of 'Lady' was wearing thin. Edgar and Flora at least were outspoken about the way their mother exhausted their goodwill and falsified all emotions, which was what Leonard had always thought. He and Virginia found two-hour visits to her pink, overheated hotel room difficult, what with the 'constant innuendoes about the goodness of Herbert & Harold; inference that L. neglects her; hints that I [Virginia] have taken him away from his family; absorbed him in mine.' Mrs Woolf followed them out to the stairs, making Leonard reiterate that she was looking better. 'Sure Len? Sure I look better?'[54]

She was much loved by her grandchildren, and family occasions were the breath of life to her. She had marked Leonard and Virginia's silver wedding by ordering for them a huge cake from Lyons, with icing-sugar decorations designed by herself, and an electric coffee-maker. 'Oh dear, what a thing real family life is!'[55] For Mrs Woolf it was the only real thing.

While the letter war with Gollancz raged, Leonard had a telephone message that his mother, now eighty-seven, had been taken into hospital following a fall. The family had her moved to the London Clinic, and Leonard visited her there daily. Virginia went with him, sometimes waiting outside the Clinic holding Sally on a lead, sometimes sitting in the corridor outside Mrs Woolf's room. All her children took turns to sit with her, apart from Harold (who was probably in Chile, where he was making good money in artificial fertilisers).

Leonard told Virginia it was like watching an animal die. At about eight o'clock in the evening of 2 July 1939 she did die; Herbert was with her. Leonard and the others arrived just too late. Dr Rau, in attendance,

---

54 VW Diary 28 April 1939
55 VW to Vanessa, Letters 26 Aug 1937

was in tears. On 5 July Leonard worked in the morning, then went to his mother's interment, kept a lunch date with John Lehmann, and attended with Virginia a service of remembrance in the Berkeley Street Synagogue.

In the spirit of apostolic honesty, Leonard banned in himself false sentiment, and in most of what he wrote about his mother, he focussed on her limitations. But when he came to write of her death, he wrote about what his own limitations must have been for her: 'I had no patience with her invincible, optimistic sentimentality, and my unsentimentality, which seemed to her hardness and harshness, distressed her. There was no quarrel or rift between us . . . but, though she would never have admitted it even to herself, I was, I think, her least-loved son.' There is something primitive in the heart and brain 'which makes us peculiarly, primordially sensitive to the mother's death. As the coffin is lowered into the grave, there is a second severing of the umbilical cord.'[56]

Marie Woolf's estate amounted to around £4,000. There were fewer grandchildren born when she made her Will; Herbert, as her executor and a stickler for exactitude, was inclined to give out legacies only to those she named. Leonard was sure her intentions would have been to leave the same to all her grandchildren, and he prevailed. Herbert could be a pain, but it was he and his wife Freda who went, with Philip, to Balls Pond cemetery in November to check their mother's grave, and who paid the Berkeley Street Synagogue £200 for the permanent planting of all the family graves.

Leonard was ready with help for the living. He contributed to the education of Philip's son Cecil, which 'took a load of trouble off our shoulders',[57] as Philip wrote; and in the summer of their mother's death, Philip was enlisting Leonard's help in finding Cecil a job in publishing, having failed to secure him an apprenticeship in the printing trade. Philip suspected that 'although they were very nice . . . there was a slight touch of "Damn the bloody Jews" about it'.[58]

*

56 *Downhill All the Way*
57 11 June 1932
58 14 Aug 1939

The Woolfs decided to move to 37 Mecklenburgh Square, on the eastern boundary of Bloomsbury. The Bedford Estate was developing parts of Tavistock Square for offices, and the noise and dust were intolerable. The intention was to let 52 Tavistock Square until their lease ran out, but there were no takers. Leonard negotiated, for £600 a year, a nine-and-a-half-year lease on the Mecklenburgh Square house. The solicitors Dolland and Pritchard were moving with them, and would occupy the ground and most of the first floor for £200 a year.

They moved into 37 Mecklenburgh Square in mid-August 1939. The removals firm took five days, being required to pack the books in their exact sequence, dismantle the bookshelves, reassemble them in the new house, and put up the books in their original order. The Press, as before, was in the basement. The Woolfs had ample quarters for themselves on the upper storeys. Leonard had a new kitchen put in; he had wiring installed for electric fires, and gas-geysers for two new bathrooms. R.H.Tawney was a neighbour in the Square, as was John Lehmann.

Back at Rodmell at the end of the month, the brick standings for yet another greenhouse were going up. Virginia just could not bear what she saw as more ugliness, and staged a protest. Leonard at once ordered the brickwork to be dismantled. This display of passive aggression did not appease her: 'What annoys me is L's adroitness in fathering the guilt on me' by his instant submission. They played a bad-tempered game of bowls. In the evening, it was she who knew how to effect reconciliation – not by paying tribute to him, but by inviting him to pay tribute to her. She asked: 'Do you ever think me beautiful now?' And Leonard replied, 'The most beautiful of women.'[59]

When Virginia called him from the top sitting-room to hear Hitler ranting, he was planting iris *reticulata* under an apple tree, and called back: 'I shan't come. I am planting iris and they will be flowering long after he is dead.' A few of those violet-coloured iris were still coming up every spring twenty-one years after Hitler's suicide, as he told in the last

59 VW Diary 28 July 1939

sentence of *Downhill All the Way.* He planted poplars in autumn 1939, and a new wisteria – planting for a future.

A Nazi-Soviet treaty of non-aggression was signed on 23 August 1939. The day before, Leonard sent back to Gollancz his revised typescript of *Barbarians at the Gate.* He might have withdrawn his moderate compromises, had he known that secret clauses in the Nazi-Soviet pact gave Germany and Russia a free hand in agreed spheres of influence. Poland was to be shared between them: Germany invaded Poland on 1 September, and Russia immediately afterwards. Britain and France were pledged to support Poland.

Men between eighteen and forty-one were called up into the armed forces. In anticipation of German bombing raids, a 'black-out' was ordered – no street-lighting (Rodmell had no street-lighting anyway), and no house lights visible from outside, all windows shrouded in black drapes. On the morning of Sunday 3 September the Prime Minister announced on the wireless that, since Germany had not responded to the Government's ultimatum to withdraw from Poland, Britain was at war with Germany.

Leonard published in the October 1939 issue of *PQ* an article headed 'De Profundis', written in the first week of war. 'The catastrophe which has been hanging over us for five years has now fallen.' He repudiated the 'great man' view of history. Napoleon, Hitler, even Pericles, were but 'the puppets or symbols of deep social forces', and until the world faced up to what those forces were, there would be endless wars. Peace does not begin when wars end, so long as states engage in 'embittered, uncontrolled economic and political competition for wealth and power'. Britain was as culpable as any other state. A protectionist British Empire was part of the international economic system, which was incompatible with peace.

He posited 'a federal system for parts of Europe'. Churchill, from late 1940, was discussing a similar model, with a Council of Europe and a common market – but imagining Britain as its 'godmother or broker',[60]

60 Hugo Young *This Blessed Plot: Britain and Europe from Churchill to Blair* Macmillan 1998

not a full member. Leonard in 'De Profundis' saw partial European federation combined with 'some kind of League system for the whole' – the whole of what? He did not, in 1939, foresee the future dominance of the United States.

Everyone in Britain was issued with a National Identity Card and an individual ration book with coupons to be exchanged for meagre amounts of butter, milk, cheese, meat, bacon, sugar. Petrol and clothing were obtainable on a 'points' system. Children and expectant mothers from the poorer parts of London were evacuated to the assumed safety of the countryside: 'Yesterday 18 pregnant women, accompanied by 3, 4 or 5 already born children arrived in omnibuses', Leonard wrote to John Lehmann from Monks House. 'Half an hour later 11 more pregnant women arrived ditto, but with rather fewer already born children. These had to be distributed in inhabited and uninhabited cottages.'[61] None were allocated to Monks House, and most soon returned to London, preferring to take their chances in familiar surroundings.

The Woolfs spent a week at 37 Mecklenburgh Square in October, arranging their flat, and lunched with Beatrice Webb, now over eighty; Sidney Webb was recovering from a stroke. 'She really is amazing in mind – I could see no difference at all, but I am afraid that physically she is very weak.'[62] It occurred to Beatrice Webb afterwards – and to no one but Beatrice Webb would such a thought occur, in such a fraught time – that since Leonard was beginning on the third volume of his trilogy, 'you might like to read the last chapter of our *Statutory Authorities for a Special Purpose.*'[63] She was sending him a copy.

Barbarians at the Gate finally came out as a Left Book Club Choice for November 1939. The following month, the Choice was the Dean of Canterbury's *The Socialist Sixth of the World*, club members being instructed to read them as a contrasting pair: Hewlett Johnson, the 'Red Dean', found the Soviet Union 'more truly Christian than any civilisation that has yet appeared'. John Strachey's dismissive critique was

---

61 4 Sept 1939. John Lehmann, *Thrown to the Woolfs*
62 LW to Margaret Llewelyn Davies 21 Oct 1939
63 19 Oct 1939

published in *Left News*, his central objection being that Leonard Woolf would not accept the necessity of Stalin's dictatorship as a means to defend Soviet Communism against its enemies.

The doughty Labour activist Ellen Wilkinson began her review of *Barbarians at the Gate*, unconventionally, with a description of 'Leonard Woolf's thin face, its deep lines heavy with thought, engraved there by his passion for human decency'. She went on to disagree with his views.[64] But Norman Angell, in a private letter, welcomed them: 'You have said things which, because our friends of the Left dodge them, needed saying by someone of the Left.' There was an evening at Monks House when Lehmann praised *Barbarians at the Gate* for its lucidity and persuasive force: 'Virginia was splashing gravy in large dollops over my plate as I spoke, and joined in with her emphatic praise. "You know, Leo, it's a *wonderful* book", while Leonard himself sat at the table in modest silence, with lowered eyes, like a schoolboy praised by the headmaster at an end-of-term prizegiving.'[65]

What Leonard Woolf's critics were asking was: Where exactly does he stand? Which side is he on? He had to answer this question many times in his life as a socialist, and his answers were consistent. 'Where you go wrong is thinking that freedom of thought is somehow or other a crime in a socialist and that socialism consists in a continuous mumbling and remumbling of phrases from Marx, Lenin, and Stalin and abuse of people who differ from you on any point at all.'[66] In *Barbarians at the Gate* he described himself as 'a Marxian Socialist – but only "up to a point"'. The importance of a point 'is not that it has position without magnitude, but that it is always a test of mental sanity. There is a point up to which the sane man believes a doctrine and says "yes" – beyond which he disbelieves it and says "no". (That is why the mentally sane have such an uncomfortable time in a world composed largely of doctrinal lunatics.)'[67]

*

64 *Time & Tide* 6 Jan 1940. Ellen Wilkinson, as Labour MP for Jarrow, organised the Jarrow March of unemployed men to London in 1936.

65 John Lehmann, *Thrown to the Woolfs* 1978

66 17 Nov 1937 to Gore Graham, a Communist writer.

67 *Daily Herald* 5 Nov 1937

For Angelica's twenty-first birthday on Christmas Day 1939 there was a party at Charleston. Angelica wrote to Bunny Garnett: 'Virginia got absolutely drunk in about five minutes, and shrieked and waved her arms. Everyone made speeches – Leonard's and Duncan's were the funniest.'[68]

---

68 King's College, Cambridge. Quoted in Frances Spalding, *Duncan Grant* Chatto & Windus 1997

14

Death and Life

'This page is being written on the first day of the year 1940', as once again 'hundreds of millions of the earth's population are engaged, with solemn concentration, in an organised attempt to kill one another.' Leonard was writing *The War for Peace*, partly as a riposte to E.H. Carr's *The Twenty Years Crisis 1919–1939* (1939), which included a critique of 'utopianism' in international relations. Although Carr did not mention Leonard Woolf, Leonard took it as an attack; he rehearsed his arguments in an article, 'Utopia and Reality', in the first issue of *PQ* for 1940. Professor Carr had set up a dichotomy between 'idealism' or 'utopianism' (bad, because naïve and feeble-minded) and 'realism' (good, because practical and strong-minded), using 'utopianism' to lump together people, policies and theories of which he disapproved.[1]

Leonard in *The War for Peace* attacked the dichotomy at its roots. The 'realists' were the idealistic group, in that their aims (peace and stability) could never be achieved by their methods (power politics and war). Leaders fighting to 'make the world safe for democracy' were actually fighting to impose their will. The 'self-determination' of small nations

1 See introduction by Peter Wilson to David Long and Peter Wilson (eds): *Thinkers of the Twenty Years' Crisis: Inter-War Idealism Reassessed* Clarendon Press 1995.

was determined by large powerful ones to suit themselves. There was no peculiar 'realism' in the exercise of brute power, any more than in the non-aggressive rejection of, for example, slavery and witch-burning. Scientists had shown how 'the earth-worm, the liver fluke and the flea' learn by experience. Why could not politicians?[2]

The Woolfs were snowed up in January 1940. The electricity failed, they wore socks and scarves in bed. Leonard went skating.

Virginia was revising her *Roger Fry*. There was much in Roger's story to disturb her. Roger had consigned his wife to an asylum, and almost at once embarked on a passionately sexual affair with Vanessa (not that Virginia put that in the book – but she read all the love-letters). She was laid up with headache and 'influenza' in February, and did not fully recover until Easter. She began reading Freud for the first time.

Biography was not Virginia's natural genre. When Leonard read her unrevised manuscript in March 1940 he found it unsatisfactory, and was brutally frank with her, on a walk. 'It was like being pecked by a very strong hard beak . . . It was a curious example of L. at his most rational & impersonal; rather impressive; yet so definite, so emphatic, that I felt convinced: I mean of failure' – but she felt that he was persisting for some reason of his own which she could not identify.

She was right, in that she was receiving the backlash of Leonard's necessary self-discipline in never making any criticism of her fiction. His fierceness about the Fry biography was a displacement, even though he always felt that there was 'something a little dead' about it.[3] Virginia retired to bed – swapping bedrooms with Leonard – with a temperature, while 'poor L' was 'fetching & carrying, & so serious, & with his old roadmenders bucket of red coal smouldering in him'.[4] He started building a rock garden.

Virginia was well enough to give a lecture in Brighton on 27 April, to

---

2 *The War for Peace* was published by G.Routledge & Co later in 1940. Of all LW's books, it is the one most worth reading in the light of the state of international relations in the early twenty-first century.

3 *Downhill . . .*

4 VW Diary 21 March 1940

which Leonard drove her. They had tea at Fullers cake shop and saw 'the old man with the whore, so L. called her'.[5] Earlier that day Vanessa had confided in them that her daughter Angelica was having an affair with Bunny Garnett and was going to live with him. Angelica was twenty-one, Bunny was nearly fifty, and had been her father's lover. Leonard was non-judgmental.

In February 1940 Moore, living in Cambridge, invited Leonard to a college dinner and sought advice about getting his son Nicholas into publishing. Leonard wrote to Tom Eliot, asking him to see Nicholas Moore, but declined the Cambridge dinner; he would rather see his old friend 'in slippers over your or my fire'. He reminded Moore of the long-ago weekend they had spent together at Asheham, and invited him to Monks House.

Moore came, with Desmond MacCarthy, in May 1940. 'It was the last time I was to see Moore. Desmond and Moore together, the one talking, talking, the other silent in the armchair, were inextricably part of my youth . . . I could shut my eyes and *feel* myself back in 1903.' Age had 'blunted the passion and softened the intensity' of Moore, now sixty-seven. Desmond was troubled by asthma, both his face and his mind 'age-beaten'. But that hot sunny weekend, they wove 'a cocoon of friendship and nostalgic memories.'[6]

Leonard also invited Dolland and Pritchard's typists, and Hogarth Press employees – lonely female ones – to Rodmell for weekends, to Virginia's displeasure.[7] But as he said, 'If it gives them so much happiness, we ought to put up with it from time to time.' Virginia used to say that Leonard only liked people in the mass, and she liked them singly. This was not correct.

Belgium fell to the Germans, and in June 1940 France collapsed. The British Expeditionary Force was driven back to Dunkirk, whence the

5 VW Diary 6 May
6 *The Journey . . .*
7 Nevertheless Rose Schrager was to remember Mrs Woolf's 'graciousness' and 'kindness' to her when she stayed a weekend at Monks House during the war. To LW 25 Jan 1954.

survivors retreated back over the Channel, many rescued by small boats which put out from the south coast. One of the rescued was Louie's brother Harry West,[8] who turned up at Louie's cottage in the early morning in bloody rags and exhausted; he came round to tell the Woolfs his harrowing tale. Just before he left for France, Harry looked to Leonard for help for his mother, who was unable to manage her severely handicapped ten-year-old son Tony. Leonard arranged for Tony to be taken into residential care. Later it all went wrong, with wild accusations that the home was starving Tony. Leonard then had to negotiate Tony's return, and fetched him, wrapped in blankets, in a taxi. This incident made a strong impression on him. He found the 'passionate devotion of mothers to imbecile children' very disturbing. He understood the appeal of helplessness, especially in baby animals, but was involuntarily appalled by the 'slobbering imbecility' of a human being.

He knew his reaction to the Tony incident was bizarre, but 'somehow or other it seemed sardonically to fit into the pattern of a private and public world threatened by destruction.'[9] That is not a sufficient explanation; but he took the fall of France very hard. John Lehmann, Tom Eliot and William Plomer were dining with the Woolfs in Mecklenburgh Square the day the news broke. 'He suddenly fell very silent, looking utterly overwhelmed, and we had to break off our discussion about the French collapse, for fear he should collapse himself.'[10] After the Germans took Paris, invasion from across the Channel was not possible but probable.

The Blitz – the nightly assault from the air on London and other cities by German bombers – was sustained from September 1940 until May 1941. It began for the Woolfs in Rodmell in August. They were eating lunch when 'there was a tremendous roar and we were just in time to see planes flying a few feet above the church spire, over the garden, and over our roof'. They could see the swastikas on the fuselages. Leaves were stripped from the trees, and a cottage was hit. Leonard joined the Rodmell fire service, taking his turn in patrolling the village at night.

---

8 Leonard called him 'Percy' in *Downhill . . .*
9 *Downhill . . .*
10 John Lehmann, *Thrown to the Woolfs*

The Germans stepped up their bombing attacks as a prelude to invading England. They had far more planes than the British, whose Hurricanes and Spitfires beat back the enemy in what became known as the Battle of Britain. Rodmell, like other places within ten miles of the vulnerable south coast, was declared a 'restricted area'. Road blocks were set up, and incomers checked. The Rodmell church bells were silenced, only to be rung as a signal that invasion had begun.

Thrown back on itself, the village responded with a flurry of communal activities. Leonard and Virginia went to first-aid classes at the Rectory, and Leonard gave away most of their saucepans to be melted down for making aeroplanes. The Woolfs were officially reprimanded for showing chinks of light at night, and had to amend their black-out curtaining. On 23 July Virginia gave what was remembered as a 'hilarious' account of the Dreadnought Hoax[11] to the Women's Institute, and spoke again to the WI on 23 September on 'Women and the War'; she became Treasurer in November 1940. Leonard lectured in the village hall on subjects such as Democracy.

Leonard knew that he (as a Jew and an anti-Fascist), and Virginia as well, would be on the 'black list', the *Sonderfahndunliste* compiled by the Nazi Security Police, and would be sent to a concentration camp when the Germans came. It was not only Jews who decided they would end their lives rather than capitulate. Vita and Harold Nicolson armed themselves with the means of suicide, as did Adrian Stephen, who provided a prescription for morphia for the Woolfs. Leonard also kept a can of petrol in the garage, so as to be able to put an end to their lives by means of carbon monoxide from the car exhaust. When German planes flew low over the garden, they lay down under a tree, on their faces, hands behind their heads, in the approved fashion, Leonard reminding Virginia not to clench her teeth. Day after day the raids went on, and by night searchlights probed the sky over the marshes.

Their Croft field, leased to Guy Jansen of South Farm, was lent to the village for cultivating vegetables. This arrangement took on

---

11 A practical joke played by Adrian and Virginia Stephen and their friends in 1910. They successfully impersonated the Emperor of Abyssinia and his entourage, and were ceremoniously received on board the battleship *Dreadnought.*

permanent life in 1941 as the Rodmell Horticultural Society, co-founded by Leonard ('Dig For Victory!' was a government slogan on posters everywhere), who introduced the idea of co-operative potatoes. The Woolfs themselves were self-sufficient in fruit and vegetables, with a surplus of apples, cabbages and honey. Virginia helped pick the apples, sitting 'in the heart of a tree with pale green globes hanging about me.'[12]

Leonard's diary, Tuesday 10 September 1940: 'Drove London . . . Meck Sq bombed unable to get to house.' Virginia was with him. They drove home dodging bombs, taking refuge in one of the 'pillboxes' erected for defence purposes – small square structures of brick and concrete, with slits for guns in the walls[13] – sharing a pot of tea with a young typist and a couple with a child who, bombed out of their homes, had taken up residence in the pillbox. The next day Churchill, on the wireless, warned that invasion could come in the next two weeks. There were unexploded bombs on the bank of the Ouse at Rodmell. A Messerschmitt was shot down on Mount Caburn, looking, Virginia thought, like a settled moth. She said to Leonard: 'I don't want to die yet.'[14]

In mid-September, the German Luftwaffe having lost too many planes, the invasion was called off. The Germans resumed their routine bombing of London and other large cities. Dolland and Pritchard were hanging on in the lower part of 37 Mecklenburgh Square, and their friendly clerk Rose Schrager[15] wrote informing Leonard that in their new flat the windows were blown out, ceilings were down, crockery smashed. Mess and misery were exacerbated by bureaucracy, with war-damage forms to fill in for the landlord and the Borough Council. John Lehmann remembered seeing Leonard and Virginia 'picking about among the ruins of their flat, rubble and glass everywhere', and Leonard remarking, 'Well, really, possessions are such a nuisance, per-

---

12 To Ethel Smyth 12 Oct 1940
13 A pillbox was put up on the instructions of the War Office in the Woolfs' Croft field in August 1940.
14 Diary 2 Oct 1940
15 Previously Rose Talbot

haps it will be a good thing to start clear again.' Another day John met them 'wandering along Guilford Street, both a little confused in the midst of the air raid which was taking place.' It was Virginia who touched Leonard's arm, saying quietly: 'Leo, there are aeroplanes overhead, don't you think we ought to take cover?'[16]

On Friday 18 October Leonard and Virginia drove again to London: 'Saw 52 Tav Sq in ruins.' Their former home for fifteen years was 'now just a pile of bricks'.[17] They saw, perched on the summit of the pile of rubble, a wicker chair, left behind when they moved. 'Nothing beside remained except a broken mantelpiece against the bare wall of the next-door house and above it intact one of Duncan Grant's decorations.'[18] Leonard had been trying to persuade the Bedford Estate to remit the rent, for which he was still responsible. There was now no house to pay rent for.

Mr Pritchard's staff in Mecklenburgh Square spent all their time mopping up water pouring in from burst mains through cracks in the building. Leonard decided that their books, plus the original hand-press, the printing machine, the type, and everything else salvageable should be brought to down to Rodmell before they were utterly ruined, and that the Hogarth Press must be evacuated. The Garden City Press at Letchworth in Hertfordshire, where most Hogarth publications were printed, offered two rooms at the top of the print-works as office space. The entire business of the Hogarth Press went to Letchworth, with two members of staff in lodgings nearby, and John Lehmann continually commuting, sending daily reports to Leonard.

The Press's main problem was getting enough paper (allocated during the war on a quota system). They made the International Psychoanalytical Library, the translations of Rilke, and above all Virginia's books, their priorities. They published poetry by Robert Graves, Cecil Day-Lewis, William Plomer, Hölderlin, Vita Sackville-West, Laurie Lee and R.C.Trevelyan. But their list had to be cut drastically. The dearth of new publications meant that the reading

---

16 *Thrown to the Woolfs*
17 LW to George Pritchard 18 Oct 1940
18 *The Journey . . .*

public was avid for everything and anything available and, by the end of the war, the Hogarth Press was left with little old stock.

In early November 1940 bombs broke the embankments of the Ouse in spite of the sandbags (and gun emplacements) on top of them, flooding the valley all the way from Lewes to the coast at Newhaven. 'All the gulls came and rode the waves at the end of the field', wrote Virginia to Ethel Smyth. It was, under the changing light, 'indescribably beautiful'. Exploring this inland sea in Leonard's old brown trousers and her gum boots, she fell headlong into a hole in a flooded field, and came home 'dripping like a spaniel', but elated.[19] Their possessions arrived from Mecklenburgh Square in early December. Leonard had to rent a room from Mrs Christian at Mill House, and two attics from the Bottens at Place Farm, for storage. There were nevertheless mountains of mildewed books piled up all over Monks House and filling the downstairs sitting room.

Life narrowed down. On Tuesdays Leonard cycled into Lewes with produce from the garden to sell at the weekly Women's Institute market. He went up to London two days a week for working lunches with William Robson and John Lehmann. Because of air raids, or bombs on the line, the one-hour journey from Victoria Station back to Lewes could take more than four; and the journey from Lewes to Letchworth, which involved changing stations in London, was a tedious nightmare which could take up to seventeen hours. On one of these trips, he acquired a short-haired Persian Blue kitten, named Peat.

His fire-watching duty kept him out until four in the morning. The highlight of his fire-fighting career was when hundreds of small incendiary bombs were dropped around Rodmell, setting fire to haystacks. The hose turned out to be too short, the ricks burned, and the amateur firemen stamped the flames from the surrounding stubble with their boots. The chaos in the house, the food shortages, the drudgery of fixing the evening black-out, the slow postal service, all bothered Virginia more than they bothered him.

---

19 14 Nov 1940

She was able to work, though her right hand began to shake, like Leonard's. They were marooned at Rodmell. 'But it's all so heavenly free and easy – L. and I alone', Virginia wrote in her diary on 14 October 1940. On 23 November she finished the novel that would be called *Between the Acts*, and felt happy about it. Thinking of writing next about herself and her family, she immersed herself in her parents' old letters and her father's memoirs – and was plunged into a deep reverie of introspection which gradually became a depression.

On 9 December 1940 Dr Octavia Wilberforce came to tea at Monks House. The Woolfs often saw her and her companion, the elderly Elizabeth Robins, who came from Kentucky; she was a novelist, a militant women's rights campaigner, and famous former actress, having created the great roles of Ibsen's plays on the London stage. Long ago, Robins's *Ibsen and the Actress* had been a Hogarth Essay; and in 1940, the Hogarth Press had just published her memoir.[20]

Octavia Wilberforce was a great-granddaughter of William Wilberforce, leader of the anti-slavery movement in Britain, and a third cousin of Virginia's. As a young girl before the Great War she trained as a physician, at a time when medicine for women was considered unseemly. Her father disinherited her, but she was materially assisted to qualify by, among others, Elizabeth Robins. Octavia practised in Brighton, and supervised the 'Home of Rest and Recuperation' for exhausted and overstrained women, which Elizabeth established in her Sussex farmhouse at Backsettown. Under Octavia's regime, the women were rehabilitated by means of locally produced food, fresh air, and the very opposite of the 'talking cure': mulling over their miseries was definitely not encouraged. The two women lived together at 24 Montpelier Crescent in Brighton. Leonard saw Octavia's relation to the older woman as that of a 'devoted daughter', and Elizabeth as devoted to Octavia, but equally devoted to herself, 'a dedicated egoist'.

Worried about Virginia, Leonard spoke to Octavia Wilberforce in her

---

20 *Raymond and I and our Magnetic North*

professional capacity. She was labelled 'leech Octavia' by Virginia who, in her depression, saw everyone around herself and Leonard as leeches, sucking life and energy from them. This changed after Octavia came to tea with Virginia on cold, snowy New Year's Day 1941 – Leonard had a WEA lecture – and wrote to her two days later that she should drink lots of milk and have lots of cream, both of which she could supply from her pedigree Jersey herd at Backsettown.

Virginia, thanking her, confided that she had 'lost all power over words'; and that she could not stop her hand from trembling. In her long, thoughtful reply, Octavia told her that 'every true genius has to lie fallow for a time'. And as a PS: 'I'd *most* like you to write your autobiography. But if it means an awful lot of research backwards why not leave it till after the War?' Or might she not write her father's life? Or a novel, or anything else? As for her trembling hand: 'Cold, fatigue, heavy lifting, over-smoking can all contribute to that.'

Octavia Wilberforce was confident in giving practical advice, but she was in awe of Virginia, who was five years older, intellectual, and famous. Octavia was like a socially superior and more intelligent Jean Thomas, from Twickenham days: admiring, interested, devoted. Virginia was thinking and talking obsessively about her family and her childhood, which Octavia thought a complete waste of time, 'balderdash'. Whether by her strategic steering or as a diversionary tactic of Virginia's, they began to discuss Octavia's conflicts with her own family.'If anything I tell you', Octavia wrote, 'diverts you in these grim times I'll be awfully proud. It wrings my heart that you should be depressed and if at times you want stark reality, I can give it you in chunks!!'

American *Harper's Bazaar* unexpectedly turned down one of Virginia's short stories, and from around her fifty-ninth birthday on 25 January Leonard began to be more seriously concerned. 'If I cant write, I can eat. As for writing, it's a washout', she wrote to Octavia, with whom she was discussing another idea – a history of English literature. Octavia's reply shows this good doctor somewhat at sea on literary matters. She was inclined to think, she wrote, that after the war what would be needed was 'good stuff'. The 'ordinary haphazard public' wanted 'a common guide and is that what you are out to give us? Will it be as long as Gibbon?!' The world must get back to 'some sort of settled good reading . . . I expect I'm writing nonsense but one thing I'm quite clear about it would be a great gain to have signposts – no, that's *not* exactly what you're doing, it's more the evolution of Literature that you're concerned with?'

She was back on her own ground in expressing relief 'that you can still eat; I'm quite unrepentant that you say you can't write. The longer you feel like that the better you'll write when you do get going. So just don't try.'[21] She made another semi-professional visit on the last day of January, Leonard being sharply aware that Virginia had been in 'a trough of despair' for the past ten days, as she herself conceded in her diary.

She was still revising her novel, always a dangerous process for her. But in early February 1941 she seemed better, reading for her history of literature, and alive to beauty in the form of 'a yellow woodpecker bright green against ruby red willows. Lord! How I started, and then saw coming across the marsh Leonard, looking like a Saxon Earl, because his old coat was torn and the lining flapped round his gum boots'.[22] She went with him to Cambridge in the middle of the month, visiting the Hogarth Press at nearby Letchworth, dining with Dadie Rylands at King's, and calling in at Mecklenburgh Square to see Mr Pritchard on the way home.

Elizabeth Bowen came to stay for two nights at Monks House, and Vita for one night. 'I rather think I've got a new lover, a doctor, a Wilberforce, a cousin,'[23] Virginia told Vita, to tease her. Virginia was toying again with the idea of writing a biographical sketch of Octavia Wilberforce, who was 'intrigued and flattered', and only worried that Virginia would find her dull.[24]

On 26 February Virginia gave Leonard *Between the Acts* to read, and he thought it 'the best of the novels with the exception of *The Waves*'. Yet

---

21 26 Jan 1941
22 To Ethel Smyth 1 Feb 1941
23 19 Jan 1941
24 21 Feb 1941

her diary confirms that all was not well. Depression made her more than normally intolerant of the 'infernal boredom' of village life. Tense and restless, she exhausted herself by fierce scrubbing of floors. In early March she was tentatively suggesting a visit to Ethel Smyth, and a date in April for a visit from Tom Eliot, and still wondering how she could write Octavia's story, 'englobe it somehow'.

On 14 March, a pleasant spring day, the Woolfs went to London to lunch with John Lehmann. Leonard and John were arguing about whether or not they should publish Terence Tiller's poems. Virginia was agitated, and told John she knew that *Between the Acts* was no good. Leonard gently contradicted her, saying it was one of the best things she had ever written. They agreed that John should read it.

On Tuesday 18 March Leonard went to the WI market in Lewes as usual, and gave a talk on Ceylon to the Rodmell WI. In extra-small letters, in his diary: 'V.n.w.' (Virginia not well.) He could not later remember for sure which day it was – but it was that Tuesday – that Virginia went for a walk in the water-meadows, and he went out to meet her, and found her coming back 'soaking wet, looking ill and shaken'. She said that she had slipped and fallen into one of the drainage dykes. This time she was not elated.

He wondered afterwards, thinking back, whether she had tried to drown herself. At the time he just had the all too familiar feeling of 'desperate uneasiness'.

Next day, Wednesday the nineteenth, he went to London as usual for his *PQ* meeting with William Robson.[25] On 20 March Virginia wrote to John Lehmann that she had definitely decided her book was not good enough to publish. 'Leonard doesn't agree.' Vanessa came to tea with her at Monks House while Leonard was lecturing to the WEA; and back at Charleston that evening, she wrote to her younger sister: 'You *must* be sensible, which means you must accept the fact that Leonard and I can judge better than you can . . . You're in the state where one never admits

25 Robson withdrew during the war as co-editor with LW of *PQ*, due to pressure of work: the LSE was evacuated to Cambridge, where he spent some of his time, and he was also working for the Ministry of Fuel and Power. He continued to meet LW to discuss articles for forthcoming issues.

what's the matter – but you must not go and get ill just now. What shall we do when we're invaded if you are a hopeless invalid?'

This slightly minatory appeal was tempered by her asking Virginia what she herself would have done after Julian's death, 'if you hadn't been able to keep me alive and cheerful. You don't know how much I depend on you.' Virginia should stop scrubbing floors, 'which for all I care can remain unscrubbed for ever. Both Leonard and I have always had reputations for sense and honesty so you must believe in us.'

On Monday 24 March, Leonard noted 'V sl. better.' But on the twenty-sixth, a day they spent sorting the books from Mecklenburgh Square, he felt that the situation was as dangerous as it had been in August 1913. He knew she was becoming suicidal, and had a 'terrifying decision' to make: 'I had to urge her to face the verge of disaster in order to accept the misery of the only method of avoiding it'[26] – which was to acknowledge how ill she was, and submit to a 'drastic regime'. Yet he also knew that too much pressure would drive her over that verge and into total breakdown.

Leonard did persuade her to consult Octavia Wilberforce, and the next afternoon, 27 March, they drove over to Montpelier Crescent. Octavia gave Virginia a physical examination, and advised complete rest, which had helped in the past; Virginia begged her not to prescribe a formal 'rest-cure'. Octavia then had a private word with Leonard in another room.

They had to decide whether it was better not to force the issue, and for Leonard to keep watch over her, in as normal a way as possible, in the hope that he could bring her through as he had done before. (They considered the Backsettown 'Home of Rest', but it was not suitable for severely disturbed patients.) The alternative course was for Leonard to hire nurses and force Virginia to submit to twenty-four-hour surveillance, against her will, which would possibly precipitate a florid psychotic reaction, as it had in the past. In any case Leonard was not easy in his mind about exerting authority in this way. 'The effective use

26 *The Journey* . . .

of power', he wrote in *The War for Peace*, 'means simply the power of an individual or individuals to make the life of another individual so intolerable that it has sufficient reason and intelligence to be able to kill itself', and others. The wielder of power might be a nation state or, in the case of an individual, 'a bullying husband'. Leonard and Octavia decided it was safest to take no drastic action for the time being. 'The decision was wrong and led to the disaster.'[27]

The events of the next day, Friday 28 March 1941, were described by Leonard and Louie and, at second hand, Octavia Wilberforce. Leonard, Louie remembered, talked to Virginia in her bedroom during the morning 'because it seemed to be one of her bad days again'. Then when Louie was tidying Leonard's study, Leonard asked: 'Louie, will you give Mrs Woolf a duster so that she can help you clean the room?' Louie presumed he thought it might help her to do something practical. 'I gave her a duster, but it seemed very strange. I had never known her want to do any housework with me before.' (She must have done her floor-scrubbing after Louie went home.) And indeed, Virginia soon put down the duster and went away. Leonard recalled going to visit her in her writing-lodge at about eleven, and she went back into the house with him. According to Virginia's biographer,[28] she told him she was going to do some housework and go for a walk before lunch; he told her to rest for half an hour, and went up to his study.

Louie saw her go out again to her lodge.[29] After a few minutes she came back to the house, put on her fur coat and wellington boots, took her walking stick, and walked quickly up the garden to the top gate.

When Louie rang the bell for lunch at one o'clock, 'I was in the garden', wrote Leonard, 'and thought she was in the house.' He told Louie he was just going upstairs to the sitting-room to hear the news on the radio. 'The next moment he came running down the stairs to the

---

27 *Ibid*

28 Hermione Lee, *Virginia Woolf* Chatto & Windus 1996

29 LW could see her lodge from one window in his study, but not from the balconied window. His desk was set across the width of the room, with the balconied window directly on his right.

kitchen calling me, "Louie!", he said, "I think that something has happened to Mrs Woolf! I think she must have tried to kill herself."'

Leonard had found two letters in envelopes on the mantelpiece in the sitting-room, one for him and one for Vanessa, which he thought (when in the last year of his life he wrote the last volume of his autobiography) that she must have written that day. But the letter to Vanessa was headed 'Sunday', which was the twenty-third, and the one to him was headed 'Tuesday', which could either be Tuesday 18 March, the day she fell in the dyke, or Tuesday the twenty-fifth, two days before the consultation with Octavia in Brighton. This is what she wrote to him:

> Dearest, I feel certain that I am going mad again. I feel we can't go through another of those terrible times. And I shan't recover this time. I begin to hear voices, and I can't concentrate. So I am doing what seems the best thing to do. You have given me the greatest possible happiness. You have been in every way all that anyone could be. I don't think two people could have been happier until this terrible disease came. I can't fight any longer. I know that I am spoiling your life, that without me you could work. And you will I know. You see I can't even write this properly. I can't read. What I want to say is that I owe all the happiness of my life to you. You have been entirely patient with me and incredibly good. I want to say that – everybody knows it. If anybody could have saved me it would have been you. Everything has gone from me but the certainty of your goodness. I can't go on spoiling your life any longer. I don't think any two people could have been happier than we have been. V.

It was a sad and a rational letter. It constituted, too late, the acknowledgment of breakdown which Vanessa and Leonard had looked for, as a preliminary to treating it. It told Leonard things he already knew – that she was hearing voices, could not concentrate, could not read, and was afraid she was going mad again. Suicide notes are produced at inquests. To that extent it was a public letter as well as a private one.

What stands out is her stress on his work: 'I know that I am spoiling your life, that without me you could work. And you will I know.' It is possible that, when he tried to make her face the fact that she was ill, he made the same kind of appeal as Vanessa, telling her she must allow herself to be helped both for her own sake and for his. He may have done what he most feared doing: made a false move, said a wrong word.

But maybe there were no correct moves, no right words, no appeal which could have penetrated her depression. Her most telling phrase is 'I can't fight any more.' She said the same in her letter to Vanessa: 'I have fought against it, but I can't any longer.'

Her suicide would have been premeditated whenever she had done it, even if she did it on impulse. As Leonard put it, the contemplation of death was always 'very near the surface of Virginia's mind'.[30] It could have happened before, or later, or not at all. It was not inevitable. There is the thinnest of membranes between what we might do, and what we actually do. Step through it, and there is no going back. She did it that day, leaving her lodge with discarded typed sheets all over the floor and a full waste-paper basket.[31]

Of course, if and when it came, it would be by drowning. Not the fumes in the garage, nor the morphia. An early tragi-comic story of Virginia's was based on a punting accident on a summer holiday: 'I sank and sank, the water creeping into ears, mouth and nose, till I felt it close over my head. This, methinks, is drowning.' She was seventeen when she wrote that.[32] Her fiction, from first to last, is saturated with underwater imagery. She wrote to Ethel, after watching a storm on the coast, the waves breaking over their car: 'Why does a splash of water satisfy all one's religious aspirations? And it's all I can do not to throw myself in – a queer animal rhapsody, restrained by L.'[33] She noted the suicide by drowning of 'the old woman who lived up at Mt Misery' who killed her dog before she went into the river, 'perhaps when the tide was high in the afternoon.'[34]

*

---

30 *The Journey . . .*
31 Described by LW in a letter to an enquirer 14 June 1942
32 'A Terrible Tragedy in a Duckpond', *Charleston Magazine* 1, 1990
33 26 Oct 1937
34 17 Aug 1938

When her mother-in-law was dying, Virginia thought that what was left of her at the end was just 'the pathetic animal . . . the body that wanted to live'. Leonard found himself, in his autobiography, telling in the chapter entitled 'Virginia's Death' his emblematic childhood story of trying to drown the puppy, which taught him that the struggling creature was 'like me an "I"', fighting death in the bucket of water 'as I would fight death if I were drowning in the multitudinous seas.' Characteristically he made no connection. But it is impossible that he would not torture himself with the thought that she, the 'I' that she was, 'the body that wanted to live', might have fought death before the end. Or had she been exalted, like the first time she fell in the water, in the magical flooded meadows? She had written two years before: 'Why not change the idea of death into an exciting experience? As one did marriage in youth.'[35]

When Leonard was very old, Malcolm Muggeridge in a television interview asked him what he felt about suicide. Leonard said: 'I think it's a lamentable thing as it happens, but I think if life isn't worth living one ought to commit suicide. I can't feel that I would but I've got no objection to other people doing it if they want to.'[36] Muggeridge, a committed Christian, demurred strongly, and Leonard went on: 'Oh, it's appalling – and also – you see – the process. If one had seen it, as I did, seen it with one's own eyes. It's only if there's been an appalling amount of mental torture such as she went through when she felt that she was going mad and that she couldn't control her thoughts, it was only when she got to that stage that she committed suicide, and of course the process of getting to that stage was absolutely appalling to – to watch.'

Leonard checked the house and garden and then ran out of the top gate towards the river. Louie went to find Percy Bartholomew, who fetched Wilfred Collins, the village policeman. The Ouse, which is tidal between Lewes and the sea, is an unlovely river between Rodmell and the bridge

---

35 Diary 18 Jan 1939

36 LW was a member of the Voluntary Euthanasia Legislation Society, which became the Euthanasia Society.

at Southease. There are no overhanging trees. It runs almost straight, like a canal, between bare embankments built up to protect the low-lying fields. That afternoon it was high tide, the water running fast; in those days it was dredged regularly. Leonard found Virginia's walking stick on the bank[37] about a mile up from the bridge. PC Collins dived repeatedly into the water, Frank Dean and his son brought ropes and tackle.

Leonard thought Virginia might have gone up to the ruin they called 'Mad Misery', and he and Louie went to look. They searched for her 'along the water meadows, and the river bank, and the brooks, until it was night-time and we had to give up.'[38] Vanessa came, when he got back home. Leonard told her the catastrophic news. Every single day, including this one, Leonard entered in his diary the cumulative mileage of his car, plus the mileage for that day, which on 28 March was thirteen – taking Vanessa back to Charleston. The rest of the space is obscured by a brownish-yellow stain which has been rubbed or wiped. It could be tea or coffee or tears. This smudge is unique in all his years of neat diary-keeping.

He found another letter to him, on her block in the Lodge. He thought it was what he saw her writing – though it is a finished, signed letter – when he went in to see her that morning. It was undated:

> Dearest,
>
> I want to tell you that you have given me complete happiness. No one could have done more than you have done. Please believe that. But I know that I shall never get over this: and I am wasting your life. Nothing anyone says can persuade me. You can work, and you will be much better without me. You see I can't write this

---

37 Leonard wrote to John Lehmann (21 Dec 1958) correcting him for saying in his autobiography that Virginia's walking stick had been floating in the river. But see his letter to W.A.Robson, below. The stick is now in the Berg Collection, New York Public Library.

38 Louie's memories are all from Joan Russell Noble (ed): *Recollections of Virginia Woolf by her Contemporaries* Peter Owen 1972.

even, which shows I am right. All I wish to say is that until this disease came upon me we were perfectly happy. It was all due to you. No one could have been so good as you have been from the very first day till now. Everyone knows that.

V.

Over the page, she wrote a note about letters from Roger Fry which she had used in her biography, to be returned to their recipients; and a directive: 'Will you destroy all my papers.'[39]

Leonard wrote to Vita Sackville-West that evening, not wanting her to see in the papers or hear on the wireless 'the terrible thing that has happened to Virginia'. 'It was, I suppose, the strain of the war and finishing the book and she could not rest or eat . . . She has been through hell these last days.'

His diary the following day, Saturday: 'Work Octavia came walked to river.' Octavia assured him that no one else could have kept Virginia going through the unhappy times; and that if by any accident he had gone first, 'it would have been the most heartbreaking catastrophe imaginable.' She tried to comfort him by saying that during their last interview, Virginia had said, unsolicited, 'I've been so very happy with Leonard', with 'much feeling and warmth in her face.'

A lot of letters were written the next day. Vanessa wrote to Vita 'as the person Virginia loved most I think outside her own family. I was there yesterday by chance and saw him. He was of course amazingly self controlled and calm and insisted on being left alone.'[40] Leonard wrote to John Lehmann, and to William Robson, 'My dear Willie: The most terrible thing has happened to me.' He explained about the recurrence of the old symptoms, and Virginia's belief that she would not recover. 'Yesterday she committed suicide. She drowned herself in the river, I think; I found her walking stick floating there. They have not yet found the body, but there is no real hope of anything else. She wrote me a

---

39 Had LW complied, and destroyed her letters, diaries, autobiographical writings and unpublished work, her literary afterlife and the afterlife of Bloomsbury would have been very different.

40 29 March 1941

letter saying she was going to do it.' He was not sure whether he could come up for their Wednesday lunch, but 'if you are free, perhaps you would see whether I am at the usual place in Smith Square and if I am we might lunch together.' Willie Robson replied to 'My poor and most dear Leonard' saying that of course he would be at their usual place on Wednesday.

Leonard's diary, Sunday: 'Work walked Charleston bus back.' He was too shaky to drive the car. On Monday, Lydia Keynes called in to buy some onions. He went up to London the next day and saw George Pritchard, the solicitor, and went to a Fabian Society Executive meeting. When Leonard arrived for lunch with Willie Robson in Smith Square on Wednesday, 'his eyes were red from weeping, his face haggard beyond description'. Willie told him that he would come down to Monks House at any time 'and that I would not talk if he wanted'.[41] Leonard went on to an Advisory Committee meeting. Willie wrote to Leonard again: 'The struggle you have had all these years has an epic quality. The real outcome is to be found in the books which Virginia gave to the world.'

They were still dragging the river. Leonard could make no official announcement of his wife's death. But on 1 April he wrote to the editor of *The Times*, Geoffrey Dawson: 'I feel I had better let you know the following facts, so that you may use them in *The Times* in any way you may think best . . .' The short news item in the paper about Virginia Woolf's presumed suicide, and the obituary on another page, were picked up by the BBC for the evening news, and precipitated scores of letters of condolence to Leonard, which continued to arrive as further news broke over the next weeks – not only from all their Cambridge, political and literary friends, but from the girl clerks at the Press, Rodmell village people, strangers, and former employees such as Nelly Boxall and old Sophie Farrell, who wrote: 'I have known and loved her Very Much, Eversince she was 4 years old. I can't bear to feel She has Strayed away from you all.' Mrs West's letter from 2

41 W.A.Robson to Trekkie Parsons 28 Dec 1975

Council Cottages conflated his sorrow with her own about her son Tony: 'I was very fond of dear Mrs Woolf and would do any think to help find her I told Louie to tell you . . . I know how sad my life is with my little Boy every day the same thing and no change.'[42] 'How good of you it was', wrote Sir John Maynard, chair of A.C.Imp.Q, on 4 April, 'to come to our meeting on Wednesday, and listen to all the irritating exchanges of opinions, when you had this terrible anxiety in your mind.'

Those who knew Virginia well all stressed the shining aspect of her – the words 'light' and 'lightness' recurred, and 'rare', 'distinguished', 'fine', 'lovely'. The point everyone made was, as Kingsley Martin put it, 'For thirty years you have stopped this happening, and made the finest thing imaginable of life together, and been responsible incidentally for books that are works of genius.' 'For myself and others it is the end of a world', wrote Tom Eliot. 'I want you to know that you are as constantly in my mind as in anyone's.' He sent the proofs of what he had written about Virginia for *Horizon*; for as well as writing to Leonard, and to each other, their writer friends memorialised her in print and on air.

Leonard insisted to Margaret Llewelyn Davies that Virginia would have got better this time as she had done before. 'Of course, I could have prevented it by immediately getting nurses and I suppose I ought to say I was wrong not to have done so. I have been proved wrong and yet I know myself that I would do the same again. One had to make up one's mind which would do the greater harm – to insist, in which case I knew it would be a complete breakdown at once and attempt at suicide, or to run the risk and try to prevent the last symptoms coming on. I say this to you because I know you will understand.'[43]

She did. 'Don't ever think differently', Margaret wrote, 'she would not have wished it. She did what she wished. And it was you who gave [to] her her greatest happiness in life, and enabled her to enjoy all the pleasure she got from the appreciation of her writing, and the love of her

42 13 April 1941
43 1 April 1941

friends.' Margaret recalled how long ago 'you asked me at Richmond if you were right to let her suffer. Now she is free from all suffering, and that is well . . . But how I think of *you*, dear Leonard . . . you know I love you both, and what that means.'[44]

Leonard's sister Bella, the governor's lady in the Gambia, sent a telegram on 12 April: 'Just received terribly sad news deeply grieved loving thoughts and sympathy dearest Leonard.' A letter was in the post, telling him how she and Tom had been at a governors' conference in Accra and, waiting for a plane at Freetown in Sierra Leone, they heard on the wireless Desmond MacCarthy talking about Virginia. Bella had no idea, until she received Leonard's reply, that Virginia had committed suicide. 'No one mentioned it to us – I suppose they did not like to.'[45] Bella's new life consumed her: 'I cannot tell you of the rush in which we live nor of the interesting visitors that come along all the time.' They had Lord Louis Mountbatten staying with them. It was all a far cry from Monks House, Rodmell.

John Lehmann lunched with Leonard soon after the disaster, and 'was moved by his fortitude in discussing everything that happened . . . though it was perfectly clear to me, from the moment I saw him, how deeply he had suffered.' Leonard wept, telling John about the day he met Virginia coming home dripping wet: 'I think he blamed himself for not having been more alert after that warning; but it is difficult to see what more he could have done . . .'[46]

After ten whole days of dragging the river, the search was abandoned. Vita came to see Leonard on 7 April, and sat with him in the upstairs sitting room. 'There was her needle-work on a chair', she wrote to Harold, 'and all her coloured wools hanging over a sort of little towel-horse which she had made for them. Her thimble on the table.' She told Leonard she did not like to think of him being there alone. 'He turned those piercing blue eyes on me and said, "It is the only thing to

---

44 3 April 1941. For more condolence letters, see Sybil Oldfield (ed): *Afterwords: Letters on the Death of Virginia Woolf* Edinburgh University Press 2005

45 23 May 1941

46 *Thrown to the Woolfs*

32. Harold and Mrs Woolf at Philip's wedding.

33. Bella and Tom Southorn on their wedding day in Ceylon.

4. Edgar and Flora at Philip's wedding.

35. Philip and Babs.

36. Sidney Webb.

37. Beatrice Webb.

38. George and Margaret Cole.

39. Margaret Llewelyn Davies and Lilian Harri
in Hampstead.

40. LW with Pinka, Clive and Julian Bell, VW, Auberon Duckworth, Duncan Grant and Quentin Bell.

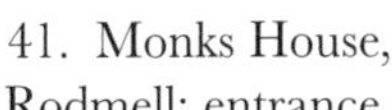

41. Monks House, Rodmell: entrance.

42. Leonard Woolf, Cassis, 1927.

43. Trekkie and Leonard in Ceylon, 1960.

44. Trekkie in Israel, 1957.

45. LW, Shelton Fernando and Ian Parsons.

46. LW and W.A. Robson at Monks House, 1954.

47. LW making his acceptance speech for the W. H. Smith Award. John Betjeman on left.

48. The *New Statesman* Board of Directors. *Left to right:* Kingsley Martin, LW, V.S. Pritchett, John Freeman, Gerald Barry, John Morgan, Jock Campbell.

50. *Far left:* Kingsley Martin.

51. *Left:* Peggy Ashcroft in Ibsen's *Rosmersholm*, 1960.

51. Cover by Carrington for LW's *Stories of the East*, Hogarth Press, 1921.

52. Colophon designed by Vanessa Bell for the Hogarth Press.

53. Leonard and Kingsley Martin, by Trekkie Ritchie.

54. LW at Monk's House, 23 August 1964, with his portrait by Henry Lamb (1912).

55. Trekkie and Leonard, June 1969.

56. LW and Edgar, 1969.

57. Virginia Browne-Wilkinson.

58. LW's nephew Cecil Woolf, son of his brother Philip.

59. LW with cacti.

60. LW portrait by Vanessa Bell, with Pinka, 1939.

61. LW with Malcolm Muggeridge.

62. LW and Coco, Monk's House.

63. LW at Monks House.

do.'"[47] To Ethel Smyth, Vita wrote: 'One expects her to come in at any minute . . . his evenings must be terrible.'[48]

His days were terrible too. 'For weeks thought and emotion were numbed.'[49] Leonard's typist friend, Rose Schrager, reported to him on 17 April that she got to the office that morning to find Mecklenburgh Square burning, the houses on either side of number 37 'completely gutted out'. The firemen had dumped all Dolland and Pritchard's furniture, books and papers out on the pavement. 'Mrs Bell's pictures, lodged in our office for safe custody, are quite untouched. I have put them in as safe a place as I can find.' Leonard was already on his way up to London: 'Home bombed'. He drove back and worked in the garden.

Vita had said to Ethel Smyth that it was better for Virginia 'to be dead than mad'. She and Vanessa were both relieved that her body had not been found. 'The river is tidal, so she has probably been carried out to sea. She loved the sea.'[50]

The day after Leonard saw Mecklenburgh Square bombed, 18 April, five teenagers bicycled out from Lewes and stopped for a picnic in the field below Asheham, on the other side of the river. They amused themselves by throwing stones at a log, trying to divert it from floating down-river on the tide. One of the boys waded out and pushed it over with a stick. It was not a log. The boys sent the girls off home and went to the police.

If the young people had not stopped by the river, Virginia's body would indeed have been carried out to sea. Angelica remembered Leonard at Charleston, 'white with exhaustion, though as always objective and dispassionate',[51] telling them how they had found her. Frank Dean thought that her body must have been wedged all that time in 'one of the holes where the fences go down to the river' to prevent cattle from straying from their fields at low tide.[52]

---

47 to Harold Nicolson 8 April 1941
48 7 April 1941
49 *The Journey . . .*
50 7 April 1941
51 Angelica Garnett, *Deceived with Kindness* Chatto & Windus The Hogarth Press 1984
52 Susan Rowland (ed): *Strike While the Iron's Hot: Frank Dean's Life as Blacksmith and Farrier in Rodmell* 1994

'The horrible business of the identification and inquest'[53] took place in the Newhaven mortuary that evening and the next day. PC Collins drove Leonard to the mortuary on both occasions. Leonard told Vanessa that these formalities were 'no more horrible than the rest', though Octavia thought identification should be a doctor's job; Virginia's body had been submerged for three weeks.

On Sunday 20 April Leonard drove to Southease, stopped and stood by the bridge, and then went to pick up Willie Robson from Lewes station. Leonard had asked him to come. They went for a walk. The next day Leonard told Willie he was going out for a few hours. He did not say why. He drove himself, alone, to the Downs Crematorium at Brighton.

The cremation was arranged by Frank Dean. Leonard and Virginia had agreed that if there were music at one's cremation, it must be the Cavatina from the B flat quartet, opus 130, by Beethoven, on account of a few bars 'of incredible beauty' which seem to 'hesitate with a gentle forward pulsing motion', as if gently propelling the dead into 'an eternity of oblivion.' But when it came to it, Leonard could not face talking to Mr Dean about Beethoven. It was as if 'the long-drawn-out horror of the previous weeks had produced in me a kind of inert anaesthesia.'[54] The crematorium laid on a recording of 'Blessed Spirits' from Gluck's *Orfeo.*

Afterwards, with surreal normality, in shock, Leonard went and had his hair cut. He drove home to Willie and explained where he had been. They went for another walk. 'He spoke with terrible bitterness', wrote Willie, 'of the fools who played the music by Gluck . . . which promised some happy reunion or survival in a future life. "She is dead and utterly destroyed" he said, and all his profound disbelief in religion and its consolations were present in those words. It was impossible to comfort him in his loneliness and sense of loss . . . I referred to her belief which he had mentioned in his letter that she

---

53 *Downhill* . . . Cause of death was recorded as 'Immersion in the river on 28 March 41 by her own act so killing herself while the balance of her mind was disturbed'.

54 *The Journey* . . .

thought she was going mad and would not recover this time, and I said we must believe that her belief was right. He denied this passionately and said "No, she could have recovered as she had done from previous attacks."'[55]

In the evening, Leonard played the Cavatina. Willie understood Leonard: he was 'a tremendously passionate man and everything he did, everything he said was highly rational in his method, but his reason was harnessed to the most profound and turbulent emotions.'[56] There survives a worn and battered sheet of A5 paper:

> They said "Come to tea and let us comfort you." But it's no good. One must be crucified on one's own private cross.
>
> It is a strange fact that a terrible pain in the heart can be interrupted by a little pain in the fourth toe of the right foot.
>
> I know that V. will not come across the garden from the Lodge, and yet I look in that direction for her. I know that she is drowned and yet I listen for her to come in at the door. I know that it is the last page and yet I turn it over. There is no limit to one's stupidity and selfishness.

His 'stupidity and selfishness' consisted in his bitter regret that she had done what she wished, exercising the self-determination which he had to respect. His Aspasia, his 'Mistress', had never dismissed him, as he had once feared she might. But in the end she abandoned him.

He buried her ashes at the foot of one of two tall elm trees just coming into leaf, standing close together on the boundary between the bowls lawn and the Croft; they always called the trees 'Leonard and Virginia'. He had a tablet made to mark the spot, with the last words of *The Waves* engraved upon it: 'Against you I will fling myself, unvanquished and unyielding, O Death!' When he rang Vanessa to tell her

55 W.A. Robson to Trekkie Parsons 28 Dec 1975
56 W.A.Robson, 'Leonard Woolf 1880–1969', BBC Radio 3, 17 Feb 1970, producer Virginia Browne-Wilkinson.

this, he 'broke down completely', and then was afraid she would think him 'sentimental'.[57]

How long since you and I went out
  Luriana, Lurilee,
To see the Kings go riding by
  Over lawn and daily lea,
With their palm leaves and cedar sheaves,
  Luriana, Lurilee.

Swing, swing, swing on a bough,
  Luriana, Lurilee,
Till you sleep in a humble heap
  Or under a gloomy churchyard tree,
And then fly back to swing on a bough,
  Luriana, Lurilee.[58]

Leonard received an anonymous letter in uneducated writing on lined paper: 'Sir, Thank the Coroner for being kind in his verdict.' Then, *The Sunday Times* misquoted the suicide note. Instead of 'I feel certain that I am going mad again. I feel we can't go through another of those terrible times', they had 'I feel I cannot go on any longer in these terrible times', i.e. because of the war. This provoked a screech of contempt in a published letter to the editor from Kathleen Hicks, wife of the Bishop of Lincoln, for this Mrs Woolf who found herself unable to carry on while others did so 'unselfishly, for the sake of others'.[59]

Leonard wrote a dignified letter to the paper correcting the quotation. Mrs Hicks sent him a badly typed letter of apology. Leonard answered it in the space at the top of her letter, mentioning that hers was unsigned, 'but I presume this was an oversight'. It was no oversight

---

57 Vanessa Bell to Vita Sackville-West 29 April 1941. Leonard had the tablet designed and made (from Hopton Wood stone), engraved and fixed by C.F.Bridgman of Lewes, monumental masons, for £11.15.0.

58 The last two stanzas of the poem by Charles Elton quoted on page 157.

59 27 April 1941

that he did not sign his own three-and-a-half lines. The bishop's wife then sent him a picture postcard of Lincoln Cathedral: 'Some people would have judged me by themselves and taken it that I meant to be rude or something' – with her signature heavily underlined. Leonard kept thinking how amused Virginia would have been.

Leonard was his wife's sole executor and residuary legatee. Patrick Pritchard, the son of old Mr Pritchard, acted for him with regard to her Will and probate. She left small bequests to Vanessa, Adrian, Clive, Duncan, Nelly Boxall and Vita – this to be one of her manuscripts, to be selected by Leonard. Her estate gross, which included her portfolio of shares, a half-share in the home and in her and Leonard's joint account, came to £14,051.3s.5d. For the purposes of probate, the annual value of royalties payable on her books was set at £102 – a massive underestimate.

Leonard had in Virginia's lifetime dealt with her foreign rights, permissions and reprints, effectively acting as her agent. The huge flow of correspondence – from academics, fans, researchers, bibliographers – began as a trickle as soon as she died, and would become a flood. Little knowing how people would be lining up to write about Virginia Woolf, Leonard wrote to his old friend Edwin Muir in autumn 1941, asking him to write a book about her work, for which he would provide biographical material. Muir replied appreciatively but tentatively; the book was not written.

Towards the end of April 1941 he heard from Alice Ritchie. 'These are hopeless times for the likes of us. I'm very ill and not likely to see much more of them – not altogether sorry.' She would like to have seen him again, but it was probably too late. 'I always thought of you as one of the most courageous men I knew.'[60] Her next letter explained that 'I am attacked by cancer, luckily in an inoperable part [the spine] . . . It would indeed be pleasant to have a talk with you again. I feel, like you, that neither absence nor silence makes any difference to so proved a friendship as ours.'

---

60 21 April 1941

Alice was staying with her younger sister Trekkie Parsons at 25 Victoria Square. Leonard went to see her there in the afternoon of 26 May, after returning Virginia's borrowed books to the London Library and attending a *PQ* meeting. He had also joined the executive committee of yet another organisation, the Anglo-Soviet Public Relations Association (ASPRA), founded after Germany attacked Russia in June, with the aim of persuading the War Cabinet that the war could be won through Anglo-Soviet co-operation. He fitted regular visits to Alice into his busy London days throughout the summer of 1941, 'watching her dying', as he said. In mid-August she was in a nursing home to have radiotherapy, and worrying about the cost: 'If I were to ask you to lend me £100 on the poor security of an unfinished book, but paying interest at 5%, what would you say?'[61] Once back at Victoria Square, she sent him 'many thanks for being so sweet about the loan (if it can be called so in the circumstances!) . . . With love, as always, Alice.'

Leonard put in two weeks editing the *New Statesman* when Kingsley Martin was away, and was elected to the board. On 6 August, instead of returning home after a typical London day, he dined and stayed the night with Willie Robson in Westbourne Park Road.[62] Willie suggested that Leonard might like to take a room in his house; Sally the spaniel would be welcome too.

It was wretched, taking the unreliable trains back to Lewes through the bombing and the black-out, and then cycling four miles in the dark to an empty house. The week after he first stayed with Willie, he went to Desmond and Molly MacCarthy (at 2 Garrick's Villas, Hampton Court); Leonard would have his own fire and armchair in his own room whenever he wanted, promised Molly. The next morning, 'Went N[ew S[tatesman] w Desmond write about the Roosevelt-Churchill meeting[63]

---

61 27 Aug 1941

62 William Robson's wife and children were living in Surrey, out of the bombing, where he joined them at weekends.

63 Churchill, anxious to have the backing of the USA in the war, met several times with President F.D.Roosevelt. After the Japanese attacked the American fleet in Pearl Harbour, Hawaii, on 7 Dec 1941, the USA declared war on Japan; Germany and Italy declared war on the USA, which then entered the war on the side of the Allies.

4.55 tr[ai]n Aylesbury stay w Philip.' Another invitation came from Stephen Spender, newly married to his second wife, the pianist Natasha Litvin: 'We have a very good cook.' Stephen Spender also had a flat at the *Horizon*[64] office, which Leonard occasionally used.

Everyone was offering or seeking safe accommodation. Adrian and Karin Stephen's daughter Ann asked Leonard if she could come to Monks House with her two babies, as the family house on the Thames estuary was in the path of the flying bombs. Leonard was not up to taking them on. Ann's sister Judith, living in the basement of 50 Gordon Square, also asked herself to stay. Instead, Leonard rented one of his cottages in the village to her and her sculptor boyfriend Leslie Humphrey.

Adrian's family constantly struck the wrong note with Leonard, and Adrian seemed unmoved by his sister's death. The whole thing, he wrote to Vanessa, 'is very unreal to me as I have been so far away from it all.' Since about 1914 (the year he married) 'I have seen her rather seldom and have never been quite sure that she wanted to see me when we did meet.'[65] (His perception of infrequent contact is not borne out by the record.) He and Karin maintained an aloofness, while feeling excluded. They were aloof even from their children. As their daughter Ann wrote to Leonard many years later, 'Something seems to have gone wrong.'[66]

Adrian's wife Karin Stephen did not write to Leonard until six months after Virginia died, 'because I thought you would not like to be troubled with letters, but you know you had my very deep sympathy'. This came at the tail of a long letter about her daughter Judith and Leslie Humphrey, of whom Leonard was seeing all too much: 'Talking to LH is like eating stale insipid food – it leaves a bad taste in the mind',[67] he wrote in his diary, in which he hardly ever vented his spleen.

Vanessa too took her sister's death with resignation. She was, as her daughter Angelica put it, not overwhelmed. 'It must have been an event

---

64 *Horizon*'s office was at 6 Selwyn House, Lansdown Terrace WC1. Spender was Connolly's assistant on the magazine.

65 April 1941. Quoted in Jean MacGibbon, *There's the Lighthouse: a Biography of Adrian Stephen* James & James 1997

66 3 June 1964

67 1 Jan 1941. Judith Stephen married the artist Nigel Henderson in 1943.

she had expected for most of her life, and now that it had happened it had lost its power to shatter.'[68] She wrote to Molly MacCarthy: 'One can only be glad that this did not happen as it so nearly did years ago – when nearly all her gifts would have been wasted. It is thanks to Leonard that it didn't. He is amazingly sensible and sane.'[69] Although they were in touch by telephone and irregular visits, Vanessa and Leonard did not grow closer – petrol was short, constant meetings seemed 'pointless' without Virginia, and Vanessa, aged sixty-two (a year older than Leonard) was becoming more reclusive.

Leonard ate frugally – mainly fish and macaroni, with eggs from his seven hens and vegetables from the garden. That first summer he was alone, Louie returned in the evenings to make his supper, and he began writing 'Garden after dinner' in his diary – something he had not felt he should do, or did not want to do, when Virginia was with him. He began to have frequent visits in the afternoons and evenings from Diana Gardner, a wood-engraver and writer,[70] who lived at Thatch Cottage in the village with her father. Diana's visits, and the familiar presences of Louie Everest and Percy Bartholomew, kept Leonard from what might have been a perilous isolation at Monks House.

Alice's last surviving letter to Leonard was from Westminster Hospital. 'I think the best thing in this prolongation of life from April has been seeing something of you again. With love, as always, Alice.'[71] She came out of hospital, but only briefly. Her sister Trekkie explained to Leonard that she was heavily 'doped' and that 'I have besought them to let her wake as little as possible now . . . I know how much you valued each other.' Alice died three days later, on 27 October. Trekkie returned his cheque, and declined, with gratitude, his suggestion that she should keep it to cover the expenses of Alice's illness. 'I shall never forget either

68 Angelica Garnett, *Deceived with Kindness*

69 20 April 1941. King's College, London

70 Diana Gardner became known through her story 'Crossing the Atlantic', and a documentary piece 'The Land Girl', both published in *Horizon*. Tambimuttu, the Ceylonese poet and editor, published a volume of her stories, *Half-Way Down the Cliffs* (Poetry London Books).

71 7 Oct 1941

that you lent it to her, or the sweet and friendly way you did it, and it certainly bought her a £100 of comfort.'[72] She herself had been ill, but hoped Leonard would soon come to lunch or dinner. Leonard had never even once seen her when he visited Alice; she had a job in a branch of the War Office in Petersham. Her husband Ian was working with the Air Ministry, interpreting photographs of European airfields.

Leonard decided he could not, in London, depend on the hospitality of friends. His diary, 11 November 1941: 'Went Cliffords Inn get flat ready.' Cliffords Inn on Fleet Street was where he and Virginia lived when they were first married. The old buildings had been replaced by modern service flats; his was number 159 on the seventh floor. He stayed there for several nights each week, and spent his evenings with friends such as Saxon Sydney-Turner. On 17 February 1942, he had 'Tea Trekkie and Ian Parsons' in his diary; but he found Trekkie alone. A few days before, he had left a present of flowers from his greenhouse – white freesias, and a red cyclamen in a pot – on her doorstep in Victoria Square.

They had not met for ten years. Trekkie had a Persian cat called Rose, whose sexual exploits served to create an instant bond between her and Leonard; and she told him about Chatto & Windus's series of miniature books for children, the Midget Books, which she was to illustrate with lithographs. He reminded her later how, on that first visit, her beauty, and the beauty of her room, 'and your mind and moods', had immediately appealed to him.

In March 1942 Leonard turned down Vita Sackville-West's new novel *Grand Canyon*. 'It is not a good book, I'm afraid', he wrote to John Lehmann, 'and I doubt whether, were it not by Vita, one would consider it.' The novel was set in the present, with the author imagining Germany winning the war. 'This is one of the most unpleasant letters I have ever had to write', Leonard told Vita, 'primarily because as an author you have always treated us so extraordinarily well that it seems almost unthinkable that the Hogarth Press should reject a book of

72 1 Nov 1941. *Love Letters: Leonard Woolf and Trekkie Ritchie Parsons 1941–1968* ed Judith Adamson Chatto and Windus 2001. All quoted correspondence between LW and TRP is from this source.

yours.' He told her *Grand Canyon* was 'profoundly defeatist' and would make 'a bad impression'.[73] (But Leonard would have felt he had to publish it, had Virginia had been there.)

This was a shocking blow to Vita, especially as Leonard had been 'profoundly moved' by her poem 'In Memoriam', published in the *Observer*. 'It expresses perfectly what was Virginia and what one felt in and to her.'[74] They had an outspoken though amicable set-to about which of Virginia's manuscripts Vita would have. Vita wanted *The Waves*, which Leonard was not prepared to part with. They agreed that she would have *Mrs Dalloway*. (She already had the manuscript of *Orlando*, which Virginia gave her.) It was difficult for Leonard to find complete manuscripts of anything at all. Virginia's papers, as he told Vita, were in 'inextricable confusion', those from Mecklenburgh Square 'heaped together in immense piles with all the books in a room at the top of the village . . . I found part of Mrs Dalloway here and part under piles of blitzed and filthy books in the other place and the same with The Years.'[75]

The Cliffords Inn flat did not last long. Leonard wanted, or thought he wanted, loneliness and silence. He patched up three rooms for himself at 37 Mecklenburgh Square and moved in, with several loads of books, in June 1942, and let the now empty basement to a medical student. 'There were no windows and no ceilings, and nothing in the house, from the roof to the water pipes, was quite sound. I got my loneliness and my silence (except when the bombs were falling) all right.'

Eliot and Forster both came down to Monks House for weekends, and he saw his sister Flora who lived nearby. John Lehmann came for a night to discuss Hogarth affairs, and found him out at the back, 'sawing wood in his old corduroys, and what I had come to call his "French poacher's" jacket'. The house struck Lehmann as cold and damp, filled with a great litter of books and papers, as well as trays of apples and jars of

73 *Grand Canyon* was also turned down by Heinemann, and published by Michael Joseph. It was not a critical success but sold 8000 copies on her reputation.
74 6 April 1941
75 14 June 1941

honey and jam. Leonard was 'a little hollow-eyed' but cheerful.[76] Kingsley Martin came for a night; Diana Gardner came round constantly; Willie Robson with eleven-year-old Elaine came for four days. With them all, he played bowls. It was a good year for plums. Maynard Keynes accepted a peerage and became Lord Keynes of Tilton; Charleston mocked, and Leonard was scathing.

Trekkie kept up the contact, telephoning him a few times without getting an answer. She gave up her job at the War Office for health reasons. 'Will you ring me up and come and see me.'[77] He called at her house with strawberries on 6 July, but did not find her in, upon which she invited him to dinner: 'I do want to see you.' Diary 21 July 1942: 'Dined Trekkie Parsons.' It is not clear whether Ian was there too. Trekkie remembered that he was 'very, very nervous. His hands were terribly shaking . . .'[78] He visited her again, and took her out to dinner at the Wellington in the Strand, and sent her flowers and fruit from Rodmell, at respectable intervals, for the rest of that summer and autumn.

'Ian is being sent away on a special job in a week or two', she wrote to him on 9 November. 'I will write and ask if I may come [to Monks House] for the night.' But it was not until 12 December that Leonard wrote in his diary: 'Work Trekkie came Walk'. She went home the next day with a load of apples. 'I keep on thinking about the light in your house and will come back and paint.'[79]

They wrote to one another over Christmas, Trekkie using 'passionate pink paper' which she hoped he admired, and she returned to Monks House on the last day of 1942. This time she stayed three nights. She made a sketch of the garden which included 'Leonard and Virginia', the two intertwined elm trees, to be worked up into a painting. A couple of days after she left, the elm beneath which Virginia's ashes were buried crashed down in a gale.

---

76 *Thrown to the Woolfs*

77 15 May 1942

78 Trekkie Parsons, (Leonard Woolf 1880–1969), BBC Radio 3, 9 Feb 1970, producer Virginia Browne-Wilkinson.

79 14 Dec 1942

15

Trekkie

Everyone liked Trekkie Parsons, or Trekkie Ritchie as she remained in her work-life. She was attractive, amusing, direct, kind. She was a good cook, and had a talent for interior design. She could be bossy, and she had a quick temper – for which she always apologised afterwards.

She was learning lithography, and Leonard quickly commissioned her to do twelve lithographic illustrations for a Hogarth children's book.[1] Her visits to Rodmell became regular. She flirted with him by proxy, sending him details of her cat Rose's yowling lust for her mate. He bought for £2 her drawing of the cyclamen he had given her. She sent him a photograph of herself and Alice as little girls, with their dolls. He gave her his early stories and poems to read. He told her she was fierce like a tiger, and gentle like a dove; and then, that she was a gentle tiger, and a fierce dove. He gave her fruit and flowers and a set of coloured eighteenth-century flower-engravings. She took to dropping in at Mecklenburgh Square on Monday evenings after her lithography class, for a boiled egg and tea and toast. By the end of February 1943 he was beginning his letters 'Dearest Tiger', and when she went away with her husband Ian in March they wrote to each other. Leonard, at sixty-two, just under two years after his wife died, was

---

1 Barbara Baker's *The Three Rings* Hogarth Press 1944

head over heels in love. As Trekkie said long afterwards, he would have fallen in love with almost anybody. He had the habit of loving.

When Leonard first loved Virginia, he had feared alienating her by his lustfulness. With Trekkie, he feared that he would bore her – or that his friends would. Willie Robson was a case in point. But as Leonard retorted in this context, he himself would be willing to go with her to the Ritz (thus defining simultaneously his own idea of extreme boringness, and Willie as first-class of his kind). Willie Robson and Trekkie got on terms fast; he endeared himself to her, and to Leonard, by buying her painting of freesias.

He was 'Dearest Leonard', and she sent him three lines of poetry:

> There's another love now
> See where he comes, like to a greedy sparrow
> Who from the poor marten his frail love snatches.

The marten [*sic* for 'martin'] was Ian. 'Did you compose the love-nest lines?' he asked her. I think you must because of the attitude to the sparrow. They are very good, but I should have thought libellous of the sparrow.'[2]

He began to fuss when he did not see her – 'whining', he called it. Trekkie was alarmed: 'I like to be an oasis, but not to create desarts [*sic*] and if there is more desart than oasis your only reasonable act is to eliminate me . . . I have you for an oasis too and now that I begin to be sure you are not a mirage I am very comfortable and hoped you were the same.' She wanted him to love her, 'but not as an epidemic disease all covered in spots and then quite cured.' His love made her happy 'but only if it makes you happy too'.[3] He was, more than most people she thought, the captain of his soul. Yes, but not of his heart, he replied: 'So I shall continue to love T.'[4] Their letters were mostly playful, though Leonard's sometimes became outpourings of worshipful longing and litanies of her perfections, as is the way of love letters, however evolved and mature the lover.

---

2 5 May 1943
3 30 May 1943
4 31 May 1943

He swung between exhilaration and despondency, seized with terror 'that next time I see you I shall find that you can't tolerate me' on account of 'the appalling insistence and persistence, which I know I possess and cannot control, which is due to some horrible fire in my entrails . . . I had hoped that age would put it out but I don't really think it does. It makes things obsess me. But only once in my life before has it made a person obsess me.'[5] The obsession of thirty years earlier superimposed its register and its codes on the new one. He called Trekkie 'Dearest tiger, Luriana.' She embodied and justified his old ideals, for he believed (in the pure spirit of *Principia Ethica*) in 'the value of art and of people and of one's relations with people. You combine all 3 values for me and as I said the you which I know to be you is the most beautiful person I've known . . . I love you.'[6]

The joy of Trekkie was that she was, supremely, different. She lived in the present. She was fresh air. Vanessa Bell painted in 1943 a group portrait of the Memoir Club, such as had been mooted years ago by Clive. She put in Duncan Grant, Leonard, herself, Clive, Bunny Garnett, Maynard, Desmond and Molly MacCarthy, Quentin Bell and Morgan Forster. She painted framed portraits of the dead – Roger Fry and Virginia – hanging on the wall behind the group. 'I am really very fond of Maynard, Desmond, Morgan and all the old Bloomsburyites', Leonard wrote to Trekkie. 'But we're terribly bony and brainy, I think, and practise a kind of bleak intellectual ruthlessness upon one another.' What he loved in Trekkie was her 'extraordinary freshness of spirit', and the poetry of her, expressed in her painting and in her love of flowers. 'It is cool and fresh and clear and beautiful, and though you can be just as intellectual and ruthless as we are, it means you are never bleak and bony as we are.'[7]

Ian and Trekkie Parsons had a strong marriage. Trekkie never implied to Leonard that she did not enjoy going away with Ian, or complained about having to be available for social occasions. But for both there were disappointments. Ian had wanted what is called a normal married life, and children. Trekkie wanted neither. She responded sharply, when

5 30 Oct 1943
6 19 Feb 1944
7 25 May 1944

Vanessa Bell's group portrait of the Memoir Club, 1943. Left to right are: Duncan Grant, LW, Vanessa Bell, Clive Bell, Bunny Garnett, Maynard Keynes, Lydia Keynes, Desmond MacCarthy, Quentin Bell, E. M. Forster. On the wall, deceased members Virginia Woolf, Lytton Strachey and Roger Fry.

asked if she had ever wanted a family, that she had 'spent her whole life trying not to have children.'[8]

She and Ian were compatible in regard to his publishing work. Trekkie was especially alive to poetry, and Ian deferred to her judgment. But her real passion was for painting, and although Ian was 'good about me wanting to paint, and as sympathetic as he can be . . . if I stopped he would soon not miss my pictures at all – and not just my pictures but all pictures.' It was for her 'as it would be for a writer living with someone who would never of their own accord read a book.'[9] Leonard was peculiarly able to supply this lack. The visual arts had not meant as much to him as literature or music.

8 Private information

9 Diary 3 April 1951. Quoted in Judith Adamson (ed): *Love Letters: Leonard Woolf & Trekkie Ritchie 1941–1968* Chatto & Windus 2001

But he had lived among people for whom painting was all in all – Vanessa Bell, Duncan Grant, Roger Fry; and his wife had been the supreme artist in another medium. He had always believed that 'the best thing in life is to be an artist and to create as you do. And if one isn't and can't, the best is to get what I get from you.'[10] He had the mental and emotional muscles to identify with Trekkie's and to allay her self-doubt.

Trekkie was a good draughtswoman, she had acquired technique at the Slade, but although she produced pleasant pictures she was not a good painter. She just missed. She lacked the raw talent. But loving her as he did, Leonard found the essential Trekkie in her work, assuring her that she was one of the rare people who, if they were peeled like an onion, would reveal 'a perfectly hard, solid object, Trekkie, an adorable Trekkie, but something far more important, an artist Trekkie . . . I'm absolutely certain that in one or two of the pictures I've seen is the hard, solid (and still adorable), master painter Trekkie.' She must get 'this solid Trekkie' into her pictures, and the pictures out into the world.'[11] He wrote her screeds of exhortation and encouragement, explaining her to herself, and himself to her. They went round galleries together – never had Leonard looked at so much art – and he took her paintings round to dealers and galleries, 'travelling' her work just as he had once 'travelled' the books of the Hogarth Press round the booksellers.

Love did not displace work. Sole editor of the *PQ* throughout the war, he contributed at article on 'Hitler's Psychology',[12] and commissioned pieces by Julian Huxley, R.H.Tawney, Harold Laski, among others, and younger writers such as Frank Pakenham and Max Beloff. William Robson contributed a major article on the Beveridge Report.[13]

---

10 2 June 1944

11 12 Aug 1943

12 *PQ* Oct–Dec 1942

13 The Beveridge Report, published December 1942, proposed a comprehensive scheme of social insurance from cradle to grave. It was the basis for the Welfare State, which included the National Health Service, put in place by the Labour Government in its post-war administration.

In April 1943 Beatrice Webb died;[14] Leonard wrote her obituary for the *Economic Journal.* Douglas Cole was now chairman of the Fabian Society, and his wife Margaret honorary secretary. Leonard became chair of the Fabian Society International Bureau, which addressed future problems of relief and reconstruction. He was also a member of the Colonial Bureau, and on the Research Planning Committee with William Robson (who after the war ended was appointed Professor of Public Administration at LSE). Leonard was pinning hope on the international forum which would replace the League of Nations, post-war.[15]

Vita Sackville-West wrote in her diary on 8 January 1943: 'Think of writing a book of four sketches – of Leonard, the two St Theresas, and a fourth unworldly person.'[16]

Leonard had in fact embarked on the least unworldly phase of his life. Trekkie was a lively, functioning woman of the world. She and Ian liked to live well. Ian was clever, confident, and a good after-dinner speaker. The Parsons' style of life had little in common with the high thinking and plain living of Leonard's friends and colleagues. Trekkie was apolitical, and while Leonard had wished Virginia to share in his political passions, he took positive pleasure in Trekkie's total ignorance of the Beveridge Report. The Parsons had a variegated circle of friends, and gave great parties where Ian played the banjo. They were known for dancing together well and stylishly – one activity where the harmony between them was unmistakeable.

Leonard did not take up dancing, but he smartened himself up. In autumn 1942 he ordered from his tailors, Jennings & Gully in Cork Street, a three-piece Harris tweed suit 'with two pairs of trowsers [*sic*]'. He always had two pairs of trousers with every suit, made to be worn with a belt, not braces. There was no need to try anything on, since he had not altered in shape or weight for years. Diana Gardner wrote a

14 Sidney Webb died in 1947

15 The term 'United Nations' was first used by President F.D.Roosevelt in 1941

16 Quoted in VG *Vita: The Life of V. Sackville-West* Weidenfeld & Nicolson. Vita ended up writing only about the 'two St Theresas', in *The Eagle and the Dove* (1943).

pen-portrait of him walking up the road from Monks House towards the end of the war, with E.M.Forster:

'[Leonard] was singularly slim, with narrow chest and hips . . . He had a famous and unforgettable face – long, narrow and craggy, with deep lines on either side of his mouth. I was always aware of his rather long top teeth and flexible lips from which issued, slowly, words of deep wisdom and slow, unforgettable humour! On either side of a high, narrow forehead, strong, iron-grey hair fell loosely. His eyes gleamed bright blue out of darkly sunburned skin.' He was wearing that day an open-necked cream shirt, the sleeves rolled loosely back over 'sun-brown sinewy arms', and greyish-green flannel trousers which were probably once half of a suit. 'His long fingers seemed faintly dusty with chalky garden soil'. He had an 'earth quality' about him, despite the fact that he was 'scrupulously clean'.[17] One of the most memorable and unique things about him was 'the equally balanced mixture of body and mind'. He seemed happy and relaxed, 'and this made him look young – as if he were an undergraduate still.'[18]

Both the Parsons drank rather a lot. With Trekkie in his life, Leonard began ordering gin, vermouth (to go with the gin), sherry and rum, plus more wine than his usual modest quota, from the Army & Navy Stores. Trekkie supplemented the stocks at Monks House on Ian's charge-account with the wine merchant Robert James of Grape Street WC2, and weaned Leonard on to patronising the same superior establishment. Ian gave Trekkie wonderful jewellery. Leonard too spent money on Trekkie. He bought her earrings for her forty-first birthday, 13 June 1943. At Christmas 1944 he had two rings from Cameo Corner in Museum Street sent to her on approval; the one she chose was set with emeralds and diamonds. In November 1947 he bought two Constable sketches from Wildenstein in New Bond Street and gave one of them to Trekkie.[19] He also bought her a Rembrandt etching.

*

17 Doubtful.
18 Diana Gardner, 'A Meeting', *Charleston Magazine* 12, 1995
19 The one he kept was 'Cumberland Landscape', 1805

In London, the lease of the house next door to the Parsons, 24 Victoria Square, came up for sale. Victoria Square is a quiet enclave of flat-fronted, stucco houses built in the 1830s, tucked away between busy streets and only two minutes' walk from Victoria Station. He and Trekkie looked over number 24 together, and he wrote the next day: 'The truth of course is that one of the strongest pulls is the thought of being so near you, dearest tiger. But I am sensible enough to see that I love you too much to come and live next door to you. I might so easily make myself just a nuisance to you . . .'[20] His spaniel Sally died of distemper a few days later, which made the idea of change easier. He went round the house with Trekkie and a builder, and on 8 September 1943 signed the lease.

There was tension, as Trekkie's closeness to Leonard found its space within her marriage. She was ill in November 1943, and in a nursing home. Just before she went in, Leonard lunched with her, Ian, and Norah Smallwood, a colleague at Chatto & Windus whose husband had just been killed in action. Norah Smallwood started out as Ian's secretary. He became her mentor, and she was a quick learner. In her thirties, she was red-haired, smart and energetic, and during the war, with Ian away, she took over the burden of production, and became a formidable editor.[21]

Trekkie had arranged to replace Leonard's Sally with a Shetland sheepdog, who arrived while she was in the nursing home. He named her Merle. 'I think she will be a perfect dog; she follows beautifully already and settles down quietly at one's feet in a bus. She is beautiful, Sally's colours [black and white], one eye brown and the other half blue and half brown . . . Thank you for Merle.'[22] It was Leonard who collected Trekkie from the nursing home on 3 December 1943 and took her home. The weekend after Christmas both she and Ian stayed

---

20 24 July 1943

21 At the end of the war she became a partner in the firm. See obituary of Norah Smallwood by John Goldsmith in *The Bookseller* 20 Oct 1984. She became chairman and managing director of Chatto & Windus in 1975, and retired in 1982. 'By then she had become an almost legendary figure in the book world, respected but also feared.'

22 20 Nov 1943

at Monks House. Ian, in his thank-you letter, thanked Leonard 'above all for your kindness to T'.

When Leonard came up to Victoria Square, he always called in to see Trekkie before he did anything else. They were in and out of each other's houses, leaving bread and milk in each other's kitchens. It was not enough for Leonard. He had the crazy idea of giving her three-quarters of Monks House as her own. He would live in the attics and she would have the rest, apart from the outside bedroom. 'The only thing we should have to share is the kitchen and bathroom until I got one in the attic . . . I would give you ½ the garden for your own (which will, I hope, show you what I think of you . . .)'[23]

Paris was liberated in August 1944, and that summer and autumn the Germans, driven back across Europe, made a final assault on London. Mr Pritchard's office had its windows blown out and the ceiling down, and the parents of Ethel Edwards, one of his young clerks, were killed when their house received a direct hit. Ethel was going to relatives in Wales, and wrote to Leonard to say goodbye: 'I always have appreciated the kindness and understanding you bestowed upon [Rose Schrager] and I in all sorts of circumstances. We both hold you in high esteem and value your friendship very much indeed . . . I hope your dear dog is very fit.'[24]

Victoria Square was damaged by a flying bomb. London was not a good place to be living on one's own, and when Ian Parsons was sent to France with the Air Force after the Normandy Landings (D-Day, 6 June 1944), Trekkie came to live on a permanent basis at Monks House until he was demobilised in the autumn of 1945. She and Leonard bicycled everywhere, Merle running alongside, searching for a weekend house to rent nearby for herself and Ian, who was posted briefly back to London in November 1944. Trekkie went to Victoria Square to be with him, while Leonard looked after her kitten Pilly. He saw her during his weekly trips to London but the break in their constant companionship was

23 18 Sept 1943
24 20 July 1944

hard. 'Come back, come back, come back; I can't do without you dearest.'[25]

Leonard never explained anything to anyone about his relationship with Trekkie. It was too ambiguous, too hard to explain. The dignity and the reality of her marriage were maintained both in life and in print, in his autobiography. Leonard did not even say anything to Vanessa. 'However', she wrote to Jane Bussy,[26] in early 1945 – 'a young woman has appeared on the scenes [*sic*], called by the rather absurd name of Trekkie Ritchie. She is married to someone in Chatto & Windus and is a painter herself . . . Well, this young woman came to stay at Rodmell when London was being fly-bombed in June, and there she still is, and that's all I know about it. But L. seems to me far happier and better and I myself think that at any rate her feelings are fairly clear', and he was looking 'more rested' than he had for years. 'But I tell you the gossip for what it's worth. I know nothing and have heard nothing.'[27]

Trekkie did her lithographical printing in the old office behind the garage, and painted in Virginia's writing-lodge. She did not share Leonard's room, but slept in the spare bedroom, next to his. When she became responsible for her elderly aunts, the visiting aunt had the spare room, and Trekkie slept in the downstairs room opening into the garden, which had been Virginia's.

Her husband Ian was Norah Smallwood's lover; one cannot say when their affair began. Trekkie became violently hostile to her. This seems irrational, in that Ian's liaison with Norah balanced Trekkie's with Leonard. It was the sexual nature of Norah's relationship with Ian which elicited Trekkie's guilt and fear. She and Ian no longer slept together. Anyone hearing this story will naturally have assumed that Leonard and Trekkie were lovers. They were, in the sense that theirs was a passionately erotic relationship. But she was almost certainly not his mistress. (Trekkie gave an interview in 1991 explicit enough to

---

25 25 Jan 1945
26 Daughter of Lytton's sister Dorothy.
27 *ibid.* 11 March 1945

dispel residual doubt in most people.)[28] They were physically close, and he tried to persuade her into bed with him, but not insistently. She, scarred by her bad first marriage, was wary of sex, and fundamentally loyal to Ian. Leonard was out of practice, and had prostate problems. He put in his anthology, published in 1967, a quotation from Montaigne's Essays: 'One had reason to remark on the unruly liberty of this member that so importunately asserts itself when we have no need of it, and so inopportunely fails us when we have need of it . . . so proudly and obstinately refusing our solicitations, both mental and manual.'

He was all too well accustomed to adoring a woman with whom he lived chastely. Small physical intimacies, such as kissing Trekkie's toe, became iconic:

> To possess all of you, body, mind and soul
> For in love there's nothing between nothing and the whole:
> 'I love your eyes, your mouth, your foot, your ear –'
> 'Not quite so fast, not quite so fast, my dear,
> You have no locus standi, no claims, I fear,
> No place or rights or privileges here.'
> 'Darling of course I know
> That this is so;
> Mine was a cry
> For what's beyond the sky;
> In this earth my claim is pretty low.
> You must allow
> Only a toe.'[29]

'To know you and love you has been the best thing in life, and if it has, as it must, the other side of it which crept into that silly poem, it isn't worth thinking about in comparison with you and what you are to

28 To Peter F. Alexander, for his book *Leonard and Virginia Woolf* St Martin's Press 1992. Judith Adamson, editor of *Love Letters*, thinks it possible however that Trekkie's usual truthfulness 'may have succumbed to a deeper need for privacy'.

29 May 1944

me.'[30] Trekkie, like Virginia, loved to be loved. She also knew how to love, and to care for the people she loved.

The Hogarth Press was, like Mecklenburgh Square, a nightmare. Nevertheless, Hogarth made some shrewd acquisitions during and just after the war – Henry Green's first novel, *Back*, in 1946, and William Sansom's novels and stories. The real problems were personal. John Lehmann wrote to Leonard on 15 October 1943 that he hardly trusted himself to put into words what he felt about 'the way you have handled our relationship in the press during the present year. I feel you are badly out of touch and your interventions either (and increasingly) irrelevant or petulant.' To which Leonard replied: 'Your attitude and language to me during the course of the last 12 months or so are absolutely inexplicable to me. I have treated you with the greatest restraint only to be met at every point with the grossest rudeness.'

All their disagreements sprung from the fact that the Hogarth Press had for decades been a cottage industry[31] operating on a shoestring, and Leonard had never altered his practices. Leonard and John quarrelled about what they should be publishing, in prolix and intense exchanges of letters, emotionally loaded 'like a lover's quarrel' – in John's view, though not in Leonard's. Their battle about the poet Terence Tiller, for example, which began when the Woolfs and John lunched together in London ten days before Virginia died, rumbled sourly on for two whole years. John felt that Leonard was incapable of appreciating new writing, and Leonard resented being treated as if he were senile. John wanted to expand and Leonard did not. In August 1944 they were offered Saul Bellow's *Dangling Man*. Leonard insisted on turning it down.

John Lehmann, at the same stage in life as were Leonard and Virginia in the dazzling early years of the Hogarth Press, suggested that he might himself found a small press for the younger authors, while remaining with Hogarth. Leonard was not having that. If the partnership was unsatisfactory, it should be terminated, and in January 1946 John

30 11 May 1944

31 '. . . what I would call not a Cottage but a Basement industry': John Lehmann, *Thrown to the Woolfs*

proposed just that. Leonard replied by return that he would exercise his right to buy John out.

A few days later he came cheerfully back to John having found a solution 'almost on my doorstep' as he disingenuously said. He had made 'a provisional arrangement' with Chatto & Windus. It happened between breakfast, over which he read John's letter, and lunchtime the same day. Ian Parsons had long had an interest in acquiring the Hogarth Press, as Alice Ritchie had told Leonard a decade before, and Leonard's closeness to Trekkie made it easy to broker the deal. In February 1946 John Lehmann quit the Hogarth Press. Chatto & Windus bought out his fifty per cent share, and the business was moved to Chatto & Windus's office in William IV Street, just off Trafalgar Square. The Hogarth Press became a limited company with Leonard, Ian and his fellow-director Harold Raymond on the board. This meant in practice that Chatto ran the Hogarth Press, while Leonard, in consultation with his board, decided what was published.

He continued to make Virginia's work his priority. He published a selection of her essays, *The Death of the Moth,* in 1942, her short stories under the title *A Haunted House* in 1944, *The Moment and Other Essays* in 1947, and *The Captain's Deathbed and Other Essays* in 1950. Just as when she was with him, he recorded their earnings in two columns – 'LW' and 'VW' – in the back of his diaries. She earned progressively more than he, and after a decade the discrepancy was tenfold. The income facilitated his life with Trekkie.

One of the first new authors Leonard took on under the new regime was A.L.Barker, with her first book of stories *Innocents* in 1947, given a dust-jacket by Duncan Grant. He also published Laurie Lee and George MacKay Brown, who was brought to him by his old friend Edwin Muir.[32] In January 1948 he heard from Dorothy Bussy (an elder sister of Lytton Strachey's, who lived in France) about a 'semi-autobiographical' story she wrote more than fifteen years before. 'I am sending it to you, my dear Leonard. Please keep my name a secret.' Leonard loved it. 'It

32 See Hugo Brunner, 'The Hogarth Press since 1946', *Charleston Newsletter* No. 6, Dec 1983

is so amusing and also terribly moving, and you have done the characters, including your own, superbly.'[33] The Hogarth Press published this story of a sixteen-year-old girl's passion for her woman teacher as *Olivia* 'by Olivia', and it became a classic.

Tom Southorn retired from the Colonial Service, and from autumn 1942 Bella, in London, was fretting to Leonard abut their younger and recently widowed sister Flora, whose life was unravelling. She and her daughter Mollie – tall and good-looking – joined the ATS,[34] and Flora subsequently wrote a book, *Two Odd Soldiers*, about their experiences, though they cannot have lasted long in the ATS. 'We had a hellish day yesterday', Bella wrote to Leonard in the last year of the war. 'No doubt you had an enquiry from the Police.' Mollie, already a problem drinker, had run away. Flora 'has made a great mistake, bringing Mollie up to be a painted conceited doll', wrote Bella. 'Please do not mention this family dirty linen to anyone.'[35]

After the war Flora went to South Africa with Mollie and Mollie's little daughter Sally. Mollie had married Peter Baker, who had a magnificent war record, published some poetry, and backed small presses. Then he turned to finance, raising capital to start up companies and shuffling his growing debts from one to company to another, while living with conspicuous extravagance. Molly was divorcing him. But Baker won a seat in Parliament before the law caught up with him, and in 1954 he was sentenced to seven years in prison for fraud and forgery.[36]

Leonard was sixty-five when the war ended. A routine was established. Trekkie spent weekends with Ian at the large and lovely house she and Leonard had found in the next village to Rodmell, Iford Grange. Leonard bicycled over frequently, and 'We cultivated our gardens passionately, the Parsons and Iford and I at Rodmell.'[37] (The gardeners

33 3 Feb 1948
34 Auxiliary Transport Service
35 29 Jan 1945
36 For details of Peter Baker's extraordinary career see *Time* magazine 13 Dec 1954.
37 *The Journey* . . .

were Leonard and Trekkie, and they collaborated on a botanical article, illustrated by her: 'The History of the Strange Stapelia'.[38]) When Ian returned to London on Mondays, Trekkie went with him. Leonard too sometimes spent Monday nights in London, and on Tuesdays saw to Hogarth Press and all his other business, before returning to Monks House with Trekkie in the afternoon and for the remainder of the week.

Maynard Keynes died on Easter Day 1946. That same spring, Morgan Forster's beloved mother died, aged ninety. He was famous, but homeless. King's College, Cambridge became his home for the rest of his life. Leonard went to dinner there in April 1948 in celebration of Morgan's seventieth birthday and G.E. Moore's seventy-fifth. The previous year Moore had had to give up the editorship of *Mind*, his main source of income. Desmond MacCarthy wrote around the friends soliciting subscriptions of £25 to help him out; Leonard sent a cheque by return of post.

Adrian and Karin Stephen were both clinically depressed. Leonard suggested to Karin that she should write a book on Freud for the Hogarth Press, 'and it seems to have given her a new lease of life'.[39] It was thought that Adrian possibly made a suicide attempt when out sailing; but he died in his sleep on 3 May 1948. Karin hung on for another five years. On 11 December 1953 their daughter Judith wrote to tell Leonard that 'mother died early this morning; and from a note which she left, there seems no doubt that she took an overdose of some kind.' Leonard's elder brother Herbert died in December 1949.

Few people are so fortunate in their later life as was Leonard Woolf. The energising effect of love made him more open, as when on 18 July 1943 he went to the Society dinner, and reported to Trekkie: 'I had not seen some of the younger members before, but the pleasant thing is that owing to the nature of the society one is on terms of complete intimacy at once.' He went back to Richard Llewelyn Davies's flat afterwards and stayed talking till two in the morning. He began seeing Tom Eliot regularly again. Leonard asked him to lunch at 24 Victoria

38 *The Geographical Magazine* (a Chatto publication) No. 17 1945–6
39 3 March 1944 to Vanessa Bell

Square, the lunch to consist of a 'mutton pie' and coffee. The joke among Leonard's friends was that in London he lived entirely on Lyons meat pies. But since 'mutton pie' features in so many of his invitations, and Trekkie was famous for her mutton pies, it seems likely that she was his supplier. (Her mutton pies were a cross between pork pies and pasties, made with flaky pastry.)

The 1940s saw the first manifestation of a phenomenon that was to be one of the features of Leonard's late life. Women whom he did not know, initially contacting him out of reverence for his wife's books, became attached to him for his own sake as an idealised figure of sympathy and wisdom. Nancy Nolan was a Dublin housewife. Leonard replied to her fan-letter about Virginia's books briefly and kindly. It was his brevity as much as his kindliness which made possible the transference. Mrs Nolan used her long letters to him as a journal or meditation, musing on the page about her family's ups and downs, consistently, for a quarter of a century. No less than six hundred of her letters to him survive. He sent her books, and photographs of Monks House and of his dogs and cats. They remained 'Mrs Nolan' and 'Mr Woolf', and the most personal note Leonard ever struck was in signing off 'Yours affectionately' in a condolence letter on the death of her husband. They never met.[40]

He shared her letters with Trekkie: 'Here is Mrs Nolan's terrifying last.'[41] When his own letters to Trekkie were over-long, he said he was as bad as Mrs Nolan. But the correspondence touched a nerve: his intrigued fondness for women who were not geniuses, and who admitted him into their confidence and into a way of thinking which he believed peculiar to the 'feminine mind'.

His sympathy with the feminine mind occasionally deflected his attention from Trekkie, landing him in relationships from which he lacked the ability to extricate himself gracefully. He preserved a letter of

40 G.B.Shaw too had regular female correspondents whom he never met, and who confided in him their daily anxieties. See Michael Holroyd *Bernard Shaw* Vol 2, *The Pursuit of Power* Chatto & Windus 1989.

41 19 July 1953

September 1947 from a young American woman: 'Honestly, Leo, I thought you were a nice guy, but when you stood me up three times running, well, buddy, that was too much.' She was no 'clinging vine' and had hoped for a pleasant friendship with no strings attached. 'So there was no need at all for you to stand me up like that, you know. I know you're busy and all that, I know too that your nerves are not made of steel, but there is no excuse to be so damnably rude as you were.' She signed off 'with tears in her eyes'.

The end of the war did not solve the problem of 37 Mecklenburgh Square. In January 1947 smoke was seeping through cracks in the walls from coal-fires in the flats next door. In May the pipe in the last functioning WC burst, flooding the basement. The house was unfit for human habitation. In spring 1948, when the pleasant exteriors of numbers 24 and 25 Victoria Square were being uniformly redecorated in cream and black, a 'sanitary notice' was served on Leonard as the landlord of 37 Mecklenburgh Square.

Leonard had only three more months of his lease remaining, which he succeeded in surrendering to the landlords, the Foundling Estate. He had never made a penny out of the house, the incessant repairs always exceeding the rents. Never has anyone so willingly parted with a property as Leonard with 37 Mecklenburgh Square. Meanwhile 24 Victoria Square was bigger than he needed. He let the top floor to a friend of Trekkie's, and the basement to his nephew Cecil, Philip's son.

In July 1946 Leonard and Trekkie took their first holiday of many alone together – two weeks in Wiltshire and Dorset. He resigned from the Labour Party Advisory Committees. G.D.H.Cole invited him to contribute a volume on world government for a series to be published by Hutchinson, but he said he was too busy. He wrote during the later 1940s booklets for the Fabian Society, and a chapter on Bloomsbury in *Flower of Cities: A Book of London.*[42] But he was mainly working on the third volume of his trilogy, *Principia Politica,* which he

42 With illustrations by Trekkie Ritchie. Max Parrish 1949

been writing all through the war with what he called 'unconscionable slowness'.

He put his Lanchester car (registration JJ 3826) back on the road in the summer of 1947. Chatto & Windus, in the name of Ian Parsons, paid the insurance. Almost at once Leonard was in trouble, summonsed for driving after midnight without lights, and receiving a hefty bill for parking at Lewes station eleven times without paying the parking fee. (There never used to be a parking fee and Leonard did not see why there should be one now.) In July 1948 he chartered a plane to take himself and Trekkie from Shoreham airfield to Penzance, at a cost of £35. In July 1949 they spent ten days in northern France; Trekkie went to Venice with Ian the day after they got back. It was as if she had two husbands, each of whom had to have a summer holiday with her, or two, and it must have been taxing.

In late 1947 and early 1948 Leonard was acting editor of the *New Statesman* while Kingsley Martin was abroad, as often in the past. Leonard was mockingly aware of the way everyone in journalism accorded undue importance to the power and influence of the press; but he acknowledged that he himself experienced 'an unusual sense of importance, a tinge of *folie de grandeur*',[43] when he sat down in the editor's chair, and he felt comfortable in it. His relationship with Kingsley Martin, however, did not mellow. Like certain married couples, neither let the other get away with anything. They found each other outrageous. Leonard, as well as sitting on the board, still wrote regularly for the paper. He also wrote many a sarcastic 'Letter to the Editor' demolishing Kingsley's editorials, supplemented by long private letters to Kingsley making the same points at length, to which Kingsley replied in kind. He would become wildly angry, and then write Leonard a placatory letter to normalise the situation.

Their chief topics of dissension were their respective attitudes to religion, to the Soviet Union and to the United States, which Kingsley attacked on account of the scale of its rearmament, post-war. An

43 *The Journey . . .*

altercation from late 1951 is illustrative. Leonard's 'Letter to the Editor': 'Sir, Week after week, every Friday, I have been reading with rapt attention and mounting excitement the thesis, reiterated and reverberating through your paper, that if only there were no Americans, we could all, under the guidance of the peace-loving, compassionate Father in Marx, Stalin, relax in peace and prosperity.'[44] Kingsley Martin wrote a personal letter of howling protest, to which Leonard replied: 'I was amused to get your letter as I expected it and could have almost written it for you.'[45] Kingsley came back again, Leonard countered his reply, and so it went on, with personal insults buried in paragraphs of gusty rhetoric. They never listened to one another, or resolved any issues. Kingsley needed Leonard's approval more than Leonard needed Kingsley's.

The paper, however, was maintaining its position. George Orwell, writing for an American readership, included Leonard Woolf in a list of the 'well-known left-wing publicists' who wrote for it, and said that 'the whole of the "enlightened" pinkish middle class reads it as a matter of habit. Its position corresponds fairly closely to that of *The New Republic* in America, but it is, I should say, a somewhat more adult paper.'[46] So far as is known, Leonard Woolf and George Orwell never met, in spite of a similar journalistic intransigence and the many parallels between the younger man's colonial experience, and his politics, with Leonard's.

They did cross swords in print. Raj Mulk Anand asked Leonard to write an introduction to his book *Letters from India.*[47] Orwell, reviewing it for *Tribune*[48] and making a play of Leonard's habit of shooting off letters to newspapers, implied that he had been provoked into yet another one, 'a rather angry letter this time which is printed as a foreword.' Leonard wrote to the editor of *Tribune*[49] to say that he had been invited by Anand to write his foreword in letter form. His only disagreement with Anand in the foreword, in fact, had been with Anand's attitude to

44 11 Nov 1951
45 15 Nov 1951
46 George Orwell, 'Britain's Left-Wing Press', *Progressive* (Madison, Wisconsin) June 1948
47 1943 Labour Book Service
48 March 1943
49 20 March 1943

the Muslim minority. By 'pretending' the Muslim problem did not exist he was 'playing into the hands of the British imperialists'. (The position of minority populations was always Leonard Woolf's concern.) He was mischievously misrepresented by Orwell.

The people now at the top were the people whom Leonard knew and had worked with. Clement Attlee was, after the General Election of 1945, Prime Minister of the first Labour Government ever to have a clear majority. Leonard went to the celebration at Party headquarters; nearly everyone he knew, as he said, was now an MP, but 'I wish the leaders were less drab', as he complained to Quentin Bell.[50] Leonard's views, as expressed in his journalism and in reports and memoranda from the Advisory Committees, had been influential. His former colleague on A.C.Imp.Q., Sir Arthur Creech-Jones, became Secretary of State for the Colonies and, when he left office, wrote to Leonard saying 'how much I owe to you and your work . . . The long preparation for power and in educating the Party has borne much fruit.'[51] In spite of this solid contribution, Leonard had little feeling of pleasure that so much of what he had campaigned for over the years was coming to pass.

Desmond MacCarthy was 'a little surprised and more depressed by your saying that your many activities seemed to you often to be futile. Are things as bad as *that*?'[52] Leonard was disabled by his bleak scepticism – as absolute as his romanticism, which found an outlet in love. Desmond, through friends in high places, was given a knighthood in 1950. Leonard was caught between his contempt for such baubles and a brute wish for public recognition which he despised in himself.

Leonard had put in a planning application to Chailey Rural District Council for converting 'the garden room, which was originally built as a workroom for a writer, into a studio with the light and space required for the work of a lithographer and artist.' The work began in January 1949. 'Yesterday I went to see Leonard who has never enough petrol to

---

50 10 Sept 1945. Hogarth Press Archive, U of Reading
51 8 April 1950
52 23 Oct 1947

come here now', Vanessa wrote to Angelica (now the mother of four daughters). 'He is building a studio!' She was not in the least shocked by the alterations to Virginia's writing-lodge, nor that they were being done for Trekkie.

In Monks House garden, on the day Vanessa visited, the iris reticulata was in bloom, and Leonard told her the story about continuing to plant them when Virginia called him in to hear Hitler ranting on the wireless. He also gave her a packet of old letters from James Russell Lowell, the American ambassador, to Vanessa and Virginia's mother, and some from Henry James. These had recently 'turned up' in the office of Dolland and Pritchard. 'Leonard so hates reading old letters that he's thankful to hand them on to me.'

Leonard also told Vanessa that he had been asked to write a joint biography of the Webbs. 'Of course it would be a terrific job taking about 3 years, he thought, but I think he's rather pleased at being asked and I tried to encourage him.'[53]

The previous week, Leonard had received a letter in Harold Laski's minuscule hand-writing, saying that at a meeting of the Trustees of the Webb Estate it was decided to ask him to be the Webbs' official biographer, with all materials at his disposal. Then he learned that R.H.Tawney had also been invited to write the biography of the Webbs. So had Laurence Hammond. Tawney was first choice, but the Trustees understood he did not want to do it. It turned out that he did. Leonard withdrew. Then Tawney withdrew. The LSE came back to Leonard, extremely embarrassed, asking would he do just Sidney. Leonard extricated himself definitively. He did however contribute an essay, 'Political Thought and the Webbs', to the book Margaret Cole was then editing, *The Webbs and Their Work*.[54]

The carry-on over the Webb biography was symptomatic. Increasingly, as Leonard withdrew from political planning for the future, he, like his old friends, became involved in the management of the past. In March 1945 he began getting Virginia's diary typed up by Kathleen

53 Vanessa Bell to Angelica Garnett 27 Feb 1949. *Selected Letters of Vanessa Bell*
54 Published by Frederick Mueller 1949

Williams, a friend of Trekkie's. 'I should like it typed on quarto, not foolscap, single spacing with fair sized margin', with carbon copies. She was a quick though not a perfectly accurate worker. He then began asking friends for any letters from Virginia that they might have, to be copied and returned.

On 26 January 1948 he heard from James Strachey, who was sorting out his brother Lytton's papers. He had already asked Leonard 'two or three times' for Lytton's letters to Virginia. Would Leonard send them so that he could get them microfilmed? Leonard complied. On 19 July Roy Harrod came to lunch at Monks House in connection with a biography of Maynard Keynes, and wrote later saying that he had seen the lubricious early Lytton/Maynard correspondence: 'I am thus the trusted repository of intimate secrets.'[55]

On 9 October 1948 Leonard heard from Vita Sackville-West, about her letters from Virginia. 'I have indeed a great quantity . . . I imagine that you would not want any of a purely personal nature but would prefer those which might deal with some literary questions or even about your travels abroad.' Vita had her own plans. Virginia's letters to date were typed out by her secretary in Virginia's lifetime, around the time of *Orlando*, though she did not tell Leonard that. Leonard replied that 'many people' thought he should publish Virginia's letters, and he was assessing the feasibility. 'The difficulty is that the really personal letters are unpublishable and . . . if one publishes only the impersonal ones, one gives a totally false impression of the character. What do you think?'[56]

Percy Bartholomew grew too old and blind to work, and after the war was replaced in Leonard's garden by Ted Warner. In July 1949 Louie's brother Harry West brought home Anneliese, a pretty eighteen-year-old girl from Pomerania whom he met when in the army of occupation in Germany, and they were married. Anneliese worked for Trekkie at Iford Grange and helped Louie out at Monks House.

---

55 17 Sept 1948. R.F.Harrod's *The Life of John Maynard Keynes* appeared in 1951, and gave no inkling of the 'intimate secrets'.

56 13 Oct 1948

Louie accepted Trekkie's position with equanimity. Leonard had a high opinion of Louie. 'Her native intelligence is extraordinary and she has that rare impersonal curiosity which the Greeks recognised as the basis of philosophy and wisdom.'[57] She came in every morning to get the breakfast for eight o'clock – eggs and bacon, and 'Louie is the only person who does it just right', said Leonard. Getting it just right included using separate pans, which were used for no other purpose, for the eggs and for the bacon – a residue, perhaps, of his Jewish upbringing. Leonard himself made the coffee. He wrote and Trekkie painted all morning, then they met for a drink and a cold lunch, left ready by Louie. He gardened every afternoon, and Trekkie went back and forth between his house and Iford Grange. Trekkie cooked the dinner, and after dinner they listened to music in the upstairs sitting-room. The routine was the same as with Virginia. It was also entirely different.

Trekkie made Leonard comfortable and overhauled his domestic arrangements. She had the exterior of Monks House colourwashed in pink – this did not last long – and had new covers made for the chairs. Louie did Leonard's washing by hand with pure soap-flakes, on account of his skin condition. Her mother, Mrs West, did his ironing, and pressed his trousers flat; he neither noticed nor cared. It was Ian who taught Anneliese to press trousers with a crease down the front, and Trekkie who made Leonard change his clothes regularly. Left to himself, he would put on the same things day after day. 'I love you even more than when I saw you five years ago', he wrote to her in September 1949. 'And in 5 years I have discovered nothing in you and I include toes which are not adorable.'

He was living a charmed life, but could not escape the ills of ageing. Dr Rau sent him to Morgan Forster's specialist, Dr Terence Millin, and on 22 January 1950 he had an operation to remove his enlarged prostate gland. Trekkie stayed at Monks House to look after the animals. She was no fair-weather friend. The water tank and the lavatory froze solid. She did not leave, but called in Frank Dean, had the cracked tank replaced, and 'the lav had to have something welded'. 'I gather from [Trekkie]',

---

57 *The Journey* . . .

wrote Vanessa, 'that one of the worst of your troubles is the skittishness of the nurses.'[58] He was in the clinic three weeks, after which he was pronounced 'quite fit' by Dr Millin. That year he became seventy, and *The Village in the Jungle* was having a new life, running as a serial in the Ceylon *Observer.*

58 Vanessa Bell to LW 26 Jan 1950

16

Disturbances

The early 1950s were years of deaths and marriages. Bella reported to Leonard on the widowed Harold's new bride, Muriel Steedman: 'She is 54, agreeable to look at and agreeable to be with. She has run for some years a tea-shop called the Bow Window in Staines.'[1] Edgar, widowed, also took a second wife, Zosia Norton. And in 1952 Quentin Bell, aged thirty-four, married Anne Olivier Popham, a clever young art historian then working with the Arts Council. (She was known as Olivier, which Leonard always wrote as 'Olivia'.) Quentin and Olivier went to live in the north of England.[2]

In May 1952, Elizabeth Robins died. Octavia moved to the Rest Home in Backsettown as director; Leonard, Robins's co-executor, also became a trustee and member of the Backsettown committee of management, a responsibility which became more and more onerous with time.

In June 1952, Desmond MacCarthy died. Leonard saw the news in the paper, feeling, as he told Molly MacCarthy, 'as if I had lost a whole piece of my life at a blow'.[3] He had not seen Desmond since the

1 27 Sept 1951
2 Quentin Bell lectured in Art Education at the University of Newcastle before becoming Professor of Fine Art at the University of Leeds.
3 10 June 1952

previous November, when Desmond was racked by an attack of asthma after a Memoir Club meeting in Gordon Square; and he had, in that anxious moment, a vivid memory of Desmond as a young man walking in the hills in Devon with Lytton, on one of Moore's reading parties. 'There are few things more terrible than such sudden visions of one's friends in youth and vigour through the miseries of age and illness.'[4] Molly MacCarthy died the following year.

Towards the end of January 1955 he heard from Marjorie Wells – the daughter-in-law of HG – that Kotelianski had died. She and the film critic Dilys Powell were Kot's chief carers. Leonard had been to see him after he had a heart attack, and Marjorie Wells told him, 'he said that for a quarter of an hour the past had come alive again.'[5] Kot had a second heart attack that very night, and a third and fatal one the next day. Leonard wrote his obituary in *The Times*[6] and a personal tribute in the *New Statesman*.[7] He had 'an uneasy feeling that, in fact, I hastened his death! He was very moved by our conversation because he got on to old times and talked about [D.H.]Lawrence and Katherine [Mansfield].'[8] Dilys Powell reassured him: 'Heaven must have sent you to Kot last week.'[9]

During the 1950s, Leonard behaved as if it were still 'before the war', complaining bitterly about bad service from shops and tradesmen. Shortages did not end with the war, and rationing continued until 1952, as did his pre-war habit of continual letter-writing about the non-arrival or unsuitability of items ordered by post. He had his coffee beans sent from Selfridges, and complained constantly about the varying weights and the faulty packaging. Selfridges ended up allocating to one assistant the sole responsibility for the weighing, packing and dispatching of Mr Woolf's beans.

---

4 *Beginning Again*
5 23 Jan 1955
6 4 Feb 1955
7 18 June 1955
8 To May Sarton
9 24 Jan 1955

The wartime culture of make-do-and-mend – margarine wrappers and short lengths of string saved, clothes patched, socks darned, old woollens unravelled to be knitted up into something else – suited his frugal nature. He did not, after the war, continue his habit of using spare diaries from a previous year, which necessitated changing every single date to fit the day of the week. But he continued to use the backs of typescripts and letters received for his carbon copies, and to re-use envelopes with economy labels. He continued to expect repairs, and the replacement of small broken parts. He found, in the later 1950s and 1960s, the assumed disposability of household articles quite intolerable. The throw-away culture was incomprehensible to him. He shot off so many letters that they clogged up the village post-box. The manager of an electrical appliances firm in Brighton with whom he had been conducting a non-stop correspondence was 'advised to give up his work and have a complete rest.'

Just before the end of the war Chailey Rural District Council (the RDC) had wanted to buy Leonard's Croft field for council housing, or 'Housing of the Working Classes', as they put it. Leonard's socialism lost out, with no contest, to his unwillingness to lose his unbroken view of the Downs. In 1951 the RDC came back to him again about the siting of a sewage pumping station on the Croft field. Leonard immediately complained to the Minister of Housing and Local Government, his friend Hugh Dalton. A public local enquiry took place in Rodmell Village Hall. Rodmell's sewage was at present discharged into an open ditch, and Leonard spoke up in favour of a scheme. But why on his land? Because, said the Council's engineer, it was the best and most economical site. The installation would be screened from Monks House by a grass mound and a hedge.

Leonard, faced with a compulsory purchase order, went into overdrive, with all the 'appalling insistence and persistence' to which he confessed, in another context, to Trekkie, and coming close to the invisible boundary between what the world calls sane and what the world calls insane. Had he been one of his own dogs, he would have called himself gruffly to heel. For well over a year Leonard peppered the Ministry, the RDC and his neighbours with intemperate letters. The village talked of little else. Finally Leonard appeared to submit to the inevitable. But then he heard that on account of the 'need for economy in local government expenditure', the Minister did not propose to confirm the compulsory purchase order at present. Leonard sent a copy of this letter to the *Sussex Express and County Herald.* He had won. Nearly five years on, when an alternative site for the sewage disposal unit was approved, Leonard, in guilt or gratitude, pledged £500 to be invested for the maintenance of the new Village Hall, being built on its existing site.

In the year of the sewage row, 1952, he stood for the East Sussex County Council. Leonard's protest had been, as he said, that of a private individual, but he was an individual with local standing: school manager, member of the Village Hall management committee, treasurer and president of the Rodmell and District Horticultural Society, president of the Lewes and District Poultry Club, a member of the National Trust, of the Ancient Monuments Society, the Society of Sussex Downsmen; and president of the Monday Literary Club in Lewes (which benefited enormously by the number of his writer friends whom he invited to come and speak).

In so far as he wished to be going anywhere, he seemed to be arriving. In January 1955 he was elected to that old-established gentleman's club in London's Pall Mall, the Athenaeum, proposed and seconded by William Robson and Gilbert Murray. In the Candidates' Book of the Athenaeum, to be signed by supporters, there were four times as many distinguished signatures as were necessary to ensure his election, among them the poet John Betjeman's.[10] Lunch at the Athenaeum made a change from the India Club off the Strand, where he got a good cheap curry.

The Hogarth Press list in the 1950s was not long but it was distinguished; the heavy sellers were Laurie Lee and Laurens van der Post. All Freud's works after 1924 had been published by Hogarth, and the first

10 In the same batch of candidates, Winston Churchill was elected to life membership, and the names of Sir William Montague Pollock, diplomat, and the artist Graham Sutherland were withdrawn for lack of sufficient support.

volume of the monumental twenty-four-volume Standard Edition of the *Complete Psychological Works of Sigmund Freud*, translated by James Strachey (with assistance) appeared in 1953. Leonard had been negotiating for this with the copyright holders, with other translators, and with Freud's American publishers, for years. He went into the office on Tuesdays, 'a small greying figure radiating intelligence, muted humour and benignity'.[11] He read the manuscripts submitted to Hogarth, and looked after his long-standing authors, with the assistance of C.Day-Lewis and, for a while, the young novelist Elizabeth Jane Howard. She found Leonard, in his dark-coloured flannel shirts (chosen, she thought, so as not to show the dirt), more attractive than Ian Parsons, and was not alone among the employees in admiring his lack of pretension and his 'practised, patient endurance' at office parties for packers and travellers.

Once he said to her, apropos of nothing: 'I often think that masterpieces are extremely boring.'[12] Dealing with the masterpieces of Laurens van der Post, he cunningly blamed the regular requirement for heavy editing on Ian Parsons, just as he blamed Ian for turning down a manuscript submitted by Laurens's wife Ingaret, who did much of the preliminary pruning of her husband's manuscripts and smoothed over the stand-offs between Leonard and Laurens.

Laurens, apropos his book *The Dark Eye in Africa*, wrote to Leonard seeking 'a real talk with you about the difference between reason and intuition'[13] – a distinction which Laurens was incapable of grasping, being a fantasist and a mythomane. This was not widely realised in his lifetime, though Leonard was aware of it – and would have smiled had he known that, after his own death, Laurens would say that his first thought when he was demobilised after the war was to go down to Monks House: 'I think I spent four days with him, in which we sat up and practically talked all day and all night long without a break, and somehow as I talked to him I felt, "Well, the war is beginning to recede

11 Peter Calvocoressi, *Threading My Way* Duckworth 1994. He joined Chatto & Windus in 1955, first as literary adviser and then as director.
12 Elizabeth Jane Howard to VG in conversation 4 Dec 2001
13 10 Feb 1955

and is behind me. I'm back in civilisation."'[14] The visit was a complete fabrication, but encapsulated for Laurens some virtual or poetic truth.

A less attractive aspect of Laurens's manipulation of the truth came in a letter to William Plomer: 'I saw Leonard yesterday and for the first time had great difficulty keeping my temper: I never knew what a fundamentally coarse and lascivious character he is. I found myself thinking suddenly, "My God, I do know why Virginia committed suicide."'[15] Leonard could, on occasion, speak crudely. When Stephen Spender as a young man naively asked him how important he thought sex was in marriage, Leonard replied: 'It depends how much importance you attach to cocks and cunts.'[16] But Laurens van der Posts's own private life was 'coarse and lascivious' to the point of criminality. It is possible that the conversation with Leonard was the other way round: Laurens had been coarse, and Leonard had responded bleakly. Such reversals are part of the armoury of fantasists, and believed by them at the time of telling.

As Leonard wrote to Lyn Irvine Newman in 1957: 'You are quite wrong about Laurens van der Post. He is not bogus: he is one of the sincerest of men. Some of what he writes is very good and some of it, in my opinion, unmitigated nonsense. But he believes it just as Christ and Freud did theirs.' But the creative wool was pulled over Leonard's eyes too, as he grew old. He accepted Laurens's *The Hunter and the Whale* (1967) as autobiographical, and 'superb', even though Laurens van der Post had never been on a whaling vessel in his life.

The authors who had been brought to the Hogarth Press by John Lehmann were mostly looked after by Norah Smallwood. Nor could Leonard, on behalf of the Hogarth Press, take any credit for the fantastic success of Laurie Lee's *Cider with Rosie* (1959). It was Norah Smallwood who got Laurie Lee to finish it, urging him on and paying

---

14 'Leonard Woolf 1880-1969' BBC Radio 3, 17 Feb 1970, producer Virginia Browne-Wilkinson.

15 1 Feb 1955. Quoted in J.D.F.Jones, *Storyteller: The Many Lives of Laurens van der Post* John Murray

16 Stephen Spender, *New York Review* 23 April 1970, reviewing *The Journey Not the Arrival Matters*

a retainer. When Lee handed in his draft, Leonard wrote him a note, dictated and signed in his absence, to the effect that he did not care much for this kind of book. 'But I think in your case we will publish it.' When John Ward, the illustrator of *Cider with Rosie*, went to meet Norah in the office, 'Leonard Woolf sat there like an old prune.'[17] *Cider with Rosie*, as well as achieving spectacular sales, won the W.H.Smith Literary Prize.

The old prune was less bold than he used to be. He turned down J.R.Ackerley's *We Think the World of You*, about how he found consolation for the loss of his homosexual lover in an intimacy with Queenie, his Alsatian bitch. Leonard found it indecent. Ackerley enquired whether it was the homosexuality, or the relationship with his dog, which was the problem. Both, said Leonard. Their friendship came to an end not because they quarrelled, but because their dogs did. Joe Ackerley came to Monks House with Queenie, who got into a 'yapping, snapping, snarling hysterical dust-up' with Leonard's Niggs.[18] Joe wrote a polite thank-you letter regretting that 'Queenie did not behave better'. But he told Trekkie that Leonard behaved monstrously, saying 'my horrible dog had attacked his beloved Queenie and I had paid no attention to this and had not even said that I was sorry.'[19]

In 1953 Leonard had his first encounter with *Encounter*,[20] co-edited by Stephen Spender, who told him that Bertrand Russell had agreed to review his *Principia Politica: A Study of Communal Psychology*, 'which is good news'. This was the 'big book' on which Leonard had been working, on and off, since soon after the death of Virginia. It was planned as the third volume of *After the Deluge*. There had been two deluges – two world wars – so he had to find another title. 'It was Maynard Keynes who said to me that what I was really trying to do in these volumes was to analyse

---

17 Valerie Grove, *Laurie Lee: the Well-Loved Stranger* Viking 1999

18 Merle died from eating rat-poison in 1952. Niggs was another 'blue beardie', from Argyll.

19 LW to William Plomer 24 Nov 1968

20 *Encounter* was under the aegis of the British Society for Cultural Freedom, affiliated to the International Congress for Cultural Freedom.

the principles of politics and that I ought to call the third volume *Principia Politica*.'[21]

Principia Politica came out in November 1953. Bertrand Russell's review was moderately good news, since they were in agreement politically, and the review in the *Economist* was bearable, the reviewer hoping for 'a constructive sequel' – implying that the present work was less than constructive. There were no ecstatic letters from the remaining old friends. Moore wrote: 'What I have enjoyed most so far is your account of how you trained your cat and dog and monkey.'[22] The Hogarth Press reissued volumes one and two of *After the Deluge* at the same time, and Leonard asked Barbara Wootton, a political activist before she was an academic, to review for *PQ* what he saw as a single extended work. Sending in her thoughtful piece (in which she dwelt, like Moore, on the 'incidental pleasures' of *Principia Politica*) she sympathised with the way he had been 'ill-served' by the newspapers.

Oxford historians, whether from the Right or from the Left, were dismissive. Hugh Trevor-Roper in *The Sunday Times*[23] found the book irrelevant and incomprehensible. A.J.P.Taylor in the *Observer*[24] found Leonard Woolf's animus against Soviet tyranny exaggerated, as did Max Beloff in the *Manchester Guardian*.[25] The anonymous reviewer for *The Times Literary Supplement* pointed out that the key concept, 'communal psychology', had already been articulated before the First World War.[26] Leonard Woolf's ideas no longer fitted the situation. This was tantamount to saying that Woolf himself was trapped in an outdated 'communal psychology'.[27] The reviewer was Professor E.H.Carr, 'against' whom Leonard had written *The War for Peace.*

---

21 *Downhill* . . .

22 18 Oct 1953

23 1 Nov 1953. Sir Duncan Wilson, an ex-ambassador, pointed out in *Leonard Woolf: A Political Biography* (NY: St Martin's Press 1978) that LW had 'reviewed sharply' Trevor-Roper's *Hitler's TableTalk* in *New Statesman* 12 May 1953.

24 1 Nov 1953

25 13 Oct 1953.

26 By Durkheim and Lebon in their work on crowd psychology, and by Wilfred Trotter in *Instincts of the Herd in Peace and War*.

27 *TLS* 30 Oct 1953

Carr also complained that Leonard Woolf was not 'academic'. The Oxford philosopher Stuart Hampshire, in Leonard's own paper, the *New Statesman*, distinguished between the generalists (always ready to produce great thoughts on great subjects) and the dons (who divide knowledge into compartments, and for whom 'all genuine knowledge is specialised knowledge'). Hampshire came down on the side of the dons, describing Leonard Woolf as straying 'through the domains of child psychology, animal psychology, anthropology and classical scholarship with the lightest possible equipment and with little reference to any detailed research.'

Leonard Woolf was a propagandist, a polemicist, a campaigner, and an ideas man. He was a public intellectual but not an academic. There was an element of 'intellectual quackery' about the academic mind-set which actually repelled him, and some 'departments of knowledge, or disciplines, as they are called in academic circles', which seemed to him 'almost completely phoney'.[28] His work had contributed to the very existence of international relations as a university subject. But not being academic – something he never set himself up to be – was the charge brought against him from that day on, as international relations, or International Relations, flourished as a university discipline. He did not append scholarly apparatus, he did not refer to the latest publications in the field, he used arguments from his own experience, from different disciplines, and from no disciplines at all.[29]

There were always academics, such as the poet William Empson, dedicated to breaking down barriers between the expert and the outsider; Empson went so far as to suggest that excessive specialisation was a threat to civil liberties.[30] But for the generality of Academe, the role of the public intellectual was performed only within Academe, in compliance with its restricted codes and conventions. Leonard Woolf was not the only writer to find himself disregarded in the second half of the

---

28 *The Journey . . .*

29 For a relatively sympathetic assessment see Peter Wilson, *The International Theory of Leonard Woolf: A Study in Twentieth-Century Idealism* Palgrave Macmillan 2003

30 See John Haffenden, *William Empson* Vol 1 *Among the Mandarins* OUP 2005

twentieth century, as the dons distanced themselves from the private scholar, the independent writer, the generalist.

In book reviews, articles, and short, single-issue books Leonard Woolf was terse. But writing *Principia Politica*, he was a dog let off the lead, running ahead, doubling back, following seductive trails. His faults, as a writer with a programme, had always been repetition, digression, and above all too much narrative political history as back-story. That is why he represented to some critics the 'Whig view of history'[31] – tracing a chain of cause and effect, with 'progress' through cataclysmic change – while himself asserting 'that I have never believed in the inevitability of progress or that man is politically rational'.[32] Indeed, his work is loud with howls of despair over the repetitions of fatal errors and the irrationality of politicians. The title of the book pressed upon him by Keynes did him no favours, eliciting unflattering comparisons with Isaac Newton, Bertrand Russell and G.E.Moore.

Leonard Woolf described *Principia Politica* in his preface as partly autobiographical and partly a study of the eternal struggle between liberty and authoritarianism, which in his case, though he would never say so, had an autobiographical subtext. He revisited in his text the concept of communal psychology, always located in the ideas and conventions prevailing shortly before one's own birth, and he acknowledged that 'like the little church at the end of my garden, I am a social and political anachronism, and so are my neighbours.' He expressed, in his account of how the world had changed, a tender fondness for the village of Rodmell and its outmoded values and behaviours.

He defended the unfashionable term 'civilisation' as indicating the intellectual, spiritual, legal and artistic values which give a viable framework to life, with inevitable and lengthy reference to the Greeks and a salutary stress on the importance of keeping religion out of politics in the interest of communal sanity. He emphasised the satisfying and sufficient pleasure of 'ordinary people' in their ordinary lives, in contrast to the 'crazy nightmare' that religion, especially the Christian stress on sin

31 Herbert Butterfield, in *The Whig View of History* (1931) had described and demolished this orientation.

32 *Downhill* . . .

and Hell (he was writing in the early 1950s) had over the centuries imposed on their mentalities. He quoted largely and lazily from his own book *Barbarians at the Gate.*

Authoritarians and dictators, he argued, employed the double-edged sword of ideology and emotional appeal, neither on its own quite doing the trick. They played on man's capacity for hatred, stronger even than fear. His already discussed chapter on the training of animals illustrated the efficacy of affect and self-interest in civilising both men and beasts. Unwilling to embrace despair, he saw 'a ray of hope' in free expression, scepticism, and the exercise of reason. (But people do not become reasonable by being hectored about how reasonable it is to be reasonable.)

The best parts of the book are inspirational and interestingly idiosyncratic, as well as intellectually attractive. If *Principia Politica* had been ruthlessly trimmed; if the chosen tone had been less magisterial, and the arguments less bulked out with historical instances; if Leonard Woolf had actually addressed the problem of power and what the community might do to contain the law-breakers, the ideologues and demagogues, and to harness the creative-destructive universe of irrational passion and emotion which he conceded to be so potent, then this would have been a spiritual and socio-political classic. Since it was not a scholarly book by the standards of academe, it should find its place among the odd, the unique, the inimitable. But *Principia Politica* remains mired in its grandiose title and aspiration.

What remained to intellectuals outside the closed shop of Academe were the higher journalism and the personal and political memoir. Leonard had always excelled at the first, and in the last decade of his life was to triumph definitively with the second. He was moving in that direction in *Principia Politica*, and began working towards the first volume of his autobiography in 1952, before *Principia Politica* was published.

In a paper he gave to the Memoir Club in 1952 Leonard spoke of Bloomsbury as history. Its downfall 'was its intolerance of everyone and everything which was not all the time amusing . . . Just as one hesitated in Moore's rooms at Cambridge to say anything amusing which was not also profound and true, so in Bloomsbury one hesitated to say anything true or profound unless it was also amusing.' He was, he said, amazed that he had ended up with the people in that room, since his genetic and social origins were so different from theirs (something to which he might not have drawn attention when he was young). 'My father's father was a Jew born in London . . . ', and he segued into a passage to be included verbatim in his first volume of autobiography, *Sowing*.

He temporarily abandoned the autobiographical project, disheartened, after the negative reception of both *Principia Politica* and, to a lesser extent, of *A Writer's Diary*, his selection from Virginia's journals. His eczema became so raw and agonising that he went into the Harley Street Nursing Home for five nights in April 1954 for intensive treatment. The month after his book appeared he suffered another assault in the form of a devastating letter from his brother Edgar, who had just read both *A Writer's Diary* and *Principia Politica*: 'It is not for me to question the decency of a man selling his wife's tragedy for gold . . . In your own book you go out of your way to disparage and hold up to ridicule our family, not because it has anything to do with the argument of your book, but because you think it adds somehow to your stature . . .' There was worse to come:

> As a boy you were mean and a bully – not that I ever allowed you to bully me, but Herbert and Harold did.
>
> I saw little of you until I went to Sweden with you in 1911, when I realized how mean you were in your outlook. After that I have seen little of you.
>
> You showed what a cad you were when you published the *Wise Virgins* – after solemnly promising not to! Desmond MacCarthy's idea of a masterpiece!
>
> Unfortunately people know I am your brother and I have the greatest objection to other people being given a lying and utterly caddish picture of our parents and our home. And I believe on good evidence you have done the same thing before.
>
> Having always been the lickspittle of greater intellects, you suffer from the deformity of the little man, who thinks it makes him greater to cry out 'See how I have risen above my degraded beginnings.'

> Unfortunately with your mean nature you'll go on the same way and delight in causing pain to all of us. But Virginia's Diary shows you up for what you are better than any words of mine.[33]

Philip, who had heard 'rumblings from 'poor E[dgar] – he can't help it', was also the recipient of the odd nasty letter from Edgar. 'I always treat him as not far from certifiable. No I could find nothing offensive to our family dignity [in *Principia Politica*]. Of course I only knew us in the shabby gentility of Putney. The criticism I personally would make is that you gave no weight to the fact of our being Jewish, which I believe is all-important. But I think we disagree on this: I remember that we took opposite views of the Palestinian situation when the Jews were liquidating the mandatory power, and I was metaphorically waving the Israeli flag.'[34]

The novelist and poet Naomi Mitchison, who had invited Leonard to her family home in Scotland the first Christmas after Virginia's death (he did not go), wrote that when reading *A Writer's Diary* what struck her was 'what a wonderful person you must have been to be married to'.[35] Isaiah Berlin wrote movingly about Virginia in the *Sunday Times*, eliciting a warm exchange between himself and Leonard. But *A Writer's Diary* like *Principia Politica* attracted some adverse reviews.

Leonard had from the beginning undertaken it 'with hesitation and misgiving',[36] reflected in his brusque cut-and-paste methods: he snipped the passages he chose (40,000 words) out of the carbon-copy pages of the typed-up diaries, sent them to the printer, and stuffed the remnants into manila envelopes. He said very little, even to Trekkie, about his disappointments over the two publications, though she realised he had to 'draw heavily on his extraordinary reserves not to be depressed.'[37]

Ian and Trekkie Parsons moved from Ifield in 1954, buying Juggs Corner, a comfortable 1930s house with a two-acre garden on the edge

---

33 27 Nov 1953
34 4 Dec 1953
35 nd. 1954
36 Anne Olivier Bell, *Editing Virginia Woolf's Diary* Bloomsbury Worship 1990
37 Diary 11 Nov 1953

of the village of Kingston, twenty-five minutes walk from Rodmell. Her talent for decorative effects was as developed as Vanessa and Duncan's; the house was light and bright, with a quirky colour sense which made her rooms unlike other people's. Her taste continued to modify the austere tradition of Monks House, with curled pile carpet and Cole's wallpaper upstairs. The interior walls on the ground floor, constructed of matchboard and asbestos sheeting, were plastered and painted. In the summer that Trekkie and Ian bought Juggs Corner, Leonard had the ultimate in conservatories erected at Monks House. It was a lean-to, stretching across two thirds of the garden side of the house, with the doors to hall and kitchen cutting through it, and extending upwards to enclose the first floor windows.

He had another new neighbour: of all people, Kingsley Martin. He and his partner Dorothy Woodman 'suddenly bought an odd-shaped cottage on the top of the Downs', called Hilltop. More than twenty years before, when it was built, the *New Statesman* had published 'a strong paragraph written by Leonard Woolf denouncing the vandal who had been wicked enough to build a house so high on the Downs.'[38] It was characteristically naïve of Kingsley to write to Leonard: 'It is exciting to think that we are going to live so near to you, and in such a spot.'[39] He apologised to Leonard, not without digs of reproach, for his part in their 'wrangles'. Leonard too apologised; although 'I always intend to follow Christ's teaching, Jehovah always breaks through.'[40] In 1956 they had, inevitably, a row over the Suez Crisis. President Nasser of Egypt nationalised the Suez Canal (whose main shareholders were the British and the French) and closed it to Israeli shipping. Britain and France, backed by the Soviet Union and opposed by the United States, attacked Egypt. Kingsley Martin in the *New Statesman* supported the policy of aggression. Leonard was emphatically against it, writing that the Left had lost the courage of 'what were' its convictions, and was encouraging dangerous thuggery.

His political activity lessened on the domestic front. A rising star in the

---

38 Kingsley Martin, *Editor: A Second Volume of Autobiography* Hutchinson 1968
39 18 Nov 1954
40 3 Aug 1956

International Bureau, and the International Secretary of the Labour Party, was Denis Healey, future Foreign Secretary and Chancellor of the Exchequer, fresh out of the army. Leonard had a hand in Healey's rise: 'Laski and I often backed a winner together. Thus I remember him and myself combining to back Denis Healey, out of a long short list, to be the new International Secretary . . . Clearly he had great talent.'[41] Healey was a devotee of Virginia Woolf's novels, and 'the great benefit of joining the Bureau', for him, was meeting Leonard Woolf. To the young man, Leonard looked even 'older than his years, a frail, trembling figure with a long brown face wrinkled like a tortoise, the inevitable brown tweed suit and knitted tie, his shock of hair still profuse, but grey.'[42]

Leonard was intrigued by show-business as he never was by the aristocracy. In 1952 he gave Bella Spewack, joint author of *Kiss Me Kate*, a five-year option on Virginia's *Orlando* for stage and film. Bella Spewack came to see him at Rodmell in June 1954, and they exchanged warm letters. 'I guarantee you'll see Orlando on the boards and with pleasure',[43] she typed in capital letters from 930 Fifth Avenue. Nothing ever came of it.

He had new friends in similar lines of business. Rodmell was no longer just an agricultural village. The Russian-born screenwriter and producer Sergei Nolbandov, then at the height of his career in British cinema, made his home in Rodmell from 1950 and became a friend. Another new Rodmell resident was Benjamin Frankel and his second wife Anna, who bought the large house called Rodmell Hill, on the other side of the Newhaven road. Frankel was a prolific composer: film music, chamber works, symphonies, a mass, jazz and revue, and songs. The Frankels exchanged visits and dinners with Leonard, and with the Parsons, as frequently as did the Nolbandovs. From April 1955 Anna Frankel began visiting Leonard without her husband at the weekends, when Trekkie was at Juggs Corner with Ian. The intimacy got out of hand.

Trekkie and Ian were in Majorca for most of May 1955. A letter from

41 Loose scrap of typescript, n.d.
42 Denis Healey, *The Time of My Life* Michael Joseph 1989
43 12 Aug 1954

Anna Frankel to Leonard tells its own story. 'Darling love, I was so utterly delighted to get your letter – I've been so homesick for you if you know what I mean. . . Darling sweetheart I can't come until late (12) on Friday evening as we are dining in town. . . If I don't get a ring, Ben will drive me round your way from the station and if there is a light outside I shall come in. I expect you will be horribly tired so if you want to go to bed *please do*. I'm entirely free on Saturday so if Friday is at all difficult don't bother – Saturday is yours anyway from mid-day to midnight. My dearest love to you, Anna.' Leonard left this among his papers along with Mrs Anna Frankel's visiting card, which had accompanied a present, probably a watch: 'For my dear love in memory of wonderful days and hoping it won't always show 6.30.'

He continued to see both Frankels until there was a bust-up, presumably about himself and Anna. When in July 1956 Ben Frankel sent Leonard his subscription to the Rodmell Horticultural Society, he expressed regret that Leonard had not accepted any of his recent invitations. Leonard replied: 'In many ways I would like to see you if we could be on easy terms, but I doubt if we can. After the "days of trouble" we agreed to meet on ordinary terms and I came twice or more. But I felt it to be extremely uncomfortable and painful both to you and Anna and to me. I am not blaming anyone – after what had happened, it was and is probably inevitable.' The Frankels left the village in 1958.

By this time Leonard and Trekkie had made another close friend in the milieu which increasingly interested him. The actor Peggy Ashcroft, whom Leonard had admired on the stage for twenty years, with her second husband Jeremy Hutchinson (Mary Hutchinson's barrister son), rented country houses in the Lewes area and became familiar visitors at Monks House and Juggs Corner. In November 1959 Leonard and Trekkie went to see Peggy Ashcroft playing Rebecca in Ibsen's *Rosmersholm*. Leonard had helped her think her way into the part, lending her a copy of Freud's essay about the play, 'Character Types'. 'I immediately discussed it with George [Devine, the director] and said I wanted to make it the centre of my interpretation.'[44] Leonard never saw

44 Quoted in Michael Billington, *Peggy Ashcroft* John Murray 1988

her on stage without writing her a perceptively praising note afterwards. Leonard despised success, 'though I want to have it', because 'most of the successful people one knows are very despicable'.[45] Peggy Ashcroft was a shining exception.

From the early 1950s, Leonard opened the garden to the public for charity on one day every year under the National Gardens Scheme.[46] Leonard's garden was a honey-trap, the place where he himself, with his dogs and cats, was at ease. Leonard in his garden enchanted children, adolescents – and women.

Anna Frankel was not the only one to be affected. His withheld sexuality had always been one source of his attraction. A visiting friend of his neighbour Evelyn Pember wrote to 'Dear Mr Woolf' in June 1956: 'I expect you don't know that I have always cared for you since I first met you, and you looked at me over the wheelbarrow. But I was unfortunately 68 on my last birthday, and you, I imagined, were somewhere in your fifties. It is not easy for me to write this; but I thought I would like you to know. Goodbye, my dear, and all my blessings.' Leonard wrote a short, graceful letter in reply, mostly about their mutual friend Mrs Pember: 'Unfortunately she has obviously never learned the great truth which should be written in letters of gold over every front door NOTHING MATTERS. . .I wish I were in my fifties, but I am 75 – not that that matters of course.'

Whether or not she observed the effects of Leonard's magnetism, and whether or nor she minded, 1957 and 1958 were difficult years for Trekkie Parsons. 'I am more and more filled with a sense of failure – in a way, a failure to produce anything, and failure in relationships.'[47] In the spring of 1958 she enjoyed, or endured, one of her usual double holidays – two weeks in northern France with Ian, who flew off home a couple of hours before Leonard arrived to join her. It was cold, and they went back earlier than planned. Trekkie had not, she felt, fallen between two stools, but 'have

---

45 To Alice Cameron 17 Jan 1962

46 The beneficiaries of the scheme were and are the Queen's Institute of District Nursing.

47 Diary 7 March 1958. Quoted in *Love Letters*

sat with half of my behind on a different stool – painting and human relationships', and both had collapsed, 'eaten away by wood worm'. She then cut out of her diary twenty-five pages, leaving only: 'I cry when I think of Ian and but for the tears feel like a dry river bed . . . I wish I could force myself not to think and think of what I hate to think of.'[48]

What she hated to think of was Ian's affair with Norah Smallwood. Trekkie just could not bear it when, for example, Norah turned up as if by coincidence when she was away with Ian. She was open with Leonard about this misery, in an ironic way. Leonard was her 'oasis'. His love sustained her. But Ian was the mainspring of her life.

The Woolf family continued its downward spiral. They knew one another's peculiarities, helped sort things out, and discussed it as little as possible. Philip, in his mid-sixties, retired from his position as agent to the Waddesdon estate at the end of 1953 and bought the mediaeval Gaulden Manor, near Lydeard St Lawrence in deepest Somerset, famous for its great hall decorated with seventeenth-century plasterwork. There were large gardens, and a lot of land, on which he put cows. The work was hard, and his wife Babs, who had rheumatoid arthritis, was depressed by the move. In September 1955 she walked into a pond and came home soaking wet – a circumstance with a heavy resonance for Leonard. Early next morning Philip came in from milking the cows and 'found her hanging from the staircase, her Alsatian dog's chain round her neck'.[49] Philip's position on suicide – that, however terrible, it was everyone's right – was the same as Leonard's. But if he grieved for his wife as Leonard grieved for his, he did not show it.

Philip was the legal guardian of his great-niece Sally, the errant Mollie's daughter. In April 1956 Mollie, who had changed her name to Diana, met the writer and actor Julian Maclaren-Ross,[50] and embarked

48 Diary 11 and 12 April 1958. Quoted in *Love Letters*

49 Marie Beesley, 'The Wilderness', unpublished memoir.

50 See Paul Willetts, *Fear and Loathing in Fitzrovia: the Bizarre Life of Writer, Actor, Soho Dandy Julian Maclaren-Ross* Dewi Lewis 2003, and J.Maclaren-Ross, *Memoirs of the Forties* Alan Ross 1965: in the early 1940s, Tambimuttu had 'some forlorn hope' that lovely seventeen-year-old Diane [*sic*] might persuade her Uncle Leonard to put money into his magazine *Poetry London*.

on a bohemian existence of moonlight flits, unpaid bills, and public drunken rows. Mollie/Diana had a son in 1957, upon which she and Maclaren-Ross were married. (He was her third husband. There had been a second failed marriage.) Philip refused to allow Sally to go to her mother even for Christmas. This caused bitterness.

Leonard never stopped thinking about Virginia. There was his own Virginia, and there was the world's Virginia. From the end of her life to the end of his, he received requests from researchers and students from all over the world, wanting to correspond with him, interview him, about Virginia Woolf. They sent him abstracts of their theses and dissertations for comment, e.g. (from a German): 'II I a) Impressionismus, Sensualismus, Symbolismus.' Some, such as Professor John Graham of the University of Western Ontario, whom Leonard first met in England in the mid 1950s, were people to whom he related as to any intelligent friend.

He was scrupulous in replying to researchers, dealing with factual questions straightforwardly. Sometimes the questions made no sense to him, as is evidenced by his reply to a request for 'philosophical material' on Virginia's 'mystical experience, the problem of reality and the integration of consciousness': 'What is the kind of material which you have in mind? I rather doubt whether there is any in existence which would reveal the sources of the ideas to which you refer.'[51] He had continually to respond to people taught to believe that artists such as his wife built on a theoretical infrastructure, and that the work could best be explicated by winkling out literary 'influences'. The 'influence' which Leonard was most frequently asked to confirm was that of the French philosopher Henri Bergson.[52] 'I doubt whether Mrs Woolf had read any Bergson'; 'I do not think that Mrs Woolf ever read Bergson at all or was influenced by him.' No, Virginia Woolf had never read her sister-in-law Karin Stephen's *The Misuse of Mind: A Study of Bergson's Attack on Intellectualism*, 'indeed the one type of book which she hardly ever read was the philosophical and the metaphysical.'

---

51 30 Aug 1950
52 LW included a critique of Bergson as an 'intellectual quack' in *Quack, Quack!*

'Virginia Woolf never met Dorothy Richardson but thought her an interesting writer'; 'there was no correspondence between Mrs Woolf and James Joyce', and no, she had not read Frazer's *The Golden Bough*, 'or not much of it'. 'My wife certainly never read Plotinus.' And no, it was unlikely that she ever read Rabindranath Tagore. 'I do not think that my wife ever read anything of Jung.' 'She was interested in psychoanalysis in a vague and general way, but I don't think she had any very definite views about it.' 'I do not think that Virginia Woolf ever really studied Freud [she first read him in 1939], though she must have looked at a good many books that we published', and she had been 'greatly impressed by him as a person when we went to see him.'

This was the other point that he had to get over to the scholars: his wife had known many of the figures mooted as 'influences', but as friends or acquaintances. She often knew more about their table manners and love lives than she did about their intellectual processes, and did not always read their books. Yes, wrote Leonard, she knew Wittgenstein: 'He stayed with Maynard Keynes one summer in a house near here and we saw a certain amount of him then. My wife did not go to his lectures . . .'

Scholars and students expected as of right to examine his wife's letters and diaries, have two-hour sessions of discussion with him, or require him to fill in questionnaires. He saw almost everyone who applied – for fifteen or twenty minutes, while he summed them up. With some he co-operated fully. It was his responsibility, as her husband, publisher and literary executor, to serve Virginia's literary afterlife. He remained courteous in circumstances where roars of outrage would have been appropriate, and was rarely more than crisp – though sometimes disingenuous, as to Professor Suzanne Henig: 'I do not think it is possible for anyone to know what first gave her the idea of the change of sex in *Orlando*.'[53] And to Jacqueline Latham, in answer to queries about *Mrs Dalloway*: 'I doubt whether there is much of anyone in Septimus or his wife. I am not sure who L. could be, it could be

53 22 Feb 1967

myself.'[54] He defended his wife's copyrights strictly, but not for money. If he approved of the work, he did not charge.

Then came the acquirers of manuscripts. Miss Frances Hamill (without, this first time, her business partner Mrs Margery Barker) came to lunch with Leonard in August 1956.

Hamill and Barker were persuasive and professional. They had been in business since 1928, dealing in manuscripts and rare books from 230 North Michigan Avenue, Chicago. Leonard agreed to sell them for £15,000 eleven items – early drafts of Virginia's novels – provided they were bought *en bloc* by either Harvard or Yale, and made available to students.

Leonard was impressed by the American students who came over to work on their theses, especially by Mary Lyon, doing her PhD at Radcliffe College on 'Virginia Woolf as a Critic', to whom he first gave lunch at the Cliffords Inn Restaurant on 8 December 1955. Soon she was helping him as well as herself, identifying the reviews Virginia had written for *The Times Literary Supplement*, to be collected for publication. They sustained a lively correspondence, and when Mary Lyon married in 1958, the year in which the Hogarth Press published Virginia Woolf's collection of essays *Granite and Rainbow*, she brought her husband to meet him, and he gave her a Trekkie Ritchie painting of cows. He never came across a similar dedication and intelligence in British students, as he told Philip, 'and I feel that if the MSS went to Cambridge or Oxford, they would be stuffed away somewhere . . . and shown from time to time to the public open under a glass case', whereas at Harvard or Yale they would be made available to students.

Hamill and Barker reported back in early 1957 that neither Harvard nor Yale would pay his price unless the originals of the diaries were included. Leonard agreed to include the diaries in the sale for $50,000, on condition that they remained in his possession for his lifetime, and that he retained the copyright, which he was leaving jointly to Angelica and Quentin. Harvard and Yale remaining unmoved, Hamill and

54 8 Sep 1965. In VW's Notebooks in the Berg Collection, NYPL, Septimus's wife Rezia is to be 'founded on L'.

Barker proposed to buy the material themselves, paying £12,500 in three instalments, to include the originals of the diaries. Leonard agreed, again with the stricture that they must be sold on only to a first-class university or library, and that the physical diaries (and the copyright) remain with him for his lifetime. He packed Virginia's diaries into two suitcases and deposited them in the Westminster Bank in Lewes, keeping the top copies of the typed-out versions in the cabinet at the foot of the stairs leading up to his study. In autumn 1958 Hamill and Barker negotiated the sale of the diaries to the Berg Collection in New York Public Library.[55]

The interest in Virginia Woolf and her friends and family having intensified after the publication of *A Writer's Diary*, the first of innumerable studies of her life and work began to appear. Leonard's article 'What is Bloomsbury?', in the third issue of *Encounter* in September 1954, was a review of J.K.Johnstone's *The Bloomsbury Group: A Study of E.M.Forster, Lytton Strachey, Virginia Woolf and their Circle.* Leonard gave his permission for John Lehmann to quote from Virginia's letters to him in his autobiography, and also on a BBC Third Programme item, 'Working with Virginia Woolf'. In October 1955 he approved of the way Jill Balcon, actor and second wife of C.Day-Lewis, read *Mrs Dalloway* on the radio, addressing her in his letter as 'My Dear Degenerate'. Other radio features about Virginia Woolf followed, and sometimes Leonard contributed.

Bloomsbury, as myth and idea, had moved into the public domain. Already their youthful selves were becoming unreal, 'people in books', while their elderly selves clung to the ownership of the past. Pippa Strachey wrote from 51 Gordon Square on 28 December 1951: 'We have been lost to each other, dear Leonard, for too long. Do let us put an end to it . . . I think of a day when we sat and conversed on the trunk of a fallen tree before you went to Ceylon and I wonder at all we have had and lost since then.'

They were harvesting the past, unsure what to display and what to

---

55 Properly the Henry W. and Albert A.Berg Collection of English and American Literature.

lock away. By autumn 1952 James Strachey had the correspondence between his brother Lytton and Virginia arranged chronologically and microfilmed, and he and Leonard thought of bringing out a jointly edited volume. The letters were 'perhaps a bit disappointing', James reported, 'though there are *some* interesting and amusing things.' But when he re-read the correspondence he found it 'a bit light-weight', and was doubtful.

But Leonard was in favour of publishing, and the Hogarth Press brought out *Virginia Woolf & Lytton Strachey: Letters* in the summer of 1956, with some names concealed, and James lamenting the necessary omission of 'some of the more atrocious pages'. Many readers agreed with Olivier Bell that the book was 'a great mistake',[56] showing Virginia and Lytton at their most affected and malicious. Bella was outraged by the revelation of the 'contempt' that Virginia had for the Woolf family. Vita was amazed, and her husband Harold Nicolson appalled, by the 'silliness, dirtiness and cattishness'. He and Vita thought that the selection misrepresented Virginia – but then they thought of her as unworldly, almost holy.

Leonard wrote to Tom Eliot that 'the whole subject of Virginia's letters has become very difficult. I should very much like to examine the ones which you have with a view to a volume of letters.'[57] As he explained to Morgan Forster, 'I have had a lot of trouble with people who want to publish her letters in various kinds of books and I think the moment has come when it would be simpler to publish a selection myself.'[58] He was asking their friends not to allow her letters to them to be published separately.[59]

Vita Sackville-West had formed a strong link with the American writer Aileen Pippett. In January 1955 she sent Leonard the proofs of her book about Virginia, *The Moth and the Star*, in which Vita had allowed her to quote copiously from Virginia's letters. Leonard was very angry. He had been promised a sight of the first draft, and of the completed

---

56 Anne Olivier Bell, *Editing Virginia Woolf's Diaries* Bloomsbury Workshop 1990
57 2 April 1955
58 28 Sept 1955
59 To TSE 2 April 1955

typescript. Neither had been forthcoming. He had never given his permission for the quotations, and did not propose to do so now. He had never even seen Virginia's letters to Vita. He stopped publication in the UK, but allowed it to go ahead in the USA, earning a grateful letter from Aileen Pippett's husband. Vita, in her turn, fulminated against Leonard's selling Virginia's manuscripts to America. 'What an odd man he is. Well, they shan't have *Mrs Dalloway* or *Orlando*; it would give me great pleasure to refuse some enormous offer, and tell Leonard that I had done so.'[60] She had been to see Leonard at Monk's House, 'rather sad, thinking of Virginia, and seeing Mrs Parsons more or less in her place.'[61]

During 1955 and 1956, Leonard was calling in Virginia's letters (including those to Vita), getting them typed, altering some names to X and Y, and returning them to their recipients, many of whom were nervous about the intimacy of Virginia's letters, and her malice. Vita proposed having Virginia's letters to herself privately printed, in a single volume, edited by her. Leonard shrewdly suggested that she did the editing work, and then let him see the typescript. Clive Bell, having reread Virginia's letters to himself, told Leonard: 'You won't be surprised to hear that all are brilliant and that the later ones are scurrilous to a degree . . . I fear they are at present unpublishable.'[62] The price of a gossip culture, dedicated to indiscretion, was turning out to be high. Maynard's brother, Geoffrey Keynes, confided in Leonard that half of Rupert Brooke's letters, which he was going through as literary executor, were now 'under seal at King's, and will never be published as far as I am concerned. They are painful and incoherent, almost mad, and really add nothing to the picture, so that I don't see that they need be published at all.'[63]

*

60 Vita died in 1963. When it was announced in *The Times* that the manuscript of *Mrs Dalloway* had been bought by the British Museum, her elder son Ben Nicolson wrote to Leonard: 'Naturally I was only delighted that it should find such a secure home.'

61 To Alvilde Lees-Milne July 1956

62 6 Aug 1955

63 20 Jan 1956

In late April 1957 Leonard and Trekkie went for ten days to Israel – the first and only visit that Leonard ever made. Leonard was never a Zionist. 'From the first moment of the Balfour Declaration [1912] I was against Zionism', he wrote, 'on the grounds that to introduce Jews into an Arab occupied territory with the ultimate prospect of establishing an independent Jewish state would lead to racial trouble.'[64] In the 1920s he had argued this strongly against the convictions of his friend the historian Lewis Namier, who sent him to have a talk with Chaim Weizmann, chief advocate of Zionism in Britain and future first President of Israel. Over three decades of political journalism, in which Leonard commented exhaustively on world events, he wrote only charily about the 'tangle', as he called it, in Palestine.

In Israel, less than a decade after the founding of the state and a year after the violence and bloodshed of the Sinai Campaign, Leonard was exhilarated. He loved the heat and sparkle of the climate, and the effervescence of the people on the streets of Tel Aviv, which reminded him of the 'busy buzz of productive ecstasy' around a beehive. Everything pleased him except the manifestations of religious orthodoxy. Finding himself in an area 'frequented by those unshaven, long-haired orthodox Jews, young men whose self-conscious, self-righteous hair and orthodoxy fill me with despair', he followed a sign to the Zoo. The long-haired monkeys seemed to gaze at him with the same self-satisfaction as the Orthodox, 'who have learned eternal truth from the primeval monkey, all the scribes and Pharisees who spend their lives making mountains of pernicious stupidity out of molehills of nonsense'. He developed with maximum intemperance a Woolfian diatribe about how the 'absurd delusions of savages' had throughout history been promoted as divine truths in order to protect the vested interests of ignorance and injustice. 'To see this process once more repeated in modern Israel is horrifying.'

The ability of believers to believe always threw Leonard Woolf into a state somewhere beyond rage and despair, and this passage in *Downhill all the Way*, exploding out of a section on zoos he had visited worldwide, earned him pained letters from readers. Their next stop was Haifa, and

64 4 April 1968 to Archbishop Fisher

the Panorama Hotel. After this visit, Leonard every year ordered boxes of oranges and grapefruits direct from Haifa through the Israel Citrus Gift Box Export Service, to be sent to friends for Christmas.

Leonard had known in Rodmell a man called Welsman, a member of the Rodmell Labour Party.[65] He lived for more than twenty-five years at Rodmell Hill (before the Nolbandovs), and worked for a shipping company in London. In the early 1950s he left England to join a kibbutz. He and Leonard kept in touch. Mr Welsman was now called Avraham Ben-Yosef, and when Leonard and Trekkie's itinerary took them to Safad, Leonard realised that Sasa Kibbutz, where Avraham Ben-Yosef worked as a shepherd, was only sixteen miles away. They hired a taxi and went to see him, and he made a return visit to dine with them, bringing a suitcase of books and pamphlets to show to Leonard. It was only when Avraham was leaving that Leonard understood that this man, who had led a sedentary life in England, had walked the sixteen miles into Safad, and proposed to walk the sixteen miles back home through the mountains that night.[66]

Leonard came home with three vivid memories of Galilee. One was of Avraham Ben-Yosef setting off on foot in the dark with his heavy suitcase. The second was of the wadi below Safad, 'so packed with wild flowers that we found twenty or thirty different species within the space of a few yards'. The third was of an unending army of small crabs climbing resolutely up the stairs of their hotel in Tiberias. On 9 May they were back in London, dining with Ian at the Goring Hotel, just round the corner from Victoria Square – the 'boring Goring' as Trekkie called it.

The visit meant a great deal to Leonard. Israel's atmosphere reminded him of London during the Blitz. 'It is impossible anywhere in

---

65 Collection of Minutes of Rodmell and Iford Labour Party, 17 Oct 1947, at Monks House: 'Mr Welsman's suggestion that German prisoners of war should be invited to attend meetings was welcomed. Mr [Quentin] Bell then opened a discussion on the present controversy regarding the length of women's skirts. No minutes were taken.'

66 Avraham Ben-Yosef returned to England twice subsequently, and visited Leonard on both occasions. In the late 1960s he left Israel to live in a commune in Japan, where he married, and changed his name to Moishe Matsuba.

Israel', he wrote, 'ever to forget that it is a small country surrounded by a ring of violently hostile Arab states, and people who consider themselves to be perpetually at war with, and pledged to destroy, Israel.'[67] In *Downhill All the Way*, written in the year of the Six-Day War, he effectively repudiated the anti-Zionist beliefs of his youth, stating that 'you must not act upon a situation which no longer exists, but upon the facts that face one. When the Jewish National Home and hundreds of thousands of Jews had been established in Palestine, when Hitler was killing millions of Jews in Europe, when the Arabs declared their intention of destroying Israel and the Israelis, Zionism and anti-Zionism had become irrelevant.' With terrorism escalating along Israel's borders, he saw the situation as 'so appalling and so delicate that no one ought to say anything to incite either side to further violence.'[68]

He had become unwell towards the end of the trip to Israel, with a cyst in his mouth. At this painful juncture, Vita came back to him about the publication of her letters from Virginia. Leonard agreed to take a look at them. Vita was sharp: 'I do hope that they will not get disarranged again as it took well over a week to put them right. You will remember that you had withdrawn some of them and I fear the result was rather a muddle.'[69] More than two months passed before Leonard told Vita he had let Ian Parsons and Norah Smallwood see the letters; and the collective decision was negative. Vita was not pleased. 'I am afraid I cannot resist saying that I feel they would go far towards undoing any harm to Virginia's reputation that may have been done by other books.'[70] She was referring, not kindly, to the reception of *A Writer's Diary* and of the Virginia/Lytton letters.

Leonard was well aware that the exposure Bloomsbury had been getting, and in some cases seeking, was counterproductive. As he wrote to Vita, he felt that 'there has been too much washing of intimate Bloomsbury linen lately', leading to 'the inevitable turn of the tide

---

67 *The Journey* . . .
68 *Ibid*
69 21 June 1957
70 25 Sept 1957

against what is called Bloomsbury'.[71] Bunny Garnett published in 1955 his memoir *The Flowers of the Forest.* Clive Bell followed up the next year with *Old Friends.* The selling-point of both books was the vivid pen-portraiture of members of the Bloomsbury circle. Chatto & Windus published them, which means that Leonard was complaisant. But when in 1959 Bunny suggested to Leonard a book of Bloomsbury Group photographs over three generations, Leonard was against the idea. 'It would be met by the usual chorus of anti-Bloomsburiensis, which is more virulent among reviewers than elsewhere . . . But apart from that it would have a slight taste of the kind of "publicity" I don't much like.'

In the 1950s he was targeted, emotionally and at long distance, by another woman obsessed initially with Virginia as a writer, and then with him as a man. Again, he became a repository of fantasies, which blossomed in the climate of his implacable calm and his few words. There are at least five hundred letters in Leonard's archive from Angela Levine, a youngish married woman living in Los Angeles, who had read everything Virginia had written and nearly all his own books. Again, he answered in a kindly, formal manner; and he sent her gingko seeds. Her letters veered between streams of consciousness on household matters in the mode of a less privileged Mrs Dalloway, and intimate raillery which betrayed a level of delusion. In her flights of fancy, she exactly mimicked Virginia's fantastical manner. 'I hope you will not mind me saying', Leonard wrote to her on 22 August 1958, 'that I am sure that I should not write to you or you to me. I am sure that it is not good for you. I think that you should quite seriously write a novel, taking it seriously and not writing to me until you have finished it.' And she most certainly should not come and see him, which is what she was proposing.

It is said[72] that Mrs Levine flew in from the USA with a potted plant, found her way to Rodmell, left the plant on his front doorstep, and went straight home again. This was worrying: 'When you first wrote to

71 27 Sept 1957

72 By Frederic Spotts, who heard it from Trekkie. *Letters of Leonard Woolf* Harcourt Brace Jovanovich 1989

me I thought you were amusing yourself with a joke and I answered, wrongly I see now, in the same vein.' This crisis over, the correspondence resumed. She meant something to him. When in early 1963 he failed to hear from her, he sent a note of enquiry. She replied: 'Thank you for the love letter. It was too. You were worried about me.'[73] And the following month: 'I am thinking about you – it seems I have been thinking about you, constantly, for five years . . . I have a small, unfurnished room in my brain labelled Mr Woolf; since it is the only one wired for electricity, I naturally spend a great deal of time there.' She came three times more to Rodmell, twice bringing her family to meet him.

Another correspondent, in 1957, expressed her identification with Virginia: '*The Waves* is my constant companion and means more to me than I could ever hope to convey in words . . . In a way I understand Virginia Woolf almost too well. For I experience similar stresses and personal tensions and "walk a tightrope" most of my life, due to being not quite in the world . . . For at times I commune with her – she becomes a part of me.' It was but a short step from this to 'You are, I am sure, an exceptionally nice person . . .' and thence to all that followed. And there were other women, who became equally fixated, and wrote to him in a similar way, over years.

On 24 October 1958 G.E.Moore, who had been awarded the Order of Merit in 1951, died in Cambridge. He too was eighty-four. Moore was buried in St Giles churchyard, next to Desmond MacCarthy and Ludwig Wittgenstein. Memorialising his friends was becoming habitual for Leonard, the survivor, and he wrote about Moore for *Encounter*. Stephen Spender was delighted with the piece. 'It is one of the best things we have ever published . . . You ought to do a volume of such essay-memoir-portraits.'[74] Leonard's five volumes of autobiography were to be vehicles for many such 'essay-memoir-portraits'.

Some professional friends, such as Leonard's first literary editor Jack Squire, fell into obscurity and poverty. Occupational pensions were

---

73 26 Jan 1963
74 28 Nov 1958

nugatory or non-existent for journalists, and writers and artists did not often make provision for their old age. Many Woolf family members too sank into poverty. There were calls for help, not only from Flora, and small sums changed hands by post regularly. There was Aunt Ada (widow of Leonard's maternal uncle Leman de Jongh), who had suffered a stroke, living with her aged sister in a suburb of Birmingham. Bella had been sending the old ladies ten shillings a week for some years, and Harold proposed sharing with Leonard and Edgar the cost of bringing their income up to twenty-six shillings a week. Leonard responded immediately to all calls for help, even if sometimes with a groan – as when he sent to Bella his five-pound contribution towards a Golden Wedding present for their Danish cousins, Martin and Emma Abrahamson: 'I wish sometimes someone would give me £5 . . .'

On 9 January 1959 Leonard went to Morgan Forster's eightieth birthday dinner at King's. Leonard already knew Noel Annan, since 1956 the Provost of King's, who was working on his book about Virginia's father Leslie Stephen. At the dinner Annan read aloud a sketch written by Lytton Strachey fifty years before, in which 'Cleanthes', a young Cambridge don, lived on the next staircase to 'Socrates' – who was Morgan Forster. Leonard's own Aspasia Papers would have caused even more of a stir.

The primacy for him of the Athens of Pericles and its luminaries received a knock that year when he read Isaiah Berlin's *Two Concepts of Liberty*; he wrote to Berlin, enquiring whether he thought there was the conscious idea of individual liberty in Pericles' Athens, and strongly pressing for an answer in the affirmative. Isaiah Berlin replied that in his opinion the *polis* was the sole source of authority and rights, and that individual rights was a mediaeval idea. Although their attitudes on most topics (including Zionism) had differed, there was respect and liking between them, and in 1959 Leonard commissioned Berlin to write a book for the Hogarth Press. He eventually wrote seven books for the Press – the first, *Vico and Herder*, though not forthcoming until 1976, was dedicated to the memory of Leonard Woolf. Leonard never ceased to brood on ancient Athens. After reading one of Moses Finlay's books on ancient Greece, he asked him: 'What has always puzzled me is how did a person like Socrates live? I have never conceived of him as a landowner or as earning anything professionally.'[75] That was a good and nasty question, replied Professor Finlay. His guess was that Socrates was supported by his friends and disciples.

Leonard rarely changed his obdurate mind. Margery Perham[76] was working on the second volume of her biography of Lord Lugard[77] when she wrote to Leonard to say how much she admired the 'imagination and intellectual courage' of his *Empire and Commerce in Africa*, but wondered whether, looking back, he would be inclined to modify any of his views. It was so long since he wrote the book, replied Leonard, that he did not remember much of what was in it: 'I daresay too that I was unfair to Lugard but not entirely . . . I don't think I can have been altogether wrong about him.'

He did not change his views about colonial self-government. An article he wrote for *Encounter*[78] provoked a hostile letter from a white Rhodesian. Obviously, replied Leonard, Africans would make a mess of governing themselves – but then so, in their own continent, had Europeans. The 1950s saw the atrocious treatment by the British of the Kikuyu rebels in Kenya. The 'obstinate stupidity' of white supremacists in Africa was to Leonard 'staggering'.[79]

In 1959 Leonard resigned his co-editorship of *PQ* while remaining on the board. His autobiography was consuming his energies. In March he was asking James Strachey about his own letters to Lytton. James replied that he had in his possession Leonard's to Lytton from 12 July 1900 to 18 November 1904, and a scattered number between 30 October 1911 and 23 April 1931. 'The mystery is about *your* letters from Ceylon . . . I can remember, unless I am imagining it, reading them. It is possible that you asked for them back and have them somewhere?' Leonard had a

---

75 5 June 1963

76 Reader in Colonial Administration at Oxford and first director of the Institute of Commonwealth Studies.

77 *Lugard: The Years of Adventure 1858–1898* Collins 1956

78 'The Colour of Our Mammies' July 1959

79 To Hugh Dakin 10 Dec 1959

rummage, and was able to tell James he had found 'several packets of letters from and to Lytton between 1904 and 1911. They are the Ceylon letters'[80] – but not so many as there should have been.

He wrote to Edgar, asking if he might include in his autobiography that 'very interesting letter about my character'. Edgar said he could, adding, 'I do not remember what I said exactly' – clearly having no awareness of what a bombshell he had delivered. Leonard wanted to include Edgar's letter because 'if one's writing a truthful autobiography, one ought, I think, to show . . . what one's family thinks of one – and what it is like.'[81]

Bella told him that Philip, after a visit to Monks House, reported finding him gardening 'and looking the picture of contented old age. May you long continue in this beatific state which falls to the lot of so few.' Her husband Tom Southorn had died, and she found life 'without Tom's perfect companionship, and handicapped by glaucoma, almost intolerable.'[82] Flora was living with her, having had a fall and fractured her hand. Bella, now over eighty, moved to 13 Belbroughton Road in north Oxford, and Flora went to live in a hotel in Crowborough, of the 'private residential type' as she described it. Such refuges became her habitat; she drifted from small cheap hotels to guest-houses in the semi-suburban parts of Sussex and Surrey. Bella, she told Leonard, 'really needs someone in the nature of nurse-companion to live with her'.[83] But then so did gallant, hapless, one-eyed Flora. In her early seventies, she had become flotsam. She was mentally unstable – she had a spell in Atkinson Morley's Hospital in south-west London – and poor.

Their brother Philip sold Gaulden Manor in 1959, and bought Wallisford Manor near Wellington, in the same county of Somerset. It may, as he asserted, have been cheaper, but it was still a major country house, and a wild undertaking for an ageing man on his own. Meanwhile Leonard had altercations with Philip's son Cecil about 24

80 11 March 1959
81 31 July 1959
82 24 Nov 1957
83 30 Aug 1958

Victoria Square: 'I was rather shocked by the condition of the basement when I went down there yesterday. What has happened to the dresser?'[84] Cecil replied that it had been temporarily taken out the back because he was redecorating the basement. His girlfriend was moving in with him – Malya Nappi, who acted, and wrote cookery books.

Ian and Trekkie felt the new couple should have a bathroom to themselves, to be incorporated into the ground-floor WC. Ian and Trekkie had an interest in the bathroom arrangements, as they had left 25 Victoria Square, and were renting a first-floor sitting-room and two bedrooms from Leonard at number 24 – moving their own furniture in, 'so that Ian feels at home there',[85] as Trekkie optimistically hoped. Cecil and Malya used to hear Ian pacing up and down, up and down, over their heads. When Leonard needed to spend a night in London, Ian had to vacate his room and sleep at his club.

On 6 August 1959 Leonard went to see Colonel C.H.N. Adams, the senior partner of Adams & Remers, his solicitors in Lewes, about the drafting of a new Will. The main change from his previous Will was that he made 'Marjorie Tulip Parsons (otherwise known as Trekkie Ritchie)' not only his residuary legatee, but his sole executor.

---

84 25 Nov 1959
85 Diary 1 April 1953

17

Letters and Lives

'Ceylon and youth! Youth and the sun and sand and palmyrah palms of Jaffna; youth and the lovely friendly Kandyan villages and villagers up in the mountains; youth and the vast lone and level plain of Hambantota, the unending jungle which tempered in me the love of silence and loneliness. Youth and the jungle!'[1]

Leonard had long wished to revisit Ceylon, since 1948 an independent sovereign state, 'before I was too old to or too dead to do so'.[2] He made the trip, with Trekkie, in 1960, arriving at Katunayaka airport in a BOAC Comet on 10 February. According to the *Daily News* of Ceylon, Leonard joked with the customs officer about getting himself a job in their Civil Service. The press was there to meet 'this slightly built and greying man' (as Leonard was described) and his private secretary (as Trekkie was described); the newspapers reminded readers of the part Leonard Woolf had played at the time of the atrocities perpetrated by the British in 1915. At the Galle Face Hotel in Colombo, Leonard was presented with the five volumes of official diaries he had kept as AGA

1 *The Journey* . . . a deliberately Conradian passage, LW having stated that Ceylon and the jungle were to him what the sea was to Conrad and his sea-captains.

2 *ibid*

in Hambantota by Shelton Fernando, permanent secretary to the Home Ministry, who became a friend. Leonard was already famous for *The Village in the Jungle*; and his official diaries were, by instruction of the Governor, Sir Oliver Goonetilleke, running serially in the *Ceylon Historical Journal*,[3] with extracts in the Ceylon *Daily Mirror*.

Leonard and Trekkie were in Ceylon for eighteen days, and the schedule was punishing for a man of nearly eighty. They met the Governor, and the Prime Minister Dr Wijayananda Dahanayaka, and visited the National Museum. They were driven around the villages of his old district – mostly linked by roads now, not jungle tracks – stayed at the Hambantota Rest House, and went to see the saltpans; and at Bundala, where a lot of people turned out to see him, he was photographed with children. The great tank at Bundala was full of flamingos and pelicans. When Leonard said he wanted to see them fly, a shot was fired into the air and they rose in their thousands.

At the kachcheri in Hambantota where he had put in so many hours he was greeted by an old man who used to accompany him on circuit, and who remembered that he had been fluent in Sinhalese. Leonard spoke, a newspaper reported, 'very softly' from a prepared script, and in between sentences 'he would look at Mrs Parsons'. He looked into the courthouse, where 'the usual murder case' was being heard, and was amused because, twelve years after independence, the proceedings were still being translated into English.

They drove up-country to Bandarawela, Nuwera Eliya, and Kandy, where they stayed as the guest of the Governor in the King's Pavilion, just up the road from the little bungalow which he had occupied as Office Assistant. 'I must admit to the discreditable enjoyment of being treated like a V.I.P. all over Ceylon.'[4] They visited the Botanical Gardens at Peradeniya, where Bella had lived with her first husband. Everywhere they went there was a party and, in Kandy, a performance by local dancers such as he had once arranged for Sir Hugh Clifford's lady friend. They were taken, in pouring rain, to the sacred sites at Sigirya,

3 Vol IX July 1959–April 1960
4 *The Journey* . . .

Polonnowua and Anuradhapura. The greatest change he found, apart from the reality of self-government, and increased prosperity, was the change in tempo. Officials toured their districts by car. There was, he felt, a loss in terms of the familiarity gained by walking alongside the villagers, sitting down under a tree and listening to them. Lastly, he and Trekkie travelled north to Jaffna, where Leonard's career had begun, and he saw the Fort, where he had lived in the bungalow on the ramparts with Tom Southorn. On their last evening in Ceylon, Mr and Mrs Shelton Fernando gave a party for them at their home in Colombo. On 1 March they were back home.

He had had misgivings before they left, principally because 'imperialism and colonialism are today very dirty words'. He had feared that the Sinhalese and Tamil administrators who had taken over from the British would be 'contemptuous if not hostile'.[5] The reverse was true; nearly every official told him that things had been 'better' under British rule. Leonard knew he was probably being told what he wanted to hear, but felt in retrospect that British rule, though often arrogant, had been 'honest'.

There was one unpleasant confrontation. The day before they flew home, Leonard was with Shelton Fernando in the Galle Face Hotel when he had a visitor – an aged man, E.R. Wijesinghe (or Wijensinhe), who had been Mudaliyar[6] of Magam Pattu when Leonard was in Hambantota. E.R.Wijesinghe had an old story to tell, and a grievance.

At the time of the rinderpest epidemic, Leonard had been called to a village in Magam Pattu where a diseased buffalo was wandering free. He met this Mudaliyar and the village headman, and told the latter to drive the buffalo towards him across the dry tank so that he could shoot it. The headman refused to do so. The beast was savage, and would attack him. Leonard passed his rifle to the Mudaliyar, drove the buffalo within range himself, and instructed the Mudaliyar to shoot it dead. Proceeding, in his role as Police Magistrate, to prosecute the owner of

---

5 *ibid*

6 The local administrator of a division within a district.

the buffalo both for letting it run untethered and for not destroying it, Leonard discovered that the owner was none other than the village headman himself. So Leonard imposed a third fine on the headman, for not doing his official duty by reporting the offender (himself) for breaking the law.

When the old Mudaliyar finished his tale, he fixed Leonard with 'a beady and baleful eye' and asked 'Was it just, Sir? Was it just?' 'Yes, Mudaliyar, it was just', replied Leonard. But he did not feel comfortable about it, and he had not felt comfortable about it at the time. 'This ambivalence with regard to law and order and justice in an imperialist society was one of the principal reasons for my resigning from the Civil Service.'[7]

The fall-out continued. Exactly a year after Leonard's visit the old Mudaliyar published a signed article in the Ceylon *Observer*[8] asserting that the real reason why Leonard Woolf had left Ceylon was 'simply that his relations with the Imperial Government were not very happy'. The Jaffna Tamil Association had asked for his dismissal, and the inhabitants of Hambantota had risen up against him. This was true, or half-true, though Leonard's reasons for leaving were other. The article included some heavy satire about Mr Woolf's 'feats of bravery' out hunting, recalling a 'hair-breadth escape from three huge thirsty elephants . . . the day when your conscience prompted you to spare a magnificent leopard which sat before you within ten yards . . .' Perhaps Mr Woolf believed that 'he had outlived everyone else of his period in Ceylon and that there would be none to contradict him . . . It would do well for Mr Woolf to know that there are others beside myself yet living in Ceylon who remember his doings.'

Leonard was effectively defended in the columns of the Ceylon *Observer*[9] by 'ADS',[10] as able a satirist as Wijesinghe. But a year later, the old

7 *The Journey* . . .

8 11 Feb 1961

9 21 Feb 1961

10 A.D.Saperamadu, a GA, who wrote an authoritative introduction to the *Diaries in Ceylon 1908–11: Records of a Public Administrator. . .and Stories from the East, Three Short Stories on Ceylon* Tisara Prakasayako (paperback) 1962. The Hogarth Press published the book the following year with hard covers and a different jacket.

Mudaliyar returned to the fight with another article,[11] almost identical to the first, but giving more examples of Mr Woolf's arrogance and unpopularity, with some new nastiness, implying cowardice about Mr Woolf's failing to shoot the leopard because 'his hands shook so much'. Again, Leonard was defended by 'ADS', with a sting in the tail for the Mudaliyar: 'Even a cursory study' of the colonial period indicated that 'the real oppressors of the people were not the white rulers so much as the local feudal rulers' such as the Mudaliyars. Ordinary people often got 'better justice' from their white rulers.[12] Leonard told Shelton Fernando that he was 'much amused' by the old Mudaliyar's article, especially as Fernando had persuaded him to delete a few lines of personal reference to him when his diaries were published in book form, so as not to hurt his feelings.

What was not edited out of the Diaries was uncomplimentary material about Benny Wijesinghe, the Mudaliyar of East Giruwa Pattu – and E.R Wijesinghe's cousin. Leonard's official diary had catalogued Benny's inadequacies and shortcomings until, on 18 January 1909: 'I have been obliged to report the Mudaliyar of East Giruwa Pattu to the Government Agent and I have recommended that he be called upon to resign. My reasons are repeated cases of neglect of duty.' On 23 June 1909 the government ordered the Mudaliyar of East Giruwa Pattu 'to be removed from Government service.'

According to 'Senex', the author of three subsequent hostile articles,[13] Leonard Woolf had mortally insulted this Benny Wijesinghe, on his first arrival in Hambantota by horse-coach from Matara, by demanding to sit up on the box-seat which Benny was already occupying. (It is not hard to guess which family was behind the spate of anonymous letters Leonard received when he was in post in Ceylon.) This time Leonard was unable to resist the impulse to answer back. The

11 *Ceylon Observer* 14 Jan 1962. *Growing*, covering LW's years in Ceylon, had just been published. Shelton Fernando was commissioned by LW to review it for *PQ*; and suggested to LW that his next volume should be called 'Mowing'.

12 *Ceylon Observer* 28 Jan 1962

13 Senex's articles ran in the *Sunday Times* of Ceylon between 24 Feb and 10 March 1963. Senex was a former civil servant called Claasz, a Burgher. He castigated LW for telling in *Growing* the story of the Burgher prostitute, as belittling to her family and to the Burgher community.

Ceylon *Observer* printed a letter, in a box, with a photograph, in which Leonard Woolf stated that there was hardly a word of truth in E.R.Wijesinghe's articles, and that he did not know why he was pursued with 'these libellous lies'. But as Shelton Fernando reminded him, 'You are a perennial subject of discussion, if not controversy, here.'[14]

He has continued to be so. To mark the centenary of his birth, an entire issue of the English Association of Sri Lanka's *English Bulletin* was taken up by a symposium of scholarly articles on Leonard Woolf – of which only one,[15] out of seven, was critical of the 'fashionable' and 'misguided' praise lavished on *The Village in the Jungle.* The centenary was marked in the Ceylon *Sunday Times* by a cool article: Leonard Woolf had failed to appreciate and understand the society in which he found himself in Jaffna.[16] The middle-class Jaffnese Tamils were educated people. He did not perceive the cultural renaissance taking place, nor the beginnings of the Home Rule movement. He saw the limitations of colonial expatriate society but lacked the moral courage not to conform. He had not bothered to find out what lay beneath what he saw as the 'gaudiness' of the Hindu religion.

This was severe but just, and true of every young colonial administrator newly arrived in Ceylon. What the article did not take into account was that he learned. He came to his own conclusions about imperialism, and conducted his life afterwards in the light of those conclusions. Towards the end of his life he regretted that he had not absorbed more of Ceylon's culture, writing to Shelton Fernando: 'The truth was that one was so busy with one's work that one had very little time for anything else.' And again: 'As you know, I never really went in to the history, although I bought books both in English and in Sinhalese about traditions and the so-called history.'[17] But the author of *The Village in the Jungle* had no reason to be apologetic.

---

14 22 June 1963

15 Rajiva Wijesinha, 'Leonard Woolf's Sacred Cow', *The English Bulletin* No 4 Dec 1980 ed D.C.R.A.Goonetilleke

16 By Dr Jane Russell, 30 Nov 1980

17 20 March 1968 and 2 May 1968

There continues in both Sri Lanka and Britain to be a stream of articles and conferences about Leonard Woolf and Ceylon, literary and political, and ranging from the journalistic and the celebratory to the academic and scholarly. As memory became history and Ceylon's disturbed political trajectory overlaid the past, the colonial period came to carry less emotional freight, and aspects of the culture of modern Sri Lanka have been recognised to owe much to the British period – not least, through the legacy of the English language (a legacy unclaimed during some intermediate decades for nationalist reasons). Interest in Leonard Woolf in Ceylon does not abate.[18]

A few years after his visit, there was a project afoot in Ceylon to make a film of *The Village in the Jungle*. He signed an agreement with Shanti Films in 1967 (in exchange for £200) and invited the gifted potter Ursula Mommens, who lived nearby in South Heighton, to go out with him to see it being made.[19] This film never got off the ground. In 1980, too late for Leonard, a Sinhalese film of *The Village in the Jungle*[20] did finally appear, directed by Lester James Pieris, with script by A.J.Gunawardana, and was featured at the Cannes Film Festival. Arthur C.Clarke, the best-selling science-fiction writer, long resident in Sri Lanka, had a cameo role as the AGA Leonard Woolf.

Leonard listed, in *The Journey Not the Arrival Matters*, his lifetime's pleasures: 'Eating and drinking, reading, walking and riding, cultivating a garden, games of every kind, animals of every kind, conversation, pictures, music, friendship, love, people.' When he celebrated his eightieth birthday on 25 November 1960, Morgan Forster sent him a case of 1949 Chateau d'Yquem. 'There are few things which have a quality which makes them stand out by themselves from their class', wrote Leonard in thanks, 'quite different things like Richebourg (Domaine de

---

18 See for example Christopher Ondaatje, *Woolf in Ceylon: An Imperial Journey in the Shadow of Leonard Woolf 1904–1911* HarperCollins Canada 2005

19 She was then married to the half-Dutch sculptor Norman Mommens, from whom Leonard commissioned 'Goliath' for his garden.

20 Its title in Sinhala is *Baddegama*.

la Romanee-Conti), Doyenne de Comice pears, Beethoven's slow movements, and Ch.d'Yquem certainly is one of them.'[21]

Much of the fun that Leonard had in his eighties came through his and Trekkie's friendship with Peggy Ashcroft at the height of her career. When they saw her in *The Taming of the Shrew*, and in *The Duchess of Malfi* and Chekhov's *The Cherry Orchard*, they dined with her and her entourage after the perfomances. In April 1961 Leonard and Trekkie went on holiday to Greece, and met up with Peggy Ashcroft in Athens. Peggy and Jeremy Hutchinson, house-hunting in Sussex, stayed sometimes at Monks House or Juggs Corner before they bought the house called Deep Thatch, at Lullington.

In summer 1962 Leonard had a letter from the American playwright Edward Albee asking permission 'to use your wife's name'[22] in the title of his new play which was opening on Broadway that autumn. He, Peggy Ashcroft and the Parsons saw *Who's Afraid of Virginia Woolf?* together in London in January 1965, after which Leonard referred Albee to his late wife Virginia's story 'Lapin and Lapinova': 'The details are quite different but the theme is the same as that of the imaginary child in your play.'[23] At the end of Albee's play about marital warfare the husband kills the imaginary child off, in an imaginary accident. Virginia's story was about a couple whose marriage was sustained by their fantasy life as besotted rabbits, Lapin and Lapinova. The husband wearies of the game, refuses to be Lapin any more, and announces the death of Lapinova. 'Lapin and Lapinova' was written early in the Woolfs' married life, based on their Mandril and Mongoose identities. She revised it for publication years later, so one cannot know whether the briskly cruel last sentence – 'So that was the end of that marriage' – was in the original version.

Ian Parsons had a coronary thrombosis in February 1965, and afterwards Trekkie and he took many more short breaks together abroad for

---

21 Chateau d'Yquem is a rich and grand dessert wine. Richebourg Domaine de la Romanée Conti is the best and probably the most expensive burgundy in the world. LW was introduced to fine wines by Ian Parsons.

22 24 July 1962

23 28 Jan 1965

his health's sake, which meant that her weekly routines with Leonard at Monks House were interrupted. In April that year Leonard went to a lunch party given by *The Sunday Times* for Raymond Mortimer's seventieth birthday: even those who seemed young to him were now old.

From 1960 Vanessa Bell rarely left Charleston. Leonard lunched with her and Duncan on 26 March 1961. Less than two weeks later, on 7 April, suffering from bronchitis, she died. Only Duncan Grant, Quentin and Angelica, and her maid were at Vanessa's burial in Firle churchyard. Her husband Clive Bell was in the London Clinic with a broken leg. Leonard went over to Charleston a few days later. He saw in *The Times* that Morgan Forster was in hospital with a slight heart attack. As he said, it was all rather depressing.

From the mid-1950s Saxon Sydney-Turner was in decline, and moved to an old people's home in north London. His flat at 28 Percy Street had to be 'thoroughly cleaned and whitewashed as Saxon's life had seriously deteriorated and had been made impecunious by his addiction to betting'.[24] A group of the friends clubbed together to buy a television set for Saxon's eightieth birthday, so that he could watch horse-racing in his room. 'I funk going to see Saxon', Leonard confessed to Saxon's lifelong friend Barbara Bagenal, enclosing his cheque, 'as I funked telephoning him when he was more alert, because I can understand hardly a word he says.'[25] Saxon was also given a copy of *Sowing*, though Raymond Mortimer wondered how he would take the portrait of himself in the character of Aristotle (from Leonard's Aspasia Papers, copied into the autobiography). Clive Bell thought he would only be glad to be in it at all. 'Saxon has resolutely refused all his life to push himself forward in any way; but he is not averse to be pushed forward a little by others. He complains that few of your reviewers [of *Sowing*] refer to him by name.'[26]

Leonard had ended his sketch of Aristotle, 'spinning his interminable cocoon', thus: 'It will be some time before we find out that he really is dead and then we shall go to the large dirty room and push and tear our

---

24 Frances Spalding, *Vanessa Bell* Weidenfeld & Nicolson 1983
25 3 Oct 1960
26 Clive Bell to LW 31 Sept 1960

way through the enormous web . . . and at last when we stand choking in the centre of it we shall find just nothing at all. Then we shall bury the cocoon.' On 4 November 1962, aged eighty-two, Saxon died in hospital following a stroke. Leonard wrote a note about him for *The Times*.[27]

Louie's husband Bert Everest died in 1961. She was married again in 1963 to Konrad Mayer, who had been a German prisoner-of-war in the camp outside Rodmell, and stayed on. Octavia Wilberforce died in December that year, and left everything to the Backsettown Trust, for which Leonard now became responsible, both as a trustee and the sole remaining executor of Elizabeth Robins. Leonard was landed with what he least liked or needed – another huge cache of boxes, trunks, packing-cases and filing-cabinets of papers and cuttings, ranging from Robins family letters from the 1840s to receipts for soda-water from the 1940s.

He entered into correspondence with the American scholar Leon Edel, a good friend of Octavia's, about the possibility of Edel writing Elizabeth Robins's life. The mass of material finally went to New York University through the good offices of Leon Edel, although he never wrote Robins's biography. The trove included more than a dozen letters from Virginia, and Edel pointed out to Leonard that those from Octavia to Elizabeth Robins dealt with 'the very last consultation'[28] and would be of great interest to any biographer of Virginia. (Edel was interested in becoming that biographer.) Leonard's labours for the Backsettown Trust, which included the affairs of the Rest Home, went on throughout the 1960s. It was an appalling burden.

On 17 September 1964 Leonard wrote to Miss Hamill that he had just been to see Clive Bell 'who is desperately ill in a nursing home and the doctors give no hope of his recovery'. Clive had cancer. He died the very next day, aged eighty-three. Trekkie was away in Scotland (and suffering from ringworm): 'Will you have to go to the funeral? I do hope not, it is so miserable.'[29] Leonard did not do funerals. But he was good

27 13 Nov 1962
28 The letters are in the Fales Collection at NYU, bought in 1964 for $12,000.
29 19 Sept 1964

at bringing the dead to life, in his endless obituary articles. As Juliette Huxley wrote to him about his contribution to the memorial volume to her husband: 'It is as near an absolute image of Aldous as one could hope to see, bringing out his unique quality, embodied in a vivid description of his appearance and gestures.'[30]

The critic and editor Cyril Connolly and his wife Deirdre came to live at Eastbourne, within easy visiting distance from Rodmell. Cyril Connolly was an avid collector of inscribed first editions of his friends' works. He bought some Hogarth Press first editions of T.S.Eliot from Leonard, and then sent them to Eliot to have them inscribed, very much *post hoc*, to their original recipient. 'I have suddenly an uneasy feeling', an embarrassed Leonard wrote to Tom, 'that I never thanked you for inscribing PRUFROCK and other rarities of mine which Cyril Conolly [*sic*] sent you and caused you, I am afraid, a good deal of trouble. I like the inscription you have written in PRUFROCK.'[31]

He wrote again about 'Prufrock' in November 1964, telling Tom how he had taken it down from the shelf to check a quotation, and read it straight through. 'It gave me great pleasure. What a good poet you are and always have been right back to 50 years ago. There is something very beautiful in Prufrock which had never been said before – completely original and you yourself.'[32] He urged Tom to bring his second wife Valerie, his former secretary, down to Monks House, but they never came. Tom Eliot had emphysema, and died in January 1965. Valerie Eliot, thanking Leonard for his letter of condolence, and apologising for her typing, 'having sprained my right hand lifting oxygen cylinders', asked rather pointedly for copies of all Tom's letters to him and to Virginia: 'In a memorandum with his Will Tom asked that I should edit his letters, and I have already written to America to ask if I may have copies of the ones you sold at Sotheby's the other day.'

Hamill and Barker scooped up (for £600) in early 1960 an 'immense quantity' of early versions of Virginia's *The Voyage Out* which Leonard

30 4 Feb 1965
31 1 Feb 1961
32 11 Nov 1964

found in the attic. The two women flew to England every year like migrating birds returning to their summer feeding-grounds, homing in on surviving members of the Bloomsbury circle and scooping up whatever they could. They had created a market in the United States, and were supplying it. For the moment, supply and demand were in equal ratio, though they were beginning to leave strategic intervals before offering their new acquisitions to the Berg Collection in New York. Leonard sold them a batch of letters to Virginia and a 'remarkable' letter from Henry James to Leslie Stephen, which he found in a drawer. In September 1964 Miss Hamill reckoned that their haul from him for that summer was worth £2,125.

By now many British writers and their heirs, aware of the generous budgets of research libraries and special collections in American universities, were selling their papers to America. In 1962 even Vita Sackville-West, for all her disapproval of Leonard's activities, sold her letters from Virginia to Hamill and Barker, along with some of her own manuscripts; they too went to the Berg. (Vita died later that year, aged seventy.) Leonard insisted on keeping copies of anything which might be useful for his autobiographies, which did not always please the buyers. Since he and Virginia had no children of their own to inherit valuable material, and all Virginia's copyrights were safely willed to Virginia's niece and nephew, it made archival and economic sense to dispose of everything responsibly in his lifetime. He got no pleasure at all out of the physical possession of old letters and papers. As he wrote to Andreas Mayor, his contact at Sotheby's, 'I am afraid that I have myself absolutely no sentimental feeling with regard to relics but I dare say it is very wrong and unpleasant.'[33]

He did not always sell. He gave over fifty letters from the Ceylonese representatives following the 1915 riots to the High Commissioner of Ceylon in London (while requesting copies of them). He had stripped away false piety, not only from conviction but as a defence against emotion: he used the back of a page from a typescript of *Beginning Again*, describing the onset of Virginia's breakdown in the Great War, as the

---

33 24 Feb 1965

carbon copy of one of his annual orders of oranges from Haifa. It was a position from which, naturally, he sometimes toppled. In 1965 he heard from a Californian couple, Margaret and Burlington Willes, proposing to purchase and manage Monks House as a literary shrine. Leonard replied that 'there is no question of Monks House being a literary shrine as I shall leave it to someone else after my death.'[34] He was not unsentimental about Trekkie.

Maynard was the first of the circle to have his life transformed into a 'Life'. R.F.Harrod's *The Life of John Maynard Keynes* had come out in 1951, and Leonard, dining at the Cranium Club nine years later, found himself sitting next to the author: 'It was rather amusing as I had not seen him for ages and I knew that he knew that I had written what Lydia [Keynes] called a "stinking" review of his book.'[35] Roy Harrod bided his time. He wrote to Leonard praising *Sowing* when it appeared – but added that 'I was very cross with you for your review of Maynard, which I thought spiteful . . . Happily for me, I subsequently got the highest tributes from writers of great distinction.'[36] Leonard replied equably that he probably did not do the book justice; but that he was not spiteful.

Harrod told Leonard that he had been advised not to divulge the homosexual content of Maynard's early letters (not revealed in his biography) to Noel Annan, the Provost of King's, as Noel was 'the most indiscreet man' in the college; the letters were under lock and key in the college library. Leonard thought Harrod had done rightly. But he persuaded Roy Harrod to be a guest at a special two-day Memoir Club meeting at Charleston in November 1961, to read aloud from that indiscreet fifty-year-old correspondence between Maynard and Lytton about the Lytton/Duncan and Duncan/Maynard sexual imbroglio. Duncan, the only survivor of the imbroglio, was unembarrassed. In between readings, there were walks on the Downs, and Frances Partridge noticed how Leonard, 'with his noble face hanging in string-like folds, walked up

34 26 June 1965
35 To Trekkie 24 April 1960
36 2 Sept 1960. Quoted in Spotts, *Letters of Leonard Woolf*

the steep hill with me, easily outpacing Angus Davidson',[37] one of the new and younger members of the Memoir Club. Frances, thinking of editing a volume of Desmond MacCarthy's letters, asked Leonard to take copies of those he had and send them to her. He still had not got round to it when she came back to him months later. He was 'bored' by the whole business of letters, he told her.

Bored he might have been, but there was no escaping from letters, nor from Lives. He heard from Michael Holroyd, who was beginning his research, with the cooperation of James Strachey, for a biography of Lytton. They met, and in late March 1963 Holroyd wrote to Leonard requesting access to Lytton's letters to him. Leonard was unwilling to do more than promise to let him see 'extracts'. With suspicious rapidity, he wrote again: 'I have looked through such letters as I have and I cannot at the moment find anything which would be of any use to you';[38] but he would have another look.

Michael Holroyd's arrival caused flutters in the depleted dovecote of Bloomsbury. Morgan Forster consulted with Leonard as to whether or not he should co-operate. Frances Partridge was disturbed by talking about the past. But in spite of themselves they all liked Holroyd. Leonard, conscious of the sexually flammable nature of his Lytton material, was not deliberately uncooperative, merely cautious. (Whenever he had no intention of complying with a request he would simply say 'It is impossible', often twice in the same short letter.) In any case, his early correspondence with Lytton, so carefully preserved by them both for posterity when they were separated by oceans, had somehow got dispersed. James Strachey in 1965 was still trying to assemble the whole of the early Lytton/Leonard correspondence, and still wondering whether Leonard might have borrowed back his own letters to Lytton from Ceylon for reference, when he was writing *Growing*. Leonard found he did indeed have his

37 Rebecca Wilson (ed): Frances Partridge, *Everything to Lose: Diaries 1939–1972* Weidenfeld & Nicolson 2000
38 3 April 1963

letters to Lytton from Ceylon – but no letters to himself *from* Lytton before 1911.[39]

On 8 October 1966 Leonard attended the banquet given by the British Psychoanalytical Society to celebrate the completion of James Strachey's Standard Edition of the Works of Sigmund Freud and, as its publisher, said a few words. James's death early the following May came as a shock. He wrote James's obituary in *The Times*, paying tribute to his years of dedication and fortitude over the Standard Edition. James and Alix Strachey were spartan and eccentric, even by Bloomsbury standards, eating out of tins and zipping themselves into suit-storage bags to sit out in their deck-chairs. James, when he died, had just been awarded the Schegel-Tieck Prize on the completion of the Standard Edition. When Leonard was asked to accept it from the German Ambassador on James's behalf, he demurred, suggesting that Alix Strachey or Anna Freud would be more suitable. Neither attended the ceremony, and Leonard filled the gap.

Every year brought a new loss. 'I am beginning to feel that I am the only survivor',[40] he wrote to Trekkie, on hearing of the death of Harold Nicolson in May 1968. He said much the same to Harold's son Nigel, adding that 'I was fond of Harold, but our relationship was rather odd. I thought of him as a complete man of the world, and my normal attitude to men of the world is very ambivalent. And then I found that under the skin he was the exact opposite for about 50% of the time.'[41]

Leonard was hesitating about authorising a biography of Virginia. Margaret Lane – in private life the Countess of Huntingdon – came to lunch at Monks House to discuss her strong wish to take it on, and they talked all afternoon. She was already an established author,[42] and Leonard wrote a concerned letter three weeks later saying he was sorry

39 To James Strachey 19 Feb 1965. This exchange is significant with regard to the mystery of the 'Pritchard Papers', see 'Aftermath'.
40 4 May 1968
41 4 May 1968
42 Fiction, and biographies of her first father-in-law Edgar Wallace, of the Brontës, and of Beatrix Potter, as well as *A Calabash of Diamonds: An African Treasure Hunt.*

to disappoint her, as he found her approach, and herself, entirely sympathetic. But it was not the moment to 'open the archives'. This was just before the publication of his first volume of autobiography; it would be 'confusing and disturbing'[43] to begin trying to write about himself and Virginia, while involving himself in a biography of her by someone else. The timing was wrong.

In 1964 he wrote to Quentin Bell about the would-be biographers: 'I usually have to give them lunch and say no. Among recent applicants have been Leon Edel,[44] the Countess of Huntingdon, and Miss Joanna Richardson.[45] I say no because I have so far myself felt that the time has not yet come for a life, that the aura of Bloomsbury or rather the fog which surrounds it has not yet sufficiently dissipated to give the biography a fair chance with the critics.' Leon Edel seemed the best so far, 'though somewhat desiccated'. Then he came to the point: 'I think that far and away the best person to do it, if it is to be done, would be you. What would you feel about this?'[46] Quentin replied by return that he thought the work 'better not be done by a member of the family or by anybody who knows as little about English literature as I do.'[47] Leonard did not take this as a 'no'. He had read Quentin's work, and was impressed by his *Ruskin (*1963). From 1965, the project was tentatively on course.

Noel Annan wrote to tell Leonard he was thinking of writing a book 'about the ideas and beliefs of the circle of friends in Bloomsbury', hoping to have private papers put at his disposal. Leonard was not prepared to let Noel have access to Virginia's letters and diaries, since Quentin would be using them for his biography. Noel came to see Leonard at Monks House for a long talk, and they dined together at the Cranium Club, after which Leonard wrote to Quentin: 'I told him I thought it would be a mistake to write on Bloomsbury but it would be a

43 28 Aug 1960

44 Edel was then deep in his 5-volume life of Henry James, published between 1953 and 1972. His *Bloomsbury: A House of Lions* was published in 1981.

45 Joanna Richardson had interviewed LW for BBC radio, and was already the author of several biographies.

46 22 Nov 1964

47 23 Nov 64

good thing to write a book on the social and intellectual revolution which took place early in the 20th century and that Bloomsbury would come into that. I think he was rather inclined to agree.'[48] In the event it was Quentin Bell who, while working on his biography of Virginia, published *Bloomsbury* in 1968 – a short monograph in the series 'Men and Movements'.[49] In his speech at the Apostles dinner that year, Leonard in his dead-pan way expressed himself perplexed to find 'Bloomsbury' sandwiched in the series between the Ballet Russe and the Nazi SS.

If the Bloomsbury circle was managing its past for posterity, so were the Fabian Society and the early Labour Party. When Douglas Cole died in 1961, his widow Margaret asked Leonard to write a personal account of him, as an aid to a future biographer. Leonard declined on the grounds that he was busy with his autobiography, and also because 'I knew Douglas off and on from 1912, but the curious thing is I never knew him really well. We worked together on things continually, but were never intimate. I felt vaguely that he never wanted any intimacy. Of course, he was nine years younger than I.'[50] He suggested Margaret Cole should contact his brother Philip, who had been Douglas's contemporary at St Paul's.

This provoked Margaret Cole into commenting on 'how bitterly you wrote of St Paul's [in *Sowing*] – as Douglas's recollections were so favourable.'[51] They then had a prolonged and scratchy exchange about his review in *PQ*[52] of her book *The Story of Fabian Socialism* – added to which, he told her, 'It is significant that Douglas in his *History of the Labour Party* says nothing at all about the advisory committees.' Margaret

48 10 April 1965. LW's suggestion may have contributed to the conception of Noel Annan's *Our Age: Portrait of a Generation* (Weidenfeld & Nicolson 1990), in which Bloomsbury is described and assessed as part of the intellectual and social background of those who came of age between the end of the Great War and 1950.

49 Weidenfeld & Nicolson. Series editor John Gross. LW reviewed Bell's book in the *New Statesman*, 31 May 1968.

50 16 Jan 1961

51 24 Jan 1961

52 No.33, 1962

Cole had written that the committees were 'in decay' in the 1920s and 1930s, whereas 'these committees did an immense amount of work . . . behind the scenes without self-advertisement', and it was largely due to them that 'the party acquired knowledge of foreign affairs and imperial problems and acquired a Labour policy in those fields (in so far as it ever did so).'[53]

Leonard could not resist harping on Margaret Cole's failure to recognise the Webbs' 'curious simplicity and sincerity, benignity and unvindictiveness.'[54] She came back at him after reading his fourth volume, *Downhill All the Way*, in spring 1967: 'I don't think what you say on that page (which is the only mention of us in the whole book) is altogether fair.'[55] The disharmony ended with Margaret Cole reading Leonard's previous volume, *Beginning Again*, and the story of Leonard and Virginia eating chocolate creams to celebrate the end of the Great War. She was moved, and sent him some chocolate creams, gift-wrapped. When it came to gift-wrapping the past for posterity, the Bloomsbury circle were pussy-cats compared with the politicals.

Leonard was making gestures about leaving the board of the *New Statesman* from 1962, but Kingsley Martin, who retired as editor in 1961 but remained on the board, persuaded him to stay on. One of their altercations of 1963 is worth noting if only because Leonard made, in the course of a memo to Kingsley, a definitive statement about the morality of means and ends. It is not at odds with G.E. Moore and *Principia Ethica*, but with an application to current events which was never in Moore's remit.

The issue was the liquidation, defended by Kingsley Martin, of dissident citizens by the Chinese government. 'It is never right', wrote Leonard, 'for an individual or government to do any vast evil as a means to some hypothetical good . . . All nuclear war is ruled out because no

53 2 July 1962
54 5 July 1962
55 8 April 1967. The offending page (220) of *Downhill All the Way* refers to the Coles 'knocking at the door' of the Fabian Society, 'and there was no gentleness or consideration when Douglas and Margaret Cole knocked at any door'.

evil, alternative to nuclear war, could be more evil than a nuclear war . . . I believe I know what is good and that some of the things which I believe are true, but I don't think my knowledge is so certain that it justifies me in injuring, torturing, or killing other people. So although up to a point I am a Marxist, I do not think that justifies me in harming in any way even a non-Marxist flea.' Kingsley, he inferred, rated economics and metaphysics above freedom. 'I rate freedom above economics and hate and distrust all metaphysics.'[56]

For all that, Leonard did not join the Campaign for Nuclear Disarmament (CND), even though Philip Noel-Baker wrote urgently from the House of Commons urging him to 'throw yourself into disarmament work'.[57] Leonard was pro-disarmament, but after a lifetime of political campaigning had come to believe that it rarely achieved much. He was against the Vietnam war, but careful to dissociate himself from 'the many people who use the Vietnam situation as an instrument of their anti-Americanism and/or Communist propaganda.' The Americans should withdraw and cut their losses, since their continued intervention 'is causing great loss and misery both to the Vietnamese and to themselves' and would not achieve its object.[58]

He wrote his last piece for *Encounter*, on Britain's entry into the European Common Market, in 1962. When in 1967 it was revealed that *Encounter* was financed by the CIA as a putative weapon for combating anti-Americanism among intellectuals, Stephen Spender and Frank Kermode severed their connection with the magazine. The Oxford economist Max Beloff asked Leonard to add his signature to a group letter to *The Times* in support of *Encounter*. Leonard said yes to Beloff – and then no: 'I find that in signing the letter you sent me I have . . . put my head into a wasp's nest. This of course is not the first time this has happened to me, but it is not the kind of place in which I like to lay my head.'[59]

He supported campaigns which he felt might achieve their object,

56 7 May 1963
57 11 May 1964 and 14 Nov 1964
58 To Cecil Woolf 11 June 1966
59 17 May 1967

such as the appeal against the prosecution for indecency of D.H.Lawrence's *Lady Chatterley's Lover* in autumn 1960. He joined the National Campaign for the Abolition of Capital Punishment, adding his name to the names of eminent others on the 'committee of honour', and attending with Peggy Ashcroft the mass meeting at the Albert Hall on 18 April 1961. The Rector of Rodmell, the Rev Gordon Naderer, was in the opposite camp, and Leonard shot off a sarcastic letter to the *Sussex Express and County Herald*: 'I am sure that many people will have been uplifted and encouraged by seeing in your last issue that Mr Naderer, who as Rector of Rodmell preaches the Gospel of Christ, so courageously comes out in favour of hanging.'[60] The trouble was, as another clergyman of Leonard's acquaintance remarked, that the paper's editor and most of its readers, unaccustomed to satire, would have taken his letter at face value. He had already crossed swords with this latest rector about the ownership of the old stone wall between Monks House garden and the churchyard. The Rector proposed replacing it with a chain-link fence – an act of vandalism, in Leonard's opinion.

His position in the village was unique. He castigated local children for nicking his apples and strawberries, but himself carried trays of fruit round to the village school. Quentin and Olivier's children, accompanying him to the annual Horticultural Show, felt they were with an important person who commanded respect. When, after eight years of fund-raising, the new Village Hall was completed, a plaque was placed in the entrance lobby to commemorate its official opening on 26 March 1960 by Leonard Woolf as the village's oldest inhabitant, and in recognition of the £500 he had given to be invested for its permanent maintenance. As his neighbour Evelyn Pember wrote to him: 'Certainly the chromosomes have danced a wild rock & roll, for when I think of English country gents around here I think of you.'

His 'appalling insistence and persistence' was undimmed. He entered into a dispute with the Zoological Society of London, of which he had been a member for decades, over whether he was, as the Society judged,

60 20 Feb 1965

a town member (one living under fifty miles from London) or, as he insisted, a country member. Rodmell was under fifty miles from London as the crow flies, but as Leonard wrote to his old acquaintance Sir Solly Zuckerman, the Secretary of the Society, 'As regards judging by the crow-flying distance, I feel that a Zoological Society should be very careful not to confuse birds with mammals. I am sure the Rodmell crow would have no objection to be considered as a resident within 50 miles whereas a mammal like myself might well object to being included in the category of crows.'[61]

A new phenomenon which aroused his uncomprehending rage was junk mail. He protested to the Postmaster General on receiving, unsolicited, 'a document from Brentford Nylons', unstamped and not in an envelope. 'Is it correct that the postal services should be used in this way?'[62] The postal services still trembled under the weight of his epic complaints to shops about 'irregularities' and 'mistakes'. He had terrible problems with his 'Gardenmaster' and its attachments (hedgecutter, saw, etc), as with garden sprays, sprinklers and lawn mowers. Boilers, fridges, cookers, went wrong or were incorrectly installed. In an order of a dozen bottles of olive oil, one arrived broken; a case of wine was one bottle short.

At the *New Statesman* board meeting of 8 January 1965, John Freeman (who had taken over from Kingsley Martin as editor), resigned, having been appointed High Commissioner in India. The candidate favoured by the board was the acting editor – a left-wing journalist in his late thirties, Paul Johnson. Leonard was opposed to him on the grounds that he was a Roman Catholic. When his opposition was leaked to the press, Leonard attempted to mend his hand, writing to Johnson: 'I was very sorry to see what one or two papers said about my attitude to your appointment. I have expressed certain opinions at Board meetings with regard to a hypothetical permanent appointment, but never anything about it or about you personally outside the Board Room.'[63] Nothing can be more personal than a man's religion. But Paul Johnson wrote a generous reply.

61 24 Feb 1961
62 7 Feb 1965
63 19 Jan 1965

After the board meeting of 17 June, Leonard wrote to Jock Campbell, the chairman: 'I still face the greatest reluctance to appointing a Roman Catholic, a communist, or any other denominationalist who subjects his will and actions in principle absolutely to an organization or party'; but he would not formally oppose the appointment as he preferred the decision to be unanimously agreed by the board. Two days later he resigned. He wrote congratulating Paul Johnson and wishing him good luck. His prejudice against a Roman Catholic in the editorial chair may not seem so very different from Harold Nicolson's prejudice against Jews in the Foreign Office. Leonard's reasoning was in tune with his distrust of all 'totalitarian' belief systems.

The board of the Hogarth Press was enlarged to include Piers Raymond (son of Chatto and Hogarth director Harold Raymond) and Peter Calvocoressi.[64] Leonard wrote formally to Ian Parsons: 'I have come to the conclusion that the time has come when I should cease to draw a salary from the Hogarth Press and [?also cease to] come to the office once a week.' Hogarth was more and more closely amalgamated with Chatto & Windus. Fewer manuscripts were being submitted specifically to the Hogarth Press. He needed the time to finish his autobiography. He would like to remain on the board: 'If I live until 1967, I shall have been in the Press for 50 years and that would be an appropriate moment for complete retirement.'[65]

Leonard was then rising eighty-five. Three years later he was still looking in at the Press once a week, before lunching at the Athenaeum with Willie Robson or new acquaintances such as Karl Miller (editor of the *Listener*) and – once – Iris Murdoch. At the Press office, his arrival was unostentatious, 'even, thanks to the great thickness of the soles of his shoes, silent', his presence made known to Norah Smallwood by the 'calmly spoken' question 'Have you got anything for me?' i.e. a manuscript to read. 'If he wanted a book to be published, it was published.'[66]

64 Publisher, author, and expert on international relations. He joined Chatto & Windus in 1955.

65 10 Oct 1965

66 Hugo Brunner 'The Hogarth Press since 1946', *Charleston Newsletter* 6 Dec 1983

One of the last was a novel by young John Goldsmith, *Mrs Mount Ascendant*; Goldsmith later had a hit with *Bullion*.

When Peter Calvocoressi went into Leonard's tiny office with a query, he always gave the impression, even if he was in the middle of something, of having all the time in the world; he had the gift 'of concentrating on the present without allowing the person you're talking to see that a quarter of your mind is on something else'.[67] Calvocoressi came to revere him, though Cecil Day-Lewis remarked that he might not have felt the same if he had known Leonard when he was younger and sharper-tongued.[68] Leonard also evolved an inspired and inspiring technique for turning books down without hurting an author's feelings. He would invite the author to come and see him in his office for a long talk, after which the author voluntarily withdrew her (it was usually her) manuscript, thanking Leonard warmly for his valuable criticism, and for opening her eyes to her own potential – thus virtually writing her own rejection letter and feeling good about it.

Philip Woolf said his doctor daughter Marie was fond of pointing out to him 'that the bad genes in the Woolf and de Jongh families (which were very obviously present) seemed to cancel out in the union of our [his and Leonard's] own parents – producing individuals only one of whom [Edgar] is fairly obviously wrong in the head; but in the next generation numbering only six there are, according to her, only two, Philippa and Clare [Clara's daughter], who are reasonably well balanced, the bad genes having reasserted themselves.'[69] It did not end with the 'next' generation. Several of Leonard's great-nephews and great-nieces were to be afflicted by what the family called 'Woolf-style depression'. What happened in the Woolf family puts Virginia's suicide in a new perspective. Couples are drawn to one another by affinities of which they are unaware. Leonard did not dissociate himself from his family

67 'Leonard Woolf 1880–1969', BBC Radio 3, 17 Feb 1970, producer Virginia Browne-Wilkinson.

68 Peter Calvocoressi to VG in conversation 3 Nov 2005

69 Philip Woolf to LW 6 June 1961

inheritance. 'I don't think I am quite as mad as Edgar but that is what mad people always think',[70] as he wrote to his niece Philippa. But he gave no inkling in his autobiographies that Virginia's depressions and suicide mirrored those in his own family. He wrote nothing at all about what follows.

Leonard's niece, Clara's daughter Betty, had a breakdown in 1960. Her agitated depression took the form of a phobia about germs, and she attempted – unsuccessfully – to gas herself and her small daughter. A criminal prosecution followed. The judge said it was a case for treatment, not punishment. She was put on probation for a year and referred to a mental hospital, from which she later emerged. That autumn Bella was in hospital in Oxford with a broken hip. She contracted pneumonia, and on 24 November she died a natural and not untimely death.[71] She was eighty-three.

Leonard's brother Philip employed what he called his 'girl gardeners', both at Gaulden and at Wellisford. Molly Wallace-Bell was a former landgirl with whom he had been infatuated ever since the war. Unfortunately for him she was a lesbian; her partner E.Armstrong was the other girl gardener. Cecil was getting married, and Philip badly wanted Leonard to come to his son's wedding. Leonard did not go, but he gave Cecil and his bride Malya some red velvet curtains from Gorringes; the young couple stayed on in the basement and ground floor at 24 Victoria Square.[72] Philip was in a poor state. He bought, with or for his girl gardeners, a small nursery garden, Nettlebed Nursery, on the outskirts of Shaftesbury in Dorset. 'By all the laws of chance I ought to have killed myself last week. I turned a complete side-somersault on my Land Rover but sustained nothing but cuts and bruises.'[73] He broke down, and went into Atkinson Morley's Hospital: 'I had been sleepwalking and doing

---

70 21 June 1961

71 Bella left £15,576. 2s.11d.

72 Duncan Grant took the top floor for a while, which was not a success with Leonard as Duncan had too many late-night callers and too often lent the key to louche friends.

73 6 June 1960

pretty dangerous things during my walks.' He had moved to Willow Cottage in the village of Stour Row, near Nettlebed Nursery.

Philip committed suicide. Over Christmas 1961, he took too many pills but survived. On 10 February 1962 he fell off a ladder. The following day, although he was seen in Shaftesbury apparently in good form, he drove off and took an overdose of pills and drank a lot of whisky near the village of Fonthill Bishop. He was seventy-one.

Flora had a slight stroke; and in 1961 an operation for cataract on her single eye failed. When Edgar arrived to take her out, he found her in a coma. 'Whether she took too many sleeping tablets no one knows . . . She is very unhappy and the whole cause is that awful Molly.' Her daughter Mollie turned up with a man, both of them drunk, and made a scene; 'eventually they were ejected but only after Molly had made a vicious assault on Flora.'[74] With unshakeable maternal loyalty, Flora would never say or hear a word against Mollie. After one of his visits to Flora, Leonard sent her letters which she had written to him in youth, to amuse her by recalling the past. 'I remember calling you "Boon"', she wrote. 'We were always very good friends, and I am glad we have remained so.'[75]

August 1962 found her in the Holloway Sanatorium at Virginia Water, taking 'fistfuls of tablets', and having electric shock treatment. It seemed to be working: Holloway, she wrote without irony, 'is Perfection'. And in a PS: 'How awful it was about Phil – and so unnecessary with 3 such exceptionally nice and devoted offspring, good health and a pleasant place to live in. I think the news, received over the telephone, was just the last shove I needed to push me right over.' Her judgment was that if Phil had had a really good radio set he would never have got so low.

On 16 October 1967 Harold, the most jovial of the Woolf brothers, or rather the one with the most amiably manic tendencies, committed suicide at the age of eighty-four by taking an overdose at his home, Walnut Tree Farm near Appledore in Kent. Harold had a cancer on his lip (which was treated). He got it into his head that he had no money.[76]

---

74 Edgar W to LW 5 Aug 1961
75 10 Oct 1961
76 Harold left £18,781

That generation of Woolfs thought people had the right to end their lives. Philip's daughter Philippa rejected this position. 'I am quite sure that it is not a rational step taken because life ceases to be worthwhile or valuable. Sanity and insanity are surely states of mind differing by the way a person interprets facts.' Philippa suggested to her Uncle Leonard that 'from what you write of Virginia's death I can only imagine that in her moments of depression things seemed so different – or her interpretation of things was so different from normal, that suicide is a logical step. But again I don't feel that one can regard this apart from a state of profound illness.'[77] This was tantamount to saying that to end your own life is, by definition, evidence of insanity. Leonard himself, to judge from his firm belief that Virginia could have 'recovered', would seem to agree with this. Yet he had an equally firm belief that she had the right to do what she did. Philippa and her sister Marie, both doctors, acknowledged that the Woolfs had a psychology, and a philosophy, of suicide.

Throughout the chain of disasters, Leonard contributed to his family a stream of modest cheques, generations of Siamese kittens, advice, hospitality, and short, forthright, friendly letters, especially to his nieces. No comment of his on these events in any letter to anyone has come to light, though he wrote to a Hogarth author and friend, Nan Fairbrother, about Philip's suicide. 'It has made me sad all day', she wrote to him, 'to think about your brother, both for you and for him.' She recalled how she and Leonard had gone together to see Philip the summer before he died – an outing which she called 'our little holiday' – 'and ironically I've thought of him as proof that one can live happily alone.'

Leonard lived happily enough alone; but he also, part-time, had Trekkie – sensible, active, loving, a little over-controlling as he moved into old age. He had his own increasingly successful life to be lived. The older he got, the less he wanted to die.

---

77 11 Nov 1965

18

Justice and Mercy

The founding in 1961 of the University of Sussex at Falmer, near Brighton (and five miles from Rodmell), had a big impact on Leonard Woolf's life. He, Trekkie and Ian became specially friendly with Asa Briggs, Sussex's first professor of history, and his wife Susan.[1] Peter Calvocoressi, Leonard's colleague at the Hogarth Press and Chatto, came to Sussex as part-time Reader in International Relations in 1965; an academic couple who also became close friends in the early 1960s were the American writer and academic William (Bill) Humphrey and his wife, from Yale.[2]

Leonard gave 160 volumes on social studies and international politics to the University of Sussex Library in 1963, plus a not quite complete run of *Political Quarterly.* He asked Asa and Susan Briggs what he should do with his stacks of old copies of *The Times*, dating back to World War I. Chuck them out, they said. He gave them his collection of 78 rpm gramophone records, the ones he had listened to with

---

1 Briggs was Vice-Chancellor of the University of Sussex 1967–76 and Chancellor of the Open University 1967–1976. Created Lord Briggs of Lewes, he went on to be Provost of Worcester College, Oxford.

2 Ian Parsons published Humphrey at Chatto & Windus. He was author of *Home from the Hill* and a regular contributor of stories to the *Saturday Evening Post.*

Virginia. In his effort to clear the clutter, he sent his collection of score-cards from the Hove cricket ground, dating from 1893, to the county club.

In June 1964, at the first degree ceremony of the University of Sussex, Leonard received an honorary degree, wearing the yellow gown of an Hon D.Litt. Professor Briggs gave the encomium: 'There is a serenity in his spirit which seems to those who know him like a gift of grace. He has meant much to his friends, and they have meant much to him. Never flattered by authority and never seeking to flatter it, acutely aware of the irony of character and of circumstances, not wishing to escape but to understand, he has made Rodmell, where he lives, a place of peace. In his beautiful garden, time is suspended. Words like "old" and "new" become clumsy and irrelevant.'

The third volume of his autobiography, *Beginning Again*, appeared in the spring of 1964, covering the beginnings of his involvement in socialism, his marriage to Virginia Stephen, and her breakdown during the Great War. This volume consolidated his project, and reviewers took the opportunity of reconsidering the two earlier volumes, positioning his work as a sustained achievement and an expanding whole. John Sparrow, the Warden of All Souls, wrote to him: 'I can hear the very sound of your voice in your prose – a good test, I think, of absolute non-affectation and unpretendingness . . . All the account of Virginia's troubles and of your devotion to her is deeply disturbing and touching.' For Sparrow as for many people, 'it was all much worse and began much earlier than I had known. How right you were to put it all down.'[3]

Leonard wrote about the nightmare times with care and simplicity, and no appeal to the reader's sympathy on his own account. He did not include anything about his collapses of health and spirits, nor about the constrictions which Virginia's frailty placed on his career. But many people wrote in the same vein as Gerald Brenan, struck by the realisation that 'we owe Virginia's books to you almost as much as to herself,

3 26 Nov 1964

for I doubt if she would have been able to write them if she had been married to anyone else.'[4]

His evocations of his wife's physical presence, her behaviour, and the impression she made on others were as clear-eyed and graphic as his pen-portraits of his Cambridge friends. Virginia was beautiful and distinguished; yet always 'to the crowd in the street there was something in her appearance which struck them as strange and laughable.' Duncan Grant, recognising the truth of this, found the descriptions of her walking down the street, with people looking and laughing, 'most moving and extraordinarily alive'.[5] Elsewhere in the volume Leonard wrote that one of her 'delusions', when she crossed the border between sanity and insanity, was that 'people laughed at her'. The logic of this suggests that her insanity (like all insanity) involved not only delusion but the stripping away of delusion. Among the many letters he received was one from Jim Bartholomew,[6] who ended with a rushed sentence about the way Mr Woolf – for they remained on formal terms – had cared for Mrs Woolf. 'I think it was marvellous I don't know how you did it but it was a great thing to have done.'

Hamill and Barker bought the typescripts of *Beginning Again*. There was no manuscript. He wrote as he spoke, straight on to the typewriter, and changed very little in the second and final version.

Beginning Again won the seventh W.H.Smith Prize in 1965. The judges, all known to Leonard, were Margaret Lane, Karl Miller and Rupert Hart-Davis. Monks House garden was invaded by the British and foreign press. 'I had my photograph taken a dozen or more times yesterday', he wrote to Trekkie (in France with Ian), 'with and without the dogs and puppy.' The dogs were Trekkie's collie Bessie, and his own Coco; the puppy was Monk, son of Coco. He was interviewed for radio, television and the newspapers. John Betjeman presented the cheque for

4 20 June 1964

5 June 1964

6 Son of Leonard's old gardener Percy, Jim Bartholomew taught printing at Brighton Technical College and became Rodmell's local historian. LW helped the Bartholomew children with their education and careers.

£1000 at a reception at the Savoy. Leonard did not alert his family. 'Until we saw you on Television we did not know anything about it',[7] complained Edgar.

Leonard said in his acceptance speech that only that August he had been handed an envelope containing a first prize of one shilling for his autumn onions. While he could not hope ever again to be handed an envelope containing a cheque for £1000 for an autumn autobiography, he did expect to get another prize for his onions, perhaps a second prize of two shillings.[8] The photograph of the event shows him speaking with a straight face, and everyone around him laughing heartily. He received a cheery postcard signed by Stephen Spender, Isaiah Berlin and Stuart Hampshire, lunching together in Princeton having just seen *The Sunday Times* with the announcement of the prize, and his photograph.

In this heady time, he made a ridiculous misjudgement. He fell for the proposition of a Major Carr of Weston-super-Mare and his 'Statistical Unit Racing Investments', which guaranteed a '100% chance of steady weekly tax-free profits'. Major Carr also had a scheme of guaranteed wins in the football pools – 'without fail', or your money back. Leonard sent in his money for both schemes, and that was the last he heard from Major Carr, who cannot have received any more eloquent letters of protest from his victims than those from Leonard Woolf.

The impulse to honour Leonard Woolf gathered momentum. In November 1965 he was elected a Fellow of the Royal Society of Literature. The Labour Prime Minister, Harold Wilson, wrote a 'Dear Leonard' letter in the spring of 1966 asking him to allow his name to go forward as a Member of the Order of the Companions of Honour (CH) in the next Birthday Honours list. Leonard declined the honour, but said how often he had thought of writing to Harold to say 'how

7 6 Nov 1965

8 Some poetic licence here, or some misreporting. There were differing newspaper reports of his comic relating of the W.H.Smith Prize to the prizes he won for his vegetables. His first prize at the Rodmell Horticultural Show that year was for spring-sown, not autumn-sown, onions. He also won third prize for a tray of mixed vegetables.

much I admire what you have done for the party and the brilliant result in the last election'.[9] He was more abrasive privately: 'Harold Wilson, whom I don't like, has done better than expected.'[10]

There was a special Apostles dinner given for him on 25 November 1966, his eighty-sixth birthday, in the private dining-room at Kettner's in Romilly Street. The idea was Dadie Rylands's, with Victor Rothschild as chief organiser. Most of Leonard's apostolic contemporaries, and some who were younger than he, were too frail to attend. The aged King's contingent, including Jack (now Sir John) Sheppard and Morgan Forster, sent regrets and love. Leonard and Morgan remained close, at long distance. Leonard wrote an affectionate, handwritten (unusual, for him) letter to Morgan for his ninetieth birthday in the New Year of 1969, and Morgan replied with equal affection. They had both done well, he wrote, and could depart in peace.

Leonard was not ready to depart. Andreas Mayor wrote to tell Trekkie how impressive he had been at the Apostles dinner: 'He went through the evening without the slightest sign of strain or fatigue . . . He looked magnificent in his purple tweeds in the midst of all the smooth dark suits – that rugged profile which might be a piece of heather-covered granite or the outline of Mr Juktas in Crete which is meant to look like the head of Zeus.' He had spoken 'with perfect ease and a relaxed and humorous command of what he wanted to say' about how the 'phenomenal' was not after all so very different from the 'real' (meaning, in apostolic code, that the pleasures and rewards of ordinary life were not inferior to those experienced 'on the heights'), and about the happiness which begins at seventy and grows steadily greater. Much of that happiness, his friends surmised, was owed to Trekkie.

Leonard's success subtly changed the dynamic of the triad of himself, Trekkie and Ian. Leonard was no longer an essentially grey eminence, whose best claim to fame was that he was the widower of a genius. Ian

9 11 May 1966. In the election of October 1964 Labour increased its majority in the House of Commons to 99.

10 To Bill Humphrey 26 Nov 1964. LW and Wilson had served together on the Fabian Executive.

wrote a formal letter to Leonard – typed on Chatto & Windus stationery, and signed in his absence – about a seemingly private matter. He had paid £95 for a coat for Trekkie's birthday. 'I gather from T that you've very kindly agreed to share this present with me, so perhaps you'd like to let me have a cheque for £47.10 at your convenience.'[11]

A month later, Leonard and Trekkie flew into New York – Trekkie, perhaps, wearing the new coat. At last, Leonard saw America. They stayed at the Barbizon-Plaza and went to the Frick, the Metropolitan Museum, to Leonard's publishers Harcourt Brace, and to the New York Public Library to meet the director of the Berg Collection, Lola Szladits; he inscribed for her the Berg's typescript of *Beginning Again.* They flew south to Charleston to look at gardens. In Washington DC they stayed at the Mayflower Hotel and saw what Leonard in his diary called 'the Melon pictures'.[12]

They were the guests of Bill and Dorothy Humphrey in Boston, and went on to Canada to stay with John Graham, professor of English at the University of Western Ontario, who was working on the manuscript of *The Waves.* His wife Angela loved and revered Leonard and kept his photograph on her desk: 'I used to write to you when I felt particularly isolated and confused', she confessed. 'These weren't letters for mailing – just letters for healing – a neurotic mechanism perhaps but it helped . . . I've told you before, I feel this freedom to burden you with thoughts and feelings that matter to me. I think you would have made a good psychoanalyst as well as a publisher of it.'[13]

Leonard enjoyed North America, he said, but he would not want to live there. Leonard's diary, 11 May 1966: 'Back to Monks, had lunch, drove Trekkie back to Juggs', and to Ian. The altered balance between Ian and Leonard was exemplified by Laurens Van der Post's invitation to him and Trekkie to hear Benjamin Britten's *The Prodigal Son* at Aldeburgh, and stay the weekend. 'We wish we could ask old Ian as well, but unfortunately our cottage is not big enough.' Ian once referred, to

11 14 March 1966

12 The National Gallery of Art in Washington was endowed by Paul Mellon. This was not his little joke. He was not great at spelling, as his typescripts attest.

13 19 Nov 1965

Nora David,[14] to 'Trekkie's extraordinary relationship',[15] but went no further.

Asa Briggs thought that Trekkie arguably had 'undue influence' on Leonard',[16] in that she could cajole him into doing anything she wanted. But she had to 'manage' both sides of her life. As they all grew older – she herself was only two years younger than the twentieth century – her dual devotion and responsibilities were borne with characteristic cheerfulness but not without strain. She was always there when Leonard needed her. Nora David was once with Trekkie when she heard that Leonard was unwell, and 'I never saw anyone get into a car quicker.'[17]

Kitty Muggeridge, wife of the journalist and broadcaster Malcolm Muggeridge and niece of Beatrice Webb, came to see Leonard in July 1966. She was writing, with Ruth Adam, the biography of her aunt, and Leonard told her about the long-ago idea that he should write about the Webbs. When he read the typescript, Leonard (while making a few corrections) wrote to Kitty: 'I have just finished reading your book with tears in my eyes . . . Beatrice comes completely to life in it.'[18]

Kitty paved the way for her husband. In early September 1966 Leonard was interviewed over three days at Monks House by Malcolm Muggeridge for BBC TV. It was meant to be a single half-hour programme, but the material was so good that it was decided to spread it between two. On film, Leonard gave Muggeridge tea in the garden: 'I'll try and pour it out without spilling it, because I have a trembling hand since birth.' His old, cultivated, Cambridge voice did not falter. The teacups rattled perilously on their saucers.

After the programme Leonard received many sad or angry letters about his adamantine stance against religion. 'I have no belief', he had said on film. 'In fact I have a strong disbelief.' His wife Virginia had gone

---

14 Her husband Dick David of the Cambridge University Press was a friend of Ian Parsons through the Publishers' Association. The two couples became close friends, and included LW.

15 Baroness David to VG 1 Nov 2001

16 Lord Briggs to VG 30 July 2003

17 Baroness David to VG 30 July 2003

18 20 March 1967. LW reviewed *Beatrice Webb: A Life* in the *New Statesman* 10 Nov 1967

for ever. He himself would be snuffed out. In reply to all the letters, he restated for the hundredth time that because religious belief made you feel better, that did not make it true. Occasionally he lost his cool: 'What astonishes me about you religious people is your extraordinary arrogance, rudeness and uncharitableness.' Trekkie did a drawing of Leonard standing on the Downs, his hands in his pockets, looking at a tall angel, complete with wings, halo, and a lily. The caption is: 'I DON'T BELIEVE A WORD OF IT.'

In January 1966 Quentin Bell committed himself to writing the biography of Virginia Woolf. The starting point was obviously her diaries. Leonard posted off his manila envelopes containing the chopped-up sections of his carbon copies. He told Quentin that, with the extracts published in *A Writer's Diary*, he now had the lot. It was not so easy. The truncated pages sometimes had the dated portion cut off, and bits were missing. Fortunately Quentin's wife Olivier was a highly trained researcher, having been employed in her youth by eminent scholars to 'get things right'.[19] She reconstituted the diaries, using Leonard's master-copy when in difficulties.

The work was made easier from early 1967 when Quentin was appointed professor of History and Theory of Art at the University of Sussex, and he and his family came to live at Cobbe's Place, within a couple of miles of, and roughly equidistant from, Charleston and Monks House. Leonard rooted out for them bundles and boxes of letters, including the copies of those he had sold. He was helpful but not controlling, exerting no pressures. Quentin sent Leonard a 'Report on Preliminary Research' after one year: the main task had been to put the 300,000 words of the diary into 'usable form'. He and Olivier were preparing a biographical index and notes as they went along. They were also sorting the Charleston papers, and were planning to interview people who knew Virginia. Olivier constructed a system of card indexes and a chronology.

*

19 *Editing Virginia Woolf's Diary* Bloomsbury Workshop 1990

In late December 1966 Vita's son Nigel Nicolson brought to Monks House a PhD student from Cornell, doing her thesis on Virginia Woolf.[20] Nigel asked Leonard if he was ready to have the Vita/Virginia letters published. Leonard prevaricated, writing three days later: 'The fact is, I find it extremely difficult to force myself to read old letters . . . Whenever one really knows the facts, one finds that what is accepted by contemporaries or posterity as the truth about them is so distorted or out of focus that it is not worth worrying about.'[21] The correspondence must await publication until after his death, when the copyright, and the decision, would be Quentin's and Angelica's.

Over and above Leonard's general distaste for old letters, reading the private correspondence of a dead spouse is perturbing. Leonard knew about Vita and Virginia. But he had not, at the time, known everything, or grasped the gamey tone of their intimacy. What he did know was Virginia's tendency to hyperbole and playfulness, and he could read 'his' Virginia in the letters to Vita. Yet reading them may have forced him into thinking in a new way about the sexual nullity of his marriage. In his bleak anthology published in 1967[22] he quoted Gorky: 'Man survives earthquakes, epidemics, the horrors of disease, and all the agonies of the soul, but for all time his most tormenting tragedy, has been, is, and will be – the tragedy of the bedroom.' At one of his last appearances at an editorial meeting of the *New Statesman*, when the idea of an issue on homosexuality was under discussion, he suddenly and surprisingly said: 'My wife was a lesbian.'

He was not ready to have this revealed to the world while he lived. He did not, in his graphic accounts of friends in his autobiography, mention their homosexuality, not even apropos of Lytton. When reproached for this in *Encounter* by Goronwy Rees, he replied on the letters page that since he was not a homosexual himself it was irrelevant to his relation to

---

20 This was Susan Kenney, later the author of many articles and essays on VW, particularly relating to her madness and suicide, and of mystery novels under the pseudonym Roz Howard – one of which, *Garden of Malice*, is not unrelated to Vita and Sissinghurst.

21 2 Jan 1967

22 *A Calendar of Consolation: A Comforting Thought for Every Day of the Year* Hogarth Press

them; and that at the time of writing it was 'still unusual to reveal facts which might be painful to living people unless it was absolutely vital to mention them.'[23]

Leonard did not change his mind-set. Before James Strachey died he gave to Lucy Norton her brother Harry Norton's letters to himself and Lytton. Leonard advised her against publishing them. 'My main reason is that they are so much about intimate psychological small beer that except for the interest in buggery I cannot imagine their being of interest to or even understandable by the general reader.' He found them hard to read himself, even though he knew everyone involved intimately. They were all dominated by the 'semi-real, semi-unreal personal drama which at that time largely owing to Lytton was imposed upon Cambridge personal relations.'[24]

With the decriminalisation in Britain of homosexual acts between consenting adults in private in 1967, the closet was unlocked. In that year, the first volume of Michael Holroyd's biography of Lytton Strachey appeared, taking the story up to 1910. It had been subjected to scrutiny from James Strachey before he unexpectedly died; thus some of the credit, or in some eyes the discredit, of the book's unprecedented sexual candour[25] was due to James. Though Leonard praised in his review Michael Holroyd's 'conscientious industry', he did not like the book very much.[26] He found it too long for its material, he told Edgar, and out of focus and distorted in the way that he described in his letter to Nigel Nicolson. Out of sympathy with the extravagantly camp culture of their youth, he thought that Holroyd treated Lytton's love-dramas too seriously.

Leonard was more positive two years later about Holroyd's second volume, praising its thoroughness, accuracy and documentation. 'He

23 To Melvyn Laski, editor of *Encounter*, 14 Feb 1968

24 9 July 1967

25 Thanks to Holroyd's elegantly discursive style, and the revelatory nature of modern biographical writing (and of tabloid journalism), the sexual content now seems more discreet than it did forty years ago.

26 'Dying of Love', *New Statesman* 6 Oct 1967

does succeed in bringing Lytton to life', he wrote in his review.[27] In all its many pages, he told Holroyd, he only noticed 'two very minor inaccuracies'.[28] A week later he wrote again saying that 'turning out some papers' he had found 'some letters from Lytton to me and also some of his poems in his own handwriting. I have had them typed out and I think it may interest you to see the typescript.'[29]

This chance find was entirely typical. Leonard's papers were chaotic. He never seems to have listed what he had in Monks House or in 24 Victoria Square in the way of old letters and papers, nor what he sold and to whom and when. He employed a variety of secretarial help for copy-typing, the typists often taking the material home, and he did not record what left his hands. In 1968 he sent some typing work to Nora David's daughter Teresa Davies, newly married and living in Wales, including a notebook of Virginia's early writings, dating from 1909. After his death the notebook was forgotten – not to be rediscovered, in a drawer, until 2002.[30]

One significance of Holroyd's biography of Lytton Strachey was that it cut though the inhibitions and anxieties which had been preoccupying the remains of the Bloomsbury circle as they exchanged, copied, mulled over, sold or secreted their yellowing packets of correspondence. The biography of Lytton made Bloomsbury sensational. It was a 'hinge' publication, opening the way for the burgeoning Bloomsbury industry as, over the decades, the nuances of their social and sexual relationships, as well as their letters and minor writings, were published, glossed and interpreted, and quality-controlled by trusts and executors, for the benefit of a world readership variously indifferent, bored, disgusted, intrigued, entranced and insatiable.

*

27 'Ménage à Cinq', *New Statesman* 23 Feb 1968

28 25 Jan 1968

29 1 Feb 1968. Holroyd incorporated some of these letters into the revised versions of his biography.

30 Published as *Carlyle's House and Other Sketches* ed. David Bradshaw, Hesperus Press 2003

Leonard's income was increased by the success of his autobiographies; Virginia's royalties added up to five times more than his own earnings, not ten times as before. He continued to manage her rights and permissions, and was quick to defend her position, writing in riposte to a dismissive reference from Sir Denis Brogan of Peterhouse, Cambridge, that 'like so many highbrow writers' he assumed that 'her reputation has been a casualty of the last war and that people no longer read her'. Leonard pointed out that sales of *To the Lighthouse* alone in 1967 were 56,653.[31] He was not avid to publish everything she left. 'I don't mind scraping out the last scrapings of the barrel, but I think one should call a halt before the scrapings are from the barrel itself',[32] he wrote, deciding that a manuscript of Virginia's, 'The Dunciad', should not be published; it could, however, be sold. In 1967 he sold more letters to Hamill and Barker, and the galleys of *The Years.*

Hamill and Barker were becoming more picky, there being now something of a glut on the market. What the two women really wanted were the crown jewels – the originals of Virginia's diaries, which they had paid for back in 1958 – in spite of the arrangement that they must remain locked up in the bank in Leonard's lifetime. They had not reckoned on his living so long. 'Might this be the year for the picking up of the diaries?' they wrote in May 1967; and tried again in 1968. No.

His fourth volume of autobiography, *Downhill All the Way*, came out in 1967. It is the least compelling of the five, even though it covers the anxious period between the two World Wars, with important passages about Virginia, and some good anecdotes and 'characters'; also lists of Hogarth publications, accounts of his journalism, of his and his wife's earnings, and of his political activities. It was written at a time when, because of success and private happiness, he was more taken up with the outside world. It brought him a tribute from William Robson, touched by Leonard's references to their collaboration on *PQ*: 'I still look back on our joint editorial partnership as the halcyon period when there

31 11 Jan 1969
32 To Quentin Bell 18 Dec 1967

was complete understanding, shared judgements, and remarkable efficiency.'[33]

The marriage of Peggy Ashcroft and Jeremy Hutchinson came apart in the mid-1960s, after twenty-five years. Jeremy Hutchinson wrote to Leonard: 'Last night Peggy told me she had talked to you, and I was so glad. She loves you so much, and has such comfort from your friendship that in the difficult and sad months ahead I know your understanding will be perhaps her greatest support.' So it was. She had always written him well-mannered, affectionate letters. In her distress over the break-up she wrote frequently to 'dearest' or 'darling' Leonard. He reminded her how fond he was of her, across the barrier of their twenty-seven years' age difference: 'Yes I *do* know', she replied, 'and I'm sure you know how fond I am of you. But perhaps you don't know how good you have been for me as well as to me.' She was grateful for 'the feeling of love and friendship that you give me'. He was 'a source of comfort and strength . . . I *shall* go on saying – and believing – "everything passes", all pain is resolved in the end, and if one learnt not to feel possessive one would never feel dispossessed.' She loved waking up at Monks House, and sitting in the garden or in the upstairs sitting room talking to him, 'and I never cease to marvel how lucky I am to have LW as a friend.'

The divorce was in 1966, and the same year Jeremy Hutchinson married June Osborn. He came with her to Monks House that spring. Leonard was not a man to take sides. In 1967 he brought out with the Hogarth Press an anthology, a *Calendar of Consolation: A Comforting Thought for Every Day in the Year.* Even the title was parodic. Innocent book-buyers were in for a shock. It is Leonard's most characteristically satirical production, and deserves to be famous. It is a calendar of disturbing thoughts, and cannot have brought comfort to Peggy Ashcroft though it may have made her laugh. The consolation offered in the ruthlessly black aphorisms and paragraphs he selected is for those for whom optimism and uplift are no consolation. Angela Graham, dis-

33 15 Aug 1967

comfited, was 'in wonder at how a man with such bleak views of life can be so alive.'[34]

Leonard's circle widened during the 1960s, not only with such as Nora and Dick David, but with Deirdre and Anthony Bland, who came to live at Iford. Deirdre and her husband Anthony, who taught at Sussex University, opened the Southover Gallery in Lewes, where Trekkie showed her pictures. Deirdre was the sister of Rupert Hart-Davis, who had been briefly married to Peggy Ashcroft in their youth. Ruth Simon, about to become Hart-Davis's third wife, wrote to Leonard: 'It is curious how at ease I feel with you, and have always felt.'[35] Leonard's social-emotional life was intense. Visitors proposed themselves constantly and brought along their weekend guests. As he wrote to Trekkie, away as rather often now, 'The volume of pleasure which one suffers is enormous and unending.'[36]

A real pleasure in 1968 was that in the spring Horticultural Show he won six firsts, one second, and one third prize – much to the delight of his new gardener, Vout Van der Keift. In the summer show they swept the board: seven first prizes, all for vegetables. The orchard was still Leonard's special care, and an ancient apple-tree which had been in the garden fifty years before, when he and Virginia bought Monks House, was finally identified as 'Mr Prothero'. In 1968 and spring 1969 Leonard ordered extravagantly large amounts of herbaceous plants for propagation: he and Vout were inaugurating a commercial operation, 'Monks House Plants'.

Leonard was, as Angela Graham said, 'so alive'. Angelica Garnett, to whom he sporadically sent cheques, said that 'I think the reason you remain so young is that you are the most honest person I know – if I ever wanted to confess my sins it is to you that I should apply. Somehow the fogs and veils that one finds impeding one's communication with most people fall to the ground with you.'[37] He never seemed like an old

34 2 Jan 1968
35 27 Sept 1962
36 21 April 1968
37 16 July 1963

person, thought Quentin's daughter Virginia (Bell) Nicholson – until one looked at his veined and wrinkled hands. He treated children as people whose opinions he valued, and gave thoughtful answers to their questions. He lived in the present and in the future. There was no old man's reminiscing. He was hospitable not only to his friends' children, but to their friends too. Shelton Fernando's son Tyrone, studying in London, brought six fellow students at once down to Monks House.

In the mid-60s he was father confessor to a young relative of Trekkie's who was having a breakdown. He had sustained her since childhood, she wrote, and now, 'You have undoubtedly saved my life'. He gave her his usual mantra, 'Nothing matters'. His own experience of depression coloured his advice: 'You get yourself into a state in which you imagine things which have no basis in reality . . . One begins for some reason to worry about something and, if one allows oneself to go on doing that, one gradually imagines all kinds of things. It is a kind of self-indulgence and one gets into a perpetual daydream. It is essential to stop this process and face the real world – which is never so bad as all that.'[38]

No welcoming flurry greeted visitors at Monks House. Leonard opened the door and, gravely and silently, let them in. It could be unnerving. The young architect Georgie Wolton, taken to tea with him (and Peggy Ashcroft) by Deirdre Bland, saw his conversational style in structural terms: most people start 'on the inside', with enquiries about the guests' journey, where they are from, what they do; and, when such questions are exhausted, move on to general topics. Leonard started straight away 'on the outside' – the political situation, for example – and worked inwards, by degrees, to the personal.[39] He disconcerted young Bernard Crick, about to be taken on at *PQ* and making a pilgrimage to Monks House, by asking him, on the threshold, with no preliminaries, whom he considered to be the greatest poet in English of the twentieth century.

Dr Elizabeth Wiskemann, a history don at the University of Sussex, told him about some 'young creatures' in their first year who were

---

38 To Gillian Tulip 4 March 1968
39 Georgie Wolton to VG 29 Feb 2004

'much excited about "Bloomsbury"'.[40] Could they come and see him? They were Clare Cherrington and her two friends Julia Flint and Kay (Catherine) Jones, who invited him to be honorary president of the Sussex University Fabian Group. He enjoyed their bright company, and they shared their academic and personal difficulties with him, as also with Trekkie. But he was perhaps not wise in writing a cheque for £900 to help Julia and Kay to buy a cottage. He was also visited by an eighteen-year-old from Streatham who wrote to him out of the blue after seeing him on television. 'In talking to you', she wrote after her first visit, 'I did not feel this terrible gap between the generations.' Leonard did not put a foot wrong. She might visit again if she wished, he told her; but the suggestion must come from her. She came again, and again.

As for the student protests of 1968, which affected Sussex as they did most other universities, 'The revolt of the young does not disturb me. I think they have been doing the same since Cain killed Abel . . . We thought in my youth that we were just as much in revolt as people do now but we were against violence and, of course, we had not the same amount of publicity in those times.'[41] What he did not agree with was the involvement of the academic staff: 'Every reasonable person who has read history must agree that rebellion is in certain circumstances justifiable, but for professors and lecturers hysterically to encourage the young to use violence against the laws and the public seems to me very dangerous. Violence practically always begets violence.'[42]

Leonard's role as counsellor to younger people was of two-way benefit: he felt privileged to be admitted into their confidence. He met Virginia Browne-Wilkinson in 1959, when she submitted a novel to the Hogarth Press, which he turned down in his uniquely encouraging way. They remained in touch and, in charge of books for the BBC's 'Woman's Hour', she came to interview him about his autobiography – or rather, she felt, he interviewed her, seeming to prolong the visit: 'I'd like to ask you to come to lunch but I hate to be an incubus to . . .

40 21 Nov 1964
41 To Patricia Hutchins 19 June 1968
42 To Anthony Bland 10 Aug 1968

people under fifty.' And almost at once, on a postcard: 'How about next Monday.'[43]

Virginia Browne-Wilkinson's lunches at Monks House became regular, and she sometimes stayed the night. Trekkie was never there on Mondays, and Jill Balcon, the actor wife of Cecil Day-Lewis, advised Virginia always to 'go on a Monday', without putting into words why. Virginia had the idea of having a bronze bust of Leonard in the garden, to balance Stephen Tomlin's head of his wife. With his agreement, she commissioned a sculptor friend to do it. He sat for twenty-five-year-old Charlotte Hewer over four weekends in June 1968. Charlotte worked in the orchard, kneeling in the daisies, with Leonard sitting in a basket-chair reading. They did not talk much. She found him a good sitter, and as a person, 'incredibly young' in spite of his old face. As an interviewer for the *Guardian* put it, 'In old age his voice is dry, his gnarled face like an animated statue coming to life when he smiles.'[44]

Though Charlotte Hewer already had a track record as a sculptor, she was earning her living as a gardener at Hillier's Nurseries,[45] so noticed and remembered what was blooming in his conservatory that summer: white and yellow datura, gloriosas, jasminum polyanthemum, gloxinias, Scarborough lilies – and cacti in the greenhouses. The head was in cold-cast bronze, and Leonard was delighted with it. (A fibreglass cast went to the National Portrait Gallery in the early 1970s.)

Louie was diagnosed with cancer. She had an operation and made a slow recovery. (Anneliese West, for whom the Parsons had built a cottage at the bottom of their land at Juggs Corner, took over the heavy work at Monks House.) With both Trekkie and Louie away, Virginia B-W spent time with Leonard at Monks House. Lunch was tinned lambs' tongues with salad from the garden, and on Sundays he roasted a shoulder of lamb, needing no help. They worked – he on the last volume of his autobiography, she on a novel in progress – and listened to music in the evenings. If he called her anything, it was 'Dearest'. Only once when,

43 Virginia Browne-Wilkinson to VG 9 Feb 2003

44 27 Dec 1968. The interviewer was Nicholas de Jongh: no direct relationship was proved between him and LW's mother's family.

45 She later made her career in landscape gardening.

with his back to her, pouring drinks for several people, he said: 'Virginia? What would you like?' did she feel the frisson of the coincidence of names. It was not uncomfortable.

On 16 February 1969 Kingsley Martin, aged seventy-two, died in Cairo, from a stroke followed by a heart attack. Leonard received the news during a weekend that Virginia B-W was staying at Monks House. They went round to Jim Bartholomew's cottage to see the report of Kingsley's death on the television. (Leonard never acquired a television set.)

Earlier that weekend, he walked with Virginia to the river, and showed her where he had found the walking stick of the other Virginia, his wife. The younger Virginia asked him if he had ever wanted to marry anyone else. 'No, no one else, ever', he replied. 'This weekend was an extraordinary sort of duet', Virginia wrote when she got home. 'Gloom, yes, but great pleasure going on steadily at the same time. Also it was very pleasant being there when you finished your book'[46] – the fifth and final volume of his autobiography, *The Journey not the Arrival Matters.*

Leonard agreed reluctantly to write about Kingsley for *PQ.*[47] His partner Dorothy Woodman wrote to him: 'He loved you, even when he disagreed most violently with you, and in the past few years at Hilltop, you gave him background and support and the happiness of sharing a real love for the garden and the Downs.'[48] They were both cat-lovers – Kingsley wrote a note full of feeling to Leonard when Troy, 'the best cat I ever had', died – and they were at one over campaigns for the preservation of the Sussex countryside. But locked into intimacy with him over decades of argument and exasperation, Leonard was as ambivalent about Kingsley Martin in death as in life. He did not go to the Memorial Meeting. With wry satisfaction, he said to Virginia B-W: 'I once made Kingsley cry – at breakfast.'

He wrote even his last volume of autobiography fast, with little revision. All five were all quite short; if bound together, they would hardly make

---

46 17 Feb 1969
47 No. 40 1969
48 24 Feb 1969

a tome. In writing them he was, as Lytton would have put it, most utterly *dans son assiette.* He was released. He wrote in other books and in his journalism about ideas, issues and events. Where he had used his own experience, it was to make sociological points. He rarely talked much about himself, for that matter, though Stephen Spender wrote that to be with him 'was to experience the very rare excitement of total communication'.[49] In a solicited puff for another's autobiography, he wrote: 'When a man writes his autobiography, he ought to give a clear spiritual X-ray of his character, and this is hardly ever done.' Leonard provided such an X-ray, although he did not suggest how much suffering he had endured; and his many omissions and elisions, invisible on the X-ray, were integral to his character.

Critics often complained about the digressions in his books, and the autobiographies were no exception. His train of thought always took the scenic route. He moved back and forth in time, following associations and connections to their conclusions before returning to the matter in hand. Anyone trying to make a chronology of his life by using the autobiographies would have a nervous breakdown. Aware that some readers found his manner too discursive, he justified his method in this last volume: 'Life is not an orderly progression, self-contained like a musical scale or a quadratic equation . . . If one is to record one's life truthfully, one must aim at getting into the record of it something of the disorderly discontinuity which makes it so absurd, unpredictable, bearable.'

The Journey Not the Arrival Matters was in essence an overview volume, apart from the grave, spare section on Virginia's last illness and suicide. The one jarring note in the book was his harping on the points of difference between himself and John Lehmann at the Hogarth Press 'in tedious and ungenerous detail', as Julian Jebb put it in his review.[50] Leonard was nettled by John Lehmann's own account in his second volume of autobiography *I Am My Brother.* Both of them, as he wrote, were prickly characters. Because of the forward-looking digressions in earlier volumes, there was some repetition of material. But he broke

49 *New York Review* 23 April 1970
50 *Sunday Times* 17 Aug 1969

new ground with breathtaking honesty when assessing the value of his life's work: 'I see clearly that I achieved practically nothing.'

The state of the world in 1969, he wrote, 'would be exactly the same if I had played pingpong instead of sitting on committees and writing books and memoranda'. In his long life, he must have 'ground through between 150,000 and 200,000 hours of perfectly useless work'. He acknowledged the 'peripheral influence' of *International Government* on the establishment of the League of Nations, and of the two Advisory Committees on the political novices of the Labour Party. But no Labour government fully supported the League, or carried through the recommendations of the Advisory Committees, even when they were adopted as official policy.[51] Injustice, cruelty, intolerance, tyranny 'fill me with a passion of disgust and horror', and he had worked for fifty-seven years to combat them. But when he thought of 'the insanity of Hitler', the cruelty and stupidity of Soviet and Chinese Communism, America's 'stupid, unjustified, bloody and useless war' in Vietnam, the unending war between Arabs and Israelis, the brutality of apartheid in South Africa and Rhodesia, 'the ebb and flow of chaos and bloodshed and bleak authoritarianism in the new African states . . . I feel acute pain, compounded, I think, of disappointment and horror and discomfort and disgust.'

But he could never, he wrote, have disengaged himself from the real world and just cultivated his garden (though he did that as well). Somewhere in him was 'a spark of fire or heat which may at any moment burst into flame and compel me violently to follow some path . . . contrary to the calculations of reason and possibility.' The 'shadow of the shadow of a dream' – the dream of defeating cruelty and barbarism – was, he wrote, a good enough carrot to keep a human donkey going.

Yet his arguments in his books against war between states and peoples were always couched as appeals to reason. Similarly paradoxical was his affinity with the wildness of animals, with social deviance, with 'madness', all of them at odds with the 'civilisation' he sought to preserve or

---

51 The failure was not his personal failure but the failure of the Left in Britain.

create. This is not so strange. Leonard's sanity was deep enough, as his wife's was not, to contain his insanity, most of the time, with inspired leaks and some messy spillages. The prerogative of 'late style', as Edward Said wrote, is to render opposites without resolving the contradictions: 'What holds them in tension, as equal forces straining in opposite directions, is the artist's mature subjectivity, stripped of hubris and pomposity.'[52]

In this last volume Leonard addressed his Jewishness, as the culture that made him what he was. 'I have always been conscious of being a Jew', he wrote to the novelist and critic Dan Jacobson in 1968, 'but in the way in which, I imagine, a Catholic is conscious of being a Catholic in England . . . I have always been conscious of being primarily British and have lived among people who without question accepted me as such.' He had of course come up against 'the common or garden anti-Semitism, from the Mosley type to the "some of my best friends have been Jews." But it has not touched me personally and only very peripherally.'[53] Yet there in perpetuity sits the Jew in the tea-shop at Kew in his own story *The Three Jews*: 'They do not like us, you know.' For the first time, in *The Journey Not the Arrival Matters*, Leonard acknowledged how much in his own character derived from his being a Jew. He had 'the inveterate, the immemorial fatalism of the Jew', who learnt 'the lessons of centuries of pogroms and ghettoes down to the gas chambers and Hitler. Thus we have learned that we cannot escape Fate . . .' Here again he is paradoxical. He had written a few pages back, apropos of his political passion, that he could never 'completely resign myself to fate'. His interior dissonances were not different in kind from everyone's, but they were demonically intense.

To work hard was another lesson 'unconsciously inculcated in Jews', almost as part of their religion. His father had absorbed this tradition and passed it on to him. All his life, he had worked 'hard and persistently. I do not claim this as a merit, but state it as a fact. Both Virginia and I looked upon work not so much as a duty as a natural

---

52 Edward Said, 'Thoughts on Late Style', *London Review of Books* 5 Aug 2004

53 3 June 1968, in response to a review of his first three volumes of autobiography in *Commentary* March 1968.

function or even a law of nature.' Thus Virginia became an honorary Jew.

What about 'Nothing matters'? He wrote in this last book that, under the eye of eternity, nothing human was of the slightest importance. But in one's personal life, 'certain things are of immense importance: human relations, happiness, truth, beauty or art, justice and mercy.' And even though what he had tried to do politically was 'completely futile and ineffective and unimportant, for me personally it was right and important that I should do it.' For Peter Calvocoressi, Leonard Woolf was 'the only man I ever met who seemed to me to be right about everything that matters.'[54] When Virginia Browne-Wilkinson, towards the end, challenged him about 'Nothing matters', he turned to her and said: 'Nothing matters, and everything matters.'

His health was good throughout the 1960s, apart from minor setbacks. On Monday 14 April 1969, in disappointing weather, Monks House garden was open to the public. Leonard wrote 'Ill', in his diary that day. Next morning Vout, the gardener, found him in an armchair in the upstairs sitting-room unable to speak intelligibly. Vout fetched his wife and Louie, and rang for an ambulance. Louie refused to allow the ambulance-men to take Leonard away to hospital. That was the last great service she did for him. Trekkie, as always on Mondays, was in London. She returned at once. Leonard was still in the armchair. He knew who she was, but could not remember her name, or his wife's name. Over the next few days his speech returned and his memory improved.

He described to Virginia B-W, when she came to see him, how he had woken in the night, knowing that something had happened to him. 'It was lovely to see you looking and sounding so much as usual', she wrote afterwards. 'All the same, I've been thinking a lot about that unpleasant night you spent on your own.' She was offering, tentatively, to 'sleep under your roof on the nights that Trekkie doesn't. I expect you really *like* being alone to the extent that you are; but if now or in the future you

---

54 *Threading My Way* Duckworth 1994

decide that you need to have someone who could telephone for a doctor and for Trekkie for you if you were took bad, and that you were prepared to put up with a bit more company than you really like' – there was nothing she would like better.[55] According to Trekkie, who read this letter out to him, Leonard was 'alarmed' and 'appalled' by the idea of Virginia nursing him. 'But I thought that if she would come for a night at weekends I could get home for a night's rest and see Ian. So we wrote to her and said this.'[56]

Whatever 'we' wrote, Leonard himself typed a letter to ' Dearest Virginia' (and posted it, unprecedentedly, in a brand new envelope): 'First I must say that whatever may happen your letter gave me intense pleasure and I can think of no one at this moment of time and my life who would have given me such pleasure by such an offer . . . But I am so fond of you and feel that you look at things so much as I do – if that is possible with almost half a century between us – that I can speak absolutely without any kind of glove, silk or wool, on.' He suggested her staying at Monks House at the weekends for a trial period of two months. 'Whatever happens, I know that my feelings for you would not alter in any way.' He was improving, though his typing was 'rather slovenly, like my brain'.[57] His brain was not so slovenly that he did not shrewdly advise her to rent out her weekend home in the Mendips for the two months' trial period.

He was able to walk in the garden. Once he insisted on driving the car back from a shopping trip to Lewes. Trekkie looked after him from Tuesday to Friday and sometimes at the weekend too, with or without Virginia, bringing Ian. ('I *hate* this house', Ian said, bumping his head on a beam coming downstairs to supper.)

Julian Jebb was setting up a fifty-minute BBC TV 'Omnibus' documentary[58] on Virginia Woolf, and wanted to interview various people –

---

55 19 April 1969
56 Trekkie Parsons, 'Account of Leonard Woolf's last illness and death', typescript, Jan 1988
57 29 April 1969
58 'A Night's Darkness, A Day's Sail'

including, of course, Leonard, who was not able to take part. He told Julian Jebb he had jaundice, suggesting an interview with Louie Mayer instead: 'She has lived in my cottage and worked for me for thirty-six years. She was devoted to my wife. She is a remarkable character and if she is allowed to get going is a remarkable talker.'[59] Angelica and Duncan came together to see him, after which Angelica wrote: 'Why is the expression of love always so damnably inadequate? If I could have hugged you 5 times as much the other day it wouldn't have been nearly enough . . . nothing is any good except the *fact* that one knows when one loves, and when one is loved.'[60] Quentin, Olivier and their son Julian came, and Quentin was able to read aloud to Leonard the early chapters of his biography of Virginia; he reached the mid-1920s.[61]

On 28 May Leonard made a note in his diary for the first time since his stroke – 'if it was a stroke'[62] – in weak and spidery handwriting: 'Work Virginia lunch.' Letting him know she could not come for one weekend in mid-June, Virginia wrote that she hoped his 'gloom' would disperse. 'It is certainly the most miserable complaint of all, depression.' Leonard could not read properly any more. It was not a question of eyesight. He found it hard to make sense of the written word. The only person he wanted to have reading aloud to him was Peggy Ashcroft, who had made for him a recording of the last words of *The Waves.*

Virginia B-W corrected the proofs of *The Journey Not the Arrival Matters*, and found for him the title of the Gluck piece which was played at his wife's cremation. When she was with him, she was unable to say what she felt on reading his account of his wife's death, so put it in a letter: 'One would have thought that it couldn't be written about, but you have written one of the most moving and restrained descriptions of apprehension and grief that anyone ever has.' He told her that he had to 'take his life in his hands to do it.'[63]

Not much more than a year before, in April 1968, he had reviewed

---

59 25 May 1969
60 14 May 1969
61 Quentin Bell's *Virginia Woolf: A Biography* was published in 2 vols in 1972.
62 TP, unpublished 'Account of Leonard Woolf's last illness and death'.
63 9 June 1969

with undimmed sarcastic verve Cynthia Asquith's 'futile and frivolous' *Diaries 1915–18* for the *Listener*. The novelist L.P.Hartley had written the introduction, and took violent exception, writing a letter of protest to which Leonard made a restrained reply. But now Leonard had to acknowledge that he could no longer write, returning Thomas Jones's *Whitehall Diary 1916–1925* to Derwent May, the *Listener*'s literary editor.

Aware that his mind was failing, he asked Virginia B-W twice to help him to end his life: he was, when it came to the crunch, a Woolf. She told the GP, Dr Rutherford, who would not connive. Leonard asked Virginia to take power of attorney on his behalf. Wisely, she referred this to Trekkie, who took it on. Virginia, who could type, answered Leonard's business letters – and, distressingly, earned Leonard's and Trekkie's rage by 'tidying' the letters and papers in his writing-room, which no one ever, ever touched. Even Louie was aghast.

He was well enough to write, or dictate, a letter to the *New Statesman* about Labour and imperialism which appeared in the issue of 13 June 1969. But in the last ten days of that month he was fretting about the £900 he had lent Julia and Kay for their cottage. Nothing further had been heard from them. Trekkie tried to sort it out, and the two young women wrote Leonard a desperately penitent letter.

In the same week he had a letter from Suzanne Henig, with whom he had corresponded generously: 'Since there is so much I want to ask you about as I finish my book [about Virginia Woolf], would it be possible for you to schedule our meeting for a little longer than the twenty minutes you gave me three years ago?'[64] Trekkie replied to this, as she did to Hugh Gibb of Dyak Films who wanted a meeting about the film rights of *To the Lighthouse*, and to someone wanting a 'chat' about plans for a film of *Orlando*. On 28 June the garden was scheduled to be open to the public. This was cancelled. The last mark Leonard made in his diary – and it was just a mark – was on the last day of June.

Leonard had said one morning when Trekkie brought him his breakfast: 'We must talk about things you do not like.' She brought to his bed the

64 20 June 1969

black tin box in which was his Will. 'It was then that I learned that he had made me his executor and residuary legate[e].' There was a Will of 1949 and a Will of 1959, almost the same except that in 1959 he made her sole executor and 'increased certain legacies'. They discussed his leaving more to Louie, to Angelica and to Quentin. 'He had left his brother Philip's two daughters and his son (Philippa, Marie and Cecil) £500 each and that was to remain unaltered.' He had also left his niece Clare £500, which they decided should be increased.[65] He feared he did not have time for a whole new Will to be drafted. Colonel Adams, his solicitor, suggested altering the existing Will in the office, and bringing it over to Monks House for him to sign. Trekkie sat with Leonard while the solicitor read out to Leonard only those parts in which there were changes; and he signed.

The downstairs sitting room, once the best room in the house, had long been a store for logs and apples, like an indoor garden shed. But weak as he was, he could get upstairs to the little sitting room almost to the end. He only wanted to see Trekkie, the beloved of more than twenty-five years, and Peggy, and Virginia B-W. Visitors were not encouraged to go to his room. Deirdre Bland, a Roman Catholic convert, managed to slip upstairs. She said, 'Leonard, when you wake up, you're going to have a wonderful surprise!' The apparently comatose man raised up his arm and said 'No, no, no, no!'[66]

He recalled, towards the end of his final volume, his father saying at Sunday lunch that as regards the rules of life, a man need only follow the advice of the prophet Micah: 'What doth the Lord require of thee, but to do justly, and to love mercy, and to walk humbly with thy God.' Although, as Leonard wrote, he had never been much concerned with God or with walking humbly with him, he believed profoundly in the two other rules. 'Justice and mercy – they seem to me the foundation of all civilised life and society, if you include under mercy toleration. This is, if course, the Semitic vision . . .' Learning, later, that the Greeks had added the vision of liberty and beauty, and putting the words of Micah

65 TP, unpublished 'Account of Leonard Woolf's last illness and death'.
66 VBW to VG 9 Feb 2003

together with the speech of Pericles in Thucydides, he found his own vision. The combination, both ethical and aesthetic, 'gives to my feeling about what I call civilisation both its intensity and also a kind of austerity'. For all his faults and fears, Leonard Woolf had an integrity of which 'intensity and also a kind of austerity' were the foundation.

He wrote in his last volume about death, recalling once more the puppy struggling in the bucket of water, and the dead Arab lying on the sand at the Pearl Fishery in Ceylon. 'I watched Alice dying of cancer in Victoria Square . . . Only a day before he died, I went to see Clive Bell, dying of cancer, no longer able to talk, but, in the room where time had stopped, his eyes watching for death, but still eager to hear from me the trivialities of the living; I saw Virginia's body in the Newhaven mortuary.'

What he felt each time, irrespective of his personal involvement, was 'the primeval sense of time stopping, the universe hesitating, waiting, in fear, regret, pity, for the annihilation or snuffing out of a life, of a living being.'

In the house where time had stopped, the night nurse woke Trekkie at 4.15 a.m. on Thursday 14 August 1969 to tell her that Leonard had died. Later Peggy Ashcroft rang Virginia: 'He's left us.'

Leonard Woolf's body was cremated the next day, the only time when both Juliette Robson and Peggy Ashcroft could be available in the immediate future. At the Downs Crematorium in Brighton, where Leonard had witnessed alone the cremation of his wife, those who loved him heard Juliette play a Bach cello partita, and Peggy read part of Milton's *Lycidas*, which he knew by heart. Afterwards everyone went back to the garden at Monks House.

Some days later, Quentin Bell wrote to Trekkie: 'I have never been quite sure whether you realised how grateful Vanessa was to you for taking Leonard out of that appalling misery and into a long and lovely autumn . . . I think you ought to know it.'[67] Trekkie was grateful for

67 28 Aug 1969

the assurance. She buried Leonard's ashes under the surviving elm – which later, like its companion, blew down in a gale. Leonard's dog Coco was a casualty. She did not settle at Juggs Corner, and was put down.

19

Aftermath

Leonard Woolf left £157,732 gross. Monks House, together with 1 and 2 Stile Cottages, was valued at £24,000.

When Ian and Trekkie read his Will, 'Ian spotted that instead of the £500 each to Philip's daughters and son, the clerk had typed £5000, and so the Will had been engrossed'.[1] As the unaltered – or *meant* to be unaltered – parts had not been read out to Leonard by his solicitor, the error had gone unnoticed. The Parsons asked Cecil and Marie, who attended the cremation, to go with them straight away to the offices of Adams and Remer, Leonard's solicitors in Lewes, to hear the Will read and have the mistake explained.

Quite understandably, Cecil and his sisters decided to take legal action to establish the validity of the Will as it stood. They added a plea of 'undue influence' on the part of Trekkie, the residuary legatee. According to Trekkie, she asked the solicitor 'if we couldn't just pay the £5000 to each and be done with it, but he said I couldn't do that properly as executor because I knew that wasn't what Leonard had intended.'[2] She could, however, to avoid unpleasantness, have made up

1 TP, unpublished 'Account of Leonard Woolf's last illness and death'.
2 *idem*

the shortfall between £500 and £5000 from her own inheritance from Leonard, as a personal gift, by a Deed of Variation.

'Leonard Woolf's Will Disputed', announced *The Times.*[3] The dispute ran on for two years amid backbiting, bitterness, and suspicion – of a QC being nobbled in a London club, of malicious delaying tactics, even (on the part of those who had not seen the Will) of the error being the other way round, i.e. that the clerk had typed £500 instead of an intended £5000. Probate could not be granted. Hamill and Barker could not collect Virginia Woolf's diaries from the Westminster Bank. No legacies could be paid out, which was hardest on Louie Mayer; the money Leonard left her was for buying her own house.

The action taken in the High Court was 'Parsons v. Hardman and Others (Sturgeon and others cited)'. Philippa was Mrs Hardman, the eldest of the siblings; Sturgeon was Leonard's sister Flora's married name. She must have come forward in their support. The day before the case was heard, they withdrew their plea of 'undue influence'.

The solution was ingenious. In the High Court on 23 July 1971, the judge pronounced for 'the force and validity' of the Will, 'save and except that sub clause 4 of clause 3 be omitted therefrom.' This was the sub clause in which the three disputed legacies were specified. In the Will as proved, there is a blank space on the page between sub clauses 3 and 5 of clause 3. It had been settled out of court, with Trekkie paying each of the three in excess of £500 but not so much as £5000. Trekkie sold 24 Victoria Square for £8000, paying Cecil compensation for vacating his flat, where as a sitting tenant he claimed a right to remain.

Monks House, its garden and land and the two cottages were also part of Leonard's legacy to Trekkie, who hoped 'that it might be kept as it was, with its contents, as Leonard and Virginia's house'. She arranged in 1972 to donate Leonard's archive – known as the Monks House Papers – to Sussex University, in return for the University buying the whole property at the probate value of £24,000. 'The arrangement did not turn out happily.'[4] The University sold off just the two cottages

---

3 30 July 1970

4 TP, 'Account of Leonard Woolf's last illness and death'.

for £22,000. Some of the contents of Monks House disappeared or went on to bonfires when it was being cleared out. The plan was to let the house furnished to visiting academics and writers. Saul Bellow came, found it uncomfortable and spooky, and did not stay long. The garden lay neglected. Finally the National Trust took over Monks House, with an endowment from the University, and after renovation and alterations it became the literary shrine that it is today.

A second unpleasantness concerned, inevitably, old letters.[5] In October 1972 the Berg in New York bought, through the reputable dealer Anthony Rota in London, a huge collection of letters, all in the same transaction. The seller was the daughter-in-law of George Pritchard, of the firm of solicitors Dolland and Pritchard. The collection included 425 letters from Leslie Stephen to his wife, eighty-four from Lytton Strachey to Leonard Woolf, thirty-one from Vanessa to Virginia, and the remainder from well-known writers to Leslie Stephen, to Leonard and Virginia Woolf, and a passionate love-letter from Leonard to Virginia. There were also twenty-seven letters between Maynard Keynes and Lytton Strachey, letters from Walter Lamb and Sydney Waterlow to Virginia, and from Moore, Forster and Keynes to Leonard. None was dated later than 1921.

Quentin and Olivier Bell read in the *Times Literary Supplement* about the Berg Collection's great acquisition. How in the world had the Pritchards come by this extraordinary cache? They communicated their concern to Trekkie. She, as Leonard's executor, explored further.

Lola Szladits, director of the Berg, had very properly enquired as to the provenance. The story was that George Pritchard died in July 1970, predeceased by his wife. Their son Patrick died soon afterwards. Mary Pritchard, Patrick's widow, provided for Dr Szladits a signed affidavit stating that the collection had been given to her father-in-law George Pritchard by Leonard Woolf. From the early 1960s until his death,

5 Both controversies were briefly discussed, in so far as he was then in possession of the facts, by Paul Levy in a lively attack on the flood of 'second-rate' books about Virginia Woolf made possible by the availability of so much material. 'Who's Ripping Off Virginia Woolf?' *Harpers & Queen* Nov 1979.

George Pritchard kept the letters at his home in Caterham, in the unlabelled deed box in which he received them. No one had ever looked properly at the letters, which were not well-ordered, until after Patrick Pritchard's death; though he knew about them, and had planned to 'write a book'.

To the Bells and the Parsons, such a gift from Leonard to George Pritchard was so unlikely as to be unbelievable. Ian Parsons took the matter up, working through the solicitor Michael Rubinstein, briefing him as to the improbability of letters between Lytton Strachey and Maynard Keynes ever having been in Leonard's possession at all. (Lytton did send on to Leonard in Ceylon letters from Keynes, among others, though these would not have been Leonard's to give away.) It was, surely, much more likely that the deed box had simply been left with George Pritchard in safe custody.

Rose Schrager, long retired, was contacted. Mr Woolf, she remembered, often stored books and papers in the Dolland and Pritchard office in Mecklenburgh Square, and Mr George rarely sent in bills either for storage or for legal work, even though Mr Woolf constantly asked for them. 'A long time ago, Mr George did mention to me that Mr Woolf had given him a package [*sic*] of letters, and when I asked, "What for?", he seemed embarrassed and replied, "Mr Woolf seems to think he owes me something", referring to the fact that he rarely made legal charges for work . . . I doubt if Mr George had any idea of their possible value.'

Rose Schrager added that if any papers had been handed to Mr George for safe keeping, 'they would have been given to me to put away in one of our huge safes . . . and I would have made a note of it on the index.'[6] Trekkie herself spoke to Rose in early December 1973. Unfortunately Rose could not remember *when* Mr George told her about Mr Woolf giving him the letters. But she did remember something else: that Mr Woolf cleared some papers from the basement and stored them 'in a little room at the side of Mr George's room.'

The partners at Dollman and Pritchard argued that if the papers had been in formal safe custody, George Pritchard would have returned

---

6 To L.A.Charlier of Dolland and Pritchard 17 July 1973

them when Leonard Woolf died. Michael Rubinstein replied that 'It really is stretching credibility too far to speculate, in the absence of any known letter of thanks from the recipient', that Mr Woolf would have given Mr Pritchard hundreds of letters 'which it would seem neither troubled to look at.'[7] But he was getting nowhere. He informed Dolland and Pritchard that Mrs Parsons did not intend to pursue the matter, 'but reserved the right to make public the facts so far as they are known to her.'

No suspicion attached to Mary Pritchard, who was at worst naïve: it was bad practice, and bad manners, not to consult with the family whose letters they were, about the proposed sale. In this she was badly advised.

There is maybe no great mystery. There is ample evidence of Leonard's groaning distaste for old letters, and he was always hopelessly vague about what was where. It is possible to imagine a scene with George Pritchard reminding him of the deed box – left perhaps in John Lehmann's former office – and Leonard, busy, preoccupied, telling him just to keep it, having no idea what was in it, in recognition of his generosity in not charging for legal services.

Leonard did not remember even the existence of the box in later years, or he would not have been puzzled, when James Strachey was collecting Lytton's correspondence, as to the whereabouts of Lytton's letters to him in Ceylon. The batch of Lytton's letters in the deed-box was the same batch as those of which he sent copies to Michael Holroyd in 1968; Leonard must have taken the trouble, some time before he stowed them away with all the rest in the deed-box, to have them typed or Xeroxed. But is there any connection at all between the Berg cache and the old family letters Leonard gave to Vanessa in 1949, saying they had 'recently turned up' in the office of Dolland and Pritchard?[8]

There have been speculations about sticky fingers. But simple explanations are generally the right ones.

*

---

7 21 Dec 1973
8 See Chapter Sixteen

Morgan Forster died in 1970. William Robson and Ian Parsons lived until 1980, and Trekkie Parsons until 1995. The two most disturbed of Leonard's siblings outlived the rest. Flora, for all her frailty, lived – most of the time in Holloway Sanatorium – until 1975. Edgar, tranquil and cheerful in his extreme old age, died in 1981, aged ninety-six.[9]

The afterlives of authors, and the careers of those who teach or write about their lives and work, are made possible by the availability of material – which in the case of Bloomsbury was massive. 'Bloomsbury books', biographies, and critical studies have proliferated. Virginia Woolf – as artist, modernist, feminist – is an iconic figure, studied in Women's Departments and English Departments in anglophone universities and beyond. The decades immediately following Leonard Woolf's death saw a new and positive wave of feminism. One of its negative aspects was a knee-jerk denigration of the male partners of significant women. Leonard Woolf and the part he played in his wife's life and death became topics for pseudo-scholarly speculation based on partial knowledge. He has been construed both as the nurturer and protector of genius, and as the oppressor or the conniver in the death of genius. There is no reason to adumbrate all the theories about his role in the marriage. They are in the public domain, and some are what he and Lytton Strachey would have described as 'very wild'.

There is a sense of something displaced in the more hostile interpretations of Leonard's role in the marriage; whatever relationship is being described, it is not solely that of Leonard and Virginia Woolf. But as with all neurotic perceptions, there is a smidgeon of truth underlying the distortions, which makes them disturbing to read. A black legend and a golden legend can be constructed around any relationship, as around any individual, and neither can ever be one hundred per cent true. All intimate relationships are freighted with ambivalences and projections. The more intimate the relationship, the more this is the case, since the importance and depth of the intimacy means the relationship has to carry a load which in other circumstances would be spread around. A

---

9 Edgar left £61,687

black legend could easily be constructed around Virginia as a wife, based on her corrosive contempt for her husband's race, his class, his family, his friends, and the work that meant so much to him, quite apart from the fact that she would not, or could not, have sex with him. But that too would be a distortion. Theirs was a real marriage. As for Leonard, he could have been happier, 'not if [he] had married someone else, but if Virginia had been other than she was.'[10]

Except in Ceylon, and apart, latterly, from specialist pockets of interest in International Studies Departments, his life, character and career have been hardly considered except in relation to his wife's. Only the publication of his *Letters* in 1989[11] and of his correspondence with Trekkie Parsons in 2001,[12] began to redress the balance. Readers of this book will have made up their own minds about the nature and quality of Leonard Woolf, the whole man.

---

10 George Spater and Ian Parsons, *A Marriage of True Minds* Chatto and Windus 1977

11 Edited and introduced by Frederic Spotts, NY: Harcourt Brace Jovanovich 1989

12 Judith Adamson (ed): *Love Letters: Leonard Woolf and Trekkie Ritchie Parsons 1941–1968* Chatto & Windus 2001

ACKNOWLEDGEMENTS

My first thanks go to Elizabeth Inglis, former director of Special Collections in the Library of the University of Sussex, who initiated me into Leonard Woolf's voluminous archive, which includes his carbon copies of most of the letters he sent; and to the present director, Dorothy Sheridan, and her kind staff, who helped me not only with the Leonard Woolf Papers but with the Monks House Papers, the Charleston Papers and the Quentin Bell Papers. Where not otherwise indicated, material by LW, or addressed to LW, is from Sussex.

Special thanks too to Leonard Woolf's niece Dr Marie (Woolf) Beesley, for her generosity and friendship, and to Anne Olivier Bell. Charles Tucker of London Beth Din undertook research into the early history of the Woolfs in Britain, as did Professor Nigel Glendinning, to both of whom I am particularly grateful, as I am for the professional expertise of picture researcher Suzanne Bosman, copy editor Robyn Karney, Jeremy Crow of the Society of Authors, my agent Bruce Hunter, Rochelle Venables, Edwina Barstow, Joe Pickering and all at Simon & Schuster.

All biographers must be thankful for WATCH (www.watch-file.com) the joint project of the universities of Reading and Texas, a database of the copyright holders of many British and American authors; and for the Location Register of English Literary Manuscripts and Letters (www.locationregister.com); not to mention Google. While these resources save much footwork and time, I am even more grateful to the following generous people for a wide variety of help, including the sharing of memories, contacts, information and insights, for practical assistance, and for the gift or loan of materials:

Judith Adamson, Belinda Allen, Gabriele Annan, R. Bailey, Vicki Berger, Michael Berry, Anthony Blond, Sandra G.Boselli, Michael Bott, Professor Douglas Brewer, Lord Briggs, Virginia Browne-Wilkinson, Peter Calvocoressi, E.M.Chilver, Anne Chisholm, Dr David Cohen, Sir Bernard Crick, Baroness (Nora) David, Marion Dell, David Dickinson, Josceline Dimbleby, Rosemary Dinnage, Valerie Eliot, Charlotte (Hewer) Evans, Lord Evans of Temple Guiting, Mary Fedden, Stephen Fein, Maggie Fergusson, Susan L.Fox, the Rt Hon John Freeman, David Frei, Henrietta Garnett, Jonathan Gathorne-Hardy, the late Jonathan Gili, Christopher Glass, Eleanor Gleadlow, Professor Paul Glendinning, Hugo Glendinning, Matthew Glendinning, Dr Simon Glendinning, Edmund Gray, Christine Groom, Charles Gunawardena, Georgina Innes, Freda K.Hamric, the late Dr Philippa (Woolf) Hardman, Suki Hardman, Dr Ross Harrison, Selina Hastings, the Rt Hon Lord Healey CH and Lady Healey, Mary Hepburn, Judith S. Herz, Jane Hill, Susan Hill, Michael Holroyd, Elizabeth Jane Howard, Lord Hutchinson of Lullington QC, the late Elizabeth Jenkins, Paul Johnson, Frances Jowell and Professor Jeffrey Jowell, Jonathan Keates, Professor Hermione Lee, Lord Lester of Herne Hill, Paul Levy and Penelope Marcus, Virginia Lindley, Professor Norman Mackenzie, Andrew MacNeillie, Joan Manning, Sue Marsh, Stephen Medcalf, Ursula Mommens, Richard Morphet, Alastair Nevin, Virginia Nicholson, the late Nigel Nicolson, Patrick O'Connor, Sybil Oldfield, Sir Christopher Ondaatje, Michael Ondaatje, Dr C.M.E.Rowland Payne, Nicholas Rankin, Dr Donald Rau, Professor Michael Roberts, Professor David Robson, Elaine Robson, Clare V. Sack, David Scrase, Richard Seebohm, John Shaw, Nathan Sivasambu, Frances Spalding, Frederic Spotts, Michael and Agnes Thambynayagam, Victoria Walsh, Alan Watkins, Annaliese West, Dr Peter Wilson, Professor Donald Winch, Joan Winterkorn, the late Amelia (Malya) Woolf, Cecil Woolf, Georgie Wolton, Jennie and Ivan Yates, Caroline and Jonathan Zoob.

In Ceylon (Sri Lanka): Ismeth Raheem, architect, antiquarian and historian, was, with his wife Delini, outstandingly generous with hospitality, introductions, materials, and information. I would also like to thank specially Dr Yasmine Gooneratne for her scholarly advice. Also Jean Arasanayagam, Katrina Luker, Robin McCarthy, Nirmala de Mel

(Quickshaws Tours Ltd), Gillian and Alwin Ratnayaka, Anna Searle (the British Council in Colombo), Dr Saroja Wettasinghe and the staff of the National Archives of Sri Lanka, Mr Chandradasa Jagoda (Government Agent, Hambantota), Professor Walter Perera, Brigadier T.T.R Silva and Captain Aruna de Silva (Jaffna); Saumya Sanaratt (Kandy Archives), and the staff of the Galle Face Hotel in Colombo.

I gratefully acknowledge the following individuals, institutions and organisations for the sight or use of material, or permission to quote from material in copyright:

First and foremost, the University of Sussex, and the Society of Authors as their representative, for published and unpublished material by Leonard Woolf, and for extracts from Leonard Woolf's *Sowing, Growing, Beginning Again, Downhill All the Way, The Journey Not the Arrival Matters.*

Also Dr Marie (Woolf) Beesley (for LW's letters from his parents and siblings); the Berg Collection of English and American Literature, The New York Public Library, Astor, Lenox and Tilden Foundations, with special thanks to Dr I. Gewirtz; the BBC Written Archives Centre; Virginia Browne-Wilkinson; the British Library; Faber & Faber Ltd (for the Estate of T.S.Eliot); the Harry Ransom Humanities Research Center, the University of Texas at Austin; Angelica Garnett; Henrietta Garnett (c Estate of Vanessa Bell 1961); Livia Gollancz (for Victor Gollancz); Margaret Hanbury (for the estate of Gerald Brenan); David Higham Associates (for Margaret Cole, John Lehmann, Kingsley Martin); the Huntington Library, San Marino, California; The Library of the *Jewish Chronicle*; the Jewish Studies Library at University College, London; Eliza Loizeau (for Peggy Ashcroft); the LSE Archives, Passfield Papers (for Beatrice and Sidney Webb); Juliet Nicolson (for the estate of V.Sackville-West); Penguin Books Ltd (for Paul Levy ed. *The Letters of Lytton Strachey* Viking 2005); the Provost and Scholars of King's College, Cambridge, and the Society of Authors as the literary representatives of the E.M.Forster estate; The Random House Group Ltd (for *The Letters of Virginia Woolf* ed. Nigel Nicolson and Joanne Trautmann, Hogarth Press, for *The Diary of Virginia Woolf* ed. Anne Olivier Bell, Hogarth Press, *Moments of Being* by Virginia Woolf, Hogarth Press, *Love Letters:*

Leonard Woolf and Trekkie Ritchie Parsons 1941-1968 ed. Judith Adamson, Chatto & Windus); Elaine Robson (for W.A.Robson); St Paul's School; The Society of Authors as the literary representative of the estate of Virginia Woolf (for 'Carlyle's House', 'The Mark on the Wall', 'An Incident in a Duckpond'); the Society of Authors as the literary representative of the estates of Clive Bell, Julian Bell, Quentin Bell and Compton Mackenzie; The Society of Authors, on behalf of the Strachey Trust (for Lytton, James, Alix, Marjorie and Philippa Strachey); the University of Reading, Archives of the Hogarth Press; Victoria University in the University of Toronto. Every effort has been made to contact all persons having any rights regarding the material used in this work. Where this has not been possible the publishers will be happy to hear from anyone who recognises their material.

Finally, my heartfelt thanks to Kevin O'Sullivan for his good humour and understanding while this book was being researched and written. As he remarked, there are – or have been – three people in this marriage.

SELECT BIBLIOGRAPHY

The many books and articles from which quotation is made in the text are documented in the footnotes. A brief list of essential background reading may however be helpful.

Students of Leonard Woolf are indebted to Leila Luedeking and Michael Edmonds for their *Bibliography of Leonard Woolf* (1992), which lists not only all his books, monographs and pamphlets but almost all his articles and reviews in newspapers, magazines and journals, signed and unsigned, published over more than half a century.

For views of his politics, see Duncan Wilson, *Leonard Woolf: A Political Biography* (1978) and Peter Wilson, *The International Theory of Leonard Woolf* (Palgrave Macmillan 2003).

Woolf's published fiction is available in modern editions: *The Village in the Jungle* (Eland 2005), *The Wise Virgins* (Persephone 2003) and *A Tale Told by Moonlight*, previously published as *Three Stories of the East* (Hesperus 2006).Not all of his non-fiction books are in print at the time of writing, but many have been reissued at intervals over the years and are available second-hand. Those most worth seeking out are:

International Government (Fabian Society 1916)

Empire and Commerce in Africa: a Study in Economic Imperialism (Allen & Unwin 1920)

Essays on Literature, History, Politics etc (Hogarth Press 1927)

After the Deluge Vol 1 (Hogarth Press 1931)

Barbarians at the Gate (Left Book Club, Gollancz 1939) Title in US: *Barbarians Within and Without*

Quack, Quack! (Hogarth Press 1935)

The War for Peace (L.W.Routledge & Sons 1940)

Principia Politica (Hogarth Press 1953)
Also his disconcerting anthology *A Calendar of Consolation: A Comforting Thought for Every Day in the Year* (Hogarth Press 1967)
(Dates refer to first British publication)

His characteristic voice is most clearly heard in his five-volume autobiography: *Sowing, Growing, Beginning Again, Downhill All the Way, The Journey Not the Arrival Matters* (Hogarth Press 1960-1969); in *The Letters of Leonard Woolf* ed. Frederic Spotts (Weidenfeld & Nicolson 1990); and in *Love Letters: Leonard Woolf and Trekkie Ritchie Parsons 1941-1968* ed Judith Adamson (Chatto & Windus 2001).

His Cambridge and later friendships can be traced in Michael Holroyd's *Lytton Strachey* (one-vol revised version, Heinemann 1994); Robert Skidelsky's *John Maynard Keynes* Vol 1 1883-1920 (Macmillan 1983); *The Letters of Lytton Strachey* ed. Paul Levy (Penguin Viking 2005); and S.P.Rosenbaum's *The Bloomsbury Group: A Collection of Memoirs and Commentary* (revised edition, University of Toronto Press 1995). For more about the least well-documented of his friends, see P.T.McSharry, 'The Bloomsbury Group, Friendship and Saxon Sydney-Turner', MA dissertation (2000), Buckingham University.

Woolf's *Diaries in Ceylon 1908-1911 and Stories from the East* were reissued by the Hogarth Press in 1963. See also Bella Sidney Woolf, *How To See Ceylon* (fifth edition, Visidunu Prakashakayo, Ceylon 2002), and Christopher Ondaatje, *Woolf in Ceylon* (HarperCollins Canada 2005).

There is a small mountain of books and articles on the life and work of Virginia Woolf. For present purposes, the following texts are the most useful for readers not wholly familiar with the territory:

Quentin Bell, *Virginia Woolf: A Biography* (2 vols, Hogarth Press 1972)
Hermione Lee, *Virginia Woolf* (Chatto & Windus 1996)
Julia Briggs, *Virginia Woolf: An Inner Life* (Allen Lane 2005)
Nigel Nicolson assisted by Joanne Trautmann (ed), *The Letters of Virginia Woolf* (vols 1- 6, Chatto & Windus 1975-1980)
Anne Olivier Bell assisted by Andrew MacNeillie (ed), *The Diary of Virginia Woolf* (vols I-V, Chatto & Windus 1977-1983)

See also:

Frances Spalding, *Vanessa Bell* (Weidenfeld & Nicolson 1983)

George Spater and Ian Parsons, *A Marriage of True Minds: An Intimate Portrait of Leonard and Virginia Woolf* (Chatto & Windus 1977), dedicated 'To Trekkie who made this book possible' and co-written by Trekkie's husband.

Peter F. Alexander, *Leonard and Virginia Woolf: A Literary Partnership* (NY: St Martin's Press 1992)

John Lehmann, *Thrown to the Woolfs* (Weidenfeld & Nicolson 1978)

Kingsley Martin, *Father Figures* and *Editor*, 2 vols of autobiography (Hutchinson 1966, 1968)

The notion that Leonard Woolf was a destructive influence in his wife's life, and on the way that it ended, was floated by Dr Phyllis Grosskurth in 'Between eros and thanatos', a review in *The Times Literary Supplement* (31 Oct 1980) of *Leave the Letters till We're Dead*, Vol VI of *The Letters of Virginia Woolf*. Grosskurth postulated a deep antipathy between the couple, arising from Virginia's dislike of Jews and of Leonard's professional milieu, and from Leonard's 'concerted attempt to undermine Virginia's confidence in herself' after he read the anti-Semitic material in *The Years*. She presented them as 'two beings locked in eternal warfare'. Did Virginia, she wondered, become 'a financial liability' to Leonard? Grosskurth speculated that he wanted her out of the way – and, just maybe, took steps in that direction. Twenty-six years on, Dr Grosskurth wrote: 'I have long regretted my impulsive and not-thought-out piece (written when I was very ill). It was an impatient reaction to my irritation with the Bloomsbury industry.'[1]

For an extended hostile interpretation of Leonard's character and of his role in the marriage, see Irene Coates, *Who's Afraid of Leonard Woolf? A Case for the Sanity of Virginia Woolf* (NY: Soho Press 1998).

1 To VG 25 May 2006.

Value of £1 sterling during LW's lifetime compared with its value in 2005

1880	£66.35
1890	£73.31
1900	£72.10
1910	£67.99
1920	£26.76
1930	£42.12
1940	£36.37
1950	£22.95
1960	£15.41
1970	£10.36

Figures from the economic history services website www.eh.net, based on the retail price index.

PICTURE CREDITS

Every effort has been made to trace the copyright holders. In the event of any inadvertent breach of copyright, the author and publisher would be pleased to include a correction in a future edition.

Plate section

1. Courtesy of Clare V. Sack; 2. The Law Society; 3. Courtesy of Clare V. Sack; 4. Suzanne Bosman (London); 5. Author photograph, 2005; 6. From LW's *Sowing*; 7. From LW's *Sowing*; 8. Courtesy of Clare V. Sack; 9. Tate Archive; 10. National Portrait Gallery, London 11. Trinity College Library, Cambridge; 12. From LW's *Sowing*; 13. From LW's *Growing*; 14; National Portrait Gallery, London; 15. Courtesy of Joan Manning; 16. Royal Geographical Society; 17–19. Author photographs, 2004. 20; University of Sussex, Special Collections; 21–23. National Portrait Gallery, London. 24. Courtesy of Anne Olivier Bell; 25–27 National Portrait Gallery, London; 28. Tate Archive; 29. Taken by Lady Ottoline Morrell, National Portrait Gallery, London; 30. Tate Archive; 31. University of Sussex, Special Collections; 32–35. Courtesy of Clare V. Sack; 36–38 National Portrait Gallery, London; 39. From Paragon Review, Archives and Special Collections, Brynmor Jones Library; 40. Tate Archive; 41. University of Sussex, Special Collections; 42. Tate Archive; 43. Courtesy of Christopher Ondaatje; 44. From LW's *The Journey not the Arrival Matters*; 45. University of Sussex, Special Collections; 46. Courtesy of Elaine Robson; 47–48. from LW's *The Journey not the Arrival Matters*; 49. Getty Images; 50. Getty Images; 51. Mander & Mitchenson Theatre Collection; 52. The Hogarth Press colophon used by permission of The Random

House Group Ltd; 53. Courtesy of Elizabeth Inglis; 54. © Richard Morphet. 55. Courtesy of Anne Olivier Bell; 56. Courtesy of Clare V. Sack; 57. Courtesy of Virginia Browne-Wilkinson; 58. Courtesy of Cecil Woolf; 59. University of Sussex, Special Collections. 60; National Portrait Gallery, London; 61; University of Sussex, Special Collections; 62. University of Sussex, Special Collections; 63. National Portrait Gallery, London

Integrated pictures

Piv Trekkie Ritchie's cartoon of LW and the Angel reproduced by kind permission of Professor Douglas Brewer; p. 74 from LW's *Growing*; p. 104 John Kent, *Guardian*, 1979; p. 229 Courtesy of the late Nigel Nicolson; p 279 Richard Kennedy, *A Boy at the Hogarth Press*, Whittington Press, 1972; p. 385 The Memoir Club by Vanessa Bell, circa 1943, NPG 6718, © Estate of Vanessa Bell, courtesy of Henrietta Garnett.

INDEX

Note: During long periods, certain people were very close to LW, and part of his life. These are Lytton Strachey (at Cambridge and, through letters, when LW was in Ceylon), his wife Virginia, to a lesser extent his sister-in-law Vanessa Bell and his eight siblings; and from 1942 until his death, Trekkie Parsons. To note every single reference to these is not practicable. Mentions of them outside the times when they were part of his daily life are all noted, and references given for all significant events or communications during the years of maximum involvement, where otherwise *passim* may be understood.